Interpersonal
Dynamics
Essays and Readings on Human Interaction

THE DORSEY SERIES IN PSYCHOLOGY

EDITOR HOWARD F. HUNT *Columbia University*

FLEISCHMAN *Studies in Personnel and Industrial Psychology* rev. ed.

FISKE & MADDI *Functions of Varied Experience*

BARNETTE *Readings in Psychological Tests and Measurements* rev. ed.

BENNIS, SCHEIN, BERLEW, & STEELE *Interpersonal Dynamics: Essays and Readings on Human Interaction* rev. ed.

RATNER & DENNY *Comparative Psychology: Research in Animal Behavior*

COURTS *Psychological Statistics: An Introduction*

DEUTSCH & DEUTSCH *Physiological Psychology*

VON FIEANDT *The World of Perception*

ROZEBOOM *Foundations of the Theory of Prediction*

KLEINMUNTZ *Personality Measurement: An Introduction*

HAMMER & KAPLAN *The Practice of Psychotherapy with Children*

MADDI *Personality Theories: A Comparative Analysis*

FREEDMAN *The Neuropsychology of Spatially Oriented Behavior*

Interpersonal Dynamics

Essays and Readings on Human Interaction

Edited by

WARREN G. BENNIS
Provost, Social Sciences and Administration
State University of New York at Buffalo

EDGAR H. SCHEIN
Professor of Organizational Psychology and Management
Massachusetts Institute of Technology

FRED I. STEELE
Assistant Professor of Administrative Sciences
Yale University

DAVID E. BERLEW
Director of Behavioral Science Center
Sterling Institute

Revised Edition · 1968
THE DORSEY PRESS, Homewood, Illinois
IRWIN-DORSEY LIMITED, Nobleton, Ontario

© THE DORSEY PRESS   1964 and 1968

REVISED EDITION

First Printing, June, 1968

Library of Congress Catalog Card No. 68–23345

Printed in the United States of America

FOREWORD

As a graduate student many years ago, I remember musing over a comment by Gordon Allport that God had not seen fit to organize natural phenomena so that they would conform to man's neat and logical ordering of the scientific disciplines. Recently C. P. Snow has given other connotations to this point in his discussion of the "two worlds."

Perhaps nowhere is the abyss between formal logic and reality more evident than in man's attempt to order knowledge about his own behavior. There are today 24 divisions within the American Psychological Association, and these are presumably logically separable from each other as well as from the subdivisions of sociology, anthropology, political science, and psychiatry. In turn, none of these gives more than a nod of recognition to the insights of the playwright, the novelist, the poet, or the historian.

In the resultant confusion of tongues, it is refreshing to come upon a sophisticated attempt to bring systematic order to an important set of behavioral phenomena without regard to disciplinary jurisdiction. When my colleagues told me so in their Preface, I realized with a start that studies of these phenomena, although they form the very core of human existence, are scattered all over the map of the behavioral sciences and the humanities. The field of interpersonal relations is not even formally recognized as a scientific discipline in its own right!

Several things become apparent as a result of this endeavor. First, and most important, there is much useful knowledge scattered all through the behavioral science literature about the many different varieties of interpersonal relationships. The fact that it is so scattered has prevented us from discovering how much, in a sense, we know already.

It is unlikely to occur to us until such a systematic analysis is undertaken that there are *common* causal relationships affecting the behavior of lovers, friends, nurses and patients, prisoners and wardens, confidence men and their victims, teachers and students, con-

sultants and clients, and mutual enemies. Since a sociologist interested in criminology has studied one of these relationships, and an
educational psychologist has studied another, a psychoanalyst another, and an organization theorist another, and so on *ad infinitum,*
the possibility of perceiving them as belonging to a *common* behavioral category is almost precluded.

A second "discovery" follows on the heels of the first: many of the
profound insights of the novelist and the poet are remarkably consistent with the knowledge.we have gained from systematic research.
It would of course be surprising if this were not so, but it is only
rarely that an attempt is made like the present one to bridge the
"two worlds." Thus the careful, critical observations of behavior reflected in the work of a first class novelist are seen to be significantly
related to the observation reflected in the report of a scientific research study. The methods are indeed different, but the slow process of accumulating useful knowledge about man's behavior is well
served by both. It is time we gave more than lip service to this fact.
The editors of this volume are to be commended for transcending
(some will say violating) the existing norms concerning the distinctions between science and the humanities, too many of which
are motivated merely by the desire to maintain status differences.

Third, the task undertaken here brings into focus some of the
glaring gaps in our knowledge about these ubiquitous phenomena.
The theoretical formulations presented in the essays by the editors
are—as they are careful to point out—only first rough approximations.
When one considers the different orientations of those who have
studied bits and pieces of interpersonal relationships, it is a genuine
tour de force to produce even a tentative theoretical framework
which ties the pieces together. Once this is done, the gaps and inconsistencies in the data become apparent. A careful perusal of these
pages will suggest dozens of significant research studies—studies
which need not stand alone, but which can contribute to the refor-
mulation or the strengthening of this theory.

Any knowledgeable critic could "nit-pick" many details of the
theory as it stands, but the breadth and depth of the formulation
challenges him instead to undertake another task, namely to offer a
better general theory. That challenge makes this an exciting book.

II

Since World War II and the Bomb, it has become increasingly
difficult for the scientist in any field to disclaim responsibility for

the uses to which knowledge is put. My colleagues have faced this issue squarely: ". . . we desire not only greater scientific attention to this field, but we *care* about improving the quality and nature of interpersonal relationships." They place themselves in the functional tradition by defining a good relationship in terms of the achievement of its primary goal, but they do not stop there. Their analysis of the "social conditions" and the "personal competencies" which appear to be essential to the achievement of the primary goals of interpersonal relationships is, for me at least, a noteworthy attempt to lay bare the assumptions and values underlying a given scientific endeavor.

Men everywhere are beginning to look toward the behavioral sciences as a source of help in creating a better world. We who identify ourselves with these sciences do mankind a disservice unless we make transparently clear a fundamental "law" of human behavior: intellectual knowledge and emotional values and needs are inextricably interwoven in all but the most trivial human acts.

Scientific endeavor is not trivial; every step of the process from the initial choice of a "field" through the design of the research to the interpretation of results is profoundly influenced by personal and cultural values. The scientist can and must take precautions to minimize the effects of these subjective factors. Perhaps the most important precaution of all—at the same time the most difficult and the least recognized—is to perceive and understand and make explicit the values underlying his own work. (Fish discover water last!) Part V of this volume provides a model which deserves emulation.

The important point about such a model, by the way, is not whether the reader agrees with it, but whether he is explicit about why and how he disagrees. It is this dialogue—carried on in the public domain—which will ultimately make possible the use of scientific knowledge about human behavior to improve the welfare of all men. If the dialogue is continuous and public, the power yielded by scientific knowledge cannot for long be used by man to exploit his fellows. If it is not, fears like those expressed by Loren Baritz in his *The Servants of Power* will turn out to be well-founded.

The furtherance of this dialogue is a second challenge which makes this an exciting book.

DOUGLAS MCGREGOR

PREFACE TO FIRST EDITION

We can divide the problems Man faces into two classes, the *non-interactional* or man-in-relation-to nature, and the *interactional* or man-in-relation-to man. This latter class involves *human* interactions which make it necessary to take into account the activities, thoughts, and feelings of the other. We have made stunning progress with respect to the noninteractional class of problems, partly because they are "stable" problems. That is, they seem to "sit still" for the engineers or scientists who adapt or create an innovation, instrument, or idea which makes a "scientific breakthrough."

When it comes to the second class of problems, the human problems, we have been notoriously incompetent. One would think, judging from the report of history, that we simply cannot progress; that unlike knowledge about physical phenomena, human knowledge is not cumulative, that parents cannot teach their children nor learn from their own parents. On the very day we are writing this preface, railroads threaten a national strike, war simmers in Vietnam, and racial tensions imperil the schools. Last year's newspapers would have carried almost identical news, with other place-names.

The trouble is that these national and international conflagrations have their counterparts at every level of human intercourse: in small groups, in marriages, in friendships, among lovers and siblings, between teachers and students, between worker and boss. Unless the protagonists are famous, the tensions go unnoticed, to be registered indirectly and anonymously in divorce rates, homicides, and gang wars or often in the more pedestrian way civilized people live with their human problems: poison pen letters, petty jealousies, unproductive relationships, prejudices, practical "jokes," destructive fantasies, unstable careers, ulcerative colitis, "frayed nerves," tranquilizers, and sleeping pills.

As human beings, we harbor moral outrage at these corrosive and destructive events. As social scientists, we consider it almost obligatory to explore and illuminate these problems. The unusual challenge lies in the fact that we do not practice as much as we know, and do not know as much as we could.

We cannot induce better practice through a book, but we can hope to enhance our understanding of those relationships that occur between small numbers of people, usually only two. We believe that this understanding is crucial, not only to improve the nature and quality of interpersonal relationships, but also to make this area more central to the sciences of man. To rephrase Pope, the proper study of man is *man-in-relation-to man.*

Two related forces went into the creation of this book. One is an intellectual and academic concern with the loosely defined field of interpersonal relations. We hope to make it more central to the discipline of social psychology, to fill an important gap that exists between the study of groups and the study of personality. At the very least we think we have succeeded in sharpening up the boundaries of the territory.

Second, we *care* about improving our interpersonal relationships. "Life Is with People," reads the felicitous title of a book, and if our vision of the world is at all accurate we foresee greater and greater reliance on our fellow men, more and more interdependencies, and hence, a more vital need to understand those enormously complex human events we call *interpersonal dynamics.*

We have edited this book with an eye to the teacher and student of interpersonal relationship as well as to the intelligent laymen. In fact, the more of the latter who come into contact with these pages, the better. For we have tried to select articles and to write our original essays in good, clear English which can be understood by an interested reader.

For the scholar and student we can foresee this book's utility in a number of ways. It might be used for courses in personality or interpersonal theory, for courses in social psychology, as a text or ancilliary text. Finally, courses in the broad area of human relations might find it a useful supplementary reading.

Let us say a final word or two in the way of acknowledgements. First, to the Sloan School of Management of M.I.T. both for providing a climate where colleagues can work profitably together, and for the fine administrative support Dean Howard Johnson has provided. Professor D. V. Brown who administered the Ford Foundation Organizational Theory Grant which made this book possible obviously deserves our full gratitude. Mary Beth Ketcham, who acted as secretary, administrator, editorial assistant and all around "Pooh-bah" gets our admiring appreciation. And to those others who helped out in one way or another, who have tried to make working on this book a pleasure rather than a chore, and who have made useful suggestions about its contents, we can scarcely show our full gratitude. These include: Clurie Bennis, Sylvan Bennis, Diane Berlew, Mary Schein, Peter Gil, Matt Miles, and John Thomas.

Cambridge, Mass.   W. G. B.
March, 1964   E. H. S.
                                                          D. E. B.
                                                          F. I. S.

PREFACE TO SECOND EDITION

The second edition of *Interpersonal Dynamics* was motivated by one primary force. We wanted to bring our message to our readers in as *interesting* and *readable* form as possible. Our basic motivations (1) to explore the rough terrain of interpersonal relations, and (2) hopefully to help improve such relations, have not changed. If anything, the reception which our volume received reassured us that there was indeed a terrain worth exploring and caring about.

We did find, however, that many of the articles included in the original edition were too abstract, dense, turgid, or confusing, however theoretically accurate they might have been. We also found, as authors, that we wanted to be stimulating *and clear*. We therefore dropped many pieces if our feedback from students and our own re-reading of them told us they fell short on clarity and readability.

In the meantime, we found many new pieces scattered in the literature which seemed to say what we wanted to say even better than some of our original selections. These have formed the bulk of the new material in the book. We have added some 18 new articles, have dropped 17 articles, and have retained 26 articles.

Our basic theoretical framework has held up reasonably well, hence we have not reorganized the sections of the book. We have edited and, in part, rewritten our introductory essays to take advantage of feedback we received from our readers and students.

A final word is in order about our "author team." The present revision had, unfortunately, to be done without the active collaboration of our colleague, David Berlew. He was serving as Chief of the Peace Corps Mission in Ethiopia at the time. We missed his contribution and look forward to joining forces with him once again on what we hope will eventually be an even better Third Edition.

Once again we wish to thank our wives, colleagues, and secretaries for their help in making this revision an actuality.

May, 1968

W. G. B.
E. H. S.
F. I. S.

TABLE OF CONTENTS

Introduction   1

PART I. **Emotional Expressions in Interpersonal Relationships** . . .   **13**

The Heterosexual Affectional System in Monkeys, *Harry F. Harlow*   43

Resolving Social Conflicts, *K. Lewin*   60

The Self-Restraint of Friends, *John E. Mayer*   65

Behavioral Study of Obedience, *Stanley Milgram*   70

Some Thoughts on Ethics of Research: after Reading Milgram's "Behavioral Study of Obedience," *Diana Baumrind*   84

The Emotionally Disturbed Child as the Family Scapegoat, *Ezra F. Vogel and Norman W. Bell*   90

Some Parallels between Sexual and Dominance Behavior of Infra-Human Primates and the Fantasies of Patients in Psychotherapy, *A. H. Maslow, H. Rand, and S. Newman*   105

Loneliness, *Frieda Fromm-Reichmann*   121

Some Social Consequences of Temporary Systems, *Philip E. Slater*   139

Materials for a Theory of Social Relationships, *Robert S. Weiss*   154

The Illusionless Man and the Visionary Maid, *Allen D. Wheelis*   163

Quasi-Courtship Behavior in Psychotherapy, *Albert E. Scheflen*   182

The Language of Emotions and Gestures, *Weston La Barre*   197

PART II. **Some Interpersonal Aspects of Self-Confirmation** **207**

On Face-Work: An Analysis of Ritual Elements in Social Interaction, *Erving Goffman*   226

The Impostor: Contribution to Ego Psychology of a Type of Psychopath, *Helene Deutsch*   249

Shooting an Elephant, *George Orwell*   267

The Uses of Fraternity, *Kenneth D. Benne*   274

The Characteristics of a Helping Relationship, *Carl R. Rogers*   287

Affiliation Motivation, Anxiety Reduction, and Self-Evaluation, *Stanley Schachter*   304

Prophecy Fails Again: A Report of a Failure to Replicate, *Jane Allyn Hardyck and Marcia Braden*   321

PART III.   Personal Change through Interpersonal Relationships ...   333

Regularized Status-Passage, *Anselm Strauss*   370
On Cooling the Mark Out: Some Aspects of Adaptation to
    Failure, *Erving Goffman*   377
Psychic Self-Abandon and Extortion of Confessions, *James
    Clark Moloney*   391
Brainwashing, *Edgar H. Schein*   406
The Special Role of Guilt in Coercive Persuasion, *E. H.
    Schein, I. Schneier, and C. H. Barker*   426
How to Change Behavior, *Timothy Leary*   440
A Narrative, *Dennis H. Lytle*   454
The Scarlet Moving Van, *John Cheever*   461
Romance at Droitgate Spa, *P. G. Wodehouse*   472
The Teacher as a Model, *Joseph Adelson*   491

PART IV.   The Instrumental Relationship   505

Social Behavior as Exchange, *George C. Homans*   523
"Banana Time"—Job Satisfaction and Informal Interaction,
    Donald F. Roy   539
The Cabdriver and His Fare: Facets of a Fleeting Relation-
    ship, *Fred Davis*   556
Psychology and the Crisis of Statesmanship, *Robert R. Blake*   568
Interpersonal Competence and Organizational Effectiveness,
    Chris Argyris   583
Businessmanship, *S. Potter*   597
Defensive Communication, *Jack R. Gibb*   606
Careers in a Deviant Occupational Group: the Dance Mu-
    sician, *Howard S. Becker*   613
The Duke's Alter Ego, *John S. Wilson*   625
The Influence of Criticalness on Creative Problem Solving
    in Dyads, *Morris B. Parloff and Joseph H. Handlon*   628

PART V.   Towards Better Interpersonal Relationships   647

Sense of Interpersonal Competence: Two Case Studies and
    Some Reflections on Origins, *Robert W. White*   674
Goals and Meta-Goals of Laboratory Training, *Warren G.
    Bennis*   680
Graduate Education in Psychology: A Passionate Statement,
    Carl R. Rogers   687
This Is Me, *Carl R. Rogers*   703
The Jonah Complex, *Abraham H. Maslow*   714
Healthy Personality and Self-Disclosure, *Sidney M. Jourard*   720
Analysis and Typology of Personality Misinterpretations,
    G. Ichheiser   731
The Nature of Competence Acquisition Activities and Their
    Relationship to Therapy, *Chris Argyris*   749

INTRODUCTION

*Well, what are you? What is it about you that you have always known as yourself? What are you conscious of in yourself: your kidneys, your liver, your blood vessels? No. However far back you go in your memory it is always some external manifestation of yourself where you come across your identity: in the work of your hands, in your family, in other people. And now, listen carefully. You in others—this is what you are, this is what your consciousness has breathed, and lived on, and enjoyed throughout your life, your soul, your immortality—*YOUR LIFE IN OTHERS.

—BORIS PASTERNAK, *Dr. Zhivago*

This is our hope: to deepen and broaden the understanding of "our life in others." We think it is of crucial importance, not only for its scientific yield, but for its potential to man's welfare. How we have attempted to realize our aim through this book is the purpose of this introductory essay.

PURPOSES OF THIS BOOK

Our main goal is to sketch out the conceptual territory and boundaries of the field of interpersonal relations more clearly, coherently, and integratively than has been done before. Our aim is to suggest a "focus of convenience" for the field.

If we are at least partly successful, then we believe that the study of interpersonal dynamics can play a major role in the behavioral sciences, rather than its present peripheral one. In other words, we hope that this volume will fill the gap which we see existing between the Cartwright and Zander[1] book of readings, *Group Dynamics*, and the Maccoby[2] et al., *Readings in Social Psychology*. We want to move the scientific study of interpersonal relations from the periphery to the center of social psychology, making it a truly *social* psychology.

Our second aim is pragmatic. This means that we desire not only

---

[1] D. Cartwright and A. Zander (eds.), *Group Dynamics: Research and Theory* (2nd ed.; Evanston, Ill.: Row, Peterson & Co., 1960).

[2] E. E. Maccoby, T. M. Newcomb, and E. L. Hartley (eds.), *Readings in Social Psychology* (3d ed.; New York: Henry Holt & Co., 1958).

greater scientific attention, but we *care* about improving the quality and nature of interpersonal relationships. Undoubtedly, it is our passionate concern for *improvement* that fuels our intellectual energies. This passion is based upon more than the moral and ideological premises presented in Part V of this volume. It is also founded on the conviction that the quality of our interpersonal relations can affect not only important arenas of social conflict (such as racial and religious tensions, international conflicts, social disorganization, etc.) but also the quality of our productive and creative efforts.

Before going on to explain the organization of this book, let us take a detailed look at the academic status of the field of interpersonal dynamics.

THE CURRENT STATE OF THE FIELD
AND OUR APPROACH TO IT

It might be useful to begin with a few words about the current academic state of interpersonal dynamics—as a field. As we do this we will be irresistibly drawn to our own views and biases. So what follows is the combination of description and viewpoint which determines our approach and orientation to the field of interpersonal dynamics.

It is a strange field: loosely organized, interdisciplinary and interstitial, i.e., tangent to or on the frontier of the behavioral sciences; it is a field without fixed boundaries or stable definitions. An analogy may help to bring it into better focus. We can compare it to a "foreign" territory, claimed by all because of its strategic importance, explored by only a few adventurers, and understood fully by none. It is not a "no-man's" land, however. It is everyman's land. And this means that long before the social scientist invaded this domain, the poets, troubadors, essayists, lyricists, and novelists were tilling its rich soil. In fact, the "humanists" have long claimed this territory for their own and have looked askance at the social scientist, referring to him as a poacher or *arriviste,* as a Point IV technocrat or as a dilettante, depending upon their mood and style.

The social scientist who does forage around in these uncharted lands not only receives abuse at the hands of the humanists, but also from his colleagues. Quite often, they will attack him harshly for losing his "scientific" bent; others, more subtly, say that he is "too dense" or that he creates a private language, bordering on neologisms. Even if his work is recognized, he is considered, at best, a soldier of fortune who should return to the fold, at worst, a fugitive.

Our analogy helps to bring into focus a number of points we can make about the current status of research and theory in the field of interpersonal dynamics:

1. There is as yet no single, comprehensive theory of interpersonal relations. Sociology, social psychology, and psychiatry have offered important insights to the understanding of its phenomena, but the area has resisted successful theoretical comprehension. "What single general proposition about human behavior have we established?" asked George Homans in 1950. His answer, alas, holds too much truth today: "And we shall find ourselves waiting for an answer."[3]

2. Because it is a new field as far as the social sciences are concerned and because of its complexity and subtlety, it tends to be treated in a discursive, exploratory, essayistic way, rather than a terse, positivistic, experimental way.

3. The third thing we can say about the field, implied in our analogy, is that despite its relevance to the behavioral sciences, it has been treated only tangentially in those fields. In social psychology, for example, we would expect it to play a fundamental role. This does not seem to be the case,[4] Social psychologists have been more interested in the group or in the individual than in interpersonal relationships. The field of psychiatry also has not yielded the expected results with respect to interpersonal theory. It has been dominated by a neuro-biophysiological philosophy of man, a reliance on the instincts and a silence regarding man's interactional behavior.[5] Anthropology and sociology fare no better, though a branch of sociology, known as the "symbolic interaction" school, has made crucial contributions to interpersonal theory. More about that later on. In summary, *the scientific study of interpersonal relations lags woefully behind the other areas of social research.*

4. Fourth, we can say that where disciplines *have* contributed to the understanding of interpersonal relations, where they have enriched its theoretical or research base, they have been "marginal" or *avant garde* groups or perhaps some sturdy iconoclasts. This is

[3]G. Homans, *The Human Group* (New York: Harcourt, Brace, Inc., 1950), p. 115.
[4]F. Heider, *The Psychology of Interpersonal Relations* (New York: John Wiley & Sons, Inc., 1958), p. 3.
[5]H. Guntrip, *Personality Structure and Human Interaction* (New York: International Universities Press, 1961), p. 17.

rather a blunt statement, one which undoubtedly requires qualification. Nevertheless, as we examined the main theoretical influences
that shaped our own interests and when we thought to detect
the theoretical origins of the papers selected for this volume it
appeared to be true. But what about the lineage of the articles
selected?

5. In the earlier edition of this volume, we relied on four major
theoretical strands which, we wrote, "shaped our thinking, which
have dominated this book, and which appear to provide the basic
structure of the field of interpersonal relations." We summarized
these influences as (1) symbolic interactionism, (2) interpersonal
theory, (3) object relations, and (4) existentialism. The readings in
this edition continue to reflect these influences but are augmented
by still another, that of an *ecological,* character. Let us review
briefly these five theoretical themes:

a) From sociology, the branch referred to earlier as *symbolic
interactionism* has been crucial. The main premise of this school is
that the data of interpersonal relations are symbols and these symbols constitute social reality. It is the language of drama, and hence
the key concept for this approach is "social role." Cooley and Mead
in the United States and Durkheim in Europe have been central in
its development; in psychology, Baldwin, James, and Dewey have
contributed to its heritage.

b) From psychiatry, we have been heavily influenced by the so-
called "Washington School," the *Interpersonal Theory* of Harry
Stack Sullivan and his associates. This branch of psychiatry has a
good deal in common with the symbolic interactionists, for both
view the processes of social communication as pivotal to their
theories.

c) In addition to the Sullivanian influence, but less visible in
this volume because of space limitations, is some of the work coming out of the English neo-Freudian school. Melanie Klein and
W. R. D. Fairbairn have impressed us with their *object relations*
point of view. Their influence can be felt only indirectly in this volume through the work of the English group theorist, W. R. Bion,
whose theories are based on some of Melanie Klein's formulations.
We have relied heavily on Bion in Part I, "Emotional Expressions in
Interpersonal Relationships." The important thing to say about the
"object relations" school is that it is an ego-psychology, i.e., it specifies an ego in relationship to its outside world, where impulses are

seen as reactions of the ego to its relevant objects, and where the inner and outer worlds are seen as reciprocal in influence.[6]

d) Finally, those students of human behavior who cannot be grouped under any simple conceptual umbrella—except perhaps *existentialism*—but who are concerned with the *self* and its actualization have to be mentioned. We have in mind the work of men such as Carl Rogers, whose influence should be obvious from a quick glance at our Table of Contents; or the writings of Maslow, Jourard, and Wheelis, who share a tremendous concern with improving the quality of relationships.

e) One interesting and new development in interpersonal dynamics has been added to this edition, practically unnoticed until after we had pruned down our selections to manageable size. There was only a hint of it making an appearance in the first edition, the highly popular article by Harry Harlow on monkeys. In this edition, we have included a new paper by Slater and a whole new section on the "communication of feeling." For the most part, these new selections can be grouped under an *ecological framework* of human interaction; that is, they tend to see man's interpersonal behavior governed by the constraints of spatial, and in fewer cases (but Slater's is a fine example), by temporal factors. For convenience, we are referring to this influence as an ecological orientation.[7]

These five sources—symbolic interactionism, Sullivanian theory, object-relations theory, existential psychology, and ecology—have fashioned the intellectual structure of this volume.[8] These choices, it should be remembered, were founded on their parent disciplines: social psychology and psychoanalytic theory. And when these five branches fuse with their parent streams, then we should have a viable scientific approach to interpersonal relations. The prospects are bright but realization perhaps not too close.

6. What are the reasons why progress has been less rapid than

---

[6]The interested reader should turn to the essay introducing Part I for a more complete statement; for a more detailed exposition of the object-relations theory, see *ibid.*

[7]E. T. Hall's recent book, *The Hidden Dimension* (New York: Doubleday, 1966), is a brilliant example of this approach and we wish long sections of this book could be reproduced here, but our own publishing ecology (limited number of pages) was a major constraint upon our desires.

[8]Attributing theoretical influences is a risky business at best. The minute one ponders about the unconscious elements then it becomes even more hazardous. And when one considers that there are *four* editors, the task becomes downright awkward. Obviously, our interests have been shaped by more than these five subfields; our backgrounds, training, and personalities must certainly be considered. These influences, however, cannot be so easily categorized and must remain silent but powerful.

one might expect in building a coherent skein of interpersonal theory? The reasons, we hazard, spring essentially from one source: the nominalistic bias of most behavioral sciences which tends to focus exclusively on convenient boundary systems such as "the skin" or "the group." This bias tends to ignore the reality of the relationship in favor of its parts. In so doing, it preserves the individual-group dichotomy of popular culture, a duality which gets the student into as much trouble as it gets him out of. A fashionable horror of "organic theories of society" coupled with the very important need of all of us to conceive of ourselves as individuals makes the individual-group dichotomy a tenacious one. Allport's remarks on personality theory bear this out:

> Virtually all the theories I have mentioned up to now conceive of personality as something integumented, as residing within the skin. There are theorists (Kurt Lewin, Martin Buber, Gardner Murphy and others) who challenge this view, considering it too closed. Murphy says that we overstress the separation of man from the context of his living. Hebb has interpreted experiments on sensory deprivation as demonstrations of the constant dependence of inner stability on the flow of environmental stimulation. Why Western thought makes such a razor-sharp distinction between the person and all else is an interesting problem. Probably the personalistic emphasis in Judeo-Christian religion is an initial factor; and as Murphy has pointed out, the industrial and commercial revolutions further accentuated the role of individuality. Buddhist philosophy, by contrast, regards the individual, society, and nature as forming the tripod of human existence. The individual as such does not stick out like a raw digit. He blends with nature, and he blends with society. *It is only the merger that can be profitably studied.*[9]

But studying the merger—the relationship—has lagged behind because of our reliance on visible and operable, and not altogether profitable, boundary systems: the individual and the group.

This lag strikes us especially when we consider the language of interpersonal relationships,[10] or rather the lack of a precise and relevant language. The problem is only partly due to the complexity of the field, although when we read Sullivan's tortuous observations of A and A' communicating to B and B' within the purview of C and C' all interacting, distorting, and attending to multifarious cues generated by a concatenation of different A's, B's, and C's, we tend to think that the complexity of interpersonal relation-

[9]G. Allport, "The Open System in Personality Theory," *Personality and Social Encounter* (Boston: Beacon Press, 1960), p. 47. Italics added.
[10]There is a discussion of the languages of interpersonal feelings in the essay introducing Part I. Here it is pointed out that two languages compete in the social sciences: the language of the *game* and the language of the *myth*. The former, according to Back is precise and formal; the latter is rich, meaningful, but ambiguous (K. W. Back, "The Game and the Myth," *Behavioral Science*, 8 [1963], pp. 66–71).

ships creates insurmountable barriers to the construction of a valid language.

The real problem has to do with the ubiquitous monadic myth of the individual. As Murray points out:

> Synthesism—or dyadic synthesism—first of all, calls for the elevation of the hardly utterable, shared values of participation in the creation and development of better forms and qualities of relationship (continuity of union, of mutual affection and respect, amid diversity of patterns of interaction) from a subordinate to a superordinate position, that is to say, the experience and fruits of affectional reciprocations, interpersonal and international, would be more highly prized than personal and national superiority and aggrandizement. To appreciate the emotional revolution involved in this transposition of values, we have only to remind ourselves that all formerly venerated models of excellence or greatness have been glorifications of a single person, a single group or nation, a single theory of religion.[11]

In any case, the individual takes priority, and we find ourselves without shared referential tools for identifying and depicting an important dimension of life: unities, ensembles, and combinations of people in interaction.[12] Certainly a married couple must *present* a "social unit" as much as a person *presents* a "self"; certainly, there must be creative *relationships* as well as creative individuals; certainly there must be *relationships* that are as permeable or closed, protean or placid, flexible or rigid, healthy or sick, as individuals. One is no more real or mystical than the other; both generate and receive human responses.

But our language as yet does not embrace these phenomena; and it will not—until the *merger* Allport talks about or the *synthesism* Murray suggests infiltrate the central domains of the behavioral sciences, rather than its interstitial crevices.

Let us summarize our orientation to the field of interpersonal relations. It is a new field, interdisciplinary and interstitial, but it is new only in the sense that it has stubbornly resisted rigorous scientific examination. There is, as yet, no single, comprehensive con-

---

[11]H. A. Murray, "Unprecedented Evolutions," *Daedalus,* 90 (1961), pp. 552–63.

[12]One exception to this is the crude and still inchoate attempt by Shepard and Bennis ("A Theory of Training by Group Methods," *Human Relations,* 9 [1956], pp. 403–14) to work out a language of interpersonal relationships. But their language, too, lacks an elegance and complexity still required. "Role" is a useful term; but aside from its omnibus and ambiguous meanings, it is thought of as certain properties residing in an *incumbent,* rather than the cluster of expectational bonds exerted upon the role incumbent. The language of *sociometry* comes fairly close, as do the philosophical speculations of Buber and the Interaction Process Analysis of Bales. Still, the "I-Thou" concept and the "who-to-whom" matrix implies two units, not one. We still hold out for the merger!

ceptual umbrella for the field. The five subfields of behavioral science disciplines from which we have drawn the most in this volume are: the symbolic interaction school of sociology, the interpersonal theories of Harry Stack Sullivan, the neo-Freudian object-relations school of psychiatry, the ecologists, and the existential psychologists and psychiatrists. None of these groups in themselves can be tightly compartmentalized or defined, but their slants or emphases show up in our own work. Finally, the main block toward developing a scientifically viable language of interpersonal relationships is partly due to the bias of Western thought that tends to focus on the individual or group. This book, *Interpersonal Dynamics*, takes the connection between the individual personality and the group—interpersonal relationships—as its pivotal concern.

ORGANIZATION OF THIS BOOK

This book consists of five parts. Each of the first four parts is oriented toward a basic aim—the *raison d'être*—of a relationship. We asked ourselves the question: why do people come together? Why do people engage in and involve others in interpersonal relationships? This question was based on the thought that *all* interpersonal relationships are oriented toward some *primary goal*, some goal or function whose presence is necessary for the relationship to exist and whose absence would seriously undermine it. Obviously, a relationship exists for more than one purpose, but there is usually a salient reason for its formation.[13] The first four parts are organized around these primary goals.

Part I is entitled "Emotional Expressions in Interpersonal Relationships." It deals with the relationship that is formed for the purpose of fulfilling *itself*, such as love, marriage, or friendship. The main transaction in the relationship is "feelings." It deals with the expressive-emotional aspects of interaction, with love, hate, ambivalence, and alienation.

Part II is entitled "Some Interpersonal Aspects of Self-Confirmation." This part encompasses those relationships that are formed for establishing social realities of two types. One type exists to aid in personal development, such as attaining personal identity; the other type exists in order to comprehend external realities. In one case, evidence is required to define the person and the relationship;

---

[13]See the essay introducing Part V for a fuller discussion and rationale for this framework.

in the other, the relationship is used to adduce evidence concerning some external matter. "Who am I?" or "Who are we?" is the subject matter for the first type. "What is that?" or "How do we feel about that?" is the subject matter for the other. In either case, the basis for the relationship is *confirmation.*

Part III is entitled "Personal Change through Interpersonal Relationships." It deals with relationships that are formed for the purpose of *change* or *influence,* that is, relationships where one or both parties come together to create a change in each other or the relationship. The change may entail anything from acquiring new behaviors to personal growth; the change may be planned and institutionalized or spontaneous. This is a broad topic, encompassing many theoretical positions and many types of change. It covers, for example, such diverse matters as psychotherapy and "brainwashing," seduction and persuasion, indoctrination and socialization. The antecedents and consequences of interpersonal change and the processes which guide them are all topics treated in Part III.

Part IV is entitled "The Instrumental Relationship." It covers those relationships that are formed in order to produce or create some goal or task, outside of the relationship itself. A conductor and his violin section, a foreman and his workers, two collaborators on a research project. these are all examples of an instrumental relationship. How the nature and quality of the interpersonal relationship affect and relate to the task is the central concern of Part IV.

To express feelings, to establish social realities—to confirm, to change and influence, and to work and create: these are the main reasons for interpersonal relationships. These four primary tasks, then, make up the content and the organizing feature for the first four parts of this volume.

We have added a fifth part: "Towards Better Interpersonal Relationships." In this part we have tried to make explicit the values, ideals, and ethics of our choices throughout the volume. In addition we have attempted two other things. We propose, or rather *envisage,* an ideal interpersonal relationship based on some normative criteria. Given that ideal, we have suggested certain social and personal conditions and capacities necessary to realize that ideal state. In short, Part V is concerned with a vision of ideal human relations and the most effective ways to reach that state.

We have tried to show our practical concern in two ways. First, Part V deals exclusively with *improving* interpersonal relationships. In this section we have focused attention on the strategic variables that affect the quality and nature of interpersonal relationships. Secondly, we have attempted to include first-rate theoretical and research papers that employ clear English. We hope that these readings, through their analytic framework, can point the way toward more intelligent actions. This belief is based on Kurt Lewin's famous *dictum:* "There is nothing so practical as a good theory."

But action does not flow ineluctably from diagnosis. As Aristotle said over two thousand years ago: "In practical matters the end is not mere speculative knowledge of what is to be done, but rather the doing of it. It is not enough to know about Virtue, then, but we must endeavor to possess it, and to use it, or to take any other steps that may make us good."[14]

The knowledge available in this book may indeed sound like "eternal verities," too abstract, too remote from an experiential basis for either emotional resonance or guides to action. In any case, the practical steps that "make us good," to use Aristotle's words, are ultimately up to the reader and to us. We can only suggest some possible alternatives.

ESSAYS AND READINGS

It might be useful now to say a word or two about the format of the five parts. The parts are practically identical in arrangement in that each contains an introductory essay and a set of readings culled from the literature. In most cases the essays attempt to provide an overview of the particular subject matter as well as to introduce the readings that follow. In writing the essays we took some liberties which we hope will add to the book's value. We attempted to sketch out some personal ideas or to attempt a new theoretical wrinkle, a luxury not often permitted by our superegos or the ordinary journal article. Each of us was responsible for a part, though we attempted to influence and help each other without losing, we hope, the distinctive individual competencies our training and background allows. Bennis was responsible for Parts I and V as well as this Introduction; Schein is responsible for Parts II and III,[15] and Steele, Part IV.

The readings represent, to our knowledge, some of the best writings in the area of interpersonal relations. They are a varied lot, going all the way from studies of rhesus monkeys to cab drivers, from fraternity houses to apocalyptic groups. The theories, research

---

[14]Aristotle, *Aristotle's Psychology,* trans. W. A. Hammond (1902).
[15]David Berlew's introductory essay remains intact.

strategics, orientations, and scope are equally varied. We have included papers by one of our students and by the president of the American Psychological Association; we have included fiction and short empirical studies; we have included papers by sociologists, psychologists, and psychiatrists of all stripes and persuasions. What they all have in common, what we strived to realize as our main criteria, was relevance, penetration, and clarification.

We did employ other criteria, however. We tried to ferret out the ignored classic; surely, this must be a dream of every anthologist. At the same time, we had to decide against the overpopular classic. We have had, too often, to sacrifice "precision" for "grasp"; and, given the state of this field, the reader will find the articles written more in the style of the essayist than the experimentalist, more in the language of the "myth" than the "game" to use Back's distinction.[16] We do have a number of rigorous, experimental studies included, to be sure. But the study that combines grasp and precision is rare, and therefore the majority of the selected readings are thoughtful, comprehensive, and essayistic. We are still working, to use Reichenbach's apt phrase, within the "context of discovery" rather than the "context of verification."

These are our criteria. Undoubtedly they were founded as well on some dubious notions about the vibrance, energy, imagination, and creativity the authors bring to their work.

We have barely scratched the surface of this "strange territory" we call interpersonal dynamics. Just as one swallow does not make a summer, one book of essays and readings does not make a "field," or even the frontier of one.

To some extent, though, we hope we have succeeded in inching forward in our pursuit of the boundaries, strategic variables, and substance of *interpersonal dynamics*. Finally, we hope we have succeeded in illuminating and creating better understanding of *your life in others*.

---

[16]Back, *op. cit.*

PART I

Emotional Expressions in
Interpersonal Relationships

*. . . I wish to show here an inward picture which does not become per-
ceptible until I see it through the external. This external is perhaps quite unobtrusive but not until I look through it, do I discover that inner picture which
I desire to show you, an inner picture too delicately drawn to be outwardly
visible, woven as it is of the tenderest moods of the soul.*

—SOREN KIERKEGAARD, *Either/Or*

This essay and the following readings in this section represent
our attempt to search out the basic emotional transactions between
people: the emotions that exist for no visible instrumental end. We
wish to reckon with, following Kierkegaard, the "tenderest moods
of the soul"; so we will be speaking of feelings that bind and
estrange, feelings that contort into angry knots of discord and those
that grow into natural affection, feelings that flow directly into
action and those that are transformed and disguised into devious
paths, feelings that overwhelm and inspire and those that depress
and disgust. This section, then, holds up an imperfect mirror to
phenomena that can be only indirectly observed and crudely measured—the raw, almost incomprehensible experiences, at the edge of
verbal awareness, we call *interpersonal feelings*.

There are four sections to this essay. Section I, which follows
immediately, discusses the perspective we bring to and the problems
we see in the study of the emotional expressions in interpersonal
dynamics. Section II samples a number of schemes and frameworks

13

for ascertaining the existence and strength of interpersonal feelings. Sections III and IV represent the core material of this essay. In Section III, we present our own typology of the emotional modalities expressed in interpersonal relationships; Section IV, in addition to introducing the readings of this part, examines three basic interpersonal expressions of feelings: "going towards" (love), "going against" (hate), and "going away" (alienation and withdrawal).

I. SOME PRELIMINARY CONSIDERATIONS

1. Scope and Definition of Interpersonal Feelings

We regard an interpersonal relationship as an irreducible element of reality. Just as we cannot have a line without the presence of two dots, we cannot have an expression of an interpersonal feeling without the existence of two people. We hope to avoid the "myth of isolation" and to stress the "connectedness" of human encounters.

Secondly we will focus only on those interactional dimensions which contain an emotional base; that is, the interdependencies and transactions that involve the expression of feelings by the participants. Thus, *this essay and the subsequent readings will be concerned with that class of human interactions where feelings are basic and pivotal in the interpersonal exchange.*

Thirdly, we regard interpersonal feelings—the emotional or affective transactions—as the basic, raw data of interpersonal relationships. We do not need to argue about whether they can be reduced to more genotypic categories, such as instincts or impulses; nor do we need or desire to assert that certain feelings are "better" or "deeper," are derivatives or causes of each other. Questions about the causal couplings of interpersonal feelings, of whether one is the obverse or precipitate of another or whether they are instinctive, acquired, or learned, need not concern us here. For our part, love is as *basic* as hate and as *real* as loneliness. What we do assert is that the expression of interpersonal feelings is basic to the existence of the relationship, that interpersonal feelings can be ascertained and measured, that they are causal elements in how people will behave, that they have real effects, and that they can be studied without recourse to a physiological or instinctual theory.[1]

These emphases—the irreducibility of the relationship, the pri-

---

[1]This is a far more complicated problem than we make it out to be. We cannot, however, be more than arbitrary at this juncture. Our oversimplified assumptions will permit us to deal with more complex issues later on.

macy of feelings and their "reality"—characterize this essay. One further thought should be added before going on. Arthur Lovejoy, the historian of ideas, coined the term "metaphysical pathos" to describe the subtle and imperceptible, even unconscious, attitudes that guide one's theoretical predilections. Nowhere is this temperamental disposition so visible as it is in the study of personality and interpersonal relations. There is only a very thin line between what one is and what one wants, between descriptive realities and normative desires. It is not only true, for example, that Hobbes and Freud developed different theories than G. Allport or Carl Rogers; they also brought to their theories a completely different world view. Our metaphysical pathos, too, tinctures this essay as well as the rest of the volume. Wherever we can, we try to make it explicit; indeed, Part V is devoted solely to some normative issues surrounding interpersonal dynamics. Our hope here is to penetrate "reality" wherever it leads us.

2. The Present State of Theory

There is as yet no single, comprehensive theory of interpersonal relations. Sociology, social psychology, and psychiatry have offered important insights to the understanding of interpersonal phenomena, but the area escapes superarrogation by one discipline.[2]

As we shall see later on in this essay, when we review the main theoretical influences feeding into the study of interpersonal feelings, we have had to draw on a wide range of disciplines and concepts. The plethora of terms used to describe interpersonal feelings testifies to the range of theories and disciplines. We find ourselves using terms such as: assumptions, needs, interpersonal response traits, orientation, impulses, and feelings. They are all used to circumscribe the class of behavioral events we are calling "interpersonal feeling."

In this section of readings, dealing with human interaction with an *affective* base, we have found the work of Harry Stack Sullivan (the so-called "Washington School of Psychiatry") and other neo-Freudian theory particularly helpful. On the other hand, in other parts of our volume, particularly Parts III and IV where we cover topics such as creativity, work, and change, the theories of the "symbolic-interactionists" (represented by the writings of Becker, Strauss, Goffman) seem more appropriate.

---

[2] See the introductory essay for a more detailed statement on the "state of theory."

3. The Languages of Interpersonal Theory, Scientific and Humanistic

It might be useful at this point to say a few words about the problem of discussing interpersonal feelings in a quasi-scientific way. This presents something of a dilemma, for interpersonal feelings have to do with man's private experiences; his visceral reactions, experiences of pain and pleasure, delight or disgust, love, fear, boredom, are all intensely private and only partially communicable. These matters have long been considered to be the domain of the humanities. Science, on the other hand, may be thought of as a device for investigating, ordering and communicating the more public of human experiences such as sense experiences and the intellectual experiences of logical thought.[3] Loosely speaking, then, the cultural elite, the humanists, have constructed a language which roughly expresses the existential situation of the individual in his world while the scientist creates a precise language which deals with objects which are independent of human beings.

Any language, though, is a process of symbolization. This is as true for poetry as it is for mathematics. What makes matters more difficult for the language of feelings is the fact that they are reflexive by nature; that is, the object of analysis, the person, does his *own* abstraction and symbolization. (The physical sciences can avoid this difficulty as they avoid the study of people.) Because of this "reflexive dilemma," the language of interpersonal feelings has stubbornly defined logical analysis or even adequate description.

Today in the social sciences, two languages compete for primacy: the language of the "game" and the language of the "myth."[4] Game languages follow the model of the physical sciences by defining all terms operationally and in formal terms. ". . . Analysis of social interaction is made in terms of moves and countermoves . . . . In all these fields the trend toward miniature systems is indicative of the model of a tight situation, rigidly defined, where individuals can be assumed to conform to a set of rules which can be completely specified."[5]

The language of the game seems most appropriate for the class of problems we referred to earlier as interactional problems devoid

---

[3] A. Huxley, "The Only Way to Write a Modern Poem about a Nightingale," *Harper's Magazine*, Vol. 227, No. 1359 (1963), pp. 62–66.

[4] K. W. Back, "The Game and the Myth," *Behavioral Science*, Vol. 8 (1963), pp. 66–71.

[5] *Ibid.*, p. 68.

of affect, where the rules are explicit, where formal models can simulate a "tight situation, rigidly defined."

But what of the problems which hold the most interest for us, interactional situations *with* affect? How would the language of the game treat the following passage from a book of fiction?

> Her back seemed mysteriously taut and hard; the body of a strange woman retains more of its mineral content, not being transmuted, through familiarity, into pure emotion. In a sheltered corner of the room we stopped dancing altogether and talked, and what I distinctly remember is how her hands, beneath steady and opaque appraisal of her eyes, in nervous slurred agitation blindly sought mine and seized and softly gripped, with infantile instinct, my thumbs. Just my thumbs she held, and as we talked she moved them this way and that as if she were steering me. When I closed my eyes, the red darkness inside my lids was trembling, and when I rejoined my wife, and held her to dance, she asked, "Why are you panting?"[6]

The language of the game could not easily untangle or encompass the range of interpersonal feelings and interactions described. Yet the excerpt is altogether unextraordinary in good fiction. This type of human experience requires a more complicated and subtle expression than the language of the game.

Back suggests as an alternate language the "language of the myth." It is a language adapted to the human capacity to grasp the complexity and nuance of vital human problems, which game languages might sacrifice to increasing precision.

> The language of the myth becomes the means of expressing those theories of social science which try to encompass an unlimited field of applicability, which appear to contain some truth but seem fated to be subject to unending controversies over interpretation. They frequently revert to the use of accepted mythology to make a point clear. Freud's theories, for example, fit closely the definition of a theory couched in the language of the myth. The concepts which he uses, such as ego, id, superego, have no precise denotable referent. The meaning derives from the experiences of the listener, and it is clear to him that something beyond the simple concepts, which are practically personifications, is meant.[7]

We cannot endorse completely Back's analysis of the two languages of social science. It is somewhat oversimplified and he tends to exaggerate the differences through polarization. At the same time, there is no denying that the language we presently use to denote the expression of interpersonal feelings falls short both of the precision of the game and the beauty of the myth.

With these three preliminary considerations spelled out, we are now in a better position to come closer to the core material of this

---

[6]J. Updike, *Pigeon Feathers* (New York: Crest Books, 1953), p. 176.
[7]Back, *op. cit.*, p. 69.

essay. In the following section, we will sample a wide array of approaches which encompass different aspects of interpersonal feelings.

II. A BRIEF SURVEY OF APPROACHES TO ASCERTAINING INTERPERSONAL FEELINGS

We said earlier that there is no single, comprehensive theory of interpersonal feelings. There are, though, a number of researchers and theoreticians who have attempted to ascertain and conceptualize the properties of interpersonal feelings through a variety of techniques. We think it would be useful at this point to sample a variety of these approaches in order to grasp the main dimensions of the field.

It will be convenient for us to organize this section in terms of the two principle ways of ascertaining interpersonal feelings. In this way we can accomplish two things at once: to acquaint the reader with these methods, but also, more basically, to examine the way theorists have conceptualized the domain of interpersonal feelings.

The two principle ways of ascertaining interpersonal feelings are some form of *self-description* and some *observation* system, whereby an observer scores interpersonal interactions, usually act-by-act.

1. Self-Rating Methods

Our main example of the use of a self-description inventory to identify and measure interpersonal feelings is FIRO, deriving its name from the "*F*undamental *I*nterpersonal *R*elations *O*rientation." The FIRO is a questionnaire developed by W. C. Schutz[8] which consists of a check list of 54 statements designed to measure an individual's propensities along three interpersonal dimensions. These three dimensions were derived partly from a factor analysis done by Schutz[9] and partly from a theoretical disposition favoring the group theories of Bion.[10]

---

[8]W. C. Schutz, *FIRO: A Three-Dimensional Theory of Interpersonal Behavior* (New York: Holt, Rinehart, & Winston, 1958); and "Interpersonal Underworld," *The Planning of Change* W. G. Bennis, K. D. Benne, and R. Chin (eds.) (New York: Holt, Rinehart, & Winston, 1961).

[9]*Op. cit.*, 1958.

[10]W. R. Bion, *Experiences in Groups and Other Papers* (New York: Basic Books, Inc., 1959). The work of D. Stock and H. Thelen, *Emotional Dynamics and Group Culture* (New York: New York University, 1958), is also associated with the FIRO dimensions.

Schutz's work starts from the assumption that each individual has different intensities of needs and different mechanisms for handling them, but that all people have three basic interpersonal needs in common:

The need for *inclusion*. This is the need to maintain a satisfactory relation between the self and other people with respect to interaction or belongingness.

The need for *control*. This is the need to maintain a satisfactory relation between oneself and other people with respect to power and influence.

The need for *affection*. This is the need to maintain a satisfactory relation between the self and other people with regard to love and affection.

Thus, *inclusion* has to do with the degree of commitment, belongingness, and participation an individual requires in human interaction; *control* has to do with the degree of influence and power an individual requires; and *affection* has to do with the degree of closeness, intimacy, an individual desires.

One additional factor has to be mentioned in order to present Schutz's theory in more or less complete form. For each dimension we can imagine that an individual *expresses* a need toward other people and that he *wants* a need fulfilled for him by another person. For example, on the inclusion dimension, we can see how one person may have a strong need to include others, to bring them into his groups easily and quickly. This same person, though, may have a low need to *want* inclusion; that is, he may not care if others include him. Thus, one aspect is what we *do* with relation to other people; this is called *expressed behavior*. The second is what we *want* from other people; this is called *wanted behavior*. Figure 1 shows the extreme types along the three dimensions.

Expressed Behavior			Wanted Behavior	
Extreme High	*Extreme Low*	*Dimension*	*Extreme High*	*Extreme Low*
Oversocial	Undersocial	*Inclusion*	Social-compliant	Countersocial
Autocrat	Abdicrat	*Control*	Submissive	Rebellious
Overpersonal	Underpersonal	*Affection*	Personal-compliant	Counterpersonal

From W. C. Schutz, Interpersonal Underworld, *The Planning of Change*, W. G. Bennis, K. D. Benne, and R. Chin (eds.) (New York: Holt, Rinehart, & Winston, 1961), p. 298.

FIG. 1. EXTREME TYPES ON THE THREE INTERPERSONAL DIMENSIONS.

A second example of the kinds of dimensions of interpersonal feeling which can be ascertained from self-descriptions is shown in

Figure 2. This list, summarized by Krech, Crutchfield, and Ballachey[11] in their recent textbook, presents twelve primary response traits (equivalent to Schutz's needs and what we are calling feel-

---

Role Dispositions

Ascendance (opposite: social timidity). Defends his rights, does not mind being conspicuous; not self-reticent; self-assured; forcefully puts self forward.

Dominance (opposite: submissiveness). Assertive; self-confident; power-oriented; tough, strong-willed; order-giving; directive leader.

Social initiative (opposite: social passivity). Organizes groups; does not stay in background; makes suggestions at meetings; takes over leadership.

Independence (opposite: dependence). Prefers to do own planning, to work things out in own way; does not seek support or advice; emotionally self-sufficient.

Sociometric Dispositions

Accepting of others (opposite: rejecting). Nonjudgmental in attitude toward others, permissive; believing and trustful; overlooks weaknesses and sees best in others.

Socioability (opposite: unsociability). Participates in social affairs; likes to be with people; outgoing.

Friendliness (opposite: unfriendliness). Genial, warm, open and approachable; approaches other persons easily; forms many social relationships.

Sympathetic (opposite: unsympathetic). Concerned with the feelings of others; displays kindly generous behavior; defends underdog.

Expressive Dispositions

Competitiveness (opposite: noncompetitiveness). Sees every relationship as a contest—others are rivals to be defeated; self-aggrandizing; noncooperative.

Aggressiveness (opposite: nonaggressiveness). Attacks others directly or indirectly; shows defiant resentment of authority; quarrelsome; negativistic.

Self-consciousness (opposite: social poise). Embarrassed when entering a room after others are seated; suffers excessively from stage fright; hesitates to volunteer in group discussions; bothered by people watching him at work; feels uncomfortable if different from others.

Exhibitionistic (opposite: self-effacing). Is given to excess and ostentation in behavior and dress; seeks recognition and applause; shows off and behaves queerly to attract attention.

D. Krech, R. S. Crutchfield, and E. I. Ballachey, *Individual in Society* (New York: McGraw-Hill Book Co., Inc., 1962), p. 106.

FIG. 2. SOME PRIMARY INTERPERSONAL RESPONSE TRAITS.

---

ings) derived from self-descriptions. These were classified into three arbitrary categories and purportedly are representative of the salient interpersonal dimensions.

---

[11]D. Krech, R. S. Crutchfield, and E. L. Ballachey, *Individual in Society* (New York: McGraw-Hill Book Co., Inc., 1962).

2. Observation: Act-by-Act Analysis

One deficiency of self-rating forms is the absence of validating data. Individuals frequently do not see themselves accurately and it is obvious that our interpersonal relations contain important areas of ignorance due to inadequate information, systematic distortions, and selective inattentions. Recently, for example, Bennis and Peabody[12] showed that self-ratings on FIRO were not significantly correlated with observers' ratings. It will be profitable to examine this discrepancy between self and observer's ratings in some detail.

Sullivan[13] explores this idea in his analysis of interpersonal communication. It is his contention that we systematically *experience* feelings which we do not admit to ourselves and which would therefore not appear as salient on any self-rating inventory. Feelings such as hostility or aggressiveness, for example, are part of the total person and are occasionally experienced. But to all intents and purposes, as the individual construes it, they are not part of the experienced self; hence, they make up the "not-self" or "denied-self."[14]

Sullivan[15] tells of a hypothetical couple, Mr. and Mrs. A. Mrs. A, according to an observer, makes a derogatory remark to her husband, Mr. A, after which Mr. A becomes quite tired. Mr. A is not aware of being offended; he is only aware of being weary. He becomes more withdrawn and preoccupied with his weariness. Under cover, according to Sullivan, Mr. A retaliates in a dominantly hostile, noncollaborative way: "A and Mrs. A are not collaborating in an exchange of hostility. She has acted against him, perhaps with full awareness of her motivation; but he "suffers weariness" while unwittingly acting against her, in his weariness ceasing to be aware of her relevance in his motivation. . . ."[16]

Mr. A, in fact, experienced, lived through, and underwent the hostile action of his wife; he reacted to it and then suffered what at first glance seemed like an irrelevant state: weariness. But if we

---

[12]W. G. Bennis and D. Peabody, "The Conceptualization of Two Personality Orientations and Sociometric Choice," *The Journal of Social Psychology*, Vol. 57 (1962), pp. 203–15.

[13]H. S. Sullivan, "Psychiatry: Introduction to the Study of Interpersonal Relations," *A Study of Interpersonal Relations, New Contributions to Psychiatry*, P. Mullahy (ed.) (New York: Hermitage Press, 1949), pp. 98–121.

[14]W. G. Bennis, "Interpersonal Communication," *The Planning of Change*, W. G. Bennis, K. D. Benne, and R. Chin (eds.) (New York: Holt, Rinehart & Winston, 1961).

[15]Sullivan, *op. cit.*

[16]Sullivan, *op. cit.*, p. 106.

studied Mr. A more closely we would see that this is not the whole story. Sullivan points out that if we had a slow-motion camera and some rather special equipment we could observe that Mr. A experienced something connected with Mrs. A's remarks. For example, we would be able to detect postural tensions in some parts of his face and increased tensions in various parts of the skeletal structure.

Now if also in our apparatus for augmenting our observational abilities, we had included a device for phonographically recording the speech and adventitious vocal phenomena produced by Mr. A, we would have found interesting data in the field of his peculiarly expressive behavior. There would appear a series of phenomena, beginning, perhaps, with an abrupt subvocal change in the flow of breath. There might appear a rudimentary sort of gasp. A rapid inhalation may be coincident with the shift in postural tension that we observed in the skeletal muscles. There may then have been a respiratory pause. When Mr. A speaks, we find that his voice has changed its characteristics considerably, and we may secure, in the record of his first sentence, phonographic evidence of a continuing shift of vocal apparatus, first towards an "angry voice" and then to one somewhat expressive of a state of weary resignation. In brief, *with refinements of observational technique* applied to the performances of Mr. A as an organism, we find that we can no longer doubt that he experienced, even if he did not perceive, the personal significance of Mrs. A's hostile remark.[17]

This discussion points to a dilemma frequently encountered by students of interpersonal behavior: the discrepancy between self-reports and expressed behavior observed by others. Both methods are obviously "valid"; self-ratings ascertain self-image and observer reports detect how others perceive the self. Carl Rogers and others make a good deal of the discrepancy between self and others' perceptions (see Part II of this volume). Our concern here, however, is not the idea of "congruence"; rather we are concerned with the range and complexity in the expression of interpersonal feelings and the need for behavioral measurements to augment the self-rating method.

A number of reliable systems for observing microscopically the act-by-act interactions between people have been developed. Perhaps the best known of these is the Interaction Process Analysis devised by Bales.[18] Figure 3 shows the system of categories used as well as a key to their meaning. Of the twelve categories, notice that only six of them deal with the social-emotional sphere of human interaction; categories 1–3 and 10–12 deal with positive and negative

---

[17]Sullivan, *op. cit.*, p. 108. Italics added.
[18]R. F. Bales, *Interaction Process Analysis* (Cambridge, Mass.: Addison-Wesley, 1950).

emotional acts respectively. The remaining six categories, 4–9, deal with instrumental problem-solving processes; numbers 4–6 signify initiating acts and 7–9 signify receiving acts. According to Bales,

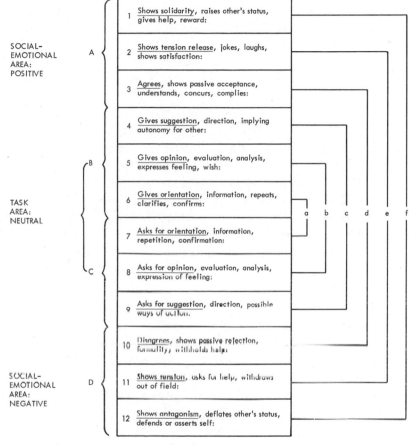

KEY:

A. Positive Reactions
B. Attempted Answers
C. Questions
D. Negative Reactions

a. Problems of Communication
b. Problems of Evaluation
c. Problems of Control
d. Problems of Decision
e. Problems of Tension Reduction
f. Problems of Reintegration

R. F. Bales, *Interaction Process Analysis* (Cambridge, Mass.: Addison-Wesley, 1950).

FIG. 3. INTERACTION PROCESS ANALYSIS.

both instrumental and social-emotional acts are necessary for effective problem solving. Our main interests in this section are the socio-emotional categories.

There are other systems more specifically geared for observing

and recording interpersonal *feelings*. Leary[19] has developed a measurement system of sixteen interpersonal variables based on the
theories of Harry Stack Sullivan. All expressed emotional behavior
can be categorized in terms of two orthogonal dimensions: hostility-
affiliation and dominance-submission. Mills[20] has developed a Sign
Process Analysis based on sign theory and sociological theory which
categorizes *objects* discussed (such as group member, "boss," etc.)
and what *valuation* is expressed toward the object, positive or negative. More recently, Mann[21] has developed an observation scheme
which is designed to assess and record the implications of each act
initiated by a group member for the state of his feelings toward
the leader of the group. Mann's scheme consists of three main areas:
(1) *Impulse Area,* which includes hostility, resisting, withdrawing,
guilt-inducing; making reparation, identifying, accepting, moving
toward; (2) *Authority Relations Area,* which includes showing dependence, independence, counterdependence; and (3) *Ego State
Area,* which includes expressing anxiety, denying anxiety, showing
self-esteem, expressing depression, and denying depression.

It is possible that Mann's interaction scheme, while focusing exclusively on expressed feelings in member-leader relations, may be
applicable to member-member relations. If so, this may be the first
comprehensive system which enables one to describe in molecular
detail emotional responses heretofore inferred. Ego states and impulse areas, most particularly, govern an important segment of interpersonal behavior. It is possible now to record these phenomena as
they are expressed.

Of course, act-by-act observational schemes have their drawbacks,
too. The problem of *inference* is perplexing. How does the observer
gauge the intent of the remark? Does he even try to or does he
look only at the effect of the remark? Does he reckon with the unconscious as well as conscious purpose? How does he score multiple
meanings? How does he deal with displacement? What about such
puzzling phenomena as silences? How unambiguous can a statement be? How does an observer determine what a unit is? Could
it be that adding atomistic and molecular units of behavior will miss
the possibly greater impact of *one* remark? All these are questions

---

[19]T. Leary, "The Theory and Measurement Methodology of Interpersonal Communication, *Psychiatry,* Vol. 18 (1955), pp. 147–61.
[20]T. M. Mills, *Group Transformation: An Analysis of a Training Group* (Englewood
Cliffs, N.J.: Prentice-Hall, 1964).
[21]R. D. Mann, *Interpersonal Styles and Group Development* (New York: John
Wiley and Sons, Co., 1967).

which the act-by-act observation schemes have to cope with in one manner or another.

It was not our intention to delve deeply into the methodological problems nor to describe in microscopic detail the self-description and observation scoring systems for ascertaining interpersonal feelings.[22] Rather our major goal was to present an array of approaches or orientations to the area. The reader has undoubtedly noticed, and may have been bothered by, the proliferation of terms coined to describe what we are calling interpersonal feelings: needs, assumptions, orientations, "who-to-whom" interactions, emotional states, impulses, interpersonal response traits, etc. Although the operational referents may vary, the terms are concerned with the same class of phenomena: emotional expression in interpersonal relationships.

Before going on to Section III of this essay, one final point should be made concerning the kinds of measurement employed to ascertain interpersonal feelings. We have argued that both the self-rating inventories and the observational systems have their advantages and limitations. We would like to demonstrate this more clearly through the use of Sullivan's interpersonal theory.[23]

We can assume, first of all, that people vary with respect to levels of awareness. We saw in the example by Harry Stack Sullivan that Mr. A was simply not aware of a feeling he experienced. But we saw how an observer could have identified the feeling Mr. A was experiencing, leading to the discrepancies between self-rating and observer ratings we commented on earlier. To complicate matters even more, it is possible that Mr. A was *concealing* something from the observer or his wife which neither could detect. After all, patients can "fool" their analysts and we have all learned to dissemble—or simply to conceal aspects of our self to others. So we not only have unconscious distortions, but also conscious *concealing*.

In order to portray this problem more graphically, the reader should turn to Figure 4.[24] Quadrant I is the area of greatest congruence, the sector of behavior where there should be no significant difference between self-rating and observer ratings. Quadrant II is the "blind area," a result of not being able to see things in ourselves which others can detect. This case is similar to the one Sullivan de-

---

[22]The interested reader should consult the original sources to gain more detailed information with respect to these scoring schemes. We merely wanted to display, not demonstrate, these schemes.

[23]Sullivan, *op. cit.*

[24]This analysis and Figure 4 are adapted from the work of J. Luft, "The Johari Window," *Human Relations Training News*, Vol. 5 (1961), pp. 6–7.

scribes, and it is this phenomenon which accounts for the discrepancy between self and other ratings. In Quadrant III is the "concealed" area, that domain of behavior that represents things *we* know but do not reveal to others. Finally, Quadrant IV is the "unknown" area, a deeply buried unconscious area that can be revealed only through depth analysis.

	Known to self	Not known to self
Known to others	I. *High congruence* "Announced self"	II. *Blind area* "Denied self"
Not known to others	III. *Concealed area* "Concealed self"	IV. *Unknown* "Unknown self"

FIG. 4.

What derivations can we make now about the ascertaining of interpersonal feelings? First, an important variable is the *"congruence" or integrity of the individual.* If he is "out of communication" with himself—i.e., Quadrant II—the self-rating inventory will not be a valid indicator of his interpersonal behavior. In fact, there should be a discrepancy between what an observer detects and what the person observes in himself. A second variable is the degree of *trust* or *psychological* safety in the situation. Lack of trust leads to the case of Quadrant III, where the individual knows something he does not reveal. In this case, a self-rating inventory would be more valid than the observer scoring—or, certainly, the scores should be discrepant. Finally, we can say that the validity of the instrument *depends on the interpersonal area to be ascertained.* A deep, unconscious motive may not be visible to the ordinary instruments used. In other words a feeling can be ascertained only if there is some social expression of it.

In conclusion, we can say that a self-rating inventory and observer scores may be equally valid in Quadrant I; observer scores would be superior in Quadrant II; self-ratings would be more valid in Quadrant III[25]; for Quadrant IV, only depth interviews or projective tests could detect these feelings.

---

[25]This, of course, depends on who is going to "see" the self-rating forms. If the person trusts the tester or if the tester is an unknown, but safe, person, then the self-rating inventory may be accurate. More complicated—but more interesting—are the games we play with ourselves, quite apart from Quadrant II where we deny seeing certain things in ourselves or Quadrant III where we conceal things from others. We are referring to that class of "self-dissembling" where we choose certain responses on a personality test, for example, knowing full well it isn't "us" we're describing, but a

III. THREE THEORETICAL APPROACHES TO INTERPERSONAL EMOTIONS

Early in this essay, in our preliminary considerations, we stated that there was no single, comprehensive theory of interpersonal relations. We also noted that our main influences have come from psychoanalytic theory, interpersonal theory, and existential theory. At this point we would like to go beyond this preliminary statement to see if we can order and organize these three streams of influence. Our hope is to identify their basic elements so that the substructure of interpersonal feelings can be more fully understood.

Theory	Source of Conflict	Source of Anxiety	Goal
Instinct theory........	Man/Nature	Lack of impulse control	Adaptation, pleasure
Interpersonal theory........	Man/Man	Lack of consensual validation	Valid communication
Existential theory........	Man/Self	Lack of meaning and/or integrity	Identity

FIG. 5. THREE APPROACHES TO INTERPERSONAL FEELINGS

We have found it convenient to divide the theoretical structure of interpersonal feelings into three branches: *instinct theory* or psychoanalytic theories associated with Freud; *interpersonal theory* or the theories associated with Harry Stack Sullivan and some neo-Freudians; and *existentialist theory* associated with May *et al.*[26] As shown in Figure 5 we can organize these theories around three features: source of conflict, source of anxiety, and goal.

1. Source of Conflict

All the above approaches imply that emotional states are aroused in order to cope with a *conflict* situation. In the case of *instinct theory,* the conflict is between man and his basic biological nature, the physical aspects of the organism. As tempting as it is to "psycholo-

---

pleasant version of ourself. It's a bit like cheating at solitaire. This case can't be explained by any of the four Quadrants in Figure 4. It is not concealing or denying *or* public. We are playing a game—not vis-à-vis others—but with ourselves, our conscious ego-ideals.

[26]R. May, *Existential Psychology* (New York: Random House, 1961).

gize" these biological conditions—and even orthodox Freudians are guilty of this—there should be no question about the basic biological nature of instinct theory.

Interpersonal theory focuses on the man-man tensions; essentially, interpersonal theory is a theory of human relations. In contrast to the instinct theory, impulses, drives, striving toward goals are considered by the interpersonal theorists as useless abstractions necessitated by the narrow bioneurological vision of psychoanalytical theory. As Sullivan said: "So if a person really thinks that his thoughts about nerves and synapses and the rest have a higher order of merit than his thoughts about signs and symbols, all I can say is, Heaven help him."[27] Interpersonal theory, then, is the study of the processes that result from man-man tensions.

Finally, *existential theory* concerns itself primarily with man in tension with his "self." Ludwig Binswanger, leader of the European existential psychiatry movement, held that the main weakness in psychoanalytic theory—a weakness he considered profound enough to prevent him from becoming a "Freudian"—was its omission of man in relation to himself.[28] But the self, as the existentialists know it, is a very complicated mechanism:

> My "being"—which by definition must have unity if it is to survive as a being—has three aspects, which we may term "self," "person," and "ego." The "self" I use as the subjective center, the experiencing of the fact that I am the one who behaves in thus and thus ways; the "person" we may take as the aspect in which I am accepted by others, the "person" of Jung, the social roles of William James; and the "ego" we may take as Freud originally enunciated it, the specific organ of perception by which the self sees and relates to the outside world . . . the point I do wish to make strongly is that *being* must be presupposed in discussions of ego and identity, and that the *centered self* must be basic to such discussions.[29]

The self is the center of existential theory and the major conflict is the self in tension with the ego and the person.

2. When the Conflict Situation Is Not Satisfactorily Resolved, Anxiety Ensues

The key concept here is *anxiety* and each approach to interpersonal feelings employs it in a crucial way. For *instinct theory*, anxiety occurs when biological impulses, the instincts, overwhelm

---

[27]H. Guntrip, *Personality Structure and Human Interaction* (New York: International Universities Press, 1961), p. 176.

[28]May, *op. cit.*, p. 32.

[29]May, *op. cit.*, p. 48.

the ego. In its most primitive form, we can observe this in Freud's writings when he asserts that: ". . . the aim of the death instinct is to undo connections and so to destroy things.[30]

In *interpersonal theory*, the presence of anxiety indicates the lack of "empathy," or at a more primitive level a "not-understood state." For Sullivan, effective human relations can occur only when individuals develop "consensual validation," a state where the primary, referential tools of communication are shared. Not to be understood is not to exist, to be destroyed. Anxiety for the *existentialist* is the threat to *being* caused by a lack of *meaning* for the self. It is that state where the self is not coterminous with the ego or the person and where the lack of integrity leads to despair and state of meaninglessness.

3. How Is Anxiety Reduced?

The organism, in *instinct theory*, avoids anxiety by reaching some desired state or goal, by seeking some adaptation or pleasure which, in turn, lessens the conflict. In other words, the ego must be able to maintain some balance between its biological impulses and the outside reality.

For the *interpersonal theorist*, anxiety is reduced when the interpersonal unit has reached a state of "valid communication." That is, when participants in an interpersonal encounter have reached the stage where they have developed methods for achieving and testing consensus, they have successfully reached the goal.

For *existentialism*, "identity" is the desired anxiety-free state. In the famous quote from Sartre, "We are our choices," he is implying that existentialism means centering on the existing- i.e., deciding— person. There is no such thing as truth or reality in existential thought aside from the human being participating and experiencing his identity.

What derivations can we make with this typology? First of all, we can say that interpersonal theory is the only one of the three approaches that makes interpersonal feelings *per se* pivotal to the theory. Instinct theory and existential theory encompass interpersonal feelings, to be sure, but only as derivatives of "deeper" motives. *Others* are important in existential theory, but only as

---

[30]S. Freud, *An Outline of Psychoanalysis* (New York: Norton, 1949), p. 20.

agents in *self-actualization; others* are important in instinct theory, but only as they lead to more effective impulse control.[31]

Our classification scheme also allows us to sort out a number of different approaches to interpersonal feelings and organize them. It should be apparent, for example, that the FIRO theory of Schutz[32] and the Sullivanian scheme of Leary[33] belong in the interpersonal theory sphere. The group theory of W. R. Bion,[34] the interaction scheme of Bales,[35] and the philosophical speculations of Martin Buber[36] must also be located there. While there are differences among these various theories, some trivial and some important, they all place primary emphasis on the relationship of man to man.

Existential theory, as we have mentioned, stresses concepts focusing on the "self." Existential psychologists such as Rogers, Maslow, and May tend to use concepts such as a "self-actualization," "existential loneliness," and "identity." It is interesting to note that when existentialists discuss loneliness, they often regard it as an affectively positive state[37]; interpersonal theorists, on the other hand, tend to treat it as a morbid, even psychotic, state.[38]

Finally, it should be stated that approaches like Mann's[39] fall into the instinct theory sector because of their reliance on the expression of impulses.

There are some difficulties with the typology which should be mentioned. Most significant for us is the fact that some interpersonal and personality theorists cannot be so easily categorized. E. Erikson, for example, falls into the "ego-psychology" school of instinct theory; on the other hand, his governing theoretical concern has been "identity." To make matters even more complicated, he is considered by some as an interpersonal theorist, his entire theory of development resting on interpersonal dimensions. We find the same problem in the work of the English branch of the neo-Freudians,

---

[31]This statement, as it now stands, is too blunt and unqualified. But the *emphasis* should be clear. The important work of the ego-psychologists (Hartmann, Kris, Erikson) and the English psychoanalysts M. Klein and W.R.D. Fairbairn stands out as an exception to this emphasis.
[32]Schutz, *op. cit.* (1958).
[33]Leary, *op. cit.*
[34]Bion, *op. cit.*
[35]Bales, *op. cit.*
[36]M. Buber, *I and Thou* (Edinburgh; T. & T. Clark, 1957).
[37]C. E. Moustakas, *Loneliness* (Englewood Cliffs, N.J.: Prentice-Hall, Inc., 1961).
[38]F. Fromm-Reichmann, "Loneliness," *Psychiatry,* Vol. 22 (1959), pp. 1–15.
[39]Man, *op. cit.*

M. Klein[40] and Fairbairn,[41] who have developed an "object relations" psychology. Where do they belong? They cannot be omitted from the interpersonal sphere. This is particularly true of Fairbairn, who places primary emphasis on object relations and who contends that libido is not primarily pleasure seeking but *object* seeking.[42]

Despite these qualifications, our classification system will help guide us in our next and final section of this essay.[43]

STYLES OF INTERPERSONAL FEELINGS

Our readings which follow are organized in terms of a classification system of interpersonal styles developed by Karen Horney.[44] It consists of three styles or modalities of how people relate to each other: *(a)* characteristically relating to others by moving *toward* them; *(b)* characteristically relating to others by moving *against* them; and *(c)* characteristically relating to others by moving *away* from them. These styles have to do with love, hate, and aloneness or alienation, and we have arranged our readings to correspond to these polarities of interpersonal expression. Let us begin by examining the interpersonal aspects of moving toward: love.

1. Going Towards: Love and Interpersonal Intimacy

In a recent book on "love," the advertising blurb reads: "Love—a short word that means so many different things. Everybody wants it; far from everybody can give it. Yet we all think we know what it means. Is it something natural that we don't need to think about, or is it art? . . . To practice the art of loving is more difficult than ever under today's pressure . . ."[45] This statement "on love"

---

[40]M. Klein, *Contributions of Psychoanalysis*, 1921–1945 (London: Hogarth Press, 1950).

[41]W. R. D. Fairbairn, *Psychoanalytic Studies of the Personality* (New York: Basic Books, 1952).

[42]Guntrip, *op. cit.*, p. 253.

[43]We cannot resist a speculation on a possible future direction of a creative synthesis in the theory of interpersonal feelings. It can be foreshadowed, we believe, in the work of Erikson, Klein, Fairbairn, Sullivan, and the ego-psychologists. All these theorists emphasize, to a greater or lesser degree, the autonomy and integration of the ego, the reality and significance of relationships and environment in personal development, and the significance of adaptation. An integration of these theories holds genuine promise for the theoretician. Since this essay was written, a brilliant beginning along these lines was made by J. D. Sutherland ("Object-Relations Theory and the Conceptual Model of Psychoanalysis," *British Journal of Medical Psychology*, Vol. 36, No. 109 [1963], pp. 109–24), who attempted to integrate ego-psychology and "object-relations theory."

[44]K. Horney, *Our Inner Conflicts* (New York: Norton, 1945).

[45]E. Fromm, *The Art of Loving* (London: Unwin, 1962), frontispiece.

represents a more-or-less average attitude toward the topic: puzzlement and confusion, chagrin and awe, yet fascination with its "curative" and harmful effects. And yet with all the cosmic and religious overtones, the concept of love, complicated and elusive as it is, must serve as one of the basic dimensions of interpersonal feelings. It *is* a complicated topic, primarily because of its rich heritage in spiritual, physical, and psychological thought. To a zoologist, like Kinsey, love can be defined in terms of orgiastic potency; to a theologian, it can be explained or understood only in terms of man's relation to God; and to a psychologist it is often either an embarrassment or a source of an argument about operational referents.

In any case, its primacy and importance in the sphere of interpersonal feelings is assured. We are pre-occupied with love because of its instinctual, human, and philosophical nature. Terms which are derivative of or synonymous with love pervade psychological literature: *libido, eros,* and object-relations from psychoanalytic theory; "intimacy" from the first phase of adulthood in Erikson's theory[46] and the second step in "group maturity" according to Bennis and Shepard.[47] Bion speaks of "pairing,"[48] Schutz of "affection,"[49] Sorokin of "altruistic love,"[50] Murray of "synthesism,"[51] Wolff of "surrender,"[52] Harlow of "heterosexual affectional systems,"[53] Fromm of "overcoming of human separateness."[54] We could multiply these examples but the point hardly requires more evidence.

It is tempting, though perhaps foolhardy, to make some tentative statement about "what love is." We invite our readers to examine the work of Allport,[55] Frankl,[56] and Fromm[57] in this respect.

These authors, alas, as thoughtful and penetrating as they are,

---

[46]E. H. Erikson, *Childhood and Society* (New York: W. W. Norton, 1960).

[47]W. G. Bennis and H. A. Shepard, "A Theory of Group Development," *Human Relations,* Vol. 9 (1956), pp. 415–37.

[48]Bion, *op. cit.*

[49]Schutz, *op. cit.* (1958).

[50]P. Sorokin, *Explorations in Altruistic Love and Behavior* (Boston: Beacon Press, 1950).

[51]H. A. Murray, "Synthesism," *Daedalus,* Vol. 90 (1961), pp. 552–63.

[52]K. Wolff, "Surrender and Religion," *Journal for the Scientific Study of Religion,* Vol. 2, (1962), pp. 36–50.

[53]H. Harlow, "The Heterosexual Affectional System in Monkeys," *American Psychologist,* Vol. 17, No. 1 (1962): See pages 43–60 of this volume.

[54]Fromm, *op. cit.*

[55]G. W. Allport, *Personality and Social Encounter* (Boston: Beacon Press, 1960).

[56]V. E. Frankl, *The Doctor and the Soul* (New York: Knopf, 1962), chap. 4.

[57]Fromm, *op. cit.*

leave us wistful, imbued still further with a Faustian restlessness. The fact is that modern psychology has failed to come to terms with love.[58] It tends to be treated in a number of ways: like a "hot potato," or starched into crisp abstractions, or elevated beyond human comprehension or capacity. But one shouldn't blame modern psychology for this "flight from tenderness" any more than the mortals who participate in the exodus.

In the essay introducing Part V of this volume we attempt to "come to terms" with love in a particularly *normative* way. For the moment, forecasting what is ahead, let us go this far: Love is a relationship between two people which allows a full and spontaneous impact. "Full and spontaneous" means: *All. Here. Now.* Love is a kind of fusion with the essence of the other person, but where the two people concerned clearly see their boundary conditions; they know where one begins and the other stops; there is no confusion about "who's who." Love is where two people can care for, show responsibility and respect for, and understand each other.[59] Love is where there is an active concern for the growth and development of the other. In addition, love is adapted to an external reality: to work, to developing a family, to relating to some external social institution.[60]

So we view love as satisfying what the psychoanalyst calls an "object relationship," what Sullivan and others would refer to as "valid communication," and what the existential theorist would term "existential union." But none of these phrases gets close to the basic, deep, potent experience which can make us competent and helpless, savage and tender, jealous and possessive, rational or insane, productive or slothful, lewd or prim, hopeful or cynical. In fact, what other human experience can account for the presence of such complex and polar emotions?[61]

At this point, it might be useful to introduce the readings that fall in this classification of "going towards." Harry Harlow's paper is a delightful study on sexual and loving behavior among monkeys.

---

[58]Allport, *op. cit.*, p. 199.

[59]Fromm, *op. cit.*, p. 25.

[60]See P. Slater "On Social Regression," *American Sociological Review* (June, 1963) pp. 339–64.

[61]We cannot avoid the "metaphysical pathos" we spoke of earlier with respect to normative wishes tincturing accurate description. The very idea of "love" is a normative concept, almost by definition. Hostility or hatred seems less so; perhaps we are more confident of its presence. Or perhaps we believe that the scientific study of hatred is more "manly" than discovering the riddle of love.

Paradoxically, while it employs rigorous scientific methods and rhesus monkeys, its findings hold the most interest for psychoanalytic theory. Lewin and Mayer in their papers develop the concept of "friendship" as a special, very important aspect of positive relationships and one that our first edition almost ignored (as does the entire field of social psychology). Both Lewin and Mayer discuss the "distancing" involved in friendship—Lewin, from the point of view of cultural differences, and Mayer, from the point of view of how friends use "openness" or "closeness" of communication to modulate tension.

It is interesting to note that the first edition had only three pieces on love, two of which we dropped. We worried then that this seminal topic was neglected. In this edition, we believe, the readings are more relevant and exciting, but we will continue to look for still better selections.

2. Going Against: Hate and Fantasy

Moving against people has to do with anger, irritation, hostility, competitiveness, exploitativeness, hate. Its biological counterpart to sex is death and its ubiquitousness is profound. In fact, hate has much in common with love: it is active; it is direct contact; it is an encounter. In fact, it is as difficult to untwine them in life as it is in science: where love is, hate is.

Its centrality to the study of interpersonal feelings is no less than love. *Thanatos* and aggression play an important part in Freud's theories; counterpersonalness is featured in Schutz's work and fight and counterpairing in the group theory of Bion. But we do not need to turn to theory or concepts to corroborate the existence of the aggressive emotion; we have only to observe our everyday experience. A section from Saul Bellow's novel, *The Victim,* brings this point out well:

> People met you once or twice and they hated you. What was the reason; what inspired it? . . . You had only to be yourself to provoke them. Why? A sigh of helplessness escaped Leventhal. If they still believed it would work, they would make little dolls of wax and stick pins in them. And why do they pick out this, that, or the other person to hate—Tom, Dick or Harry? No one can say. They hate your smile or the way you blow your nose or use a napkin. Anything will do for an excuse. And meanwhile this Harry, the object of it, doesn't even suspect. How should he know someone is carrying around an image of him (just as a woman may paste a lover's picture on the mirror of her vanity case or a man his wife's snapshot in his wallet) carrying it around to look at and hate? It doesn't even have to be a reproduction of poor Harry.

It might as well be the king of diamonds. . . . It doesn't make a bit of difference. Leventhal had to confess that he himself had occasionally sinned in this respect, and he was not obviously a malicious person. But certain people did call out this feeling. He saw Cohen, let us say, once or twice, and then, when his name was mentioned in company, let fall an uncomplimentary remark about him. Not that this Cohen had ever offended him. But what were all the codes and rules, Leventhal reflected, except an answer to our own nature? Would we have to be told "Love!" if we loved as we breathed? No, obviously. Which was not to say that we didn't love but we have to be assisted whenever the motor started missing. . . . [62]

The fictional character quoted, "the victim," communicates a desperate, fruitless complexity about the nature of hostility. He knows hostility is real, that it appears inevitable and impulsive, and that the targets of hostility, the victims, are selected without reason. We can say all this about love, too. We seem to be left with some of the same ambiguities and complexities when we try to become analytical about hate as we do about love, and perhaps for the same reasons.

There are things we do know about hostility; we know that hostility is related to "frustration," or to some tension the individual is undergoing. However, this explains both too much and too little; individuals vary tremendously in their tolerance of frustration as well as what they perceive to be frustrating. In addition, frustration is only one kind of stimulus which may lead to aggression. So the "frustration-leads-to-aggression" hypothesis is useful, though a bit too restrictive for our analytic purposes.

We prefer the broader perspective of identifying the *threatening conditions* that lead to aggression. Some of these threatening conditions are known to be related to hostility: competition, jealousy, envy, deprivation, status-anxiety, forms of social degradation, thwarted aspirations, to name only a few. We can see more clearly now that "frustration" in the usual sense it is employed is only one form of threat, "that motivational and emotional state which results from persistent blockage of goal-directed behavior."[63] We can also see that threats can emanate from without or from within. An example of the former is a feared boss or a hated rival who spitefully jeopardizes the career of a highly motivated subordinate. An example of the latter is the flood of emotion experienced by an individual during an anxiety attack. In either case, the threat imperils

---

[62]S. Bellow, *The Victim* (New York: Viking Press, Compass Books, 1958), pp. 80–81.

[63]Krech, Crutchfield, and Ballachey, *op. cit.*, p. 134.

—or is perceived to be imperilling—the ego. Thus, our formulation regarding the expression of hostility would be:

This formulation advances us a little, but we still have to know more about the elements of a threatening situation and how different types of individuals react to these stimuli. We also need to know far more than we now do regarding the people "chosen" as victims. If we can gain more understanding of the interpersonal exchanges between aggressor and victim, we will be on our way toward a theory of interpersonal relationships. This means adumbrating the complexity of the unconscious collusion between the oppressed and the aggressor and the peculiar meaning of the exchange for both.

Some light can be thrown on this issue if we examine the special case of "prejudice."[64] James Baldwin[65] points out that the reason the white man hates the Negro is because the Negro reminds him of those conflictual areas in his personality which the white man struggles to repress: sexuality, rampant impulses, id forces the white man does not "own up to." The same argument was made about anti-Semitism in Hitler's Germany. In both cases we can see that hostility was expressed to certain targets in order to alleviate inner conflict. By identifying these impulses in others and then projecting them outward, the individual is able to reduce his own anxiety. Note two factors in this process: (1) that hostility is a defensive maneuver entered into in order to avoid anxiety; (2) that the targets selected are not random, that they relate to conflicts the aggressor has and cannot consciously face.

This formulation permits us to understand more fully the role of hostility in *interpersonal* relationships. What we can detect is an interesting parallel between the origin of hostility in an individual

---

[64]We are talking here and throughout this section on "going against" of excessive or defensive hostility. We do not have in mind *appropriate* hatred or rage as that, for example, which might be directed toward a destructive person. Prejudice, by definition, implies a type of hostility which is excessive, off-target, and caused by reasons quite often unconscious to the aggressor; there is *always* some distortion of reality in prejudice. Realistic or appropriate hostility, as we define it, is based on some legal constraints and ethical codes; it is willful, directed to the appropriate source of threat, and conscious.

[65]J. Baldwin, *The Fire Next Time* (New York: Dial Press, 1963).

when he selects a particular target to discharge his anger, and the origin of hostility in a pair or group when it selects a certain target. In both cases we can identify the basis of conflict *via* understanding the victim and the peculiar meaning of the victim for the aggressors. Vogel and Bell in their research on the role of scapegoating in family settings show that the targets of hostility are not accidental, that the person selected is intimately related to the source of tension: "If the parents' most serious unresolved problems were with male figures, the child chosen to represent the family conflict was usually a male child. Similarly, sibling order could be a strong factor. If one or both parents had difficulties with older brothers, an older boy in the family might become the scapegoat."[66] Some victims of hostility are "satisfactory" and others are not. Victims are satisfactory only if they enable the attackers to alleviate some important conflict within the aggressive pair.

Another example of this unconscious maneuvering was shown by Bennis,[67] who analyzed a case of severe aggression toward a group member who emerged as an informal leader of the group while the formal leader was absent. When the formal leader returned, the substitute leader was excessively attacked for no apparent reason. We should point out that this particular person was selected as the informal leader because of his perceived resemblance to the formal leader. It was inferred that the critical rage vented toward the substitute was due to the feelings of revenge which could not be expressed openly toward the "deserting" leader. Thus the substitute leader was the victim of hostility which was felt, but unexpressed, toward the formal leader. This enabled the group to avoid, for the time being, their negative impulses toward the formal authority, a more anxiety-producing and threatening object for them than their peer.

From these examples we can detect the complicated vicissitudes of hostility. It serves a number of purposes simultaneously. First, it avoids anxiety in the organism whether a pair, a group, or a person. Second, it identifies the source of the anxiety and projects it outwards, thereby doing two things at once: discharging hostility and destroying what one can't face internally. Thirdly, the victims frequently unconsciously collude with the aggressors in becoming

---

[66]E. Vogel and N. Bell, "The Emotionally Disturbed Child as the Family Scapegoat," *The Family,* N. W. Bell and E. F. Vogel (eds.) (Glencoe, Ill.: The Free Press, 1960) pp. 382–97. See pages 90–104 of this volume.

[67]Bennis, "Defenses against 'Depressive-Anxiety' in Groups: The Case of the Absent Leader," *Merrill-Palmer Quarterly,* Vol. 7 (1961), pp. 3–30.

the target of the aggressors' rage.[68] Fourthly, and most centrally, *hostility preserves distance and precludes a full and spontaneous relationship between the oppressed and the attacker.* This is equally true for the "co-operating oppressors" (the husband and wife who scapegoat a child) as it is between couple and child. Continued scapegoating causes a lack of communication, which in turn prevents discovery of the sources of their conflicts. But as long as the conflict is not discovered and "worked through," the scapegoating continues.

And now we can return to Saul Bellow's victim and his profound questions: "People met you once or twice and they hated you. What was the reason; what inspired it?" We are still unable to formulate a satisfactory answer for him. What may be put into clearer focus, though, is the idea that in a relationship of hate, neither the victim nor the aggressor can influence or change the nature of their emotional exchange until their own relationship is more fully understood. There is an essential helplessness for the victim; he cannot "do anything" when he is used and exploited as a target for "projective identification";[69] the aggressor is equally helpless for he dimly perceives that the anxiety he is attempting to ward off may have only peripheral relevance to the victim.

So far we have discussed hostility as an altogether undesirable state, as a defense against anxiety and as a "distancing" factor in interpersonal relationships. There are, of course, positive and productive aspects of hostility. Freud[70] believed that civilization springs from instinctual renunciation; repressed aggression leads to work under many conditions and sublimation and substitution are often channeled into the service of "good works." More recently, Semrad *et al.*[71] have contended that hostility may lead to increased productivity in group settings. Mills[72] shows, in an ingenious experiment,

---

[68]This is highly speculative as well as complicated. In the study by Bennis (*op. cit., Merrill-Palmer Quarterly,* 1961) referred to earlier, it was found that the two individuals who drew the most hostility during the formal leader's absence were attacked because they persisted in reminding the group of his absence. In both cases the fathers of these two men died during their childhood. Thus, it seemed possible that they were evoking hostility as a way of draining off guilt associated with an earlier loss, a loss for which they feel in some degree responsible.

[69]The concept of "projective identification" developed by Melanie Klein appears to fit all the cases under the heading of "prejudice." M. Klein, "On Identification," *New Directions in Psychoanalysis* (New York: Basic Books, 1956), chap. 13.

[70]S. Freud, *Civilization and Its Discontents* (London: Hogarth, 1930).

[71]E. Semrad and J. Arsenian, "On the Concept of Billets" (Boston: Massachusetts Mental Health Center, 1958), unpublished manuscript.

[72]Mills, *op. cit.*

that certain forms of hostility—toward the person in authority—may be extremely functional for work in interpersonal settings.

Let us review the papers that are included in this edition under the "going against" section. First, the experiment by Milgram (see page 70 reveals some perplexing findings about "destructive obedience."[73] It raises some issues—including the ethics of science (summarized in Baumrind's letter included in this edition)—which leave the editors aroused and uncertain. In fact, we struggled for some time (before printing this in the first edition) among ourselves but finally decided that the results of this experiment, extraordinary and cruel as they are, throw light on a very important issue. Published after the first edition went to press, Diana Baumrind explores some of the ethical questions which confronted us when the first edition was published in 1963. The Maslow *et al.* paper illustrates a powerful mind attempting to show some connections between human nature and animal behavior. Many readers have probably skimmed through Lorenz's work on aggression, but many will be surprised to read the fascinating (and almost unnoticed) findings of Maslow and his colleagues which were reported *before* ethology became as popular as it is today. We retained from the first edition only the Harlow paper and the Vogel and Bell paper on the intricate dynamics of hostility and scapegoating in the family. The reader response to both of these articles reflects, we suspect, not only their high quality but their seminal character.

Both love and hate, as we said earlier, share some common properties. They both mobilize affect and involvements, they represent the basic currency in interpersonal exchanges. Let us go on to the third modality now, "moving away."

3. Going Away: Isolation and Withdrawal

In his essay "On Narcissism," Freud[74] pointed to the "introversion of the libido": the fact, often observed in the clinic, that people seemed to have withdrawn their attention and feelings from the external world to themselves. Horney describes this type of interpersonal style in the following manner:

> The underlying principle . . . is never to become so attached to anybody or anything that he or it becomes indispensable. Another pronounced need is for

---

[73]S. Milgram, "Behavioral Study of Obedience," *Journal of Abnormal and Social Psychology,* Vol. 67, No. 4 (1963), pp. 371–78. See pp. 70–84 of this volume.

[74]S. Freud, "On Narcissism: An Introduction," *Collected Papers, IV* (London: Hogarth, 1953).

privacy. The person is like the person in a hotel room who rarely removes the "Do Not Disturb" sign from his door. His independence, like the whole phenomenon of detachment of which it is a part, has a negative orientation; it is aimed at not being influenced, coerced, tied, obligated.[75]

Loneliness, withdrawal, isolation, estrangement, alienation are all words that seem descriptive of this interpersonal style; catatonic stupor, depression, and psychosis are all clinical correlates of what we have in mind by "going away."

Let us be clear about what we do *not* mean by "isolation and withdrawal." We do not mean that condition of life where a person broadens and deepens his humanity through an experience of "loneliness." Moustakas,[76] for example, tells us movingly about his "gripping, painful, exhilarating, and beautiful experience of being utterly alone and separated from others." We do not mean isolation or withdrawal caused by "reality factors," such as moving into a strange city or the self-imposed withdrawal due to "role imprisonment." Woodrow Wilson wrote to friends about his own loneliness caused by holding public office which brought him only "irreparable loss and desperate suffering."[77] We do not mean by withdrawal those temporary aberations sometimes noticed as a pathological reaction to stress and referred to by Greenson[78] and Strassman, Thaler, and Schein,[79] as "apathy." We do not have in mind, when we talk of isolation and withdrawal, those individuals who think of themselves as "mavericks" or "independent thinkers" who refuse to conform or those individuals who view themselves as vigilantes of dissent.

When we talk of "going away" what we have in mind is a characteristic orientation toward the outside world and interpersonal relationships which can be summarized by Sartre's: "Hell is other people." We have in mind a *chronic* withdrawal from involvement with the environment, a loss of contact with external reality. The kind of loneliness and isolation we have in mind is similar to Fromm-Reichmann's notion of loneliness (p. 121, this volume): it is nonconstructive and disintegrative. So we are not discussing here "independence" or "autonomy" or "self-actualization" or any of those "peak experiences" an individual reports when he is "at one" with

[75]Horney, *op. cit.*

[76]Moustakas, *op. cit.*

[77]*Ibid*, p. 82.

[78]R. R. Greenson, *Psychoanalytic Quarterly,* Vol. 18 (1949).

[79]H. D. Strassman, M. B. Thaler, and E. H. Schein, "A Prisoner of War Syndrome: Apathy as a Reaction to Severe Stress," *American Journal of Psychiatry,* Vol. 112 (1956).

himself. We are referring to that state of human affairs, possibly as ubiquitous as love and hate, which realizes its aims through reduced contact with external reality.

It is something of a contradiction to talk of isolation and withdrawal as an *interpersonal* style. The "moving against and moving towards" styles are in contact with their environments, while the "moving away" style is detached and dead insofar as other people are concerned. There are, however, at least three types of "going away" which evolve in an interpersonal context with resulting unique interactions.

1. First we can mention *narcissistic withdrawal,* or what Slater refers to as "the withdrawal in strength." The narcissist doesn't "need" people in the conventional sense; he appears autonomous and ingenious, a man with power, fascination, and charisma.[80] The paradox is that the narcissist—the most inward of men—seems to have a certain seductive fascination for most people and it is upon him that other men lean;[81] he is the one that others seek to follow and emulate.[82] The narcissist does not lean on others, so the relationship which ensues is a "tilted" one, one without reciprocation, but interpersonal nevertheless. The interesting thing here is that most people simply will not leave the narcissist "alone," a point Slater makes with brilliant insistence.

2. The main point of Slater's essay has to do with *social regression,* a form of interpersonal withdrawal which draws the social anxiety of the group because of its violations—real and fantasied—of group and societal norms. It is a form of libidinal contraction, a withdrawal in concert with someone else, which denies the existence of others and imperils the integrity of social institutions. An example of social regression might be a violation of the incest taboo where a brother and sister engage in sexual relations; or where a man and woman "live in sin." What is important for us to note is the social and interpersonal aspects of this withdrawal and how the libidinal contraction tends to intensify the expression of interpersonal feelings of the withdrawing unit.[83]

3. The last form of withdrawal we will mention here was covered

---

[80]We should point out that this is true only when the ego strength of the narcissist is strong and adaptive. See Philip Slater's, "On Social Regression," *American Sociological Review* (June 1963) pp. 334–64.

[81]Freud, *op. cit.,* 1953.

[82]J. Adelson, "The Teacher as a Model," *American Scholar,* Vol. 30 No. 3 (1961), pp. 383–406. See p. 491 this volume.

[83]In the Thomas Mann story, "The Blood of the Walsungs" (*Stories of Three Decades* [New York: Knopf, 1936], pp. 279–319), note that the dyadic withdrawal of the twins ended in sexual intercourse.

in the first edition of *Interpersonal Dynamics* by Bateson *et al.* in their brilliant analysis of communication difficulties.[84] Their theoretical framework identifies the kinds of communication patterns set up in families (although painfully noticeable in other social patterning, such as authority relations in organizations) which can lead to various forms of psychoses. We can refer to this type of withdrawal as the "double-bind," withdrawal caused by a complete inability to understand the mixed signals induced by ambivalence. So when the mother tells her child to "go to bed," the child can interpret this message in various ways—such as "get the hell out of my sight!" or "Darling, you'd better get the proper amount of sleep." Or when the boss asks his subordinate if he's too autocratic, the subordinate may not understand whether he should respond with submission or rebellion. And so on.

The readings in the "going away" section reflect our interest in the interpersonal aspect of withdrawal and isolation. The Fromm-Reichmann piece is the best example we have found of a psychiatric approach to loneliness. (The Bateson *et al.* and Slater papers, which appeared in the first edition, are also good examples of social forms of withdrawal.) In this edition, we have included a new, still unpublished paper by Slater on nonpermanent relations (typically induced by a terrifying rate of social mobility) and a new, also unpublished paper by Robert Weiss on certain deficiencies in social relations, illustrated by parents without partners. In addition, we have reprinted the delightful, bittersweet fable (reminiscent of Thurber's best writing) by Allen Wheelis, the psychoanalyst turned writer.

We have added a new section to this edition of *Interpersonal Dynamics,* based on our own evaluation as well as some readers' responses. We felt that a new section was needed to supplement the triadic—going towards, away, and against. This new section presents the modes of *expressing* these feelings. Thus, we decided to include a paper by the anthropologist LaBarre on the language and gesture of emotion, particularly some of its cross-cultural variations, and finally, an interesting paper on the meaning of posture and "proxemics" in psychotherapeutic settings.

Our knowledge is still meager; we know very little. Fromm-Reichmann says:

---

[84]Gregory Bateson, Don D. Jackson, Jay Haley, and John Weakland, "Toward a Theory of Schizophrenia," *Behavioral Science* (Oct. 1956), pp. 251–64.

. . . loneliness is one of the least satisfactory conceptualized psychological phenomena, not even mentioned in most psychiatric textbooks. Very little is known among scientists about its genetics and psychodynamics, and various different experiences which are descriptively and dynamically as different from one another as culturally determined loneliness, self-imposed aloneness, compulsory solitude, isolation, and real loneliness are all thrown into the one terminological basket called "loneliness."[85]

These words of Fromm-Reichmann could be applied to all three interpersonal styles examined in this essay: love, hate, *and* isolation. We are also left, alas, with a distinct feeling that our analysis of aggression was more convincing than our discussion of love. Who can say why? What we are left with now, at the close of this essay, is an awesome feeling that we have barely scratched the surface of our topic and that we must again turn for help outward to the poet and inward to ourselves.

THE HETEROSEXUAL AFFECTIONAL SYSTEM IN MONKEYS[*1]

Harry F. Harlow

The inspiration for this address came from observational data obtained from seven guinea pigs—two males and three females in a colony and two females brought in temporarily. Observations were provided by my ten-year-old daughter Pamela. These observations were made with love and endearment, and the behavior observed was endearment and love. Furthermore, these observations were made at a level of objectivity difficult for an adult to attain in this field.

Male and female guinea pigs are very fond of each other. They stare blissfully into the limpid pink or ruby or midnight-blue pools of each other's eyes. They nuzzle and they cuddle and the end production is not characterized by rush or rape. After all, one does not have to hurry if there is no hurry to be had. This, Pamela has wit-

[85]Fromm-Reichmann, *op. cit.* See p. 121 of this volume.
[*]"The Heterosexual Affectional System in Monkeys," Harry F. Harlow. Reprinted from the *American Psychologist* (January 1962). Used by permission.
[1]This research was supported by funds received from the Graduate School of the University of Wisconsin, from the Ford Foundation, and from Grant M-4528, National Institutes of Health.

nessed several times. A caged, virgin adult female was brought by a friend for mating. Twirp, Pamela's large, black, gentle male, was put into the cage with the new female. He purred, nuzzled her, brushed up against her, smelled and licked her, and gradually conquered the frightened animal. A half-hour later they were snuggled up next to each other, peaceful and content, and they lived in bliss for several weeks until another friend brought in her female and Twirp repeated his patient, gentle approach. Twirp has convinced me that some male guinea pigs, at least, are endowed with an innate sense of decency, and I am happy to say that this is the way most male monkeys behave. I presume that there are some men who have as deep a depth of dignity as guinea pigs.

The guest stands, unfortunately, ended peaceful coexistence in the colony. For many months the five adult guinea pigs had lived amiably in one large cage, with Twirp in command and the second male playing second fiddle. While Twirp was host to the visiting females, White Patch commanded the permanent harem. When Twirp was reintroduced to the colony cage, it took but ten seconds to discover that he would not be tolerated. White Patch bared his teeth and lunged at Twirp, and to save the males, a new cage was acquired.

This led to various divisions of the females and led Pamela to discover particular male guinea pigs like particular female guinea pigs, and they squeal piteously when separated, even when the female is so bulging with babies that she can offer the male nothing in terms of drive reduction. Particular female guinea pigs like particular male guinea pigs. Tastes seem fairly stable, for even after weeks of peaceful residence with the unfavored male, the female will still attempt to get to her favorite male, and after weeks of quiet residence with unfavored females, the male will still try to get to his favorite female.

The females, like the males, defend their rights. In the happy one-cage days two females were separated from the group to care for their litters. White Thrush, in an advanced stage of pregnancy, lived alone with the males. When Chirp was returned to the colony cage after three weeks of maternal chores, both males approached enthusiastically, making friendly gestures. But Hell hath no fury like a female guinea pig spurned, and White Thrush would not tolerate infidelity. She hissed at Chirp, and lunged, and as Chirp fled from the cage, White Thrush pursued, teeth bared. The males also pursued, clucking and purring in anticipation. The males won, and

White Thrush sulked the rest of the day. Guinea pigs apparently have a well-developed heterosexual affectional system.

Sex behavior in the guinea pig has been intensively investigated, and there are exhaustive studies on what has been called the sex drive, but I know of no previous mention of or allusion to the guinea pig's heterosexual affectional system. No doubt this stems from the paradigm which has been established for research in this area.

In a typical experiment a male guinea pig and a female guinea pig in estrus are taken from their individual cages, dropped into a barren chamber, and observed for 15 minutes. In such a situation there is a high probability that something is going to happen and that it will happen rapidly and repeatedly. The thing that happens will be reliable and valid, and all that one needs to do to score it is to count. It is my suggestion that from this time onward it be known as the "flesh count." Sometimes I wonder how men and women would behave if they were dropped naked into a barren chamber with full realization that they had only fifteen minutes to take advantage of the opportunities offered them. No doubt there would be individual differences, but we would obtain little information on the human heterosexual affectional system from such an experiment.

Sex is not an adventitious act. It is not here today and gone tomorrow. It starts with the cradle, and as a part of the human tragedy it wanes before the grave. We have traced and are tracing the development of the heterosexual affectional system in monkeys.

We believe that the heterosexual affectional system in the rhesus monkey, like all the other affectional systems, goes through a series of developmental stages—an infantile heterosexual stage, a preadolescent stage, and an adolescent and mature heterosexual stage. Although these stages are in considerable part overlapping and cannot be sharply differentiated in time, we would think of the infantile stage as lasting throughout the first year and being characterized by inadequate and often inappropriate sexual play and posturing. The preadolescent stage, beginning in the second year and ending in the third year in the female and the fourth year in the male, is characterized by adequate and appropriate sexual play and posturing, but incompleteness. The adolescent and adult stage is characterized by behaviors which are similar in form but give rise to productive outcomes which are also reproductive.

Since in this paper sex is an unavoidable issue, we present illustrations of normal adult macaque monkey sex behavior. Sexual invitation may be initiated by the female, as in Figure 1, by a present pattern with buttocks oriented toward the male, tail elevated, and the female looking backward with a fear-grimace (not threat) pattern involving flattened ears and lip smacking. As you can see, this

FIG. 1. INITIAL RESPONSE TO FEMALE SEXUAL-PRESENT POSTURE. THE MALE SUBSEQUENTLY ACCEPTED THE INVITATION.

FIG. 2. INITIAL RESPONSE TO MALE SEXUAL-PRESENT POSTURE. THE FEMALE (No. 48) SUBSEQUENTLY APPROACHED AND GROOMED THE MALE.

pattern need not involve rape nor even rush on the part of the male. The male may also solicit, as in the case of the animal in the foreground of Figure 2; this animal has assumed a posture soliciting either grooming or more intimate favors. These patterns seldom elicit violent, uncontrolled, reflex behaviors. Normal male and female overt sex behavior is shown in Figure 3, the male having assumed the complex sex posture involving ankle clasp, dorsoventral mounting, and clasp of the female's buttocks. The partner demonstrates the complete female sexual pattern of elevating the buttocks, lowering the head, and looking backward. There have been millions of rhesus monkeys for millions of years, and there will be more in the future.

FIG. 3. NORMAL MALE AND FEMALE SEXUAL POSITIONING.

We have traced the development of the infantile heterosexual stage during the first year of life in two test situations using observational techniques. One is our playroom, illustrated in Figure 4, which consists of a room 8 feet high with 36 feet of floor space. In this room are a platform, ladder, revolving wheel, and flying rings to encourage the infants' adaptation to a three-dimensional world, and there is an assortment of puzzles and toys for quieter activities. Two groups of four infants each, half of each group male and half female, have been observed in the playroom daily over many months. The second apparatus is shown in Figure 5. This is the playpen situation, and it consists of four large living cages and adjoining pens. Each living cage houses a mother and infant, and a three-inch by five-inch opening in the wall between cage and playpen units enables the infants to leave the home cage at any time but restrains the mothers. The playpen units are separated by wire-mesh panels which are removed one or two hours a day to allow the infants to interact in pairs during the first 180 days and both in pairs and in groups of four during the next half-year of life. Again, we are referring to data gathered from two playpen setups, each housing four infants and their real or surrogate mothers. Insofar as the infantile heterosexual stage is concerned, it makes little or no difference from which situation we take our data.

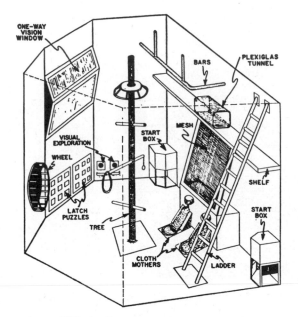

FIG. 4. PLAYROOM TEST SITUATION.

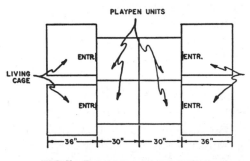

FIG 5. PLAYPEN TEST SITUATION.

The outstanding finding in both the playroom and playpen is that male and female infants show differences in sex behavior from the second month of life onward. The males show earlier and more frequent sex behavior than do females, and there are differences in the patterns displayed by the sexes. The males almost never assume the female sex-posture patterns, even in the earliest months. The females, on the other hand, sometimes display the male pattern of sex posturing, but this is infrequent after ten months of age. Predominantly, females show the female pattern, and exceptional instances are to other females, not males. Frequency of sex behavior for both males and females increases progressively with age. There is no latency period—except when the monkeys are very tired.

The early infantile sexual behaviors are fragmentary, transient, and involve little more than passivity by the female and disoriented grasping and thrusting by the male. Thus, the male may thrust at the companion's head in a completely disoriented manner or laterally across the midline of the body, as in Figure 6. However, it is our opinion that these behaviors are more polymorphous than perverse.

FIG. 6. IMMATURE MALE AND FEMALE SEXUAL POSTURING,
PLAYROOM OBSERVATION.

Thus, as soon as the sexual responses can be observed and measured, male and female sexual behaviors differ in form. Furthermore, there are many other behaviors which differ between males and females as soon as they can be observed and measured. Figure 7 shows the development of threat responses by males and females in the playroom, and these differences are not only statistically significant, but they also have face validity. Analysis of this behavior shows that males threaten other males and females but that females are innately blessed with better manners; in particular, little girl monkeys do not threaten little boy monkeys.

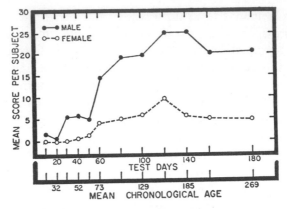

FIG 7. FREQUENCY OF THREAT RESPONSES BY MALES
AND FEMALES IN THE PLAYROOM.

The withdrawal pattern—retreat when confronted by another monkey—is graphed for the playroom in Figure 8, and the significance is obvious. Females evince a much higher incidence of passive responses, which are characterized by immobility with buttocks oriented toward the male and head averted, and a similar pattern, rigidity, in which the body is stiffened and fixed.

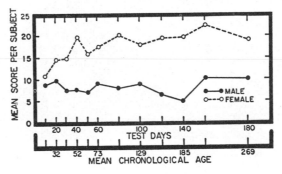

FIG. 8. FREQUENCY OF WITHDRAWAL RESPONSES BY
MALES AND FEMALES IN THE PLAYROOM.

In all probability the withdrawal and passivity behavior of the female and the forceful behavior of the male gradually lead to the development of normal sex behaviors. The tendency for the female to orient away from the male and for the male to clasp and tussle at the female's buttocks predisposes the consorts to assume the proper positions. The development of the dorsally oriented male sex-behavior pattern as observed in the playroom situation is shown in Figure 9 and may be described as a composite yearning and learning curve.

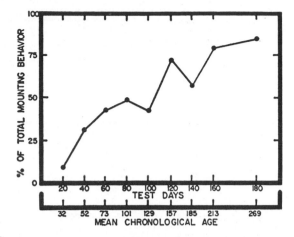

FIG. 9. PERCENTAGE OF ALL MALE MOUNTS (IMMATURE AND MATURE) IN THE PLAYROOM THAT SHOWS DORSAL ORIENTATION (MATURE PATTERN).

Infant male and female monkeys show clear-cut differences in behavior of far greater social significance than neonatal and infantile sex responses. Grooming patterns, which are basic to macaque socialization, show late maturation, but as is seen in Figure 10, when they appear, they sharply differentiate the two sexes. Caressing is both a property and prerogative of the females. Basic to normal

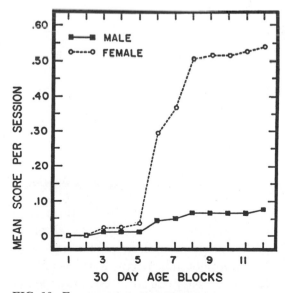

FIG. 10. FREQUENCY OF GROOMING RESPONSES MADE BY MALES AND FEMALES IN THE PLAYROOM.

macaque socialization is the infant-infant or peer-peer affectional
system, and this arises out of and is dependent upon the play patterns which we have described elsewhere and only mention here.
As is shown in the solid lines of Figure 11, play behavior in the
playroom is typically initiated by males, seldom by females. How-

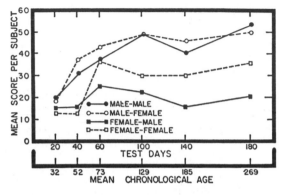

FIG. 11. FREQUENCY OF PLAY-INITIATIONS BY MALES AND FEMALES TO MONKEYS OF
THE SAME (MALE-MALE, FEMALE-FEMALE) AND OTHER SEX (MALE-FEMALE, FEMALE-
MALE). OBSERVATIONS ARE FROM THE PLAYROOM.

ever, let us not belittle the female, for they also serve who only
stand and wait. Contact play is far more frequent among the males
than the females and is almost invariably initated by the males.
Playpen data graphed in Figure 12 show that real rough-and-tumble
play is strictly for the boys.

I am convinced that these data have almost total generality to
man. Several months ago I was present at a school picnic attended
by 25 second-graders and their parents. While the parents sat and
the girls stood around or skipped about hand in hand, 13 boys
tackled and wrestled, chased and retreated. No little girl chased
any little boy, but some little boys chased some little girls. Human
beings have been here for two million years, and they'll probably
be here two million more.

These secondary sex-behavior differences probably exist throughout the primate order, and, moreover, they are innately determined
biological differences regardless of any cultural overlap. Because
of their nature they tend automatically to produce sexual segregation during middle and later childhood, but fortunately this separation is neither complete nor permanent. Behavioral differences
may very well make it easy through cultural means to impose a

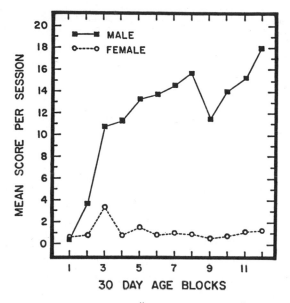

FIG. 12. FREQUENCY OF OCCURRENCE OF "ROUGH-AND-TUMBLE" PLAY FOR TWO MALES
AND TWO FEMALES IN THE PLAYROOM THROUGH THE FIRST YEAR OF LIFE.

sexual latency period in the human being from childhood to puberty. We emphasize the fact that the latency period is not a bio
logical stage in which primary sex behavior is suppressed, but a
cultural stage built upon secondary behavioral differences.

We believe that our data offer convincing evidence that sex behaviors differ in large part because of genetic factors. However,
we claim no originality for the discovery of intersex behavioral differences. In 1759 Laurence Sterne in his book *Tristram Shandy*
described male and female differences at the most critical period
in Tristram Shandy's development; indeed, it would not be possible
to conceive of a more critical period.

"*Pray, my dear,* quoth my mother, *have you not forgot to wind
up the clock?*———— *Good G————!* cried my father, making an
exclamation, but taking care to moderate his voice at the same
time————*Did ever woman, since the creation of the world, interrupt a man with such a silly question?*"[2]

Men and women have differed in the past and they will differ in
the future.

---

[2]Sterne, Laurence. *The Life and Opinions of Tristram Shandy, Gentleman,* J. A.
Work (ed.), (New York: Odyssey Press, 1940), p. 5.

It is possible that the listener has been dismayed by the frequent reference to sex and the relatively infrequent reference to affection. Out of these infantile behavior patterns, both sexual and nonsexual, develop the affectional bonds and the social ordering that appear to be important or even essential to the full development of the heterosexual affectional system of macaques. Traumatic affectional errors, both transient and prolonged, may have devastating effects upon subsequent social and sexual behaviors.

For some years we have been attempting to establish experimental neuroses in infant monkeys by having them live on unfriendly and inconsistent mother surrogates. One preparation was a rejecting mother that on schedule or demand separated her baby when a wire frame embedded in her spun-nylon covering was displaced violently upward and backward. The baby was disturbed, but as soon as the frame was returned to its resting position, the baby returned to cling to its surrogate mother as tightly as ever. Next we developed an air-blast mother with a series of nozzles down the entire center of her body which released compressed air under high pressure—an extremely noxious stimulus to monkeys. The blasted baby never even left the mother, but in its moments of agony and duress, clung more and more tightly to the unworthy mother. Where else can a baby get protection? Apparently our infant had never read Neal Miller's theory that avoidance gradients are precipitous and approach gradients gradual and tenuous, for love conquered all.

We next devised a shaking mother, which on schedule or demand shook her infant with unconscionable violence until its teeth chattered. The infant endured its tribulations by clinging more and more tightly. At the present time we believe we may be on the threshold of success through Jay Mowbray's creation of the porcupine mother, which extrudes brass spikes all over its ventral surface. Preliminary studies on two infants suggest that they are emotionally disturbed. Whether or not we eventually succeed, the fact remains that babies are reluctant to develop experimental neuroses, and at one time we even wondered if this were possible.

During the time that we were producing these evil mothers, we observed the monkeys which we had separated from their mothers at birth and raised under various mothered and nonmothered conditions. The first 47 baby monkeys were raised during the first year of life in wire cages so arranged that the infants could see and hear and call to other infants but not contact them. Now they are five to seven years old and sexually mature. As month after month and year after year have passed, these monkeys have appeared to be less and less normal. We have seen them sitting in their cages strangely mute, staring fixedly into space, relatively indifferent to people and other monkeys. Some clutch their heads in both hands and rock back and forth—the autistic behavior pattern that we have seen in babies raised on wire surrogates. Others, when approached or even left alone, go into violent frenzies of rage, grasping and tearing at their legs with such fury that they sometimes require medical care.

Eventually we realized that we had a laboratory full of neurotic monkeys. We had failed to produce neurotic monkeys by thoughtful planning and creative research, but we had succeeded in producing neurotic monkeys through misadventure. To err is human.

Because of housing pressures some of these monkeys and many of our surrogate-raised monkeys lived in pairs for several years while growing to sexual maturity, but we have seldom seen normal sex behavior, and we certainly have not had the validating criterion of newborn baby monkeys. Instead, these monkeys treat each other like brother and sister, proving that two can live in complete propinquity with perfect propriety as long as no one cares.

Their reason for being, as we saw it, was to produce babies for our researches, and so at this point we deliberately initiated a breeding program which was frighteningly unsuccessful. When the older, wire-cage-raised males were paired with the females at the peak of estrus, the introduction led only to fighting, so violent and vicious that separation was essential to survival. In no case was there any indication of normal sex behavior. Frequently the females were the aggressors; even the normal praying mantis waits until the sex act is completed.

Pairing such cloth-surrogate-raised monkeys as were sexually mature gave little better end results. Violent aggression was not the rule, and there was attempted sex behavior, but it was unreproductive since both the male and female behaviors were of the infantile type we have already described.

At this point we took the 17 oldest of our cage-raised animals, females showing consistent estrous cycles and males obviously mature, and engaged in an intensive re-education program, pairing the females with our most experienced, patient, and gentle males, and the males with our most eager, amiable, and successful breeding females. When the laboratory-bred females were smaller than the sophisticated males, the girls would back away and sit down facing the males, looking appealingly at these would-be consorts. Their hearts were in the right place, but nothing else was. When the females were larger than the males, we can only hope that they misunderstood the males' intentions, for after a brief period of court-ship, they would attack and maul the ill-fated male. Females show no respect for a male they can dominate.

The training program for the males was equally unsatisfactory. They approached the females with a blind enthusiasm, but it was a misdirected enthusiasm. Frequently the males would grasp the females by the side of the body and thrust laterally, leaving them working at cross purposes with reality. Even the most persistent attempts by these females to set the boys straight came to naught. Finally, these females either stared at the males with complete con-tempt or attacked them in utter frustration. It became obvious that they, like their human counterparts, prefer maturer men. We re-alized then that we had established, not a program of breeding, but a program of brooding.

We had in fact been warned. Our first seven laboratory-born babies were raised in individual cages while being trained on a learning test battery. William Mason planned to test their social behaviors subsequently, and great care had been taken to keep the babies socially isolated and to prevent any physical contacts. Neo-natal baby monkeys required 24-hour-a-day care, and infant mon-keys need ministrations beyond a 40-hour week. We had assigned the evening care to Kathy, a maternal bit of fluff who had worked for several years as a monkey tester while studying to become an elementary school teacher.

Checking on his wards one night near 10 P.M., Mason found Kathy sitting on the floor surrounded by seven baby monkeys, all eight of the primates playing happily together. Before the horrified scientist could express his outrage, Kathy had risen to her full height of five feet two. Already anticipating the carping criticisms which he was formulating, she shook her finger in his face and spoke with conviction: "Dr. Mason, I'm an education student and I know that it is improper and immoral to blight the social development of little children. I am right and you are wrong!"

Although we were angry with Kathy, we did think there was a certain humor in the situation and we did not worry about our monkeys. We simply transferred Kathy to an office job. Alas, she could not have been more right and we could not have been more wrong! We have already described the social-sexual life of these 7 monkeys and the next 40 to come.

Two years later we had more than theoretical reasons to be disturbed because Mason tested a group of these isolation-raised monkeys, then between 2.5 and 3.5 years of age, and found evidence of severe social abnormalities, which might be described as a sociopathic syndrome. He matched the laboratory-raised monkeys on the basis of weight and dentition patterns with monkeys that had been born and raised in the wild for the first 12 to 18 months, then captured and subjected to various kinds of housing and caging treatments for the next year or two. In the test situations the laboratory-raised monkeys, as compared with feral monkeys, showed infantile sexual behavior, absence of grooming, exaggerated aggression, and absence of affectional interaction as measured by cooperation.

We are now quite certain that this sociopathic syndrome does not stem from the fact that the baby monkeys were raised in the laboratory but from *how* they were raised in the laboratory. Our infants raised in the laboratory by real monkey mothers and permitted opportunity for the development of normal infant-infant affection demonstrate normal male and female sexual behavior when they enter the second year of life. Furthermore, our playroom and playpen studies show that infant monkeys raised on cloth mothers but given the opportunity to form normal infant-infant affectional patterns also develop normal sexual responses.

In a desperate attempt to assist a group of 18 three- to four-year-old cloth-surrogate-raised monkeys, half of them males and half females, we engaged in a group-psychotherapy program, placing these animals for two months on the monkey island in the Madison Zoo, as shown in Figure 13. Their summer vacation on the enchanted island was not without avail, and social grooming responses rapidly developed and were frequent in occurrence. After a few days of misunderstanding, patterns of social ordering developed, and a number of males and females developed friendship patterns. Unfortunately, sexual behavior was infrequent, and the behavior that was observed was completely inadequate—at least from our point of view. In desperation we finally introduced our most experienced, most patient, and most kindly breeding male, Smiley (the male in Figures 1 and 2), and he rapidly established himself as king of the island and prepared to take full advantage of the wealth of opportunity which surrounded him. Fortunately, the traumatic experiences he encountered with unreceptive females have left no apparent permanent emotional scars, and now that he has been returned to our laboratory breeding colony, he is again making an important contribution to our research program. If normal sexual behavior occurred, no member of our observational team ever saw it, and had a female become pregnant, we would have believed in parthenogenesis.

FIG. 13. GROUP OF CLOTH-SURROGATE-RAISED MONKEYS ON THE MONKEY ISLAND IN THE MADISON ZOO.

But let us return to the monkeys that we left on the island and the older ones that we left in their cages. A year has passed, and the frustrations that both we and our monkeys experienced are in some small part nothing but a memory. We constructed larger and more comfortable breeding cages, and we designed a very large experimental breeding room 8 feet by 8 feet by 8 feet in size with appropriate platforms and a six-foot tree. Apparently we designed successful seraglios for I can report that not all love's labors have been lost. It does appear that the males are completely expendable unless they can be used in a program of artificial insemination. Certainly we can find no evidence that there is a destiny that shapes their ends unless some Skinnerite can help us with the shaping process. We have, however, had better success with some of the females, particularly the females raised on cloth surrogates.

Even so, one of the wire-caged-raised females is a mother and another is pregnant. Three cloth-surrogate females are mothers and four or five are expectant. We give all the credit to three breeding males. One, Smiley, does not take "no" for an answer. Smiley has a way with females. Patient, gentle, and persuasive, he has overcome more than one planned program of passive resistance. One female did not become pregnant until the fifth successive month of training. Month after month she has changed, and now she is mad about

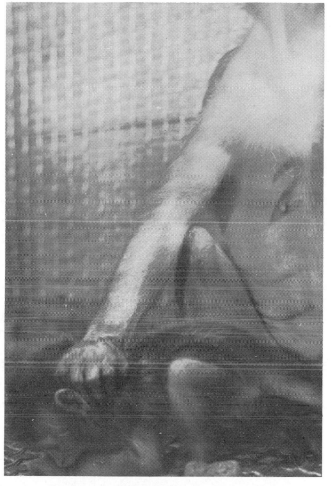

FIG. 14. TYPICAL BEHAVIOR OF UNMOTHERED MOTHER TOWARD HER INFANT. MOTHER IS LOOKING UPWARD WHILE CRUSHING HER BABY AGAINST THE CAGE FLOOR.

the boy. Male No. 342 behaves very much like Smiley. Even when females threaten him, he does not harm them. Given time, he has been able to overcome more than one reluctant dragon, and he is a master of the power of positive suggestion.

Breeding male No. 496 has helped us greatly, particularly with the younger, cloth-surrogate-raised females. His approach differs from that of Smiley and No. 342. His technique transcends seduction, and in contract bridge terms it may be described as an approach-forcing system.

Combining our human and male-monkey talents, we are winning the good fight and imparting to naive and even resistant female monkeys the priceless gift of motherhood. Possibly it is a Pyrrhic victory. As every scientist knows, the solution of one scientific problem inevitably leads to another, and this is our fate (Figure 14). Month after month female monkeys that never knew a real mother themselves becomes mothers—helpless, hopeless, heartless mothers devoid, or almost devoid, of any maternal feeling.

RESOLVING SOCIAL CONFLICTS*
Kurt Lewin

THE SOCIAL DISTANCE BETWEEN INDIVIDUALS IN THE UNITED STATES AND IN GERMANY

Considering the structure of the individual as a social being, there seem to be the following differences between the typical American and typical German. The average *"social distance"* (the term used as in sociology) *between different individuals seems to be smaller in the United States so far as the surface regions, or, as one may say, the "peripheral regions," of the personality are concerned.* That means the American is more willing to be open to other individuals and to share certain situations with other individuals than the German.

Quite commonly strangers on the street may greet one another with a smile, a behavior unusual in Germany. People waiting for the bus may start to discuss the weather, and in the train, conversation between strangers starts more easily than in Germany. (There is certainly a difference between the people of a large and a small town, both in the United States and Germany. The Englishman, at least outside of England, may be even more reserved in such situations than a German.) The American seems more friendly and more ready to help a stranger. It is more customary in the United States

Pp. 18–22, 23–25, *Resolving Social Conflicts* by Kurt Lewin. Copyright 1948 by Harper & Row, Publishers, Incorporated. Reprinted by permission of the publishers.

to invite a visitor, who is not a personal friend, to lunch or to one's home, than in Germany under similar circumstances. Nearly every German coming to the United States admires the natural ease and the efficiency with which the American generally take care of all the minor difficulties a newcomer has to face.

In boarding houses one finds people sitting in their rooms with the door wide open, so that anyone might step in. The American seems to have decidedly less need for privacy in certain regions of life. It is possible to find the office door of even a president of a college open all day; so everybody can see with whom he is conversing and in what manner he is acting. Such behavior would be unthinkable in Germany even for an unimportant official, one of whose techniques in getting respect and showing his importance is to let people wait a long time in front of his closed door. In the United States it would be bad taste to let other persons wait, however great the difference in the social status of the persons involved may be. This difference between the United States and Germany is very striking, and is an expression of the democratic attitude toward the equal rights of everybody and of the greater general accessibility of the American.

The average American talks less loudly than the German, both in a private conversation, and in public. It may well be that this is due to the fact that the peripheral regions of the U-type are more accessible. Besides the G-type tends, as we will see, to a more emotional and aggressive behavior.[1]

Nevertheless, the average "social distance" between persons in the United States seems not to be smaller in every respect, but only in regard to more peripheral layers of the person. The more intimate "central" regions of personality seem to be at least as separated between different persons, and at least as difficult to get access to as among Germans. For instance, relations between boys and girls might progress in the United States more easily up to a certain point, whereas the step leading to an intimate relationship seems to be more clearly marked than in Germany. In Germany, there is a more gradual transition in social relationships from the very peripheral to the very intimate. Germans entering the United States

---

[1]The "layering" of personality structure in terms of accessibility of social distance is graphically shown in Figure 1. Essentially, Lewin is saying that the outer boundaries (peripheral) are easier to penetrate in the American (U-type) and relatively inaccessible at the deeper levels of personality. The German (G-type) shows the opposite boundary system: low accessibility at the peripheral areas and more possibilities for reaching the core areas of personality. [Eds.]

notice usually that the degree of friendly and close relation, which one may achieve as a newcomer within a few weeks, is much higher than under similar circumstances in Germany. Compared with Germans, Americans seem to make quicker progress towards friendly relations in the beginning, and with many more persons. Yet this development often stops at a certain point; and the quickly acquired friends will, after years of relatively close relations, say good-by as easily as after a few weeks of acquaintance.

AN OPERATIONAL DEFINITION OF SOCIAL DISTANCE

If one wants to express these facts with topological and dynamic concepts, one has to ask what "social distance" between persons means from an operational point of view.

Two groups of facts seem to be possible for an operational definition of social distances:

1. One can start with the difference between the more "peripheral" and the more "central" regions of the person, taking the operational definition from the many kinds of experiments in which the relation of an activity to these different layers have proved to be of primary importance (experiments on psychological satiation, emotions, quasi-needs). The more central regions are defined as the more intimate, personal regions. In these regions, the individual usually is more sensitive than in the peripheral.

2. The second definition could make use of the way social distances generally are proved in sociology: The person A is asked whether he would share certain situations (like traveling in the same car, playing games together, dancing together, marrying) with a certain person B. The differences in social distance can be defined as different degrees of intimacy of the situation which the person is willing to share with the other.

A certain distance, therefore, means, dynamically speaking, the accessibility of certain situations or activities of the person B for the person A, and the non-accessibility for more intimate situations. This accessibility to certain situations or activities is equivalent (or very closely related) to the possibility of B to communicate with certain, but not with the more central, layers of A.

So far as the state of the person A is concerned, a smaller social distance to B than to C means that more central regions of A are open to B than to C. The statement about the typical American compared with the typical German would mean that, *ceteris paribus,* the peripheral layers of the American show less resistance against communication from another person.

One can represent the greater "openness" by co-ordinating to the peripheral layers themselves or to their boundaries less resistance against communicative actions from outside. Figure 1 represents the state of the typical American (U-type, Figure 1a) compared with the German (G-type, Figure 1b).

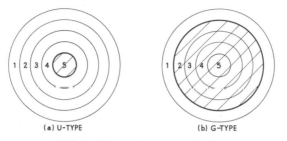

(a) U-TYPE   (b) G-TYPE

FIG. 1. PERSONALITY STRUCTURE.

The thickness of the boundary lines between the personality layers represents the difference in accessibility. The hatched area corresponds to the "private" region of the person.

In the diagram, the degree of resistance against communication from outside is represented by stronger boundaries (heavier lines) around the layer in question. I distinguish arbitrarily the same number of layers within the person.

Using such means, one would have to symbolize the U-type, let us say, by four peripheral regions with easily permeable boundaries. Only the very central (fifth) region is insulated from communication to a high degree. In the G-type only the most peripheral region (first) is easily accessible. The more central are relatively difficult of approach. A major boundary lies already between the regions 1 and 2 (Figure 1b).

The facts available seem not to permit a statement about the relative permeability of every region. But they do seem to permit statements about position of the first main resistance against *invasion* from outside.

EMOTION, FRIENDSHIP, AND FRICTION

A second fact could be mentioned which is somewhat related to the same structural differences. The American is much less likely to respond with anger, or at least with open anger, to the hundred small misfortunes of everyday life. Several facts seems to converge to this effect. The American reacts generally to such accidents more from the point of view of action (he considers what has to be done next in order to remedy the situation), the German more from a moral point of view (he considers whose fault it was). Furthermore, such incidents are less likely to touch central regions of the person. In other words, the range of events which correspond to the peripheral, non-private regions, seems to be comparatively greater for the American. This is entirely in line with our basic statement. As the private field includes more layers for the G-type, he is likely to act more emotionally.

This fact is of especial importance for the interrelationship between several persons. One can ask how many layers of two persons (A and B, Figure 2) can come in contact with each other without touching the "private" regions. Communication between regions can be represented by overlapping, or by a common boundary of the regions in question. From our basic assumption, it follows that more regions can overlap in the U-type than in the G-type before private regions are touched. For instance, the overlapping of the three outer layers does not involve a communication between the private regions of the U-type (Figure 2a), whereas such overlapping would involve private regions of the G-type (Figure 2b).

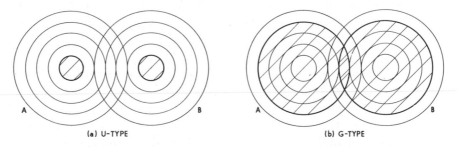

(a) U-TYPE   (b) G-TYPE

FIG. 2. TWO PERSONS (A AND B) IN COMMUNICATION.

This should have two results: It should make possible *relatively close relations between persons of the U-type without a deep personal friendship*. On the other hand, these persons should be *less in danger of personal friction*. Such friction occurs more easily if personal regions are touched. The facts mentioned seem to be well in line with both conclusions.

ACTIONS AND IDEALS

The fact that there are more regions which are not considered "private" by the American does not mean that these peripheral regions are considered of less importance by him. On the contrary, if one considers the structure of the person as a whole, our basic assumption implies that the relative weight of the non-private regions is greater for a person of the U-type than for the G-type. The facts mentioned above point already in this direction.

A second fact can be mentioned here. The peripheral layers of personality include what one can call the "motoric" or "executive" region of a person. This region is the outer layer of the person, the one closest to the environment. It corresponds to the appearance and action of the person. That the relative weight of the appearance seems to be greater for the U-type was mentioned above. The *actions* are relatively more emphasized in the U-type. The American, as compared with the German, emphasizes achievement more than ideology or status. In science he emphasizes practice more than theory. The U-type prefers to make extensive "empirical" collection of facts. The greater relative weight which the central regions, and therefore the ideals and other "irreal" facts have for the German, is of fundamental importance for so-called German idealism as against American pragmatism. A similar difference in attitude between Germans and Americans is striking in the fields of politics and religion.

THE SELF-RESTRAINT OF FRIENDS*

John E. Mayer

In the spring of 1954 a group of 88 college women, mostly juniors and seniors, who were attending a large metropolitan college were asked to place themselves in a number of imaginary situations and to indicate how they would react. One of the situations, upon which the following analysis is based, was as follows:

Suppose that a good friend of yours *has just met* a boy whom she seems to be quite interested in. For one reason or another you have an unfavorable opinion of him.

What do you think you would do in such a situation? That is, would you tell your friend how you felt? If yes, why? If not, why not?

Fifteen per cent said they would discuss their feelings with their friend; 20 per cent said they would not; while 65 per cent qualified their answers, indicating that under certain conditions they would

*From "The Self-Restraint of Friends: A Mechanism in Family Transition," *Social Forces*, Vol. 35 (1957), pp. 230–38. Abridged and reprinted by permission of the author and *Social Forces*.

act one way but under other conditions they would act otherwise. Before considering some of these conditions, what are some of the main reasons given by respondents for either expressing or withholding their opinions?

REASONS FOR EXPRESSING OPINION

Those who say they would discuss the matter with the friend, under some or all conditions, reveal that the relationship between them and their friend overshadows that between the friend and the suitor. In more formal terms, X, the friend in question, simultaneously occupies the role of a good friend and a person in a courtship relationship; the question of which role shall receive priority is solved by this group of respondents in favor of the former.

This emphasis is indicated in a number of ways. Some point out that the unrestricted sharing of feelings is one of the prerogatives of a friendship relationship. A few go further and believe that such sharing is obligatory.

> It so happens that recently a friend of mine started going steady with a boy I do not like. I think it my duty, as a good friend, to freely express my opinions. As a friend, she knows I am only interested in her welfare, and to keep from her my true feelings is more the actions of an enemy.

Others are more inclined to stress what may be the unhappy consequences of remaining silent.

> If a good friend of mine met a boy that I disapproved of for one reason or another, I would definitely tell her. This is true especially if she did not see the faults herself. . . . My reasons for telling her my opinions are that I would not like to see her make a mistake or be unhappy.

REASONS FOR WITHHOLDING OPINION

It is equally apparent that those who place restraints upon the expression of their feelings are responding primarily to X's other role—that of someone in a courtship relationship.

In accounting for their own reticence, their responses are peppered with moral directives: "It's none of my business"; "I have no right to interfere." Sometimes reference is made as to how the girl friend should conduct herself in this situation. "It's up to her to discover the boy's assets and liabilities." "One has the right to pick and choose one's boy friends." Such sentiments clearly reflect the norms that regulate the relationship between those who are courting and those in the immediate social environment, e.g., friends, relatives. When it comes to choosing a marriage partner it is accepted that others will minimize their influence, while at the same time it is incumbent upon those involved to reach their own decision and to take full responsibility for their choice.

While some of the respondents appeal directly to what they feel are intrinsically "right" and "wrong" ways of acting, others are more concerned with the possible consequences of violating the norms. A danger is that their friends might resent hearing their opinion and, even worse, that the friendship might be seriously jeopardized.

> If I spoke my mind, she might resent it and feel that I am attempting to domineer and influence her.
> I would not tell my friend how I felt because the quickest way to lose a good friend and make an enemy is to say something about the fellow she likes.

Foremost Considerations in Reaching a Decision

The large majority of respondents—and the majority would have probably been even larger if the students had been questioned further—did not give undisputed precedence to one alternative while completely subordinating the other. In varying degrees they were sensitive to the demands of both relationships and were, consequently, pulled in opposing directions at the same time. They resolved their dilemma, at least on paper, by examining more closely various aspects of the situation described and then specifying the conditions under which they would take one course rather than the other. In the following are some of the considerations they felt would be the most relevant in helping them to decide whether to voice an opinion or to maintain silence.

1. How involved are the couple? The closer the attachment, the more cautious are friends apt to become in publicizing their low estimate of the boy. When the two people are quite absorbed in each other, to speak one's mind without careful forethought is viewed as "interfering," "inflicting one's opinion," and "sticking one's nose into other people's business."[1]

2. How close are the friends? In general, the closer the association, the smaller are the barriers to communication.

> If it were an honest and close friendship I would tell her my opinions. . . .
> Yes, I would tell her if she was a very good friend of mine and if we discussed things openly together in the past.

---

[1] The tendency of friends to curb their influence, which continues throughout the courtship period, reaches its climax after the couple are married. It is expected that, above all, marriage should be a private relationship between husband and wife and that many of its internal aspects should not be revealed to others. However much the spouses may work toward this end, the withdrawal action of friends—their long practiced self-restraint—is instrumental in making it a private relationship.

3. Who brings up the subject? Respondents feel considerably less restraint when they are asked for their views.

> I would not volunteer information. However, my friend would probably ask me and then I would answer *tactfully*.

But even though one's opinion is solicited, this is no guarantee that it will be truthfully given.

> If she were to ask me my opinion about him I would simply say, "I don't know him well enough to say whether or not I like him; but I think he's nice."

4. What is the basis of one's dislike? A primary question concerns the reliability of one's unfavorable impression of the boy.

> If I felt that my opinion was well-grounded I would express my thoughts very objectively to the girl. If I just had a feeling about the fellow, I would give him time to prove or disprove my opinion of him.

Even though early impressions are repeatedly confirmed, there still remains the question of whether the basis of one's dislike is serious enough to warrant bringing it out into the open.

> Sometimes you meet people, and for no particular reason they "strike you the wrong way." In such a case I would not express my opinion concerning the boy. If on the other hand, there are outstanding characteristics, such as nastiness, stinginess, assuming a dominant air, etc., which make the boy dislikable and a bad companion then I would express my opinion.

In actuality, respondents are faced with more than simply reaching a yes or no decision as to whether or not they should give voice to their sentiments. If it is decided that conditions warrant speaking up, there still remains the question as to how much of one's opinion should be expressed. Opinion, like color, runs through many gradations, and to convey a negative opinion is not necessarily to impart its full strength.

As might be expected, there is a marked tendency to convey a less damaging impression than is actually felt, and for this purpose a variety of techniques is used. Some respondents would simply understate the intensity of their negative estimate of the boy, while others would respond frankly but cushion the blow with an enthusiastic account of his assets. Another technique, designed to minimize the impact of one's opinion, is to cast serious doubts upon its reliability; e.g., "It is only my opinion and I certainly could be wrong."

In sum, communication between friends tends to be curtailed in varying degrees under the following conditions: when the couple are engrossed in each other, when the friendship between the girls is only a casual one, when the friend's opinion is not solicited, and when the friend feels her low regard for the boy may lack substance.

Since such conditions as these occur with some regularity in the social life of individuals, their net effect in silencing adverse opinion may well be considerable.

The Self-Restraint of Friends

Focusing upon the pattern of self-restraint identified above, it is of interest how early in the relationship of the couple this pattern tends to become invoked. When a romance is well advanced, with the partners heading toward marriage, not to interfere is a well-recognized obligation. However, it will be recalled that, in the situation presented to the respondents, the couple had only recently met, and presumably the romance was still in its initial stages. Yet, even at this point, there was a marked tendency to withhold negative comment.

The strength of this tendency is suggested by the fact that upon occasion it competes successfully with the interaction patterns obtaining between good friends. It is between friends that the flow of opinion and sentiment, both favorable and unfavorable, tends to be less censored and restricted than in most other types of associations. Such patterns of communication, often of long duration, are apt to be well established and not easily swept aside; for them to be interrupted suggests the existence of a counterbalancing force of considerable magnitude.

Finally, the tentative nature of the preceding remarks should be kept in mind. For one thing, the answers of a group of respondents to a hypothetical situation are not necessarily infallible indicators of their behavior in the actual situation. Furthermore, there is the question of the extent to which the same patterns would appear within other sectors of the population. In particular, to what extent would the tendency toward self-restraint manifest itself within other groups, e.g., males, different age groups, different social levels?[2]

---

[2]Because of the tradition of greater male independence and self-reliance, males will presumably be even more restrained from influencing their friends. If true, this suggests a number of interesting implications. Because males who are seeking mates may be subject to a lesser degree of control, it is possible that they will depart more from the standards of their friends. As a result, the latter may be less favorably disposed toward their friends' wives than females will be toward their friends' husbands. Accordingly, one would expect that after the marriage there would be a greater likelihood of strain arising between male as compared to female friends, and that more of the male friendships would be discontinued as a result. From the standpoint of the married couple, their joint friendship circle would possibly include, for the same reason, a smaller proportion of the husband's than of the wife's pre-marital friends.

BEHAVIORAL STUDY OF OBEDIENCE*
Stanley Milgram

Obedience is as basic an element in the structure of social life as one can point to. Some system of authority is a requirement of all communal living, and it is only the man dwelling in isolation who is not forced to respond, through defiance or submission, to the commands of others. Obedience, as a determinant of behavior, is of particular relevance to our time. It has been reliably established that from 1933–45 millions of innocent persons were systematically slaughtered on command. Gas chambers were built, death camps were guarded, daily quotas of corpses were produced with the same efficiency as the manufacture of appliances. These inhumane policies may have originated in the mind of a single person, but they could only be carried out on a massive scale if a very large number of persons obeyed orders.

Obedience is the psychological mechanism that links individual action to political purpose. It is the dispositional cement that binds men to systems of authority. Facts of recent history and observation in daily life suggest that for many persons obedience may be a deeply ingrained behavior tendency, indeed, a prepotent impulse overriding training in ethics, sympathy, and moral conduct. C. P. Snow points to its importance when he writes:

> When you think of the long and gloomy history of man, you will find more hideous crimes have been committed in the name of obedience than have ever been committed in the name of rebellion. If you doubt that, read William Shirer's "Rise and Fall of the Third Reich." The German Officer Corps were brought up in the most rigorous code of obedience . . . in the name of obedience they were party to, and assisted in, the most wicked large scale actions in the history of the world.[1]

While the particular form of obedience dealt with in the present study has its antecedents in these episodes, it must not be thought all obedience entails acts of aggression against others. Obedience serves numerous productive functions. Indeed, the very life of so-

---

*From *Journal of Abnormal and Social Psychology,* Vol. 67, No. 4 (1963), 371–78. Used by permission.
[1]C. P. Snow, "Either/Or," *Progressive,* Feb., 1961, p. 24.

ciety is predicated on its existence. Obedience may be ennobling and educative and refer to acts of charity and kindness, as well as to destruction.

General Procedure

A procedure was devised which seems useful as a tool for studying obedience.[2] It consists of ordering a naive subject to administer electric shock to a victim. A simulated shock generator is used, with 30 clearly marked voltage levels that range from 15 to 450 volts. The instrument bears verbal designations that range from Slight Shock to Danger: Severe Shock. The responses of the victim, who is a trained confederate of the experimenter, are standardized. The orders to adminster shocks are given to the naive subject in the context of a "learning experiment" ostensibly set up to study the effects of punishment on memory. As the experiment proceeds the naive subject is commanded to administer increasingly more intense shocks to the victim, even to the point of reaching the level marked Danger: Severe Shock. Internal resistances become stronger, and at a certain point the subject refuses to go on with the experiment. Behavior prior to this rupture is considered "obedience," in that the subject complies with the commands of the experimenter. The point of rupture is the act of disobedience. A quantitative value is assigned to the subject's performance based on the maximum intensity shock he is willing to administer before he refuses to participate further. Thus for any particular subject and for any particular experimental condition the degree of obedience may be specified with a numerical value. The crux of the study is to systematically vary the factors believed to alter the degree of obedience to the experimental commands.

The technique allows important variables to be manipulated at several points in the experiment. One may vary aspects of the source of command, content and form of command, instrumentalities for its execution, target object, general social setting, etc. The problem, therefore, is not one of designing increasingly more numerous experimental conditions, but of selecting those that best illuminate the *process* of obedience from the sociopsychological standpoint.

---

[2] S. Milgram, "Dynamics of Obedience" (Washington, D.C.: National Science Foundation, January 25, 1961), mimeo.

Related Studies

The inquiry bears an important relation to philosophic analyses of obedience and authority (Arendt,[3] Friedrich,[4] Weber,[5]), an early experimental study of obedience by Frank,[6] studies in "authoritarianism" (Adorno, Frenkel-Brunswik, Levinson, & Sanford,[7]; Rokeach,[8]), and a recent series of analytic and empirical studies in social power (Cartwright[9]). It owes much to the long concern with *suggestion* in social psychology, both in its normal forms (e.g., Binet,[10]) and in its clinical manifestations (Charcot[11]). But it derives, in the first instance, from direct observation of a social fact; the individual who is commanded by a legitimate authority ordinarily obeys. Obedience comes easily and often. It is a ubiquitous and indispensable feature of social life.

METHOD

Subjects

The subjects were 40 males between the ages of 20 and 50, drawn from New Haven and the surrounding communities. Subjects were obtained by a newspaper advertisement and direct mail solicitation. Those who responded to the appeal believed they were to participate in a study of memory and learning at Yale University. A wide range of occupations is represented in the sample. Typical subjects were postal clerks, high school teachers, salesmen, engineers, and laborers. Subjects ranged in educational level from one who had not finished elementary school, to those who had doctorate and other professional degrees. They were paid $4.50 for their participation in the experiment. However, subjects were told that payment was simply for coming to the laboratory, and that the money was theirs

---

[3]H. Arendt, "What Was Authority?" in *Authority*, C. J. Friedrich (ed.) (Cambridge: Harvard Univ. Press, 1958), pp. 81–112.

[4]C. J. Friedrich (ed.), *Authority* (Cambridge: Harvard Univ. Press, 1958).

[5]M. Weber, *The Theory of Social and Economic Organization* (Oxford: Oxford Univ. Press, 1947).

[6]J. D. Frank, "Experimental Studies of Personal Pressure and Resistance," *J. Gen. Psychol.*, Vol. 30 (1944), pp. 23–64.

[7]T. Adorno, Else Frenkel-Brunswik, D. J. Levinson, and R. N. Sanford, *The Authoritarian Personality* (New York: Harper, 1950).

[8]M. Rokeach, "Authority, Authoritarianism, and Conformity," in *Conformity and Deviation*, I. A. Berg and B. M. Bass (eds.) (New York: Harper, 1961), pp. 230–57.

[9]D. Cartwright (ed.), *Studies in Social Power* (Ann Arbor: Univ. of Michigan Institute for Social Research, 1959).

[10]A. Binet, *La Suggestibilité* (Paris: Schleicher, 1900).

[11]J. M. Charcot, *Oeuvres Complètes* (Paris: Bureaux du Progrès Médical, 1881).

no matter what happened after they arrived. Table 1 shows the proportion of age and occupational types assigned to the experimental condition.

TABLE 1

DISTRIBUTION OF AGE AND OCCUPATIONAL TYPES IN THE EXPERIMENT

Occupations	20–29 Years n	30–39 Years n	40–50 Years n	Percentage of Total (Occupations)
Workers, skilled and unskilled........	4	5	6	37.5
Sales, business, and white-collar......	3	6	7	40.0
Professional........................	1	5	3	22.5
Percentage of total (age)............	20	40	40	

Note: Total $n = 40$.

Personnel and Locale

The experiment was conducted on the grounds of Yale University in the elegant interaction laboratory. (This detail is relevant to the perceived legitimacy of the experiment. In further variations, the experiment was dissociated from the university, with consequences for performance.) The role of experimenter was played by a 31-year-old high school teacher of biology. His manner was impassive, and his appearance somewhat stern throughout the experiment. He was dressed in a gray technician's coat. The victim was played by a 47-year-old accountant, trained for the role; he was of Irish-American stock, whom most observers found mild-mannered and likable.

Procedure

One naive subject and one victim (an accomplice) performed in each experiment. A pretext had to be devised that would justify the administration of electric shock by the naive subject. This was effectively accomplished by the cover story. After a general introduction on the presumed relation between punishment and learning, subjects were told:

But actually, we know *very little* about the effect of punishment on learning, because almost no truly scientific studies have been made of it in human beings.

For instance, we don't know how *much* punishment is best for learning—and we don't know how much difference it makes as to who is giving the punishment, whether an adult learns best from a younger or an older person than himself—or many things of that sort.

So in this study we are bringing together a number of adults of different occupations and ages. And we're asking some of them to be teachers and some of them to be learners.

We want to find out just what effect different people have on each other as teachers and learners, and also what effect *punishment* will have on learning in this situation.

Therefore, I'm going to ask one of you to be the teacher here tonight and the other one to be the learner.

Does either of you have a preference?

Subjects then drew slips of paper from a hat to determine who would be the teacher and who would be the learner in the experiment. The drawing was rigged so that the naive subject was always the teacher and the accomplice always the learner. (Both slips contained the word "Teacher.") Immediately after the drawing, the teacher and learner were taken to an adjacent room and the learner was strapped into an "electric chair" apparatus.

The experimenter explained that the straps were to prevent excessive movement while the learner was being shocked. The effect was to make it impossible for him to escape from the situation. An electrode was attached to the learner's wrist, and electrode paste was applied "to avoid blisters and burns." Subjects were told that the electrode was attached to the shock generator in the adjoining room.

In order to improve credibility the experimenter declared, in response to a question by the learner: "Although the shocks can be extremely painful, they cause no permanent tissue damage."

Learning Task.   The lesson administered by the subject was a paired-associate learning task. The subject read a series of word pairs to the learner, and then read the first word of the pair along with four terms. The learner was to indicate which of the four terms had originally been paired with the first word. He communicated his answer by pressing one of four switches in front of him, which in turn lit up one of four numbered quadrants in an answer-box located atop the shock generator.

Shock Generator.   The instrument panel consists of 30 lever switches set in a horizontal line. Each switch is clearly labeled with a voltage designation that ranges from 15 to 450 volts. There is a 15-volt increment from one switch to the next going from left to right. In addition, the following verbal designations are clearly indicated for groups of four switches going from left to right: Slight Shock, Moderate Shock, Strong Shock, Very Strong Shock, Intense Shock, Extreme Intensity Shock, Danger: Severe Shock. (Two switches after this last designation are simply marked XXX.)

Upon depressing a switch; a pilot light corresponding to each switch is illuminated in bright red; an electric buzzing is heard; an electric blue light, labeled "voltage energizer," flashes; the dial on the voltage meter swings to the right; various relay clicks are sounded.

The upper left-hand corner of the generator is labeled Shock Generator, Type ZLB, Dyson Instrument Company, Waltham, Mass. Output 15 Volts–450 Volts.

Details of the instrument were carefully handled to insure an appearance of authenticity. The panel was engraved by precision industrial engravers, and all components were of high quality. No subject in the experiment suspected that the instrument was merely a simulated shock generator.

Sample Shock. Each naive subject is given a sample shock on the shock generator, prior to beginning his run as teacher. This shock is always 45 volts, and is applied by pressing the third switch of the generator. The shock is applied to the wrist of the naive subject, and has its source in a 45-volt battery wired into the generator. This further convinces the subject of the authenticity of the generator.

Shock Instructions. The subject is told to administer a shock to the learner each time he gives a wrong response. Moreover—and this is the key command—the subject is instructed to "move one level higher on the shock generator each time the learner flashes a wrong answer." He is also instructed to announce the voltage level before administering a shock. This serves to continually remind subjects of the increasing intensity of shocks administered to the learner.

Preliminary and Regular Run. Pretests revealed that the procedure of reading words and administering shocks requires some practice before it can be handled smoothly. Therefore, immediately preceding the regular run, the teacher is given a preliminary series of 10 words to read to the learner. There are 3 neutral words in the practice series (i.e., words that the learner answers correctly), so that shocks are administered for 7 of the words, with the maximum shock at 105 volts (moderate shock). Almost all subjects master the procedure by the time the preliminary run is over.

Subjects are then presented with a second list, and are told that the procedure is the same as for the first list; the experimenter adds, however: "When you get to the bottom of the list, repeat it over again, and continue giving shocks, until the learner has learned all the pairs correctly." The experimenter instructs the subject to, "start from 15 volts and increase the shock level one step each time the learner gives a wrong answer."

Feedback from the Victim.   In all conditions the learner gives a predetermined set of responses to the word pair test, based on a schedule of approximately three wrong answers to one correct answer. In the present experimental condition no vocal response or other sign of protest is heard from the learner until Shock Level 300 is reached. When the 300-volt shock is administered, the learner pounds on the wall of the room in which he is bound to the electric chair. The pounding can be heard by the subject. From this point on, the learner's answers no longer appear on the four-way panel.

At this juncture, subjects ordinarily turn to the experimenter for guidance. The experimenter instructs the subject to treat the absence of a response as a wrong answer, and to shock the subject according to the usual schedule. He advises the subjects to allow 5–10 seconds before considering no response as a wrong answer, and to increase the shock level one step each time the learner fails to respond correctly. The learner's pounding is repeated after the 315-volt shock is administered; afterwards he is not heard from, nor do his answers reappear on the four-way signal box.

Experimenter Feedback.   At various points in the experiment the subject may turn to the experimenter for advice on whether he should continue to administer shocks. Or he may indicate that he does not wish to go on. It was important to standardize the experimenter's responses to these inquiries and reactions.

If the subject indicated his unwillingness to go on, the experimenter responded with a sequence of "prods," using as many as necessary to bring the subject into line.

Prod 1: Please continue, *or* Please go on.
Prod 2: The experiment requires that you continue.
Prod 3: It is absolutely essential that you continue.
Prod 4: You have no other choice, you *must* go on.

The prods were always made in sequence: Only if Prod 1 had been unsuccessful could Prod 2 be used. If the subject refused to obey the experimenter after Prod 4, the experiment was terminated. The experimenter's tone of voice was at all times firm, but not impolite. The sequence was begun anew on each occasion that the subject balked or showed reluctance to follow orders.

Special prods. If the subject asked if the learner was liable to suffer permanent physical injury, the experimenter said: "Although the shocks may be painful, there is no permanent tissue damage, so please go on." [Followed by Prods 2, 3, and 4 if necessary.]

If the subject said that the learner did not want to go on, the experimenter replied: "Whether the learner likes it or not, you must go on until he has learned all the word pairs correctly. So please go on." [Followed by Prods 2, 3, and 4 if necessary.]

Dependent Measures

The primary dependent measure for any subject is the maximum shock he administers before he refuses to go any further. In principle this may vary from 0 (for a subject who refuses to administer even the first shock) to 30 (for a subject who administers the highest shock on the generator). A subject who breaks off the experiment at any point prior to administering the thirtieth shock level is termed a *defiant* subject. One who complies with experimental commands fully, and proceeds to administer all shock levels commanded, is termed an *obedient* subject.

Further Records. With few exceptions, experimental sessions were recorded on magnetic tape. Occasional photographs were taken through one-way mirrors. Notes were kept on any unusual behavior occurring during the course of the experiments. On occasion, additional observers were directed to write objective descriptions of the subjects' behavior. The latency and duration of shocks were measured by accurate timing devices.

Interview and Dehoax. Following the experiment, subjects were interviewed; open-ended questions, projective measures, and attitude scales were employed. After the interview, procedures were undertaken to assure that the subject would leave the laboratory in a state of well being. A friendly reconciliation was arranged between the subject and the victim, and an effort was made to reduce any tensions that arose as a result of the experiment.

RESULTS

Preliminary Notions

Before giving an account of the experimental results, it is instructive to consider how persons predict others will perform when commanded to administer powerful shocks to another person. Fourteen Yale seniors, all psychology majors, were provided with a detailed description of the experimental situation. They were asked to reflect carefully on it, and to predict the behavior of 100 hypothetical subjects. More specifically, they were instructed to plot the distribution of obedience of "100 Americans of diverse occupations, and ranging in age from 20 to 50 years," who were placed in the experimental situation.

There was considerable agreement among the respondents on the expected behavior of hypothetical subjects. All respondents predicted that only an insignificant minority would go through to the end of the shock series. (The estimates ranged from 0 to 3%; i.e., the most "pessimistic" member of the class predicted that of 100 persons, 3 would continue through to the most potent shock available on the shock generator—450 volts.) The class mean was 1.2%. The question was also posed informally to colleagues of the author, and the most general feeling was that few if any subjects would go beyond the designation Very Strong Shock.

Result of Experiment I

Subjects Accept Situation. With few exceptions subjects were convinced of the reality of the experimental situation, that they were administering shocks to another person, and the most potent shocks were extremely painful. In the post-experimental interview subjects were asked: "How painful to the learner were the last few shocks that you administered to him?" Subjects were instructed to indicate their answers on a printed 14-point scale ranging from "Not at all painful" to "Extremely painful." The modal response was 14 (Extremely painful) with the mean at 13.42.

Signs of Extreme Tension. Many subjects showed signs of nervousness in the experimental situation, and especially upon administering the more powerful shocks. In a large number of cases the degree of tension reached extremes that are rarely seen in socio-psychological laboratory studies. Subjects were observed to sweat, tremble, stutter, bite their lips, groan, and dig their fingernails into their flesh. These were characteristic rather than exceptional responses to the experiment.

One sign of tension was the regular occurrence of nervous laughing fits. Fourteen of the 40 subjects showed definite signs of nervous laughter and smiling. The laughter seemed entirely out of place, even bizarre. Full-blown, uncontrollable seizures were observed for 3 subjects. On one occasion we observed a seizure so violently convulsive that it was necesssary to call a halt to the experiment. The subject, a 46-year-old encyclopedia salesman, was seriously embarrassed by his untoward and uncontrollable behavior. In the post-experimental interviews subjects took pains to point out that they were not sadistic types, and that the laughter did not mean they enjoyed shocking the victim.

Distribution of Scores. It had been conjectured that persons would not, in general, agree to administer shocks beyond the level designated as Very Strong Shock. The distribution of maximum shocks for this experiment is shown in Table 2. The obtained distribution of scores deviates radically from the prediction.

TABLE 2

DISTRIBUTION OF BREAKOFF POINTS

Verbal Designation and Voltage Indication	*Number of Subjects for Whom This Was Maximum Shock*
Slight Shock:	
15	0
30	0
45	0
60	0
Moderate Shock:	
75	0
90	0
105	0
120	0
Strong Shock:	
135	0
150	0
165	0
180	0
Very Strong Shock:	
195	0
210	0
225	0
240	0
Intense Shock:	
255	0
270	0
285	0
300	5
Extreme Intensity Shock:	
315	4
330	2
345	1
360	1
Danger: Severe Shock:	
375	1
390	0
405	0
420	0
XXX	
435	0
450	26

Upon command of the experimenter, each of the 40 subjects went beyond the expected breakoff point. No subject stopped prior to administering Shock Level 20. (At this level—300 volts—the victim kicks on the wall and no longer provides answers to the teacher's multiple-choice questions.)

Of the 40 subjects, 5 refused to obey the experimental commands beyond the 300–volt level. Four more subjects administered one further shock, and then refused to go on. Two broke off at the 330-volt level, and 1 each at 345, 360, and 375 volts. Thus a total of 14 subjects defied the experimenter. It is instructive to reprint their remarks at the point of defiance, as transcribed from the tape recordings:

[0124] I think he's trying to communicate, he's knocking. . . . Well it's not fair to shock the guy . . . these are terrific volts. I don't think this is very humane. . . . Oh, I can't go on with this; no, this isn't right. It's a hell of an experiment. The guy is suffering in there. No, I don't want to go on. This is crazy. [Subject refused to administer more shocks.]

[0123] He's banging in there. I'm gonna chicken out. I'd like to continue, but I can't do that to a man. . . . I'm sorry I can't do that to a man. I'll hurt his heart. You take your check. . . . No really, I couldn't do it.

These subjects were frequently in a highly agitated and even angered state. Sometimes, verbal protest was at a minimum, and the subject simply got up from his chair in front of the shock generator, and indicated that he wished to leave the laboratory.

Of the 40 subjects, 26 obeyed the orders of the experimenter to the end, proceeding to punish the victim until they reached the most potent shock available on the shock generator. At that point, the experimenter called a halt to the session. (The maximum shock is labeled 450 volts, and is two steps beyond the designation: Danger: Severe Shock.) Although obedient subjects continued to administer shocks, they often did so under extreme stress. Some expressed reluctance to administer shocks beyond the 300-volt level, and displayed fears similar to those who defied the experimenter; yet they obeyed.

After the maximum shocks had been delivered, and the experimenter called a halt to the proceedings, many obedient subjects heaved sighs of relief, mopped their brows, rubbed their fingers over their eyes, or nervously fumbled cigarettes. Some shook their heads, apparently in regret. Some subjects had remained calm throughout the experiment, and displayed only minimal signs of tension from beginning to end.

DISCUSSION

The experiment yielded two findings that were surprising. The first finding concerns the sheer strength of obedient tendencies manifested in this situation. Subjects have learned from childhood that it is a fundamental breach of moral conduct to hurt another

person against his will. Yet, 26 subjects abandon this tenet in following the instructions of an authority who has no special powers
to enforce his commands. To disobey would bring no material loss
to the subject; no punishment would ensue. It is clear from the remarks and outward behavior of many participants that in punishing
the victim they are often acting against their own values. Subjects
often expressed deep disapproval of shocking a man in the face of
his objections, and others denounced it as stupid and senseless. Yet
the majority complied with the experimental commands. This outcome was surprising from two perspectives: first, from the standpoint of predictions made in the questionnaire described earlier.
(Here, however, it is possible that the remoteness of the respondents
from the actual situation, and the difficulty of conveying to them
the concrete details of the experiment, could account for the serious
underestimation of obedience.)

But the results were also unexpected to persons who observed the
experiment in progress, through one-way mirrors. Observers often
uttered expressions of disbelief upon seeing a subject administer
more powerful shocks to the victim. These persons had a full acquaintance with the details of the situation, and yet systematically underestimated the amount of obedience that subjects would
display.

The second unanticipated effect was the extraordinary tension
generated by the procedures. One might suppose that a subject
would simply break off or continue as his conscience dictated. Yet,
this is very far from what happened. There were striking reactions
of tension and emotional strain. One observer related:

I observed a mature and initially poised businessman enter the laboratory smiling and confident. Within 20 minutes he was reduced to a twitching, stuttering
wreck, who was rapidly approaching a point of nervous collapse. He constantly
pulled on his earlobe, and twisted his hands. At one point he pushed his fist
into his forehead and muttered: "Oh God, let's stop it." And yet he continued
to respond to every word of the experimenter, and obeyed to the end.

Any understanding of the phenomenon of obedience must rest on
an analysis of the particular conditions in which it occurs. The following features of the experiment go some distance in explaining
the high amount of obedience observed in the situation.

1. The experiment is sponsored by and takes place on the
grounds of an institution of unimpeachable reputation, Yale University. It may be reasonably presumed that the personnel are competent and reputable. The importance of this background authority

is now being studied by conducting a series of experiments outside of New Haven, and without any visible ties to the university.

2. The experiment is, on the face of it, designed to attain a worthy purpose—advancement of knowledge about learning and memory. Obedience occurs not as an end in itself, but as an instrumental element in a situation that the subject construes as significant, and meaningful. He may not be able to see its full significance, but he may properly assume that the experimenter does.

3. The subject perceives that the victim has voluntarily submitted to the authority system of the experimenter. He is not (at first) an unwilling captive impressed for involuntary service. He has taken the trouble to come to the laboratory presumably to aid the experimental research. That he later becomes an involuntary subject does not alter the fact that, initially, he consented to participate without qualification. Thus he has in some degree incurred an obligation toward the experimenter.

4. The subject, too, has entered the experiment voluntarily, and perceives himself under obligation to aid the experimenter. He has made a commitment, and to disrupt the experiment is a repudiation of this initial promise of aid.

5. Certain features of the procedure strengthen the subject's sense of obligation to the experimenter. For one, he has been paid for coming to the laboratory. In part this is canceled out by the experimenter's statement that: "Of course, as in all experiments, the money is yours simply for coming to the laboratory. From this point on, no matter what happens, the money is yours."[12]

6. From the subject's standpoint, the fact that he is the teacher and the other man the learner is purely a chance consequence (it is determined by drawing lots) and he, the subject, ran the same risk as the other man in being assigned the role of learner. Since the assignment of positions in the experiment was achieved by fair means, the learner is deprived of any basis of complaint on this count. (A similar situation obtains in Army units, in which—in the absence of volunteers—a particularly dangerous mission may be assigned by drawing lots, and the unlucky soldier is expected to bear his misfortune with sportsmanship.)

7. There is, at best, ambiguity with regard to the prerogatives of a psychologist and the corresponding rights of his subject. There

---

[12]Forty-three subjects, undergraduates at Yale University, were run in the experiment without payment. The results are very similar to those obtained with paid subjects.

is a vagueness of expectation concerning what a psychologist may require of his subject, and when he is overstepping acceptable limits. Moreover, the experiment occurs in a closed setting, and thus provides no opportunity for the subject to remove these ambiguities by discussion with others. There are few standards that seem directly applicable to the situation, which is a novel one for most subjects.

8. The subjects are assured that the shocks administered to the subject are "painful but not dangerous." Thus they assume that the discomfort caused the victim is momentary, while the scientific gains resulting from the experiment are enduring.

9. Through Shock Level 20 the victim continues to provide answers on the signal box. The subject may construe this as a sign that the victim is still willing to "play the game." It is only after Shock Level 20 that the victim repudiates the rules completely, refusing to answer further.

These features help to explain the high amount of obedience obtained in this experiment. Many of the arguments raised need not remain matters of speculation, but can be reduced to testable propositions to be confirmed or disproved by further experiments.[13]

The following features of the experiment concern the nature of the conflict which the subject faces.

10. The subject is placed in a position in which he must respond to the competing demands of two persons: the experimenter and the victim. The conflict must be resolved by meeting the demands of one or the other; satisfaction of the victim and the experimenter are mutually exclusive. Moreover, the resolution must take the form of a highly visible action, that of continuing to shock the victim or breaking off the experiment. Thus the subject is forced into a public conflict that does not permit any completely satisfactory solution.

11. While the demands of the experimenter carry the weight of scientific authority, the demands of the victim spring from his personal experience of pain and suffering. The two claims need not be regarded as equally pressing and legitimate. The experimenter seeks an abstract scientific datum; the victim cries out for relief from physical suffering caused by the subject's actions.

12. The experiment gives the subject little time for reflection. The conflict comes on rapidly. It is only minutes after the subject

---

[13]A series of recently completed experiments employing the obedience paradigm is reported in S. Milgram "Some Conditions of Obedience and Disobedience to Authority," *Human Relations,* 1964.

has been seated before the shock generator that the victim begins his protests. Moreover, the subject perceives that he has gone through but two-thirds of the shock levels at the time the subject's first protests are heard. Thus he understands that the conflict will have a persistent aspect to it, and may well become more intense as increasingly more powerful shocks are required. The rapidity with which the conflict descends on the subject and his realization that it is predictably recurrent may well be sources of tension to him.

13. At a more general level, the conflict stems from the opposition of two deeply ingrained behavior dispositions: first, the disposition not to harm other people, and second, the tendency to obey those whom we perceive to be legitimate authorities.

SOME THOUGHTS ON ETHICS OF RESEARCH: AFTER READING MILGRAM'S "BEHAVIORAL STUDY OF OBEDIENCE"*

Diana Baumrind

Certain problems in psychological research require the experimenter to balance his career and scientific interests against the interests of his prospective subjects. When such occasions arise the experimenter's stated objective frequently is to do the best possible job with the least possible harm to his subjects. The experimenter seldom perceives in more positive terms an indebtedness to the subject for his services, perhaps because the detachment which his functions require prevents appreciation of the subject as an individual.

Yet a debt does exist, even when the subject's reason for volunteering includes course credit or monetary gain. Often a subject participates unwillingly in order to satisfy a course requirement. These requirements are of questionable merit ethically, and do not alter the experimenter's responsibility to the subject.

---

*Reprinted from the *American Psychologist,* Vol. 19 (1964), pp. 421–23.

Most experimental conditions do not cause the subjects pain or indignity, and are sufficiently interesting or challenging to present no problem of an ethical nature to the experimenter. But where the experimental conditions expose the subject to loss of dignity, or offer him nothing of value, then the experimenter is obliged to consider the reasons why the subject volunteered and to reward him accordingly.

The subject's public motives for volunteering include having an enjoyable or stimulating experience, acquiring knowledge, doing the experimenter a favor which may some day be reciprocated, and making a contribution to science. These motives can be taken into account rather easily by the experimenter who is willing to spend a few minutes with the subject afterwards to thank him for his participation, answer his questions, reassure him that he did well, and chat with him a bit. Most volunteers also have less manifest, but equally legitimate, motives. A subject may be seeking an opportunity to have contact with, be noticed by, and perhaps confide in a person with psychological training. The dependent attitude of most subjects toward the experimenter is an artifact of the experimental situation as well as an expression of some subjects' personal need systems at the time they volunteer.

The dependent, obedient attitude assumed by most subjects in the experimental setting is appropriate to that situation. The "game" is defined by the experimenter and he makes the rules. By volunteering, the subject agrees implicitly to assume a posture of trust and obedience. While the experimental conditions leave him exposed, the subject has the right to assume that his security and self-esteem will be protected.

There are other professional situations in which one member—the patient or client—expects help and protection from the other—the physician or psychologist. But the interpersonal relationship between experimenter and subject additionally has unique features which are likely to provoke initial anxiety in the subject. The laboratory is unfamiliar as a setting and the rules of behavior ambiguous compared to a clinician's office. Because of the anxiety and passivity generated by the setting, the subject is more prone to behave in an obedient, suggestible manner in the laboratory than elsewhere. Therefore, the laboratory is not the place to study degree of obedience or suggestibility, as a function of a particular experimental condition, since the base line for these phenomena as found in the laboratory is probably much higher than in most other settings.

Thus experiments in which the relationship to the experimenter as an authority is used as an independent condition are imperfectly designed for the same reason that they are prone to injure the subjects involved. They disregard the special quality of trust and obedience with which the subject appropriately regards the experimenter.

Other phenomena which present ethical decisions, unlike those mentioned above, *can* be reproduced successfully in the laboratory. Failure experience, conformity to peer judgment, and isolation are among such phenomena. In these cases we can expect the experimenter to take whatever measures are necessary to prevent the subject from leaving the laboratory more humiliated, insecure, alienated, or hostile than when he arrived. To guarantee that an especially sensitive subject leaves a stressful experimental experience in the proper state sometimes requires special clinical training. But usually an attitude of compassion, respect, gratitude, and common sense will suffice, and no amount of clinical training will substitute. The subject has the right to expect that the psychologist with whom he is interacting has some concern for his welfare, and the personal attributes and professional skill to express his good will effectively.

Unfortunately, the subject is not always treated with the respect he deserves. It has become more commonplace in sociopsychological laboratory studies to manipulate, embarrass, and discomfort subjects. At times the insult to the subject's sensibilities extends to the journal reader when the results are reported. Milgram's (1963) study is a case in point. The following is Milgram's abstract of his experiment:

This article describes a procedure for the study of destructive obedience in the laboratory. It consists of ordering a naive S to administer increasingly more severe punishment to a victim in the context of a learning experiment. Punishment is administered by means of a shock generator with 30 graded switches ranging from Slight Shock to Danger: Severe Shock. The victim is a confederate of E. The primary dependent variable is the maximum shock the S is willing to administer before he refuses to continue further. 26 S's obeyed the experimental commands fully, and administered the highest shock on the generator. 14 S's broke off the experiment at some point after the victim protested and refused to provide further answers. The procedure created extreme levels of nervous tension in some S's. Profuse sweating, trembling, and stuttering were typical expressions of this emotional disturbance. One unexpected sign of tension—yet to be explained—was the regular occurrence of nervous laughter, which in some S's developed into uncontrollable seizures. The variety of interesting behavioral dynamics observed in the experiment, the reality of the situation for the S, and the possibility of parametric variation within the framework of the procedure, point to the fruitfulness of further study [p. 371].

The detached, objective manner in which Milgram reports the emotional disturbance suffered by his subject contrasts sharply with his graphic account of that disturbance. Following are two other quotes describing the effects on his subjects of the experimental conditions:

I observed a mature and initially poised businessman enter the laboratory smiling and confident. Within 20 minutes he was reduced to a twitching, stuttering wreck, who was rapidly approaching a point of nervous collapse. He constantly pulled on his earlobe, and twisted his hands. At one point he pushed his fist into his forehead and muttered: "Oh God, let's stop it." And yet he continued to respond to every word of the experimenter, and obeyed to the end [p. 377].

In a large number of cases the degree of tension reached extremes that are rarely seen in sociopsychological laboratory studies. Subjects were observed to sweat, tremble, stutter, bite their lips, groan, and dig their fingernails into their flesh. These were characteristic rather than exceptional responses to the experiment.

One sign of tension was the regular occurrence of nervous laughing fits. Fourteen of the 40 subjects showed definite signs of nervous laughter and smiling. The laughter seemed entirely out of place, even bizarre. Full-blown, uncontrollable seizures were observed for 3 subjects. On one occasion we observed a seizure so violently convulsive that it was necessary to call a halt to the experiment . . . [p. 375].

Milgram does state that,

After the interview, procedures were undertaken to assure that the subject would leave the laboratory in a state of well-being. A friendly reconciliation was arranged between the subject and the victim, and an effort was made to reduce any tensions that arose as a result of the experiment [p. 374].

It would be interesting to know what sort of procedures could dissipate the type of emotional disturbance just described. In view of the effects on subjects, traumatic to a degree which Milgram himself considers nearly unprecedented in sociopsychological experiments, his casual assurance that these tensions were dissipated before the subject left the laboratory is unconvincing.

What could be the rational basis for such a posture of indifference? Perhaps Milgram supplies the answer himself when he partially explains the subject's destructive obedience as follows, "Thus they assume that the discomfort caused the victim is momentary, while the scientific gains resulting from the experiment are enduring [p. 378]." Indeed such a rationale might suffice to justify the means used to achieve his end if that end were of inestimable value to humanity or were not itself transformed by the means by which it was attained.

The behavioral psychologist is not in as good a position to ob-

jectify his faith in the significance of his work as medical colleagues
at points of breakthrough. His experimental situations are not sufficiently accurate models of real-life experience; his sampling techniques are seldom of a scope which would justify the meaning with
which he would like to endow his results; and these results are hard
to reproduce by colleagues with opposing theoretical views. Unlike
the Sabin vaccine, for example, the concrete benefit to humanity of
his particular piece of work, no matter how competently handled,
cannot justify the risk that real harm will be done to the subject. I
am not speaking of physical discomfort, inconvenience, or experimental deception per se, but of permanent harm, however slight.
I do regard the emotional disturbance described by Milgram as
potentially harmful because it could easily effect an alteration in
the subject's self-image or ability to trust adult authorities in the
future. It is potentially harmful to a subject to commit, in the
course of an experiment, acts which he himself considers unworthy,
particularly when he has been entrapped into committing such acts
by an individual he has reason to trust. The subject's personal responsibility for his actions is not erased because the experimenter
reveals to him the means which he used to stimulate these actions.
The subject realizes that he would have hurt the victim if the current were on. The realization that he also made a fool of himself
by accepting the experimental set results in additional loss of self-
esteem. Moreover, the subject finds it difficult to express his anger
outwardly after the experimenter in a self-acceptant but friendly
manner reveals the hoax.

A fairly intense corrective interpersonal experience is indicated
wherein the subject admits and accepts his responsibility for his
own actions, and at the same time gives vent to his hurt and anger
at being fooled. Perhaps an experience as distressing as the one
described by Milgram can be integrated by the subject, provided
that careful thought is given to the matter. The propriety of such
experimentation is still in question even if such a reparational experience were forthcoming. Without it I would expect a naive,
sensitive subject to remain deeply hurt and anxious for some time,
and a sophisticated, cynical subject to become even more alienated
and distrustful.

In addition the experimental procedure used by Milgram does
not appear suited to the objectives of the study because it does not
take into account the special quality of the set which the subject
has in the experimental situation. Milgram is concerned with a very

important problem, namely, the social consequences of destructive obedience. He says,

Gas chambers were built, death camps were guarded, daily quotas of corpses were produced with the same efficiency as the manufacture of appliances. These inhumane policies may have originated in the mind of a single person, but they could only be carried out on a massive scale if a very large number of persons obeyed orders [p. 371].

But the parallel between authority-subordinate relationships in Hitler's Germany and in Milgram's laboratory is unclear. In the former situation the SS man or member of the German Officer Corps, when obeying orders to slaughter, had no reason to think of his superior officer as benignly disposed towards himself or their victims. The victims were perceived as subhuman and not worthy of consideration. The subordinate officer was an agent in a great cause. He did not need to feel guilt or conflict because within his frame of reference he was acting rightly.

It is obvious from Milgram's own descriptions that most of his subjects were concerned about their victims and did trust the experimenter, and that their distressful conflict was generated in part by the consequences of these two disparate but appropriate attitudes. Their distress may have resulted from shock at what the experimenter was doing to them as well as from what they thought they were doing to their victims. In any case there is not a convincing parallel between the phenomena studied by Milgram and destructive obedience as that concept would apply to the subordinate-authority relationship demonstrated in Hitler Germany. If the experiments were conducted "outside of New Haven and without any visible ties to the university," I would still question their validity on similar although not identical grounds. In addition, I would question the representativeness of a sample of subjects who would voluntarily participate within a noninstitutional setting.

In summary, the experimental objectives of the psychologist are seldom incompatible with the subject's ongoing state of well-being, provided that the experimenter is willing to take the subject's motives and interests into consideration when planning his methods and correctives. Section 4b in *Ethical Standards of Psychologists* (APA, undated) reads in part:

Only when a problem is significant and can be investigated in no other way is the psychologist justified in exposing human subjects to emotional stress or other possible harm. In conducting such research, the psychologist must seriously consider the possibility of harmful aftereffects, and should be prepared to remove them as soon as permitted by the design of the experiment.

Where the danger of serious aftereffects exists, research should be conducted only when the subjects or their responsible agents are fully informed of this possibility and volunteer nevertheless [p. 12].

From the subject's point of view procedures which involve loss of dignity, self-esteem, and trust in rational authority are probably most harmful in the long run and require the most thoughtfully planned reparations, if engaged in at all. The public image of psychology as a profession is highly related to our own actions, and some of these actions are changeworthy. It is important that as research psychologists we protect our ethical sensibilities rather than adapt our personal standards to include as appropriate the kind of indignities to which Milgram's subjects were exposed. I would not like to see experiments such as Milgram's proceed unless the subjects were fully informed of the dangers of serious aftereffects and his correctives were clearly shown to be effective in restoring their state of well being.

REFERENCES

American Psychological Association. *Ethical Standards of Psychologists: A Summary of Ethical Principles.* Washington, D. C.: APA, undated.

Milgram, S. "Behavioral Study of Obedience," *Journal of Abnormal Social Psychol.*, Vol. 67 (1963), pp. 371–78.

THE EMOTIONALLY DISTURBED CHILD AS THE FAMILY SCAPEGOAT*

Ezra F. Vogel and Norman W. Bell

The phenomenon of scapegoating is as old as human society. Sir James Frazer records, in *The Golden Bough,* numerous instances, reaching back to antiquity, of public scapegoats, human and other. He views the process of scapegoating as one in which ". . . the evil influences are embodied in a visible form or are at least supposed to be loaded upon a material medium, which acts as a vehicle to draw them off from the people, village, or town." The scapegoat's function ". . . is simply to effect a total clearance of all the ills that have been infesting a people." Frazer was dealing with the phenomenon at the level of a society, tribe, village, or town. It is the purpose of this paper to examine the same phenomenon within families, by viewing an emotionally disturbed child as an embodiment of certain types of conflicts between parents. This pattern is a special case of a common phenomenon, the achievement of group unity through the scapegoating of a particular member. It is, perhaps, more widely known that a group may achieve unity through projection of hostilities to the outside, but there are also a large number of cases where members of a particular group are able to achieve unity through scapegoating a particular member of that group. Thus, the deviant within the group may perform a valuable function for the group, by channeling group tensions and providing a basis for solidarity.

The notion that the family is in large part responsible for the emotional health of the child is a compelling one in contemporary behavioral science. By and large, however, the research has focused largely on the mother-child relationship, and the independent variable by which the mother-child relationship and the child-rearing practices are usually explained is the personality and developmental history of the mother. Recently, an attempt has also been made to treat the father-child relationship, again largely in terms of the personality and developmental history of the father. While in clinical practice there is some awareness of family dynamics, in the literature, the family has largely been treated simply as a collection of personalities, and the child's personality development has been seen almost exclusively as a direct result of the separate personalities of his parents. Rarely is the interaction of parents treated as a significant independent variable influencing childhood development. Even when broader cultural patterns have been considered, childhood development has been related to child-rearing practices and socialization into the culture, with little consideration of the family as the mediating unit.

Data for this paper are derived from the intensive study of a small group of "disturbed" families, each with an emotionally disturbed child, and a matched group of "well" families without clinically manifest disturbance in any child. Of the nine families in each group, three were Irish-American, three Italian-American, and three old-American. The families were seen by a team including psychi-

*"The Emotionally Disturbed Child as the Family Scapegoat," pp. 382–97. Reprinted with permission of the publisher, from *The Family*, (eds.) N. W. Bell and E. F. Vogel. Copyright 1960 by The Free Press, a Corporation. Abridged and all references omitted.

atrists, social workers, psychologists, and social scientists. The disturbed families, on which this paper is based, were seen weekly in the offices of a psychiatric clinic and in their homes over periods ranging from one to four years. Detailed information was gathered about the members' developmental histories and character structure, but even more specific data were obtained about current processes.

The present paper is concerned with how a child in the family, the emotionally disturbed child, was used as a scapegoat for the conflicts between parents and what the functions and dysfunctions of this scapegoating are for the family.

In all the disturbed families it was found that a particular child had become involved in tensions existing between the parents. In the "well" families used for control purposes, either the tensions between the parents were not so severe or else the tensions were handled in such a way that the children did not become pathologically involved. In general, both parents of the emotionally disturbed child had many of the same underlying conflicts, but in relationship to each other they felt themselves to be at opposite poles, so that one spouse would act out one side of the conflict and the other would act out the other side of the conflict. They had developed an equilibrium in which they minimized contact with each other and minimized expressions of affect, particularly hostility, which they strongly felt for each other, and this made it possible for them to live with each other. But this equilibrium had many difficulties, the most serious of which was the scapegoating of a child.

1. SOURCES OF TENSION THAT LEAD TO SCAPEGOATING

It is our contention that scapegoating is produced by the existence of tensions between parents which have not been satisfactorily resolved in other ways. The spouses in the disturbed families had deep fears about their marital relationship and about the partner's behavior. They did not feel they could predict accurately how the other would respond to their own behavior. Yet, the other's response was of very great importance and was thought to be potentially very damaging. The partners did not feel they could deal with the situation by direct communication, because this might be too dangerous, and they resorted to manipulations of masking, evading, and the like. This atmosphere of tension has several sources. One of the sources was the personality problems of each spouse, but in the present analysis the focus will be on the group sources of the tension. These tensions usually have several sources. At a very general level, one of the main sources of tension was conflict in cultural value orientations. Value orientations are abstract, general conceptions of the nature of human nature and man's relationship to it, of man's relation to man, of the most significant time dimension, and of the most valued type of activity. All societies have preferences and alternative preferences to these basic dimensions; these preferences are expressed within a wide range of phenomena. In complex ways, they are related to personality and social structure and to more specific values. When people are in the process of acculturation, as was the case with the families of Irish and Italian backgrounds, many possibilities for value-orientation conflict arise. Any one individual may have been socialized into conflicting or confused patterns, and be unsuccessful in bridging the gap. Marriage partners may have been socialized into different patterns and be working on different assumptions. All our disturbed families had problems of these sorts. Some were trying to shift quickly to a set of orientations they had not thoroughly internalized, and without having neutralized previous orientations. Others were trying to live by conflicting orientations.

A common example of the cultural value conflicts was the conflict centered around the problems of individual performance. There were considerable pulls toward the American middle-class achievement patterns. In families which had partially internalized both sets of value orientations, it was impossible to live up to both sets of values, and whichever the family chose, this meant that certain conflicts would result.

Another source of tension was the relations of the family and the larger community. Disturbed families usually had problems in this area, rejecting and/or being rejected by the community. In some cases, a family had very severe disapproval of a very close-knit ethnic neighborhood directed at them. In other cases, families had moved from ethnic neighborhoods to more fashionable suburbs and suffered in their own eyes by comparison to their new neighbors. Consequently, their social relationships with these neighbors were often minimal; when they did exist, they were usually strained or else one spouse had fairly good relationships with some friends and the partner had poor relationships with these friends. All families, to a greater or lesser extent, had problems in their relationships with families of orientation. Typically, the wife was strongly attached to her parents and antagonistic towards her husband's family, while the husband was attached to his parents and antagonistic to his wife's family. If either spouse was critical of his in-laws, the partner typically defended his own parents and became more critical of his in-laws. If one spouse was critical of his own parents, the partner was often friendly to them. The unbalanced attachments to parents and parents-in-law were not resolved. Changes usually produced more tension, but the basic sources of strain remained unchanged.

2. THE SELECTION OF THE SCAPEGOAT

The tensions produced by unresolved conflicts were so severe that they could not be contained without some discharge. It is not surprising that some appropriate object was chosen to symbolize the conflicts and draw off the tension. Conceivably, some person or group outside the family could serve in this capacity. However, in these disturbed families, the parents had by and large internalized the standards of the surrounding community sufficiently so that they had great difficulty in finding a legitimate basis for scapegoating outsiders. In addition, most of these families had very tenuous ties with the community, and since they were very concerned about being accepted, they could not afford to antagonize their associates. While some of the families did, at times, have strong feelings of antagonism toward various members of the community in which they lived, they could rarely express this antagonism directly. Even if at times they were able to manifest their antagonism, this usually led to many additional complications, and the family preferred to scapegoat its own child.

Channeling the tensions within the family did not lead to difficulties with the outside, but usually the latent hostilities between the husband and wife made it very difficult to deal with problems openly between them. There was always danger the partner might become too angry, which would lead to severe and immediate difficulties. A number of factors made a child the most appropriate object through which to deal with family tensions. First of all, the child was in a relatively powerless position compared to the parents. While he was dependent on the parents and could not leave the family, he was not able effectively to counter the parents' superior power. Although the parents' defenses were fairly brittle in comparison with those of well parents, still their defenses were much stronger than those of their children. Because the child's personality is still very flexible, he can be molded to adopt the particular role which the family assigns to him. When the child does take on many of the characteristics which the parents dislike in themselves and each other, he becomes a symbolically appropriate object on which to focus their own anxieties. Since the person scapegoated often develops such severe tensions that he is unable to perform his usual task roles, it is important that those family members performing essential, irreplaceable functions for the family not be scapegoated. The child has relatively few tasks to perform in the family, compared to the parents or other elders, and his disturbance does not ordinarily interfere with the successful performance of the necessary family tasks. The "cost" in dysfunction of the child is low relative to the functional gains for the whole family.

In all cases, with partial exception of one family, a particular child was chosen as the scapegoat, while other children were relatively free of pathology. The selecting of a particular child is not a random matter; one child is the best symbol. Just as a dream condenses a variety of past and present experiences and a variety of emotional feelings, the scapegoat condenses a variety of social and psychological problems impinging on the family.

Who is selected as the scapegoat is intimately related to the sources of tension. Where value-orientation conflicts existed, the child chosen was the one who best symbolized these conflicts. For example, if the conflicts revolved about achievement, a child who failed to achieve according to expectations could become the symbol of failure. Alternatively, a child might be an appropriate object because he was achieving independently and thus violating norms of loyalty to the group.

The position of the child in the sibling group frequently became a focus for the unresolved childhood problems of the parents. If the parents' most serious unresolved problems were with male figures, the child chosen to represent the family conflict was usually a male child. Similarly, sibling order could be a strong factor. If one or both parents had difficulties with older brothers, an older boy in the family might become the scapegoat.

In two cases, the sex or sibling position of the child seemed to be particularly important in the selection of a particular child as the family scapegoat. In one of these cases, the mother was the oldest of three siblings and had considerable feelings of rivalry with her next younger sister which had never been effectively resolved. Although the father had two older siblings, they were so much older that to him they were a separate family. In his effective family environment, he was the older of two children and had considerable

feelings of rivalry toward a younger brother who displaced him and
for whom he subsequently had to care. This couple has three children, and there was an unusual amount of rivalry between the oldest and the second sibling. Both the parents sided very strongly
with the oldest child. They were continuously conscious of the
middle child bothering the older, for which they severely criticized
this middle child. There are many striking parallels, even to small
details, in the relationship between the parents and their next
younger siblings and the relationship between their oldest child
and the next younger sibling.

Another pattern revolved about the identification of a child with
a parent whom he resembled. This was found in all families, sick
and well, in one form or another; but in the disturbed families, the
child was seen as possessing very undesirable traits, and although
the parent actually possessed the same traits, the focus of attention
was the child and not the parent. In one family, in particular, this
pattern was striking. The father and the eldest son had very similar
physical characteristics; not only did they have the same first names
but both were called by the same diminutive name by the mother.
At times, the social worker seeing the mother was not certain
whether the mother was talking about her husband or her son. The
wife's concerns about the husband's occupational adequacy were
not dealt with directly, but the focus for her affect was the child
and his school performance. In fact, the son was criticized by his
mother for all the characteristics which she disliked in her husband,
but she was unable to criticize her husband directly for these characteristics. She channeled all her feelings, especially anxiety and
hostility, to the child, although her husband had similar problems.
Furthermore, in order to control her feelings toward her husband,
she remained very aloof and distant and was not able to express to
him her positive or negative feelings. While she channeled many
criticisms and anxieties through the child, she also expressed many
of her positive feelings to the child, thereby leading to severe
Oedipal conflicts. The husband was not happy about his wife being
so aloof from him, but on the other hand he found that by co-operating with his wife in criticizing the child, he was able to keep the
burden of problems away from himself. He thus joined with the
wife in projecting his own difficulties and problems onto the child
and in dealing with them as the child's problems rather than as his
own.

In three of the families, the scapegoat had considerably lower intelligence than did the other children in the family. In all these families, there were serious conflicts about the value of achievement, and the parents had great difficulty themselves in living up to their own achievement aspirations. In all these three cases, the parents were unable to accept the fact that their children had limited abilities, and they continually held up impossible standards for these children. Although all three children had I.Q.'s in the 80's or below and had failed one grade or more, all three mothers stated that they intended that their children should go to college. At the beginning of therapy, one of the mothers hoped her son would attend medical school and become a doctor; another had begun to put away a small amount of money from a very tight budget for her daughter's college education, even though the daughter's intelligence was that of a moron. At the beginning of therapy, none of the parents was able to deal directly with his own difficulties in achievement. In contrast, in one of the families, there were two children in the family who had very low intelligence, one of whom had failed a grade in school, but the family scapegoat was a boy who had normal intelligence. In this case, the parents, who had average intelligence, had resolved their conflicts about achievement by denying that they were interested in achievement and accepting their social position. This child of slightly higher intelligence and greater physical activity was seen by them as a very aggressive child who was always doing too much, and the parents were continually worried that he was "too smart."

In a number of cases, the disturbed child either had a serious physical disease when he was young or a striking physical abnormality such as a hare lip, bald spots in the hair, or unusually unattractive facial features. The mere existence of some such abnormality seemed to draw attention to one particular child, so that if there were some sorts of anxieties or problems in the family at all, the child with the physical peculiarities seemed to become the focus of the family problems. Here again, however, it was not the mere existence of a physical defect but its meaning in the life of the family which gave it its significance. For example, in some families there was a feeling that they had committed certain sins by not living up to their ideals, for instance by using contraceptives. This was a very common problem, since many families could not possibly live up to the two opposing sets of ideals which they had at least partially internalized. The child's physical abnormality became a symbol of the family's sin of not having lived up to some partially-internalized values, and the malformed child was seen as a sinful child who was not living up to the standards of the group. Since the family's relationship with the community was often tenuous, the fact that one of their children had physical abnormalities that made the child the focus of neighborhood ridicule served to make the parents increasingly ashamed of the child's physical characteristics and to focus increasingly more attention on this child. For example, one of the main concerns of the family with the unusually ugly child was that other children were continually teasing her about her appearance. However, the concern was less for the child herself, and more for the whole family. Her problems symbolized the parents' past and present problems with the neighborhood; rather than sympathize with the child, they abused her all the more. In another case in which a female child's physical illness became a focus of the family's problems, the parents were extremely concerned about her safety, which was again related in part to the potential dangers in social relationships with the outside world. As a result of the girl's illness, the family became much more cautious than was necessary, and on some occasions they were even reluctant to accept medical advice that she could participate in certain activities without danger to her health. The continual contacts that the child had with middle-class professional personnel through hospitalization and clinic visits led her to accept certain middle-class American values more than did the rest of the family, and the family was continually expressing the feeling that she had different attitudes after hospitalization and contact with hospital personnel. The disliked attitudes ascribed to the child were in general those of middle-class American culture. Not only abnormalities but general body type could become the symbol to call forth scapegoating. In two families, the spouses had many problems in their sexual life. Rather than face these maladjustments directly, the problems were expressed through concern about the masculinity and normality of a slender, graceful son.

While the general process of symbolization of a scapegoat is very similar to the dream symbolization, there is one problem in the family selection of a scapegoat which is not met in the selection of a dream symbol, and that is the problem of availability. While in dreams, any symbolic representation is open to the dreamer, in the family only a very small number of children are available as the potential scapegoats. Hence, when there is a serious family problem and no child is an appropriate symbol of the problem, there must be considerable cognitive distortion in order to permit the most appropriate one available to be used as a scapegoat. For example, in one family which was very concerned about the problems of achievement, the focus of the family's problems was the eldest son. Although he was receiving passing grades in school, whereas the parents had had very poor school records, the parents were very critical of his school performance. Because of this pressure, the child worked hard and was able to get somewhat better marks on his next report card. However, the mother stoutly maintained that her son didn't deserve those grades, that he must have cheated, and she continued to criticize him for his school performance.

The other aspect of the problem of availability resulted from the fact that the parents apparently have had tensions since early in marriage. As nearly as it was possible to reconstruct the marital history, it appeared that the spouses had selected each other partly on the basis of the fact that they shared many of the same conflicts and understood each other quite well. Not long after marriage, however, they seemed to have become polarized in their conflicts, so that one parent represented one side of the conflict and the other represented the other side. This seems to have given each of the spouses a way of handling his own conflicts and allowed each to remain fairly consistent and well integrated by projecting difficulties onto the partner. However, it also led to very severe difficulties in the marital relationship and created many tensions which were quickly displaced onto the first available and appropriate object, very often the first child. Since the eldest child was the first one available for scapegoating, he often seems to have been assigned this role and, once assigned, has continued in it. Perhaps because of his prior availability and his closer involvement in the adult world, he is a more appropriate object for the scapegoating. In the one case in which a child was able to escape the scapegoat role by decreasing his attachment to the home, the next most appropriate child was used in the scapegoat role.

3. INDUCTION OF THE CHILD INTO THE SCAPEGOAT ROLE

If the child is to be a "satisfactory" scapegoat, he must carry out his role as a "problem child." The problem behavior must be reinforced strongly enough so that it will continue in spite of the hostility and anxiety it produces in the child. This delicate balance is possible only because the parents have superior sanction power over the child, can define what he should or should not do, and control what he does or does not do. This balance necessarily requires a large amount of inconsistency in the ways parents handle the child.

The most common inconsistency was between the implicit (or unconscious) and the explicit role induction. In all cases, certain behavior of the child violated recognized social norms. In some instances stealing, fire-setting, expressions of hostility, or unco-operativeness affected the child's relationships with people outside the family. In other instances, bed-wetting, resistance to parental orders, or expression of aggression to sibling affected relationships in the family. But in all instances, while the parents explicitly criticized the child and at times even punished him, they supported in some way, usually implicitly, the persistence of the very behavior which they criticized. This permission took various forms: failure to follow through on threats, delayed punishment, indifference to and acceptance of the symptoms, unusual interest in the child's symptom, or considerable secondary gratification offered to the child because of his symptom. The secondary gratification usually took the form of special attention and exemption from certain responsibilities. While the parents had internalized social norms sufficiently to refrain from violating the norms themselves, they had not sufficiently internalized them to prevent giving encouragement to their children for acting out their own repressed wishes. The wish to violate these norms was transferred to the child, but the defenses against this wish were never as strong in the child.

Another type of inconsistency seen was that one parent would encourage one type of behavior, but the other parent would encourage an opposing type of behavior. The result again was that the child was caught in the conflict. This also permitted one spouse to express annoyance to the other indirectly without endangering the marital relationship. For example, in one case, the father objected to the son's leaving toys lying around and would violently explode at the child for such behavior, implying that the mother was wrong in permitting him to do this. The mother realized that the father exploded at such behavior and did not stop the father since she "knew he was right." Nevertheless, she often indicated that the child need not bother picking up the toys, since she felt that he was too young to have to do such things by himself and that the father was too strict. If the mother's encouragement of the behavior annoying to the father was explicit, there would be danger that the father's hostility would be directed at the mother rather than the child. By keeping the encouragement implicit the mother was able to deny that she had encouraged the child. The father was usually willing to accept this denial, even if he did not believe it, rather than risk an explosion with his wife. In some instances, however, the other spouse was angered or felt compelled to criticize the other for not handling the child properly. Then the encouragement of the child to behave in a certain way would have to become more subtle to avoid criticism of the other spouse, another delicate balance to maintain. A parent had to give sufficient encouragement to the child to perform the act, without making it so obvious that his spouse felt obliged to criticize him.

In addition to the inconsistent pressures resulting from the difference between explicit and implicit expectations and from the differences between the expectations of the two parents, the child also had to deal with changes in each parent's expectations. From the parent's conscious point of view this inconsistency resulted from an attempt to reconcile two conflicting desires: teaching the child to behave properly and not being "too hard on the child." When a parent was consciously attempting to teach the child proper behavior, he was extremely aggressive and critical. At other times, the parent felt he had been too critical of the child and permitted him to behave in the same way without punishment, and would be extremely affectionate and supportive. While the explanation given for this inconsistency was that he wanted to teach the desired behavior without being "too hard on the child," its latent function was to prevent the child from consistently living up to the ostensibly desired behavior and to preserve the disliked behavior. The period of not being "too hard on the child" served to reinforce the disapproved behavior and the period of "being firm" permitted the parents to express their anxieties and hostility. This balance was also very delicate since it was always possible that negative sanctions would become so severe that the child would refuse to behave in such a way that parents felt he could legitimately be punished.

The delicacy of this balance was perhaps best exemplified by the problem of bed-wetting. Parents complained about bed-wetting, but at the same time they could not bring themselves to do anything to alter the child's behavior. If the therapists could get both parents to be firm at the same time, the child would usually stop bed-wetting. Very soon, however, by putting a rubber sheet on the bed, or buying special night clothes "just in case he wets," the child was encouraged again to wet. One mother succeeded several times in finding methods to stop her son's wetting, but immediately stopped using them "since he's stopped now." In several cases, the parents would alternate in being concerned and trying to be firm and being unconcerned and implicitly encouraging the behavior, at all times remaining inconsistent, one with the other. It seemed clear that whether or not the child wet his bed was a relatively sensitive index of just where the balance of rewards from the parents lay. In general, however, the implicit demands carried the greater sanction power and the child continued with the behavior of which the parents unconsciously approved and consciously disapproved. Presumably, the sanctions of the parents against bed-wetting would increase as the child grew older, and the balance would become delicate only at that later time.

Since these conflicting expectations existed over a long period of time, it is not surprising that the child internalized these conflicts. Once a child was selected as a deviant, there was a circular reaction which tended to perpetuate this role assignment. Once he had responded to his parents' implicit wishes and acted in a somewhat disturbed manner, the parents could treat him as if he really were a problem. The child would respond to these expectations and the vicious cycle was set in motion. Both the child and the parents, then, had complementary expectations. The particular role assigned to the child was appropriately rewarded. It is difficult, if not impossible, to distinguish just at what point the parents began treating the child as if he were a problem and at what point the child actually did have internalized problems. There does not seem to be any sudden development of the child's problems; rather, it is a process occurring over a period of time. By the time the family was seen in the clinic, the vicious cycle was well established, and the child had internalized his disturbed role to such an extent that it was difficult to effect change only by removing external pressures. This was, of course, particularly true for older and more disturbed children. The fact that the child becomes disturbed adds stability to the role system, so that once set in motion, scapegoating did not easily pass from one child to another. In the well families, when scapegoating did take place, it was less severe and did not become stabilized with one child as a continual scapegoat.

4. THE RATIONALIZATION OF SCAPEGOATING

When a scapegoating situation was established, a relatively stable equilibrium of the family was achieved. However, there were difficulties in maintaining the equilibrium. Parents had considerable guilt about the way they treated the child, and when the child was identified as disturbed by neighbors, teachers, doctors, or other outside agencies, pressure was brought to bear for some action to be taken. When called upon to explain, parents did not have much difficulty in explaining why they were so concerned about the child, but they did have great difficulty in rationalizing their aggressive and libidinal expressions to the children.

One way in which the parents rationalized their behavior was to define themselves, rather than the children, as victims. They stressed how much difficulty there was coping with all the problems posed by their child. For example, mothers of bed-wetters complained about the problems of keeping sheets clean and the impossibility of the child staying overnight at friends' or relatives' homes. Such rationalizations seemed to relieve some of the guilt for victimizing the children and served as a justification for continued expressions of annoyance toward the children.

Another way was to emphasize how fortunate their children really were. For most of these parents, the standard of living provided for their children was much higher than the standard of living they enjoyed when they were children. One of the central complaints of these parents, particularly the fathers, was that the children wanted too much and got much more than the parents ever got when they were children. This was seen by the parents as a legitimate excuse for depriving their children of the toys, priviliges, and other things they wanted, and for refusing to recognize the children's complaints that they were not getting things. A closely related type of rationalization stems from the change of child-rearing practices over the past generation. The parents felt that their parents were much stricter than they were with their children and that children nowadays "get away with murder." Many of the parents had acute conflicts about how strict to be with children, and when the parents did express aggression to the children, they often defined it as beneficial strictness and "giving the child a lesson." Since their own parents were much more severe with them, their own children don't realize "how good they have it."

The parents also used various specific norms to justify their behavior. Even though the parents may be giving implicit encouragement to break these norms, the fact that these social norms are explicitly recognized gives the parents a legitimate basis for punishing the children. As long as the permission for disobeying the sanctions is implicit, it is always possible for the parents to deny that they are really giving it. In general, these parents were reluctant to admit that their child had an emotional disturbance or that he was behaving the way he was because of certain inner problems. They generally interpreted the disturbed child's behavior as willful badness. They felt that the child could behave differently if he really wanted to. Hence, what was needed, in their view, was not consideration, advice, and help, but a "lesson" in how to behave, i.e., severe reprimands and punishment; but even this they could not give. At times, the parents attempted to deny completely that they were scapegoating this particular child. They insisted very rigidly that "we treat all the children just the same." At other times, the parents insisted that this one particular child was just different from all others, implying that this child deserved punishment and that they were good parents since their other children have turned out so well.

Frequently, the mothers expressed, although inconsistently, unusually strong affection for a son. They justified this almost invariably in the same way: the child had problems and difficulties and thus needed more help and care than the other children. However, what they considered care and protection far exceeded the usual limits. This can be seen, for example, in the mother who carried her twelve-year-old son from the bed to the bathroom so that he could avoid bed-wetting, in the mother who continually fondled her adolescent son and called him "lovie," and in the frequent slips of the tongues by a variety of family members which identified the mother and son as spouses. Fathers, on the other hand, often had special attachments to, and fondness for, daughters.

All these attempts of the parents to rationalize their behavior had a very defensive quality and showed the difficulty these parents had in reconciling their own behavior with general social norms about child-rearing. In the more severely disturbed families, the pressing nature of their problems required serious distortion of social norms, but in the mildly disturbed families, more attention was given to the social norms, and attempts were made to express emotions in more acceptable ways. In any event, much energy was required to keep the balance stable, a state which required co-ordination of many subtle and inconsistent feelings and behaviors. It was, in effect, an "armed truce," and the danger of an explosion was constantly present.

SOME PARALLELS BETWEEN SEXUAL AND DOMINANCE BEHAVIOR OF INFRA-HUMAN PRIMATES* AND THE FANTASIES OF PATIENTS IN PSYCHOTHERAPY†

A. H. Maslow, H. Rand, and S. Newman.

It is our purpose in this paper to present some parallels between human and infra-human primates in respect to dominance-subordination, and to male and female sexuality and character, that have arisen in our own work.

What appears openly in the behavior of these animals often shows an astonishing resemblance to the content of secret human wishes and fantasies, dreams, myths, characterological adaptations, neurotic and psychotic acts and symptoms, as well as overt and covert social and psychological interactions, especially between parent and child, male and female, therapist and patient, and, in general, between the strong and the weak, the rulers and the ruled. Thus, this resemblance offers a perspective on aspects of human psychology not easily accessible to behavioral observation.

We wish to stress as strongly as we can that we are dealing with interesting and suggestive *parallels*, not with proofs of anything. Monkeys and apes prove nothing whatsoever about human beings; but they *suggest* a great deal, as we can testify. These parallels have certainly enriched our perceptions, giving another dimension to many human psychological problems, enabling us to see much that we had not noticed before. They have also raised many questions, speculations, and hypotheses which were new for us and which, of course, await validation by other techniques.

---

*No effort has been made to survey the entire literature on this subject; this paper is based almost entirely on the investigations of the senior author listed in the references (2–16).

†Adapted from an address given before the Massachusetts Psychological Association, February 16, 1960.

This is quite definitely an intellectual game we are playing and is quite appropriate, even perhaps necessary, at the idea-producing level of scientific work. It is certainly necessary to be cautious in science and we wish to be, too (especially by our stress on *parallels*). But it is not well to be *only* cautious. A certain boldness in the forward elements of science, in speculation and theories, is also needed.

THE DOMINANCE-SUBORDINATION SYNDROME IN INFRA-HUMAN PRIMATES

This syndrome may be generalized to all infra-human primates and, indeed, in its basic schema, to most other animals. It has been described for all vertebrate classes from the teleost fishes to the human being (except for amphibians). For our purposes, however, it is most useful, to begin with, to concentrate on the *Old World* monkeys and baboons in whom the syndrome is seen most nakedly in its sado-masochistic form. Apes and New World monkeys vary in certain respects described in a previous communication (8) and may be postponed for later consideration.

In brief, it is observed that when a pair of monkeys is introduced to each other for the first time, they will, without exception, form at once into a dominance-subordination hierarchy; i.e., one will assume the status of boss or overlord and the other will become the subordinate one. Under experimental conditions this status is independent of gender. Either male or female can become either the dominant or the subordinate individual. Where there is a real discrepancy in size, the larger one will usually be the dominant. Sexual dimorphism, therefore, almost always guarantees male dominance in the wild. In the laboratory, however, one can select as one pleases. If a female is selected who is larger than the male, she becomes dominant and he becomes subordinate. So also when two males or two females are paired; the larger one ordinarily becomes dominant. Since prior to these experiments only observations in the wild or in herds or flocks were available, we can understand why it should have been believed that dominance was an exclusively male prerogative. When the factor of size is ruled out by pairing equally large monkeys, more subtle determinants emerge into view. Sureness, lack of hesitation, a confident posture, cockiness—in short, what the observer is irresistibly impelled to call self-confidence— determines the issue. It is as if the animals somehow knew at first glance which was dominant and which subordinate. Since there are two animals involved, sometimes it looks as if this occurs by one animal conceding dominance, sometimes by one animal assuming or taking dominance, but more often these two attitudes are assumed simultaneously. Characteristically one maintains a level stare and the other drops his eyes or looks off to a corner. The postures become different, the subordinate one assumes a craven and appeasing attitude, his tail drooping, his belly closer to the floor. He looks hesitant and uncertain. He may chatter in fear or back into a corner or get out of the way.

Often, however, the difference in status shows itself very soon by a pseudo-sexual act. The subordinate animal, whether male or female, presents (assumes the female sexual position); the dominant one, whether male or female, mounts. This must be called pseudo-sexual because most often it is a token act. Sexual excitement may not be seen. Erection may be absent in the mounting male. There may be no pelvic thrusts or they may be weak and nominal. The head may be mounted instead of the pelvis, etc. There may be no penetration. The only desideratum at times seems to be getting above the subordinate, regardless of its posture or position. Sometimes the subordinate animal goes eagerly or willingly into this situation, sometimes reluctantly. In a few cases, reluctant subordination shows itself by an assumption of a face-to-face sexual position rather than the presenting for dorso-ventral mounting. This kind of dominance mounting and subordinate presenting probably occurs more often at the beginning of a relationship rather than after status has been stabilized.

DOMINANCE-SUBORDINATION IN HUMANS

In sub-primate species, dominance may involve actual use of physical strength, as it does, for example, in the gang or group of pre-adolescent or adolescent boys. Punching or formal boxing may establish a boy in the dominance hierarchy; often the combat takes the form of wrestling, which is won when the winner lies on top of the loser for specified amounts of time, frequently defined by counting, or by admission of defeat ("say 'uncle'").

But the very *threat* of use of force, or an obvious external evidence—bigger size, obvious self-confidence, strong muscles, swagger, strutting or cockiness—may be enough, as it is in monkeys. This again we may observe among boys—also in pre-adolescents in both sexes, for example, when some girls may try to measure up their strength against boys but eventually acknowledge that boys are

stronger. This is also accepted tacitly by most children in regard
to their parents and other adults.

In later life also the struggle for dominance manifests itself in all
areas of interpersonal relationships, in overt behavior, in dreams,
fantasies, neurotic and psychotic symptoms. However, in the sexual
realm especially we can see parallels between our data from primates and human behavior patterns and fantasies.

If maturation does not result in a healthy integration under the
hegemony of genitality, masculine sexual activity may be identified with dominance, control, manipulation, aggression, and even
sadistic behavior. This may extend over a wide range of phenomena.
At the extreme, the partner may be bound and actual pain inflicted.
Or he may be immobilized, made passive, manipulated, dominated,
used. Here, as in the dominance struggle of the primates, the power,
dominance, and aggression aspects overshadow the genital drives
and only use them to channel through. The pattern of the struggle is basically non-sexual, regardless of the gender of the participants. Thus in the dominance struggle there are several possible
combinations:

1. Male-male relationship.
2. Female-female relationship.
3. Male-female relationship in which the man is dominant.
4. Male-female relationship in which the woman is dominant.

Cases 3 and 4 are often deceptive and masquerade frequently as
the "normal" genital adjustment. Yet even here, in the behaviorally
"normal" sexual act, dominance and subordination fantasies are
often found:

1. A case of a homosexual woman, whose strong masculine aspirations appeared in the course of treatment, who spontaneously found herself in her first
heterosexual experience on top of her male partner, feeling herself as the
thrusting, dominant one.
2. A male patient with an anaesthetic penis seeks out sexual intercourse to
feel powerful; he has repetitive fantasies of wielding a whip over a harem of
women.
3. A patient reports fantasies of sucking the breast during "normal" intercourse. Even though his behavior is dominant his fantasy is submissive.
4. An active homosexual woman feels that the climax of her seductive
campaign has been reached when an innocent girl succumbs sexually, *not*
when she herself has sexual pleasure. Indeed, it is almost irrelevant for her.

In the behaviorally "normal" (to the eye of the camera) sexual
intercourse, the fantasies may express a dominant-subordinate impulse rather than a love, a sex, or reproductive impulse. One way
in which this is commonly reflected is in the use of the words screw-

ing and fucking to express overpowering aggression, contempt, conquest, assumption of the dominant status, or even cruelty. These words are used in many non-sexual situations. "Did I get screwed," a man may exclaim to say that he was taken advantage of. "I got raped" (or "shafted"), a man or woman may say in situations in which he or she was taken advantage of, fooled, swindled, or exploited; or of an irritatingly superior or hoity-toity woman, males are apt to say, "She ought to be raped," as if this would humble her properly.

Human adults—consciously, preconsciously, and unconsciously—frequently perceive and describe the sexual act in terms of the infantile perception of it as the male ("overpowering, cruel, bad") doing something harmful to the female ("helpless, unwilling, weak"). The child may perceive his father as killing the mother or hurting her in the act. So also when he sees animals copulating.

The perception of the sexual act may be sado-masochistic and manipulative in its essence and express itself correspondingly in language.

This is the (masturbation) fantasy of a dominant woman:

> She is an oriental queen, all powerful. She is surrounded by huge male slaves, almost naked. She selects one for a sexual partner and commands him to serve her. He does this in the way that she prefers, she on her back and he above her. She likes the feeling of being crushed by his weight. He is very potent and with a huge penis performs to her complete satisfaction. She lets herself go entirely in an orgiastic way.
>
> But after it is over, because he has committed lèse majesté, she commands that he be decapitated, which is done. He does not protest but recognizes that this is inevitable, proper, and suitable. She then commands another slave to do the same.

This woman is frigid in actual sexual intercourse. She has the common rape and prostitution fantasies. Apparently these enable her to surrender enough to enjoy sexuality. Several of these high-dominance women who were sexually neurotic, and who "dominatized" the sexual act, managed some compromise pleasure in sexuality by such fantasies as the following:

1. By being in the above position, and insisting that the man remain immobile, these women could image that *they* were the males and that *they* had the penis ("as if it were part of *my* body and I were entering him").

2. The fantasy that the penis was attached to her body and that she was "screwing" him has been reported by some females even though they assumed the below position.

3. That the man was really "serving" her, was her slave, working hard, sweating, and grunting at his job of pleasing her rather than himself, while she saw herself as taking her ease, not working, making no effort, and secretly using him.

4. By stretching and pulling the clitoris to resemble a penis in masturbation.

5. By decontaminating the "surrender," i.e., refusing to submit (even though sexually submitting) by refusing to enjoy it, by hiding the enjoyment, by contemptuous gestures, e.g., smoking casually during the act, yawning, laughing contemptuously at his excitement.

MODES OF ADJUSTMENT OF THE SUBORDINATED ONES

In Animals

"Presentation" to the dominant animal may range from a kind of symbolic gesture of recognition of the other's superiority to actual *"giving up"* of the male role in an acute situation and thus trying to escape injury and punishment by the other animal.

The completely subordinate animal flees to a far corner of the cage when food is thrown in, and thus makes it clear that he is not competing for it. To obtain food it may often engage in what Kempf (1) called "prostitution behavior"; i.e., it may present itself sexually to the dominant one. This it does also to avoid attack or to obtain protection. These presentations are frequently merely nominal, vestigial—one is tempted to say "symbolic." They are different from real sexual behavior in heat. The following responses have been observed in the subordinate animal in a dominance mounting: fear, apprehension, disinterest, mere complaisance, annoyance, impatience, passivity, cringing, waxy flexibility, or attempts at flight. In many cases (but not in all) the response pattern indicates that being dominance-mounted is unpleasant.

Sexual presentation and subordination may serve as a *means* for achieving several aims that can be summarized under the headings of self-preservation and handling fear in threatening situations. This includes warding off attacks, avoiding punishment, obtaining access to food, and other benefits and privileges.

In Man

Man learns subordinate patterns of behavior from early childhood on. While he is factually helpless he learns to submit to his parents and to other adults. He has to do this, for his (or her) very survival depends on parental care. Also, threatening situations and fears can be handled by the child only with the help of parents (or their substitutes). The child can assert its will only if the parents let him do so and are not threatened by his asserting his will. By and large, he can strive for security when he is young only by being and becoming the object of parental love and care. He cannot really be the *subject* of masculine assertive behavior towards the parents unless they let him—or when they do not realize that he is asserting himself by various covert compromise formations, e.g., apparent inability to get the good grades in school that his parents demand.

This helpless situation, as long as the child is young, leaves deep impressions both upon the human individual and upon the cultural, artistic, and social aspects of mankind.

The adult, too, may use the subordinate pattern as a means of handling threats, escaping punishment, and obtaining favors and approval. In other words, such an adult will not assert his will, will not fight, compete, or challenge, but rather will try to escape dangers by "degrading" himself, by surrendering or ingratiation, by voluntary subordination and appeasement. This is not an all-or-none situation—there are many intermediate grades. A monkey that has to submit unwillingly may, for instance, retain some degree of dominance by facing his sexual partner rather than presenting his rear. Such compromise formations are common also in humans. Complete subordination is rare. An effort is made to preserve as much self-assertion, will, and freedom as is possible under the circumstances.

Ingratiation, continuing smilings, being unable to win, some forms of kindness—all these can be seen as attempts at avoiding danger by voluntarily accepting dominance and making clear that one is no threat to the dominant one. Other techniques are appeasement, submissiveness, fawning, humility, propitiation, meekness; lack of demandingness or challenge, whimpering, cringing, showing fear, whining, compliance, wheedling, reducing; appealing *via* incapacity, helplessness, fearfulness, or illness; dependence, the call to pity, the giving of constant admiration, being "good"; looking up to, adoration, worship; passivity, the "you are always right" technique. These are all accommodations whereby the subordinate child, the weaker one, can adapt himself to living with the sado-masochistic parent, the strong one. Observe that these are also customary techniques whereby a weak minority group can accommodate to a stronger group.

That these subordinance techniques ("presenting techniques") can all be seen as sexualized is obvious, for most of these techniques may also be called "feminine," even in our culture, and *are* in fact feminine in more traditional sado-masochistic cultures where women are valued less than men.

Weakness can appease strength and avert its dangers by sexualizing itself and by offering in a symbolic way a sexual service to the strong. Also strength and would-be strength may assert itself and prove itself *via* sexual channels.

Why does presenting and its variations work so well in appeasing and forestalling the wrath of the strong? We do not really know. We know that it does work and that we have infra-human parallels which force us to think of at least the possibility of instinctoid sources. For instance, the ethologists have described for us the "chivalry reflex" in the wolf and in the dog. Two animals may be fighting hard, even to the death. However, if one *concedes* defeat by rolling over and exposing its throat and belly, not fighting any longer, the conqueror will no longer attack but will turn away. In one or another isomorphic form, something of the sort can be seen in many other species. In the infra-human primates, it is sexual presenting which apparently has the same meaning, or at least the same appeasing and life-saving effect.

In some lower species, this is the mechanism that differentiates male from female objects for the attacking male. If it fights back, it's a male and fighting ensues; if it doesn't fight back but instead assumes another kind of posture, varying with the species, it is a female and sexual activity ensues. In some birds, the females indicate subordinance not only by assuming a sexually inviting position, but also by soliciting food from the male in the way that a half-grown fledgling does. No instance is known in which a male does this in the wild. Here also human parallels strongly suggest themselves. The appeal to many males of admitted fear, helplessness, passivity, receptiveness, etc., in the female or in the child suggests a parallel to the chivalry reflex. Most males, especially immature males, in our culture are not sexually drawn to the female who is strong, assertive, self-confident, self-sufficient, and if he *is*, we may suspect that his feminine component is attracted to her masculine component; that is, at the unconscious and fantasy level, this may simply be a reversal of roles, for the strong woman can also be drawn to the dependent male as a man is to a woman or perhaps as a mother is to a son. Even this reminds us of the chivalry reflex. (Of course, we must not forget that in the human beings we find, in our own culture at least, that psychologically mature and strong males can be drawn to psychologically mature females who may look too "strong" for the average, more delicate male.)

DOMINANCE, SUBORDINATION, MASCULINITY, FEMININITY

The young or neurotic human being in many cultures has a tendency to identify or confuse subordinate status with feminine status and the dominant status with masculine status.

The man in subordinate status, whether willingly or unwillingly arrived at, in relation to a boss, superior officer, or anybody who gives him orders, may react as if he had been made female, as if even justifiable orders were like being mounted or raped. He may respond to a realistic situation as if he had been ordered to become feminine, i.e., to present. This, as in the monkeys, is without relationship to gender; i.e., it may happen in response to either male or female boss. Some respond to this subordination by submitting willingly or even eagerly but these are often despised.

Army lingo examples: Such a person or act is called "brownnose," "being cornholed," "asskisser," "asslicker," "being browned." The phrase "he is prostituting himself" also applies. Other men may fight against this as if against an assault upon their masculinity, even when the demands or orders are perfectly natural or justifiable. That is, such dominance relations are sexualized just as sexual relations are seen as dominance-subordination metaphors.

Furthermore, in those cultures which value masculinity more than femininity, being pushed into subordinate status means being degraded or demoted. In such cultures this attitude is shared by both men and women. Women who feel that their femininity is synonymous with inferior status or subordination may repudiate their femininity in various unconscious ways or unconsciously emulate the male, or they may in their striving for esteem or status or self-respect fantasy being male. This is as if they thought that the only way to be strong or capable or intelligent or successful were to be male. So also, following the same assumption, the woman in order to be a good female may feel it necessary to give up her strength, intelligence, or talent, fearing them as somehow masculine and defeminizing.

This has been observed overtly in female children who will openly demand some phallic equivalent, e.g., will urinate in the standing position. In adults, this is not seen overtly very often (exceptions are in psychotics or in some female homosexuals) but is rather seen in fantasy or dreams of contempt or hostility or desexualizing and castrating of the male, or of various forms of resistance to being pushed into the female position, either literally or figuratively.

HOMOSEXUALITY

We have learned from Evelyn Hooker to speak of the many kinds of homosexualities and to give up monistic explanations and theories. However, the homosexual behavior that is so easily and parsimoniously explained in monkeys, that is, as a function of dominance and subordination status, can also be paralleled in *some* forms of human homosexuality, overt as well as covert. The dominating Lesbian certainly exists, and she so strongly identifies the female sexual role with total domination by the male, with obliteration of her personality, her self-hood, that she could not possibly accept the role of "weakness." Feeling herself to be so strong she identifies with the conquering male. So also for the pansy type of male homosexual who feels himself to be so weak that he cannot possibly fit into *his* distorted image of the dominant male, the raper, the exploiter, the selfish, arrogant taker of what he wants. But also his sexual presenting can be a way of protecting himself or winning favors, as in men's prisons. The same mechanism may be seen in the "normal" man.

An unconsciously passive, fearful man, ingratiating and appeasing his therapist, had the following dream: "I was following a narrow snowy path someplace in the wilds of Alaska. Suddenly there is a huge frightening bear standing on his hind legs in front of me, blocking the path. In terror I turn around and put my rear up to him, eagerly and quickly fitting his penis into my anus in the hope that he won't attack me. It works and I can go on." He was disturbed by this dream, seeing it as homosexual.

Let us say that at least *one* factor in the complex web of human homosexuality is the dominance-subordination determinant in its sado-masochistic version, in the version that so many children report and adults covertly fantasy, that "Daddy is killing Mommy" or, upon watching animals copulate, "He is hurting her." Some males cannot stand to identify with the hurter and/or prefer to identify with the hurtee. Some females cannot or will not identify with the hurtee and/or prefer to identify with the hurter. Presumably in such cases differentiating sex from dominance, instead of confounding them, should cure *this* aspect of the illness.

SEXUALIZING OF THE TRANSFERENCE

The actual subordination of the therapeutic patient, his factual weakness, his necessary humility, the lowering of self-esteem implied in asking someone for help and in exposing oneself in all one's shame and embarrassment, leads not only to the customary hostility fantasies and verbalizations, but also encourages a sexualization of the relationship. Whatever character style or defenses the patient has lived by will reveal themselves here in a sexual translation, most often in a dominatized form. That is, it will be either of raping, castrating, or otherwise dominating the analyst or, more frequently, of winning his love by offering oneself to him as a sexual object (although, of course, there are also many other fantasied ways of winning his love). All this can be independent of the gender of either the analyst or the patient, just as in monkeys. "Presenting to the analyst" this may be called, and must very frequently be isomorphic with the ways in which long ago, as a child, the patient "presented" to his parents, especially to the one seen as more powerful (regardless of gender). It may be hypothesized that any therapeutic atmosphere or technique which minimized the factual status of subordination would reduce sexualization of the relationship.

The patient, a 23-year-old single man, had been for most of his life fearful of older men, especially those in the authoritative position. He was never conscious of any hostile feelings, wishes, or fantasies toward these men; toward the original man, his father, he had the same attitude. In fact, if someone criticized his father he would passionately defend him. In analytic treatment the patient developed the same attitudes toward the analyst. He came in one day with the following dream:

He is in some kind of prison atmosphere where he is to be forced to submit to penile intercourse by some big man. The man approaches him ready to penetrate him and the dream ends.

In association to the dream the patient suddenly remembered something that had occurred the day before and represented for the first time a conscious, hostile fantasy toward an older man. When he left the analyst's office and got into his car, he saw the analyst's car nearby. His fantasy was that he wanted to crash his car into the rear of the analyst's car. This fantasy had apparently been transient and had gone into repression. The dream apparently was a projected retaliative gesture.

RELIGIOUS OBLATION

We may speak not only of the "feminine aspects of Christianity" in the Nietzschean sense (and of other religions as well), but also we can get a richer understanding of the oblative and homonomous aspects of all religious experience, and especially of the conversion experience, by separating the fusion of sexuality and dominance-subordination (pride-humility). The conversion experience as depicted by James, Begbie, and many others is often described in a clearly sexual way, but also as a giving up of pride and autonomy in favor of surrender and oblation, with ensuing peace of mind in the "successful" cases. The necessary giving up of will and of self-sufficiency, as presented in these accounts, can be understood better if we are clearly aware of the simultaneous and ambitendent urges to rule and be ruled, to dominate and to submit, and if we are also aware of the delights of surrender. In the Western male, these are felt especially as dangerous to the (unevolved) conception of masculinity, are felt even as a castration, as a becoming feminine, as a homosexual reaction; i.e., they are sexualized.

A patient in homosexual panic ran away and hid in a hotel room in another city. He couldn't sleep and felt frightened much of the time. Suddenly during the night, as he lay in bed on his back, he felt the weight of a presence on top of him. He submitted to it lovingly and felt "This is God." He felt peaceful and slept deeply for the first time in months. Next morning, he awoke refreshed and relaxed and determined to serve God by good works, which he now does. He returned to his wife and is heterosexual with her.

We may hypothesize that man's bisexual or ambitendent urges (to be masculine and feminine simultaneously, or, what amounts to the same thing, to master and to submit) are generally dangerous to him because he interprets femininity as submission and submission as feminine, feels himself thereby castrated, lower in self-esteem, emasculated. He generally has few outlets for, or legitimate expressions of, his feminine-submitting, or oblative impulses. *But,* it seems to be somewhat more possible for him to satisfy these tendencies without threat to his picture of himself as masculine, if he can surrender to a God, to some omnipotent, omniscient figure, where rivalry is out of the question. Kneeling before a God is less an unmanly act then kneeling before a rival or competitor or peer. It is "suitable" in the gestalt psychological sense, appropriate, "fitting and proper," called for; it is not a defeat.

And, of course, this satisfying oblation is also possible before a human if that person is seen as Godlike enough, "great" enough, e.g. Napoleon, Hitler, on the one hand; Lincoln, Schweitzer, on the other.

It is also interesting to observe that most women in most cultures that we know are apt to be more religious (in this sense) than their men are. They seem to be less threatened by oblation, and to be more able to enjoy it in an uncomplicated way. So also are women apt to be less destroyed and less rebellious, made less "neurotic," by conquest of their society from without. Their admiration for the conqueror is less threatening to their integrity as persons than it is in men who must fight against their oblative tendencies or else lose self-respect. Or to put it in another way, being raped (in whatever sense) is less psychologically damaging to women than to men. Women are more able to permit themselves to "relax and enjoy it" than men are.

HEALTHY DIFFERENTIATION OF DOMINANCE FROM SEXUALITY: DESEXUALIZATION

One hoped-for effect of depth therapy is to separate and unconfound these two areas of life, and to keep them differentiated, to learn that the penis is in fact not a club or a sword or a rending instrument, that the vagina is not a garbage pail or a biting mouth or an engulfing well, that the above or below position in the sexual act is meaningful only for sexual convenience and pleasure, that taking orders from a superior is not equivalent to being raped, that sexual oblation to stronger people is not necessary to avert their anger. It is hoped for the woman that her sexual surrender becomes *not* a giving up of her ego or self-respect; it is *not* a conquest in which by surrendering she concedes her slavish status thereafter. The male must learn that by penetrating his wife, he has neither conquered nor asserted mastery nor committed a sadistic act. Nor has she thereby conceded submission in other areas of life. Nor need he feel guilty or fearful after the sexual act if he can feel that he is welcomed rather than resented, if he has not conquered but collaborated. And so on.

What all this amounts to is the differentiation of sex from dominance and subordination. It seems likely that this is really, *fully* possible only for the human being, although there seem to be some approaches to this separation in the chimpanzee.

A paper (8), whose theoretical implications have been overlooked, called attention to the qualitative differences in what was called "dominance-quality" in the three large families of infra-human primates. Briefly, all the New World monkeys show a laissez-faire quality of dominance. All the Old World monkeys and baboons show the kind of sado-masochistic or dominating, tyrannical quality of dominance we have mostly talked about in this paper. The anthropoid apes (of whom we really know only the chimpanzees) show a more friendly, altruistic, cooperative quality of dominance. We do not have enough data, even on the chimpanzee, to be very confident of this. But what we *do* have indicates that there is absolutely less pseudo-sexual behavior, less dominance-sexual equivalence, less dominance mounting, and the like in chimpanzees. Certainly there is less bullying, cringing, and cowering.

This suggests (nothing more, of course) that the dominance-sexual fusion is a lower evolutionary development than the differentiation of sex from dominance and parallels our suspicion that such a differentiation in the human being may be a correlate or epiphenomenon of greater psychological maturity or development. Considering the importance of such a speculation, it certainly calls for more investigation than it has received.

The obverse implication is that the confounding of sex and dominance in the human being may be an evidence of immaturity or of neurosis, of the loss of a distinctively human capacity, of mild psychopathology, of human diminution.

HEALTHY FEMININITY AND MASCULINITY

Of course, there are many theoretical possibilities here, and all fascinating. We mention one only because we have data that bear on this puzzle. It *may* turn out that healthy growth or psychotherapy in the human being has as its hoped-for consequence *not* the abolition of the dominance-subordination relationships as between male or female at their deepest levels, or between parents and children. What may rather be the case is a change in what has been called "dominance-quality" from the baboon quality to the chimpanzee quality. In chimpanzees, the dominance-subordination syndrome can also be seen but it has taken on an entirely different flavor, one of kind and fostering and responsible strength which is at the service of the weak; older-brotherly dominance it was called. By this time the words "dominance" and "subordination" become misnomers and can be very misleading. Substitutes might be, for instance, "kind and loving strength" and "trusting dependence."

In any case, in the human being, the healthy shift is away from devaluation of the subordinate status with mutual hostility toward an accepting and loving attitude. Concomitant with this is a de-sexualizing of the statuses of strength and weakness and of leadership; so either man or woman can be, without anxiety and without degradation, either weak or strong, as the situation demands. Either must be capable of both leadership or surrender; e.g., a therapist has to be motherly; unfortunate mothers must be ready also to father their children.

We have in essence been concerned with the old problem of bisexuality, of the conflict between "maleness" and "femaleness" in either male or female, penis envy, castration anxieties, masculine protest, and phallic masculinity.

Without trying at this point to spell out consequences in detail, we may point to the following pregnant fact. There is evidence available to indicate that the sexual hormones produce not only sexual but also dominance desires. That is to say, the same hormones may produce both the sexual syndrome and the dominance-subordination syndrome. No wonder they are so intimately interconnected. Indeed, the problem then is transformed into understanding how they become separated, independent, e.g., how position in the sexual act becomes detached from dominance-subordination meaning, how the penis can become *only* a sexual tool and not a power weapon, how the anus can become only a defecating organ and no more a sexual receptacle, how an employee can come to take necessary orders without feeling feminized-subordinated.

POSTSCRIPT

For those of you who enjoy the game of theoretical speculation and manipulation, there is much here to play with. For instance, with respect to Freudian theory, we have opened up the possibility of combining oedipal theory and castration theory in a single and unified system. They can both be pushed into the more general phrasing of "the mutual accommodations of the strong and the weak to each other and the pathological sexualization of these accommodations." We have opened up another possibility with respect to Freudian and Adlerian theory, namely, that they may be, in the respects we have dealt with, isomorphic parallel languages, at an archaic level saying the same thing, one from the sexual side of the fusion, the other from the dominance side of the same fusion. The so far mysterious problem of the definition of healthy masculinity and femininity have been touched on, and this is clearly *one* way of playing with this mystery. We have only barely mentioned the thread of sexualization that can be plucked out of the web of inter-class and caste relationships. We have bypassed altogether the intricate questions of the relationships of culture to our primate inheritance, even though we are quite convinced that the study of infra-human primates has much to teach the sociologist. We imply another approach to the psychoanalytic theory of instincts and still another toward the understanding of sadism-masochism, of authoritarianism, of hypnosis, of the need for achievement, of the definition of the various types of love, of religious oblation, even of the servant problem. And so on and so on.

REFERENCES

1. KEMPF, E. J. "The Social and Sexual Behavior of Infra-Human Primates," *Psychoanalytic Review*, Vol. 4 (1917), pp. 127–54.

2. MASLOW, A. H. "The Authoritarian Character Structure," *Journal of Social Psychology*, Vol. 18 (1943), pp. 401–11.

3. MASLOW, A. H. "The Comparative Approach to Social Behavior," *Social Forces*, Vol. 15 (1937), pp. 487–90.

4. MASLOW, A. H. "The Determination of Hierarchy in Pairs and in a Group," *Journal of Genetic Psychology*, Vol. 49 (1936), pp. 161–90.

5. MASLOW, A. H. "The Dominance Drive as a Determiner of the Social and Sexual Behavior of Infra-Human Primates. I. Observations at Vilas Park Zoo," *Journal of Genetic Psychology*, Vol. 48 (1936), pp. 261–77.

6. MASLOW, A. H. "Dominance-Feeling, Behavior and Status," *Psychological Review* Vol. 44 (1937), pp. 404–20.

7. MASLOW, A. H. "Dominance-Feeling, Personality and Social Behavior in Women," *Journal of Social Psychology*, Vol. 10, (1939), pp. 3–39.

8. MASLOW, A. H., "Dominance-Quality and Social Behavior in Infra-Human Primates," *Journal of Social Psychology*, Vol. 11 (1940), pp. 313–24.

9. MASLOW, A. H. "Individual Psychology and the Social Behavior of Monkeys and Apes," *Int. J. Individ. Psychol.*, Vol. 1 (1935), pp. 47–59.

10. MASLOW, A. H. *Motivation and Personality*, New York: Harper, 1954.

11. MASLOW, A. H. "Power Relationships and Patterns of Personal Development," in *Problems of Power in American Democracy*, (ed. A. KORNHAUER). Detroit, Mich.: Wayne University Press, 1957.

12. MASLOW, A. H. "Self-Esteem (Dominance-Feeling) and Sexuality in Women," *Journal of Social Psychology*, Vol. 16 (1942), pp. 259–94.

13. MASLOW, A. H. *The Social Personality Inventory: A Test for Self-Esteem in Women* (with manual). Stanford, Calif.: Stanford University Press, 1942.

14. MASLOW, A. H. "A Test for Dominance-Feeling (Self-Esteem) in Women," *Journal of Social Psychology*, Vol. 12 (1940), pp. 255–70.

15. MASLOW, A. H. "A Theory of Sexual Behavior in Infra-Human Primates," *Journal of Genetic Psychology*, Vol. 48 (1936) pp. 310–38.

16. MASLOW, A. H. AND FLANZBAUM, S.: "The Experimental Determination of the Dominance Behavior Syndrome," *Journal of Genetic Psychology*, Vol. 48 (1936), pp. 278–309.

LONELINESS*

Frieda Fromm-Reichmann

I am not sure what inner forces have made me, during the last years, ponder about and struggle with the psychiatric problems of loneliness. I have found a strange fascination in thinking about it— and subsequently in attempting to break through the aloneness of thinking about loneliness by trying to communicate what I believe I have learned.

Perhaps my interest began with the young catatonic woman who broke through a period of completely blocked communication and obvious anxiety by responding when I asked her a question about her feeling miserable. She raised her hand with her thumb lifted, the other four fingers bent toward her palm, so that I could see only the thumb, isolated from the four hidden fingers. I interpreted the signal with, "That lonely?," in a sympathetic tone of voice. At this, her facial expression loosened up as though in great relief and grati-tude, and her fingers opened. Then she began to tell me about her-self by means of her fingers, and she asked me by gestures to respond in kind. We continued with this finger conversation for one or two weeks, and as we did so, her anxious tension began to decrease and she began to break through her noncommunicative isolation; and subsequently she emerged altogether from her loneliness.

I have had somewhat similar experiences with other patients; and so I have finally been prompted to write down what I have learned about loneliness from my work with the patients and from other experiences of my own.

The writer who wishes to elaborate on the problems of loneliness is faced with a serious terminological handicap. Loneliness seems to be such a painful, frightening experience that people will do prac-tically everything to avoid it. This avoidance seems to include a strange reluctance on the part of psychiatrists to seek scientific clari-fication of the subject. Thus it comes about that loneliness is one of

*Excerpted from Frieda Fromm-Reichmann, "Loneliness," reprinted by special permission of The William Alanson White Psychiatric Foundation, Inc., from *Psy-chiatry* Vol. 22, No. 1 (Feb., 1959), pp. 1–15. Copyright 1959 by The William Alanson White Psychiatric Foundation, Inc.

the least satisfactorily conceptualized psychological phenomena, not even mentioned in most psychiatric textbooks. Very little is known among scientists about its genetics and psychodynamics, and various different experiences which are descriptively and dynamically as different from one another as culturally determined loneliness, self-imposed aloneness, compulsory solitude, isolation, and real loneliness are all thrown into the one terminological basket of "loneliness."

Before entering into a discussion of the psychiatric aspects of what I call real loneliness, I will briefly mention the types of loneliness which are *not* the subject of this paper. The writings of modern sociologists and social psychologists are widely concerned with culturally determined loneliness, the "cut-offness and solitariness of civilized men"—the "shut-upness," in Kierkegaard's phrase[1] which they described as characteristic of this culture. While this is a very distressing and painful experience, it is by definition the common fate of many people of this culture. Unverbalized as it may remain, it is nevertheless potentially a communicable experience, one which can be shared. Hence it does not carry the deep threat of the un-communicable, private emotional experience of severe loneliness, with which this paper will be concerned.

I am not here concerned with the sense of solitude which some people have, when, all by themselves, they experience the infinity of nature as presented by the mountains, the desert, or the ocean—the experience which has been described with the expression, "oceanic feelings."[2] These oceanic feelings may well be an expression of a creative loneliness, if one defines creativity, with Paul Tillich, in the wider sense of the term, as "living spontaneously, in action and reaction, with the contents of one's cultural life."[3]

I am also not concerned in this paper with the seclusion which yields creative artistic or scientific products. In contrast to the dis-integrative loneliness of the mental patient, these are states of constructive loneliness, and they are often temporary and self-induced, and may be voluntarily and alternately sought out and rejected. Nearly all works of creative originality are conceived in such states of constructive aloneness; and, in fact, only the creative person who is not afraid of this constructive aloneness will have free command

[1]Søren Kierkegaard, *The Concept of Dread,* translated by Walter Lowrie; Princeton, N.J., Princeton Univ. Press, 1944; p. 110. See also Erich Fromm, *Escape from Freedom;* New York, Rinehart, 1941.

[2]Sigmund Freud, *Civilization and its Discontents;* London, Hogarth, 1939; see, for instance, p. 8.

[3]Paul Tillich, *The Courage to be;* New Haven, Yale Univ. Press, 1952; p. 46.

over his creativity. Some of these people, schizoid, artistic personalities in Karl Menninger's nomenclature, submit to the world, as a product of their detachment from normal life, "fragments of their own world—bits of dreams and visions and songs that we—out here—don't hear except as they translate them."[4] It should be added that an original, creative person may not only be lonely for the time of his involvement in creative processes, but subsequently *because* of them, since the appearance of new creations of genuine originality often antedates the ability of the creator's contemporaries to understand or to accept them.

I am not talking here about the temporary aloneness of, for instance, a person who has to stay in bed with a cold on a pleasant Sunday afternoon while the rest of the family are enjoying the outdoors. He may complain about loneliness and feel sorry for himself, for to the "other-directed" types of the culture, "loneliness is such an omnipotent and painful threat...that they have little conception of the positive values of solitude, and even at times are very frightened at the prospect of being alone."[5] But however much this man with a cold may complain about loneliness, he is, needless to say, not lonely in the sense I am talking about; he is just temporarily alone.

While the loneliness of the person who suffers the sense of loss and of being alone following the death of someone close to him is on another level, it too does not concern me here. Freud and Abraham have described the dynamics by which the mourner counteracts this aloneness by incorporation and identification; this can often be descriptively verified by the way in which the mourner comes to develop a likeness in looks, personality, and activities to the lost beloved one.[6] By such incorporation and identification the human mind has the power of fighting the aloneness after the loss of a beloved person. Somewhat similar is the sense of lonesomeness which lovers may suffer after a broken-off love affair. Daydreams, fantasies, and the love songs of others—or sometimes original compositions—help the unhappy lover to overcome his temporary solitude: "Out of my great worry I emerge with my little songs," as the German poet Adelbert von Chamisso put it.

[4]Karl Menninger, *The Human Mind;* New York, Knopf, 1930; p. 79.
[5]Rollo May, *Man's Search for Himself;* New York, Norton, 1953; p. 26. See also David Reisman, *The Lonely Crowd;* New Haven, Yale Univ. Press, 1950.
[6]Sigmund Freud, *The Ego and the Id;* London, Hogarth, 1935; pp. 36–37. Freud, "Mourning and Melancholia," in *Collected Papers* 4:152–70; London, Hogarth, 1934; see especially p. 160. Karl Abraham, "Notes on the Psycho-Analytical Investigation and Treatment of Manic-Depressive Insanity and Allied Conditions," Ch. 6; in *Selected Papers on Psycho-Analysis,* London, Hogarth, 1937.

The kind of loneliness I am discussing is nonconstructive, if not disintegrative, and it shows in, or leads ultimately to, the development of psychotic states. It renders people who suffer it emotionally paralyzed and helpless. In Sullivan's words, it is "the exceedingly unpleasant and driving experience connected with an inadequate discharge of the need for human intimacy, for interpersonal intimacy."[7] The longing for interpersonal intimacy stays with every human being from infancy throughout life; and there is no human being who is not threatened by its loss.

I have implied, in what I have just said, that the human being is born with the need for contact and tenderness. I should now like to review briefly how this need is fulfilled in the various phases of childhood development—if things go right—in order to provide a basis for asking and answering the question, What has gone wrong in the history of the lonely ones? That is, what has gone wrong in the history of those people who suffer from their failure to obtain satisfaction of the universal human need for intimacy?

The infant thrives in a relationship of intimate and tender closeness with the person who tends him and mothers him. In childhood, the healthy youngster's longing for intimacy is, according to Sullivan, fulfilled by his participation in activities with adults, in the juvenile era by finding compeers and acceptance, and in preadolescence by finding a "chum." In adolescence and in the years of growth and development which should follow it, man feels the need for friendship and intimacy jointly with or independently of his sexual drive.[8]

A number of writers have investigated what may happen, at various stages of development, if the need for intimacy goes unsatisfied. For example, René Spitz demonstrated the fatal influence of lack of love and of loneliness on infants, in what he called their "anaclytic depression."[9] An interesting sidelight on this is provided by experiments in isolation with very young animals, in which the effect of isolation can be an almost completely irreversible lack of development of whole systems, such as those necessary for the use of vision in accomplishing tasks put to the animal.[10] Sullivan and Suttie have

---

[7]Harry Stack Sullivan, *The Interpersonal Theory of Psychiatry;* New York, Norton, 1953; p. 290.

[8]*Ibid.*, pp. 261–62.

[9]René Spitz and Katherine M. Wolf, "Anaclytic Depression," pp. 313–42; in *Psychoanalytic Study of the Child*, Vol. 2; New York, International Univ. Press, 1946.

[10]John C. Lilly has referred to these experiments in "Mental Effects of Reduction of Ordinary Levels of Physical Stimuli on Intact, Healthy Persons," *Psychiatric Research Reports*, No. 5; American Psychiatric Association, June, 1956.

noted the unfortunate effects on future development if a person's early need for tenderness remains unsatisfied, and Anna Freud, in her lecture at the 1953 International Psychoanalytic meetings in London, described sensations of essential loneliness in children under the heading of "Losing and Being Lost."[11]

Both Sullivan and Suttie have particularly called attention to the fact that the lonely child may resort to substitute satisfactions in fantasy, which he cannot share with others. Thus his primary sense of isolation may subsequently be reinforced if, despite the pressures of socialization and acculturation, he does not sufficiently learn to discriminate between realistic phenomena and the products of his own lively fantasy. In order to escape being laughed at or being punished for replacing reports of real events by fictitious narratives, he may further withdraw, and may continue, in his social isolation, to hold on to the uncorrected substitutive preoccupation. An impressive example of the results of such a faulty development has been presented by Robert Lindner, in his treatment history of Kirk Allen, the hero of the "true psychoanalytic tale," "The Jet-Propelled Couch."[12]

Incidentally, I think that the substitutive enjoyment which the neglected child may find for himself in his fantasy life makes him especially lonely in the present age of overemphasis on the conceptual differentiation between subjective and objective reality. One of the outcomes of this scientific attitude is that all too frequently even healthy children are trained to give up prematurely the subjective inner reality of their normal fantasy life and, instead, to accept the objective reality of the outward world.

The process by which the child withdraws into social isolation into his substitutive fantasies may occur if the mothering one weans him from her caressing tenderness before he is ready to try for the satisfactions of the modified needs for intimacy characteristic of his ensuing developmental phase. As Suttie has put it, separation from the direct tenderness and nurtural love relationship with the mother

---

[11]Sullivan, *op. cit.;* Ian D. Suttie, *The Origins of Love and Hate;* New York, Julian Press, 1952. Anna Freud, *Internat. J. Psycho-Anal.* (1953) 34:288; (1954) 35:283.

An interesting description by a layman of the impact of loneliness in childhood is given by Lucy Sprague Mitchell in her *Two Lives: The Story of Wesley Clair Mitchell and Myself* (New York, Simon and Schuster, 1953). In this book she vividly contrasts her own childhood loneliness with the affection, approval, and security her husband had as a child.

[12]Robert Lindner, *The Fifty-Minute Hour: A Collection of True Psychoanalytic Tales;* New York, Rinehart, 1955; pp. 221–93.

may outrun the child's ability for making substitutions.[13] This is a rather serious threat to an infant and child in a world where a taboo exists on tenderness among adults. When such a premature weaning from mothering tenderness occurs, the roots for permanent aloneness and isolation, for "love-shyness," as Suttie has called it, for fear of intimacy and tenderness, are planted in the child's mind; and the defensive counterreactions against this eventuality may lead to psychopathological developments.

Zilboorg, on the other hand, has warned against psychological dangers which may arise from other types of failure in handling children—failures in adequate guidance in reality testing. If the omnipotent baby learns the joy of being admired and loved but learns nothing about the outside world, he may develop a conviction of his greatness and all-importance which will lead to a narcissistic orientation to life—a conviction that life is nothing but being loved and admired. This narcissistic-megalomanic attitude will not be acceptable to the environment, which will respond with hostility and isolation of the narcissistic person. The deeply seated triad of narcissism, megalomania, and hostility will be established, which is, according to Zilboorg, at the root of the affliction of loneliness.[14]

The concepts of Sullivan, Suttie, and Zilboorg are all based on the insight that the person who is isolated and lonely in his present environment has anachronistically held on to early narcissistic need fulfillments or fantasied substitutive satisfactions. According to Sullivan and Suttie, it may be the fulfillment of his early needs which has been critical; or, according to Zilboorg, the failure may have been in meeting his needs later on for adequate guidance in reality testing.

Karl Menninger has described the milder states of loneliness which result from these failures in handling infants and children in his "isolation types of personality"—that is, lonely and schizoid personalities.[15] The more severe developments of loneliness appear in the unconstructive, desolate phases of isolation and real loneliness which are beyond the state of feeling sorry for oneself—the states of mind in which the fact that there were people in one's past life is more or less forgotten, and the possibility that there may be interpersonal relationships in one's future life is out of the realm of expectation or imagination. This loneliness, in its quintessential form,

---

[13]Suttie, *op. cit.*, pp. 87–88.
[14]Gregory Zilboorg, "Loneliness," *The Atlantic Monthly*, January, 1938.
[15]Menninger, *op. cit.*

is of such a nature that it is incommunicable by one who suffers it. Unlike other noncommunicable emotional experiences, it cannot even be shared empathically, perhaps because the other person's empathic abilities are obstructed by the anxiety-arousing quality of the mere emanations of this profound loneliness.[16]

I wonder whether this explains the fact that this real loneliness defies description, even by the pen of a master of conceptualization such as Sullivan. As a matter of fact, the extremely uncanny experience of real loneliness has much in common with some other quite serious mental states, such as panic. People cannot endure such states for any length of time without becoming psychotic—although the sequence of events is often reversed, and the loneliness or panic is concomitant with or the outcome of a psychotic disturbance. Subject to further dynamic investigation, I offer the suggestion that the experiences in adults usually described as a loss of reality or as a sense of world catastrophe can also be understood as expressions of profound loneliness.

On the other hand, while some psychiatrists seem to think of severe psychotic loneliness as part of, or as identical with, other emotional phenomena, such as psychotic withdrawal, depression, and anxiety, I do not agree with this viewpoint, in general. I shall elaborate on the interrelationship between loneliness and anxiety later. So far as psychotic withdrawal is concerned, it constitutes only seemingly a factual isolation from others; the relationship of the withdrawn person to his interpersonal environment, and even his interest in it, is by no means extinguished in the way that is true of the lonely person. So far as depressed patients are concerned, every psychiatrist knows that they complain about loneliness; but let me suggest that the preoccupation with their relationships with others, and the pleas for fulfillment of their interpersonal dependency-needs—which even withdrawn depressives show—are proof that their loneliness is not of the same order as the state of real detachment I am trying to depict.

The characteristic feature of loneliness, on which I shall elaborate later, is this: It can arouse anxiety and fear of contamination which may induce people—among them the psychiatrists who deal

---

[16]Some attention has been given to this interference of anxiety with the freedom of utilizing intuitive abilities by a seminar in which I participated, dealing specifically with intuitive processes in the psychiatrist who works with schizophrenics. See "The 'Intuitive Process' and its Relation to Work with Schizophrenics," introduced by Frieda Fromm-Reichmann and reported by Alberta Szalita-Pemow; *J. Amer. Psychoanal. Assn.* (1955) 3.7–18.

with it in their patients—to refer to it euphemistically as "depression." One can understand the emotional motivation for this definition, but that does not make it conceptually correct.

People who are in the grip of severe degrees of loneliness cannot talk about it; and people who have at some time in the past had such an experience can seldom do so either, for it is so frightening and uncanny in character that they try to dissociate the memory of what it was like, and even the fear of it. This frightened secretiveness and lack of communication about loneliness seems to increase its threat for the lonely ones, even in retrospect; it produces the sad conviction that nobody else has experienced or ever will sense what they are experiencing or have experienced.

Even mild borderline states of loneliness do not seem to be easy to talk about. Most people who are alone try to keep the mere fact of their aloneness a secret from others, and even try to keep its conscious realization hidden from themselves. I think that this may be in part determined by the fact that loneliness is a most unpopular phenomenon in this group-conscious culture. Perhaps only children have the independence and courage to identify their own loneliness as such—or perhaps they do it simply out of a lack of imagination or an inability to conceal it. One youngster asked another, in the comic strip "Peanuts," "Do you know what you're going to be when you grow up?" "Lonesome," was the unequivocal reply of the other.

Incidentally, one element in the isolation of some lonely psychotics may be the fact that, perhaps because of their interpersonal detachment, some of them are more keen, sensitive, and fearless observers of the people in their environment than the average non-lonely, mentally healthy person is. They may observe and feel free to express themselves about many painful truths which go unobserved or are suppressed by their healthy and gregarious fellowmen. But unlike the court jester, who was granted a fool's paradise where he could voice his unwelcome truths with impunity, the lonely person may be displeasing if not frightening to his hearers, who may erect a psychological wall of ostracism and isolation about him as a means of protecting themselves. Cervantes, in his story, "Man of Glass," has depicted a psychotic man who observes his fellowmen keenly and offers them uncensored truths about themselves. As long as they look upon him as sufficiently isolated by his "craziness," they are able to laugh off the narcissistic hurts to which he exposes them.[17]

I would now like to digress for a moment from the subject of real,

---

[17]Cervantes Saavedra, "Man of Glass," pp. 760–96; in *The Portable Cervantes*, translated and edited by Samuel Putman; New York, Viking Press, 1951.

psychotogenic loneliness to consider for a moment the fact that while all adults seem to be afraid of real loneliness, they vary a great deal in their tolerance of aloneness. I have, for example, seen some people who felt deeply frightened at facing the infinity of the desert, with its connotations of loneliness, and others who felt singularly peaceful, serene, and pregnant with creative ideas. Why are some people able to meet aloneness with fearless enjoyment, while others are made anxious even by temporary aloneness—or even by silence, which may or may not connote potential aloneness? The fear of these latter people is such that they make every possible effort to avoid it—by playing bridge, by looking for hours at television, by listening to the radio, by going compulsively to dances, parties, the movies. As Kierkegaard has put it, ". . . one does everything possible by way of diversions and the Janizary music of loud-voiced enterprises to keep lonely thoughts away. . . ."[18]

Perhaps the explanation for the fear of aloneness lies in the fact that, in this culture, people can come to a valid self-orientation, or even awareness of themselves, only in terms of their actual overt relationships with others. "Every human being gets much of his sense of his own reality out of what others say to him and think about him," as Rollo May puts it.[19] While alone and isolated from others, people feel threatened by the potential loss of their boundaries, of the ability to discriminate between the subjective self and the objective world around them. But valid as this general explanation for the fear of loneliness may be, it leaves unanswered the question of why this fear is not ubiquitous.

Generally speaking, I believe that the answer lies in the *degree* of a person's dependence on others for his self-orientation, and that this depends in turn on the particular vicissitudes of the developmental history. Here, you may recall, I am talking about aloneness, and not what I term real loneliness; and whether the same holds true for loneliness, I do not know. Only an intensive scrutiny of the developmental history of the really lonely ones might give the answer; and the nature of real loneliness is such that one cannot communicate with people who are in the grip of it. Once they emerge from it, they do not wish—or they are unable—to talk about their loneliness or about any topic which is psychologically connected with it, as I suggested earlier.

Descriptively speaking, however, one can understand why people are terrified of the "naked horror"—in Binswanger's term—of real

[18]Kierkegaard, *op. cit.*, p. 107.
[19]Rollo May, *Man's Search for Himself;* New York, Norton, 1953; p. 32.

loneliness. Anyone who has encountered persons who were under the influence of real loneliness understands why people are more frightened of being lonely than of being hungry, or being deprived of sleep, or of having their sexual needs unfulfilled—the three other basic needs which Sullivan assigns to the same group as the avoidance of loneliness. As Sullivan points out, people will even resort to anxiety-arousing experiences in an effort to escape from loneliness, even though anxiety itself is an emotional experience against which people fight, as a rule, with every defense at their disposal.[20] Needless to say, however, the person who is able to do this is not fully in the grip of true, severe loneliness, with its specific character of paralyzing hopelessness and unutterable futility. This "naked horror" is beyond anxiety and tension; defense and remedy seem out of reach. Only as its all-engulfing intensity decreases can the person utilize anxiety-provoking defenses against it. One of my patients, after she emerged from the depths of loneliness, tried unconsciously to prevent its recurrence by pushing herself, as it were, into a pseudo-manic state of talkativeness, which was colored by all signs of anxiety.

Another drastic defensive maneuver which should be mentioned is compulsive eating. As Hilde Bruch's research on obesity has shown, the attempt to counteract loneliness by overeating serves at the same time as a means of getting even with the significant people in the environment, whom the threatened person holds responsible for his loneliness.[21] The patient I have just mentioned, who resorted to pseudo-manic talkativeness as a defense against loneliness, told me that her happiest childhood memory was of sitting in the darkened living room of her home, secretly eating stolen sweets. In her first therapeutic interview, she said to me, "You will take away my gut pains [from overeating], my trance states [her delusional states of retreat], and my food; and where will I be then?" That is, if she gave up her defenses against her loneliness, where would she be then?

Sullivan, it should be added, thought that loneliness—beyond his description of it in terms of the driving force to satisfy the universal human need for intimacy—is such an intense and incommunicable experience that psychiatrists must resign themselves to describing it in terms of people's defenses against it. Freud's thinking about it

---

[20]Sullivan, *op. cit.*, p. 262.
[21]Hilde Bruch, *The Importance of Overweight;* New York, Norton, 1957; "Developmental Obesity and Schizophrenia," *Psychiatry* (1958) 21:65–70.

seems to point in the same direction, in his references to loneliness and defenses against it in *Civilization and its Discontents.*[22]

PATIENT'S DESCRIPTION OF LONELINESS

One of our patients at Chestnut Lodge, as she emerged from a severe state of schizophrenic depression, asked to see me because she wished to tell me about the deep state of hopeless loneliness and subjective isolation which she had undergone during her psychotic episodes. But even though she was now in fine command of the language, and even though she came with the intention of talking, she was just as little able to tell me about her loneliness in so many words as are most people who are engulfed in or have gone through a period of real psychotic loneliness. After several futile attempts, she finally burst out, "I don't know why people think of hell as a place where there is heat and where fires are burning. That is not hell. Hell is if you are frozen in isolation into a block of ice. That is where I have been."

I don't know whether this patient was familiar with Dante's description of the ninth and last, or frozen circle of the Inferno. It is in essence quite similar to the patient's conception of hell—the "lowest part of the Universe, and farthest remote from the Source of all light and heat," reserved for the gravest sinners, namely those "who have done violence to their own kindred (like Cain who slew Abel), and those who committed treachery against their native land." Among others, Dante met there "two sinners that are frozen close together in the same hole."[23]

Despite the difficulty of communicating about loneliness, every now and then a creative patient succeeds in conveying his experience of essential loneliness artistically after having emerged from it. Mary Jane Ward succeeded in doing so in her novel, *The Snake Pit.*[24]

The most impressive poetic document of loneliness from a mental patient of which I know has been written by Eithne Tabor, a schizophrenic patient at St. Elizabeths Hospital:

Panic

And is there anyone at all?
And is
There anyone at all?
I am knocking at the oaken door . . .

---

[22]Freud, *op. cit.*

[23]*The Divine Comedy of Dante Alighieri: The Caryle Wiksteed Translation;* New York, Modern Library, 1932; p. 169.

[24]Mary Jane Ward, *The Snake Pit;* New York, Random House, 1946.

And will it open
Never now no more?
I am calling, calling to you—
Don't you hear?
And is there anyone
Near?
And does this empty silence have to be?
And is there no-one there at all
To answer me?

I do not know the road—
I fear to fall.
And is there anyone
At all?[25]

Another patient, after her recovery, wrote the following poem, "The Disenchanted," which she dedicated to me:

The demented hold love
In the palm of the hand,
And let it fall
And grind it in the sand.
They return by darkest night
To bury it again,
And hide it forever
From the sight of men.[26]

In another poem, "Empty Lot," also written after her recovery, she depicted symbolically what loneliness feels like:

No one comes near here
Morning or night.
The desolate grasses
Grow out of sight.
Only a wild hare
Strays, then is gone.
The landlord is silence.
The tenant is dawn.[27]

All these poems have—only seemingly coincidentally—a common feature: They are not entitled "Loneliness," but "Panic," "The Disenchanted," and "Empty Lot." Is this because of the general inclination of the word-conscious and word-suspicious schizophrenic to replace direct communications and definitions by allusions, symbols, circumlocutions, and so on? Or is it an unconscious expression of the fear of loneliness—a fear so great that even naming it is frightening? If one remembers that fear of loneliness is the common fate of the

[25]Eithne Tabor, *The Cliff's Edge: Songs of a Psychotic;* New York, Sheed and Ward, 1950; p. 36, Reprinted by permission of the author.
[26]*Ibid.*
[27]*Ibid.*

people of this Western culture, be they mentally healthy or disturbed, it seems that the choice of the titles of these poems is determined by this fear.

ENFORCED AND EXPERIMENTAL ISOLATION

There are two sources of verification for the assumption that severe loneliness cannot ordinarily be endured more than temporarily without leading to psychotic developments—if it does not, in fact, occur as an inherent part of mental illness. One source of verification is found in the psychoses which develop in people undergoing an experience of enforced isolation, the other in the psychosis-like states ensuing from experimentally induced states of loneliness.

Three types of nonexperimental isolation may be differentiated. The first is the voluntary isolation which comes about in the course of polar expeditions, or in the lives of rangers at solitary outposts. Such isolation may be tolerated without serious emotional disturbances. Courtauld's "Living Alone Under Polar Conditions" may be mentioned as representative to some degree.[28] Courtauld, who was isolated on the Greenland icecap in a weather station, writes that there is no objection, in his judgment, to a solitary voluntary mission if one is certain of adequate measures for one's safety and of ultimate relief. He recommends, however, that only persons with active, imaginative minds, who do not suffer from a nervous disposition and are not given to brooding, and who can occupy themselves by such means as reading, should go on polar expeditions.

The second type of isolation is represented by solitary seafarers, who seem to be in a considerably more complex situation than the polar isolates or solitary rangers. Most of the solitary sailors seem to suffer from symptoms of mental illness. Slocum, for instance, developed hallucinations of a savior who appeared in times of particular stress—a reflection, probably, of his inner conviction that he would survive.[29]

The third group consists of those who are subjected to solitary confinement in prisons and concentration camps. They are, of course, seriously threatened by psychotic developments, and they do frequently become victims of mental illness.

Christopher Burney has written a report about his survival, with-

---

[28]A. Courtauld, "Living Alone Under Polar Conditions," *The Polar Record*, No. 4, July, 1932; Cambridge, The University Press.
[29]Joshua Slocum, *Sailing Alone Around the World:* London, Rupert-Hart-Davis, 1948.

out mental illness, of eighteen months of solitary confinement by the Germans during World War II.[30] His isolation was made worse by cold, physical and emotional humiliation, and a near-starvation diet. On the few occasions when he had an opportunity for communication, ". . . I found that the muscles of my mouth had become stiff and unwilling and that the thoughts and questions I had wanted to express became ridiculous when I turned them into words."[31] "Solitude," he says, "had so far weaned me from the habit of intercourse, even the thin intercourse of speculation, that I could no longer see any relationship with another person unless it were introduced gradually by a long overture of common trivialities."[32]

Burney describes the systematic devices he developed to counteract the danger of becoming mad; he forced himself to divide his lonely days into fixed periods, with a daily routine made up of such items as manicuring his fingernails with a splinter of wood he had managed to peel from his stool, doing physical exercises, pacing up and down his cell, counting the rounds he made, and whistling a musical program made up of every tune he could remember. He forced himself to divide the eating of his one meager meal per day between noon and evening, despite the craving of his hungry stomach. On one of the rare occasions when he was allowed to go outside for exercise, he brought back with him to his cell a snail; "It was company of a sort, and as it were an emissary from the world of real life. . . ."[33] He disciplined his mind to work on intellectual and spiritual problems, whose starting point had frequently to come from the torn and ancient sheets of newspaper, or sometimes pages of books, given him for toilet paper.

Secretly routinizing his life proved to be an important safeguard for his mental equilibrium. The importance of this device can be measured by the degree to which Burney felt threatened by even small changes, such as a change in the sequence of receiving first soup and then bread, to receiving first bread and then soup. He also felt being moved from one cell to another as a threat to his equilibrium, even though the new cell, as such, was obviously preferable to the old one.

While Burney survived his ordeal without mental illness, he was aware, toward the end of the eighteen months of solitary confine-

---

[30]Christopher Burney, *Solitary Confinements* New York, Clerke and Cockeran, 1952.
[31]*Ibid.*, p. 86.
[32]*Ibid.*, p. 105.
[33]*Ibid.*, p. 109.

ment, that isolation was threatening his mental health. "As long as my brain worked," he says, "solitude served a purpose, but I could see that it was slowly exhausting the fuel with which it had started, and if it stopped from inanition I would have nothing left but cold and hunger, which would make short work of me. Metaphysics were not enough: they are an exercise, weakening rather than nourishing; and the brain requires food of real substance."[34] The intensity of the effort it had taken to stay adjusted to his solitary life may be measured by the fact that, at the first opportunity to communicate, he did not dare to talk, "because I thought it quite probable that if I opened my mouth I should show myself to be mad."[35] "I tried to talk . . . and succeeded a little, but constantly had to check my tongue for fear of uttering some impossibility."[36]

The reports of Ellam and Mudie, and Bernicot include statements similar to these last remarks of Burney's.[37] As Lilly says, in discussing these accounts, "The inner life becomes so vivid and intense that it takes time to readjust to the life among other persons and to re-establish one's inner criteria of sanity."[38]

One more remark about Burney's experience: I believe that his unquestioning, matter-of-fact belief in the spiritual validity of the political convictions which were the cause of his imprisonment may have been an additional factor which helped him to survive his ordeal without becoming mentally ill. In this sense, his confinement was more of a piece with the voluntary isolation of the polar explorers than, for example, with the imprisonment of a delinquent. The delinquent prisoner is not likely to have the determination and devotion to a cause which helped Burney to stay mentally sound, even though he was deprived of the opportunity to work or to receive stimulation through reading—which for many others seem to have been the two most effective antidotes or remedies for the humiliation of confinement and the rise of disintegrating loneliness.

My suggestion that Burney's conviction and determination were factors in his remaining mentally healthy raises a question about the inner emotional factors which determine whether a person can tolerate isolation or will be particularly vulnerable to its dangers. So far, I have not succeeded in finding specific psychodynamic or de-

---

[34]*Ibid.*, p. 150.
[35]*Ibid.*, p. 151.
[36]*Ibid.*, p. 152.
[37]Patrick Ellam and Colin Mudie, *Sopranino;* New York, Norton, 1953. Louis Bernicot, *The Voyage of the Anahita;* London, Rupert-Hart-Davis, 1953.
[38]Lilly, *op. cit.,* p. 4.

scriptive data which could be helpful in differentiating between people who react to solitude with or without succumbing to psychotic loneliness. However, it should be possible to learn more by interrogating persons who have exposed themselves voluntarily to a life of solitude and isolation.

The last important source of insight into the psychodynamics of loneliness is the significant experimental work of Donald Hebb and his group at McGill University[39] and of John C. Lilly at the National Institute of Mental Health,[40] who have exposed their subjects to experimentally created states of physical and emotional isolation. Both investigators have brought about marked temporary impairments of people's emotional reactions, mental activities, and mental health by cutting down the scope of their physical contact with the outside world through experimental limitations of their sensory perception and decreased variation in their sensory environment. In the Canadian experiments the aim has been to reduce the *patterning* of stimuli to the lowest level; while the National Institute of Mental Health experiments have endeavored to reduce the *absolute intensity* of all physical stimuli to the lowest possible level.

The subjects of the McGill experiments spent twenty-four hours a day, with time out for eating and elimination, on a comfortable bed with a foam rubber pillow. Although communication was kept to a minimum, an amplifier connected with earphones was provided, through which an observer could test the subject verbally. Other noises were masked by fans and the humming of air-conditioners. The subjects wore translucent goggles which transmitted diffused light but prevented patterned vision, and gloves and cardboard cuffs reaching from below the elbow to beyond the fingertips. The most striking result of these experiments was the occurrence of primarily visual, but also auditory, kinesthetic, and somesthetic hallucinatory experiences. The subjects, even though they had insight into the objective unreality of these experiences, found them extremely vivid.

In Lilly's experiments at the National Institute of Mental Health, the subject was immersed, except for his head, in a tank of water as such temperature that he felt neither hot nor cold. In fact, he

---

[39]W. H. Bexton, Woodburn Heron, and T. H. Scott, "Effects of Decreased Variation in the Sensory Environment," *Canadian J. Psychol.* (1954) 8:70–76; Woodburn Heron, "The Pathology of Boredom," *Scientific American* (1957) 196:52-56. Woodburn Heron, W. H. Bexton, and Donald O. Hebb, "Cognitive Effects of a Decreased Variation in the Sensory Environment," *Amer. Psychologist* (1953) 8:366 (abstract).
[40]Lilly, *op. cit.*

tactually could feel the supports which held him, and a blacked-out mask over his whole head, but not much else. The sound level was also low, and the total environment was an even and monotonous one. Lilly has reported the various stages of experience through which subjects go, with, eventually, the projection of visual imagery.

LONELINESS AND ANXIETY

My impression is that loneliness and the fear of loneliness, on the one hand, and anxiety, on the other, are sometimes used interchangeably in our psychiatric thinking and in our clinical terminology; for instance, it is probably true that what psychiatrists describe as separation-anxiety can also be described as fear of loneliness. Furthermore, most authors agree, explicity or implicity, with the definition of anxiety as a response to the anticipated loss of love and approval by significant people in one's environment. Tillich expresses a similar idea when he postulates the ability to accept acceptance in spite of the anxiety of guilt as the basis for the courage of confidence.[41] Does that not imply that man with his imperfections is threatened by loneliness if his anxiety prevents him from accepting acceptance? And does this in turn not mean that anxiety is closely related to the fear of isolation or loneliness? Or, when Tillich says that "the anxiety of meaninglessness is anxiety about the loss of an ultimate concern," is that not synonymous with Binswanger's depiction of loneliness as a state of need in which people are bare of any interest in any goal?[42]

Yet I suspect that if we psychiatrists can learn to separate the two dynamisms more sharply from one another, we will come to see that loneliness in its own right plays a much more significant role in the dynamics of mental disturbance than we have so far been ready to acknowledge. I find good reason for this hypothesis in my own experience with my patients and on the basis of the many reports about other patients which I have heard from my colleagues.

This, in turn, makes me wonder about the origin of this conceptual merger between anxiety and loneliness. I have already suggested that this may have been brought about originally by the fear of loneliness, which the psychiatrist, of course, shares with his nonprofessional fellowmen. But perhaps this is an oversimplification. Perhaps a contributing factor is the ever-increasing insight of psychiatrists into the enormous psychodynamic significance of anxiety

[41]Tillich, *op. cit.*, p. 164.
[42]*Ibid.*, p. 47.

for the understanding of human psychology and psychopathology, which has brought about such a degree of preoccupation with this universal emotional experience that it has limited our ability to study other ubiquitous emotional experiences adequately. For instance, the neglect accorded loneliness has also existed, to a lesser degree, for grief, which has, by and large, been mentioned only as a part of mourning, depression, and melancholia; as far as I know, nowhere, except in Sullivan's writings, has its significance as an independent emotional experience in its own right been recognized.[43] Hope, as an outcome of memories of previous satisfaction, as a stimulus for efforts focused upon positive goals, and as a means of relieving tension, has only recently been introduced as an important concept by Thomas French.[44] The psychodynamics of realistic worry in its own right have been recently investigated for the first time by Judd Marmor.[45] Very little is known about the psychodynamics of pain. Envy is a universal human experience whose significance as an independent emotional experience has again been noted only by Sullivan, as far as I know.[46] And above all, real loneliness has only quite rarely been mentioned, in so many words, in the psychiatric literature. Thus I believe that the suggestion is justified that the interrelation of loneliness and anxiety be thoroughly scrutinized, with the goal of accomplishing a new and more precise differentiation between the two dynamisms.

PHYSICAL LONELINESS

I would like to add to this discussion of emotional loneliness a word about physical loneliness. The need or at least the wish, to have, at times, physical contact with another is a universal human phenomenon, innate and constant, from the time when the human infant leaves the womb and is physically separated from his mother. Physical and emotional disturbances in infants due to consistent lack of physical contact have been repeatedly described, and such a wise and experienced psychotherapist as Georg Groddeck has repeatedly elaborated on the topic of loneliness for nonsexual physical contact in adults.

---

[43]Harry Stack Sullivan, *Clinical Studies in Psychiatry;* New York, Norton, 1956; pp. 105–12.

[44]Thomas French, *The Integration of Behavior, Vol. I: Basic Postulates;* Chicago, Univ. of Chicago Press, 1952.

[45]Judd Marmor, "The Psychodynamics of Realistic Worry," pp. 155–263; in *Psychoanalysis and the Social Sciences,* Vol. 5; New York, International Univ. Press, 1958.

[46]Sullivan, *Clinical Studies in Psychiatry, op. cit.,* p. 128–38.

In the middle and upper social strata of Western culture, physical loneliness has become a specific problem, since this culture is characterized by so many obsessional taboos with regard to people's touching each other, or having their physical privacy threatened in other ways. I agree with Gorer's suggestion that American drinking habits can be understood as a means of counteracting the threats of physical loneliness.[47]

People who give massages or osteopathic treatment are quite aware of the fact that their treatment, irrespective of the specific physical ailment for which it is primarily applied, often helps their patients emotionally by relieving their physical loneliness. Pointing in the same direction is the pacifying influence which an alcohol back rub often has on mental patients, and the eagerness with which many of them ask for it.

SOME SOCIAL CONSEQUENCES OF TEMPORARY SYSTEMS*

Philip E. Slater

Social change brings pain and costs as well as relief and benefits. What will life be like in a society based on temporary systems? How will people relate to one another? To what extent will such an organizational pattern simply accentuate conditions already present in our society?

One obvious effect of the widespread extension of temporary systems would be a sharp increase in geographic mobility. If task forces are to be organized on a temporary basis around specific problems there is no particular reason why their formation should be locally restricted. Individuals will be brought together on the basis of talent and availability, and geographic location will be less important as an impediment than prior commitments. We will then become a nation of itinerants, moving continually on an irregular and perhaps even nonrecurrent circuit of jobs. What is mildly characteristic of the academic world today will become accelerated

---

[47]Geoffrey Gorer, *The American People;* New York, Norton, 1948; p. 130.
*"Some Social Consequences of Temporary Systems" by Philip E. Slater from *The Temporary Society* by W. G. Bennis and P. E. Slater. Copyright © 1968 by Warren G. Bennis and Philip E. Slater. Reprinted by permission of Harper & Row, Publishers.

and general throughout the economy. While work may become more meaningful, will not the reverse be true of "private life"?

We know something about the effects of mobility, for we live in what is undoubtedly the most mobile society that has ever existed anywhere in the world. It is true that there have been many societies that continually moved from place to place. But these nomadic tribes moved as a group, and usually over a fixed route. They carried their possessions, their relationships, their entire way of life along with them, unchanged. In most cases, even the land did not really change since every part of the route was reencountered at predictable intervals, save in times of climatic or military cataclysm (which although they make history, are grossly unrepresentative). They were just as rooted to the land as a peasant farmer, but to a corridor instead of a region.

Mobility in modern society is quite another matter. Here individuals or family units are plucked out of their social context and transplanted. They may never live in the same place twice. While they may stay within the same society (although these boundaries may also weaken in the future), they must form new relationships, adapt to a new physical environment, new norms, and so on. Those who remain behind must repair the social fissure that the transients have created.

The consequences of mobility for our culture are profound. George Pierson has argued with great force that most of what is distinctively American can be traced to it (1964, pp. 119 ff.). Optimism, conservatism, other-directedness, individualism, equalitarianism, superficiality, identity-diffusion, gregariousness, alienation, homogeneity, money-mindedness, loneliness, nostalgia, anxiety, conformity, activity, achievement-orientation, pragmatism, love of novelty, materialism, youth worship—all of these real or imagined qualities bear some relationship to this tendency of modern Americans to uproot themselves at relatively frequent intervals.

But we must distinguish between those characteristics which spring directly from the effects of mobility itself, and those which derive from mechanisms designed to soften these effects. Thus moving about frequently tends to detach the individual from enduring and significant relationships—this is a primary effect. But the difficulty of continually forming new bonds and breaking old ones might be mitigated by developing ways of accelerating the process of acquaintance: an informality, and easy friendliness, a capacity for ready, if superficial, relationship. This would be a secondary effect—one which need not automatically occur, but which might evolve as a compensatory mechanism.

PRIMARY CONSEQUENCES OF TEMPORARY SYSTEMS

We can hypothesize two primary and three secondary consequences of increased mobility and temporary systems, all of them little more than extrapolation from existing conditions. First, the process of individuation, of the separation of the individual from those permanent groups which provide him with ready-made values and traits, and from which he derives his identity, will accelerate. His ability to say "I am a ——" prior to the completion of his education or training will disappear utterly. His experience will become more unique, his knowledge and work more narrowly specialized, his social existence more atomized.

The second effect will be a concomitant feeling—acute and pervasive—of alienation, of anomie, of meaninglessness. These feelings will, as usual, be misconstrued as a function of everyone having become alike, although the striving toward uniformity is actually a secondary phenomenon, an attempt to *counteract* the feelings of alienation and anomie. On the contrary, these feelings arise when the individual is deprived of a permanent, contextual group toward whom he feels a bond of likeness, heightened by one or two points of specialization which define his role in that group.

Human beings are all equipped with the same emotional repertoire, the same basic needs, the same basic defenses. Out of those they evolve more idiosyncratic structures which we call personality or, when they are based on shared definitions of meaning, culture. These differences help maintain boundaries between individuals and between groups but at the cost of some violence to the emotional life of the individual. His body may tell him, as a human being, to respond in a given way to a punch in the nose, or a sexual stimulus, or a loss, or a rejection, but he may have learned, as a member of a specific culture, or as one playing a special role within that culture, not to react in this human way, but rather in some way which defines him more uniquely.

To be more unique, in other words, is to be less human, more of a social artifact. One man learns to lose the capacity to respond to a given situation with love, another with anger, another with jealousy, another with tears, and so on. This process of emotional crippling we call personality development. Its positive side is a hypertrophy of other responses which permit a kind of emotional specialization within the group. In a permanent group the individual can sense his likeness with others, while the self-alienation that arises from his specialized response system is mitigated by his close and constant contact with other specialists, who express his needs and feelings for him as he does for them. In a culture in which a man cannot weep, his women may weep for him. If he is a group jester and not supposed to feel gloomy, there will be some dour compatriot to do this for him, and so on. And where the group as a whole warps human feeling in a given direction, defining its differentness from other groups, his similarity with those around him palliates his sense of alienation from his feelings.

When an individual loses a more or less permanent role in a permanent group, his specialization becomes pointless and somewhat burdensome. He becomes a part in search of a whole, feeling neither enough like others to avoid a sense of being alone and lost, nor sufficiently included in a stable pattern of differentiation to have a sense of himself as a distinguishable entity embedded in a pattern of other such entities. In a society which places a value on individualism this inability to experience oneself leads paradoxically to a cry for *more* uniqueness, more eccentricity, more individuation, thus exacerbating the system.

The only conceivable solution to this problem is, to put it bluntly, the obliteration of differences: the maximization of uniformity, of homogeneity, of sameness among people. This is based, however, on two assumptions. The first assumption is that we accept mobility as a given. It might be felt that the price paid for mobility, for flexibility, for democracy in fact, is too high—that we should try and find ways to bring the entire movement of our time to a sudden and grinding halt before everything of value in human life is lost. I do not regard this as possible, nor am I certain it is desirable. Before settling for the manifold ills that mankind has borne throughout history we owe ourselves the resolution at least to peer into the unknown and imagine what it might hold, and what might be made of it.

The second assumption is the more crucial, since if it does not obtain, few people would wish to accept the first. Homogenization could only be tolerated if people are uniformly transformed into full human beings, rather than remaining specialized semi-persons as we are now constituted. Fantasies of uniformity have always made the negative assumption that such uniformity would be a similarity of limitedness—that all humans will become robots, or assume the specialized posture of a gregarious suburbanite, or that of a submissive peasant, or whatever. In other words, we imagine with horror that all humans will be forced to accept some specialized stance now voluntarily adopted by a few. But such a homogenization would not be viable, since (a) it would retain the same constraints under which we now suffer without providing the compensatory mechanisms of vicarious expression, the sense of separate-although-embedded identity, (b) the advantages of a social division of labor would be lost, and the society as a whole would suffer from the loss of variety, the lack of human resources. This does not mean that such a system cannot be essayed—we can see attempts to evolve this kind of uniformity in segments of our own society— it only means that a society so structured will fail. A viable society must somehow avail itself of a great variety of contradictory human responses. If members of that society are to be limited in the ways they can respond, then it is necessary that they be limited in different ways—otherwise generalized shortages will (and do) arise. Conversely, if a society is to function with similar participants, each one must be complex and unrestricted in available response patterns. They must have the capacity to be introverted *and* extroverted, controlled *and* spontaneous, independent *and* dependent, gregarious *and* seclusive, loving *and* hostile, strong *and* weak, and so on.

This is, of course, utopian. Human beings will never achieve this degree of humanness; nor will complete uniformity ever be achieved, happily. We are merely saying that insofar as uniformity is sought, incompleteness must be eschewed. Less variety from person to person requires more variety within each person. The individual will be more changeable, less predictable from moment to moment, from situation to situation, less able to play the same tune all his life long. Wardrobes may, taken as a whole, be more similar, but each one far more varied, and the variety of dress in any given social situation much greater than today.

SECONDARY CONSEQUENCES OF TEMPORARY SYSTEMS

I. Interchangeability

The first secondary consequence has already been dealt with indirectly. If one must make and break relationships rapidly then it becomes increasingly important that people be as interchangeable as possible, and this is most simply achieved through uniformity. It is, of course, a basic principle of mass production and has extended itself in a variety of ways throughout our culture, leading to complaints of dullness and monotony. One revealing expression of the principle is the motel. An American today can travel almost anywhere in the country and stop at a motel to find himself in an entirely familiar environment. He would indeed be hard put to distinguish one from another. As relationships become increasingly temporary the need to establish such instant familiarity will correspondingly increase.

But people are not motels, for the most part, and we have already pointed out the necessity for an enrichment of the individual before interchangeability will be viable. No such problem exists for the motel: the human need for variety in physical surroundings is extremely limited, even trivial, and we may expect the monotony of our physical environment to maintain its accelerative rate of growth, only slightly damped by self-conscious remedial measures.

Interchangeability is a threatening concept. It violates every principle of association known to man and conjures up an image of social chaos. Yet it is only a logical extension of the evolution of associational principles up to this moment.

The most primitive and elemental principle of association is territoriality, which simply states that the greater the physical distance between A and B, the less important they are to each other. It exists in pure form almost nowhere at the human level, and almost everywhere at the animal level (cf. Hall, 1966, pp. 7–37; Lorenz, 1966; Scott, 1958 pp. 206 ff.). Although alloyed with other principles it is still of vital importance in human society today. If we make the necessary modification, for moving units, of substituting propinquity of *pathways* for static propinquity, it is still the most powerful single factor in human relationships, from marital choice (Koller, 1962) to interfamilial relationships (Festinger *et al.*, 1950; Whyte, 1956, pp. 365–86). It lingers as an important bond even when the propinquity is made artificial by temporal separation (Mead, 1964, pp. 131–41).

The limitations of territoriality are obvious: it is impossible to construct any large-scale organization on this principle alone since there is no way to achieve centralization. Village A can relate to village C only through intermediate village B, and if A and C are equidistant from B, there is no basis for assigning greater weight to one or the other.

But all existing human societies, however primitive, share at least one other associational principle which redresses this deficiency.

This principle is kinship, which states that the greater consanguineal distance (always to some extent arbitrarily defined by the culture) between A and B, the less important they are to each other. This principle is modeled after the territorial one but is liberated from dependence upon the physical environment. When it is combined with exogamous marriage rules it cuts across the territorial principle, permitting multiple loyalties and the coalescence of larger social units.

Both of these principles are universal today, but in modern urban societies they have been severely intruded upon by a third, as Simmel observed some time ago in his analysis of "social circles" (Simmel, 1964, pp. 127 ff.). This principle, which is capable of infinite subdivision, but which we might crudely label the principle of common interest, states that the fewer the interests shared by A and B the less important they are to each other. (The interests may, but need not, be utilitarian.) This principle goes further than kinship in detaching association from fixed external conditions. While the kinship principle is based in part on cultural definitions, the common interest principle is entirely so based, and hence is totally manipulable in cultural terms. It not only permits still larger and more complex social systems, but also adds an element of flexibility; territories and kin relationships cannot change, but interests can and do.

The growth of temporary systems will tend further to limit the spheres of territoriality and kinship. But it also challenges the common interest principle in its traditional form. The concept of interchangeability inaugurates a fourth principle, which we might call the principle of temporary relevance. It is not really new, but merely an extension of the common interest principle. It eliminates *any fixed basis* for human relationships, although the temporary bases derive from common interest. Thus any permanence in human association will depend upon the survival of the earlier principles.

Now it can be seen from this progression that each principle frees human relationships more and more from dependence upon external constraints, permitting more freedom of choice and a wider range of possible encounters. What is threatening about interchangeability is *(a)* the introduction of transitoriness as a necessary rather than accidental feature of social life, and *(b)* the apparent violation of our popular belief that people choose to relate to one another on the basis of the intrinsic qualities of the other person. The first threat is a real one which we will discuss later on in detail.

The second is in large part illusory, based on a sentimental misconception of social relationships.

Obviously the principles of territoriality and kinship ignore the intrinsic qualities of the individual altogether. This is expressed in a number of adages and homilies to the effect that one can choose one's friends but not one's relatives or neighbors (although the latter is only partially true today). Choice is thus offered as a sop to compensate for the loss of stability, security, and permanence. The choice is not really an individual one, however, and is in that sense an illusion. We are conditioned by our culture and by our early socialization experiences to make certain kinds of choices with fair predictability. Our interest patterns bring us into contact with similar individuals whom we then "choose." The principle of temporary relevance faces up to this reality with rather brutal honesty.

But it must be remembered that total interchangeability will never be achieved. If it could be, temporary systems would not be necessary, for they assume at least a technical specialization. But such temporary working groups will have little else reliably in common besides their task—again, by definition. They cannot serve as a social circle, nor will it be easy to enter and leave other circles on so rapid a basis, at least as they are now constituted. It will be increasingly necessary to take people as one finds them—to relate immediately, intensely, and without the basis of traditional social props, rituals, and distancing mechanisms. Distance will be provided by transience, and the old patterns of gamesmanship, of extended, gradual and incomplete unmasking will become appropriate. By the time the individual reaches his "here-is-the-real-me" flourish he will find himself alone again. It seems clear that one of the unintended functions of "sensitivity training" or "basic encounter" groups is an anticipatory socialization mechanism for a world of temporary systems, since they emphasize openness, "feedback," immediacy, communication at a "feeling" level, the "here-and-now," more awareness of and ability to express "deeper" feelings, and so on. Group members often express surprise and chagrin at their capacity to respond with warmth and intensity to individuals they would in other situations have regarded with indifference, fear, or contempt. After the initial shock has worn off the inevitability of preference hierarchies is rediscovered, but a sense of the degree to which opportunities for significant relationships are wasted by casual stereotyping is usually retained. Such an awareness would be a precondition of a society of temporary systems.

II. Other-Directedness

Another secondary consequence of temporary systems would be the development of more flexible normative mechanisms. This again represents the intensification of an existing trend rather than a new departure. Mobility and change rule out the efficacy of any permanent system of social control. *External controls* depend upon the permanent embeddedness of the individual in the same social unit—a condition which has largely vanished from the civilized world. *Internalized controls of a fixed kind* rapidly become irrelevant to a changing social environment. Our society has long required, and obtained, a system of internalized controls which incorporates moral relativism—what Riesman has called "other-direction." The individual must at one and the same time be capable of self-restraint while recognizing that groups vary in what they consider desirable and undesirable social behavior (Riesman *et al.*, 1955, pp. 37–38). He must be acutely sensitive and responsive to group norms while recognizing the essential arbitrariness, particularity, and limited relevance of all moral imperatives.

This idea is offensive to many and has generated a whole tradition of angry nostalgia among postwar critics of American society. Riesman himself, while not in the least responsible for the gross distortions of his basic argument, shares in this nostalgia to a certain degree. His use of the term "gyroscope" to describe the conformity mechanism of the inner-directed man (Riesman *et al.*, 1955, pp. 31 ff.) betrays this sentiment (A less flattering metaphor would be a wind-up toy.). For the inner-directed individual is programmed at birth to display a limited range of responses in all situations, regardless of environmental variation, and while this may well be considered heroic, it is, like all heroic manifestations, excessively simple-minded. Even computers have achieved a higher degree of sophistication.

A society organized around temporary systems promises even greater virtuosity in flexible self-controls and further reduction in the shrinking store of half-heartedly embraced moral absolutes. It is important to recognize, however, that we are not heralding the disappearance of the "superego" (or whatever one wishes to label human normative responses). Anyone who interprets contemporary trends in terms of a "loosening" of social restraints on impulse is reading the signals with one eye closed. The simple (and largely ineffectual) "no" of the Puritan divine made far fewer inroads on

instinctual expression and created for fewer moral dilemmas than
the "fun morality" Wolfenstein discusses (1963, pp. 168–75). More
play in work also means more work in play, until all acts become
both playful and instrumental, public and private, and no sphere
of human expression is altogether uncontaminated.

III. Intensification and Dedifferentiation of the Marital Relationship

One of the more tiresome cliches of family sociology is that the
modern family has somehow declined in significance, having been
stripped of so many of its earlier functions. To this calamity is then
attributed a host of social problems, notably divorce.

It is a mistake only a sociologist could make. For if we concentrate our attention on the marital bond it becomes immediately
apparent that the hazards to which it is currently subject flow from
a surfeit rather than a loss of functions. These functions, however,
are primarily emotional. Two married persons in a stable and permanent social context need seek little from each other. Psychological and interpersonal needs can be satisfied in a variety of other relationships—kin, neighborhood, friendship. In many societies and
subcultures deeply entrenched patterns of sex segregation make
intimate communication between the sexes difficult or impossible—
men and women literally live in different worlds. Wherever this
stability begins to break down, husband and wife tend to increase
their emotional demands upon each other. Elizabeth Bott was probably the first to point out this effect, observing that couples in "close-
knit" relational networks maintained a rigid division of labor, were
deeply involved in external bonds, and placed little emphasis on
shared interests, joint recreation, or a satisfying sexual relationship.
Couples in "loose-knit" networks, on the other hand, showed little
division of labor, emphasized marital "togetherness," and were
highly self-conscious about childrearing techniques (Bott, 1957, p.
198). The transition from working-class to middle-class status and
from "urban villager" to suburban environments tends to bring
about a loosening of relational networks and is therefore usually
associated with an increase in the intensity and intimacy of the marital bond, and a decrease in marital and parental role differentiation
(Komarovsky, 1964; Young and Willmott, 1964; Slater, 1961; Litwak,
1966, p. 14).

Although sociologists have generally argued, with good reason,
that higher income, education, and other attributes of middle-class
standing are stabilizing forces for marriage (but cf. Hillman, 1962),

one would anticipate that the greater burden placed on the marital bond by the reduction of alternative intimate and enduring relationships would augment the rate of marital dissolution. In a non-mobile society one expects of marriage only a degree of compatibility. Spouses are not asked to be lovers, friends, and mutual therapists. But it is increasingly true of our own society that the marital bond is the closest, deepest, most important, and putatively most enduring relationship of one's life. Paradoxically, therefore, it is increasingly likely to fall short of the demands placed upon it and be dissolved. As emotional alternatives are removed, its limitations become less and less tolerable. The social ties of modern Americans are becoming so ephemeral that a permanent point of reference seems essential, and this perhaps accounts for the heroic effort made in our society—through marriage manuals, counselors, psychotherapists, magazine articles, and so on—to find ways of enabling the marriage relationship to bear the enormous emotional burdens placed on it.

The future of marriage in a society of temporary systems remains ambiguous. There is no inherent reason why families could not remain permanent in such a society—moving as a unit when moves occur. Yet there are several strains which such family mobility creates, and which tend to pull it apart in the absence of compensatory mechanisms. The family as a whole cannot be as easily included in the temporary system framework as the single individual. Many large corporations with mobile executives have recognized this problem, but their attempts to remedy it have been rather ambivalent. By trying to include the wife and family in organization thinking they have acted alternately to stabilize and to rupture the marital bond: the former through including the family in corporation activities, providing therapeutic facilities, and so on; the latter by demanding that the husband's organizational commitment always come first, and by penalizing the husband for the wife's personality and behavior. As Whyte observes, in his discussion of these practices, "divorce rarely disqualifies a man," since the wife may have been "outgrown" by her rising executive husband (Whyte, 1962, pp. 118 ff.).

The most obvious strain in a society based on temporary systems would be produced by the wife having a career of her own. This would mean that at any moment competing job requirements or opportunities might threaten to separate them geographically. This is an increasing problem in the academic world, where more and more professional couples are appearing. Unless the wife is willing to assume a consistently ancillary status it is often difficult for the couple both to find desirable positions in the same community. It is perhaps for this reason that there has been a decrease in the entry of educated women into the profession. Yet the dedifferentiation of marital roles accompanying mobility constitutes a powerful force for feminine parity, and a mobile society must either accept the pull of competing careers or the push of feminine discontent. Our society has tended, with some ambivalence, toward the latter, and the result has been (in addition to much outcry, argument, and public discussion) an exaggerated investment of feminine achievement motivation into the childrearing process. While the social costs of either solution are high, it is difficult to envision a more serious risk than that which results from children having to validate their mothers' competence through their own successes, "creativity," and mental health.

Even if this problem could somehow be eliminated, pressures on the marital bond through time would remain. It is not merely a question of the executive "outgrowing" the wife. The male who participates intensively in a series of temporary systems would be changed by each, and each would make a different set of emotional demands upon him. Different aspects of his personal repertory would be exaggerated or muted in each new system, and his wife would somehow be forced to adapt to these in the context of maintaining the one stable and permanent adult relationship in both their lives.

As noted earlier, contemporary transformations in social relationships largely take the form of converting spatial effects into temporal ones. The idea of temporary systems itself assumes such a conversion, for as routine tasks become automated, those requiring human participation will increasingly relate to the boundaries of current experience—to invention, ambiguity, unusual synthesis, catastrophic changes, and so on. This means that the skills required will include larger quantities of creativity, imagination, social perception, and personal insight, and will hence draw upon all layers of the personality with maximum involvement and commitment. Such involvement will tend to drive other social affiliations out—temporary systems will inherently be what Coser calls "greedy organizations" (Coser, 1967). But only temporarily so, by definition. Instead of partial commitment to a relatively large number of groups over a relatively long period of time, we will see relatively total commitment to a single group over a short time period—the organizational equivalent of "serial monogamy" replacing a kind of permanent polygamy.

The metaphor reminds us that some sociologists have imagined the marital relationship to be undergoing a similar alteration—decreasing its temporal span as it increases its intensity. Time imposes a limit previously maintained by other important relationships (kin, neighborhood, friendship). Is this the pattern which will become characteristic of the future? Will the serial monogamy of adolescent "going steady" relationships become a model for the entire society? Will marriage itself become a temporary system, situationally specific, tied to a particular locality and task?

The principal barrier to this solution is the childrearing process. It is in fact difficult to imagine ways of integrating the raising of children with temporary systems. Not only the constant separations and changes of parents, but even the geographical moves themselves would have damaging consequences. For our society is one which depends upon the autonomy of the childhood peer-group as a way of "quarantining" cohorts. If this were not so, a child moving from place to place with his family would not suffer the social impairment that we know he does in the United States. Peer-group relations are simply too important, and the child who must continually make and break them is operating with an enormous handicap.

But this is assuming a transitional state in which some individuals are operating under the new system and some are not. What if *everyone* were geared to temporary systems and interchangeability? Then every boy in the neighborhood would be the "new boy," or would very recently have been, and every child would have rotating parents. Could children adjust to such a general state of affairs, or would it produce shallow, superficial, unreliable, "psychopathic" adults (cf. Slater, 1964, pp. 20 ff.)? Would the society then become transformed into something totally different? Would such individuals care about the kinds of issues we are concerned with here? Would it matter if they did not? We must be careful not to define as intrinsically pathogenic the conditions which generate deviant behavior in our own society—not to impose upon the limitless opportunities of the future those treasured axioms which are the product of the social pathology of our own era. Could a world of "superficial," fickle, unscrupulous, but nonaggressive individuals make the world any more dangerous than it is? Threaten the demise of culture any more? All we can say with any confidence about the assumptions under which we normally operate is that they have enabled us to manipulate the environment a good deal and to make the earth almost uninhabitable. An objective comparison between the joys and dangers of primitive as against civilized life invariably ends in a toss-up.

We can reasonably assume that: (1) the more the infant child is initially dependent upon a small number of nurturing agents the more disturbing will be their loss; (2) loss of the mother between six months and a year would probably interfere with the development of personality characteristics necessary for adequate functioning in a mobile society (Caplan, 1955, pp. 123–55); (3) any attempt to meet the problem of multiple parents (one assumes the child would normally remain with the mother) by de-emphasizing paternal participation in the socialization process would generate serious difficulties for male personality development (Burton and Whiting, 1961). If these difficulties can be met, the viability of a matching familial form of temporary system is simply an open question.

One must remember, however, that social mechanisms do not emerge full-blown, but arise out of other such mechanisms. One could object to any hypothetical social arrangement on the grounds that the transition to it would be intolerable, leading to attempts to thwart and counteract the direction of change. This seems highly likely in the case of the kinds of trends we have been discussing. It is hard to conceive of any mixture of the family structures juxtaposed here that would not be considerably more disturbing than a pure type of either. This will help to generate unusual modifications and syntheses that we can not possibly envision now.

We may also anticipate an increase in the opposition to those basic assumptions which precipitate technological change in our society. There will be more questioning of the utilitarian axioms of our lives as the traditional ideas of progress continue to tarnish, and as some underdeveloped countries, operating with different assumptions, leapfrog into a less cultured and more satisfying modernity. There will be even more emphasis on hedonistic, experience-oriented approaches to life, with or without drugs. There will be more nostalgia, more revivals, more clinging to real and imagined pasts. There will be more world-rejecting fantasies of static, loving, bucolic utopian communities, many of which will be carried into action.

We cannot begin to weight these factors properly and imagine into what combinations they will be molded. What I have tried to do in this chapter is to suggest some of the forces at work in generating change, some of the strains which they must inevitably create, and some hypothetical "solutions" to what are fundamentally insoluble dilemmas of social life.

REFERENCES

BOTT, ELIZABETH. *Family and Social Network*. London: Tavistock, 1957.

BURTON, R. V. AND WHITING, J. W. M. "The Absent Father and Cross-Sex Identity." *Merrill-Palmer Quarterly*, Vol. 7, 1961, pp. 85–95.

CAPLAN, G. *Mental Health Aspects of Social Work in Public Health*. Berkeley: University of California School of Social Welfare, 1955.

FESTINGER, L., SCHACTER, S. AND BACK, K. *Social Pressures in Informal Groups*. N.Y.: Harper, 1950.

HALL, E. T. *The Hidden Dimension*. Garden City, N.Y.: Doubleday, 1966.

HILLMAN, KAREN G. "Marital Instability and Its Relation to Education, Income, and Occupation: An Analysis Based on Census Data," in *Selected Studies in Marriage and the Family* (eds. R. F. WINCH, R. McGINNIS, AND H. R. BARSINGER), pp. 111–26. N. Y.: Holt, Rinehart & Winston, 1962.

KOLLER, M. R. "Residential and Occupational Propinquity," in *Selected Studies in Marriage and the Family* (eds. R. F. WINCH, R. McGINNIS, AND H. R. BARSINGER), pp. 472–77. N.Y.: Holt, Rinehart & Winston, 1962.

KOMAROVSKY, MIRRA. *Blue Collar Marriage*. N.Y.: Random House, 1964.

LITWAIS, E. "Technological Innovation and Ideal Forms of Family Structure in an Industrial Democratic Society." Unpublished manuscript, University of Michigan School of Social Work, Feb., 1966.

LORENZ, K. *On Aggression*. N.Y.: Harcourt, Brace, 1966.

MEAD, MARGARET. "We Are All Third Generation," in *The Character of Americans* (ed. M. McGIFFERT), pp. 131–41. Homewood, Ill.: Dorsey, 1964.

PIERSON, G. W. "The M-Factor in American History," in *The Character of Americans* (ed. M. McGIFFERT), pp. 118–30, Homewood, Ill.: Dorsey, 1964.

RIESMAN, D., GLAZER, N., AND DENNY, R. *The Lonely Crowd*. Garden City, N.Y.: Doubleday, 1955.

SCOTT, J. P. *Animal Behavior*. Chicago: University of Chicago Press, 1958.

SIMMEL, G. *Conflict and the Web of Group-Affiliations*. N.Y.: The Free Press, 1964.

SLATER, P. E. "Prolegomena to a Psychoanalytic Study of Aging and Death," in *New Thoughts on Old Age* (Ed. R. KASTENBAUM), pp. 19–40. N.Y.: Springer, 1964.

SLATER, P. E. "Parental Role Differentiation." *American Journal of Sociology*, Vol. 67 (1961) pp. 296–308.

WHYTE, W. H., JR. *The Organization Man*, pp. 365–86. Garden City, N.Y.: Doubleday, 1956.

WHYTE, W. H., JR. "The Wife Problem," in *Selected Studies in Marriage and the Family* (eds. R. F. WINCH, R. McGINNIS, AND H. R. BARSINGER). N.Y.: Holt, Rinehart & Winston, 1962.

WOLFENSTEIN, MARTHA. "Fun morality: An Analysis of Recent American Child-Training Literature," in *Childhood in Contemporary Cultures* (eds. M. MEAD AND M. WOLFENSTEIN), pp. 168–78. Chicago: University of Chicago Press, 1963.

MATERIALS FOR A THEORY OF
SOCIAL RELATIONSHIPS[*]

Robert S. Weiss

A number of theories of the socioemotional functions of social ties are explicit, or seem implicit, in current work. The problem is, of course, central in study of human experience. It is that of what we gain through relationships. It may be of value to review two of the theories, since in combination they served as initial orientations for the work reported here.[1]

The first theory proposes that individuals possess a "fund of sociability," a readiness and need to interact with others, which may be distributed in various ways, but is in any event of constant amount.[2] In this view individuals might with equal satisfaction engage in a great deal of intense contact with a few others, or in a more limited amount of less intense contact with a great many others. Difficulty would be encountered only if the demands on the fund were too great or the opportunities for expenditure from the

[*]This paper is based on work on the functions of social ties supported by a grant from NIMH, number MH409214-02, and from the Social Security and Welfare Administration of the Department of Health, Education, and Welfare, Grant Number 294. The paper appeared as a section of "Social Relationships and the Aged Individual," *Daedalus*, (Winter 1967).
[1]Other approaches, distinct from those discussed here, include: Peter Blau's emphasis on the goal-directed nature of relationships, also a theme in the work of George Homans; instinct theories, which perhaps should not be included in a listing of current work; the division of relationships or components of relationships into those which are security seeking and those which are satisfaction seeking, which occurs in the work of both Karen Horney and Harry Stack Sullivan; a variety of sociologically functionalist views, new versions of which are constantly appearing; and the views of Freud, which seem to see behavior as an expression of biological energy which may be directed or diffused through a variety of devices.

[2]The fund-of-sociability idea has been put forward most recently by Joel I. Nelson in "Clique Contacts and Family Orientations," *American Sociological Review*, Vol. 31, No. 5 (October 1966), pp. 663–72. He points out that a similar statement is contained in the work of Elizabeth Bott, *Family and Social Network* (Tavistock, 1957). The theory was considered but rejected by Theodore Caplow and Robert Forman in their "Neighborhood Interaction in a Homogenous Community," *American Sociological Review*, Vol. 15, No. 2 (June 1950), pp. 357–66. A theory which, though not identical, resembles that of a fund-of-sociability is contained in Philip Slater's "On Social Regression," *American Sociological Review*, Vol. 28, No. 3 (June 1963), pp. 339–64. This paper discusses alternative deployments of what is assumed to be a constant amount of libidinal energy.

fund too limited or, possibly, if the channels available for expenditure were for some reason uncongenial.

The second theory might be characterized as the theory of the mediating primary group. This theory distinguishes between primary relationships, which are close, frequent, face-to-face, and accompanied by warmth and commitment, and secondary relationships, which are essentially instrumental. (Examples of the latter would include relationships required by work—with the exception of some relationships with colleagues of long standing; memberships in formal organizations; and emotionally unimportant relationships with acquaintances, individuals who provide services, and the like.) The theory proposes that our beliefs, attitudes, and understandings are formed in good part through interaction with other members of the primary groups to which we belong. It holds that without any primary group affiliations we would drift into a state of normlessness or anomie. Participation in other sectors of the society expresses the goals and values established in primary group interaction, but an individual might withdraw from secondary contacts and yet not find himself in difficulty so long as he continued to be an active participant in one or more primary groups.[3]

The first empirical materials I want to present come from a study of the Parents Without Partners organization.[4] This is a national association of fairly autonomous local chapters, each providing a variety of programs for parents who are for any reason alone. For about a year a colleague and I attended meetings of the Boston chapter, participated in programs, and interviewed current and former members. Two research questions concerned us: first, what loss had these individuals sustained with the dissolution of their marriage; and second, in what way did membership make up for the loss?

Our initial hypothesis, on beginning the study, was based on an

---

[3]The ideas referred to here have a long history in both German and American sociology. A valuable review is given by Edward Shils in "The Study of the Primary Group," Daniel Lerner and Harold Lasswell (eds.), *The Policy Sciences* (Stanford, Calif.: Stanford University Press, 1951), pp. 44–69. See also Elihu Katz and Paul Lazarsfeld, "The Rediscovery of the Primary Group; Case Histories of the Intervening Variable," *Personal Influence* (Free Press, 1955), pp. 34–42. A recent example of the tendency to see all close relationships as of a kind is Nicholas Babchunk and Alan P. Bates, "The Primary Relations of Middle-Class Couples; A study in Male Dominance," *American Sociological Review*, (June 1963), pp. 377–84.

[4]My associate in this work was Father Carroll Bourg, S.J., now at the Society for Christ in Baltimore, Maryland. We would like to acknowledge the help of Professor Donald Klein of the Institute for Applied Behavioral Sciences, National Training Laboratories, in Washington, D.C., and of the research committee of the Boston chapter of Parents Without Partners, Inc.

underlying view which combined elements of the two theories just described. We assumed that individuals require a certain amount of "primary" contact—which we interperted as contact in which emotions might be expressed—and this amount may be obtained either through a great deal of interaction within a single relationship or through less intense interaction within a number of relationships. We therefore anticipated that members of the organization would report that they had been lonely and restless after the dissolution of their marriage, but that the interchange with other members which accompanied immersion in organizational activity had made up some part of the loss.

We found that although Parents Without Partners offered single parents assistance with a host of difficulties they were likely to encounter in their social life and in their roles as parents, most members seemed to have joined simply because they were lonely. Loneliness seemed to have been experienced by the great majority of members who talked about the matter. In addition, it seemed clear that loneliness was a direct consequence of the loss of the marital relationship, rather than a secondary consequence of the change in social role or increase in financial strain which might have accompanied the dissolution of the marriage. A qualification of this assertion is that this seemed not to have been true, or to have been true to a lesser extent, when the marriage had not been the only source of emotional interchange in the individual's life; an example would be a woman who had been extremely close, before the dissolution of her marriage, to her sister, girl friend, or mother.[5]

Another problem which might be associated with the absence of a marital tie, in addition to loneliness, was a tendency to over-respond to a perceived setback or slight, sometimes with depression, sometimes with anger. Members of the organization often considered themselves and each other to be unusually touchy, and indeed we were on more than one occasion led to agree with them. We were led to speculate about the existence of a syndrome of emotional isolation, whose symptoms would include both loneliness and oversensitivity.

For some individuals, membership in PWP was of great help. For others it seemed to be of little value, or whatever value it had

----

[5]There are a number of descriptions in the literature of marriages in which both husband and wife maintain close relationships with same-sex peers or in which the wife remains close to her mother. See, for example, Mirra Komarovsky, *Blue-Collar Marriage* (New York: Random House, 1962).

was outweighed by dissatisfactions. Among those who were helped by the organization, many reported that the chief contribution of the organization to their well-being was that it provided a means for them to meet others in the same situation as themselves, with whom they could exchange experiences and, in some cases, become friends. Men and women differed a good deal here. Men were apt to put more stress on service to the organization or on dating and less emphasis on friendships. But if we consider only female members, then the sponsorship of friendships or friendship-like relationships might be seen as the chief contribution the organization made to their well-being.[6]

The interesting question was whether these friendships, or the combination of friendships and participation in organizational activities, would compensate for the absence of marriage, at least in relation to loneliness. On this point our findings were unequivocal: they did not. Members remained lonely; friends and activities, perhaps particularly discussion groups, helped in that they made the loneliness easier to manage, but they did not end it, nor even appreciably diminish it.[7] One woman described the uses and limitations of friendship in these words: "Sometimes I have the girls over, and we talk about how hard it is. Misery loves company, you know."

Our work to this point made it clear that friendships, however valuable they may be in other ways, do not supply the functions once supplied by marriage. Therefore, either the functions of friendship are qualitatively different from those of marriage, or if they are qualitatively the same, they are supplied in distinctly lesser quantity.

---

[6]The difference in friendship-like relationships formed by men and by women may perhaps be communicated by saying that where women developed commitments to each other, men developed commitments to the Parents Without Partners organization. Women would call each other frequently, sometimes daily, to chat, would exchange visits, and would spend evenings in a group, just because they liked being with each other. Men rarely called or visited each other except on organizational business, but organizational business could become extensive enough to cause a man to spend a good part of his evenings and weekends participating with other men and with the more active women in the management of the community. The amount of organizationally sponsored sociability engaged in by active men and by active women seemed to be about the same, but the definitions of the relationships they formed were somewhat different. In this connection it is significant that women outnumbered men among members by a ratio of about four to one.

[7]For both men and women loneliness could be allayed, though perhaps only temporarily, by dating. Our data here are not as dense as we would wish, but there is much evidence that dating did seem to be substitutive, for a time at least, for the particular function of the marital tie whose absence is signalled by loneliness. The remarkable capacity of a new dating relationship to combat loneliness, despite the apparent absence of a basis for effective emotional integration, may depend on the development of an illusion of sympathetic understanding, to which both participants contribute energetically, but which on continued acquaintance is dispelled.

To decide between these alternatives we required a situation where individuals maintained effective marriages but were without friends. Our expectation was that if marriage and friendship provide different functions, then we should find individuals whose lives lacked friendships to be experiencing distress, despite the existence of a marriage. If on the other hand marriage provided the same functions as friendship, but more intensely, we should find these individuals getting along almost as well as anyone else, with perhaps some marginal distress due to the absence of quantitatively less important friendships.

For the last two years we have been slowly gathering data about the experiences of newcomer couples, beginning with a pilot study of half a dozen couples who had moved to the Boston suburbs from at least two states away, and continuing with a more intensive study of two additional newcomer families.[8] These newcomers to the Boston area provided us with a group of individuals who were temporarily without friends.

We found in all but two of our newcomer couples that after a period of time without friends the wife experienced severe distress, while the primary difficulty for the working husband seemed to have been an inability to understand what was happening to his wife. The housebound wife's distress was different in quality, but comparable in intensity, to the distress reported as having followed the dissolution of a marriage. One way of describing the qualitative difference is that the dissolution of a marriage seems to result in a sense of emotional isolation, while the absence of friends, for the woman who stays at home, seems to result in a sense of social isolation. The absence of anyone who shares the woman's problems, interests, and concerns—who cares about the same things she cares about—seems to lead to a loss of engagement with the homemaking tasks which would otherwise be the focus of her energies. Despite the warmth which may exist in her marriage, she is likely to become painfully bored, as the subjective concomitant of a loss of investment in her activities. One newcomer wife who had in her former home been extremely active and had considered herself reasonably happy found herself drinking a great deal, possibly compulsively; another, even more at a loss, proposed that the family return to the area of her parents' home, whatever the damage this would do to her husband's career. The other newcomer wives who had similarly

------

[8]My associate in this work is Elizabeth Hartwell.

severe initial difficulties did manage to establish friendships after a time, and then the initial period seemed to them to have been simply an unhappy phase, about which they had perhaps made too much fuss.

The husbands escaped the newcomer blues because they found men at work with whom they could talk about the things that concerned them: the job, news events, sports, driving patterns and other customs of the new area, and so on. Their jobs prevented social isolation. Two of the men with whom we worked, an Army sergeant and a production supervisor, listed for us the people with whom they chatted during the day, and the number was impressive. Of the exceptional wives, one was married to a man who had moved his family into a neighborhood just being developed, where everyone was a newcomer, and it was easy for his wife to form friendships with other wives in exactly her situation. He did this because in a previous move he had bought a house in an old neighborhood, where friendship circles were already formed, and had found that his wife became so bored that she began a schedule of night school courses which forced him to stay home alone with the children much of the week. The other exceptional wife had no children and was therefore able to solve the problem of social isolation neatly by going to work.

Taking all our cases into account we may generalize that in the absence of social ties in which central life concerns are shared, individuals will experience a sense of social isolation. We may conclude that just as friends do not make up for a lost marriage, so marriage does not make up for lost friends.[9]

These findings are incompatible with the idea that relationships are relatively undifferentiated in function, since it is clear that friendship and marriage provide distinct functions. The findings also are not compatible with the idea that the essential distinction among relationships is between those which are primary and those which are secondary, since marriage and friendship seem each to fit in the primary category, and yet their functions are different. We are led to another theory of the nature of social ties which proposes that individuals require that a number of distinct functions be supplied

---

[9]In none of the couples we have thus far studied have we found that husbands and wives share enough so that the shop talk of the one matters greatly to the other. An exception to this generalization may be couples in which both husband and wife are trained in the same profession. A colleague's wife, herself a Ph.D., reports that although she and her husband have moved several times, she has never experienced "newcomer blues," since she is able to participate with her husband in his work.

by the relationships they integrate with others, and that failure in any regard will result in distress. It also seems the case that relationships tend to specialize in the function they fulfill, in the sense that emotional integration but not social integration is provided by marriage, while the converse is true for friendship. In addition, just as relationships specialize by function, so they seem to specialize in their assumptions; and, in fact, it may well be the specialization of assumptions which leads to specialization of function. In a relationship of multiple functions—an office romance would be an example of such a relationship—the participants relate to each other at different times in terms of different sets of assumptions. They ordinarily will choose assumptions appropriate to whatever setting they are in, but they also develop a signal system involving vocabulary, voice tone, and gesture, which, along with its other functions, communicates the set of assumptions operative at any given time. When we find such multi-function relationships, it may be analytically justifiable to speak of a plurality of relationships involving the same two individuals.

The specialization of relationships is probably always incomplete. Undoubtedly there is a certain level of emotional integration in every friendship, though ordinarily not a great deal. At times, however, either or both participants in a friendship may respond to a need for emotional exchange, and the friendship assumptions may be flooded out temporarily; one likely consequence of such sudden redefinition is apt to be uneasiness between the participants when they attempt to reinstate the former assumptions. In general, in our observation to date, marriage tends to provide more than one function, but few other relationships do to any great extent. In addition, the resistance to redefinition of relational assumptions are ordinarily strong enough that an individual can only temporarily redefine the assumptions of one or more of his remaining relationships to serve as replacements for a lost relationship.

To this point I have described just two forms of functional relationship. On the basis of our work with Parents Without Partners, we believe we can identify five interactional systems, all of which are necessary for individual well-being, and which differ in assumptions, content, and functions. We may find in time that this category system must be modified in some way, but so far it has seemed adequate. We have named the five types of social ties by what seems to be the function each provides the individual who maintains it: emotional integration, social integration, opportunity for nurturance, reassurance of worth, and provision of assistance.

1. *Emotional integration* is provided by relationships in which emotions are expressed and reacted to in a way which is stabilizing for the participants. Maintenance of such a relationship seems to require both frequency and regularity of interaction, as well as acceptance that emotional expression is appropriate to the relationship. This function is provided by marriage; by dating relationships at least for a time; among some women by relationships with a close friend, a sister, or mother; and among some men in certain situations between "buddies."[10]

2. *Social integration* is provided by relationships in which participants share concerns, because of similar situations or because they are striving for the achievement of similar objectives. Such relationships permit the development of a shared interpretation of experience, as well as the exchange of information and ideas. Within these relationships one finds companionship and an opportunity for an exchange of services, especially in the area of mutual interest. This function is provided both by friendships and by relationships among colleagues; among women, more frequently the first, while among men, more frequently the second.[11]

3. *Opportunity for nurturance* is provided by relationships in which the adult takes responsibility for the well-being of a child, and so can develop a sense of being needed. Responsibility for children seems to add to the value of the goals of a wide variety of activities in an individual's life.[12]

4. *Reassurance of worth* is provided by relationships which attest to an individual's competence in some role. Colleague relationships

---

[10]For a discussion of this function of marriage see Robert O. Blood, Jr. and Donald Wolfe, *Husbands and Wives* (Free Press, 1960), particularly their chapter 7, "Understanding and Emotional Well-Being." That it is not intrinsic to marriage is one conclusion of Mirra Komorovsky's *Blue-Collar Marriage, op. cit.* A different relationship which may provide the same function is described in "Buddy relations and combat performance," by Rodger Little, *The New Military*, edited by Morris Janowitz (Russell Sage, 1964.) Mr. Little writes, "A buddy had to 'understand' in a deeply personal sense. Buddies became therapists to one another. . . ."

[11]Studies of retired men suggest that they experience a boredom and restlessness very similar to the condition we have found among newcomer wives. See Eugene A. Friedmann and Robert J. Havighurst, *The Meaning of Work and Retirement* (Chicago, 1954.) Nicholas Babchuck and Alan Bates have some interesting comments on the content of friendships between middle-class couples, *op. cit.*

[12]In a somewhat cursory search of the sociological literature, I have found only a very few discussions of the motivations of parents in having children. One suggestion has been that children are a consumption item, like a second car or a swimming pool, which may represent one way of disposing of surplus funds. There seems very little recognition in the general literature, however, that having children may contribute to the well-being of the parents. The literature on adoption may be richer, but to this point I have not been able to find corroboration for the assessments made on the basis of our work with Parents Without Partners.

function in this way for some men, particularly men whose work is difficult or highly valued. Relationships within the family may function in this way for other men, for whom competence depends not on particular skills, but rather on the ability to support a family, and for whom respect depends on recognition of competence as a breadwinner. For women who work this function may be provided by relationships with colleagues; for women who stay home, relationships with husbands, children, and acquaintances who recognize their homemaking skill may provide this function.[13]

5. *Assistance* is provided by a wide variety of relationships when there is urgent need, but primarily by neighbors and by close kin other wise. Only within close kin ties, especially lineal ties, may one expect assistance which is not severely limited in time and extent.[14]

Although our on-going research has thus far produced only limited evidence which bears on this, it is our conjecture that the absence of any one of the functions necessary to well-being is signalled by a distinct form of distress, different in kind but not in degree, from the symptoms which accompany other deficits.

We conjecture that deficits and symptoms are associated in this way: the absence of emotional integration results in loneliness; of social integration in boredom; of opportunity for nurturance in a sense of emptiness or pointlessness; of reassurance of worth in a sense of worthlessness; and of assistance in a sense of vulnerability or of having been abandoned. This schedule of causes and conditions is an attempt to represent in a compact, if overly pat, way what seem to be differences in the quality of the distress reported as accompanying different deficits. It is difficult to say, at least at this point, that some deficits are more disorganizing than others; that absence of emotional integration, for example, is more disorganizing than absence of opportunity for nurturance. One can cite, in this connection, childless couples who were as downcast by difficulty in arranging for an adoption as any lonely person might be by

---

[13]In at least one discussion virtually all motivation for work is reduced to a need for "ego-recognition"; see Rensis Likert, *New Patterns of Management* (New York: McGraw-Hill, 1961.) See also, for data regarding the analogous valuings of housework, Robert S. Weiss and Nancy M. Samuelson, "Feelings of Worth among American Women," *Marriage and Family Living* (November, 1957).

[14]The importance of help in the relationships of parents and grown children is attested to by, among others, Marvin Sussman, "The Help Pattern in the Middle-Class Family," in Sussman (ed.), *Source Book in Marriage and the Family*, (New York: Houghton-Mifflin, 1962.) See also, for the subjective experience of being symbolically without kin, "Christmas in an Apartment Hotel," Mark Benney, Robert Weiss, Rolf Meyersohn, and David Riesman, *American Journal of Sociology*, (November 1959).

difficulty in finding love. Any deficit seems to create a condition of dissatisfaction marked by restlessness and occasional bouts of acute distress.

In continuing work we are attempting to give more substance to this discussion of the assumptions, content, and functions of relationships, and the deficits associated with their absence. We have already encountered as a complicating feature the coexistence of relationships which lead, for example, to pressure on marriages from commitments to kin. We assume that in still other ways we will find the framework sketched here to need elaboration.

THE ILLUSIONLESS MAN AND THE VISIONARY MAID*

Allen B. Wheelis

Once upon a time there was a man who had no illusions about anything. While still in the crib he had learned that his mother was not always kind; at two he had given up fairies; witches and hobgoblins disappeared from his world at three; at four he knew that rabbits at Easter lay no eggs; and at five on a cold night in December, with a bitter little smile, he said goodbye to Santa Claus. At six when he started school, illusions flew from his life like feathers in a windstorm: he discovered that his father was not always brave or even honest, that Presidents are little men, that the Queen of England goes to the bathroom like everybody else, and that his first grade teacher, a pretty round-faced young woman with dimples, did not know everything, as he had thought, but thought only of men and did not know much of anything. At eight he could read, and the printed word was a sorcerer at exorcising illusions—only he knew there were no sorcerers. The abyss of hell disappeared into the even larger abyss into which a clear vision was sweeping his beliefs. Happiness was of course a myth; love a fleeting attachment, a dream of enduring selflessness glued onto the instinct of a rabbit. At twelve he dispatched into the night sky his last unheard prayer. As a young man he realized that the most generous act is self-serving, the most disinterested inquiry serves interest; that lies are told by printed words, even by words carved in stone; that art begins with a small "a" like everything else, and that he could not escape the ruin of value by orchestrating a cry of despair into a song of lasting beauty; for beauty passes and deathless art is quite mortal. Of all those people who lose illusions he lost more than anyone else, taboo and prescription alike; and as everything became permitted nothing was left worthwhile.

He became a carpenter, but could see a house begin to decay in the course of building—perfect pyramid of white sand spreading out irretrievably in the grass, bricks chipping, doors sticking, the first tone of gray appearing on white lumber, the first film of rust on bright nails, the first leaf falling in the shining gutter. He became then a termite inspector, spent his days crawling in darkness under old houses, lived in a basement room and never raised the blinds, ate canned beans and frozen television dinners, let his hair grow and his beard. On Sundays he walked in the park, threw bread to the ducks—dry French bread, stone-hard, would stamp on it with his heel, gather up the pieces, and walk along the pond, throwing it out to the avid ducks paddling after him, thinking glumly that they would be just as hungry again tomorrow. His name was Henry.

One day in the park he met a girl who believed in everything. In the forest she still glimpsed fairies, heard them whisper; bunnies hopped for her at Easter, laid brilliant eggs; at Christmas hoofbeats shook the roof. She was disillusioned at times and would flounder, gasp desperately, like a fish in sand, but not for long; would quickly, sometimes instantly, find something new, and actually never gave up any illusion, but would lay it aside when necessary, forget it, and whenever it was needed, back it would come. Her name was Lorabelle, and when she saw a bearded young man in the park, alone among couples, stamping on the hard bread, tossing it irritably to the quacking ducks, she exploded into illusions about him like a Roman candle over a desert.

"You are a great and good man," she said.

"I'm petty and self-absorbed," he said.

"You're terribly unhappy."

"I'm morose . . . probably like it that way."

"You have suffered a great deal," she said. "I see it in your face."

"I've been diligent only in self-pity," he said, "have turned away from everything difficult, and what you see are the scars of old acne shining through my beard; I could never give up chocolate and nuts."

"You're very wise," she said.

"No, but intelligent."

They talked about love, beauty, feeling, value, life, work, death—and always she came back to love. They argued about everything, differed on everything, agreed on nothing, and so she fell in love with him. "This partakes of the infinite," she said.

But he, being an illusionless man, was only fond of her. "It partaketh mainly," he said, "of body chemistry," and passed his hand over her roundest curve.

"We have a unique affinity," she said. "You're the only man in the world for me." "We fit quite nicely," he said. "You are one of no more than five or six girls in the county for me." "It's a miracle we met," she said. "I just happened to be feeding the ducks." "No, not chance; I couldn't feel this way about anybody else."

"If you'd come down the other side of the hill," he said, "you'd be feeling this way right now about somebody else. And if I had fed squirrels instead of ducks I'd be playing with somebody else's curves."

"You're my dearest darling squirrel," she said, "and most of all you're my silly fuzzy duck, and I don't know why I bother to love you—why are you such a fool? Who dropped you on your head?—come to bed!" On such a note of logic, always, their arguments ended.

She wanted a wedding in church with a dress of white Alençon lace over cream satin, bridesmaids in pink, organ music, and lots of people to weep and be happy and throw rice. "You'll be so handsome in a morning coat," she said, brushing cobwebs off his shoulders, "oh and striped pants, too, and a gray silk cravat, and a white carnation. You'll be divine." "I'd look a proper fool," he said, "and I'm damned if I'll do it." "Oh please! It's only once." "Once a fool, voluntarily, is too often." "It's a sacrament." "It's a barbarism." "Symbols are important." "Then let's stand by the Washington Monument," he said, "and be honest about it."

"You make fun," she said, "but it's a holy ceremony, a solemn exchange of vows before man and God."

"God won't be there, honey; the women will be weeping for their own lost youth and innocence, the men wanting to have you in bed; and the priest standing slightly above us will be looking down your cleavage as his mouth goes dry; and the whole thing will be a primitive and preposterous attempt to invest copulation with dignity and permanence, to enforce responsibility for children by the authority of a myth no longer credible even to a child."

So . . . they were married in church: his hands were wet and his knees shook, he frowned and quaked; but looked divine, she said, in morning coat and striped pants; and she was serene and beautiful in Alençon lace; the organ pealed, weeping women watched with joy, vows were said, rice thrown, and then they were alone on the back seat of a taxi, her lips seeking his, murmuring, "I'm so happy, darling, so terribly happy. Now we'll be together always."

"In our community," he said, "and for our age and economic bracket, we have a 47.3 per cent chance of staying together for twenty years."

She found for them a white house on a hill in a field of red poppies and white daisies, with three tall maple trees. There they lived in sunlight and wind, and she began to fill their life with fragile feminine deceptions, worked tirelessly at them, and always there was something new. She concealed the monotony of eating by variety, never two meals the same, one morning French toast in the shape of their house, the next a boiled egg with smiling painted face and a tiny straw hat; cut flowers on the table, color and sweetness blooming from a Dutch vase, as if unrelated to manure; Italian posters on the wall as if they had traveled; starched white curtains at the windows, as if made of a brocade too rich and heavy to bend; morning glories covering the outhouse with royal purple. When he came home at night she would brush the cobwebs from his hair, make him bathe and shave and dress—to appear as if he had not worked in dirt. She made wonderful sauces, could cook anything to taste like something else, created a sense of purity by the whiteness of tablecloth, of delicacy by the thinness of crystal, would surround a steak with parsley as if it were not flesh but the bloom of a garden, supported her illusions with candlelight and fine wine, and smiled at him across the table with lips redder than real. In the bedroom candlelight again, and yet another nightgown to suggest a mysterious woman of unknown delights, and a heavy perfume, as if not sweat but sweetness came from her pores.

Being an illusionless man, he admitted that he liked these elegant mirages, found them pleasant, that it was good to sleep with her fine curves under his hand, her sweet smells in his nose, that he slept better now than when he lived alone. He became less gloomy, but not much.

One Sunday afternoon, walking hand in hand in sunshine through the poppies and daisies, he noticed her lips moving. "What are you saying?" he said. "Do you love me?" "I'm fond of you," he said; "love is an illusion." "Is there anybody else? I'm terribly jealous." "Jealousy is the illusion of complete possession." "Do other women attract you?" "Yes." "Some men are not like that." "Some men are liars," he said.

She became pregnant, bought baby clothes, tried out names, was always singing. "Please be happy," she said. "By 1980 the world population will . . ." "Oh be quiet!" he said.

She prepared a room for the baby, hung curtains, bought a crib, read books, became apprehensive. "Will he be all right? What do you think? Will he be a good baby? He doesn't have to be pretty, you know, that's not so important, but I'd like him to be intelligent. And will he have two eyes and the right number of fingers and toes? I want him to have everything he needs and nothing too much. What do you think?" "Some minor congenital aberrations are inevitable," he said; "the major malformations are less. . . ." "Don't say such things," she said. "Why do you scare me?" "I was just. . . ." "Oh . . . and will I know what to do?" she said, ". . . how to take care of him? What do you think? Will I be any good at it?"

One night he felt her lips moving in his hair. "Praying?" he said. "Yes." "What did you ask?" "That someday you will say you love me."

She felt weak, became sick; in bed she looked pale and scared. "Will the baby be all right?" she said. "Don't ever leave me. What are you thinking? Tell me." She began to bleed, was terrified, lay very still, but lost the baby anyway.

She was depressed then, her face motionless and dark. "I lost it because you don't love me," she said.

"There is no established correlation," he said, "between the alleged state of love, or lack of it, and the incidence of miscarriage."

"I'm not wanting statistics," she screamed.

"What then?"

"Nothing. Everything. It's not enough . . . just being 'fond.' I hate fondness. What's the matter with you? It wouldn't have happened . . . I want to be loved!"

"You're being hysterical," he said, "and you're not finishing your sentences."

Suddenly, all at once, she looked at him with a level detached gaze and did not like what she saw. "You were right," she said; "you *are* petty and self-absorbed. What's worse, you have a legal mind and there's no poetry in you. You don't give me anything, don't even love me, you're *dull.* You were stuck in a hole in the ground when I found you, and if I hadn't pulled you out you'd be there still. There's no life in you. I give you everything and it's not enough, doesn't make any difference. You can't wait to die, want to bury yourself now and me with you. Well I'm not ready yet and I'm not going to put up with it any longer, and now I'm through with you and I want a divorce."

"You've lost your illusions about me," he said, "but not the having of illusions. . . ."

"While you," she said, "have lost your illusions about everything, and can't get over being sore about it."

". . . they'll focus now on someone else. . . ."

"Oh I hope so!" she said; "I can hardly wait."

". . . you waste experience."

"And you waste *life!*"

He wouldn't give her a divorce, but that didn't matter; for she couldn't bear the thought of his moving back to that basement, and anyway, she told herself, he had to have someone to look after him; so they lived together still and she cooked for him when she was home and mended his clothes and darned his socks, and when he asked why, she said, with sweet revenge, "Because I'm fond of you, that's all. Just fond."

She got a job with a theater, typed scripts and programs, worked nights in the box office, let her hair grow into a long silken curtain curled up at the bottom below her shoulders, wore loose chiffon blouses with clown sleeves, trailed filmy scarves from her neck, and fell in love with an actor named Cyrus Anthony de Maronodeck. Her a's broadened and she affected a way of turning her head with so sudden a movement that it could not go unnoticed; no longer did she walk in or out of a room, she strode.

"Cyrus is so *interesting!*" she said, "makes everything an adventure, concentrates energy and passion into a moment until it glows!" She struck a pose: " 'When I die,' he says, 'I may be dead for a long time, but while I'm here I'll live it to the hilt.' " "A philosopher, too," Henry said.

One Sunday night Cyrus borrowed a thousand dollars from Lorabelle for his sick mother; and the following day it transpired that he had borrowed also the weekend receipts from the box office and had taken his leave of the company. For several days Lorabelle wouldn't believe it, waited for word from him, bit her fingernails—until he was apprehended in Laredo crossing the border with a blonde.

She worked next in a brokerage house operating an enormous and very intelligent machine which tapped and hummed and whirred and rotated, sent its carriage hopping up and down and side to side, performed seventeen mathematical calculations without ever a mistake, took pictures of everything and had illusions about nothing—but Lorabelle did, and presently fell in love with her boss, Mr. Alexander Orwell Mittelby, a sixty-year-old man who loved her with a great passion, she told Henry, but who was married and unfortunately could not get a divorce because his wife was a schizophrenic, had a private nurse in constant attendance; the shock of divorce, Mr. Mittelby had said, would kill her.

"Alex is unique," Lorabelle told Henry, "simply not like the rest of us . . . not at all. He has no interest in himself, has grown beyond that. I've never met a man so mature, so genuinely wise. 'All my personal goals lie in the past,' he told me; 'the only thing left is to seek the common good.' He has no patience with personal problems, complexes . . . that sort of thing . . . sees the romantic protest for what it is: adolescent complaining. Oh Henry, I wish you could know him. He faces life with so much courage—such a gallant careless courage. 'Despair is a luxury,' he says, 'and I can't afford it.' "

Lorabelle wore short tight skirts, high needle-like heels, jeweled glasses, and her hair bouffant; she read the *Wall Street Journal* and *Barron's Weekly*, studied the new tax legislation, spoke out for laissez faire in discussion groups, and at an Anti-World-Federalist dinner chanced to meet Mrs. Mittelby, who was not schizophrenic at all, but a plain shrewd woman with a wrinkled face, gray hair, and a very sharp tongue. Lorabelle stared at her with deepening shock. "My husband's secretaries," Mrs. Mittelby said, "always seem stunned by my sanity . . . then seek other employment."

In her depression Lorabelle turned away from people, rented a cabin on an island, left Henry to look after himself, came home only on weekends, spent her days walking on deserted beaches, her nights alone writing an autobiographical novel by lamplight. "It's really a kind of self-analysis," she said, "but I want so much to make it beautiful."

After a few months she fell in love with a fisherman. "His name is Jim," she said to Henry. "That's all, just Jim. And he's like his name, exactly: simple, strong, uncomplicated. I wish you could know each other."

"Bring him to dinner!" Henry shouted. "Let him live here! Give him my clothes, my bed!"

"Don't be angry. You'd like him; you couldn't help it. He's so kind, so gentle, so much a part of the elements: in his eyes the wind and the ocean—you can see them!—in his hand the strength, the toughness . . . the grip on the helm in a storm, in his bearing the straightness of the tall pointed firs, in his character the solid rock of the coast."

"If he had a foundation," Henry said, "he'd be a house with a swimming pool."

Lorabelle cut her hair short, wore boots and a sou'wester, scanned the sky for weather signs, studied navigation charts, hung a tide table on the wall. "I want a divorce," she said. "No." "Why? You don't love me." "To protect you from your own bad judgment. You'd be married six times before you were forty if you were free." "Then I'll run away with him," she said.

And she would have, but the sheriff got there first, arrested Jim for bigamy: plain Jim had three last names and a wife with each, and while he sat in jail the three of them squabbled for the fishing boat, which was all he owned.

Lorabelle gave up the cabin, burned her manuscript, and moved back home; wept and wailed and could not be consoled. "There's something wrong with *my* sanity," she said. "I can't do it myself. I'd better see a psychoanalyst." "You'll get a whopping transference," Henry said.

She went to a Dr. Milton Tugwell, took to analysis with great facility, worked quickly through her depression, went four times a week and wished it were more. "I'm so terribly lucky," she said to Henry. "There are so many analysts, you know—good, bad, indifferent—I had no way of knowing . . . and he turns out to be the *one* analyst for me. No one else would be right."

"It really is a kind of miracle, isn't it?" Henry said.

"No, really! I mean it. There's a special affinity between us, I felt it the very first session. We speak the same language; sometimes he knows what I'm thinking before I say it—sometimes even before I know I'm thinking it. It's amazing. And he has the most astonishing memory, remembers *everything*. And the way—Oh Henry! if you could only know him, hear him talk!—the way he fits these things together! things you'd never realize were connected. . . ."

Dr. Tugwell made many excellent interpretations: Lorabelle learned about her orality, anality, penis envy, oedipus complex, and, as a kind of bonus, had many insights also into Henry and shared them with him, surprised at his lack of responsiveness.

One night at the theater she saw Dr. Tugwell in the company of a tall gray-haired woman with a hard face. His wife, Lorabelle thought, and something clicked for her, an insight all on her own: *Dr. Tugwell was unhappy with this woman.* So this was the source of that sad note in his voice. He deserved better. She wanted to make him happy, as a woman; and she could, she knew she could. She looked narrowly at Mrs. Tugwell. Then it occurred to her (the analysis must be taking effect, she thought; this was her second insight in an hour) that Dr. Tugwell might have some special feeling of this sort for her, and the more she thought about it the more obvious it became.

When in her next hour she talked of these matters, Dr. Tugwell said nothing except, "What comes to mind about that?" and she was disappointed, but then realized that he could not speak, that he was the prisoner of a professional commitment which required him to stifle his feeling for her. She walked in the meadow on the hill in sunshine, and knew in her heart what must be hidden in his; and someday, she thought, when the analysis was over maybe he would get a divorce and Henry would give her a divorce, and she and Dr. Tugwell would meet on a different basis. She picked a daisy, pulled the petals, and it came out right. Softly she tried his name on her lips, "Milton, darling," and blushed, "sweetest Milt . . . honey," felt him walk beside her, his hand slip around her waist, heard his deep beloved voice begin, "Lorabelle, there is something I must tell you. . . ."

The analysis lasted longer than any of her affairs, perhaps because, paying for her sessions, she valued them more than meetings with lovers, or perhaps because her illusions did not encounter anything hard enough in Dr. Tugwell's silence to cause breakage; but after five years Henry came to the end of his resources and tolerance, said he would pay for no more sessions. This proved him cruel and unfeeling, Lorabelle thought, and reported it triumphantly to Dr. Tugwell who, strangely, regarded it as reasonable.

Lorabelle wept through the last hour, tears making lakes in her ears, overflowing on the pillow, dripping from her chin as she stood up, shaking, to face him, her voice quavering as she thanked him for the changes in her, breaking as she said goodbye. Yet at that very moment she had the comfort of a secret vision: now that she was no longer his patient he was free to become her lover. But days passed and he didn't call; weeks and the vision was shaken; a month and she was desolate. She went back to see him; and this time, sitting in a chair before him, feeling oddly dislocated, really did see him. There along the wall was the green couch on which she had lain for so many hours, from which she had looked up at the blank ceiling, had raved, rambled, complained, and wept; and there—shrinking back slightly from the violence of her disappointment—was the man of her dreams who had listened, out of sight, behind the couch: dark suit of expensive cloth and cut, perfectly pressed, dark tie, silk shirt with white-on-white design, high cordovan sheen on calf-skin loafers, shell-rimmed glasses flashing a nervous glare. There was strain in his voice, she thought; he used jargon, was more detached than he need have been: a continuing transference problem, he said . . . not infrequent . . . might require further analysis . . . unresolved father attachment . . . he had committed her hours . . . could do nothing now . . . sorry . . . perhaps later . . . call him in three months.

For weeks Lorabelle stayed home in deep silent gloom, wouldn't eat, wouldn't dress; but bounced back finally, as she always did, got a job selling tickets at a carousel, and there met Adelbert Bassew, big game hunter—"What a man!" she exclaimed to Henry; "six feet six, all fire and brawn. Imagine!"—who asked her on a safari. And so it continued through the days and weeks of their lives, year after year: Catholic Church, Christian Science, yoga; Al, Bob, and Peter; Paris, Rome, and Nairobi; technocracy, mysticism, hypnotism; short hair, long hair, wig; and whenever she would say, in that rapturous tone of hers, "I realize now . . .," Henry would know she had abandoned one illusion and was already firmly entrapped by the next. They became poor on her pursuits, lived in a basement; her illusions became sillier, shabbier, until finally she was sending in box-tops from cereal packages. Crow's feet appeared around her eyes, white hair among the gold; her skin became dry and papery. But as she got older something about her stayed young: the springing up of hope, the intoxicating energy, the creation of a new dream from the ruin of the old. From the despair of disillusion always she would find her way back: to a bell-like laughter with the rising note of an unfinished story, to a lilt of voice like the leap of water before rapids, to a wild dancing grace of legs and hips like a horse before a jump, to the happy eyes so easily wet with sympathy or love.

But these same years made Henry older than his actual age, more withdrawn, bitter, morose; his face haggard, lined; his hair gray. Every day he got up and went to work, but did nothing else—would not read a book or walk in the park or listen to music. In the evenings he would drink; but gin nourished no illusion, brought no pleasure, only numbness and finally sleep. Lorabelle felt anger and pity and contempt, all at the same time, and would rail at him. "Just look at yourself: drunk, dirty, head hanging like a sick cat . . . How can you stand yourself? What are you trying to do? make me feel guilty? . . . Well I don't. Playing the martyr? Is that it? What's the matter with you? Why don't you find someone else if you're so unhappy with me?"

Henry would shrug, thinking there are no happy marriages and it would be no different with anyone else; but sometimes, far at the back of his unhappy mind, he would come upon the truth: he stayed with her because, with all her witless pursuit of illusions, she nevertheless stirred him—like the wren, trapped under a house, that had flown in his face: he had caught it in his hand, felt the terrified struggle, the concentration of heat, the tremolo of heartbeat too faint and fast to count. Lorabelle brought him no comfort; but, holding her, he felt life, and would not give it up. And sometimes in the midst of her railings Lorabelle would know that she stayed with Henry— not simply, as she said, because he wouldn't give her a divorce—but because he was a rock and she leaned on him.

But even rocks may crumble, and one Monday morning Henry did not move when the alarm went off; he lay still, eyes open, looking at the empty face of the clock, thinking numbly of millions of termites burrowing in wood who would suffer no further interference from him.

He stayed in bed most of the day, ate little, drank much, said nothing. The next day was the same, and the next, and so all week; and on Friday it occurred to Lorabelle that—Henry having apparently retired from business—she must earn the living. After her morning coffee, therefore, she sat down at her desk to compose the fourth line of a jingle about soap flakes; first prize would bring a thousand dollars. Next she invented a hatpin that could neither fall out of a hat nor prick a finger; drew a careful sketch of the device, and addressed it to the U. S. Patent Office; this might make a fortune, she thought. Then she collected all her green stamps: not many, she mused, but enough for a present for Henry. She prepared his lunch on a tray, found him lying in bed staring at the ceiling; he would say nothing and would not eat. She put on her best dress, arranged flowers by his bed, and kissed him on the nose. "I'll be back soon," she said.

It was a beautiful day, the sun shining, wind moving here and there among the trees like playful strokes of a great invisible brush.

"I know he will be all right," she said to herself, and posted her jingle and her invention, saying a little prayer for each. She went then to a fortune-teller, an old West Indian woman, who told her that someone dear to her was ill and would die. Lorabelle was shocked and left immediately, bought three sweepstakes tickets in Henry's name to fight the prediction, said another prayer, went on to the supply house and got a pipe and slippers for her green stamps. For a dollar she bought jonquils—because they were pretty and would make him happy—then counted her money. With the two dollars that were left she bought a steak to tempt his appetite.

At home she found him in pyjamas sitting at the table drinking gin. "Oh sweetheart!" she said, "you break my heart . . . I won't have it, I just won't have it . . . you understand? Cheer up now. I've got presents for you." She put the pipe in his hand, brought tobacco, put the slippers on his bare feet—"There! You see? Aren't they nice? And so warm. A perfect fit! You like them?"—but he said nothing. She began to sing, trying not to cry, then broke off: "Oh, and I have something else . . . another wonderful surprise, you'll see. Now don't come in the kitchen," she added, unnecessarily. She broiled the steak, put it on a heated plate, garnished it with water cress, put jonquils on the tray, a chef's cap on her head, lighted candles, and brought it in singing the Triumphal March from *Aida,* placed it before him with a flourish and a sweeping low bow. He turned away. "Oh please, do eat it," she cried; "I got it just for you. It's delicious, you'll see! Try it . . . it would be so good for you."

"Where's the gin?" he said.

"Don't drink any more; you'll get sick. I'm so worried. Eat now. You'll feel better, I know you will, really . . . I just know it. Here, let me feed you."

She cut a bit of steak, waved it under his nose, held it to his mouth, touched his lips; he knocked it away, the fork clattering to the floor, the morsel skittering into a corner. She picked them up, took away the tray. In the kitchen she threw the fork at the calendar, kicked the garbage can, wept; then she composed herself and went back, humming, to the living room; Henry had not moved. Lorabelle put up a card table, took newspaper clippings from her purse, spread out maps of the city: she was working on a treasure hunt. Only three clues had been published, and already she had an idea where the treasure might be. The first prize was five thousand dollars; tomorrow she would take a shovel and go digging.

"Where's the gin?" Henry said.

"There isn't any more, sweetheart. And a good thing because

you've had too much . . . you're drunk, you're ruining your health."

"Give me some money," he said tonelessly.

"We haven't any."

He got up, walked unsteadily to the table where she was sitting, opened her purse and took out her wallet. A few coins fell to the table, rolled on the floor; there were no bills. He turned her handbag upside down; an astrology chart tumbled out, then a Christian Science booklet, a handbill from the Watchtower Society, *Palmistry in Six Easy Lessons,* dozens of old sweepstakes tickets and the three new ones, *Love and the Mystic Union,* fortunes from Chinese cookies (one of which, saying "He loves you," she snatched away from him), a silver rosary, a daily discipline from the Rosicrucians, the announcement of a book titled *Secret Power from the Unconscious through Hypnosis*—but no money. He shook the bag furiously and threw it in a corner, surveyed the litter before him with unblinking bloodshot eyes, his face expressionless. "Stupid fool!" he said thickly. "Purse full of illusions . . . suitcase full of illusions . . . whole goddamned lousy life full of illusions . . ." He turned away, stumbled back to the table, put the empty gin bottle to his mouth, turned it over his head, broke it on the hearth.

"Oh my dear," Lorabelle cried, her eyes wet, "you keep waiting for the real thing, but this is all there is." He turned ponderously, facing her, eyes like marble; she came to him. "These are the days . . . and nights . . . of our years and they're passing—look at us! We're getting old—and what else is there?"

"Bitch!"

She faltered, raising her arm, but recovered and went on to touch the side of his head where the hair was gray. "Do please come back to life; I don't want you to die; I'd be so lonely. I'd forget all the bad times and remember all the wonderful things . . . where have they gone? . . . you feeding the ducks, stamping on the bread—so sweet you were!"

"Get out."

The gray stonelike face above her did not move, not even the eyes. A death mask, she thought; the fortune-teller was right. "Oh my dear! I feel so sad." She cried, lowered her head; with a convulsive movement she caught his hand, pressed it to her heart. "It hurts so," she said. "For years you've been cutting yourself off . . . more and more. I'm the only one still holding you, and now you're drifting away. Don't die, sweetheart, let me help you, hold on to me!"

He freed his hand and hit her in the face, sent her crashing into the wall, started after her, thinking, "Where's that broken bottle?" realized with a sense of numb strangeness that he wanted to kill her . . . paused. She stood looking at him, tears running down her face, then left the room. He turned back to the table, sat heavily, observed the hand that had hit her; the fingers felt numb. Before him on the table was the hatpin she had worked with that morning: long sharp pin, black plastic ball at one end, at the other an odd device of safety pins and scotch tape. "Illusion!" he said, grabbing it up in clenched fist and driving it deep into the table; the plastic ball broke, the base of the pin went through his hand, stuck out three inches on top. There was no blood. His hand hung there in mid-air, quivering slightly, like an insect pinned to a card. He moved his fingers: a white crab without a shell, he thought, impaled on a boy's stick. Blood appeared around the pin; the feeling of numbness crept up his arm; he wanted a drink, didn't want to die yet, wasn't ready. Numbness came now to the other arm. He began tugging at the pin, ten cold crab legs fumbling around a spike.

The next morning he shaved, got dressed, and ate breakfast; felt restless, wanted to do something but didn't know what. "Will you go for a walk with me?" he said. Lorabelle was tired, her eyes red, hadn't slept, but was never altogether without hope. "Yes," she said.

They walked by rivers, over bridges, through forests, sat in dry grass and watched a tiny squirrel at the tip of a branch in a fir tree; walked through meadows, by cliffs, over dunes, along the beach, saw two sea stars in a tide pool waving their arms at each other; walked on streets between high buildings, through crowds, watched a little girl feeding pigeons by a fountain. Lorabelle was silent and dejected, her hair scraggly, her shoulders stooped. Something was moving inside Henry, pressing him; he wanted to say something but didn't know what.

That evening as they sat together in their basement room, silent and unhappy, the phone rang. Henry, having known since child-hood that a telephone ring means requests, burdens, and obligations, did not move; and for the first time Lorabelle—to whom the same sound meant love, opportunity, adventure—did not answer. Henry looked up, saw that she was exhausted: "Let it ring," he said. She nodded, but couldn't bear the sense of someone calling unheeded, began to hope as she walked, walked faster as she hoped, was soon running lest she be too late, and a few moments later was exclaim-ing in astonishment and joy: "What? . . . No! . . . Really? . . . Yes! yes! oh yes . . . he's right here . . . No, I have it . . . So much! That's wonderful! . . . Marvelous!" then flung herself in Henry's arms, weeping, laughing, "You've won the Irish Sweepstakes! $137,000! Can you imagine! My God . . .!'"

Henry was pleased, but confused and vaguely disturbed; said it was hers not his, since she had bought the ticket. "No, no," she said, "I bought it in your name, and it's yours, and I'm so happy I could cry. . . ." She wiped her tears. ". . . you need it, darling, more than I . . . because I've always known about miracles but you haven't known, but now maybe you will, a little, and I'm so glad it happened for you. Isn't it marvelous?"

"It won't be much after taxes."

"Oh but still a lot," she said, "a very great deal. Just think . . .! We'll go to Paris and live in the Ritz, and you'll have a dark blue suit and a gray silk tie and cufflinks of lapis and maybe a black stick with a little silver. You'll stand very straight and swing the stick lightly, back and forth, as we stroll on the *Boulevard St. Germain* and the *Rue St. Honoré,* and I'll be so proud." She sat on his lap, eyes glistening, hugged him, kissed the gray hair by his ear. "Then we'll get a Citroën and drive down the Loire, and come finally to beautiful sand and water. Oh, and Monte Carlo! We'll stand around the casino watching the Texas oilmen and the pretty girls and the diamond bracelets; we'll hold hands and look on at roulette and moisten our lips and be like poor cautious tourists, and nobody will know we're rich. Then you'll toss out a ten thousand dollar bill: 'Red,' you'll say. That's all, just that: 'Red,' in a quiet voice, and people will fall silent and stare, and the croupier's hand will tremble, and the wheel will spin and oh! . . . it won't matter whether it's red or black because it's just money either way, not love, and we'll go to Rome and rent a villa, and when. . . ."

"We're broke," he said, "long before Rome. In Genoa we couldn't pay the hotel bill. Remember? Had to sell your jewels . . . and my walking stick."

"Oh no!" she said, "there you go, already sad. . . . Then we remembered the *other* bank account—how could you forget?—found we had plenty of money . . . We go on to Rome, rent a villa and in the evening sit on the terrace holding hands, flowers blooming all around us, and to the west on the crest of a hill seven cypress trees in a row, an orange sun sinking between the black trunks, the whole sky a brilliant golden drum; and you'll feel a throbbing of your heart and a kind of singing rapture, and you'll press my hand and say, 'I love you.' "

Henry was touched by her fantasy and felt some lightness of heart: it would be nice to have some money, he thought—how incredible!—and maybe they really would enjoy a trip. That night they slept in each other's arms and the next day the windfall was gone: it had been a mistake; the officials were terribly sorry; it was another man with the same name and almost the same telephone number, who owned a candy store and had five children, weighed three hundred pounds, and was pictured in the newspaper with his family, seven round beaming faces. Lorabelle was in dispair, but Henry was tranquil, still felt that lightness of heart. He comforted Lorabelle and stroked her finally to sleep in the evening, her wet face on his shoulder. It was an illusion, he thought, and for a while I believed it, and yet—curious thing—it has left some sweetness. Throughout the night he marveled about this—could it be he had won something after all?—and the next day, crawling under the rotting mansion of a long-dead actor, he looked a termite in the eye and decided to build a house.

He bought land by the sea and built on a cliff by a great madrona tree which grew out horizontally from the rock, a shimmering cloud of red and green; built with massive A-frames, bolted together, stressed, braced, anchored in concrete to withstand five-hundred-mile winds, a house—in the best illusory style, he thought wryly—to last forever. But the cliff crumbled one night in a storm during a twenty-four foot tide; Lorabelle and Henry stood by hand in hand in the rain and lightning, deafened by crashing surf and thunder, as the house fell slowly into the sea while the great madrona remained, anchored in nothing but dreams. They went then to live in an apartment, and Henry worked as a carpenter, built houses for other people, began planning another house of his own.

One evening after dinner Henry was sitting at the table, smoking a pipe, working on blueprints; across the room Lorabelle, at her desk, bent over a "Who Am I?" contest. ("We might win $3,500," she had said; "just think of it! Wouldn't that be marvelous? Oh the things we will do . . .!") She was humming now, a waltz from *Die Fledermaus*. Henry looked up, observed the happy face bent to the illusory task, the golden hair streaked with gray falling across her cheek, the wrinkles of laughter now indelible around her eyes, the putting of pencil to mouth like a child, puzzled . . . laid down his pipe. "I love you, Lorabelle," he said. She looked up, startled: "What . . . did you say?" "I love you," he said. She blushed, started to rise, the pencil falling from her hand: "But . . . but . . . you said it was an illusion." It is, he thought, because love claims the future and can't hold it; but claims also the present, and we have that. Not wanting to confuse her or start an argument, he said only, "I love you anyway." She ran to him, weeping with joy, "Oh Henry, I'm so happy, so terribly happy! This is all we lacked . . . all we'll ever need." He took her and the moment in his arms, kissed her, and said nothing.

He built a house on a plateau in a sheltered valley, protected from wind and water; blasted a gigantic hole in solid granite, floated the house on a bubble of pure mercury for earthquakes, built walls of reinforced concrete seven feet thick, doors and cabinets of stainless steel, pipes and lightning rods of copper, roof of inch-thick slate. "Oh, Henry, I'm so proud!" Lorabelle said. "I'd like to see what could happen to this house." "You'll see," he said darkly. It cost a fortune and they couldn't meet the payments; the bank took it over, sold it to a university as a seismographic station; Henry and Lorabelle moved to an attic in the city.

One afternoon Lorabelle came home in a rapturous mood. "Oh, Henry, I've met the most wonderful man! A graduate student of Far Eastern studies and . . . you know, sort of a mystic himself . . . such a spiritual quality . . . name is Semelrad Apfelbaum . . . gives seminars on Buddhism." "Sounds like the real thing all right," Henry said bitterly. After dinner Lorabelle put on a diaphanous dress of black chiffon with a flowing lavender scarf, a gold chain around her neck, a sapphire on her finger, perfume in her hair. "Where are you going?" Henry said. "To meet Semelrad," she said; "he's so wonderfully kind, and so generous . . . is going to tutor me privately till I catch up with the class." "You're not going anywhere," Henry said. "I'm not a child, Henry," Lorabelle said with dignity. "But you *are*—precisely," Henry said. Lorabelle reminded him that theirs was a relationship of equality, with the same rights, that she must live her own life, make her own decisions, her own mistakes if need be; and when this failed to convince him she tossed back her head, affected great hauteur, and marched out of the room. Henry caught her at the door, turned her over his knee, applied the flat of his hand to the bottom of his delight; and it was perhaps that same night—for she did not go out—that Lorabelle got pregnant, and this time didn't lose it: the baby was born on Christmas, blue eyes and golden hair, and they named her Noel.

Henry built a house of solid brick in a meadow of sage and thyme, and there Noel played with flowers and crickets and butterflies and field mice. Most of the time she was a joy to her parents, and some of the time—when she was sick or unkind—she was a sorrow. Lorabelle loved the brick house, painted walls, hung pictures, and polished floors; on hands and knees with a bonnet on her head she dug in the earth and planted flowers, looked up at Henry through a wisp of hair with a happy smile; "We'll never move again," she said. But one day the state sent them away and took over their house to build a freeway. The steel ball crashed through the brick walls, bulldozers sheared away the flower beds, the great shovels swung in, and the house was gone. Henry and Lorabelle and Noel moved back to the city, lived in a tiny flat under a water tank that dripped continuously on the roof and sounded like rain.

Henry and Lorabelle loved each other most of the time, tried to love each other all the time, to create a pure bond, but could not. It was marred by the viciousness, shocking to them, with which they hurt each other. Out of nothing they would create fights, would yell at each other, hate, withdraw finally in bitter silent armistice; then, after a few hours, or sometimes a few days, would come together again, with some final slashes and skirmishes, and try to work things out—to explain, protest, forgive, understand, forget, and above all to compromise. It was a terribly painful and always uncertain process; and even while it was under way Henry would think bleakly, "It won't last, will never last; we'll get through this one maybe, probably, then all will be well for a while—a few hours, days, weeks if we're lucky—then another fight over something—what?—not possible to know or predict, and certainly not to prevent . . . and then all this to go through again; and beyond that still another fight looming in the midst ahead, coming closer . . . and so on without end." But even while thinking these things he still would try to work through the current trouble because, as he would say, "There isn't anything else." And sometimes there occurred to him, uneasily, beyond all this gloomy reflection, an even more sinister thought: that their fights were not only unavoidable but also, perhaps, necessary; for their passages of greatest tenderness followed hard upon their times of greatest bitterness, as if love could be renewed only by gusts of destruction.

Nor could Henry ever build a house that would last forever, no more than anyone else; but he built one finally that lasted quite a while, a white house on a hill with lilac and laurel and three tall trees, a maple, a cedar, and a hemlock. It was an ordinary house of ordinary wood and the termites caused some trouble and always it needed painting or a new roof or a faucet dripped or something else needed fixing, and he grew old and gray and finally quite stooped doing these things, but that was all right, he knew, because there wasn't anything else.

Noel grew up in this house—a dreamy, soft-spoken girl, becoming more and more beautiful—wore her long hair in pigtails, practiced the piano, sang in a high true voice, played in the meadow, caught butterflies among the lilac. At nineteen she fell in love with Falbuck Wheeling who wore a tattered brown leather jacket and roared in on a heavy motorcycle dispelling peace and birds and butterflies, bringing noise and fumes and a misery Henry felt but could not define. Falbuck had a hard bitter face, said little, would sit at the kitchen table sullen and uncomfortable, and Henry could never get him into conversation because whatever the subject—literature, government, justice—Falbuck would sit staring at him, silent and disbelieving, until finally with a few labored and nasty words he would assert some rottenness behind the facade; then, as if exhausted by this excursion into communication, he would get up, taking Noel as if he owned her, and roar away. Noel spent her days with him, and soon her nights, wore jeans and an old army shirt with the tails hanging out, let her hair hang loose and tangled, smoked cigarettes in a long black holder. Henry and Lorabelle talked earnestly to this wild, changed girl, now hardly recognizable as their daughter, advised caution and delay, but to no avail: she married Falbuck and went to live with him in a tiny room over a motorcycle shop. Henry and Lorabelle were left alone in the house on the hill, in peace now, with butterflies and the sound of wind in the three trees, and wished she were back.

Every morning Henry took his tools and went to his work of building houses—saw the pyramid of white sand spreading out in the grass, the bricks chipping, the doors beginning to stick, the first tone of gray appearing on white lumber, the first leaf falling in the bright gutter—but kept on hammering and kept on sawing, joining boards and raising rafters; on weekends he swept the driveway and mowed the grass, in the evenings fixed the leaking faucets, tried to straighten out the disagreements with Lorabelle; and in all that he did he could see himself striving toward a condition of beauty or truth or goodness or love that did not exist, but whereas earlier in his life he had always said, "It's an illusion," and turned away, now he said, "There isn't anything else," and stayed with it; and though it cannot be said that they lived happily, exactly, and certainly not ever after, they did live. They lived—for a while—with ups and downs, good days and bad, and when it came time to die Lorabelle said, "Now we'll never be parted," and Henry smiled and kissed her and said to himself, "There isn't anything else," and they died.

QUASI-COURTSHIP BEHAVIOR IN PSYCHOTHERAPY*

Albert E. Scheflen

For nearly a decade our research group[1] has been making a comparative study of different methods of psychotherapy.

We discovered that certain interchanges were performed in a startlingly similar fashion or form, whether the therapist was an active interventionist or an orthodox psychoanalytic listener. For instance, the structure we clinically know as rapport shows the same basic elements of posture, voice, and movement, regardless of who the participants are. In other words, we came to recognize that human behavior is patterned and systematic. It is made up of regular, standard gestalten or units which are arranged in lawful configurations.

One of these regular structures that invariably appeared in psychotherapy included behaviors like those found in American courtship. The ethics of psychotherapy have traditionally proscribed sexual behavior, and most of the therapists we studied were unaware that they behaved in ways which could be identified as sexual in therapy sessions. When we interviewed them about it, they spoke defensively, saying that if indeed they showed such actions they did not intend to; they must have unresolved personal problems or untoward countertransference reactions. So at first we thought that these little-known elements of courtshiplike behavior were undesirable contaminants of psychotherapy. But there were reasons to assume that this was not the case. First of all, some few therapists

*Reprinted by special permission of The William Alanson White Psychiatric Foundation, Inc., Vol. 28 (1965), pp. 245–55. Copyright by The William Alanson White Psychiatric Foundation, Inc.

[1]This research was supported by the Commonwealth of Pennsylvania. It was carried out in continuous corroboration with Ray L. Birdwhistell, whose thinking helped shape many of the ideas and observations. Drawings for this paper were done by Sherl Winter and editorial work by Alice Schwar. [Drawings for this volume adapted from the original.]

Ray L. Birdwhistell, J. D. Van Vlack, cinematographer, and the author constituted the film analysis team. The clinical team consisted of Catherine L. Bacon, O. Spurgeon English, Warren W. Hampe, and Max Katz, and at times Morris Brody, George Devereux, John Rosen, and others.

were quite aware of such behaviors and considered them a necessary part of their technique. Second, we saw these behaviors in all the psychotherapies we examined and in nearly all other interactions as well. Behavior this universal could not be written off as untoward or incidental.

THE METHOD OF RESEARCH

From general systems theory[2] we have a model for conceptualizing the organization of living systems. Components are organized into units which, in turn, are part of larger systems. Even more recently it has become evident that behavior is integrated analogously; that is, standard units are integrated into larger units which, in turn, make up still larger units.

Such an arrangement of behavioral units in a hierarchy of levels has been applied to animal behavior by the ethologists.[3] It has long been held by gestalt theorists that human behavior is perceived in gestalten.[4] In the last generation methods have been worked out in structural linguistics for determining the units of speech behavior and their arrangement in larger units,[5] analogous to the hierarchies of levels of material systems. And in both the American[6] and British[7] schools of anthropology the realization has been growing that *all behavior—not only speech—is patterned this way*. So we now know why the gestalt theorists could find that people perceive units, not merely qualities of behavior; for these units are coded in a cultural and institutional tradition, and each generation learns them by conscious and unconscious processes.

These strands of development were formalized as a method of research at Palo Alto in 1956 by Gregory Bateson, Ray Birdwhistell, Henry Brosin, Frieda Fromm-Reichmann, Charles Hockett, and Norman McQuown, and since then have been developed further by Ray Birdwhistell and the author. This approach to human behavior

---

[2]W. Ross Ashby, "General Systems Theory as a New Discipline," *General Systems,* Vol. 3, (1958), pp. 1–6. Ludwig von Bertalanffy, "An Outline of General Systems Theory," *British J. Philosophy of Science,* Vol. 1 (1950), p. 134. Bertalanffy, *Problems of Life* (New York: Harper, 1960).

[3]Konrad Lorenz, *King Solomon's Ring* (New York: Crowell, 1952). Peter H. Klopfer, *Behavioral Aspects of Ecology* (Englewood Cliff, N. J.: Prentice-Hall, 1962.

[4]Kurt Koffka, *Principles of Gestalt Psychology* (New York: Harcourt, 1935).

[5]Henry A. Gleason, *An Introduction to Descriptive Linguistics* (New York: Holt, Rinehart, and Winston, 1955). Charles F. Hockett, *A Course in Modern Linguistics* (New York: Macmillan, 1958).

[6]See, for example, Ruth Benedict, *Patterns of Culture* (New York: Mentor Books, 1946).

[7]See, for example, E. E. Evans-Pritchard, *Social Anthropology* (London: Cohen and West, 1951).

is known as "context analysis." Its principles and procedures have been described in other publications by Birdwhistell[8] and myself.[9] While I shall not detail the approach in this paper, it is this method that I applied to understanding the quasi-courting behaviors to be described here.

COMPONENT ELEMENTS IN COURTSHIP
BEHAVIOR AND THEIR QUALIFIERS

Once we had, through some observations of American courtship, become conscious of courting and courtinglike elements in kinesic behavior, we were surprised to see them in any interaction we observed. They appeared not only among lovers, but in psychotherapy sessions, business meetings, parties, conferences, and so on. Certainly all of these interactions were not supposed to end in sexual consummation. It seemed that either Americans court whenever they come together, regardless of what they are doing, or else these subtle sexual behaviors had some qualifying signals that modified their function. This latter possibility is the one I am going to develop. I shall begin by describing the basic courtship elements as they appear in interactions, and then describe the qualifiers that are combined with them in those situations that are not to be taken as seductive or sexual.

Basic Elements of Courtship

Some of the common activities of early courtship in America are courtship readiness, positioning for courtship, and actions of appeal or invitation.

Courtship readiness. Courtship behaviors occur after a participant has come into a specific state of readiness. People in high courtship readiness are often unaware of it and, conversely, subjects who think they "feel" very sexually active often do not evidence courtship readiness at all. Courtship readiness is most clearly evidenced

[8]Ray L. Birdwhistell, Chapter 3, in *The Natural History of an Interview*, edited by Norman McQuown (New York: Grune & Stratton, 1965). Birdwhistell, "Paralanguage: 25 Years after Sapir," in *Lectures on Experimental Psychiatry*, edited by Henry Brosin (Pittsburgh: Univ. of Pittsburgh Press, 1961). Birdwhistell, "The Frames in the Communication Process," paper read to the American Society of Clinical Hypnosis, October 10, 1959.

[9]Albert E. Scheflen, "Communication and Regulation in Psychotherapy," *Psychiatry*, Vol. 26 (1963), pp. 126–36. Scheflen, "Natural History Method in Psychotherapy: Communicational Research," in *Methods of Research in Psychotherapy*, edited by Louis A. Gottschalk and Arthur H. Auerbach (New York: Appleton-Century-Crofts, 1965). Scheflen, *Stream and Structure of Communicational Behavior* (Philadelphia: Commonwealth Mental Research Foundation, 1965).

by a state of high muscle tonus. Sagging disappears, jowling and bagginess around the eyes decrease, the torso becomes more erect, and pot-bellied slumping disappears or decreases. The legs are brought into tighter tonus, a condition seen in "cheesecake" and associated with the professional model or athlete. The eyes seem to be brighter. Some women believe their hair changes. Skin color varies from flush to pallor—possibly depending upon the degree of anxiety. It is possible that changes in water retention and odor occur.

Preening often accompanies these organismic changes, sometimes only as token behaviors. Women may stroke their hair, or glance at their makeup in the mirror, or sketchily rearrange their clothing. Men usually comb or stroke their hair, button and readjust their coats, or pull up their socks. Some preening behaviors which have been observed in psychotherapy sessions are shown in Figure 1.

(A) Tie Preen
(B) Sock Preen
(C) Hair Preen

A   B   C

FIG. 1. SOME PREENING BEHAVIOR OF MALE PSYCHOTHERAPISTS.

Positioning for courtship. Courtship, after the earliest steps, occurs in the assumption by the courting partners of postures which have a standard relationship. The partners turn their bodies and heads so as to face each other in a vis-à-vis or tête-à-tête configuration. They tend to lean toward each other and place their chairs or extremities in such a way as to block off others.[10] Figure 2 shows the vis-à-vis positioning used in courtship. It also depicts the courtship position which is used when the parties open the position of the upper half of their bodies to include a third person, but form a closed circle with their legs. When courting partners orient themselves vis-à-vis and come into closer physical proximity, they usually adopt an intimate mode of conversation.

---

[10]This relationship does not obtain at times when the partners share some mutual interest as a step in courtship—for example, when a man takes his girl to the movies. In these instances both partners are oriented outward, but they usually adopt the same bodily posture in mirror-imaged relationship.

Actions of appeal or invitation. The assumption of one participant of a vis-à-vis orientation with courtship readiness may be considered an invitation to courtship or to related activities. Other activities also appear to invite reciprocation in courtship. In addition to complementary or invitational statements and soft or draw-

(A) With Two People
(B) With Third Party Present

A   B

FIG. 2. POSITIONING FOR COURTSHIP.

ling paralanguage, characteristic bodily motions are seen. Flirtatious glances, gaze-holding, demure gestures, head-cocking, rolling of the pelvis, and other motions are well known. In women, crossing the legs, slightly exposing the thigh, placing a hand on the hip, and exhibiting the wrist or palm are also invitational. Protruding the breast and slow stroking motions of the fingers on the thigh or wrist also are common. Some of these activities, seen in psychotherapy sessions, are illustrated in Figure 3.

(A) Presenting the Palm, with Hair
     Preening
(B) Rolling the Hip
(C) Presenting and Caressing the Leg

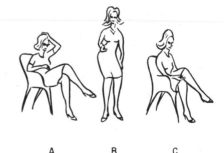

A   B   C

FIG. 3. APPEALING OR INVITATIONAL BEHAVIORS OF WOMEN PATIENTS.

Qualifiers of Courting Behavior

Two boys are wrestling. They may be fighting for domination or to defeat each other; but they also may have a quite different purpose. Their wrestling may not, even over years of repetition, progress to victory for either boy. Neither is hurt or humiliated. Instead of showing anger, both may laugh and show evidence of considerable pleasure. The spectators seem to know from the beginning that injury and victory are not the aims of this interaction.

Characteristic signals that the sexual elements of behavior which I have described are not to be taken literally as courtship include the following:

References to the inappropriate context. Partners in a quasi-courtship may make references to the inappropriateness of the situation for sexuality by reminding each other that other people are present or by reminders of taboos or ethical considerations. They may also remind each other that they are together to conduct the business at hand. In psychotherapy, the patient may be encouraged to feel her sexual feelings fully, yet be cautioned, by reference to the context, not to act them out. More often than not, such references are nonverbal. A gesture or movement of the eyes or head toward the setting or toward others is as effective as any verbal statement of inappropriateness.

Incomplete postural-kinesic involvement. After the earliest steps in a courtship the partners move into vis-à-vis relationship of posture and adopt an intimate mode of conversation, excluding others from their relationship. In quasi-courtship this relationship of postures is incomplete. The participants may face each other, but turn their bodies so that they face partly away from each other, or they may extend their arms so as to encompass others. Or they may cast about the room with their eyes or project their voices so as to be clearly audible to third parties. When no third parties are present, quasi-courting people may face, look at, or project to unseen third parties. This story of divided loyalties is told in Figure 4. In Figure 4A the

A   B

FIG. 4. MULTIPLE POSTURAL RELATIONSHIPS IN QUASI-COURTING.

woman, in vis-à-vis positioning with a man, turns in search behavior to another man passing by. In Figure 4B, the couple on the right are in a semiclosed tête-à-tête position, but the girl is touching the other man with her ankle. This kind of division of the body in multiple simultaneous relationships we have called splitting.[11]

Omission or incompleteness of key courting behaviors. The behaviors may be modified so as to leave out characteristic courting elements. This is done by failing to complete typical courting actions or by conducting them only in certain communicative modalities so that the gestalt required for a courting unit is not completed. For example, in courtship a man may lean forward, touch his partner, soften his facial expression, and, in soft paralanguage, verbalize his love. In quasi-courting he may say the words while leaning slightly away from her, smile only by retracting the corners of his lips without crinkling his eyes, and use a matter-of-fact tone of voice.

Disclaimers. Participants in quasi-courting may try to reduce ambiguity and indicate noncourtship by lexical disclaimers. They may reassure the partners and others that their interest is not sexual. They may seem to court while talking about their love for another partner, or they may intellectualize the flirtation in a discussion of great books.

Bizarreness of performance of the courtship elements. Sometimes in an interaction where seduction is inappropriate, the courtship elements appear without the above qualifiers. But instead, the elements are performed in a bizarre, histrionic manner, which seems improper to middle-class eyes, and which can appear to be a burlesque of courtship. When I first saw this in schizophrenic patients I thought such actions were psychotic. But broader observation shows this variant to be characteristic of teen-agers and men and women of the lower social class. The bizarre pattern is used by those who do not use the other qualifiers. If, indeed, this is a class difference, then my choice of the word "bizarre" represents a middle-class value judgment. It is logical that quasi-courting forms might differ between the classes, since their dating and courtship patterns are known to differ markedly.[12]

---

[11]See Scheflen, *Stream and Structure of Communicational Behavior,* in footnote 9.

[12]There is an American middle-class tendency to combine romantic love, which historically was a platonic concept, with active sexuality. It may be this combination that necessitates signals for differentiating courting and quasi-courting. Qualifiers seem to be learned by middle-class children first in their relations with older relatives and later in the characteristic middle-class dating pattern with its ritualistic line-spieling flattery, dance programs, and nonprogressing courtshiplike routines. But the non-upwardly-mobile lower class, which separates romantic love and sexuality, has no developed dating pattern of this kind and apparently lacks the pattern of quasi-courting well known in the middle class. For discussions of middle-class dating patterns, see the following: D. D. Bromley and F. H. Britten, *Youth and Sex: A Study of 1300*

THE QUASI-COURTING COMPLEX AS AN ENTITY

Quasi-courting can be distinguished from actual courtship by three major characteristics: (1) The *integration of components.* With elements of courtship are included the qualifiers that state, in essence, "This activity is not to be taken literally as seduction." (2) The *contexts of appearance.* Quasi-courting is identified also by the fact that it occurs in contexts in which courting or sexual behavior is inappropriate. (3) The *progression.* The ultimate progression in the interactional sequences determines whether the pattern is one of courtship or quasi-courtship. The quasi-courting pattern does not proceed to sexual consummation even in the later history of a given relationship.[13]

It is possible to postulate a state of quasi-courting readiness which includes a few aspects of courtship readiness but is observably different. For example, women may imitate the appearance of high tonus of courtship readiness by wearing nylon hose and high-heeled shoes which throw the foot into flexion and tighten the hamstrings, and may adopt a particular type of provocative, slightly bizarre attire and cosmetics that give the impression of "sexiness." Such devices appear to solicit quasi-courting rather than courting, and experienced men recognize that "sexy" women are not necessarily sexual, and are perhaps even likely to be frigid.

Quasi-courting occurs in nearly any situation—at least among the middle class—in which the members know each other and are engaged in a common objective. The sequence can be observed in the classroom, dining room, and meeting hall, and between parents and children, hosts and guests, teachers and students, doctors and patients. It occurs between men and women and between members of the same gender. The intensity and duration vary from the briefest

---

College Students (New York: Harper, 1938). Rayanne D. Cupps and Norman S. Hayner, "Dating at the University of Washington," *Marriage and Family Living*, Vol. 9 (1947), pp. 30–31. Winston Ehrmann, *Premarital Dating Behavior* (New York: Holt, 1959), C. Kirkpatrick and T. Caplow, "Courtship in a Group of Minnesota Students," *Amer. J. Sociology*, Vol. 51 (1945), pp. 114–25. Robert T. Ross, "Measures of the Sex Behavior of College Males Compared with Kinsey's Results," *J. Abnormal and Social Psychology*, Vol. 45 (1950), pp. 753–55. Geoffrey Gorer, *The American People: A Study in National Character* (New York: Norton, 1948).

[13]This is why there is a serious risk of misinterpreting component behaviors of any pattern when they are observed out of context. If, for example, you hear only that two men exchanged kisses, without knowing that the context was a French military ceremony, you might wrongly interpret the kissing as homosexual. This is the shortcoming of the currently popular isolation-of-variables method of research in which this or that element of behavior is studied as an isolate.

of kinesic interchanges (in formal activities such as psychotherapy) to the most elaborate, continuous, and intense rituals in situations such as the cocktail party. In the upper middle-class social context, in fact, quasi-courting takes on the quality of a deliberate game for enhancing attractiveness and social interest. Quasi-courting across marital lines is common. It does not produce signs of anxiety or force interruption so long as certain rules are observed.[14]

Often a quasi-courting relationship is at some point converted into an actual courtship. I have no observational data on this eventuality, but I would guess that some special signals or statements would be required to indicate the transition. On the other hand, a courtship may at some point be converted into a quasi-courtship. This would be indicated by the addition of the qualifiers. But by and large, in a quasi-courting sequence, *the qualifiers are enacted from the beginning.*

The occurrence of any deviance highlights and clarifies the lawfulness of the normal structure. For instance, an interactant may perform courting when it is inappropriate to do so, or perform overly intense quasi-courting as a means of forcing another participant to withdraw from relationship. Or the qualifiers may be deliberately kept unclear in order to produce an ambiguity between courtship and quasi-courtship, thereby confusing the other participant or forcing him to declare his intentions.

QUASI-COURTING SEQUENCES IN PSYCHOTHERAPY

Quasi-courting has occurred in all the psychotherapies we have observed from psychoanalytic to active interventionalistic—in family, group, and individual types. In the more psychoanalytic or more conventional psychotherapies the quasi-courting is covert—that is, merely postural and kinesic. The fact that it is nonlexical probably reflects the tendency of such therapists to be unaware of its use. This covert, automatic type of quasi-courting is like that found in any American interaction and functions to maintain the integration of the group—a point which I shall discuss later. Some psychotherapists, however, use quasi-courting openly and explicitly to bring the patient to face certain conflicts and to make special definitions of the relationship conscious. In these cases the quasi-courting is

---

[14]The alarm bell rings when one party begins excluding others by seeking isolation or forming full and complete vis-à-vis postures with a partner, prolonging a quasi-courting involvement with one particular partner, or manifesting sexual responsivity, tactile contact, and so on.

overt, with lexical and tactile components. The illustrations in Figures 5, 6, and 7 from psychotherapy sessions are of the covert type usual in America.[15] I shall return to the overt uses at the end of the paper.

Figure 5 shows a sequence which occurred at the very beginning of a ninth session in which two male therapists were treating a young schizophrenic girl.

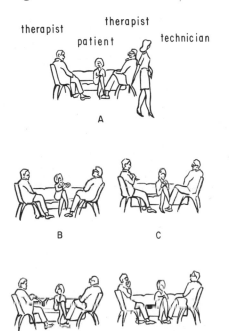

FIG. 5. QUASI-COURTING SEQUENCE THAT REESTABLISHED AN INTERRUPTED DOCTOR-PATIENT RELATIONSHIP.

At the beginning of the sequence (5A) the therapist on the viewer's left turns to watch an attractive research technician walk across the room. The patient begins to preen (5B). The therapist turns back to the patient and also preens (5C, 5D), but he then disclaims courtship by an ostentatious look of boredom and a yawn (5E). Immediately afterward, the patient tells him she is interested in an attractive male aide.

The sequence depicted in Figure 6 occurred in an initial inter-

---

[15]The examples are taken from therapy sessions in which more than two persons were involved. We prefer to study sequences of quasi-courting in a larger group because behaviors of additional interactants form a context in which to test function.

view conducted by a British family therapist with a British family. The situation at the beginning of the sequence is shown in 6A. Next to the therapist are the patient (a young schizophrenic), her mother, her mother's mother, and her father. Whenever—and this occurs many times during the session—the therapist is in a conversation with either the daughter or the grandmother, the mother moves

FIG. 6. Quasi-courting sequence that ended in
a realignment of relationships.

into courtship readiness and begins coquettish expressions and movements. She crosses her legs and extends them, places her hand on her hip, and learns forward (6B). Invariably the therapist responds by preening and turning to the mother, asking her a question (6C). Both of the other women immediately place a leg across the space between the mother and therapist, "boxing in" the mother (6D). The mother then "decourts";[16] she goes out of courting tonus,

---

[16]Decourting is a term we use to indicate the withdrawal from a courtship or quasi-courtship. It includes, of course, cessation of courtship readiness and withholding of courting behaviors. But the effect can be more profound and include actually becoming unattractive, withdrawing from relationship entirely, and so on. Decourting accounts for many of the well-known phenomena in which men and women who are ordinarily deemed attractive suddenly appear unattractive or even repellent. Often the other person attributes such changes, if he tries to explain them at all, as due to ill health, weight loss or weight gain, or something of the sort.

sits back, and stops her coquettish behavior (6E). The daughter and grandmother "box in" the flirtatious mother after a signal (foot-waving) from the father (6D).[17]

The next example occurred in a first session of family therapy. The situation was as follows: The young daughter had at the beginning of the session shown very high courtship readiness toward

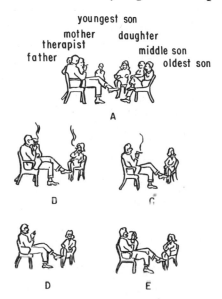

FIG. 7. ANOTHER TYPE OF REALIGNMENT FOLLOWING A QUASI-COURTING SEQUENCE.

the therapist. But when he avoided glancing at or speaking to her, she gradually lost tonus and came to appear disinterested and remote. As the therapist continued to focus his attention upon the parents, two of the other children, who seemed always to take their cues from their sister, also began to show signs of losing interest. It seemed at this point that the key to avoiding losing three of the family members called for tactical inclusion of this girl. But the father was holding the therapist in a compelling monologue which allowed no interruption. It was at this point that the therapist began the quasi-courting sequence, which is shown in Figure 7.

In 7A the quasi-sexual sequence between the therapist and the daughter begins with their holding gazes. In 7B the gaze-holding continues while they drag on their cigarettes in perfect synchrony. In 7C the daughter pulls away from the therapist's

[17]By American standards, this mother appeared to be courting, since qualifiers of the American type were absent. The monitoring by her family makes this conjecture probable.

gaze and sharply turns her head to her left, placing her arm across her lap as a barrier. In 7D she continues to avoid his gaze and begins to decourt. As she does so, she turns to her mother (7E), moving into synchronous smoking with her instead of with the therapist. She also from then on sits in the same posture as her mother. Thus, she ends the quasi-courting, moving into a relationship with her mother—not with the therapist. But she does not, from this point on, any longer dissociate herself from the group.

QUASI-COURTING AS A SYSTEMS-MAINTAINING DEVICE

One can ask: *"In what situations does quasi-courting appear?* and *What does it do in the interaction whenever it appears?*

Withdrawal or exclusion.   In the examples taken from the psychotherapy sessions, a certain context was evident at each appearance of quasi-courting: Some member of the group had withdrawn or had been excluded.

This happened in many other quasi-courting sequences that we have observed, both in psychotherapy and in other interactions. I think that the following generalizations are justified. In a twosome, quasi-courting is likely whenever one or the other of the participants turns away, withdraws, or appears preoccupied. In a larger group (such as a family in therapy, a party, or a meeting), quasi-courting appears in these same situations, and also when some member of the group has been ignored or excluded by others. If any group is to be maintained, a participant who is excluded or who dissociates himself is likely to be called back into relationship by the others. At the social level, then, quasi-courting is one kind of system-maintaining mechanism.[18] But it is only one such device. A withdrawing member might be called back with admonition, exhortation, tactile contact, and a host of other mechanisms. Shortly I shall discuss what specific conditions elicit quasi-courting rather than one of the other mechanisms.

Gender confusion.   Ambiguity arises when some participant behaves in a way that is inappropriate to his gender—for instance, when a woman acts very aggressive and domineering or a man behaves passively and femininely. Ambiguity can also arise about gender identification when the situation is such that some group member is placed in a position usually occupied by a member of the opposite sex—for instance, when two males are alone together at an intimate table in a nightclub. In such situations quasi-courting

---

[18]See Scheflen, "Communication and Regulation in Psycotherapy," in footnote 9. Also, Ray L. Birdwhistell, personal communication.

may appear. Here it seems to be a way of affirming gender or determining which member will fill some generally feminine or masculine role in the relationship. The quasi-sexual behavior generally
leads to heightening the signals of gender identification.

What Does Quasi-Courting Do in Interaction?

A person is said to be attractive when he has a compelling effect
upon the behavior of a partner or group. Certainly everyone has
experienced the effect of the arrival of an attractive person at a
dull business meeting. Attractiveness is elicited in others, and the
resulting interactions build up to provide an increased attentiveness
and readiness to relate by the whole group.[19] Thus a group can
become animated and cohesive enough to work together to complete
a dull or tedious task.

*I am suggesting that a great many different designations have
been previously applied to what is a single basic state of a human
organism.* This state is necessary to group cohesion and the completion of tasks that are not immediately gratifying. Some of the
different terms used to describe this state are attractiveness, attentiveness, sociability, readiness to relate, and quasi-courtship. I shall
also suggest that this favorable state is in some way a derivative
of sexualness—whatever that may be physiologically and psychologically—and indicative of some optimal state between immediate sexual preoccupation and marked sexual inhibition.

I presume that this is what is meant by the psychoanalytic concept of genitality[20]—a personality state that is considered a sublimation of sexual interest and characterized by such qualities as co-
operativeness, creativity, and the like. Conversely, in psychoanalytic
theory, pregenitality—in many respects comparable to our definition
of decourting—is associated with withdrawal, narcissism, suspicious-
ness, and other qualities inimical to group interests.

It is postulated, then, that quasi-courting is that set of system-

---

[19]This state can be put into terms that make it precisely definable and measurable.
In our research we use a concept of modes of communication, as described by Ray L.
Birdwhistell in Chapter 3 in *The Natural History of an Interview* (see footnote 8);
and also in personal communications. The alertness and attentiveness associated with
quasi-courting are usually seen as belonging to the *interpersonal* mode. Here an interactant projects his voice appropriately to the distance which lies between him and
his partner, converges his eyes appropriately, and uses a moderate to high muscle
tonus. On the other hand, an interactant who mumbles to himself, falls into hypotonus,
seems to converge on his own body, and so on, is said to be in the *intrapersonal* mode.
This mode is often seen in decourting persons.
[20]Sigmund Freud, "New Introductory Lectures on Psychoanalysis," *Standard Edition of the Complete Psychological Works*, Vol. 22 (London: Hogarth, 1964). Otto
Fenichel, *The Psychoanalytic Theory of the Neuroses* (New York: Norton, 1945).

maintaining devices that is used when the insufficiency in sociability
or attentiveness is due to some inhibition of this sexually derived
state.[21]

The foregoing postulation can be supported by observing the contexts in which decourting occurs—that is, the contexts in which existing states of courtship or courtship readiness disappear into dis-
sociation, unattractiveness, and loss of attentiveness. There are five
contexts in which I have often seen this occur: (1) When gender
confusion persists. For example, a woman engages a man with
preening and other quasi-courting behavior, but he responds with
high-pitched voice, cocked head, and eye flutter. The woman may
decourt if he persists in refusing her signals of gender identification.
(2) When there is ambiguity about whether the situation is one of
courtship or quasi-courtship. For example, a man moves actively
toward and into vis-à-vis with a woman without clear qualifiers. She
may decourt until he moves partly out of vis-à-vis and adds other
disclaimers. (3) When the other person quasi-courts too intensely.
The duration and frequency of courtship elements may approach
some disruptive level, or the context may be inappropriate even for
evident, clearly signaled quasi-courting. (4) When the group is
already in a high state of alertness or quasi-sexual tension and can
tolerate no more. If the quasi-courting member persists in his behavior, despite monitoring and disapproval of the group, the other
members may have to decourt to drop the level of tension. (5) When
other group members actively interfere with quasi-courting. For
example, in a family session whenever the daughter showed appealing behaviors, the mother engaged in monitoring activities until
the girl finally gave up and decourted.

Such contexts lead to an extinguishing of quasi-courtship readiness, and a decrease of attentiveness, relatedness, and other qualities necessary to sustain group participation. These unfavorable
states are correctable by proper quasi-courting sequences.

If it is true that quasi-courting is introduced and accepted in a
group in which there is a lack of alertness and interpersonal relatedness, and is not accepted in a group in which these qualities are
already high, then one can surmise that for any group, at any

<hr>

[21]The theoretical assumption behind this way of conceptualizing these organismic
states accords with current thinking in psychoanalysis and other fields. It presumes
there is an underlying state for sociability and relatedness that is basically libidinal or
derived from sexualness. It is, of course, possible that sexualness is, rather, another
derivative or activity that occurs in some basic organismic set of alertness.

point in an interaction, there is an optimal range of relatedness, alertness, and quasi-courting states. It can further be postulated, in the manner that is characteristic for describing stable systems, that reductions below the allowable minimum induce more quasi-courting, and that any threatened increase above some allowable maximum reduces it. The idea is thus derived that quasi-courting functions as a cybernetic type of governor for maintaining a favorable range of relatedness.

In the field of psychotherapy technique, this is not a new idea— in individual-centered terms, at least. Psychotherapists think of patients as having optimal states of transference or of sexual and dependent involvement. If they become too remote from the therapist, or so over-involved as to impair their lives outside the sessions, the therapist must exert an influence to remedy this. Traditionally psychotherapists have devices, so far not clearly described, for further engaging a patient or for cooling him off, to keep him within this favorable range. It appears that quasi-courting is one such device.

THE LANGUAGE OF EMOTIONS AND GESTURES*

Weston La Barre

The anthropologist is wary of those who speak of an "instinctive" gesture on the part of a human being. One important reason is that a sensitivity to meanings which are culturally different from his own stereotypes may on occasion be crucial for the anthropologist's own physical survival among at least some groups he studies, and he must at the very least be a student of this area of symbolism if he would avoid embarrassment.[1] He cannot safely rely upon his own culturally subjective understandings of emotional expression in his

---

*From "The Cultural Basis of Emotions and Gestures," *Journal of Personality*, Vol. 16 (1947), pp. 49–68. Abridged and reprinted by permission of the author and *Journal of Personality*.

[1] The notorious Massey murder in Hawaii arose from the fact that a native beach boy perhaps understandably mistook the Occidental "flirting" of a white woman for a *bona fide* sexual invitation. On the other hand, there are known cases which have ended in the death of American ethnographers who misread the cultural signs while in the field.

relations with persons of another tribe. The advisability and the value of a correct reading of any cultural symbolism whatsoever has alerted him to the possibility of culturally arbitrary, quasi-linguistic (that is, noninstinctual but learned and purely agreed-upon) meanings in the behavior he observes.

GESTURES EXPRESSING AGREEMENT AND DISAGREEMENT

A rocking of the skull forward and backward upon its condyles, which rest on the atlas vertebra, as an indication of affirmation, and the rotation upon the axis vertebra for negation have so far been accepted as "natural" and "instinctive" gestures that one psychologist at least[2] has sought an explanation of the supposedly universal phenomenon in ascribing the motions of "yes" to the infant's seeking of the mother's breast, and "no" to its avoidance and refusal of the breast. This is ingenious, but it is reckoning without one's host, since the phenomenon to be explained is by no means as widespread ethnologically, even among humans, as is mammalian behavior biologically.

Indeed, the Orient alone is rich in alternatives. Among the Ainu of northern Japan, for example, our particular head noddings are unknown:

the right hand is usually used in negation, passing from right to left and back in front of the chest; and both hands are gracefully brought up to the chest and gracefully waved downwards—palms upwards—in sign of affirmation.[3]

The Semang, pygmy Negroes of interior Malaya, thrust the head sharply forward for "yes" and cast the eyes down for "no."[4]

The Abyssinians say "no" by jerking the head to the right shoulder, and "yes" by throwing the head back and raising the eyebrows. The Dyaks of Borneo raise their eyebrows to mean "yes" and contract them slightly to mean "no." The Maori say "yes" by raising the head and chin; the Sicilians say "no" in exactly the same manner.[5]

A Bengali servant in Calcutta rocks his head rapidly in an arc from shoulder to shoulder, usually four times, in assent; in Delhi a Moslem boy throws his head diagonally backward with a slight turning of the neck for the same purpose; and the Kandyan Singhalese bends the head diagonally forward toward the right, with an indescribably

---

[2]E. B. Holt, *Animal Drive and the Learning Process* (New York, 1931), p. 111, and personal conversations.

[3]A. H. S. Landor, *Alone with the Hairy Ainu* (London, 1893), pp. 6, 233–34.

[4]W. W. Skeat and C. O. Blagden, *Pagan Races of the Malay Peninsula* (2 vols.; London, 1906).

[5]Otto Klineberg, *Race Differences* (New York, 1935), p. 282.

graceful turning in of the chin, often accompanying this with a cross-legged curtsey, arms partly crossed, palms upward—the whole performance extraordinarily beautiful and ingratiating. Indeed did my own cultural difference not tell me it already, I would know that the Singhalese manner of receiving an object (with the right hand, the left palm supporting the right elbow) is not instinctive, for I have seen a Singhalese mother *teaching* her little boy to do this when I gave him a chunk of palm-tree sugar. I only regretted, later, that my own manners must have seemed boorish or subhuman, since I handed it to him with my right hand, instead of with both, as would any courteous Singhalese. Alas, if I had handed it to a little Moslem beggar in Sind or the Punjab with my *left* hand, he would probably have dashed the gift to the ground, spat, and called me by the name of an animal whose flesh he had been taught to dislike, but which I have not—for such use of the left hand would be insulting, since it is supposed to be confined to attending to personal functions, while the right hand is the only proper one for food.

THE POINTED FOREFINGER

Those persons with a passion for easy dominance, the professional dog lovers, must often be exasperated at the stupidity of a dog which does not respond to so obvious a command as the pointed forefinger. The defense of man's best friend might be that this "instinctively" human gesture does not correspond to the kinaesthesias of a nonhanded animal. Nevertheless, even for an intelligent human baby, at the exact period when he is busily using the forefinger in exploring the world, "pointing" by an adult is an arbitrary, sublinguistic gesture which is not automatically understood and which must be *taught*. I am the less inclined to berate the obtuseness to the obvious of either dog or baby, because of an early field experience of my own. One day I asked a favorite informant of mine among the Kiowa, old Mary Buffalo, where something was in the *ramada* or willow-branch "shade" where we were working. It was clear she had heard me, for her eighty-eight-year-old ears were by no means deaf; but she kept on busying both hands with her work. I wondered at her rudeness and repeated the request several times, until finally with a puzzled exasperation which matched my own, she dropped her work and fetched it for me from in plain sight: she had been repeatedly pointing with her lips in approved American Indian fashion, as any Caucasian numbskull should have been able to see.

EXPRESSIONS OF JOY AND SADNESS

Some time afterward I asked a somewhat naive question of a very great anthropologist, the late Edward Sapir: "Do other tribes cry and laugh as we do?" In appropriate response, Sapir himself laughed, but with an instant grasping of the point of the question: in which of these things are men alike everywhere, in which different? Where are the international boundaries between physiology and culture? What are the extremes of variability, and what are the scope and range of cultural differences in emotional and gestural expression?

Smiling, indeed, I have found may almost be mapped after the fashion of any other culture trait; and laughter is in some senses a geographic variable. On a map of the Southwest Pacific one could perhaps even draw lines between areas of "Papuan hilarity" and others where a Dobuan, Melanesian dourness reigned. In Africa, Gorer noted that:

laughter is used by the Negro to express surprise, wonder, embarrassment and even discomfiture; it is not necessarily, or even often, a sign of amusement; the significance given to "black laughter" is due to a mistake of supposing that similar symbols have identical meanings.[6]

Thus it is that even if the physiological behavior be present, its cultural and emotional functions may differ. Indeed, even within the same culture, the laughter of adolescent girls and the laughter of corporation presidents can be functionally different things; so too the laughter of an American Negro and that of the white he addresses.

The behaviorist Holt "physiologized" the smile as being ontogenetically the relaxation of the muscles of the face in a baby replete from nursing. Explanations of this order may well be the case, if the phenomenon of the smile is truly a physiological expression of generalized pleasure, which is caught up later in ever more complex conditioned reflexes. And yet, even in its basis here, I am not sure that this is the whole story: for the "smile" of a child in its sleep is certainly in at least some cases the grimace of *pain* from colic, rather than the relaxation of pleasure. Other explanations such as that the smile is *phylogenetically* a snarl suffer from much the same *ad hoc* quality.

Klineberg writes:

It is quite possible, however, that a smile or a laugh may have a different mean-

---

[6]Geoffrey Gorer, *Africa Dances* (New York, 1935), p. 10.

ing for groups other than our own. Lafcadio Hearn has remarked that the Japanese smile is not necessarily a spontaneous expression of amusement, but a law of etiquette, elaborated and cultivated from early times. It is a silent language, often seemingly inexplicable to Europeans, and it may arouse violent anger in them as a consequence. The Japanese child is taught to smile as a social duty, just as he is taught to bow or prostrate himself; he must always show an appearance of happiness to avoid inflicting his sorrow upon his friends. The story is told of a woman servant who smilingly asked her mistress if she might go to her husband's funeral. Later she returned with his ashes in a vase and said, actually laughing, "Here is my husband." Her White mistress regarded her as a cynical creature; Hearn suggests that this may have been pure heroism.[7]

Many in fact of these motor habits in one culture are open to grave misunderstanding in another. The Copper Eskimo welcome strangers with a buffet on the head or shoulders with the fist, while the northwest Amazonians slap one another on the back in greeting. Polynesian men greet each other by embracing and rubbing one another's back; Spanish-American males greet one another by a stereotyped embrace, head over right shoulder of the partner, three pats on the back, head over reciprocal left shoulder, three more pats. In the Torres Straits islands "the old form of greeting was to bend slightly the fingers of the right hand, hook them with those of the person greeted, and then draw them away so as to scratch the palm of the hand; this is repeated several times."[8] The Ainu of Yezo have a peculiar greeting; on the occasion of a man meeting his sister, "The man held the woman's hands for a few seconds, then suddenly releasing his hold, grasped her by both ears and uttered the Aino cry. Then they stroked one another down the face and shoulders."[9] Kayan males in Borneo embrace or grasp each other by the forearm, while a host throws his arm over the shoulder of a guest and strokes him endearingly with the palm of his hand. When two Burd males meet, "they grasp each other's right hand, which they simultaneously raise, and each kisses the hand of the other."[10] Among the Andaman Islanders of the Gulf of Bengal:

When two friends or relatives meet who have been separated from each other for a few weeks or longer, they greet each other by sitting down, one on the

[7]Lafcadio Hearn, "The Japanese Smile," in *Glimpses of Unfamiliar Japan* (2 vols.; New York, 1894), quoted in Klineberg.

[8]A. C. Haddon (ed.), *Report on the Cambridge Expedition to the Torres Straits* (5 vols.; Cambridge, 1904), IV, 306; Thomas Whiffen, *The North West Amazons* (London, 1905), p. 259.

[9]R. Hitchcock, "The Ainos of Yezo," in *Papers on Japan*, pp. 464–65. See also Landor, pp. 6, 233–34.

[10]J. Perkins, "Journal of a Tour from Oroomish to Mosul, through the Koordish Mountains, and a Visit to the Ruins of Nineveh, "*Journal of the American Oriental Society*, Vol. 2 (1851), p. 101; Charles Hose & William MacDougall, *The Pagan Tribes of Borneo* (2 vols.; London, 1912), I, 124–25.

lap of the other, with their arms around each other's necks, and weeping or
wailing for two or three minutes till they are tired. Two brothers greet each
other in this way, and so do father and son, mother and daughter, and husband and wife. When husband and wife meet, it is the man who sits in the
lap of the woman. When two friends part from one another, one of them
lifts up the hand of the other towards his mouth and gently blows on it.[11]

Some of these expressions of "joy" seem more lugubrious than
otherwise. One old voyager, John Turnbull, writes as follows:

The arrival of a ship brings them to the scene of action from far and near.
Many of them meet at Matavai who have not seen each other for some length
of time. The ceremony of these meetings is not without singularity; taking a
shark's tooth, they strike it into their head and temples with great violence, so
as to produce a copious bleeding; and this they will repeat, till they become
clotted with blood and gore.

The honest mariner confesses to be nonplussed at this behavior.

I cannot explain the origin of this custom, nor its analogy with what it is intended to express. It has no other meaning with them than to express the
excess of their joy. By what construction it is considered symbolical of this
emotion I do not understand.[12]

Quite possibly, then, the weeping of an American woman "because
she is so happy" may merely indicate that the poverty of our gamut
of physiological responses is such as to require using the same response for opposite meanings. Certainly weeping does obey social
stereotypes in other cultures. Consider old Mary Buffalo at her
brother's funeral: she wept in a frenzy, tore her hair, scratched her
cheeks, and even tried to jump into the grave (being conveniently
restrained from this by remoter relatives). I happened to know that
she had not seen her brother for some time, and there was no particular love lost between them: she was merely carrying on the way
a decent woman should among the Kiowa. Away from the grave,
she was immediately chatting vivaciously about some other topic.
Weeping is *used* differently among the Kiowa. Any stereotypes I
may have had about the strong and silent American Indian, whose
speech is limited to an infrequent "ugh" and whose stoicism to pain
is limitless, were once rudely shattered in a public religious meeting.
A great burly Wichita Indian, who had come with me to a peyote
meeting, after a word with the leader which I did not understand
(it was probably permission to take his turn in a prayer) suddenly
burst out blubbering with an abandon which no Occidental male
adult would permit himself in public. In time I learned that this

---

[11]A. R. Radcliffe-Brown, *The Andaman Islanders* (Cambridge, 1922), p. 117 and
p. 74 n. 1.
[12]John Turnbull, *A Voyage Round the World* (London, 1813), pp. 301-2.

was a stereotyped approach to the supernatural powers, enthusiastic weeping to indicate that he was as powerless as a child, to invoke their pity, and to beseech their gift of medicine power. Everyone in the tipi understood this except me.

So much for the expression of emotion in one culture, which is open to serious misinterpretation in another: there is no "natural" language of emotional gesture. To return a moment to the earlier topic of emotional expression in greetings: West Africans in particular have developed highly the ritual gestures and language of greeting. What Gorer says of the Wolof would stand for many another tribe:

> The gestures and language of polite intercourse are stylized and graceful; a greeting is a formal litany of question and answer embracing everyone and everything connected with the two people meeting (the questions are merely formal and a dying person is stated to be in good health so as not to break the rhythm of the responses) and continuing for several minutes; women accompany it with a swaying movement of the body; with people to whom a special deference is due the formula is resumed several times during the conversation; saying goodbye is equally elaborate.[13]

But here the sublinguistic gesture language has clearly emerged into pure formalisms of language which are quite plainly cultural.

ONE GESTURE, MANY MEANINGS

The allegedly "instinctive" nature of such motor habits in personal relationships is difficult to maintain in the face of the fact that in many cases the same gesture means exactly opposite, or incommensurable things, in different cultures. Hissing in Japan is a polite deference to social superiors; the Basuto applaud by hissing, but in England hissing is rude and public disapprobation of an actor or a speaker. Spitting in very many parts of the world is a sign of utmost contempt; and yet among the Masai of Africa it is a sign of affection and benediction, while the spitting of an American Indian medicine man upon a patient is one of the kindly offices of the curer. Urination upon another (as in a famous case at the Sands Point, Long Island, country club, involving a congressman since assassinated) is a grave insult among Occidentals, but it is part of the transfer of

---

[13]Gorer, p. 38. Cf. Hollis, *The Masai, Their Language and Folklore* (Oxford, 1905), pp. 284–87; E. Torday and T. A. Joyce, *Notes ethnographiques sur les peuples communément appelés Bakuba, ainsi que sur les peuplades apparentées, les Bushonga* (Brussels, 1910), pp. 233–34, 284, *et passim.* West Africans have developed the etiquette and protocol of greeting to a high degree, adjusting it to sex, age, relative rank, relationship degrees, and the like. Probably there is more than a trace of this ceremoniousness surviving in American Negro greetings in the South.

power from an African medicine man in initiations and curing rituals. As for other opposite meanings, Western man stands up in the presence of a superior; the Fijians and the Tongans sit down. In some contexts we put on more clothes as a sign of respect; the Friendly Islanders take them off. The Toda of South India raise the open right hand to the face, with the thumb on the bridge of the nose, to express respect; a gesture almost identical among Europeans is an obscene expression of extreme disrespect. Placing to the tip of the nose the projecting knuckle of the right forefinger bent at the second joint was among the Maori of New Zealand a sign of friendship and often of protection;[14] but in eighteenth-century England the placing of the same forefinger to the right side of the nose expressed dubiousness about the intelligence and sanity of a speaker— much as does the twentieth-century clockwise motion of the forefinger above the right hemisphere of the head. The sticking out of the tongue among Europeans (often at the same time "making a face") is an insulting, almost obscene, act of provocative challenge and mocking contempt for the adversary, so undignified as to be used only by children; so long as Maya writing remains undeciphered we do not know the meaning of the exposure of the tongue in some religious sculptures of the gods, but we can be sure it scarcely has the same significance as with us. In Bengali statues of the dread black mother goddess Kali, the tongue is protruded to signify great raging anger and shock; but the Chinese of the Sung dynasty protruded the tongue playfully to pretend to mock terror, as if to "make fun of" the ridiculous and unfeared anger of another person.[15] Modern Chinese, in South China at least, protrude the tongue for a moment and then retract it, to express embarrassment at a *faux pas*.

Kissing, as is well known, is in the Orient an act of private loveplay and arouses only disgust when indulged in publicly: in Japan it is necessary to censor out the major portion of love scenes in American-made movies for this reason. Correspondingly, some of the old *kagura* dances of the Japanese strike Occidentals as revolting overt obscenities, yet it is doubtful if they arouse this response in Japanese onlookers. Manchu kissing is purely a private sexual act,

[14]Klineberg, pp. 286–87, citing J. Lubbock, *Prehistoric Times* (New York, 1872); E. Best, *The Maori* (2 vols.; Wellington [N. Z.], 1924); R. H. Lowie, *Are We Civilized?* (New York, 1929); and A. C. Hollis, *The Masai, Their Language and Folklore* (Oxford, 1905), p. 315.
[15]*Chin P'ing Mei* (Shanghai, n. d.), Introduction by Arthur Waley. The 16th-century Chinese also had the expressions to act "with seven hands and eight feet" for awkwardness, and "to sweat two handfuls of anxiety."

and though husband and wife or lovers might kiss each day, they would do it stealthily since it is shameful to do in public; yet Manchu mothers have the pattern of putting the penis of the baby boy into their mouths, a practice which probably shocks Westerners even more than kissing in public shocks the Manchu.[16] Tapuya men in South America kiss as a sign of peace, but men do not kiss women because the latter wear labrets or lip plugs. Nose-rubbing is Eskimo and Polynesian; and the Djuka Negroes of Surinam[17] show pleasure at a particularly interesting or amusing dance step by embracing the dancer and touching cheek to cheek, now on one side, now on the other—which is the identical attenuation of the "social kiss" between American women who do not wish to spoil each other's makeup.

In the language of gesture all over the world there are varying mixtures of the physiologically conditioned response and the purely cultural one, and it is frequently difficult to analyze out and segregate the two. The Chukchee of Siberia, for example, have a phenomenal quickness to anger, which they express by showing the teeth and growling like an animal—yet man's snout has long ceased being functionally useful in offensive or defensive biting as it has phylogenetically and continuously retreated from effective prognathism. But this behavior reappears again and again: the Malayan pagans, for example, raise the lip over the canine tooth when sneering and jeering. Is this instinctual reflex or mere motor habit? The Tasmanians stamped rapidly on the ground to express surprise or pleasure; Occidentals beat the palms of the hands together for the same purpose ordinarily, but in some rowdier contexts this is accompanied by whistling and a similar stamping of the feet. Europeans "snort" with contempt; and the non-Mohammedan primitives of interior Malaya express disgust with a sudden expiration of the breath. In this particular instance, it is difficult to rid oneself of the notion that this is a consciously controlled act, to be sure, but nevertheless at least a symbolic "sneeze" based upon a purely physiological reflex which does rid the nostrils of irritating matter. The favorite gesture of contempt of the Menomini Indians of Wisconsin—raising the clenched fist palm down up to the level of the mouth, then bringing it swiftly downwards, throwing forth the thumb and first two fingers—would seem to be based on the same "instinctual" notion of rejection.

---

[16]S. M. Shirokogoreff, *Social Organization of the Manchus* (Extra Vol. III, North China Branch, Royal Asiatic Society, Shanghai, 1924), pp. 122–23.
[17]M. C. Kahn, "Notes on the Saramaccaner Bush Negroes of Dutch Guiana," *American Anthropologist*, Vol. 31 (1929), p. 473.

PART II

Some Interpersonal Aspects of Self-Confirmation

INTRODUCTION

American psychology has only recently acknowledged the important role played by human relationships in man's search for a sense of personal identity and personal worth. Perhaps Harry Stack Sullivan and Carl Rogers more than any other writers have been responsible for this humanizing trend in our psychological tradition. One of the most important contributions of this trend has been the emphasis it has placed on the individual's potential for personal development and growth. This essay will examine some of the interpersonal processes relevant to such personal development.

In this essay we shall discuss what we believe to be two major components or subprocesses of self-confirmation. We shall call the first of these the process of *self-evaluation*. All of us have beliefs about our relative and our ultimate worth. We feel superior to some persons but inferior to others. We may or may not feel "worthy." Most of us expend considerable energy trying to maintain or change our beliefs about how good we are. It is this continual process of self-evaluation and re-evaluation that determines an individual's level of self-esteem or sense of personal worth.

We shall refer to the second major component of self-confirmation as the process of *self-definition*. Just as we have beliefs about our worth, so we also have beliefs about who we are and what we are. Some persons, particularly adolescents, seem to be engaged in a desperate struggle to define themselves. Others appear to be concerned primarily with maintaining or preserving beliefs about themselves. Still other persons seem to know what they are now, but are intent on discovering what they might become. In every case, however, attempts to define the self result in certain beliefs about the self, or what we shall refer to as a "self-image" or "identity."[1]

The first section of this essay will examine some of the interpersonal aspects of *self-evaluation*. Our primary focus will be on *re-evaluation* of self, or the possibility of change in level of self-esteem after adolescence. However, the section begins with a discussion of the initial development of self-esteem, and an examination of some critical elements of parent-child interaction. After a description of several possible outcomes of early relationships, we turn to a consideration of strategies for maintaining self-esteem. The first section closes with a consideration of self-exposure as a strategy for testing possibly invalid assumptions about self-worth, and an examination of some problems involved in obtaining useful "evaluative" feedback.

The second section of the essay examines the relevance of interpersonal relationships to the process of *self-definition*. The section begins with a brief examination of some ways an identity is formed, and then takes up problems of maintaining an identity or self-image. The second section closes with consideration of the possibility of enlarging or extending one's personal identity. The concept of "selflessness" and the role of "descriptive" feedback from other persons are discussed in this context.

SELF-EVALUATION

A. The Development of Self-Esteem

The basic unit of interaction that concerns us is a very simple one. One person acts and in doing so intentionally or unintentionally exposes a part of his self—something of what he is, or thinks he is, or hopes he is. A second person responds to the first person's act and to his exposed self. Very frequently his reactions convey approval or disapproval, acceptance or rejection. In this simple unit of social interaction lies one of the keys of the process of self-evaluation.

The process of learning about ourselves begins very early in life. Clearly not all of it involves social interaction. The infant explores

---

[1]"Identity," "self-concept," and "self-image" are used interchangeably in this eassy.

his body and experiences recurrent organic sensations which lead to the evolution of a sense of bodily self. He interacts with his physical environment and learns the distinction between what is himself and what is not himself. But the infant also learns very quickly that some of his actions elicit responses of approval, attention, love. Others seem to go unnoticed. Still others are responded to with withdrawal, coldness, or irritation. As he progresses from infancy to young childhood, he discovers more and more evaluative elements in the responses of others to his behavior or to his self.

The result of these different responses to his acts soon becomes quite apparent. Acts that elicit responses of attention or approval or affection tend to occur more and more frequently. Behavior that elicits withdrawal or coldness or rejection occurs less and less frequently.[2] Gradually the overt personality of the child, as manifested in his behavior, is shaped by the people with whom he interacts.

However, because of the human capacity for self-consciousness, the process of personality formation is not entirely a matter of simple reinforcement. The child's patterns of behavior arouse responses *within himself* leading to a set of perceptions of himself which become stable. Once a self as a stabilizing concept begins to emerge, the child associates certain of his acts with this self, even if others ignore or punish them. In this case the acts may become a covert part of the child's self, and others' responses to those acts become judgments of parts of the child's self.

Most of us who are parents set an impossible task for ourselves: we want our children to believe that our love for them is unconditional but we also want them to behave in a reasonable acceptable manner. To accomplish the latter we must respond differentially to their behaviors, to the different parts of their selves that are manifested in their behavior. We must communicate approval in response to some, disapproval in response to others. A child must inevitably experience our disapproval as a withholding or withdrawal of love, *and therefore our love as conditional,* regardless of our intentions and real feelings.

It may be helpful to think rather crudely of the evolution of a "good self" and a "bad self." We behave, and in doing so we always manifest or expose a part of our self. In some cases our behavior

---

[2]There are, of course, exceptions to this general tendency, such as when a child resists or aggresses against his parents, or tests their love by being "bad," or more pathological cases where the child acts in order to obtain a response—any response—in order to establish an *existence,* regardless of the evaluation of these elicitative acts.

elicits a response from others that we perceive as accepting, approving, loving. Thus we learn that certain parts of our selves are acceptable and lovable. Subjectively, we experience these parts of our self as our "good self." In other instances, our acts elicit reactions we perceive as disapproving, rejecting, unloving. When this happens we learn that certain parts of our self are not acceptable or lovable to others. These we experience as our "bad self."[3]

What we have described is congruent with Freud's notions about self-esteem or self-love as outlined in his paper. "On Narcissism: An Introduction".[4] Freud argued that the infant cathects his ego, or loves himself as he is. Thus he is completely acceptable to himself and his self-love or self-esteem is maximal. However, as the infant becomes a child he learns the difference between what he is and what his parents (and society) want him to be. He learns that certain parts of himself are no longer acceptable and lovable to his parents. Two things then happen. First, his libido deserts his ego and cathects an idealized image of his self that he feels would be completely accepted and loved by his parents, i.e., his ego ideal. He no longer loves and accepts himself for what he is, but rather loves and accepts himself only to the extent that he approximates his ego ideal. Effectively, then, the acceptance or rejection of others determines his acceptability to himself, or his self-esteem. Second, he tends to repress or suppress those parts of his self that are not consonant with his ego ideal. They become his "bad" self, unacceptable and unlovable to others and thus to himself.

Types of Outcomes of Parental Strategies.   Generally speaking, we can conceive of three types of outcomes of early experiences with acceptance and rejection:

1. A person may learn that no matter how he behaves or tries to "be," he cannot be assured of the love and esteem of other people. He becomes convinced of his own worthlessness, or at the very least, has serious doubts about his lovability. Maternally deprived and rejected children will often fall in this category.

There are several behavior patterns we might expect from the individual with very low self-esteem. He may simply give up. This might take the form of deep depression and suicidal tendencies, or

---

[3]Those parts of the "bad self" which we selectively *inattend-to* would comprise what Sullivan calls the "not self."

[4]S. Freud, "On Narcissism: An Introduction," in *Collected Papers*, Vol. IV, Joan Riviere (trans.) (London: Hogarth Press, 1956).

of acting out good and bad impulses alike without regard for the reactions of other people or of society generally. Such a person might exhibit his "bad self," either to confirm his feelings of worthlessness or to receive the punishment he feels he deserves.

The person who has not given up, who has accepted himself as a person with some worth, will behave quite differently. He may expose to other people as little of his self as possible to avoid the feedback that will confirm his fears. Or he may behave narcissistically by exposing only the best things about his self, or things that are not really his self at all, and demand the approval and love of others. But as long as there is a glimmer of hope, exposing much of his real self is a terrible risk because one bit of negative feedback, real or perceived, may serve to extinguish that glimmer.

2. A second outcome of early experience, at the opposite extreme from the first, is to learn that love is unconditional, that whatever one does or feels—or *is*—he is loved and is therefore worthy of love. In our society, given the socialization practices we employ, this outcome is rarely observed. A person with such high self-esteem will be capable of responding naturally and spontaneously, as a whole person, in any situation. The possibility that relationships after childhood can lead to such an outcome will be discussed later in this essay.

3. It is with the third outcome, somewhere between the first and second, that most of us must live. We have learned that we are loved and are worthy of love at certain times but not at other times. Whether we are loved or not depends on how we are behaving, what parts of ourselves we are exposing. As we pass childhood this becomes translated into a feeling that certain things about us are acceptable and lovable, whereas other things are not. This outcome tends to be associated with several behavioral strategies designed to maintain or preserve self-esteem.

B. Maintaining Self-Esteem

The feeling or expectancy that if someone knew everything about us they could not accept or love us has profound implications for behavior. There appear to be three primary effects. First, it leads to a tendency to *hide* those parts of our self which we feel are less than totally acceptable. We relate to others as part persons rather than whole persons.

Second, the feeling that parts of our self are unlovable often results in a tendency to *pretend* we are something we are not, to wear masks, to erect facades.[5] Pretending has a number of advantages over hiding. For one thing it includes hiding; we can play a part that does not include "bad" parts of our self. We can even act out or expose our "bad self," but as part of the role we are playing, not as part of us.[6] If we are rejected while playing a part we are comforted by our belief that it is not our real self that has been found wanting.[7]

Third, doubts concerning self-worth encourage *cautious and ritualized behavior*. To respond spontaneously and naturally involves the risk of unintentional exposure of "bad" parts of the self and the possibility that fears of unacceptability will be confirmed. Thus there is a tendency not to be spontaneous or natural but to be guarded and deliberate in any new situation that may arise. Often persons who are reserved or aloof are in fact exercising caution.

All three of the effects described above are essentially strategies designed to avoid the rejection anticipated if more of the self were visible to others. Fear of rejection in this case stems not so much from the possible frustration of affiliative needs as from possible confirmation of the person's fears of being unacceptable to others. Maintaining self-esteem is a life-long concern for most of us, and for many of us the possibility of even a single instance of rejection by another presents a terrible threat and one to be carefully guarded against.

C. Re-evaluation of Self

1. *Self-Exposure.*   The same strategies or behavior tendencies that serve to maintain self-esteem also prevent any real self-growth. There can be no basic change in self-esteem without testing the assumption that if others knew certain things about us we would be unloved. That assumption cannot be tested except by exposing

[5]Carl Rogers in *On Becoming a Person* (Boston: Houghton-Mifflin, 1961), chap. 18., subsumes both hiding and pretending under the more general heading of "incongruence." People are incongruent, according to Rogers, when there is a lack of correspondence or match between (1) what they are experiencing and their awareness of it, or (2) their awareness and what they communicate about their awareness to other persons. In the first instance, they are hiding from or deluding themselves; in the second they are hiding from or deluding others.

[6]Erving Goffman focuses on impression making and pretense in his book, *The Presentation of Self in Everyday Life* (Garden City, N.Y.: Doubleday Anchor, 1959). In his brilliant paper, "On Face-Work: An Analysis of Ritual Elements in Social Interaction," (page 226, this volume) he analyzes social rituals that facilitate both "hiding" and "pretending."

[7]Helene Deutsch analyzes some of the subtle dynamics of pretending and being exposed in her excellent paper, "The Impostor: Contribution to Ego Psychology of a Type of Psychopath," (page 249, this volume).

all of the self to others and observing their reaction. We may discover that others accept and love us even after we have exposed
our "bad self" to them. If so, relearning or re-evaluation of self
can occur, leading to a greater sense of personal worth. Of course,
we may also have our fear that we are unworthy of love confirmed
by others and thus experience a loss of self-esteem.

2. *Validity of Assumptions about Self-Worth.* What chance is
there that a person's doubts about his self-worth are realistic? If his
doubts are unwarranted, testing through self-exposure should logically lead to their dissipation or extinction. But if they are realistic
fears, greater exposure of self may lead only to their reinforcement
and a further loss of self-esteem.

There are several reasons for expecting doubts about self-worth
to be unrealistic, mostly stemming from the fact that the most serious of these doubts originate in infancy and early childhood. First,
some of the most persistent assumptions about the acceptability or
unacceptability of parts of the self are formed before the child's
faculties for making fine discriminations have fully developed, resulting in a tendency for him to over generalize.[8] For example, a
child who feels threatened with loss of love for hitting other children may "learn" to believe that any of the aggressive impulses he
feels make him unworthy of love.

Second, a child cannot be objective about his parent's love for
him and may see the threat of loss of love where in fact it does not
exist. His perceptions may be distorted or autistic due to immature
notions of causality, a vague conception of time, intense affect, or
a simple lack of experience and the perspective it provides. This
can lead to invalid assumptions, as when a child assumes that
something he did caused his mother to desert him, when in fact she
had to go to the hospital.

A third reason we can expect many assumptions about self-worth
to be invalid is that they are frequently based on the reactions of
just one or two persons, usually the parents. Parents may find something about their child unacceptable because they are intolerant
and not capable of loving any other human unconditionally, or because the child has become involved in his parent's neurosis.[9] In
other cases, changing standards of behavior make it impossible for

---

[8]For an illuminating and thorough discussion of the characteristics of learning that
occurs during infancy and early childhood, see D. C. McClelland, *Personality* (New
York: Holt, Rinehart and Winston, 1951), pp. 441–58.

[9]For an enlightening discussion of neurotic interaction between parent and child,
see E. Vogel and N. Bell, "The Emotionally Disturbed Child as the Family Scapegoat," in this volume, page 90.

parents to accept their children, and for their children to accept themselves. Because of changed attitudes toward sex in our society, for example, strictly brought up young people often experience guilt and loss of self-esteem for behaving in ways that are unacceptable to their parents but perfectly acceptable among their peers.

Finally, the simple fact that what may be quite unacceptable in a child may be acceptable or even desirable in an adolescent or adult may lead to incorrect assumptions about self-worth. A child may feel threatened by loss of love if he is willful or overly independent as a child. However, this same independence in the male adult may lead to acceptance and success.

To summarize, the probability that an individual's doubts about his self-worth are based on adequate evidence of his unacceptability to a number of relatively unconflicted persons who know him well is very low.

3. *Evaluative Feedback.* By "evaluative feedback" we mean social cues or "reflected self-appraisals" useful for evaluation or re-evaluation of the self. Not all persons are concerned with self-improvement. Persons with low self-esteem, for example, are primarily concerned with *reassurance.* They tend to search others' responses to them only for clues of approval or disapproval, acceptance or rejection. Narcissists seek the compliments, admiration, and applause of other persons in a desperate and continuous effort to dispel doubts about their ultimate worth as human beings. There is little concern among such people for realistic self-appraisal or self-improvement.

For most persons, however, evaluative feedback serves a potentially useful function. Through self-exposure and feedback persons can test assumptions about their acceptability or lovability and thereby develop greater self-esteem. Evaluative feedback makes it possible to develop and maintain a realistic conception of one's competencies and liabilities, strengths and weaknesses. Finally, evaluative feedback serves as a basis for self-improvement; unless we become aware of our weaknesses and shortcomings, we cannot set about overcoming them.

There are two general classes of social responses that people tend to use as feedback for purposes of evaluating self-worth. When people interact, however formally or impersonally, they frequently give off very subtle cues regarding their feelings about the other person. We can call this *indirect feedback.* The second class, which we will call *direct feedback,* consists of verbal statements explicitly describing one person's perceptions of or reactions to another.

There are several points of interest concerning the nature and use of indirect feedback. It is often ambiguous. A smile may be a polite social habit, but it may also convey warmth and approval. Aloofness may indicate disapproval, but it may also indicate an individual's fear of intimacy. The problem of ambiguous feedback is magnified by the fact that people tend to see what they expect to see, to be particularly sensitive to those cues in their environment which confirm their expectancies. Thus, if a person expects others to find him unacceptable, he will tend to see smiles as polite only and aloofness as rejection.

Indirect feedback tends to be overgeneralized. The feeling that we are being rejected, if the cues are subtle, may develop gradually. If so, it is difficult to associate someone's rejection of us with a specific act, or one small part of our self that we exposed. Rather, we tend to experience the incident as a rejection of our whole self, or all those parts of our self about which we have doubts.

Indirect feedback does not allow for justification or explanation. It frequently happens that we find something about another person unacceptable until we understand why he is that way, until he has a chance to explain his self to us.

Just as frequently the feedback may reveal more about the giver than the receiver. If inaccurate feedback is communicated indirectly, there is little chance it will be questioned or corrected by others. If the reason for another's reaction to us cannot be openly explored, there is no way to determine whether or not the feedback was justified.

It should be clear that indirect feedback is not very useful, and can be harmful, for purposes of self-evaluation. The person receiving the feedback must draw inferences from subtle, often ambiguous, cues without the opportunity to explore the exact meaning of or reasons for the feedback.

Direct feedback is potentially more useful for evaluating self-worth. However, even direct feedback can be useless if it does not reflect frank appraisals or reactions.

One major reason for lack of frankness is our cultural taboo on criticizing another person, particularly to his face. We tend to admire people who claim, "There is some good in everyone, and I look for that," or, "If I do not have something good to say about someone, I do not say anything at all."[10] These are high-sounding

---

[10]A parallel to this is the anti-intellectual component: "What I don't know won't hurt me"; "Let sleeping dogs lie," etc.

sentiments, but they also convey the message that it is wrong to look critically at another person and even worse to communicate criticism. Maslow has noted that even our definitions of love do not ordinarily include the obligation to feedback or criticize.[11]

One result of our tendency to say only positive things to each other is that we cannot really trust others to be honest with us. If people suppress their criticism and look for something polite or tactful to say, even positive feedback becomes suspect and therefore of little benefit. It is little wonder that we often are not comforted by others' reassurances that they accept and love us despite what we have exposed of our self.

Because of the taboo we place on face-to-face criticism, negative feedback tends to be accompanied by strong emotions on the part of both giver and receiver. Many persons will level criticism only if they first become angry. As a result we learn to react defensively or strike back, responding to the threat we have learned to associate with criticism. Because of our emotional response we tend to experience the criticism as a rejection of our whole self and thus something to be warded off or discredited at all costs.

We cannot blame the scarcity of direct evaluative feedback entirely on social custom. Frequently people ask others to evaluate them, but at the same time give off subtle cues that they do not really want to hear anything other than reassurance. On the other hand, we sometimes withhold feedback because we do not want another person to change. We get used to others being the way they are, our relationships with them stabilize and become comfortable, and we may even obtain satisfaction from their weaknesses and imperfections. In fact it is likely that we use other people, particularly hated or scapegoat targets, in a defensive way to keep our own anxiety at a minimum. Evaluative feedback, even though it might be helpful to the other person, would only upset a satisfying

---

[11]A. H. Maslow, "Summer Notes on Social Psychology of Industry and Management at Non-Linear System, Inc., Del Mar, California," unpublished manuscript (1962).

Maslow goes on to point out the irony of our willingness to let someone go on making the same mistake over and over, ostensibly out of kindness, but really because we are afraid of hurting him and being struck back. As contrast, he cites the Bruderhof where one aspect of Christian love is to be honest with others, even when it hurts. If a faculty member is a bad teacher because he mumbles on and on it is considered to be a brotherly duty, and an expression of caring, to tell him so (*ibid*, pp. 5–6.).

Retaliation is one main factor that inhibits feedback. Another is the danger that if one exposes a perception or feeling about another, he *may* have to change it. Or even more: he may have to get *closer* to the target of criticism. (In the essay introducing Part I, we pointed to the "distancing" function of the stereotype—or untested perception.)

relationship. Finally, people are frequently *afraid* to offer even helpful criticism. They are afraid that they might hurt the other person and/or might be hurt themselves by an act of retaliation on his part.

4. *Facilitating Relationships.* The prototype of a relationship that facilitates positive self-re-evaluation or increased self-esteem is one in which unconditional love is combined with direct feedback.

Some relationships between adults come to approximate this state. A relationship of this sort begins when people trust each other enough to start exposing more and more of themselves to each other. Each person exposes his self in small increments, tentatively, waiting for a response. If the response is disapproval or rejection, the relationship freezes at that point, is terminated, or the testing begins anew. If each exposure is met with acceptance, there is a continual build-up of trust, a growing confidence that they will not hurt each other intentionally. The process is mutually reinforcing, since when one person trusts enough to make himself vulnerable by exposing himself, trust is generated in the other person.

A successful relationship from the standpoint of an increase in self-esteem is one where the individuals are committed to openness and trust in their human transactions, and find themselves accepted or loved. There is concrete evidence of each individual's acceptability, with a corresponding increase in self esteem.

Let us briefly summarize what we have said about the process of self-evaluation. Experiences with acceptance and rejection during infancy and childhood are basic to the development of our self-esteem as adults. However, re-evaluation of self with a consequent increase in self-esteem can occur after childhood, usually as a result of testing assumptions about self-worth through exposing the self to others and obtaining feedback. Relearning of this type depends primarily on direct feedback that is both honest and unambiguous. Thus, while exposure of self can be an effective strategy for confirming self-worth, it must occur in the context of a relationship that can tolerate honest expression of feelings.

SELF-DEFINITION

In this section we are concerned with a second major component of self-confirmation—the process of self-definition. Every person has certain beliefs about who or what he is; taken together, these beliefs are a person's self-image, or identity. Here we shall focus on interpersonal processes that bear on how such beliefs are formed, how they are maintained, and how they change.

A. Identity Formation

Erik Erikson has defined identity formation in the following manner: ". . . identity formation . . . is a lifelong development largely unconscious to the individual and to his society. Its roots go back all the way to the first self-recognition: in the baby's earliest exchange of smiles there is something of a self-realization coupled with a mutual recognition."[12]

With respect to identity formation, it may be useful to examine some ideas of G. H. Mead, who perhaps more than any other theorist before or since views the self as predominantly a social product, Mead[13] emphasized the importance of face-to-face interaction with others: from the time we are very young children, we constantly act toward others and they respond to us. One result of the continuous exchange between ego and alter is that we learn about our selves; each act directed toward us contains cues about how others see and experience us as individuals. Thus our beliefs about our self, our self-image, are in large measure a reflection of others' perceptions of us. The phrases "looking glass self" coined by Cooley and "reflected self-appraisal" by Sullivan are graphic statements of this process.

Not all beliefs about self are formed as a result of face-to-face interaction. Festinger[14] has used the term "social comparison process" to describe another way people appraise and evaluate different aspects of their selves. In some cases it may be more efficient, or less risky, to compare our self to another person whose social stimulus value is known to us. In this way, we may develop certain beliefs about our selves without benefit of direct feedback from other persons. It seems probable that as we pass from childhood into adolescence and adulthood, more and more of our beliefs about our self are formed indirectly, through some form of social comparison process.

B. Maintaining an Identity

Festinger[15] has distinguished between what he calls *physical* and *social* reality. Beliefs and opinions about physical reality can be

---

[12]E. Erickson, "The Problem of Ego Identity," in *Identity and Anxiety*, Stein, Vidich, and White (eds.) (Glencoe, Ill.: Free Press 1960), p. 47.

[13]G. H. Mead, *Mind, Self, and Society* (Chicago, Univ. of Chicago Press, 1934).

[14]L. Festinger, "A Theory of Social Comparison Processes," *Human Relations*, Vol. 7 (1954), pp. 117–40.

[15]L. Festinger, "Informal Social Communication," *Psychological Review*, Vol. 57 (1950), pp. 271–82.

validated by physical measurement: we can test our belief that glass is fragile by striking it with a hammer. Social reality cannot be tested by physical means. There is no physical measurement, for example, that can tell us decisively whether Republicans or Democrats are most adept at handling problems of foreign policy. Festinger goes on to assert that beliefs, attitudes, or opinions about social reality are correct, valid, or proper only to the extent they are anchored in a group of people with similar beliefs.

Many beliefs about self fall into the category of social reality. There are no physical means of determining whether we are in fact a leader of men, good-looking, or exceptionally tactful. Therefore, validation or confirmation of many beliefs about who or what we are must ultimately depend upon social consensus.

There are at least two varieties of beliefs that must be socially validated and confirmed if an individual's self-image or identity is to remain secure: (1) beliefs about the self, about who and what we are, and (2) beliefs about the nature of social reality.

1. *Beliefs about Self.* An individual's self-image is confirmed when other persons' responses to him indicate that their beliefs about who and what he is correspond with his own. There is a mutual recognition of his self, and the validity of his self-image is confirmed. Under conditions that provide consistent social confirmation of all aspects of the self, a strong and integrated identity or self-image will develop and be sustained. As a result there is less need to search for responses that confirm the self, or to shield one's self from disconfirming responses. There is greater freedom to respond spontaneously to a situation, to *be*, without a binding concern for the consistency or recognizability of the self-image that is presented. Operating from such a position of strength, a person can dare to *hear* feedback about who he is and what he is, and thus can continually test the validity of his beliefs about his self.

The psychological importance of maintaining a consistent self-image is evident from the existence of elaborate social rituals that function primarily to reduce the probability of disconfirmation, particularly in casual social contacts. "Being tactful," for example, consists essentially of responding to other people in a way that does not challenge the validity of the self they are publicly presenting. The two papers by Erving Goffman included in this volume are excellent analyses of such rituals.

The "identity diffusion" and uncertainty that results when the self is not confirmed by others, or when it is disconfirmed, has been described by a number of authors. In his moving essay, "The Therapeutic Despair,"[16] Leslie Farber writes of his *despair* when a patient refuses to confirm him in his role as therapist or healer by getting well. Erik Erikson has suggested that *identity crises* result when other people, or society, are willing to recognize a person only as something he cannot or does not want to be. He points out that social confirmation of *some* identity, even a negative one, is often preferable to a lack of confirmation and the uncertainty and confusion that results: ". . . many a late adolescent, if faced with continuing diffusion, would rather be nobody or somebody bad, or indeed, dead—and this totally, and by free choice—than be not-quite-somebody."[17]

Finally, in his perceptive and fascinating tale[18] about a young British Colonial officer, George Orwell graphically illustrates the relationship between identity diffusion and *susceptibility to influence*. Unhappy with his role but desperate ". . . to avoid looking a fool," the young officer acts out the oft-quoted wisdom that "people become what you expect them to be."[19]

2. *Beliefs about Reality.*[20] It is important to most people to believe that they are rational and objective, that their world view is "realistic" and accurate. This element of self-image is confirmed through validation of various beliefs or assumptions about the world. When these beliefs and assumptions involve social reality, their validation depends upon interaction with other persons who share a common image of the nature of reality.

Confidence in one's self as someone who has valid beliefs about the nature of reality is prerequisite for discovery, for daring to see the world in new ways. We depend on people with such confidence to lead in defining and redefining social reality, to raise questions even about beliefs supported by social consensus. Persons who lack confidence in the validity of their perceptions and beliefs will feel pressures to conform, to accept the beliefs of others as more valid than their own. However, in a heterogeneous society no man can be a complete conformist; the validity of many of our beliefs is

[16]L. Farber, "The Therapeutic Despair," *Psychiatry,* Vol. 1 (1958), pp. 7–20.
[17]Erikson, *op. cit.,* p. 62.
[18]Included in this volume, page 267.
[19]See the essay introducing Part III for a more complete discussion of the relationship between self-confirmation and susceptibility to influence or personal change.
[20]In this part we are focusing on social processes relevant to definition of self. See the description of a "Type B" relationship in the essay introducing Part V for a discussion of interpersonal processes which lead to both self-definition and defintion of external reality.

challenged by the different beliefs of other people, other groups. Nevertheless, the effort we expend to make sure we have some social support for our views is evidence of our dependence on shared perceptions and beliefs for confirmation of a core part of the self.

One of the most common ways we confirm our views that are not universally held is by associating with people who *do* share and thus confirm our perceptions, attitudes, opinions, and beliefs. Persons who have lived for an extended period in an alien culture often speak of their relief at having their world view confirmed upon their return home. Festinger, Riecken, and Schachter[21] and Hardyck and Braden[22] have provided penetrating descriptions of the reactions of apocalyptic groups to disconfirmations of some important beliefs and expectations. In the case of members of the "Lake City" group described by Festinger *et al.*, the reaction to disconfirmation was to proselytize and attract new members to the group in order to restore the individual's confidence in his beliefs and thus prevent identity-diffusion, if not disintegration. In contrast, the highly cohesive "True Word" group discussed by Hardyck and Braden apparently provided the social confirmation required for individual members to maintain their beliefs in the face of physical disconfirmation without proselytizing. In both cases, however, one clear implication is that lack of confirmation of important beliefs about the environment threatens certain beliefs about the self and leads to defensive rather than reality-testing strategies.

People also respond to a lack of social support or confirmation of their perceptions and beliefs by changing them to conform to those of their most salient reference group.[23] The paper by Schachter which follows this essay provides unusual documentation of the way people use very subtle social cues to "test reality" and to adjust the appropriateness of their emotional responses.

C. Identity Extension

In this section we are concerned with identity change, specifically the growth or extension of identity or self-image.

1. *Self-Realization.* The verb "to realize" has more than one meaning. Among other things, it implies both *knowing* and *making concrete or real*, suggesting two ways that a self-image might be

---

[21]L. Festinger, H. W. Riecken, Jr., and S. Schachter, *When Prophecy Fails* (Minneapolis: Univ. of Minnesota, 1956).

[22]Page 321 this volume.

[23]See the essay introducing Part III.

extended. Self-realization, as we conceive of it, involves both becoming consciously aware of the self as it presently exists, and extending the self to include latent potentialities. The discussion of self-esteem in an earlier section of the essay is directly relevant to the first aspect of self-realization: self-awareness. There we suggested that doubts about self-worth can lead to repression as well as suppression of certain parts of the self; hiding, pretending, and caution are strategies for self-delusion as well as for deluding others. Here we are more concerned with self-realization in the sense of discovering what the self *can* be.

2. *Self-Realization through "Selflessness."* For us, the key to self-realization, to discovering what the self *can* be is selflessness: we become our self only as we can forget our self. Fingarette has described selflessness in the following terms:

. . . "selflessness" is a characteristic mystic concept associated with the "enlightened" state . . . It does not mean the absence of a self in the psychoanalytic sense of that term, nor does it refer to the absence of the ego or of the "self-representations," or to the loss of ability to distinguish "inner" and "outer" as in hallucination or estrangement . . . "Selflessness," being a term in a "subjective" language, expresses the lack of conscious awareness of self. But this is true in a sense which cannot be made unambiguous in ordinary language. We can point to the unawareness in question by referring to its psychological conditions: it is that "normal" unselfconsciousness characteristic of experience which is primarily nonanxious and motivated by neutralized drives functioning within the non-conflictful portions of the ego. It is an unselfconsciousness akin to the normal unawareness of our breathing.[24]

A person capable of selflessness must be sure enough of his worth as an individual, self-accepting enough, that he does not need to hide, or pretend, or be cautious; instead he can respond openly, spontaneously, and naturally to new situations and new people. Only by temporarily suspending the conscious desire for consistency, the need to be what we know we can be successfully and safely, can we find out what *else* we might be. Only by responding *unselfconsciously*, momentarily freed from too great dependence on what we have been, can we discover what variety there is within us.

It should be emphasized that while selflessness connotes a lack of conscious awareness of self in action, it is a *suspension* of awareness, not the incapacity to be aware. It is this distinction that differentiates the person capable of selflessness from the schizo-

---

[24]H. Fingarette, "The Ego and Mystic Selflessness," in *Identity and Anxiety*, Stein, Vidich, and White (eds.) (Glencoe Ill.: Free Press, 1960), pp. 580–81.

phrenic. Although the term "selflessness" often has been used to describe only the rather esoteric states of the religious mystic or drug addict, it is probable that most persons with some "nonconflictful portions of the ego" can behave selflessly, or unselfconsciously, in some situations.

Selflessness also implies the capacity to observe one's self in a detached and objective fashion. A person's first impulse in the face of critical feedback from the environment is to defend the self, to preserve the status quo, to look out for his self-interests. Under these conditions it is difficult, if not impossible, to evaluate feedback objectively and use it constructively. Selflessness, on the other hand, suggests the capacity to become temporarily detached from one's self, to stand back and look at the self as another person might. If the ability to behave unselfconsciously is the first step toward identity extension, then the capacity to view our behavior objectively is certainly the second.

3. *Facilitating Relationships.* Selflessness and self-realization can occur to the degree that a person feels worthy in a relationship. The parties to the relationship will feel that they are accepted, that the other has made a positive decision concerning their value of them. There will be a feeling that this decision is final and will stand in the face of any new aspects of the self that might emerge.

Furthermore, the persons involved will feel they are accepted for what they are; their images of each other will neither be too grandiose nor too modest. Expectations of each other will be realistic.

Finally, there will be an implicit assumption that one person will not deliberately hurt the other to satisfy his own needs, a quality of a relationship often called *trust.*

It appears, therefore, that self-definition and self-evaluation interact with each other. The person has to be something in order to be evaluated, and the person has to be positively evaluated in order to be something new.

In the papers that follow this essay, Carl Rogers and Kenneth Benne describe with considerable insight and wisdom some characteristics of interpersonal relationships that further selflessness and self-growth.

4. *Descriptive Feedback.* Learning about our self from others' responses to us does not stop with the end of childhood and the initial development of a sense of identity. During our discussion of self-evaluation, we suggested that low self-esteem is associated

with a tendency to perceive only the evaluative elements in others' responses to us—the approval or disapproval, acceptance or rejection. The need to maintain a certain level of self-esteem seems to take precedence over all else, and doubt about self-worth stimulates "selfishness" or "selfconsciousness," rather than selflessness. Most people, however, at least in some areas can become temporarily self-detached to observe the reactions of others to their self. They can go beyond the evaluated feedback to the descriptive cues that can help them discover *what* they are rather than just how acceptable they are.

The distinction between indirect and direct feedback, made in connection with evaluative feedback, is also relevant here. However, whereas indirect feedback is of little use, and may even be harmful, for purposes of self-evaluation, it plays an extremely important role in self-definition. Others' responses to our behavior, often nonverbal, may contain information they might not be able to express more directly. Nevertheless, it frequently is not enough. Persons who attend human relations training laboratories such as those sponsored by the National Training Laboratories[25] almost invariably express a desire to be told point blank how other people perceive them. This is particularly true of persons with a relatively strong sense of personal worth who are not worried about, or even particularly interested in, others' *evaluations* of them.

The shortage of useful descriptive feedback stems partly from difficulty in predicting whether the person to receive the descriptive feedback will respond to it as just that, or whether he will scan it only for its evaluative content. Psychologists face this problem when they try to feed back the results of psychological tests; teachers face a similar dilemma when they discuss a student's work with him, or counsel a student on possible careers. All too often persons who want and can make good use of descriptive feedback are denied it because the person who might help them has had a bad experience with someone who could hear only the evaluative elements in the feedback he was given.

SUMMARY

This essay represents an attempt to point up some of the interpersonal aspects of self-confirmation. We have focused on self-evaluation and self-definition as two processes critical to self-confir-

---

[25] E. H. Schein and W. G. Bennis, *Personal and Organizational Change Through Group Methods* (New York: Wiley, 1964).

mation and having important interpersonal ramifications. Rather than try to draw conclusions, it seems more appropriate to close with an illustration that dramatizes many of the points we have made.

As part of a research project, forty-five young managers in a large utility company were interviewed extensively about their career problems. Nearly all of the men had been hired right out of college as management trainees, and had been working for this particular organization for six years. As one might expect, a variety of complaints and problems were unearthed, but one in particular stood out because of the intense frustration associated with it.

Several of the young managers had been quite successful up to the time they began their business careers, and as a result they had no reason to believe they would not continue to be successful. Each had, at the beginning of his career, rather high expectations of what he would accomplish. The image each had of himself was that of a highly competent person who would rise to the top among a group of his peers.

Before long, however, their experiences in the company began to challenge their self-images. They did not move ahead particularly fast, only keeping pace with or falling behind the majority of their peers. This experience was quite at odds with the expectations they had. The environment offered several possible rationalizations for failure. Because of a period of business regression, promotions were frozen. The company was automating various functions, cutting back on the total number of employees and thus the number of management positions. The company was consolidating small work units into larger ones, giving more responsibility to individual managers, but eliminating managerial positions in the process.

The basic dilemma these men expressed was whether or not in the face of feedback from their environment they should re-evaluate themselves and re-adjust their self-images to be more consistent with the cues they were receiving. Many of their colleagues were quick to perceive and accept the evaluative cues contained in the company's response to them and to re-evaluate themselves accordingly. Others, less confident of their worth as individuals, sought only reassurance, rationalizing or denying their predicament. These men could do neither, at least not on the basis of the impersonal and frequently ambiguous feedback available to them. They did express a desperate need for respected superiors to give them absolutely objective, point-blank feedback on their potential as managers. With honest, direct feedback they could trust, they felt they could decide whether to modify their self-image appropriately, or to try to confirm their self-image in another company. However, they were unable to persuade their superiors to be absolutely honest and open with them; the superiors apparently either felt they would be hurting rather than helping their subordinate by leveling with him, or they had been taught it was poor management. In any case, the organization failed to recognize the capacity these men had to use direct feedback constructively, with the result that the men in question were unable to resolve their dilemma.

Clearly there are no simple solutions to the dilemmas the young managers are confronting. Self-esteem and self-image are the hard-core of personality, but we have little control over their development, and lack the knowledge and techniques to influence or alter them reliably. Recently, however, there has been an increasing awareness of the importance of interpersonal processes, and a growing concern with "creative human relationships," or relationships that facilitate personal growth. This section, indeed this entire book, is a reflection of that concern.

ON FACE-WORK: AN ANALYSIS OF RITUAL ELEMENTS IN SOCIAL INTERACTION*

Erving Goffman

Every person lives in a world of social encounters, involving him either in face-to-face or mediated contact with other participants. In each of these contacts, he tends to act out what is sometimes called a *line*—that is, a pattern of verbal and nonverbal acts by which he expresses his view of the situation and through this his evaluation of the participants, especially himself. Regardless of whether a person intends to take a line, he will find that he has done so in effect. The other participants will assume that he has more or less willfully taken a stand, so that if he is to deal with their response to him he must take into consideration the impression they have possibly formed of him.

The term *face* may be defined as the positive social value a person effectively claims for himself by the line others assume he has taken during a particular contact.[1] Face is an image of self delineated in terms of approved social attributes—albeit an image that

*Excerpted from Erving Goffman, "On Face-Work: An Analysis of Ritual Elements in Social Interaction." Reprinted by special permission of The William Alanson White Psychiatric Foundation, Inc., *Psychiatry*, Vol. 18, No. 3 (Aug. 1955), pp. 213–31. Footnotes renumbered. Copyright 1955 by The William Alanson White Psychiatric Foundation Inc.

[1]For discussions of the Chinese conception of face, see the following: Hsien Chin Hu, "The Chinese Concept of 'Face,'" *Amer. Anthropologist* (1944) n.s. 46:45–64. Martin C. Yang, *A Chinese Village;* New York, Columbia Univ. Press, 1945; pp. 167–72. J. Macgowan, *Men and Manners of Modern China;* London, Unwin, 1912; pp. 301–12. Arthur H. Smith, *Chinese Characteristics;* New York, Fleming H. Revell Co., 1894; pp. 16–18. For a comment on the American Indian conception of face, see Marcel Mauss, *The Gift* (Ian Cunnison, tr.); London, Cohen & West, 1954; p. 38.

others may share, as when a person makes a good showing for his profession or religion by making a good showing for himself.

A person tends to experience an immediate emotional response to the face which a contact with others allows him; he cathects his face; his "feelings" become attached to it. If the encounter sustains an image of him that he has long taken for granted, he probably will have few feelings about the matter. If events establish a face for him that is better than he might have expected, he is likely to "feel good"; if his ordinary expectations are not fulfilled, one expects that he will "feel bad" or "feel hurt." In general, a person's attachment to a particular face, coupled with the ease with which disconfirming information can be conveyed by himself and others, provides one reason why he finds that participation in any contact with others is a commitment. A person will also have feelings about the face sustained for the other participants, and while these feelings may differ in quantity and direction from those he has for his own face, they constitute an involvement in the face of others that is as immediate and spontaneous as the involvement he has in his own face. One's own face and the face of others are constructs of the same order; it is the rules of the group and the definition of the situation which determine how much feeling one is to have for face and how this feeling is to be distributed among the faces involved.

A person may be said to *have*, or *be in*, or *maintain* face when the line he effectively takes presents an image of him that is internally consistent, that is supported by judgments and evidence conveyed by other participants, and that is confirmed by evidence conveyed through impersonal agencies in the situation. At such times the person's face clearly is something that is not lodged in or on his body, but rather something that is diffusely located in the flow of events in the encounter and becomes manifest only when these events are read and interpreted for the appraisals expressed in them.

The line maintained by and for a person during contact with others tends to be of a legitimate institutionalized kind. During a contact of a particular type, an interactant of known or visible attributes can expect to be sustained in a particular face and can feel that it is morally proper that this should be so. Given his attributes and the conventionalized nature of the encounter, he will find a small choice of lines will be open to him and a small choice of faces will be waiting for him. Further, on the basis of a few known attributes, he is given the responsibility of possessing a vast number of others. His coparticipants are not likely to be conscious of the character of many of these attributes until he acts perceptibly in such a way as to discredit his possession of them; then everyone becomes conscious of these attributes and assumes that he willfully gave a false impression of possessing them.

Thus while concern for face focuses the attention of the person on the current activity, he must, to maintain face in this activity, take into consideration his place in the social world beyond it. A person who can maintain face in the current situation is someone who abstained from certain actions in the past that would have been difficult to face up to later. In addition, he fears loss of face now partly because the others may take this as a sign that consideration for his feelings need not be shown in the future. There is nevertheless a limitation to this interdependence between the current situation and the wider social world: an encounter with people whom he will not have dealings with again leaves him free to take a high line that the future will discredit, or free to suffer humiliations that would make future dealings with them an embarrassing thing to have to face.

A person may be said to *be in wrong face* when information is brought forth in some way about his social worth which cannot be integrated, even with effort, into the line that is being sustained for him. A person may be said to *be out of face* when he participates in a contact with others without having ready a line of the kind participants in such situations are expected to take. The intent of many pranks is to lead a person into showing a wrong face or no face, but there will also be serious occasions, of course, when he will find himself expressively out of touch with the situation.

When a person senses that he is in face, he typically responds with feelings of confidence and assurance. Firm in the line he is taking, he feels that he can hold his head up and openly present himself to others. He feels some security and some relief—as he also can when the others feel he is in wrong face but successfully hide these feelings from him.

When a person is in wrong face or out of face, expressive events are being contributed to the encounter which cannot be readily woven into the expressive fabric of the occasion. Should he sense that he is in wrong face or out of face, he is likely to feel ashamed and inferior because of what has happened to the activity on his account and because of what may happen to his reputation as a participant. Further, he may feel bad because he had relied upon the encounter to support an image of self to which he has become emotionally attached and which he now finds threatened. Felt lack of judgmental support from the encounter may take him aback, confuse him, and momentarily incapacitate him as an interactant. His manner and bearing may falter, collapse, and crumble. He may become embarrassed and chagrined; he may become shamefaced. The feeling, whether warranted or not, that he is perceived in a flustered state by others, and that he is presenting no usable line, may add further injuries to his feelings, just as his change from being in wrong face or out of face to being shamefaced can add further disorder to the expressive organization of the situation. Following common usage, I shall employ the term *poise* to refer to the capacity to suppress and conceal any tendency to become shamefaced during encounters with others.

In our Anglo-American society, as in some others, the phrase "to lose face" seems to mean to be in wrong face, to be out of face, or to be shamefaced. The phrase "to save one's face" appears to refer to the process by which the person sustains an impression for others that he has not lost face. Following Chinese usage, one can say that "to give face" is to arrange for another to take a better line than he might otherwise have been able to take,[2] the other thereby gets face given him, this being one way in which he can gain face.

As an aspect of the social code of any social circle, one may expect to find an understanding as to how far a person should go to save his face. Once he takes on a self-image expressed through face he will be expected to live up to it. In different ways in different societies he will be required to show self-respect, abjuring certain actions because they are above or beneath him, while forcing himself to perform others even though they cost him dearly. By entering a situation in which he is given a face to maintain, a person takes on the responsibility of standing guard over the flow of events as they pass before him. He must ensure that a particular *expressive order* is sustained—an order which regulates the flow of events, large or small, so that anything that appears to be expressed by them will be consistent with his face. When a person manifests these compunctions primarily from duty to himself, one speaks in our society of pride; when he does so because of duty to wider social units, and receives support from these units in doing so, one speaks of honor. When these compunctions have to do with postural things, with expressive events derived from the way in which the person

---

[2]Smith, *op. cit.*, p. 17.

handles his body, his emotions, and the things with which he has physical contact, one speaks of dignity, this being an aspect of expressive control that is always praised and never studied. In any case, while his social face can be his most personal possession and the center of his security and pleasure, it is only on loan to him from society; it will be withdrawn unless he conducts himself in a way that is worthy of it. Approved attributes and their relation to face make of every man his own jailer; this is a fundamental social constraint even though each man may like his cell.

Just as the member of any group is expected to have self-respect, so also he is expected to sustain a standard of considerateness; he is expected to go to certain lengths to save the feelings and the face of others present, and he is expected to do this willingly and spontaneously because of emotional identification with the others and with their feelings.[3] In consequence, he is disinclined to witness the defacement of others.[4] The person who can witness another's humiliation and unfeelingly retain a cool countenance himself is said in our society to be "heartless," just as he who can unfeelingly participate in his own defacement is thought to be "shameless."

The combined effect of the rule of self-respect and the rule of considerateness is that the person tends to conduct himself during an encounter so as to maintain both his own face and the face of the other participants. This means that the line taken by each participant is usually allowed to prevail, and each participant is allowed to carry off the role he appears to have chosen for himself. A state where everyone temporarily accepts everyone else's line is established.[5] This kind of mutual acceptance seems to be a basic

---

[3]Of course, the more power and prestige the others have, the more a person is likely to show consideration for their feelings, as H. E. Dale suggests in *The Higher Civil Service of Great Britain* (Oxford, Oxford Univ. Press, 1941), p. 126n. "The doctrine of 'feelings' was expounded to me many years ago by a very eminent civil servant with a pretty taste in cynicism. He explained that the importance of feelings varies in close correspondence with the importance of the person who feels. If the public interest requires that a junior clerk should be removed from his post, no regard need be paid to his feelings; if it is a case of an Assistant Secretary, they must be carefully considered, within reason; if it is a Permanent Secretary, his feelings are a principal element in the situation, and only imperative public interest can override their requirements."

[4]Salesmen, especially street "stemmers," know that if they take a line that will be discredited unless the reluctant customer buys, the customer may be trapped by considerateness and buy in order to save the face of the salesman and prevent what would ordinarily result in a scene.

[5]Surface agreement in the assessment of social worth does not, of course, imply equality; the evaluation consensually sustained of one participant may be quite different from the one consensually sustained of another. Such agreement is also compatible with expression of differences of opinion between two participants, provided

structural feature of interaction, especially the interaction of face-to-face talk. It is typically a "working" acceptance, not a "real" one, since it tends to be based not on agreement of candidly expressed heartfelt evaluations, but upon a willingness to give temporary lip service to judgments with which the participants do not really agree.

The mutual acceptance of lines has an important conservative effect upon encounters. Once the person initially presents a line, he and the others tend to build their later responses upon it, and in a sense become stuck with it. Should the person radically alter his line, or should it become discredited, then confusion results, for the participants will have prepared and committed themselves for actions that are now unsuitable.

Ordinarily, maintenance of face is a condition of interaction, not its objective. Usual objectives, such as gaining face for oneself, giving free expression to one's true beliefs, introducing depreciating information about the others, or solving problems and performing tasks, are typically pursued in such a way as to be consistent with the maintenance of face. To study face-saving is to study the traffic rules of social interaction; one learns about the code the person adheres to in his movement across the paths and designs of others, but not where he is going, or why he wants to get there. One does not even learn why he is ready to follow the code, for a large number of different motives can equally lead him to do so. He may want to save his own face because of his emotional attachment to the image of self which it expresses, because of his pride or honor, because of the power his presumed status allows him to exert over the other participants, and so on. He may want to save the others' face because of his emotional attachment to an image of them, or because he feels that his coparticipants have a moral right to this protection, or because he wants to avoid the hostility that may be directed toward him if they lose their face. He may feel that an assumption has been made that he is the sort of person who shows

---

each of the disputants shows "respect" for the other, guiding the expression of disagreement so that it will convey an evaluation of the other that the other will be willing to convey about himself. Extreme cases are provided by wars, duels, and barroom fights, when these are of a gentlemanly kind, for they can be conducted under consensual auspices, with each protagonist guiding his action according to the rules of the game, thereby making it possible for his action to be interpreted as an expression of a fair player openly in combat with a fair opponent. In fact, the rules and etiquette of any game can be analyzed as a means by which the image of a fair player can be expressed, just as the image of a fair player can be analyzed as a means by which the rules and etiquette of a game are sustained.

compassion and sympathy toward others, so that to retain his own face, he may feel obliged to be considerate of the line taken by the other participants.

By *face-work* I mean to designate the actions taken by a person to make whatever he is doing consistent with face. Face-work serves to counteract "incidents"—that is, events whose effective symbolic implications threaten face. Thus poise is one important type of face-work, for through poise the person controls his embarrassment and hence the embarrassment that he and others might have over his embarrassment. Whether or not the full consequences of face-saving actions are known to the person who employs them, they often become habitual and standardized practices; they are like traditional plays in a game or traditional steps in a dance. Each person, subculture, and society seems to have its own characteristic repertoire of face-saving practices. It is to this repertoire that people partly refer when they ask what a person or culture is "really" like. And yet the particular set of practices stressed by particular persons or groups seems to be drawn from a single logically coherent framework of possible practices. It is as if face, by its very nature, can be saved only in a certain number of ways, and as if each social grouping must make its selections from this single matrix of possibilities.

The members of every social circle may be expected to have some knowledge of face-work and some experience in its use. In our society, this kind of capacity is sometimes called tact, *savoir-faire*, diplomacy, or social skill. Variation in social skill pertains more to the efficacy of face-work than to the frequency of its application, for almost all acts involving others are modified, prescriptively or proscriptively, by considerations of face.

If a person is to employ his repertoire of face-saving practices, obviously he must first become aware of the interpretations that others may have placed upon his acts and the interpretations that he ought perhaps to place upon theirs. In other words, he must exercise perceptiveness.[6] But even if he is properly alive to sym-

---

[6]Presumably social skill and perceptiveness will be high in groups whose members frequently act as representatives of wider social units such as lineages or nations, for the player here is gambling with a face to which the feelings of many persons are attached. Similarly, one might expect social skill to be well developed among those of high station and those with whom they have dealings, for the more face an interactant has, the greater the number of events that may be inconsistent with it, and hence the greater the need for social skill to forestall or counteract these inconsistencies.

bolically conveyed judgments and is socially skilled, he must yet be willing to exercise his perceptiveness and his skill; he must, in short, be prideful and considerate. Admittedly, of course, the possession of perceptiveness and social skill so often leads to their application that in our society terms such as politeness or tact fail to distinguish between the inclination to exercise such capacities and the capacities themselves.

I have already said that the person will have two points of view— a defensive orientation toward saving his own face and a protective orientation toward saving the others' face. Some practices will be primarily defense and others primarily protective, although in general one may expect these two perspectives to be taken at the same time. In trying to save the face of others, the person must choose a tack that will not lead to loss of his own; in trying to save his own face, he must consider the loss of face that his action may entail for others.

In many societies there is a tendency to distinguish three levels of responsibility which a person may have for a threat to face that his actions have created. First, he may appear to have acted innocently; his offense seems to be unintended and unwitting, and those who perceive his act can feel that he would have attempted to avoid it had he foreseen its offensive consequences. In our society one calls such threats to face *faux pas, gaffes,* boners, or bricks. Secondly, the offending person may appear to have acted maliciously and spitefully, with the intention of causing open insult. Thirdly, there are incidental offenses; these arise as an unplanned but sometimes anticipated by-product of action—action which the offender performs in spite of its offensive consequences, although not out of spite. From the point of view of a particular participant, these three types of threat can be introduced by the participant himself against his own face, by himself against the face of the others, by the others against their own face, or by the others against himself. Thus the person may find himself in many different relations to a threat to face. If he is to handle himself and others well in all contingencies, he will have to have a repertoire of face-saving practices for each of these possible relations to threat.

THE BASIC KINDS OF FACE-WORK

The Avoidance Process. The surest way for a person to prevent threats to his face is to avoid contacts in which these threats are likely to occur. In all societies one can observe this in the avoidance relationship[7] and in the tendency for certain delicate transactions to be conducted by go-betweens.[8] Similarly, in many societies, members know the value of voluntarily making a gracious withdrawal before an anticipated threat to face has had a chance to occur.[9]

Once the person does chance an encounter, other kinds of avoidance practices come into play. As defensive measures, he keeps off topics and away from activities which would lead to the expression of information that is inconsistent with the line he is maintaining. At opportune moments he will change the topic of conversation or the direction of activity. He will often present initially a front of diffidence and composure, suppressing any show of feeling until he has found out what kind of line the others will be ready to support for him. Any claims regarding self may be made with belittling modesty, with strong qualifications, or with a note of unseriousness; by hedging in these ways he will have prepared a self for himself that will not be discredited by exposure, personal failure, or the unanticipated acts of others. And if he does not hedge his claims about self, he will at least attempt to be realistic about them, knowing that otherwise events may discredit him and make him lose face.

Certain protective maneuvers are as common as these defensive ones. The person shows respect and politeness, making sure to extend to others any ceremonial treatment which might be their due. He employs discretion; he leaves unstated facts which might implicitly or explicitly contradict and embarrass the positive claims made by others.[10] He employs circumlocutions and deceptions, phrasing his replies with careful ambiguity so that the others' face

---

[7]In our own society an illustration of avoidance is found in the middle- and upper-class Negro who avoids certain face-to-face contacts with whites in order to protect the self-evaluation projected by his clothes and manner. See, for example, Charles Johnson, *Patterns of Negro Segregation;* New York, Harper, 1943; ch. 13. The function of avoidance in maintaining the kinship system in small preliterate societies might be taken as a particular illustration of the same general theme.

[8]An illustration is given by K. S. Latourette, *The Chinese: Their History and Culture* (New York, Macmillan, 1942): "A neighbor or a group of neighbors may tender their good offices in adjusting a quarrel in which each antagonist would be sacrificing his face by taking the first step in approaching the other. The wise intermediary can effect the reconciliation while preserving the dignity of both" (Vol. 2: p. 211).

[9]In an unpublished paper Harold Garfinkel has suggested that when the person finds that he has lost face in a conversational encounter, he may feel a desire to disappear or "drop through the floor," and that this may involve a wish not only to conceal loss of face but also to return magically to a point in time when it would have been possible to save face by avoiding the encounter.

[10]When the person knows the others well, he will know what issues ought not to be raised and what situations the others ought not to be placed in, and he will be free

is preserved even if their welfare is not.[11] He employs courtesies, making slight modifications of his demands on or appraisals of the others so that they will be able to define the situation as one in which their self-respect is not threatened. In making a belittling demand upon the others, or in imputing uncomplimentary attributes to them, he may employ a joking manner, allowing them to take the line that they are good sports, able to relax from their ordinary standards of pride and honor. And before engaging in a potentially offensive act, he may provide explanations as to why the others ought not to be affronted by it. For example, if he knows that it will be necessary to withdraw from the encounter before it has terminated, he may tell the others in advance that it is necessary for him to leave, so that they will have faces that are prepared for it. But neutralizing the potentially offensive act need not be done verbally; he may wait for a propitious moment or natural break—for example, in conversation, a momentary lull when no one speaker can be affronted—and then leave, in this way using the context instead of his words as a guarantee of inoffensiveness.

When a person fails to prevent an incident, he can still attempt to maintain the fiction that no threat to face has occurred. The most blatant example of this is found where the person acts as if an event which contains a threatening expression has not occurred at all. He may apply this studied nonobservance to his own acts—as when he does not by any outward sign admit that his stomach is rumbling —or to the acts of others, as when he does not "see" that another has stumbled.[12] Social life in mental hospitals owes much to this process; patients employ it in regard to their own peculiarities, and visitors employ it, often with tenuous desperation, in regard to

---

to introduce matters at will in all other areas. When the others are strangers to him, he will often reverse the formula, restricting himself to specific areas he knows are safe. On these occasions, as Simmel suggests, ". . . discretion consists by no means only in the respect for the secret of the other, for his specific will to conceal this or that from us, but in staying away from the knowledge of all that the other does not expressly reveal to us." See *The Sociology of Georg Simmel* (Kurt H. Wolff, tr. and ed.); Glencoe, Ill., Free Press, 1950; pp. 320–21.

[11]The Western traveler used to complain that the Chinese could never be trusted to say what they meant but always said what they felt their Western listener wanted to hear. The Chinese used to complain that the Westerner was brusque, boorish, and unmannered. In terms of Chinese standards, presumably, the conduct of a Westerner is so gauche that he creates an emergency, forcing the Asian to forgo any kind of direct reply in order to rush in with a remark that might rescue the Westerner from the compromising position in which he had placed himself. (Smith, *op. cit.*, ch. 8, "The Talent for Indirection.") This is an instance of the important group of misunderstandings which arise during interaction between persons who come from groups with different ritual standards.

[12]A pretty example of this is found in parade-ground etiquette which may oblige those in a parade to treat anyone who faints as if he were not present at all.

patients. In general, tactful blindness of this kind is applied only to events which, if perceived at all, could be preceived and interpreted only as threats to face.

A more important, less spectacular kind of tactful overlooking is practiced when a person openly acknowledges an incident as an event that has occurred, but not as an event that contains a threatening expression. If he is not the one who is responsible for the incident, then his blindness will have to be supported by his forbearance; if he is the doer of the threatening deed, then his blindness will have to be supported by his willingness to seek a way of dealing with the matter which leaves him dangerously dependent upon the cooperative forbearance of the others.

Another kind of avoidance occurs when a person loses control of his expressions during an encounter. At such times he may try not so much to overlook the incident as to hide or conceal his activity in some way, thus making it possible for the others to avoid some of the difficulties created by a participant who has not maintained face. Correspondingly, when a person is caught out of face because he had not expected to be thrust into interaction, or because strong feelings have disrupted his expressive mask, the others may protectively turn away from him or his activity for a moment, to give him time to assemble himself.

The Corrective Process. When the participants in an undertaking or encounter fail to prevent the occurrence of an event that is expressively incompatible with the judgments of social worth that are being maintained, and when the event is of the kind that is difficult to overlook, then the participants are likely to give it accredited status as an incident—to ratify it as a threat that deserves direct official attention—and to proceed to try to correct for its effects. At this point one or more participants find themselves in an established state of ritual disequilibrium or disgrace, and an attempt must be made to re-establish a satisfactory ritual state for them. I use the term *ritual* because I am dealing with acts through whose symbolic component the actor shows how worthy he is of respect or how worthy he feels others are of it. The imagery of equilibrium is apt here because the length and intensity of the corrective effort is nicely adapted to the persistence and intensity of the threat.[13] One's face, then, is a sacred thing, and the expressive order required to sustain it is therefore a ritual one.

[13]This kind of imagery is one that social anthropologists seem to find naturally fitting. Note, for example, the implications of the following statement by Margaret

The sequence of acts set in motion by an acknowledged threat to face, and terminating in the re-establishment of ritual equilibrium, I shall call an *interchange*.[14] Defining a message or move as everything conveyed by an actor during a turn at taking action, one can say that an interchange will involve two or more moves and two or more participants. Obvious examples in our society may be found in the sequence of "Excuse me" and "Certainly," and in the exchange of presents or visits. The interchange seems to be a basic concrete unit of social activity and provides one natural empirical way to study interaction of all kinds. Face-saving practices can be usefully classified according to their position in the natural sequence of moves which comprise this unit. Aside from the event which introduces the need for a corrective interchange, four classic moves seem to be involved.

There is, first the challenge, by which participants take on the responsibility of calling attention to the misconduct; by implication they suggest that the threatened claims arc to stand firm and that the threatening event itself will have to be brought back into line.

The second move consists of the offering, whereby a participant, typically the offender, is given a chance to correct for the offense and re-establish the expressive order. Some classic ways of making this move are available. On the one hand, an attempt can be made to show that what admittedly appeared to be a threatening expression is really a meaningless event, or an unintentional act, or a joke not meant to be taken seriously, or an unavoidable, "understandable" product of extenuating circumstances. On the other hand, the meaning of the event may be granted and effort concentrated on the creator of it. Information may be provided to show that the creator was under the influence of something and not himself, or that he was under the command of somebody else and not acting for himself. When a person claims that an act was meant in jest, he may go on and claim that the self that seemed to lie be-

---

Mead in her "Kinship in the Admiralty Islands" (*Anthropological Papers of the American Museum of Natural History,* 34:183–358): "If a husband beats his wife, custom demands that she leave him and go to her brother, real or officiating, and remain a length of time commensurate with the degree of her offended dignity" (p. 274).

[14]The notion of interchange is drawn in part from Eliot D. Chapple, "Measuring Human Relations," *Genetic Psychol. Monograph* (1940) 22:3–147, especially pp. 26–30, and from A. B. Horsfall and C. A. Arensberg, "Teamwork and Productivity in a Shoe Factory," *Human Organization* (1949) 8:13–25, especially p. 19. For further material on the interchange as a unit see E. Goffman, "Communication Conduct in an Island Community," unpublished Ph.D. dissertation, Department of Sociology, University of Chicago, 1953, especially chs. 12 and 13, pp. 165–95.

hind the act was also projected as a joke. When a person suddenly finds that he has demonstrably failed in capacities that the others assumed him to have and to claim for himself—such as the capacity to spell, to perform minor tasks, to talk without malapropisms, and so on—he may quickly add, in a serious or unserious way, that he claims these incapacities as part of his self. The meaning of the threatening incident thus stands, but it can now be incorporated smoothly into the flow of expressive events.

As a supplement to or substitute for the strategy of redefining the offensive act or himself, the offender can follow two other procedures: he can provide compensations to the injured—when it is not his own face that he has threatened; or he can provide punishment, penance, and expiation for himself. These are important moves or phases in the ritual interchange. Even though the offender may fail to prove his innocence, he can suggest through these means that he is now a renewed person, a person who has paid for his sin against the expressive order and is once more to be trusted in the judgmental scene. Further, he can show that he does not treat the feelings of the others lightly, and that if their feelings have been injured by him, however innocently, he is prepared to pay a price for his action. Thus he assures the others that they can accept his explanations without this acceptance constituting a sign of weakness and a lack of pride on their part. Also, by his treatment of himself, by his self-castigation, he shows that he is clearly aware of the kind of crime he would have committed had the incident been what it first appeared to be, and that he knows the kind of punishment that ought to be accorded to one who would commit such a crime. The suspected person thus shows that he is thoroughly capable of taking the role of the others toward his own activity, that he can still be used as a responsible participant in the ritual process, and that the rules of conduct which he appears to have broken are still sacred, real, and unweakened. An offensive act may arouse anxiety about the ritual code; the offender allays this anxiety by showing that both the code and he as an upholder of it are still in working order.

After the challenge and the offering have been made, the third move can occur: the persons to whom the offering is made can accept it as a satisfactory means of re-establishing the expressive order and the faces supported by this order. Only then can the offender cease the major part of his ritual offering.

In the terminal move of the interchange, the forgiven person conveys a sign of gratitude to those who have given him the indulgence of forgiveness.

The phases of the corrective process—challenge, offering, acceptance, and thanks—provide a model for interpersonal ritual behavior, but a model that may be departed from in significant ways. For example, the offended parties may give the offender a chance to initiate the offering on his own before a challenge is made and before they ratify the offense as an incident. This is a common courtesy, extended on the assumption that the recipient will introduce a self-challenge. Further, when the offended persons accept the corrective offering, the offender may suspect that this has been grudgingly done from tact, and so he may volunteer additional corrective offerings, not allowing the matter to rest until he has received a second or third acceptance of his repeated apology. Or the offended persons may tactfully take over the role of the offender and volunteer excuses for him that will, perforce, be acceptable to the offended persons.

An important departure from the standard corrective cycle occurs when a challenged offender patently refuses to heed the warning and continues with his offending behavior, instead of setting the activity to rights. This move shifts the play back to the challengers. If they countenance the refusal to meet their demands, then it will be plain that their challenge was a bluff and that the bluff has been called. This is an untenable position; a face for themselves cannot be derived from it, and they are left to bluster. To avoid this fate, some classic moves are open to them. For instance, they can resort to tactless, violent retaliation, destroying either themselves or the person who had refused to heed their warning. Or they can withdraw from the undertaking in a visible huff—righteously indignant, outraged, but confident of ultimate vindication. Both tacks provide a way of denying the offender his status an an interactant, and hence denying the reality of the offensive judgment he has made. Both strategies are ways of salvaging face, but for all concerned the costs are usually high. It is partly to forestall such scenes that an offender is usually quick to offer apologies; he does not want the affronted persons to trap themselves into the obligation to resort to desperate measures.

It is plain that emotions play a part in these cycles of response, as when anguish is expressed because of what one has done to another's face, or anger because of what has been done to one's own. I want to stress that these emotions function as moves, and fit so precisely into the logic of the ritual game that it would seem difficult to understand them without it.[15] In fact, spontaneously expressed feelings are likely to fit into the formal pattern of the ritual interchange more elegantly than consciously designed ones.

MAKING POINTS—THE AGGRESSIVE USE OF FACE-WORK

Every face-saving practice which is allowed to neutralize a particular threat opens up the possibility that the threat will be willfully introduced for what can be safely gained by it. If a person knows that his modesty will be answered by others' praise of him, he can fish for compliments. If his own appraisal of self will be checked against incidental events, then he can arrange for favorable incidental events to appear. If others are prepared to overlook an affront to them and act forbearantly, or to accept apologies, then he can rely on this as a basis for safely offending them. He can attempt by sudden withdrawal to force the others into a ritually unsatisfactory state, leaving them to flounder in an interchange that cannot readily be completed. Finally, at some expense to himself, he can arrange for the others to hurt his feelings, thus forcing them to feel guilt, remorse, and sustained ritual disequilibrium.[16]

When a person treats face-work not as something he need be prepared to perform, but rather as something that others can be counted on to perform or to accept, then an encounter or an undertaking becomes less a scene of mutual considerateness than an arena in which a contest or match is held. The purpose of the game is to preserve everyone's line from an inexcusable contradiction, while scoring as many points as possible against one's adversaries and making as many gains as possible for oneself. An audience to the struggle is almost a necessity. The general method is for the person to introduce favorable facts about himself and unfavorable facts about the others in such a way that the only reply the others will be able to think up will be one that terminates the interchange in a

---

[15]Even when a child demands something and is refused, he is likely to cry and sulk not as an irrational expression of frustration but as a ritual move, conveying that he already has a face to lose and that its loss is not to be permitted lightly. Sympathetic parents may even allow for such display, seeing in these crude strategies the beginnings of a social self.

[16]The strategy of maneuvering another into a position where he cannot right the harm he has done is very commonly employed but nowhere with such devotion to the ritual model of conduct as in revengeful suicide. See, for example, M. D. W. Jeffreys, "Samsonic Suicide, or Suicide of Revenge Among Africans," *African Studies* (1952) 11:118–22.

grumble, a meager excuse, a face-saving I-can-take-a-joke laugh, or an empty stereotyped comeback of the "Oh yeah?" or "That's what you think" variety. The losers in such cases will have to cut their losses, tacitly grant the loss of a point, and attempt to do better in the next interchange. Points made by allusion to social class status are sometimes called snubs; those made by allusions to moral respectability are sometimes called digs; in either case one deals with a capacity at what is sometimes called "bitchiness."

In aggressive interchange the winner not only succeeds in introducing information favorable to himself and unfavorable to the others, but also demonstrates that as interactant he can handle himself better than his adversaries. Evidence of this capacity is often more important than all the other information the person conveys in the interchange, so that the introduction of a "crack" in verbal interaction tends to imply that the initiator is better at footwork than those who must suffer his remarks. However, if they succeed in making a successful parry of the thrust and then a successful riposte, the instigator of the play must not only face the disparagement with which the others have answered him but also accept the fact that his assumption of superiority in footwork has proven false. He is made to look foolish; he loses face. Hence it is always a gamble to "make a remark." The tables can be turned and the aggressor can lose more than he could have gained had his move won the point. Successful ripostes or comebacks in our society are sometimes called squelches or toppers; theoretically it would be possible for a squelch to be squelched, a topper to be topped, and a riposte to be parried with a counterriposte, but except in staged interchanges this third level of successful action seems rare.[17]

THE CHOICE OF APPROPRIATE FACE-WORK

When an incident occurs, the person whose face is threatened may attempt to reinstate the ritual order by means of one kind of strategy, while the other participants may desire or expect a practice of a different type to be employed. When, for example, a minor

---

[17]In board and card games the player regularly takes into consideration the possible responses of his adversaries to a play that he is about to make, and even considers the possibility that his adversaries will know that he is taking such precautions. Conversational play is by comparison surprisingly impulsive; people regularly make remarks about others present without carefully designing their remarks to prevent a successful comeback. Similarly, while feinting and sandbagging are theoretical possibilities during talk, they seem to be little exploited.

mishap occurs, momentarily revealing a person in wrong face or out of face, the others are often more willing and able to act blind to the discrepancy than is the threatened person himself. Often they would prefer him to exercise poise,[18] while he feels that he cannot afford to overlook what has happened to his face and so becomes apologetic and shamefaced, if he is the creator of the incident, or destructively assertive, if the others are responsible for it.[19] Yet on the other hand, a person may manifest poise when the others feel that he ought to have broken down into embarrassed apology—that he is taking undue advantage of their helpfulness by his attempts to brazen it out. Sometimes a person may himself be undecided as to which practice to employ, leaving the others in the embarrassing position of not knowing which tack they are going to have to follow. Thus when a person makes a slight *gaffe,* he and the others may become embarrassed not because of inability to handle such difficulties, but because for a moment no one knows whether the offender is going to act blind to the incident, or give it joking recognition, or employ some other face-saving practice.

COOPERATION IN FACE-WORK

When a face has been threatened, face-work must be done, but whether this is initiated and primarily carried through by the person whose face is threatened, or by the offender, or by a mere witness,[20] is often of secondary importance. Lack of effort on the part of one person induces compensative effort from others; a contribution by one person relieves the others of the task. In fact, there

---

[18]Folklore imputes a great deal of poise to the upper classes. If there is truth in this belief it may lie in the fact that the upper-class person tends to find himself in encounters in which he outranks the other participants in ways additional to class. The ranking participant is often somewhat independent of the good opinion of the others and finds it practical to be arrogant, sticking to a face regardless of whether the encounter supports it. On the other hand, those who are in the power of a fellow-participant tend to be very much concerned with the valuation he makes of them or witnesses being made of them, and so find it difficult to maintain a slightly wrong face without becoming embarrassed and apologetic. It may be added that people who lack awareness of the symbolism in minor events may keep cool in difficult situations, showing poise that they do not really possess.

[19]Thus, in our society, when a person feels that others expect him to measure up to approved standards of cleanliness, tidiness, fairness, hospitality, generosity, affluence, and so on, or when he sees himself as someone who ought to maintain such standards, he may burden an encounter with extended apologies for his failings, while all along the other participants do not care about the standard, or do not believe the person is really lacking in it, or are convinced that he is lacking in it and see the apology itself as a vain effort at self-elevation.

[20]Thus one function of seconds in actual duels, as well as in figurative ones, is to provide an excuse for not fighting that both contestants can afford to accept.

are many minor incidents in which the offender and the offended simultaneously attempt to initiate an apology.[21] Resolution of the situation to everyone's apparent satisfaction is the first requirement; correct apportionment of blame is typically a secondary consideration. Hence terms such as tact and *savoir-faire* fail to distinguish whether it is the person's own face that his diplomacy saves or the face of the others. Similarly, terms such as *gaffe* and *faux pas* fail to specify whether it is the actor's own face he has threatened or the face of other participants. And it is understandable that if one person finds he is powerless to save his own face, the others seem especially bound to protect him. For example, in polite society, a handshake that perhaps should not have been extended becomes one that cannot be declined. Thus one accounts for the *noblesse oblige* through which those of high status are expected to curb their power of embarrassing their lessers,[22] as well as the fact that the handicapped often accept courtesies that they can manage better without.

Since each participant in an undertaking is concerned, albeit for differing reasons, with saving his own face and the face of the

---

[21]See, for instance, Jackson Toby, "Some Variables in Role Conflict Analysis" [*Social Forces* (1952) 30:323–37]: "With adults there is less likelihood for essentially trivial issues to produce conflict. The automatic apology of two strangers who accidentally collide on a busy street illustrates the integrative function of etiquette. In effect, each of the parties to the collision says, 'I don't know whether I am responsible for this situation, but *if* I am, you have a right to be angry with me, a right that I pray you will not exercise.' By defining the situation as one in which both parties must abase themselves, society enables each to keep his self-respect. Each may feel in his heart of hearts, 'Why can't that stupid ass watch where he's going?' But overtly *each plays the role of the guilty party* whether he feels he has been miscast or not" (p. 325).

[22]"Regardless of the person's relative social position, in one sense he has power over the other participants and they must rely upon his considerateness. When the others act toward him in some way, they presume upon a social relationship to him, since one of the things expressed by interaction is the relationship of the interactants. Thus they compromise themselves, for they place him in a position to discredit the claims they express as to his attitude toward them. Hence in response to claimed social relationships every person, of high estate or low, will be expected to exercise *noblesse oblige* and refrain from exploiting the compromised position of the others.

Since social relationships are defined partly in terms of voluntary mutual aid, refusal of a request for assistance becomes a delicate matter, potentially destructive of the asker's face. Chester Holcombe, *The Real Chinaman* (New York, Dodd, Mead, 1895) provides a Chinese instance: "Much of the falsehood to which the Chinese as a nation are said to be addicted is a result of the demands of etiquette. A plain, frank 'no' is the height of discourtesy. Refusal or denial of any sort must be softened and toned down into an expression of regretted inability. Unwillingness to grant a favor is never shown. In place of it there is seen a chastened feeling of sorrow that unavoidable but quite imaginary circumstances render it wholly impossible. Centuries of practice in this form of evasion have made the Chinese matchlessly fertile in the invention and development of excuses. It is rare, indeed, that one is caught at a loss for a bit of artfully embroidered fiction with which to hide an unwelcome truth" (pp. 274–75).

others, then tacit cooperation will naturally arise so that the participants together can attain their shared but differently motivated objectives.

One common type of tacit cooperation in face-saving is the tact exerted in regard to face-work itself. The person not only defends his own face and protects the face of the others, but also acts so as to make it possible and even easy for the others to employ face-work for themselves and him. He helps them to help themselves and him. Social etiquette, for example, warns men against asking for New Year's Eve dates too early in the season, lest the girl find it difficult to provide a gentle excuse for refusing. This second-order tact can be further illustrated by the widespread practice of negative-attribute etiquette. The person who has an unapparent negatively valued attribute often finds it expedient to begin an encounter with an unobtrusive admission of his failing, especially with persons who are uninformed about him. The others are thus warned in advance against making disparaging remarks about his kind of person and are saved from the contradiction of acting in a friendly fashion to a person toward whom they are unwittingly being hostile. This strategy also prevents the others from automatically making assumptions about him which place him in a false position and saves him from painful forbearance or embarrassing remonstrances.

Tact in regard to face-work often relies for its operation on a tacit agreement to do business through the language of hint—the language of innuendo, ambiguities, well-placed pauses, carefully worded jokes, and so on.[23] The rule regarding this unofficial kind of communication is that the sender ought not to act as if he had officially conveyed the message he has hinted at, while the recipients have the right and the obligation to act as if they have not officially received the message contained in the hint. Hinted communication, then, is deniable communication; it need not be faced up to. It provides a means by which the person can be warned that his current line or the current situation is leading to loss of face, without this warning itself becoming an incident.

Another form of tacit cooperation, and one that seems to be much used in many societies, is reciprocal self-denial. Often the person does not have a clear idea of what would be a just or acceptable apportionment of judgments during the occasion, and so he volun-

[23]Useful comments on some of the structural roles played by unofficial communication can be found in a discussion of irony and banter in Tom Burns, "Friends, Enemies, and the Polite Fiction," *Amer. Sociol. Rev.*, (1943) 18:654–62.

tarily deprives or depreciates himself while indulging and complimenting the others, in both cases carrying the judgments safely past what is likely to be just. The favorable judgments about himself he allows to come from the others; the unfavorable judgments of himself are his own contributions. This "after you, Alphonse" technique works, of course, because in depriving himself he can reliably anticipate that the others will compliment or indulge him. Whatever allocation of favors is eventually established, all participants are first given a chance to show that they are not bound or constrained by their own desires and expectations, that they have a properly modest view of themselves, and that they can be counted upon to support the ritual code. Negative bargaining, through which each participant tries to make the terms of trade more favorable to the other side, is another instance; as a form of exchange perhaps it is more widespread than the economist's kind.

A person's performance of face-work, extended by his tacit agreement to help others perform theirs, represents his willingness to abide by the ground rules of social interaction. Here is the hallmark of his socialization as an interactant. If he and the others were not socialized in this way, interaction in most societies and most situations would be a much more hazardous thing for feelings and faces. The person would find it impractical to be oriented to symbolically conveyed appraisals of social worth, or to be possessed of feelings— that is, it would be impractical for him to be a ritually delicate object. And as I shall suggest, if the person were not a ritually delicate object, occasions of talk could not be organized in the way they usually are. It is no wonder that trouble is caused by a person who cannot be relied upon to play the face-saving game.

FACE AND SOCIAL RELATIONSHIPS

When a person begins a mediated or immediate encounter, he already stands in some kind of social relationship to the others concerned, and expects to stand in a given relationship to them after the particular encounter ends. This, of course, is one of the ways in which social contacts are geared into the wider society. Much of the activity occurring during a encounter can be understood as an effort on everyone's part to get through the occasion and all the unanticipated and unintentional events that can cast participants in an undesirable light, without disrupting the relationships of the participants. And if relationships are in the process of change, the object will be to bring the encounter to a satisfactory close without altering the expected course of development. This perspective nicely accounts, for example, for the little ceremonies of greeting and farewell which occur when people begin a conversational encounter or depart from one. Greetings provide a way of showing that a relationship is still what it was at the termination of the previous coparticipation, and, typically, that this relationship involves sufficient suppression of hostility for the participants temporarily to drop their guards and talk. Farewells sum up the effect of the encounter upon the relationship and show what the participants may expect of one another when they next meet. The enthusiasm of greetings compensates for the weakening of the relationship caused by the absence just terminated, while the enthusiasm of farewells compensates the relationship for the harm that is about to be done to it by separation.[24]

It seems to be a characteristic obligation of many social relationships that each of the members guarantees to support a given face for the other members in given situations. To prevent disruption of these relationships, it is therefore necessary for each member to avoid destroying the others' face. At the same time, it is often the person's social relationship with others that leads him to participate in certain encounters with them, where incidentally he will be dependent upon them for supporting his face. Furthermore, in many relationships, the members come to share a face, so that in the presence of third parties an improper act on the part of one member becomes a source of acute embarrassment to the other members. A social relationship, then, can be seen as a way in which the person is more than ordinarily forced to trust his self-image and face to the tact and good conduct of others.

THE NATURE OF THE RITUAL ORDER

The ritual order seems to be organized basically on accommodative lines, so that the imagery used in thinking about other types

---

[24]Greetings, of course, serve to clarify and fix the roles that the participants will take during the occasion of talk and to commit participants to these roles, while farewells provide a way of unambiguously terminating the encounter. Greetings and farewells may also be used to state, and apologize for, extenuating circumstances—in the case of greetings for circumstances that have kept the participants from interacting until now, and in the case of farewells for circumstances that prevent the participants from continuing their display of solidarity. These apologies allow the impression to be maintained that the participants are more warmly related socially than may be the case. This positive stress, in turn, assures that they will act more ready to enter into contacts than they perhaps really feel inclined to do, thus guaranteeing that diffuse channels for potential communication will be kept open in the society.

of social order is not quite suitable for it. For the other types of social order a kind of schoolboy model seems to be employed: if a person wishes to sustain a particular image of himself and trust his feelings to it, he must work hard for the credits that will buy this self-enhancement for him; should he try to obtain ends by improper means, by cheating or theft, he will be punished, disqualified from the race, or at least made to start all over again from the beginning. This is the imagery of a hard, dull game. In fact, society and the individual join in one that is easier on both of them, yet one that has dangers of its own.

Whatever his position in society, the person insulates himself by blindness, half-truths, illusions, and rationalizations. He makes an "adjustment" by convincing himself, with the tactful support of his intimate circle, that he is what he wants to be and that he would not do to gain his ends what the others have done to gain theirs. And as for society, if the person is willing to be subject to informal social control—if he is willing to find out from hints and glances and tactful cues what his place is, and keep it—then there will be no objection to his furnishing this place at his own discretion, with all the comfort, elegance, and nobility that his wit can muster for him. To protect this shelter he does not have to work hard, or join a group, or compete with anybody; he need only be careful about the expressed judgments he places himself in a position to witness. Some situations and acts and persons will have to be avoided; others, less threatening, must not be pressed too far. Social life is an uncluttered, orderly thing because the person voluntarily stays away from the places and topics and times where he is not wanted and where he might be disparaged for going. He co-operates to save his face, finding that there is much to be gained from venturing nothing.

Facts are of the schoolboy's world—they can be altered by diligent effort but they cannot be avoided. But what the person protects and defends and invests his feelings in is an idea about himself, and ideas are vulnerable not to facts and things but to communications. Communications belong to a less punitive scheme than do facts, for communications can be by-passed, withdrawn from, disbelieved, conveniently misunderstood, and tactfully conveyed. And even should the person misbehave and break the truce he has made with society, punishment need not be the consequence. If the offense is one that the offended persons can let go by without losing too much face, then they are likely to act forbearantly, telling themselves that they will get even with the offender in another way at another time, even though such an occasion may never arise and might not be exploited if it did. If the offense is great, the offended persons may withdraw from the encounter, or from future similar ones, allowing their withdrawal to be reinforced by the awe they may feel toward someone who breaks the ritual code. Or they may have the offender withdrawn, so that no further communication can occur. But since the offender can salvage a good deal of face from such operations, withdrawal is often not so much an informal punishment for an offense as it is merely a means of terminating it. Perhaps the main principle of the ritual order is not justice but face, and what any offender receives is not what he deserves but what will sustain for the moment the line to which he has committed himself, and through this the line to which he has committed the interaction.

Throughout this paper it has been implied that underneath their differences in culture, people everywhere are the same. If persons have a universal human nature, they themselves are not to be looked to for an explanation of it. One must look rather to the fact that societies everywhere, if they are to be societies, must mobilize their members as self-regulating participants in social encounters. One way of mobilizing the individual for this purpose is through ritual; he is taught to be perceptive, to have feelings attached to self and a self expressed through face, to have pride, honor, and dignity, to have considerateness, to have tact and a certain amount of poise. These are some of the elements of behavior which must be built into a person if practical use is to be made of him as an interactant, and it is these elements that are referred to in part when one speaks of universal human nature.

Universal human nature is not a very human thing. By acquiring it, the person becomes a kind of construct, built up not from inner psychic propensities but from moral rules that are impressed upon him from without. These rules, when followed, determine the evaluation he will make of himself and of his fellow-participants in the encounter, the distribution of his feelings, and the kinds of practices he will employ to maintain a specified and obligatory kind of ritual equilibrium. The general capacity to be bound by moral rules may well belong to the individual, but the particular set of rules which transforms him into a human being derives from requirements established in the ritual organization of social encounters. And if a particular person or group or society seems to have a unique character all its own, it is because its standard set of human-nature elements is pitched and combined in a particular way. Instead of much pride, there may be little. Instead of abiding by the rules, there may be much effort to break them safely. But if an encounter or undertaking is to be sustained as a viable system of interaction organized on ritual principles, then these variations must be held within certain bounds and nicely counterbalanced by corresponding modifications in some of the other rules and understandings. Similarly, the human nature of a particular set of persons may be specially designed for the special kind of undertakings in which they participate, but still each of these persons must have within him something of the balance of characteristics required of a usable participant in any ritually organized system of social activity.

THE IMPOSTOR: CONTRIBUTION TO EGO PSYCHOLOGY OF A TYPE OF PSYCHOPATH*

Helene Deutsch

For psychoanalytic research in the field of psychopathy, the year 1925 constitutes a historical milestone, as it was then that Aichhorn published his book, *Wayward Youth*,[1] and Abraham his paper, "The History of a Swindler."[2] Whereas Aichhorn drew his knowledge from many years of observation and from the therapy of numerous cases, Abraham based his psychoanalytic findings on the study of one psychopath of a certain type. Abraham's paper has remained one of the classics of psychoanalytic literature. Following his example, I consider it especially valuable to single out from the many varieties of psychopathic personality one particular type and to attempt to understand him. The type I have chosen is the impos-

---

*Reprinted in its entirety from Helene Deutsch, "The Impostor: Contribution to Ego Psychology of a Type of Psychopath," *Psychoanalyt. Quart.*, Vol. 24, No. 4: (1955), 483–505. Used by permission.
[1] A. Aichhorn, *Verwahrloste Jugend*, Vienna, International Psychoanalytischer Verlag, 1925. (Translation: *Wayward Youth*, New York, Viking Press, 1935.)
[2] K. Abraham, Die Geschichte eines Hochstaplers in Lichte psychoanalytischer Erkenntnis, Imago, 11:355–370, 1925. (Translation by Strachey, A. *Psychoanalyt. Quart.*, 4:570–587, 1935.)

tor. I will restrict myself to the undramatic kind of impostor and leave the others—more fascinating ones—to a later publication.

About twenty years ago, the head of a large agency for the treatment of juvenile delinquents persuaded me to interest myself in a fourteen-year-old boy and, if possible, to lead him into analysis. The boy came from an exceedingly respectable family. His father, a business magnate, was a well-known philanthropist to whom the agency was indebted for major financial assistance. A typical American business man, he was entirely committed to the financial aspects of life. His sincerity and altruism gave him a dignity which everyone respected. He never pretended to be something he was not, and his business acumen was accompanied by a great sense of social responsibility. Son of a poor Lutheran clergyman, the manners and morals of his pious father were engrained in his character.

This father's hard work, perseverance, and—judging from his reputation—financial genius had made him one of the richest men in the community. He loved to stress the fact that he was a "self-made man," and it was his great ambition to leave his flourishing business to his sons for further expansion. At home he was a tyrant who made everyone tremble and subject to his command. His wife was a simple woman from a poor family, not very beautiful nor gifted with any sort of talent. He had simply married an obedient bed companion and housewife, let her share his material goods and, in part, his social prominence, and supported various members of her family.

Jimmy, the patient, was born late in the marriage. At his birth, his older brother was eleven, the next ten years old. The mother, always anxious, but warmhearted and tender, devoted herself completely to her youngest child. She indulged him endlessly, her chief interest being to please him. All his wishes were fulfilled and his every expression of displeasure was a command to provide new pleasures. In such an atmosphere, narcissism and passivity were bound to flourish. These were the foundations, the powerful predisposing factors for the boy's further development. The growing brothers abetted the mother's coddling, and for them the little boy was a darling toy to whom everything was given without expecting anything in return.

The father did not concern himself with the boy during the first three or four years of his life. In those days, Jimmy escaped the paternal tyranny, and the older brothers' battle against the despot took place outside the little boy's sphere of living. As the two older boys entered adolescence, this battle became more intense and ended in full rebellion. The younger brother, an introverted, artistically inclined boy, exchanged home for boarding school; the older, mechanically gifted, soon became independent and left the family.

The father was not a man to accept defeat. He simply renounced the older sons and, with his boundless energy, turned to his youngest, thus transferring the boy from his mother's care into his own. He partially retired from business but continued the pursuit of his financial and philanthropic activities from home. Jimmy, then four years old, spent the major part of the day with his father and heard his conversations with visitors who were all in a subordinate position to his father and in many cases financially dependent on him. The father became to him a giant, and the boy reacted to his father's efforts to make him active and aggressive and to arouse intellectual interests in him with some anxiety, yet with positive signs of compliance. A strong unity developed, and the process of the boy's identification with his father, which the latter had mobilized, was in full flower.

When Jimmy was seven, his father became the victim of a serious chronic illness resulting in five years of invalidism, during which time he lived at home in a wing removed from the central part of the house. Whether this illness was pulmonary tuberculosis or lung abscess never became clear. The boy saw very little of his father and the most vivid memory of this sickness was his father's malodorous sputum. According to Jimmy's report, his father remained alive only to spit and to smell bad.

Around this time a change took place in Jimmy. He developed a condition which appears to have been a genuine depression. He stopped playing, ate little, and took no interest in anything. Then— in a striking way—he became very aggressive, tyrannized his mother, and attempted to dominate his brothers. His first truancy was to run away to a nearby woods and refuse to come home. He created for himself a world of fantasy and described in a pseudological fashion his heroic deeds and the unusual events in which he had played a prominent role. These pseudologies, typical for his age, may well have been the precursors of Jimmy's future actions. While his mother—"for the sake of peace" and not to disturb the sick father— continued giving in to him in everything, his brothers now ridiculed him and relegated him to the role of a "little nobody."

In the course of the next few years, Jimmy had some difficulties in school. Though he was intelligent and learned quickly, he found it hard to accept discipline, made no real friends, was malicious and aggressive without developing any worthwhile activity—"a sissy," as he characterized himself. Since the father's name carried weight in the community, Jimmy felt with partial justification that nothing could happen to him, his father's son. He was not yet guilty of asocial acts, not even childish stealing.

When he was twelve years old, his once beloved father died. Jimmy did not feel any grief. His reaction was manifested in increased narcissistic demands, the devaluation of all authority, and in a kind of aggressive triumph: "I am free; I can do whatever I want." Soon afterward, his asocial acts began to occur.

Before we discuss his pathology, let us say a few words about this boy's relationship to his father, which suffered such a sudden break. In this alliance with his father, which began in his fifth year, the spoiled, passive little boy became in part the father's appendage. Identification with the powerful father created a situation in which the ego was simultaneously weakened and strengthened. When he had been in competition with the father, he was forced to feel small and weak; however, when he accepted as a criterion of his own value his father's verdict: "You are my wonderful boy," and his plans for the future: "You will be my successor," Jimmy's self-conception and ego image resembled his marvelous father, and his narcissism—originally cultivated by his mother—received new powers from his relationship with his father. In his seventh or eighth year Jimmy lost this "wonderful" father (not yet by death, but by devaluation), and his *own* conception of himself as a "wonderful boy" suffered a heavy blow.

The events of later years give more understanding of what took place in this period which was so fateful for him. As mentioned before, I first saw Jimmy when he was fourteen years old.

First Phase of Treatment

I was determined to resist accepting Jimmy for treatment. I had never had any experience in treating juvenile delinquents, associating such cases with Aichhorn and his school, which I considered outside my sphere. I yielded, however, to the pressure of the boy's mother, whom I knew and respected, and to the pleas of the heads of the social agency. Because of the uncertainty of my approach and in contrast to my usual habit, I made notes of Jimmy's behavior. They contain the results of four to six interviews. At the time they seemed somewhat sterile to me, and yet, regarding them in the light of later insights, they are extraordinarily illuminating. The interviews took place in 1935.

Jimmy was a typical young psychopath. He was increasingly unable to submit to the discipline of school. There was a repetitive pattern in his pathological acting out. At first he ingratiated himself by doing quite well; after a time he became insolent and rebellious toward his superiors, seduced his friends to break discipline, tried to impress them by the extravagance of his financial expenditures, and started quarrels and fights only to escape in a cowardly fashion under the ridicule of his companions. He forged checks with his mother's or older brother's signature and disrupted the school and the neighborhod by his misdeeds. Every attempt to bring about his adaptation by changing schools ended in truancy. Toward me he behaved very arrogantly. With an obvious lack of respect, he stated that he had not come of his own accord. He claimed nothing was wrong with him; that it was "the others" who would benefit by treatment.

He admitted he had again run away from school, and that this had been bad for him, and insisted that his trouble started when he began to "grow very fast." He wanted to remain a little boy; when he was little he was his father's pet. His father used to say, "Just wait until you are grown up; *we* (father and he) will show the world."

Jimmy complained that the boys laughed at him, but "You know," he said, "I can defend myself." Sometimes he was sincere and admitted that essentially he was helpless and weak: "You know, they never took me seriously at home. For my big brothers I was sort of a puppet, a joke. I was always a kid whose ideas did not count and whose performance was laughable."

School was like home. He had difficulties because not to learn meant showing them, "I can do what I want and do not have to obey." He forgot everything he learned, so "Why learn," he asked, "if I forget it?" He told me that his father had cursed his brothers: "I will show them," he had said, "they will end up in the gutter without my help." But to his father, Jimmy was different; father based all his hopes on him. When he was a little boy he felt that nothing could happen to him because his father was very powerful. Everything was subject to his father, and together they were allies against all hostile influences. His father's sickness changed all this.

The big promise, "We will show them," could not be redeemed. The brothers were now stronger than he. They ridiculed him, and he was waiting to be grown up; then he would show them!

In school it was always the same story. The teachers and especially the headmasters were "no good." They pretended to be something they were not. Of course he did not wish to obey them. He knew at least as much as they did, but they refused to acknowledge it. The boys were no good. Some might have been but they were led on by the others. And all this was instigated from "above" because "they" knew that he would not let himself be put upon.

In this short period of observation, I learned that Jimmy was infuriated by not being acknowledged as someone special; some of his complaints had an uncanny, paranoid character. During our meetings, Jimmy played the undaunted hero, but with no trace of any emotion. One got an impression of great affective emptiness in him. All his asocial acts were his means of showing that he was something special. Stealing, debts were ways of obtaining money for the purpose, one might say, of buying narcissistic gratifications. He rebelled against all authority and devalued it. The moment he perceived that the methods he employed no longer sustained his prestige, his displeasure quickly mounted and drove him away.

With me he was overbearing, arrogant, cocksure. One day he came with the question: "Are you a Freudian?" He then proceeded, most unintelligently, to lecture me about analysis with catchwords he had picked up, or remarks based on titles he had seen. For instance: "That thing about civilization is particularly idiotic," or "The old man (meaning Freud) isn't even a doctor." When I tried to point out to him that, after all, he did not know anything and that I believed he talked so big because he was afraid, he stopped coming; as usual, a truant.

He presented such a typical picture of a juvenile delinquent that I felt concern about his future, wondering whether he would eventually become a criminal. His lack of affect, inability to form human relationships, and paranoid ideas led me to consider the possibility of an incipient schizophrenia.

Second Phase of Treatment

I did not see Jimmy for eight years, but remained in contact with several people close to him. Some of the news about him was reassuring. He nevertheless confronted those around him with one problem after another. These were truancies in a more adult sense.

He accepted positions which he did not keep, responsibilities he failed to meet. He made promises and broke them, with serious consequences to himself and to others. He accepted financial commitments, but neglected them so that they ended in failure. He provoked situations ominous not only for himself but also for those whom he had lured into these situations with false promises—which to him, however, were real. Up to the time he came of age, his misdeeds were regarded as youthful indiscretions by the executors of the family estate. At twenty-one, he assumed that he was now financially independent and had already made financial commitments in the most extravagant ventures, when, to his fury, he was placed under legal guardianship.

With his customary bravado, Jimmy volunteered for military service during the war. He reported for duty on his new, shiny motorcycle. Soon he was the center of admiration among his comrades. Neither he nor they had any doubt that he would become one of the heroes of the war. He had, after all, volunteered to protect his fatherland, and his grandiose spending, his hints at connections with military authorities left no doubt that he was someone quite special. In this atmosphere he thrived until one day the news came that a commanding officer, noted for his severity, was to attend inspection. Jimmy had sufficient orientation in reality to realize that one cannot fool military authorities. The "hero" turned into a truant. But in military life, that was not so easy. One does not desert, as one does in civilian life under the auspices of an approving family. On the contrary, one is punished for such actions, and Jimmy could never tolerate punishment. He had an attack of anxiety—which was genuine—and a delusional state—which was not. He was declared to be sick, taken to a hospital, and from there was sent home.

The anxiety had been real, and his fear frightened him. His dream of being a hero was shattered. It is quite possible that under more favorable circumstances, Jimmy, like so many other heroes of wars and revolutions, might have made his pathology serve a glorious career. Now he remembered that years ago a woman had predicted just this kind of fear, and he came straight to me for help.

He was in so-called analysis, although it was actually more a supportive therapy, for eight years. The success of this treatment, while limited, was nevertheless important for him. During that period I witnessed many episodes in his pathological acting out and gained some insight into its nature. What kept him in treatment, however, was his anxiety which had increased since the war episode. It was evident that the defensive function of his acting out had been sufficiently threatened by reality that it was no longer adequate to hold internal dangers in check.

During the eight years which had elapsed since my first contact with Jimmy, he had been put through high school and prep school by the combined efforts of tutors, teachers, advisors, the head of the child guidance clinic, and his financial managers. They had even succeeded in having him admitted to a college where he stayed half a year. His intelligence and ability to grasp things quickly had, of course, been a help, but further than this he could not go. His narcissism did not permit him to be one of many; his self-love could be nourished only by feeling that he was unique. This desire for uniqueness did not, however, make him a lonely, schizoid personality. He was oriented toward reality, which to him was a stage on which he was destined to play the leading role with the rest of humanity as an admiring audience. There were for him no human relationships, no emotional ties which did not have narcissistic gratification as their goal. His contact with reality was maintained, but it was not object libido which formed the bridge to it. He was always active, and he surrounded himself with people; he sent out "pseudopodia," but only to retract them laden with gifts from the outside world.

After Jimmy left college, it was necessary to find him a job, to settle him in some field of work. All attempts at this, of course, failed. As in his school days, he could not tolerate authority and had no capacity for sustained effort. Success had to be immediate; he had to play the leading role from the start. He decided to become a gentleman farmer. A farm was purchased for him and he worked zealously on the plans for the farm. The preliminary work was done, the livestock was in the barn, and Jimmy even behaved as a socially responsible person. He created several positions at the farm for his former cronies; the fact that they knew as little about farming as he did was to him beside the point. His adaptation to reality had come to its end, and the enterprise was doomed to failure. Jimmy, however, acquired an elegant country outfit, saw to it that his clothing was saturated with barnyard smells, dyed his hair and eyebrows blond, and appeared among a group of former acquaintances in a New York restaurant as a "country gentleman." His farm project was soon involved in various difficulties, and his protégés deserted him; he was in debt and financial ruin seemed imminent when his guardians came to his rescue and he was saved by his fortune.

In another episode, Jimmy was a great writer. Here his pseudo-contact with others was even more intense. He presided over a kind of literary salon where intellectuals gathered about his fireplace, with Jimmy in the center. Short stories were his specialty for, of course, he lacked the capacity for prolonged, patient creativity. He knew how to make life so very pleasant for his literary admirers that they remained within his circle. He had even drawn several well-known writers into his orbit. He already visualized himself as a great writer and brought a sample of his productivity for me to read. When I seemed somewhat critical (his writing was pretentious and quite without originality), he was furious and told me that I simply did not understand modern literature.

He soon gave up his literary career to become a movie producer. He made connections with men in the industry and spent considerable sums of money, but the result was always the same. At one time he became an inventor and even succeeded in inventing a few small things. It was fascinating to watch the great ado over these little inventions and how he used them to appear a genius to himself and to others. He had calling cards printed with the identification "inventor" on them and set up a laboratory to work out his discoveries. This time, he chose as his collaborator an experienced physicist, and, within a short period, succeeded in making this man believe that Jimmy was a genius. With uncanny skill, he created an atmosphere in which the physicist was convinced that his own achievements were inspired by Jimmy, the genius. His pretense that he was a genius was often so persuasive that others were taken in for a short time. Jimmy's self-esteem was so inflated by these reactions from his environment that occasionally he was able to achieve things which to some degree justified the admiration which he himself had generated.

In the course of his treatment, I succeeded in getting Jimmy through college. His success in temporarily impressing his teachers as an outstanding student of philosophy was almost a farce. Actually he knew little beyond the titles and the blurbs on the jackets of the books, but on this basis he was able to engage for hours in polemics, and it was some time before he was found out. In these activities Jimmy did not impress us as a real imposter. His transformations from a pseudo-imposter into a real one were only transitory. For instance, he made certain connections by using the name of the abovementioned collaborator; another time, he altered his name in such a way that it was almost identical with the name of a celebrity in a particular field. He was not an extravagant imposter; his pretenses were always close to reality but were nevertheless a sham.

For the purposes of comparison, it may serve to summarize briefly the stories of impostors who are closely related to the type described. They differ only in the stability of their chosen roles. A fascinating example is the well-known case of Ferdinand Demara, which was much discussed several years ago.[3] After running away from home, Demara became, in turn, a teacher of psychology, a monk, a soldier, a sailor, a deputy sheriff, a psychiatrist, and a surgeon—always under another man's name. With almost incredible cleverness and skill, he obtained each time the credentials of an expert and made use of knowledge acquired ad hoc so brilliantly that he was able to perpetrate his hoaxes with complete success. It was always by accident, never through mistakes he had made, that he was exposed as an impostor. In his own estimation, he was a man of genius for whom it was not necessary to acquire academic knowledge through prolonged studies, but who was able to achieve anything, thanks to his innate genius.

Reading his life history, one sees that he was perpetually in pursuit of an identity which would do justice to his narcissistic conception of himself in terms of "I am a genius" and which at the same time would serve to deny his own identity. This denial of his own identity appears to me to be the chief motive for his actions, as is true in the case of other impostors. In the course of his masquerading, Demara did much capable work and could bask in the sunshine of his successes. His parents had wanted to finance his way through college and medical school but he was never interested in a conventional way of life. When interviewed by reporters he acknowledged his enormous ambition and his need to take "short cuts." He declared that he would like for a change to use his own name but that he could not because of all that had happened. Whenever Demara resumes his activities, one may presume it will be possible only under a usurped name or not at all. His statement that he cannot use his own name—however rational it may sound—is nevertheless the expression of a deeper motive.

Another famous impostor of recent years is the "physicist" Hewitt, who, under the name of Dr. Derry, began teaching theoretical physics, mathematics, and electrical engineering in numerous universities with great success, without ever having finished high school.[4]

[3]J. McCarthy, "The Master Impostor," *Life*. January 28, 1952.
[4]H. Brean, "Marvin Hewitt Ph(ony) D," *Life*, April 12, 1954.

Like Jimmy, he sometimes used his own name but, again like Jimmy, under false colors. He impersonated two different actual doctors of philosophy in physics, masqueraded as a nationally known man, and took responsible positions under various names. He had been unmasked twice, yet tried again to achieve success under still another physicist's name.

In Hewitt's life history, there are many analogies to Jimmy's history. Hewitt's need for admiration was as great as Jimmy's, and the narcissistic motive behind his masquerading was equally evident. At the beginning of his career as an impostor, Hewitt was somewhat unsure of himself, but when he found himself being admired, his personality unfolded its full capacities. He was able to create for himself an atmosphere of power and prestige. When he felt that his masquerading was becoming too dangerous, he abandoned his project, changed his name, and embarked on another masquerade which became a new source of narcissistic satisfaction. Sometimes he was presented with an opportunity to work under his own name, as he was a gifted and really brilliant man who could have had a successful career. Such offers he always turned down; he could work only under another name, in an atmosphere of tension, in the precarious situation of imminent exposure. Like Jimmy, he regarded himself as a genius and courted situations in which he would be exposed as the counterpart of a genius a liar, an impostor.

Demara, Hewitt, and Jimmy appear to be victims of the same pathological process of the ego—only the level of their functioning is different. Demara changed the objects of his identifications perhaps because he was driven by fear of impending unmasking. The objects whose names he temporarily bore corresponded to his high ego-ideal, and he was able to maintain himself on the high level of the men he impersonated. His manifold talents and his intelligence were outstanding, his capacity for sublimation was but little impaired. It was not lack of ability, but psychopathology which made him an impostor.

Hewitt had a much more consolidated ego-ideal. His interests were, from the beginning, oriented toward physics; his talent in this direction even made him a child prodigy; his path was marked out. But he rejected any success which he could realistically achieve through work and perserverance under his own name and preferred *pretending* under the mask of a stranger's name. The objects of his identification were physicists of repute, men who already were what he would have liked to become. In this as in the other cases,

I consider the incapacity to accept the demands imposed by the discipline of study, and the lack of perseverance, to be a secondary motive for becoming an impostor.

Jimmy, in his striving for an ego-ideal, appears to us like a caricature of Demara and Hewitt. In contrast to them, he was unable to find objects for successful identification because his limited capacity for sublimation and his lack of talent made this impossible for him. He was able to satisfy his fantasies of grandeur only in naive acting out, pretending that he was *really* in accordance with his ego-ideal. On closer examination, I was struck by the resemblance of his acting out to the performance of girls in prepuberty.

Various identifications which later in puberty can be explained as defense mechanisms and which one meets in schizoid personalities as expressions of a pathologic emotional condition, prove, on closer inspection, to have a specific character in prepuberty. They remind us strongly of the play of small children, and seem to be an "acting out" of those transitory, conscious wishes that express the idea, "That's what I want to be like." It is noteworthy that this acting out has a concrete and real character, different from mere fantasying.[5]

Jimmy, too, acted out his transitory ideal which never became fully established. Compared with Dr. Greenacre's "psychopathic patients,"[6] Jimmy's ideals did not have the character of magic grandeur and were not so unattached to reality. Quite the contrary, Jimmy always turned to external reality to gratify his narcissistic needs. His emptiness and the lack of individuality in his emotional life and moral structure remind us furthermore of the "as-if" personalities.[7] In contrast to these, Jimmy's ego did not dissolve in numerous identifications with external objects. He sought, on the contrary, to impose on others belief in his greatness, and in this he often succeeded. His only identifications were with objects which corresponded to his ego-ideal—just like the impostor Hewitt, only on a more infantile level. Another difference is that the "as-if" patients are not aware of their disturbance, whereas Jimmy, while firmly pretending that he *was* what he pretended to be, asked me again and again, sometimes in despair: "Who am I? Can *you* tell me that?"

In spite of these individual differences between the various types, I believe that all impostors have this in common: They as-

[5]H. Deutsch, *The Psychology of Women*, New York: Grune & Stratton, 1944, Vol. I., p. 9.

[6]P. Greenacre, "Conscience in the Psychopath," *Trauma, Growth, and Personality*, New York, W. W. Norton & Co. Inc., 1952, p. 167.

[7]H. Deutsch, "Some Forms of Emotional Disturbance and Their Relationship to Schizophrenia," *Psychoanalyt. Quart.*, 11:301–21, 1942.

sume the identities of other men not because they themselves lack the ability for achievement but because they have to hide under a strange name to materialize a more or less reality-adapted fantasy. It seems to me that the ego of the impostor, as expressed in his own true name, is devaluated, guilt laden. Hence he must usurp the name of an individual who fulfills the requirements of his own magnificent ego-ideal. Later we shall see that Jimmy's fear of being unmasked as an impostor increased when he began to be successful under his own name and figure.

As his treatment proceeded, Jimmy's fears increased as his acting out lessened. With this change of behavior he entered a new phase in this therapy, the phase of anxiety. It was this phase which revealed more of the nature of the process. But this does not mean that the phase of acting out was free of anxiety. It was anxiety that brought him to me, and anxiety kept him with me. In time, his increasing anxieties assumed a more hypochondriacal character. He examined his body, his pulse, and so on and wanted to be certain that a physician could be reached. It was not difficult to assume that a man whose personality was limited by an unsuccessful identification with his father repeated his father's disease in hypochondriacal symptoms.

By and by, Jimmy gave up his grotesque acting out, and his behavior became increasingly realistic. First, he founded an institute for inventions. This project was still in accordance with his fantasy of being a great inventor. Because he had associated himself with a friend who, despite his naive belief in Jimmy, was genuinely gifted scientifically and had already achieved recognition, and because of the considerable sums of money available, Jimmy gradually worked his way toward acquiring a going concern. Here, for the first time in his life, he functioned well and enjoyed a certain solid respect. He limited his acting out to founding a colony for artists in which he acted the role of a "brilliant connoisseur of art"; also he set up for himself some sort of an "altar" at home. He married a girl with an infantile personality who blindly believed in his genius and adored him. When she began to have doubts, he simply sent her away and threatened her with divorce. Love he never experienced; even from his children he expected gratifications for his narcissism and he hated them when they failed him in this respect.

The condition which now confronted us seemed paradoxical: The more effectively he functioned in reality, the more anxiety he developed. In the days when he had really been a swindler, he never feared exposure. Now that he worked more honestly and pretended less, he was tortured by the fear that his deceit might be discovered. He felt like an impostor in his new role—that of doing honest work. Obviously he remained an impostor after all, and, in his very real personal success, he now had an inner perception of his inferiority. In the beginning, we had had the suspicion that Jimmy always feared his own inferiority and that he was hiding his anxiety behind a bloated ego-ideal. It could now be better understood why he inquired after his identity, why he had the depersonalized feeling, "Who am I really?" In this, he reminds us of those more or less neurotic individuals who, having achieved success, experience like Jimmy the same inner motivation.

Jimmy's anxieties gradually acquired a phobic character. His professional activities were impeded by a fear of leaving town and of being too far from home. This evidently represented a counterphobic mechanism against his earlier running away.

Thus we may speak of a certain success in his treatment which was never a psychoanalysis. In my forty years of practice, I have never seen a patient as little capable of transference as Jimmy. He and I sometimes talked of "hot air therapy," for I called his grandiose acting out "hot air" until it was greatly devalued. At the same time, I appealed to his narcissism by showing him what he could really achieve. In this way we continued for eight years. About two years ago, I passed him on to a colleague who is continuing the therapy.

Reviewing Jimmy's pathological behavior chronologically, the connection between his preadolescent delinquency and his later acting out becomes clear. By the phrase he used when he came to see me as a fourteen-year-old, "I became grown up too fast," he meant to say that he did not yet feel capable of playing the role his father had assigned to him for a time when he would be grown up. His high ego-ideal, cultivated by the father, and an identification with the "great father" did not permit him—despite a certain degree of insight—to wait for the process of growing up to take place. He demanded that the world treat him not according to his achievements but according to his exalted ego-ideal. The refusal of his environment to do so was an attack on himself, on his grandeur, on his ego-ideal. This feeling that hostile elements were aligned against him grew at times into paranoid reactions. He responded to these insults in a way which brought him to the borderline of real criminal behavior, but when he began to feel that he was defeated, he ran away.

Perhaps, if he had had enough aggression at his disposal, he would have continued his career as a criminal. An appeal to his conscience was fruitless, as, after all, he considered himself to be a victim and his actions as self-defense. Maybe this is true of all juvenile delinquents. Social injustice and a desire to avenge oneself for it is often given as a reason for delinquent behavior. In Jimmy's case, such a rationalization could not be used.

His passivity led him in another direction. Instead of fighting for his narcissistic "rights," he found less dangerous and more regressive methods of asserting his ego-ideal. What he was not, he could become by pretending. Only when this was made impossible for him—first through external reality (the army), then through his treatment—was he overwhelmed by anxiety and feelings of inferiority, and one could then realize the defensive function of his pathological behavior.

We suspect that Demara and Hewitt, the other two impostors mentioned, were also hiding such an ego through identification with someone else's ego, by means of what might be called a nonego ego. In these cases of a more solidly constructed imposture, the inner anxiety is partly projected to the outside, and the impostor lives in perpetual fear of discovery. Jimmy did not fear such discovery, for he had not assumed another's name. What threatened him was that if his pretending were to be unmasked, he would be laughed at as he was once ridiculed by his brothers and later by his schoolmates. He developed real anxiety only when he gave up pretending, so that both he and others were confronted with his "true" ego.

Let us consider the causes of Jimmy's pathology. Dr. Greenacre[8]—in agreement with other writers—finds etiological factors in the emotional deprivation of psychopaths and delinquents. Her emphasis rests on the combination of both indulgence and severity on the part of the parental figures; this is in accordance with Wilhelm Reich's conception of the character structure of the psychopath.[9] The emotional climate of Jimmy's childhood was different, but evidently no less disastrous. Whereas Dr. Greenacre's patient was emotionally deprived, Jimmy was overloaded with maternal love. I knew the mother very well, and I know that she was one of those masochistic mothers who, loving and warmhearted, completely surrender themselves for the benefit of others. She was a masochistic

[8]Greenacre, *op. cit.*
[9]W. Reich, *Charakteranalyse.* Vienna, Published by the author, 1933. (Translation: *Character Analysis,* New York, Orgone Institute Press, 1945.)

victim not only of the despotic father but also of her children, especially Jimmy. Her last child's every wish was granted. Any active striving he had was paralyzed through premature compliance; every need for wooing and giving was smothered by the mother's loving initiative in meeting his demands.

I believe that the emotional overfeeding of a child is capable of producing very much the same results as emotional frustration. It contributes to an increase of infantile narcissism, makes adaptation to reality and relationship to objects more difficult. It creates intolerance of frustration, weakens the ego's ability to develop constructive defenses, and is in large measure responsible for passivity.

Jimmy's relationship with his father was very well suited to strengthen the predisposition created by the mother. The powerful, despotic personality of the father contributed to Jimmy's passivity, and the father's narcissism prepared the ground for Jimmy's later, fateful identification with him.

These attitudes of the parents created a predisposition for the pathological development of the boy. But it was a traumatic experience which activated this predisposition. The father's sickness and isolation caused an abrupt interruption of the normal maturing process of Jimmy's ego. The frustration stemming from the fact that Jimmy was no longer able to feel himself to be part of a great father crippled his ego which was not yet strong enough to endure the brutal attack of separation. The enforced awareness of his self as being distinct from that of his father was anachronistic in his development. The normal process of identification had not yet reached that degree of maturity from which further development would have been possible.

Simultaneously with the separation from his father came the devaluation of that powerful figure. Consequently, the character of his identification also underwent a change. What had so far strengthened his ego was no longer available. With the devaluation of the father, a shadow fell across his own identified ego. The fact that the traumatic event occurred in the latter part of latency was decisive for Jimmy's psychopathology. As we know, this period is of utmost importance for the maturation of the ego apparatus, for the establishment of a less rigid superego, and for the capacity to cope with reality. In a normal, gradual development of a boy in latency, not harmed by trauma, Jimmy would have transferred his identification with the father onto other suitable objects. Eventually his ego would have been ready to assimilate the identification into the self and to achieve a reliable degree of inner stability. His ambivalent sexual relationship to the father would have yielded to tender love, and a path toward reality and toward the formation of constant object relationship would have been made.

The pathogenic force of this trauma was due to two factors: (1) its suddenness, and (2) its daily repetition during the four years that preceded his father's death. As a result, regressive forces in the ego replaced progress in development, and the whole process of sublimation was impaired.[10] The boy was incapable of goal-oriented endeavor because he was unable to postpone reaching an attempted goal. The fact that his relationship to the father never became desexualized was revealed in his masturbatory fantasies of a passive-feminine-masochistic character and in his fears of homosexuality. His relationship to his mother became submerged in his identification with her as his father's debased sexual object. The manifestations of this identification could be traced back from his recent masturbatory fantasies to that period of his childhood in which he had been enuretic.[11]

It is interesting to observe pathology in what is commonly agreed to be normal. The world is crowded with "as-if" personalities and even more so with impostors and pretenders. Ever since I became interested in the impostor, he pursues me everywhere. I find him among my friends and acquaintances, as well as in myself. Little Nancy, a fine three-and-a-half-year-old daughter of one of my friends, goes around with an air of dignity, holding her hands together tightly. Asked about this attitude she explains: "I am Nancy's guardian angel, and I'm taking care of little Nancy." Her father asked her about the angel's name. "Nancy" was the proud answer of this little impostor.

Having referred to "normal impostors," I should clarify my conception of the term "impostor." The pathological impostor endeavors to eliminate the friction between his pathologically exaggerated ego-ideal and the other, devaluated, inferior, guilt laden part of his ego in a manner which is characteristic for him; he behaves as if his ego-ideal were identical with himself, and he expects everyone else to acknowledge this status. If the inner voice of his devaluated ego on the one hand, and the reactions of the outside world on the other hand, remind him of the unreality of his ego ideal, he still

---

[10]There are psychopaths endowed with great capacities for sublimation and creativeness, although their ego functioning is gravely impaired.

[11]J. J. Michaels, *Disorders of Character,* Springfield, Ill.: Charles C Thomas, 1955.

clings to this narcissistic position. He desperately tries—through pretending and under cover of someone else's name—to maintain his ego-ideal, to force it upon the world, so to speak.

A similar conflict, though in a milder form, seems to exist also in the normal personality. In the complex development of a normal individual there are certain irregularities, and only seldom can a successful harmony be attained. Perhaps the identity between the ego-ideal and the self is achieved only by saints, geniuses, or psychotics. As one's ego-ideal can never be completely gratified from *within*, we direct our demands to the external world, *pretending* (like Jimmy) *that we actually are what we would like to be.* Very often we encounter paranoid reactions in normal personalities which result from the fact that their environment has refused to accept an imposture of this sort.

Both history and belletristic literature are rich in impostors. Thomas Mann's story about the impostor Felix Krull shows the most profound understanding of this type.[12] It is amazing to consider how the psychological genius of a writer is able to grasp intuitively insights at which we arrive laboriously through clinical empiricism. The passivity, the narcissistic ego-ideal, the devaluation of the father's authority, and the complicated processes of identification of the impostor Felix Krull are very well understood by Mann; and even the profound similarity between the shabby Krull and the wealthy, distinguished prince whose name and existence Krull, the impostor, takes over, is well understood by the writer.

I wish to close by repeating what I stated at the beginning. The case here discussed represents only a certain type of psychopath. I believe that such an individual typological approach to the large problem of psychopathy may prove very fruitful.

---

[12]T. Mann, *Bekenntnisse des Hochstaplers Felix Krull,* Frankfurt: Fischer Verlag, 1954. (Translation: *Confessions of Felix Krull,* New York: Alfred A. Knopf, 1955.)

SHOOTING AN ELEPHANT*

George Orwell

In Moulmein, in Lower Burma, I was hated by large numbers of people—the only time in my life that I have been important enough for this to happen to me. I was sub-divisional police officer of the town, and in an aimless, petty kind of way anti-European feeling was very bitter. No one had the guts to raise a riot, but if a European woman went through the bazaars alone somebody would probably spit betel juice over her dress. As a police officer I was an obvious target and was baited whenever it seemed safe to do so. When a nimble Burman tripped me up on the football field and the referee (another Burman) looked the other way, the crowd yelled with hideous laughter. This happened more than once. In the end the sneering yellow faces of young men that met me everywhere, the insults hooted after me when I was at a safe distance, got badly on my nerves. The young Buddhist priests were the worst of all. There were several thousands of them in the town and none of them seemed to have anything to do except stand on street corners and jeer at Europeans.

All this was perplexing and upsetting. For at that time I had already made up my mind that imperialism was an evil thing and the sooner I chucked up my job and got out of it the better. Theoretically—and secretly, of course—I was all for the Burmese and all against their oppressors, the British. As for the job I was doing, I hated it more bitterly than I can perhaps make clear. In a job like that you see the dirty work of Empire at close quarters. The wretched prisoners huddling in the stinking cages of the lock-ups, the grey, cowed faces of the long-term convicts, the scarred buttocks of the men who had been flogged with bamboos—all these oppressed me with an intolerable sense of guilt. But I could get nothing into perspective. I was young and ill-educated and I had had to think out my problems in the utter silence that is imposed on every Englishman in the East. I did not even know that the British Empire is dying, still less did I know that it is a great deal better than the younger empires that are going to supplant it. All I knew was that I was stuck between my hatred of the empire I served and my rage against the evil-spirited little beasts who tried to make my job impossible. With one part of my mind I thought of the British Raj as an unbreakable tyranny, as something clamped down, in *saecula saeculorum,* upon the will of prostrate peoples; with another part I thought that the greatest joy in the world would be to drive a bayonet into a Buddhist priest's guts. Feelings like these are the normal by-products of imperialism; ask any Anglo-Indian official, if you can catch him off duty.

One day something happened which in a roundabout way was enlightening. It was a tiny incident in itself, but it gave me a better glimpse than I had had before of the real nature of imperialism— the real motives for which despotic governments act. Early one morning the sub-inspector at a police station the other end of the town rang me up on the 'phone and said that an elephant was ravaging the bazaar. Would I please come and do something about it? I did not known what I could do, but I wanted to see what was happening and I got on to a pony and started out. I took my rifle, an old .44 Winchester and much too small to kill an elephant, but I thought the noise might be used in *terrorem.* Various Burmans stopped me on the way and told me about the elephant's doings. It was not, of course, a wild elephant, but a tame one which had gone "must." It had been chained up, as tame elephants always are when their attack of "must" is due, but on the previous night it had broken its chain and escaped. Its mahout, the only person who could manage it when it was in that state, had set out in pursuit, but had taken the wrong direction and was now twelve hours' journey away, and in the morning the elephant had suddenly reappeared in the town. The Burmese population had no weapons and were quite helpless against it. It had already destroyed somebody's bamboo hut, killed a cow and raided some fruit-stalls and devoured the stock; also it had met the municipal rubbish van and, when the driver jumped out and took to his heels, had turned the van over and inflicted violences upon it.

The Burmese sub-inspector and some Indian constables were waiting for me in the quarter where the elephant had been seen. It was a very poor quarter, a labyrinth of squalid bamboo huts, thatched with palm-leaf, winding all over a steep hillside. I remember that it was a cloudy, stuffy morning at the beginning of the rains. We began questioning the people as to where the elephant had gone and, as usual, failed to get any definite information. That is invariably the case in the East; a story always sounds clear enough at a distance, but the nearer you get to the scene of events the vaguer it becomes. Some of the people said the elephant had gone in one direction, some said that he had gone in another, some professed not even to have heard of any elephant. I had almost made up my mind that the whole story was a pack of lies, when we heard yells a little distance away. There was a loud, scandalized cry of "Go away, child! Go away this instant!" and an old woman with a switch in her hand came round the corner of a hut, violently shooing away a crowd of naked children. Some more women followed, clicking their tongues and exclaiming; evidently there was something that the children ought not to have seen. I rounded the hut and saw a man's dead body sprawling in the mud. He was an Indian, a black Dravidian coolie, almost naked, and he could not have been dead many minutes. The people said that the elephant had come suddenly upon him round the corner of the hut, caught him with its trunk, put its foot on his back, and ground him into the earth. This was the rainy season and the ground was soft, and his face had scored a trench a foot deep and a couple of yards long. He was lying on his belly with arms crucified and head sharply twisted to one side. His face was coated with mud, the eyes wide open, the teeth bared and grinning with an expression of unendurable agony. (Never tell me, by the way, that the dead look peaceful. Most of the corpses I have seen looked devilish.) The friction of the great beast's foot had stripped the skin from his back as neatly as one skins a rabbit. As soon as I saw the dead man I sent an orderly to a friend's house nearby to borrow an elephant rifle. I had already sent back the pony, not wanting it to go mad with fright and throw me if it smelt the elephant.

The orderly came back in a few minutes with a rifle and five cartridges, and meanwhile some Burmans had arrived and told us that the elephant was in the paddy fields below, only a few hundred yards away. As I started forward practically the whole population of the quarter flocked out of the houses and followed me. They had seen the rifle and were all shouting excitedly that I was going to shoot the elephant. They had not shown much interest in the elephant when he was merely ravaging their homes, but it was different now that he was going to be shot. It was a bit of fun to them, as it would be to an English crowd; besides they wanted the meat. It made me vaguely uneasy. I had no intention of shooting the elephant—I had merely sent for the rifle to defend myself if necessary—and it is always unnerving to have a crowd following you. I marched down the hill, looking and feeling a fool, with the rifle over my shoulder and an ever-growing army of people jostling at my heels. At the bottom, when you got away from the huts, there was a metalled road and beyond that a miry waste of paddy fields a thousand yards across, not yet ploughed but soggy from the first rains and dotted with coarse grass. The elephant was standing eight yards from the road, his left side towards us. He took not the slightest notice of the crowd's approach. He was tearing up bunches of grass, beating them against his knees to clean them and stuffing them into his mouth.

I had halted on the road. As soon as I saw the elephant I knew with perfect certainty that I ought not to shoot him. It is a serious matter to shoot a working elephant—it is comparable to destroying a huge and costly piece of machinery—and obviously one ought not to do it if it can possibly be avoided. And at that distance, peacefully eating, the elephant looked no more dangerous than a cow. I thought then and I think now that his attack of "must" was already passing off; in which case he would merely wander harmlessly about until the mahout came back and caught him. Moreover, I did not in the least want to shoot him. I decided that I would watch him for a little while to make sure that he did not turn savage again, and then go home.

But at that moment I glanced round at the crowd that had followed me. It was an immense crowd, two thousand at the least and growing every minute. It blocked the road for a long distance on either side. I looked at the sea of yellow faces above the garish clothes—faces all happy and excited over this bit of fun, all certain that the elephant was going to be shot. They were watching me as they would watch a conjurer about to perform a trick. They did not like me, but with the magical rifle in my hands I was momentarily worth watching. And suddenly I realized that I should have to shoot the elephant after all. The people expected it of me and I had got to do it; I could feel their two thousand wills pressing me forward, irresistibly. And it was at this moment, as I stood there with the rifle in my hands, that I first grasped the hollowness, the futility of the white man's dominion in the East. Here was I, the white man with his gun, standing in front of the unarmed native crowd—seemingly the leading actor of the piece; but in reality I was only an absurd puppet pushed to and fro by the will of those yellow faces behind. I perceived in this moment that when the white man turns tyrant it is his own freedom that he destroys. He becomes a sort of hollow, posing dummy, the conventionalized figure of a sahib. For it is the condition of his rule that he shall spend his life in trying to impress the "natives," and so in every crisis he has got to do what the "natives" expect of him. He wears a mask, and his face grows to fit it. I had got to shoot the elephant. I had committed myself to doing it when I sent for the rifle. A sahib has got to act like a sahib; he has got to appear resolute, to know his own mind and do definite things. To come all that way, rifle in hand, with two thousand people marching at my heels, and then to trail feebly away, having done nothing—no, that was impossible. The crowd would laugh at me. And my whole life, every white man's life in the East, was one long struggle not to be laughed at.

But I did not want to shoot the elephant. I watched him beating his bunch of grass against his knees, with that preoccupied grandmotherly air that elephants have. It seemed to me that it would be murder to shoot him. At that age I was not squeamish about killing animals, but I had never shot an elephant and never wanted to. (Somehow it always seems worse to kill a *large* animal.) Besides, there was the beast's owner to be considered. Alive, the elephant was worth at least a hundred pounds; dead, he would only be worth the value of his tusks, five pounds, possibly. But I had got to act quickly. I turned to some experienced-looking Burmans who had been there when we arrived, and asked them how the elephant had been behaving. They all said the same thing: he took no notice of you if you left him alone, but he might charge if you went too close to him.

It was perfectly clear to me what I ought to do. I ought to walk up to within, say, twenty-five yards of the elephant and test his behavior. If he charged, I could shoot; if he took no notice of me, it would be safe to leave him until the mahout came back. But also I knew that I was going to do no such thing. I was a poor shot with a rifle and the ground was soft mud into which one would sink at every step. If the elephant charged and I missed him, I should have about as much chance as a toad under a steam-roller. But even then I was not thinking particularly of my own skin, only of the watchful yellow faces behind. For at that moment, with the crowd watching me, I was not afraid in the ordinary sense, as I would have been if I had been alone. A white man mustn't be frightened in front of "natives"; and so, in general, he isn't frightened. The sole thought in my mind was that if anything went wrong those two thousand Burmans would see me pursued, caught, trampled on and reduced to a grinning corpse like that Indian up the hill. And if that happened it was quite probable that some of them would laugh. That would never do. There was only one alternative. I shoved the cartridges into the magazine and lay down on the road to get a better aim.

The crowd grew very still, and a deep, low, happy sigh, as of people who see the theatre curtain go up at last, breathed from innumerable throats. They were going to have their bit of fun after all. The rifle was a beautiful German thing with cross-hair sights. I did not then know that in shooting an elephant one would shoot to cut an imaginary bar running from ear-hole to ear-hole. I ought, therefore, as the elephant was sideways on, to have aimed straight at his ear-hole; actually I aimed several inches in front of this, thinking the brain would be further forward.

When I pulled the trigger I did not hear the bang or feel the kick—one never does when a shot goes home—but I heard the devilish roar of glee that went up from the crowd. In that instant, in too short a time, one would have thought, even for the bullet to get there, a mysterious, terrible change had come over the elephant. He neither stirred nor fell, but every line of his body had altered. He looked suddenly stricken, shrunken, immensely old, as though the frightful impact of the bullet had paralysed him without knocking him down. At last, after what seemed a long time—it might have been five seconds, I dare say—he sagged flabbily to his knees. His mouth slobbered. An enormous senility seemed to have settled upon him. One could have imagined him thousands of years old. I fired again into the same spot. At the second shot he did not collapse but climbed with desperate slowness to his feet and stood weakly upright, with legs sagging and head drooping. I fired a third time. That was the shot that did for him. You could see the agony of it jolt his whole body and knock the last remnant of strength from his legs. But in falling he seemed for a moment to rise, for as his hind legs collapsed beneath him he seemed to tower upward like a huge rock toppling, his trunk reaching skywards like a tree. He trumpeted, for the first and only time. And then down he came, his belly towards me, with a crash that seemed to shake the ground even where I lay.

I got up. The Burmans were already racing past me across the mud. It was obvious that the elephant would never rise again, but he was not dead. He was breathing very rhythmically with long rattling gasps, his great mound of a side painfully rising and falling. His mouth was wide open—I could see far down into caverns of pale pink throat. I waited a long time for him to die, but his breathing did not weaken. Finally I fired my two remaining shots into the spot where I thought his heart must be. The thick blood welled out of him like red velvet, but still he did not die. His body did not even jerk when the shots hit him, the tortured breathing continued without a pause. He was dying, very slowly and in great agony, but in some world remote from me where not even a bullet could damage him further. I felt that I had got to put an end to that dreadful noise. It seemed dreadful to see the great beast lying there, powerless to move and yet powerless to die, and not even to be able to finish him. I sent back for my small rifle and poured shot after shot into his heart and down his throat. They seemed to make no impression. The tortured gasps continued as steadily as the ticking of a clock.

In the end I could not stand it any longer and went away. I heard later that it took him half an hour to die. Burmans were bringing dahs and baskets even before I left, and I was told they had stripped his body almost to the bones by the afternoon.

Afterwards, of course, there were endless discussions about the shooting of the elephant. The owner was furious, but he was only an Indian and could do nothing. Besides, legally I had done the right thing, for a mad elephant has to be killed, like a mad dog, if its owner fails to control it. Among the Europeans opinion was divided. The older men said I was right, the younger men said it was a damn shame to shoot an elephant for killing a coolie, because an elephant was worth more than any damn Coringhee coolie. And afterwards I was very glad that the coolie had been killed; it put me legally in the right and it gave me a sufficient pretext for shooting the elephant. I often wondered whether any of the others grasped that I had done it solely to avoid looking a fool.

THE USES OF FRATERNITY*

Kenneth D. Benne

Many people find it a contradiction to emphasize group experience as a condition of eliciting and stabilizing individuality in members of our mass society. Such an emphasis often evokes defensive and anxious responses against both "groups" and "conformity." The anxiety seems deepest in those intellectuals most committed to the battle for individualism and freedom, who see a radical disjunction, if not a downright contradiction, between "group" and "individual," between "fraternity" and "freedom." As the cohorts of a specious "togetherness" grow stronger and more vocal, anxiety is transmuted into despair. Yet this despair-engendering disjunction is not a valid one, although it disturbs many democratic-minded American intellectuals.

A clarification of the meaning and uses of "fraternity" may help. The traditional literature of democracy gives us relatively little aid. Liberty and equality have been extensively compared and contrasted, analyzed, berated and defended, but fraternity has remained neglected. Connoting as it does the relations of siblings, and by extension any peer relation, fraternity has stood in Western minds under the shadow of parent-child relations and, by extension, of leader-follower or, in bureaucratic forms, superior-subordinate relations.

The normative orientation of our democratic culture, including its qualified commitment to "brotherhood," was shaped within a Hebraic-Christian religious heritage. In this heritage, the ideal relation, in the first instance, is between parent and child—the relation of God to man—and, only secondarily, a peer relation—the relation of man to man. In the former, the themes of dependence and counterdependence, often posturing as independence, predominate. As the Bible enjoins man to function in the image of God, personal maturity is conceived in terms of independence, autonomy, self-suffi-

*Reprinted in its entirety from Kenneth D. Benne, "The Uses of Fraternity," *Daedalus: Journal of the American Academy of Arts and Sciences,* Spring, 1961, pp. 233–46. Used by permission.

ciency. It is difficult to keep in focus the alternative ideal of maturity—the ability to function autonomously, creatively, and productively in interdependence—an ideal more consonant with the democratic value of fraternity. The second lacks the "reality" of the first, not only in the secular thinking about processes of maturation and socialization by psychotherapists and teachers, by parents and publicists, but also in the religious thinking of priests and rabbis.

In contemporary scientific studies of human development, their main line, as inspired by Freud, is for the most part firmly within this religiously shaped tradition. In Freudian thought the "representative anecdote" (to use Kenneth Burke's term) for characterizing the agony of maturation is the Oedipus myth. In this view, both the central problem and the dynamism of personal maturation remain within the parent-child relation and the various surrogates of this relation. Freud might have evolved a different version of the process of human development had he instead taken the parable of Joseph and his brethren as "representative anecdote." If he had, the place of peer relations in man's development would have been illuminated. The values and dis-values of peer-group membership in eliciting a man's talents and stabilizing his orientations would have moved from the periphery to the center of our awareness. Joseph's relations with Jacob and Rachel would still have been important, but equally so would his peer relations.

Our traditional thinking on human relations has developed a vast literature on leadership but only a tiny one on membership. "Members" tend to dissolve into a faceless host of followers, and so fail to be studied in their own right. Nor is it surprising that the thinking about an individual's socialization has been dominated by parent-child and teacher-pupil relations. Correspondingly, it has neglected the problems of peer relations within the processes of education and socialization. This imbalance of attention is no accident, and it represents more than a cognitive difficulty, one that goes considerably deeper into the values of our culture. Before it can be overcome, Americans will have to do more than acquire additional concepts and knowledge of groups and peer-group relations. Yet the relative emphasis on the influence of parents (or parent-surrogates) and peer groups in the processes of socialization seems to be undergoing a fundamental change within our increasingly bureaucratized and suburbanized culture.

David Riesman has observed in the adult community of our culture a continued habit of mind once considered characteristic of adolescence.[1] Possessed of no inner convictions, or torn by pulls and counter-pulls as to right orientations, many adults, when faced with alternatives, turn to their peers in determining what opinions to hold, what conduct to adopt. "Other-directedness" replaces "inner-directedness." The "normal" takes the place of the "normative." The peer group has become, and tends to remain, the principal arbiter of adult choices and evaluations.

William H. Whyte has dissected the governing values of the managerial elites and sub-elites in our suburbs and exurbs.[2] He, too, notes a decline of inner direction. The chief aim of life is to satisfy the demands of "the organization," its Kafkaesque internal needs, and its needs in public relations, which are often contradictory. Organizational policies (more and more determined by group processes) are elevated to the status once occupied in the Protestants' system of values by theology and the ways of the fathers.

These changes in the guiding values of adults are bound to bring correlative changes in the rearing of children. Indeed, shifts in these patterns must have been occurring far earlier in order to have made the alleged changes in character patterns noted in many contemporary adults. One theme runs through much of the already large and growing literature on the patterns of early socialization in American culture. The influence of peer groups in adolescent attitudes, orientations, and the criteria of taste and morality (always a strong one) is being accentuated in contemporary "teen-age" culture. And the role of the peer group, as against the family group, in validating the self seems to be gaining ground in children well below the age of adolescence.

The purveyors of the instruments of enculturation—popular music, magazines, comic books, television programs—are well aware of the emergence of a distinctive "youth" market and are exploiting it. They realize that the peer group has gained as an arbiter of youthful taste and conduct. Even a casual examination of the products prepared for this market indicates a "new" image of hero and heroine, for whom the peer group, not the adult, is the source of criteria for self-validation, for determining success or failure. Youthful heroes and heroines accept the authoritative limits to their actions set by

---

[1] See particularly David Riesman (with Reul Denny and Nathan Glazer), *The Lonely Crowd* (New Haven: Yale University Press, 1950); also David Riesman, *Individualism Reconsidered* (Glencoe: The Free Press, 1954).

[2] William H. Whyte, *The Organization Man* (New York: Simon and Schuster, 1956).

their parents more to humor or conciliate them than through any conviction that they may be right. Nor do they respect such limits in a spirit of healthy rebellion that projects an alternative rightness.

A favorite approach by young people in persuading parents as to a new idea about clothing, recreation, or privileges is that all the others in their age group now possess and enjoy whatever they are asking for. It is hard for parents to resist this appeal, since their own choices of what is needed in a good home are made on the same consensual basis. One story shows a convergence in the process of consensual validation on the part of two generations. The parents in a suburban town were widely entreated by their fifth-grade children to extend bedtime on the basis that all the others in the fifth grade were enjoying this new freedom. The parents got together and adopted a common standard for negotiating with their children. It is difficult to say how typical this way of dealing with a "value-issue" between children and parents actually is. Probably its main atypicality lies in the highly conscious way in which the processes of consensual validation were employed by the parents.

The trends in our culture seem to elevate the peer group as an influence in both early and continuing socialization and to diminish both the influence of parents and parental surrogates in early socialization and also that of internalized parent figures (in the form of superego and ego ideal) on continuing processes of socialization in adults. Whether the effects of these trends are admirable or not, they respond to a social reality—the fact of persuasive change, which moves all men away from a reliance upon fixed traditions as the validators of choice and conduct.

Today, socialization and resocialization are not complete, in any sense of the word, at the end of adolescence. Adults are pressed by a changing reality to make and remake major choices as to career, outlook on the world, or political and ethical orientations. Previous choices are being continually upset. Adults who do not avoid the reality of the choices confronting them, though they frequently do so, turn for guidance to some source other than fixed traditions. Consensual validation by some groups or groups of peers is a realistic adjustment to this situation. It is not something that can be abolished by preaching against it.

If we accept the trend as actual and in some measure based on reality, that does not, however, support the near despair of many democratic intellectuals; the values of individuality or of liberty, in a positive rather than a negative sense, need not fall prey to the trend. Stripped of its sophistications, the claim that they must runs like this: if in early experience peer-group influences become a socializing force with a much greater influence than they once had, the values of individuality and freedom in our culture are doomed. The argument assumes that peer-group influences cannot be utilized to elicit, strengthen and develop individual resourcefulness and talent. It assumes also the triumph of "equality in mediocrity." In this degraded sense, equality is stripped of its normative meaning of uninhibited access to resources for various patterns of individual or subgroup development, and it becomes instead a uniformity or sameness among people.

These assumptions bring our attention back to the relation of fraternity to liberty and equality. The part fraternity has played within the traditional drama of socialization may help to explain the fixation which impels many people to oppose peer-group influences on "individuality" and "equality."

In traditional patterns of socialization, peer-group influences have been related dialectically to those of parents or parent-surrogates—that is, they have been assumed to operate in opposition to the legitimate influences of parents or parent-surrogates. Ideally, if the dialectic were completed, out of the conflict there should come a synthesis, in which children could become the productive partners of their parents or teachers. The normative orientation of our culture and the dominant social organization which has fostered it have so far operated against the completion of this dialectic.

Peer groups among siblings within a family are often formed to resist objectionable parental directives or influences. The normal rivalry for parental approval is then suppressed in the interest of a united front. Any group with the primary goal of defense against authority develops rigid codes of loyalty and standards of uniform behavior. The range of individual variation among its members is narrowed. Their distrust of deviations from group codes is augmented when, outside the defensive or offense alliance, the members are rivals. There is something clandestine in the affairs of such associations; vows of secrecy are rigidly enforced. Thus, the function of fraternity in its earliest manifestations within a traditional family has been to reward the standardization of its members and to punish individual variations.

In this respect, the situation is not different in the nonfamilial adolescent peer group, which also functions both offensively and defensively in the dialectical process of transferring authority away from the family. Again, the function of fraternity has traditionally been identified with group standards which punish individual variations and which tend to reward conformity to a type. The enemy here is not only powerful: it carries with it legitimacy, which in part the rebels themselves accept. Mechanisms for handling guilt get involved with this brave banding together to defy authority.

The profusion of adult peer groups, or voluntary associations, have likewise served offensive and defensive purposes in resisting the pressures of the dominant society, such as the purposes of immigrants striving to maintain the ethnic patterns of the old country against the pressures of the dominant Anglo-Saxon, white, Protestant culture. Groups like the religious denominations within a religiously pluralistic society have traditionally been enrolled for attack and defense, however ambivalent their professed ethic of brotherhood may have made them in recognizing this motivation. Upwardly mobile vocational groupings—labor unions, for example—have developed a semi-military internal organization in their struggles to heighten the social and economic status of their members.

In the light of these experiences, it is hardly surprising that peer-group solidarity and loyalty should be considered as inherently opposed to individual variations in taste, thought, or conduct. The uses of fraternity that we know first and best have been to reduce and narrow, rather than to widen and enhance, the range of members' individual variations in expression and development. Fraternity in this view *is* opposed to liberty, and peer group to individuality.

But this opposition is neither inherent nor necessary in peer-group experience. Cohesion and the suppression of individual variations are not inevitable concomitants in the life of a group. A group organized for purposes other than simple offense or defense against authority develops an internal division of labor, the better to achieve its common purpose. Differences in ability and talent lend strength to a group, if the talents complement one another in relation to its goal. A good baseball team cannot be made up entirely of pitchers; it requires a variety of abilities, in the interest of the game. The emphasis is on achievement, not on defense or offense against authority. Where the accepted goal of a group requires complementary and variegated abilities, variations in individual behavior are rewarded rather than punished, encouraged rather than condemned.

The principle of complementarity among members has forced itself upon the attention of students of group life. The rationalization of life that has accompanied the bureaucratization of work, of health and social services, and of education has necessitated the deliberate formation of groups—in contrast with families, agrarian neighborhoods, or guilds, which were not consciously built. This process has made objective studies of the formation and operation of groups both possible and necessary. Men who are to build groups must know something about how they work; they cannot depend on traditions.

Study has drawn attention to some characteristics of groups other than those related to early socialization and has focused on groups in which the engrossing drama of counterdependence and dependence is not so focal or so deep. A comparison of the operation of authority-subordinate relations with that of peer relations in the lives of various groups is now possible.

It is easy to see in problem-solving and activity groups—as in all those formed for achieving a task—that group processes may be applied to elicit, reward and develop differing abilities for whatever the goal requires. But this observation about the operation of task groups falls far short of answering questions about peer-group experiences in releasing individual talent. The effects of group participation on the value systems and life orientations of the members are also important. Many peer-group influences on children and adults in contemporary organizations with a well-rationalized task are now working toward destroying individuality rather than developing distinctive styles and talents. Contemporary group experiences often educate members against a value system which would lead them to continue to develop their own abilities. The functional rationalization of society has often led to an increase in the irrationality of its members. If teachers or other group leaders focus primarily or solely on rationalizing the task of problem-solving aspects of group life, they may fail to recognize the deeply "miseducative" effects of these group-experiences on their members.[3]

Peer-group experiences, however, can not only help members to work more effectively with others but also to develop the basic attitudes and values that aid the growth of an autonomous and ra-

---

[3]Paul Goodman's comment on "progressive education" is eloquent on this point. "This radical proposal, aimed at solving the dilemmas of education in the modern circumstances of industrialism and democracy, was never given a chance. It succeeded in destroying the faculty psychology in the interests of educating the whole person, and in emphasizing group experiences, but failed to introduce learning-by-doing with real problems. The actual result of the gains has been to . . . foster adjustment to society as it is" (*Growing Up Absurd* [New York: Random House, 1960], p. 225).

tional individual. Some of these values are: an awareness and acceptance of self in its limitations and uniqueness; a validation of self as capable (within limits) of creative accomplishment; a commitment to build and maintain an interdependence with others, in which help can be both given and received; and a positive appraisal of the differences and conflicts among members as potentially productive of growth and progress. These values are either absent or are being destroyed in many natural processes of socialization today. Yet the peer group, which is rising in importance as a means of early and continuing socialization, can strengthen a value system that supports creative individuality, the practice of liberty and genuine equality.

People learn value systems, in the first instance, as they form relations with others. These relations in turn develop norms, with corresponding rationales, which the individual then internalizes. If people, young or old, can build groups with standards that reward and strengthen honest self-expression and self-acceptance, creativity, mutual helpfulness, and the capacity to cope with conflicts (within the self or with others), then the members of such groups will assimilate these values as conditions of membership.

Conformity is not necessarily stultifying; in itself, it does not define the standards of a group. To understand the power of conformity is to become aware of the wide range of purposes, for good or bad, this power can serve. Thoreau, the advocate of individuality and civil disobedience, learned his values in association with others. He found them through his conforming to certain values within his family and in the New England culture of his day. His own values were shared by many of the Unitarians of his time, and were certainly not unknown to his own peer group in Concord. In short, he had group support for recognizing, respecting, articulating, and asserting his individuality.

The pressures for conformity need not suppress individuality unless the standards of the group reward its suppression and punish its expression. Fraternity can be applied either to destroy or to build the personal values and orientations necessary for the practice of liberty and equality. Theoretically, there is no essential incompatibility, therefore, between peer-group influences and the development of individual potentialities. These influences can build the basic values in individuals that are necessary for the social nurture of unique potentialities, and the major obstacles are practical ones that can be overcome.

Since 1947, the present writer, together with an increasing number of university colleagues, has tried to help people build training groups that to some degree embody growth-releasing and growth-sustaining standards. The members of such a group are asked to construct their own miniature society, the only requirement being that they jointly observe and analyze and jointly seek to learn from their own experiences. The training leader helps the group to carry out this requirement. Such groups succeed—though often painfully—in constructing a peer group which to some degree embodies the standards discussed above, and some members do acquire values consonant with these standards. The degree of cohesion and individual involvement is often higher in training groups than in other kinds of associations to which the members have belonged. Training groups demonstrate that, at least under special circumstances, the practical difficulties of making fraternity serve the disciplines of liberty and equality can be overcome.[4]

What are some of these practical difficulties? Groups must develop trust in the honesty and helpful intention of the training environment and its leader. Peer groups normally unite (defensively or offensively) against the symbols of authority, and from this fact flow the identity-destroying effects of the group on its members, its punishment of individual variations, its exaltation of uniformity. In training groups, the members must resolve their normal resistance to authority if the group is to relax that defensiveness and support a wide range of individual variations. In this process the dominant normative orientations of our culture toward authority-subordinate relations and toward peer relations are reviewed and revised by the members. The "authority figure" must also be disciplined to accept the rigorous testing he must undergo in order to earn trust. As the group overcomes its distrust and works out its relation with him, its defensiveness relaxes, and there develops not only a toleration of individual differences but also the active encouragement to express them creatively.

Group members must struggle through and beyond the habit of stereotyping one another, to develop a mode of perceiving one another in all the bewildering and fascinating multiplicity that personalities freed from stereotyping present. The behavioral correlate

---

[4]National Training Laboratories, *Explorations in Human Relations Training* (Washington, D.C.: National Education Association, 1953); Kenneth D. Benne and Warren G. Bennis, *What Is a Training Group?* Boston University Human Relations Center Research Reports and Technical Notes, No. 21.

is the achievement of a sense of real encounter. Members make at
least a little progress beyond the bloodless interchanges that characterize so many of our relations with others, and move toward
the often frightening but growth-releasing encounter of person with
person.[5] Conflict as well as agreement characterize this new level
of human relations. Members come to see the microcosmic world
they are building and also the larger social world as inherently
ambiguous and paradoxical; but the ambiguities and paradoxes are
now faced in a setting of mutual trust and security. For the realistic
acceptance of conflict and ambiguity is one condition of creative
response to environment. Some of the members of training groups
learn this fundamental truth.

The writer has worked with a number of training groups composed of managers from industrial and governmental bureaucracies.
The conflicts with which such organization men struggle are not
essentially different from those of teachers and social workers,
priests and psychiatrists, though their roles may differ. One experience from a training group of industrial managers may give the
flavor of conversation in such a group, and will illustrate a problem
with which the organization man must often contend.

A member confessed to the group that he was not actually interested in getting ahead in his company and that he had to hide
this from his colleagues, so as not to be considered queer. At first,
this confession produced a punishing response from other members;
on the surface, they had accepted the normal assumption that the
road to self-validation was to rise in the bureaucratic structure, and
to question it appeared somehow subversive. As some members
began to take the side of the deviant one, conflict developed and
sub-groups formed; these argued over the proper hierarchy of values
for a manager who was also a person. In time, it became clear that
the real focus of the conflict was within each person and that it concerned the legitimacy of the organizational demands as related to

---

[5]It was in conducting training groups that the author discovered the experiential meaning of Martin Buber's fundamental distinction between collectivity
and community. "Collectivity is not a binding but a bundling together: individuals
packed together, armed and equipped in common, with only as much life from
man to man as will inflame the marching step. But community . . . is the being no
longer side by side but with one another of a multitude of persons. And this multitude, though it also moves toward one goal, yet experiences everywhere a turning
to, a dynamic facing of, the other, a flowing from I to thou. . . . Collectivity is based
on an organized atrophy of personal existence, community on its increase and confirmation in life lived toward one another." Martin Buber, *Between Man and Man*
(Boston: Beacon Press, 1955), p. 31. See also Buber's earlier work, *I and Thou*
(Edinburgh: R. and R. Clark, 1937).

their own unique needs. Various conflicts in personal values were brought out and clarified, and differing strategies for changing the system were discussed. The man who opened the discussion discovered he was not so much of a deviant among managers as he had believed.

It is not surprising that in many of the quandries brought out in such a training group the members should regress to an adolescent attitude, for it is in adolescence that nonfamilial peer-group identifications first gain their power. Though they are not necessarily valid ones, choices made then are now thrust up into consciousness again and reviewed. Such choices might be concerned with career, outlook on life and the world, the falsities in the adult world, or the identity and adequacy of self. These are questions that are normally of great concern to many adolescents, but adults in training groups revive them with a new earnestness.

A training group of adults thus provides a lens for examining the true nature of the fateful choices which our culture has led people to make in their adolescence. Contemporary adolescents might raise different questions in a training group, for the world has changed. In a middle-aged adult group, however, the results of some of the stresses and strains of our culture that were operative in their adolescence can be observed.

Many crippling constructions of a self-image are revealed, reviewed, and revised in training groups. Among them are those masculine self-images that deny and suppress feminine components in the male, and female self-images that deny and suppress correlative male components. One of the most stultifying effects of our culture comes from the stereotyping that forces people to deny parts of themselves. These false constructions make for a waste of energy in the defense of an invalid self-image before one's self and the world. Abraham Maslow has said that the acceptance of one's total nature is one of the most dependable criteria of a creative personality.[6] It is a plausible hypothesis that today both peer groupings and families support this form of crippling self-rejection.

The training group, of course, is only one example of the current attempts to use peer-group experience to support a valid self-acceptance and the acceptance of one's individual limitations and potentialities. The group is perhaps a unique attempt to foster a value

[6]Abraham Maslow, "Creativity in Self-Actualizing People," in H. H. Anderson (ed.), *Creativity and Its Cultivation* (New York: Harper, 1959).

system that supports continuing realization of these potentialities, an experimental attempt to apply fraternity in an "unorthodox" manner and for "unorthodox" ends.

Another example of a like use in fraternity is the reported effort of detached group workers to establish rehabilitating relations with youth gangs.[7] This process presents difficulties like those encountered by the trainer in a training group. The worker, like the trainer, does not try to deny the importance of peer-group experience in the personal lives of the gang members. He recognizes that it has a value, even under the constricting and stultifying form of the gang. He must begin by affirming the personal value of fraternity. By implication, he does not affirm *a priori* the adequacy of the values of the adult environment, against which the gang is in revolt. He comes in, not to break up the gang, but to gain a special kind of membership in it that will enable him to work with it toward remaking its standards in patterns that release growth. This is the same problem that the training-group leader faces in struggling toward a mutual relation with the training group. In both situations, trust of the authoritative adult environment, or of the leader as surrogate of that environment, must be achieved before the group can give up its fixation on primitive offensive or defensive goals and its slavish reliance on standards that inhibit the growth of its individual members.

A closely related example comes from the experimental efforts of social workers in Boston to construct neighborhood peer groups around physically or emotionally handicapped youngsters.[8] One criterion in choosing the peers is the nature of the boy's or girl's handicap. These workers are trying to learn more about how to construct and utilize peer groups as part of the rehabilitation of handicapped persons in general. Equally important are some of the reported effects on normal children who work with the handicapped ones in peer relations. The workers consciously endeavor not only to assist the rehabilitation of the handicapped member but also to help the other members to grow in the process. Growth comes from acquiring a new shared outlook of acceptance of their differences. In a sense, the handicapped person dramatizes the dif-

---

[7]See, for example, *Reaching the Fighting Gang* (New York: New York City Youth Board, 1960).

[8]See Richard Bond, Virginia Burns, Ralph Kolodny, and Marjory Warren, "The Neighborhood Peer Group," *The Group,* Vol. 17, No. 2, (1954) and Ralph Kolodny, Samuel Waldfogel, and Virginia Burns, "Summer Camping in the Treatment of Ego-Defensive Children," *Mental Hygiene,* Vol. 44, No. 2 (1960).

ferences and deviations that are inherent in every individual, though in more subtle forms.

In a boys' group, for example, the boys are expected to show tenderness as well as robustness. This is a hard but important thing for male children in our culture to learn to do. As members work through the dramatic differences between themselves and the handicapped member, other differences, not so dramatic, in themselves and others tend to be accepted also. The adult worker is needed to help the group accomplish these new insights, but he must work with the group in such a way as not to destroy its peer character. Again, a new and difficult role for the authority figure in socializing processes is indicated. He must exert a reeducative influence within a group, without destroying the group's peer character, on which its reeducative value depends.

Thus the practical difficulties in utilizing fraternity to develop the disciplines of liberty and equality can be overcome, at least in specially created settings. True, the experimental demonstrations of this fact have accomplished little when measured against the magnitude of the social problem to be solved, but their results have been encouraging enough to warrant extended effort along analogous lines. It is important that the experimentation not be limited in the future to the educational, semitherapeutic and therapeutic contexts to which it has thus far been confined. Our society has drifted into patterns of early and continuing socialization which elevate peer-group influences to a new prominence. In this drift, values of individuality, of liberty and equality, have been eroded and in some cases lost. Our inherited normative orientation and our unanalyzed experiences with peer groups in our own socialization frequently block us from seeing that the best hope for maintaining, strengthening and extending these eroded values may well lie in transforming the quality of peer-group experiences.[9]

To make peer-group experiences serve individuality, leaders in socialization must re-analyze and re-evaluate the normative orientations of our culture toward valid processes of socialization and

---

[9]The ideal of a mature personality argued for in this essay is not really very different from David Riesman's "autonomous person," Paul Goodman's "independent" or Erich Fromm's "productive" personality. What the present discussion adds may be the search for ways of deliberately creating the social (or group) conditions which make the development of such personalities most likely within the limitations and compulsions of an industrial society. This search has led the writer to reassess the potentialities of a means often used "naturally" to defeat the development of the kinds of personalities desired.

valid ideals of personal maturity. They must achieve an understanding of the uses and abuses of fraternity.

Relations with authority will never disappear from work and citizenship or from early and continuing process of socialization. However, the role of authority in socialization must be reconceived. Authority figures must learn a new respect for peer-group processes as potentialities for either growth or stultification. Like training-group leaders and detached group workers, authority figures must translate this respect into actions appropriate to the social affiliations they control and direct. This translation will require the relatively novel utilization of authority to enhance the normative content of peer-group life without destroying its essential character. The first step in endowing group life with creative responsibilities may well be a realistic revaluation, both cognitive and affective, of the uses and abuses of fraternity.

THE CHARACTERISTICS OF A HELPING RELATIONSHIP*

Carl R. Rogers

I have long had the strong conviction—some might say it was an obsession—that the therapeutic relationship is only a special instance of interpersonal relationships in general, and that the same lawfulness governs all such relationships. This was the theme I chose to work out for myself when I was asked to give an address to the convention of the American Personnel and Guidance Association at St. Louis, in 1958.

Evident in this paper is the dichotomy between the objective and the subjective which has been such an important part of my experience during recent years. I find it very difficult to give a paper which is either wholly objective or wholly subjective. I like to bring the two worlds into close juxtaposition, even if I cannot fully reconcile them.

My interest in psychotherapy has brought about in me an interest in every kind of helping relationship. By this term I mean a relationship in which at least one of the parties has the intent of pro-

*Excerpted from Carl R. Rogers, *On Becoming A Person* (Boston: Houghton Mifflin, 1961), chap. 3, pp. 39–58, "The Characteristics of a Helping Relationship." Used by permission.

moting the growth, development, maturity, improved functioning, improved coping with life of the other. The other, in this sense, may be one individual or a group. To put it in another way, a helping relationship might be defined as one in which one of the participants intends that there should come about, in one or both parties, more appreciation of, more expression of, more functional use of the latent inner resources of the individual.

Now it is obvious that such a definition covers a wide range of relationships which usually are intended to facilitate growth. It would certainly include the relationship between mother and child, father and child. It would include the relationship between the physician and his patient. The relationship between teacher and pupil would often come under this definition, though some teachers would not have the promotion of growth as their intent. It includes almost all counselor-client relationships, whether we are speaking of educational counseling, vocational counseling, or personal counseling. In this last-mentioned area it would include the wide range of relationships between the psychotherapist and the hospitalized psychotic, the therapist and the troubled or neurotic individual, and the relationship between the therapist and the increasing number of so-called "normal" individuals who enter therapy to improve their own functioning or accelerate their personal growth.

These are largely one-to-one relationships. But we should also think of the large number of individual-group interactions which are intended as helping relationships. Some administrators intend that their relationship to their staff groups shall be of the sort which promotes growth, though other administrators would not have this purpose. The interaction between the group therapy leader and his group belongs here. So does the relationship of the community consultant to a community group. Increasingly the interaction between the industrial consultant and a management group is intended as a helping relationship. Perhaps this listing will point up the fact that a great many of the relationships in which we and others are involved fall within this category of interactions in which there is the purpose of promoting development and more mature and adequate functioning.

The Question

But what are the characteristics of those relationships which *do* help, which do facilitate growth? And at the other end of the scale is it possible to discern those characteristics which make a relationship unhelpful, even though it was the sincere intent to promote growth and development? It is to these questions, particularly the first, that I would like to take you with me over some of the paths I have explored, and to tell you where I am, as of now, in my thinking on these issues.

THE ANSWERS GIVEN BY RESEARCH

It is natural to ask first of all whether there is any empirical research which would give us an objective answer to these questions. There has not been a large amount of research in this area as yet, but what there is is stimulating and suggestive. I cannot report all of it but I would like to make a somewhat extensive sampling of the studies which have been done and state very briefly some of the findings. In so doing, oversimplification is necessary, and I am quite aware that I am not doing full justice to the researches I am mentioning, but it may give you the feeling that factual advances are being made and pique your curiosity enough to examine the studies themselves, if you have not already done so.

Studies of Attitudes

Most of the studies throw light on the attitudes on the part of the helping person which make a relationship growth-promoting or growth-inhibiting. Let us look at some of these.

A careful study of parent-child relationships made some years ago by Baldwin[1] and others at the Fels Institute contains interesting evidence. Of the various clusters of parental attitudes toward children, the "acceptant-democratic" seemed most growth-facilitating. Children of these parents with their warm and equalitarian attitudes showed an accelerated intellectual development (an increasing I.Q.), more originality, more emotional security and control, less excitability than children from other types of homes. Though somewhat slow initially in social development, they were, by the time they reached school age, popular, friendly, non-aggressive leaders.

Where parents' attitudes are classed as "actively rejectant" the children show a slightly decelerated intellectual development, relatively poor use of the abilities they do possess, and some lack of originality. They are emotionally unstable, rebellious, aggressive,

---

[1] A. L. Baldwin, J. Kalhorn, and F. H. Breese, "Patterns of Parent Behavior," *Psychol. Monogr.*, Vol. 58, No. 268 (1945), pp. 1–75.

and quarrelsome. The children of parents with other attitude syndromes tend in various respects to fall in between these extremes.

I am sure that these findings do not surprise us as related to child development. I would like to suggest that they probably apply to other relationships as well, and that the counselor or physician or administrator who is warmly emotional and expressive, respectful of the individuality of himself and of the other, and who exhibits a nonpossessive caring, probably facilitates self-realization much as does a parent with these attitudes.

Let me turn to another careful study in a very different area. Whitehorn and Betz[2] investigated the degree of success achieved by young resident physicians in working with schizophrenic patients on a psychiatric ward. They chose for special study the seven who had been outstandingly helpful, and seven whose patients had shown the least degree of improvement. Each group had treated about fifty patients. The investigators examined all the available evidence to discover in what ways the A group (the successful group) differed from the B group. Several significant differences were found. The physicians in the A group tended to see the schizophrenic in terms of the personal meaning which various behaviors had to the patient, rather than seeing him as a case history or a descriptive diagnosis. They also tended to work toward goals which were oriented to the personality of the patient, rather than such goals as reducing the symptoms or curing the disease. It was found that the helpful physicians, in their day by day interaction, primarily made use of active personal participation—a person-to-person relationship. They made less use of procedures which could be classed as "passive permissive." They were even less likely to use such procedures as interpretation, instruction or advice, or emphasis upon the practical care of the patient. Finally, they were much more likely than the B group to develop a relationship in which the patient felt trust and confidence in the physician.

Although the authors cautiously emphasize that these findings relate only to the treatment of schizophrenics, I am inclined to disagree. I suspect that similar facts would be found in a research study of almost any class of helping relationship.

Another interesting study focuses upon the way in which the

[2]B. J. Betz, and J. C. Whitehorn, "The Relationship of the Therapist to the Outcome of Therapy in Schizophrenia," *Psychiat. Research Reports # 5. Research Techniques in Schizophrenia.* (Washington, D.C., American Psychiatric Association, 1956), pp. 89–117; also "A Study of Psychotherapeutic Relationships between Physicians and Schizophrenic Patients, *Amer. J. Psychiat.,* Vol. III (1954), pp. 321–31.

person being helped perceives the relationship. Heine[3] studied individuals who had gone for psychotherapeutic help to psychoanalytic, client-centered, and Adlerian therapists. Regardless of the type of therapy, these clients report similar changes in themselves. But it is their perception of the relationship which is of particular interest to us here. When asked what accounted for the changes which had occurred, they expressed some differing explanations, depending on the orientation of the therapist. But their agreement on the major elements they had found helpful was even more significant. They indicated that these attitudinal elements in the relationship accounted for the changes which had taken place in themselves: the trust they had felt in the therapist; being understood by the therapist; the feeling of independence they had had in making choices and decisions. The therapist procedure which they had found most helpful was that the therapist clarified and openly stated feelings which the client had been approaching hazily and hesitantly.

There was also a high degree of agreement among these clients, regardless of the orientation of their therapists, as to what elements had been unhelpful in the relationship. Such therapist attitudes as lack of interest, remoteness or distance, and an over-degree of sympathy, were perceived as unhelpful. As to procedures, they had found it unhelpful when therapists had given direct specific advice regarding decisions or had emphasized past history rather than present problems. Guiding suggestions mildly given were perceived in an intermediate range—neither clearly helpful nor unhelpful.

Fiedler, in a much quoted study,[4] found that expert therapists of differing orientations formed similar relationships with their clients. Less well known are the elements which characterized these relationships, differentiating them from the relationships formed by less expert therapists. These elements are: an ability to understand the client's meanings and feelings; a sensitivity to the client's attitudes; a warm interest without any emotional over-involvement.

A study by Quinn[5] throws light on what is involved in under-

[3] R. W. Heine, "A Comparison of Patients' Reports on Psychotherapeutic Experience with Psychoanalytic, nondirective, and Adlerian Therapists," unpublished doctoral dissertation, University of Chicago, 1950.

[4] F. E. Fiedler, "Quantitative Studies on the role of Therapists Feelings toward Their Patients," in O. H. Mowrer (ed.), *Psychotherapy: Theory and Research* (New York: Ronald Press, 1953), chap. 12.

[5] R. D. Quinn, "Psychotherapists' Expressions as an Index to the Quality of Early Therapeutic Relationships," unpublished doctoral dissertation, University of Chicago, 1950.

standing the client's meanings and feelings. His study is surprising in that it shows that "understanding" of the client's meanings is essentially an attitude of *desiring* to understand. Quinn presented his judges only with recorded therapist statements taken from interviews. The raters had no knowledge of what the therapist was responding to or how the client reacted to his response. Yet it was found that the degree of understanding could be judged about as well from this material as from listening to the response in context. This seems rather conclusive evidence that it is an attitude of wanting to understand which is communicated.

As to the emotional quality of the relationship, Seeman[6] found that success in psychotherapy is closely associated with a strong and growing mutual liking and respect between client and therapist.

An interesting study by Dittes[7] indicates how delicate this relationship is. Using a physiological measure, the psychogalvanic reflex, to measure the anxious or threatened or alerted reactions of the client, Dittes correlated the deviations on this measure with judges' ratings of the degree of warm acceptance and permissiveness on the part of the therapist. It was found that whenever the therapist's attitudes changed even slightly in the direction of a lesser degree of acceptance, the number of abrupt GSR deviations significantly increased. Evidently when the relationship is experienced as less acceptant the organism organizes against threat, even at the physiological level.

Without trying fully to integrate the findings from these various studies, it can at least be noted that a few things stand out. One is the fact that it is the attitudes and feelings of the therapist, rather than his theoretical orientation, which is important. His procedures and techniques are less important than his attitudes. It is also worth noting that it is the way in which his attitudes and procedures are *perceived* which makes a difference to the client, and that it is this perception which is crucial.

"Manufactured" Relationships

Let me turn to research of a very different sort, some of which you may find rather abhorrent, but which nevertheless has a bearing upon the nature of a facilitating relationship. These studies have

[6]J. Seeman, "Counselor Judgments of Therapeutic Process and Outcome," in C. R. Rogers, and R. F. Dymond (eds.), *Psychotherapy and Personality Change* (University of Chicago Press, 1954), chap. 7.

[7]J. E. Dittes, "Galvanic Skin Response as a Measure of Patient's Reaction to Therapist's Permissiveness," *J. Abnorm. & Soc. Psychol.,* Vol. 55 (1957), pp. 295–303.

to do with what we might think of as manufactured relationships.

Verplanck,[8] Greenspoon[9] and others have shown that operant conditioning of verbal behavior is possible in a relationship. Very briefly, if the experimenter says "M'hm," or "Good," or nods his head after certain types of words or statements, those classes of words tend to increase because of being reinforced. It has been shown that using such procedures one can bring about increases in such diverse verbal categories as plural nouns, hostile words, statements of opinion. The person is completely unaware that he is being influenced in any way by these reinforcers. The implication is that by such selective reinforcement we could bring it about that the other person in the relationship would be using whatever kinds of words and making whatever kinds of statements we had decided to reinforce.

Following still further the principles of operant conditioning as developed by Skinner and his group, Lindsley[10] has shown that a chronic schizophrenic can be placed in a "helping relationship" with a machine. The machine, somewhat like a vending machine, can be set to reward a variety of types of behaviors. Initially it simply rewards—with candy, a cigarette, or the display of a picture—the lever-pressing behavior of the patient. But it is possible to set it so that many pulls on the lever may supply a hungry kitten—visible in a separate enclosure—with a drop of milk. In this case the satisfaction is an altruistic one. Plans are being developed to reward similar social or altruistic behavior directed toward another patient, placed in the next room. The only limit to the kinds of behavior which might be rewarded lies in the degree of mechanical ingenuity of the experimenter.

Lindsley reports that in some patients there has been marked clinical improvement. Personally I cannot help but be impressed by the description of one patient who had gone from a deteriorated chronic state to being given free grounds privileges, this change being quite clearly associated with his interaction with the the machine. Then the experimenter decided to study experimental extinction, which, put in more personal terms, means that no matter

---

[8]W. S. Verplanck, "The Control of the Content of Conversation: Reinforcement of Statements of Opinion," *J. Abnorm. & Soc. Psychol.*, Vol. 51 (1955), pp. 668–76.

[9]J. Greenspoon, "The Reinforcing Effect of Two Spoken Sounds on the Frequency of Two Responses," *Amer. J. Psychol.*, Vol. 68 (1955), pp. 409–16.

[10]O. R. Lindsley, "Operant Conditioning Methods Applied to Research in Chronic Schizophrenia," *Psychiat. Research Reports # 5. Research Techniques in Schizophrenia* (Washington, D.C.: American Psychiatric Association, 1956) pp. 118–53.

how many thousands of times the lever was pressed, no reward of any kind was forthcoming. The patient gradually regressed, grew untidy, uncommunicative, and his grounds privilege had to be revoked. This (to me) pathetic incident would seem to indicate that even in a relationship to a machine, trustworthiness is important if the relationship is to be helpful.

Still another interesting study of a manufactured relationship is being carried on by Harlow and his associates,[11] this time with monkeys. Infant monkeys, removed from their mothers almost immediately after birth, are, in one phase of the experiment, presented with two objects. One might be termed the "hard mother," a sloping cylinder of wire netting with a nipple from which the baby may feed. The other is a "soft mother," a similar cylinder made of foam rubber and terry cloth. Even when an infant gets all his food from the "hard mother" he clearly and increasingly prefers the "soft mother." Motion pictures show that he definitely "relates" to this object, playing with it, enjoying it, finding security in clinging to it when strange objects are near, and using that security as a home base for venturing into the frightening world. Of the many interesting and challenging implications of this study, one seems reasonably clear. It is that no amount of direct food reward can take the place of certain perceived qualities which the infant appears to need and desire.

Two Recent Studies

Let me close this wide-ranging—and perhaps perplexing—sampling of research studies with an account of two very recent investigations. The first is an experiment conducted by Ends and Page.[12] Working with hardened chronic hospitalized alcoholics who had been committed to a state hospital for sixty days, they tried three different methods of group psychotherapy. The method which they believed would be most effective was therapy based on a two-factor theory of learning; a client-centered approach was expected to be second; a psychoanalytically oriented approach was expected to be least efficient. Their results showed that the therapy based upon a learning theory approach was not only not helpful, but was somewhat deleterious. The outcomes were worse than those in the

[11]H. F. Harlow, "The Nature of Love," *Amer. Psychol.,* Vol. 13 (1958), pp. 673–85.

[12]E. J. Ends, and C. W. Page. "A Study of Three Types of Group Psychotherapy with Hospitalized Male Inebriates," *Quar. J. Stud. Alcohol,* Vol. 18 (1957) pp. 263–77.

control group which had no therapy. The analytically oriented therapy produced some positive gain, and the client-centered group therapy was associated with the greatest amount of positive change. Follow-up data, extending over one and one-half years, confirmed the in-hospital findings, with the lasting improvement being greatest in the client-centered approach, next in the analytic, next the control group, and least in those handled by a learning theory approach.

As I have puzzled over this study, unusual in that the approach to which the authors were committed proved *least* effective, I find a clue, I believe, in the description of the therapy based on learning theory.[13] Essentially it consisted (a) of pointing out and labeling the behaviors which had proved unsatisfying, (b) of exploring objectively with the client the reasons behind these behaviors, and (c) of establishing through re-education more effective problem-solving habits. But in all of this interaction the aim, as they formulated it, was to be impersonal. The therapist "permits as little of his own personality to intrude as is humanly possible." The "therapist stresses personal anonymity in his activities, i.e., he must studiously avoid impressing the patient with his own (therapist's) individual personality characteristics." To me this seems the most likely clue to the failure of this approach, as I try to interpret the facts in the light of the other research studies. To withhold one's self as a person and to deal with the other person as an object does not have a high probability of being helpful.

The final study I wish to report is one just being completed by Halkides.[14] She started from a theoretical formulation of mine regarding the necessary and sufficient conditions for therapeutic change.[15] She hypothesized that there would be a significant relationship between the extent of constructive personality change in the client and four counselor variables: (a) the degree of empathic understanding of the client manifested by the counselor; (b) the degree of positive affective attitude (unconditional positive regard) manifested by the counselor toward the client; (c) the extent to which the counselor is genuine, his words matching his own internal feeling; and (d) the extent to which the counselor's response

---

[13]C. W. Page, and E. J. Ends, "A Review and Synthesis of the Literature Suggesting a Psychotherapeutic Technique Based on Two-Factor Learning Theory," unpublished manuscript, loaned to the writer.

[14]G. Halkides, "An Experimental Study of Four Conditions Necessary for Therapeutic Change," unpublished doctoral dissertation, University of Chicago, 1958.

[15]C. R. Rogers, "The Necessary and Sufficient Conditions of Psycho-Therapeutic Personality Change," *J. Consult. Psychol.*, Vol. 21 (1957), pp. 95–103.

matches the client's expression in the intensity of affective expression.

To investigate these hypotheses she first selected, by multiple objective criteria, a group of ten cases which could be classed as "most successful" and a group of ten "least successful" cases. She then took an early and late recorded interview from each of these cases. On a random basis she picked nine client-counselor interaction units—a client statement and a counselor response—from each of these interviews. She thus had nine early interactions and nine later interactions from each case. This gave her several hundred units which were now placed in random order. The units from an early interview of an unsuccessful case might be followed by the units from a late interview of a successful case, etc.

Three judges, who did not know the cases or their degree of success, or the source of any given unit, now listened to this material four different times. They rated each unit on a seven point scale, first as to the degree of empathy, second as to the counselor's positive attitude toward the client, third as to the counselor's congruence or genuineness, and fourth as to the degree to which the counselor's response matched the emotional intensity of the client's expression.

I think all of us who knew of the study regarded it as a very bold venture. Could judges listening to single units of interaction possibly make any reliable rating of such subtle qualities as I have mentioned? And even if suitable reliability could be obtained, could eighteen counselor-client interchanges from each case—a minute sampling of the hundreds or thousands of such interchanges which occurred in each case—possibly bear any relationship to the therapeutic outcome? The chance seemed slim.

The findings are surprising. It proved possible to achieve high reliability between the judges, most of the inter-judge correlations being in the 0.80's or 0.90's, except on the last variable. It was found that a high degree of empathic understanding was significantly associated, at a .001 level, with the more successful cases. A high degree of unconditional positive regard was likewise associated with the more successful cases, at the .001 level. Even the rating of the counselor's genuineness or congruence—the extent to which his words matched his feelings—was associated with the successful outcome of the case, and again at the .001 level of significance. Only in the investigation of the matching intensity of affective expression were the results equivocal.

It is of interest too that high ratings of these variables were not associated more significantly with units from later interviews than with units from early interviews. This means that the counselor's attitudes were quite constant throughout the interviews. If he was highly empathic, he tended to be so from first to last. If he was lacking in genuineness, this tended to be true of both early and late interviews.

As with any study, this investigation has its limitations. It is concerned with a certain type of helping relationship, psychotherapy. It investigated only four variables thought to be significant. Perhaps there are many others. Nevertheless it represents a significant advance in the study of helping relationships. Let me try to state the findings in the simplest possible fashion. It seems to indicate that the quality of the counselor's interaction with a client can be satisfactorily judged on the basis of a very small sampling of his behavior. It also means that if the counselor is congruent or transparent, so that his words are in line with his feelings rather than the two being discrepant; if the counselor likes the client, unconditionally; and if the counselor understands the essential feelings of the client as they seem to the client—then there is a strong probability that this will be an effective helping relationship.

Some Comments

These then are some of the studies which throw at least a measure of light on the nature of the helping relationship. They have investigated different facets of the problem. They have approached it from very different theoretical contexts. They have used different methods. They are not directly comparable. Yet they seem to me to point to several statements which may be made with some assurance. It seems clear that relationships which are helpful have different characteristics from relationships which are unhelpful. These differential characteristics have to do primarily with the attitudes of the helping person on the one hand and with the perception of the relationship by the "helpee" on the other. It is equally clear that the studies thus far made do not give us any final answers as to what is a helping relationship, nor how it is to be formed.

How Can I Create a Helping Relationship?

I believe each of us working in the field of human relationships has a similar problem in knowing how to use such research knowledge. We cannot slavishly follow such findings in a mechanical way or we destroy the personal qualities which these very studies show to be valuable. It seems to me that we have to use these studies, testing them against our own experience and forming new and further personal hypotheses to use and test in our own further personal relationships.

So rather than try to tell you how you should use the findings I have presented I should like to tell you the kind of questions which these studies and my own clinical experience raise for me, and some of the tentative and changing hypotheses which guide my behavior as I enter into what I hope may be helping relationships, whether with students, staff, family, or clients. Let me list a number of these questions and considerations.

1. Can I *be* in some way which will be perceived by the other person as trustworthy, as dependable or consistent in some deep sense? Both research and experience indicate that this is very important, and over the years I have found what I believe are deeper and better ways of answering this question. I used to feel that if I fulfilled all the outer conditions of trustworthiness—keeping appointments, respecting the confidential nature of the interviews, etc.—and if I acted consistently the same during the interviews, then this condition would be fulfilled. But experience drove home the fact that to act consistently acceptant, for example, if in fact I was feeling annoyed or skeptical or some other non-acceptant feeling, was certain in the long run to be perceived as inconsistent or untrustworthy. I have come to recognize that being trustworthy does not demand that I be rigidly consistent but that I be dependably real. The term "congruent" is one I have used to describe the way I would like to be. By this I mean that whatever feeling or attitude I am experiencing would be matched by my awareness of that attitude. When this is true, then I am a unified or integrated person in that moment, and hence I can *be* whatever I deeply *am*. This is a reality which I find others experience as dependable.

2. A very closely related question is this: Can I be expressive enough as a person that what I am will be communicated unambiguously? I believe that most of my failures to achieve a helping relationship can be traced to unsatisfactory answers to these two questions. When I am experiencing an attitude of annoyance toward another person but am unaware of it, then my communication contains contradictory messages. My words are giving one message, but I am also in subtle ways communicating the annoyance I feel and this confuses the other person and makes him distrustful,

though he too may be unaware of what is causing the difficulty. When as a parent or a therapist or a teacher or an administrator I fail to listen to what is going on in me, fail because of my own defensiveness to sense my own feelings, then this kind of failure seems to result. It has made it seem to me that the most basic learning for anyone who hopes to establish any kind of helping relationship is that it is safe to be transparently real. If in a given relationship I am reasonably congruent, if no feelings relevant to the relationship are hidden either to me or the other person, then I can be almost sure that the relationship will be a helpful one.

One way of putting this which may seem strange to you is that if I can form a helping relationship to myself—if I can be sensitively aware of and acceptant toward my own feelings—then the likelihood is great that I can form a helping relationship toward another.

Now, acceptantly to be what I am, in this sense, and to permit this to show through to the other person, is the most difficult task I know and one I never fully achieve. But to realize that this *is* my task has been most rewarding because it has helped me to find what has gone wrong with interpersonal relationships which have become snarled and to put them on a constructive track again. It has meant that if I am to facilitate the personal growth of others in relation to me, then I must grow, and while this is often painful it is also enriching.

3. A third question is: Can I let myself experience positive attitudes toward this other person—attitudes of warmth, caring, liking, interest, respect? It is not easy. I find in myself, and feel that I often see in others, a certain amount of fear of these feelings. We are afraid that if we let ourselves freely experience these positive feelings toward another we may be trapped by them. They may lead to demands on us or we may be disappointed in our trust, and these outcomes we fear. So as a reaction we tend to build up distance between ourselves and others—aloofness, a "professional" attitude, an impersonal relationship.

I feel quite strongly that one of the important reasons for the professionalization of every field is that it helps to keep this distance. In the clinical areas we develop elaborate diagnostic formulations, seeing the person as an object. In teaching and in administration we develop all kinds of evaluative procedures, so that again the person is perceived as an object. In these ways, I believe, we can keep ourselves from experiencing the caring which would exist if we recognized the relationship as one between two persons. It is a real achievement when we can learn, even in certain relationships or at certain times in those relationships, that it is safe to care, that it is safe to relate to the other as a person for whom we have positive feelings.

4. Another question the importance of which I have learned in my own experience is: Can I be strong enough as a person to be separate from the other? Can I be a sturdy respecter of my own feelings, my own needs, as well as his? Can I own and, if need be, express my own feelings as something belonging to me and separate from his feelings? Am I strong enough in my own separateness that I will not be downcast by his depression, frightened by his fear, nor engulfed by his dependency? Is my inner self hardy enough to realize that I am not destroyed by his anger, taken over by his need for dependence, nor enslaved by his love, but that I exist separate from him with feelings and rights of my own? When I can freely feel this strength of being a separate person, then I find that I can let myself go much more deeply in understanding and accepting him because I am not fearful of losing myself.

5. The next question is closely related. Am I secure enough within myself to permit him his separateness? Can I permit him to be what he is—honest or deceitful, infantile or adult, despairing or over-confident? Can I give him the freedom to be? Or do I feel that he should follow my advice, or remain somewhat dependent on me, or mold himself after me? In this connection I think of the interesting small study by Farson[16] which found that the less well adjusted and less competent counselor tends to induce conformity to himself, to have clients who model themselves after him. On the other hand, the better adjusted and more competent counselor can interact with a client through many interviews without interfering with the freedom of the client to develop a personality quite separate from that of his therapist. I should prefer to be in this latter class, whether as parent or supervisor or counselor.

6. Another question I ask myself is: Can I let myself enter fully into the world of his feelings and personal meanings and see these as he does? Can I step into his private world so completely that I lose all desire to evaluate or judge it? Can I enter it so sensitively that I can move about in it freely, without trampling on meanings which are precious to him? Can I sense it so accurately that I can catch not only the meanings of his experience which are obvious to him, but those meanings which are only implicit, which he sees only

---

[16]R. E. Farson, "Introjection in the Psychotherapeutic Relationship," unpublished doctoral dissertation, University of Chicago, 1955.

dimly or as confusion? Can I extend this understanding without limit? I think of the client who said, "Whenever I find someone who understands a *part* of me at the time, then it never fails that a point is reached where I know they're *not* understanding me again . . . What I've looked for so hard is for someone to understand."

For myself I find it easier to feel this kind of understanding, and to communicate it, to individual clients than to students in a class or staff members in a group in which I am involved. There is a strong temptation to set students "straight," or to point out to a staff member the errors in his thinking. Yet when I can permit myself to understand in these situations, it is mutually rewarding. And with clients in therapy, I am often impressed with the fact that even a minimal amount of empathic understanding—a bumbling and faulty attempt to catch the confused complexity of the client's meaning—is helpful, though there is no doubt that it is most helpful when I can see and formulate clearly the meanings in his experiencing which for him have been unclear and tangled.

7. Still another issue is whether I can be acceptant of each facet of this other person which he presents to me. Can I receive him as he is? Can I communicate this attitude? Or can I only receive him conditionally, acceptant of some aspects of his feelings and silently or openly disapproving of other aspects? It has been my experience that when my attitude is conditional, then he cannot change or grow in those respects in which I cannot fully receive him. And when—afterward and sometimes too late—I try to discover why I have been unable to accept him in every respect, I usually discover that it is because I have been frightened or threatened in myself by some aspect of his feeling. If I am to be more helpful, then I must myself grow and accept myself in these respects.

8. A very practical issue is raised by the question: Can I act with sufficient sensitivity in the relationship that my behavior will not be perceived as a threat? The work we are beginning to do in studying the physiological concomitants of psychotherapy confirms the research by Dittes in indicating how easily individuals are threatened at a physiological level. The psychogalvanic reflex—the measure of skin conductance—takes a sharp dip when the therapist responds with some word which is just a little stronger than the client's feeling. And to a phrase such as, "My you *do* look upset," the needle swings almost off the paper. My desire to avoid even such minor threats is not due to a hypersensitivity about my client. It is simply due to the conviction based on experience that if I can free him as completely as possible from external threat, then he can

begin to experience and to deal with the internal feelings and conflicts which he finds threatening within himself.

9. A specific aspect of the preceding question but an important
one is: Can I free him from the threat of external evaluation? In
almost every phase of our lives—at home, at school, at work—we
find ourselves under the rewards and punishments of external judgments. "That's good"; "that's naughty." "That's worth an A"; "that's
a failure." "That's good counseling"; "that's poor counseling." Such
judgments are a part of our lives from infancy to old age. I believe
they have a certain social usefulness to institutions and organizations such as schools and professions. Like everyone else I find myself all too often making such evaluations. But, in my experience,
they do not make for personal growth and hence I do not believe
that they are a part of a helping relationship. Curiously enough a
positive evaluation is as threatening in the long run as a negative
one, since to inform someone that he is good implies that you also
have the right to tell him he is bad. So I have come to feel that the
more I can keep a relationship free of judgment and evaluation,
the more this will permit the other person to reach the point
where he recognizes that the locus of evaluation, the center of responsibility, lies within himself. The meaning and value of his experience is in the last analysis something which is up to him, and
no amount of external judgment can alter this. So I should like to
work toward a relationship in which I am not, even in my own feelings, evaluating him. This I believe can set him free to be a self-
responsible person.

10. One last question: Can I meet this other individual as a person who is in process of *becoming*, or will I be bound by his past
and by my past? If, in my encounter with him, I am dealing with
him as an immature child, an ignorant student, a neurotic personality, or a psychopath, each of these concepts of mine limits what he
can be in the relationship. Martin Buber, the existentialist philosopher of the University of Jerusalem, has a phrase, "confirming the
other," which has had meaning for me. He says "Confirming means
. . . accepting the whole potentiality of the other. . . . I can recognize in him, know in him, the person he has been . . . *created* to
become. . . . I confirm him in myself, and then in him, a relation
to this potentiality that . . . can now be developed, can evolve."[17]
If I accept the other person as something fixed, already diagnosed

---

[17]M. Buber, and C. Rogers, "Transcription of Dialogue Held April 18, 1957, Ann
Arbor, Mich.," unpublished manuscript.

and classified, already shaped by his past, then I am doing my part to confirm this limited hypothesis. If I accept him as a process of becoming, then I am doing what I can to confirm or make real his potentialities.

It is at this point that I see Verplanck, Lindsley, and Skinner, working in operant conditioning, coming together with Buber, the philosopher or mystic. At least they come together in principle, in an odd way. If I see a relationship as only an opportunity to reinforce certain types of words or opinions in the other, then I tend to confirm him as an object—a basically mechanical, manipulable object. And if I see this as his potentiality, he tends to act in ways which support this hypothesis. If, on the other hand, I see a relationship as an opportunity to "reinforce" *all* that he is, the person that he is with all his existent potentialities, then he tends to act in ways which support *this* hypothesis. I have then—to use Buber's term—confirmed him as a living person, capable of creative inner development. Personally I prefer this second type of hypothesis.

Conclusion

In the early portion of this paper I reviewed some of the contributions which research is making to our knowledge *about* relationships. Endeavoring to keep that knowledge in mind I then took up the kind of questions which arise from an inner and subjective point of view as I enter, as a person, into relationships. If I could, in myself, answer all the questions I have raised in the affirmative, then I believe that any relationships in which I was involved would be helping relationships, would involve growth. But I cannot give a positive answer to most of these questions. I can only work in the direction of the positive answer.

This has raised in my mind the strong suspicion that the optimal helping relationship is the kind of relationship created by a person who is psychologically mature. Or to put it in another way, the degree to which I can create relationships which facilitate the growth of others as separate persons is a measure of the growth I have achieved in myself. In some respects this is a disturbing thought, but it is also a promising or challenging one. It would indicate that if I am interested in creating helping relationships I have a fascinating lifetime job ahead of me, stretching and developing my potentialities in the direction of growth.

AFFILIATION MOTIVATION, ANXIETY REDUCTION, AND SELF-EVALUATION*

Stanley Schachter

Let us recapitulate the major findings of the studies presented thus far:

1. The affiliative tendency is positively related to the states of anxiety and hunger.

2. The relationship between anxiety and the affiliative tendency is independent of the opportunity to communicate, for it remains positive in a variety of conditions ranging from completely free communication to absolutely no verbal communication.

3. The affiliative tendency is highly directional. Anxious subjects want to be only with those in a similar plight.

4. There are individual differences in the propensity to affiliate under conditions of anxiety—a patent truism, but a remarkably effective discriminator is ordinal position of birth.

The interpretive implications of this series of findings have left us with two possible interpretations of the basic relationship between anxiety and the affiliative tendency. Under conditions of anxiety, the choice of "Together" is prompted by needs for anxiety reduction or by self-evaluative needs, or both. These alternatives, though initially plausible, are in a sense residual interpretations, for they are the explanatory possibilities remaining after a series of analytic experiments has ruled out the major alternative explanations. However, both of these residual interpretations have clear-cut implications of their own which permit direct testing of their explanatory power. If the presumed anxiety-reducing property of group membership is a potent determinant of the choice of "Together," it should be anticipated that being with others will actually reduce anxiety. If evaluative needs are major determinants of the relationship between anxiety and affiliation, it should be anticipated

*Reprinted from Stanley Schachter, *The Psychology of Affiliation*, chap. 8, pp. 103–25, "Anxiety Reduction and Self-Evaluation." Abridged and used by permission of the publishers, Stanford University Press. Copyright 1959 by the Board of Trustees of the Leland Stanford Junior University.

that being with others will lead to homogeneity of emotional intensity among the group members and to relative stability of emotion. This expectation derives from the set of assumptions which indicate that social evaluation is possible only when there is relative homogeneity among the members of a reference group. Assuming evaluative needs and granting a situation in which evaluation is possible only through social comparison processes, it follows from the above that if discrepancies exist among group members, pressures will arise to reduce such discrepancy. If both the evaluative and anxiety-reducing alternatives are operative, it should be anticipated that under anxiety-producing conditions being together with others will lead to both anxiety reduction and relative homogeneity of anxiety intensity.

In order to test these several alternatives, Wrightsman[1] designed and conducted an experiment in which he experimentally produced a state of anxiety and then varied the social surroundings of his subjects. In some conditions, subjects were brought together to wait on their participation in the anxiety-provoking experiment; in a comparison condition, subjects waited in complete isolation. In this study, four subjects, previously unacquainted, were scheduled for each experimental group. As each subject arrived, he or she was met by a female assistant dressed as a nurse who showed each subject to a completely private room. In his own room, the subject was seated at a sterile-looking table on which was arrayed a variety of hypodermic needles, cotton swabs, alcohol, medicine bottles, slides, ampules, and syringes. The subject seated, the nurse asked him to fill out a brief questionnaire and told him that he would receive information about the experiment via the loudspeaker in his room. She then left the room, leaving the subject completely alone. In a few minutes, the loudspeaker in each room opened up with a tape-recorded talk, the essential features of which are the following:

We have asked you to come today to serve as a subject in an experiment concerned with the relation of glucose level to the efficiency of mental activity. . . . Briefly, what we will do is to drastically change the level of glucose in your blood, to see how this changes your ability to solve mental problems and tasks. The normal supply of glucose carried in the blood is around sixty to ninety milligrams per hundred cubic centimeters of blood. First we will take a blood sample from you to determine just how much we can change the glucose level and still avoid harmful effects or damaging results. This sample

[1] L. S. Wrightsman, "Effects of Waiting with Others on Changes in Level of Felt Anxiety," *Journal of Abnormal Social Psychology*, Vol. 61 (1960), pp. 216–22.

need be only a drop of blood and it will be collected by pricking your finger. This sample will be placed under a microscope for a quick check of the approximate glucose level. Then we will change your glucose level. In some cases we will raise it upward, by injection of a glucose-additive. In other cases we will lower the glucose level through the use of a drug which serves as a glucose-depressant.

As we want to test the immediate effects of change in glucose-level on how you react to a series of problems that follow, it is necessary for us to administer the depressant-drug and glucose-additive in a manner that gets the substance into the blood and the cells as quickly as possible. Therefore we will give you an injection or a series of injections of about one and one-half cubic centimeters with a hypodermic needle. These will be administered to you so that they enter the bloodstream immediately and because of this they are likely to be more painful than routine injections. Only a nurse or technician will be present with you during the injection period.

Although I can't tell you much more about the experiment, in all fairness I should warn you that the injection of the drug will cause you to feel drowsy and lacking in energy—sort of slowed down or a "woozy" feeling—but you should be able to maintain your ability to respond. With some subjects such a feeling may be maintained for several hours before passing away. If your glucose level is raised, the new concentration will be abnormally high, at an absolute maximum amount near the point which brings on glucose-shock, fainting, and similar symptoms of hyperglycemia or diabetes. But such changes, if they occur, will cause no permanent harm.

Before beginning, we have a set of questions which we would like you to answer. When you get your copy, please write your name at the top of the first sheet, read the directions carefully, and give the most accurate answer you can to each question. Thank you.

Following this, a brief questionnaire was distributed to all subjects with the rationale that it was necessary to get additional information about the subjects in order to understand their reactions during the experiment. The chief item on this questionnaire was a question designed to measure anxiety level which read:

For normative purposes, the research committee would like you to indicate just how at-ease or ill-at-ease you feel about being a subject in an experiment involving the taking of a blood test and hypodermic injection and involving changes in one's physiological state.

Please assign a number anywhere from 0 to 100 to indicate your feeling. The number 0 would indicate that you felt completely at-ease and felt no concern over having a blood test and a drug-injection and participating in the experiment. The number 100 would indicate that you felt extremely ill-at-ease and were very concerned about taking a blood test and injection and participating in this experiment. You may choose any number from 0 through 100.

This question answered, the subjects were assigned to one of the three experimental conditions—"Alone," "Together Talk," or "Together No-Talk."

Alone. When a subject had answered this last question, the nurse reentered the room, collected the questionnaire, and simply said, "You are to wait here till we are ready to use you. You can study or read or smoke if you like. There will be only a short wait." The nurse then left the room, leaving the subject completely alone for five minutes. In this condition, then, there are four subjects, each in a private room and having no contact with one another, each exposed at the same time to the same anxiety-provoking instructions and each awaiting injection in isolation.

Together Talk. Having answered the questionnaire, all four subjects were brought together in a common room and told, "You are to wait here until we are ready to use you. You can study or read or smoke if you like. If you want to talk, that's okay. You can talk about the experiment or anything you like. There will be only a short wait." The experimenter and nurse then left the room for a five-minute period. During this five-minute period the group was observed through a one-way mirror.

Together No Talk. All four subjects were brought together in a common room and told, "You are to wait here until we are ready to use you. You can study or read or smoke if you like. However, please do *not* talk. Part of the experiment is of a verbal nature and we want only your own ideas to be given. Therefore it is important that you not talk about the experiment or anything else. There will be only a short wait." And again the experimenters left the room for a five-minute period and observed the group during this time. All groups obeyed these "no-talk" instructions completely.

After this five-minute wait, the subjects in all conditions were told that the experiment was about to begin and were asked to fill out a final questionnaire designed again to measure anxiety level. The chief items of this questionnaire were the following:

1. A measure in which the subjects are asked to estimate their degree of uneasiness on a 0-100 point scale.

2. A six-point scale ranging from "1. I feel completely calm" to "6. I feel extremely uneasy" in response to the question, "How nervous and uneasy do you feel about taking part in this experiment involving hypodermic injections?"

3. Finally, the subjects were given the option of deciding for themselves whether or not they wished to take part in the experiment.

These questions answered, the experiment was over and an explanation and catharsis session ensued.

In each condition there was a total of seventeen groups, each consisting of four subjects. In each condition there was a total of seven all-male groups and ten all-female groups. All subjects were psychology student volunteers, receiving extra course credit for participation in the experiment. In all of the data to be presented, the trends revealed are precisely the same for male and female groups and the data from the two sets of groups will be pooled in all tables.

ANXIETY REDUCTION

If the anxiety-reduction hypothesis is correct, it should be anticipated that there will be greater anxiety reduction in the "Together" conditions than in the "Alone" condition. Table 1 presents the rele-

TABLE 1

EFFECTS OF BEING ALONE OR WITH OTHERS ON ANXIETY

Condition	No. of Groups	No. of Subjects	Anx 2	% Subjects Refusing to Continue	Pre-Waiting-Period Index	Post-Waiting-Period Index	Changes in Anx Pre-Post Index
Alone.............	17	68	2.79	14.9	41.35	37.16	−4.19
Together No-Talk...	17	68	2.91	8.8	42.76	36.59	−6.17
Together Talk......	17	68	2.85	14.7	43.69	37.26	−6.43

vant data. It should be noted first that the groups are similar in their initial level of anixety. Scores on the pre-waiting-period index (the first measure requiring the subjects to estimate their degree of uneasiness on a 0-100 point scale) are much the same in the three conditions. And following the experimental treatments the picture remains much the same: though there is a general trend to anxiety reduction with time, the terminal level of anxiety is almost identical in the three conditions. For none of the measures does any of the possible between-condition comparisons even approach statistical significance. It would appear that being with others has no particular anxiety-reducing effect.

It will be recalled, however, that in the earlier experiments the relationship between anxiety and the affiliative tendency was restricted almost entirely to subjects who were first-born and only children. It is reasonable, then, to suggest that anxiety reduction, if indeed it is a consequence of being with others, would be stronger for early than for later-born subjects. Such an effect could, of course, be obscured in the data presented in Table 1, which lumps together the data of all subjects. The data for the two sets of subjects are presented separately in Table 2. For tabular convenience, this table

TABLE 2

RELATIONSHIP OF ORDINAL POSITION TO ANXIETY REDUCTION

Condition	N	First-Born and Only Subjects Pre-Waiting Period Index	Post-Waiting Period Index	Anxiety Reduction Pre-Post Indices	Gross Change	N	Later-Born Subjects Pre-Waiting Period Index	Post-Waiting Period Index	Anxiety Reduction Pre-Post Indices	Gross Change	First vs. Later P Value* Anxiety Reduction	Gross Change
Alone†	41	42.07	38.56	−3.51	4.24	26	39.89	35.42	−4.47	6.00	n.s.	n.s.
TNT	33	43.24	33.91	−9.33	9.94	35	42.37	39.11	−3.26	4.17	.06	.07
TT†	32	39.81	31.47	−8.34	10.84	35	47.77	42.91	−4.86	6.57	n.s.	.05
P value* Alone vs. TNT				< .05	< .05				n.s.	n.s.		
P value Alone vs. TT				< .05	< .01				n.s.	n.s.		

*All levels of confidence computed by the Mann-Whitney U test.
†The total N in these conditions is slightly smaller than in Table 1 owing to the elimination of twins and adopted children.

presents only the data gathered in the pre- and post-waiting-period administrations of the 0-100 point scale of "uneasiness." Although the data on the remaining two measures are not presented here, the trends are precisely the same on all measures of anxiety.

The columns in Table 2 labeled "Anxiety Reduction" contain the algebraic means of the changes in anxiety level from pre- to post-waiting-period administrations of the uneasiness measure. The minus sign, of course, indicates a decrease of anxiety. It will be noted immediately that there is greater anxiety reduction for first-born subjects in the "Together" conditions than for first-born subjects in the "Alone" condition. No such effect is evident for later-born subjects for whom the degree of anxiety reduction seems much the same in the three experimental conditions. It would appear, then, that being with others does have anxiety-reducing effects for first-born and only subjects. This finding, of course, agrees neatly with the consistent tendency, in the earlier experiments, for anxious first-born subjects to choose "Together." This pair of complementing facts gives strong support to the hypothesis that one of the determinants of the "Together" choice is the anxiety-reducing property of being with other people.

The relationship at issue, however, may not be quite as simple as the last paragraph would indicate. The columns labeled "Gross Change" in Table 2 contain the arithmetic means of the changes in anxiety level. These figures represent the absolute magnitude of change, regardless of whether a change indicates anxiety reduction or increase. Again, first-borns in "Together" conditions change considerably more than do first-borns in the "Alone" condition. And again there are no between-condition differences of any consequence among the later-born subjects. It should be noted, however, that while anxiety reduction is greatest in the "Together No-Talk" condition, gross change is greatest in the "Together Talk" condition. Comparison of the magnitude of the two sets of scores would indicate that the gross change in the "Together No-Talk" condition is made up of anxiety-reducing scores to a somewhat greater extent than in the "Together Talk" condition. Furthermore, it should be noted, on the right-hand side of the table, that when first- and later-borns *within* the "Together Talk" condition are compared, the two groups differ significantly in gross change but not in anxiety reduction. Though certainly the magnitudes of the differences in the several comparisons just made are not great, they do at least suggest that for first-borns in the "Together Talk" condition, anxiety reduction is not an inevitable consequence of being with others. First-born subjects, as suggested by the gross-change data, are more influencible than later-born subjects. If the tenor of a group discussion were to be really terrifying and anxiety provoking, it might indeed be anticipated that the anxiety of first-borns would be greater than that of later-borns.

Let us summarize these findings so far. For first-born subjects, anxiety reduction is a consequence of being together with other people in a similar plight. For such subjects, the simple physical presence of other people, as in the "pure" "Together No-Talk" condition, is anxiety reducing. Allowing the subjects to communicate with one another may somewhat complicate the relationship, for first-born subjects are more influencible than later-born subjects. It is suggested that when communication is allowed, the effect on anxiety of being with others will depend on the nature of the communication.

THE SOCIAL EVALUATION OF ANXIETY

Before examining Wrightsman's data for indications of social evaluation of anxiety, let us review the scheme evolved[2] from the large number of studies on social determinants of opinion and ability evaluation. It has been hypothesized, first, that a drive exists in man to evaluate his opinions and abilities, i.e., to determine the "rightness" or "wrongness" of an opinion and the "goodness" or "badness" of an ability. Secondly, it is hypothesized that when an objective, nonsocial means (e.g., a reality check or reference to an authoritative source) of evaluation is not available, evaluation will be made by comparison with the opinions and abilities of other people. Finally, it is hypothesized that stable and precise evaluation by social comparison is possible only when the opinions and abilities available for comparison are not too divergent from one's own; the tendency to compare oneself with others decreases as the discrepancy in opinion or ability increases.

From these several hypotheses it may be derived that when discrepancies of opinion or abilities exist among the members of a group, pressures will arise to reduce such discrepancies. In interpersonal settings, such pressures to uniformity can be manifested in three ways. When discrepancies exist, tendencies will arise to: (1) change one's own opinion or ability to bring oneself closer to

[2]L. Festinger, "A Theory of Social Comparison Process," *Hum. Relat.*, Vol. 7 (1954), 117–40.

other group members; (2) change others in the group so as to bring
them closer to oneself; and (3) cause one to cease comparing oneself to those in the group who are extremely different from oneself.
This schema has proven particularly useful in understanding social
determinants of opinion and ability evaluation, and numerous experiments have demonstrated the operation of these tendencies
as they relate to such variables as degree of discrepancy, cohesiveness, and importance of issue.

Now if the suggestion that the emotions, like the opinions and
abilities, are evaluated by means of social comparison processes is
correct, it should be anticipated that these same manifestations of
pressures to uniformity will be evident in situations where discrepancies of emotional state exist. In such situations, too, there should
be indications of self change, of attempts to influence others and
bring them closer to one's own position, and of the rejection, as
comparison points, of those who deviate too far from one's own
position. In the brief discussion of "gross change" which terminated
the preceding section of this chapter, it was suggested that the relatively large gross change in the "Together Talk" condition was an
indication of on-going social influence. But, let us ask first, do such
changes really indicate influencibility or are they merely random
changes suggesting that people are simply more flighty when in one
another's presence than when they are alone? If random "flighti-
ness" is the appropriate explanation, no particular change in the
final as compared with the initial dispersion of scores on the "0 to
100 uneasiness" scale should be anticipated; if influencibility is the
proper explanation, it should be expected that the final scores on
this scale will be more homogenous than the initial scores, for presumably people are being influenced toward one another's position—
and this, of course, is precisely the result that the self-evaluation
schema demands, for the effects of tendencies to bring oneself into
closer conformity to others and to influence others to closer agreement with oneself would necessarily result in homogenization of
emotional state.

As an index of the degree of homogenization in each group, the
range of scores on post-waiting-period administration of the "0 to
100" point scale is simply divided by the range of scores in the
pre-waiting-period administration of this same scale. For example,
a group of subjects who before the waiting period gave scores of
40, 60, 80, and 90 and after the waiting period scores of 45, 60, 70,

and 85 would have an index of .80. The lower the score, the greater the degree of social influence and homogenization.

TABLE 3

Effect of Being with Others on Homogenization of Anxiety

Condition	N	Mean Initial Range	Mean Index of Homogenization
Alone............17		67.06	.980
TNT............17		65.29	.841
TT...............17		66.65	.831
TT vs. Alone:		$t = 2.37$	
		$p = .03$	
TNT vs. Alone:		$t = 2.08$	
		$p = .05$	

Data derived from these computations are presented in Table 3. The indices of homogenization for both "Together" conditions are noticeably smaller than the figure obtained for the "Alone" condition. These decreases in dispersion are significantly smaller than 1.00 (the point at which the initial and final ranges are identical) at the .01 level for "Together Talk" and the .02 level of confidence for the "Together No-Talk" condition. The fact that both "Together" conditions differ significantly from the "Alone" condition is an indication that this decrease in dispersion is not a result of some pure artifact such as a tendency for those who initially chose extreme scores to be more moderate in their second judgment.

It would certainly appear, then, that social influence does take place and that homogenization of anxiety is a clear consequence of being with others. The fact that the "Together No-Talk" index is almost as low as the "Together Talk" index could lead one to speculation about self-evaluative needs and pressures to uniformity so great that subjects soundlessly search out and accommodate to cues as to how others are responding; or it could lead to a search for an artifact. And one possible artifact does suggest itself from the fact that the measure used has zero as a built-in floor and that there is a general tendency for anxiety to decrease with time, with the "Together" groups decreasing overall slightly more than the "Alone" groups. This combination of factors might lead to lower indices of homogenization in the "Together" conditions. If such an artifact is at work, it should be expected that there will be a sizeable correlation between the magnitude of anxiety decrease and the index of homogenization. Examination of the "Together Talk" data makes it clear that such an artifact has at best a trivial impact. In this condition some groups increase in anxiety level and other groups decrease. The changes in anxiety level vary from a mean increase of 5.00 to a decrease of 26.75, and there is only a small and non-significant correlation between the magnitude of anxiety decrease and the index of homogenization. In the "Together No-Talk" groups, on the other hand, there is fairly consistent decrease of anxiety level in all groups (mean change varies from 0 to a decrease of 18.75) and the correlation between anxiety reduction and homogenization is $+ .57$, significant at the .02 level of confidence. It may be concluded, then, that the decrease in dispersion in "Together Talk" groups is a result of social-influence processes, while a similar decrease in "Together No-Talk" groups is at least in part artifactually produced.

So far, in support of the suggestion that the emotions, like the opinions, are subject to social influence and evaluation, it has been demonstrated that emotional states of group members grow more alike as a result of interaction, an indication that, as with opinions and abilities, tendencies to self change and to influence others are active when discrepancies among group members exist.

Let us examine Wrightsman's experiment next for indications of the operation of the final tendency postulated—the tendency to cease comparison with those in the group who are extremely different from oneself. It has been hypothesized that the tendency to compare oneself with others decreases as the discrepancy increases. It should follow from this that in the "Together Talk" condition of this experiment, when the initial range of anxiety is great there should be relatively little change and little homogenization of state of anxiety, for in such groups discrepancy is so great that comparison may cease. Further, it should be anticipated, again in the "Together Talk" condition, that when the initial range of scores is small there will be little change and little further homogenization, for when the discrepancy is small, evaluation is immediately possible and influence processes will cease. Only for intermediate ranges of discrepancy should there be strong indications of social influence and homogenization. It is anticipated, then, that in the "Together Talk" condition there will be a non-monotonic relationship, peaking at intermediate ranges, between the initial range of anxiety scores and the degree of homogenization.

In the "Alone" condition, there should of course be no relationship between initial range and degree of homogenization. Subjects in this condition are completely isolated and have no idea of how other people are reacting. There should therefore be little change and no homogenization no matter what the initial range of these arbitrarily designated "groups" of subjects.

For the "Together No-Talk" condition, it is of course impossible to make any clear-cut prediction. If the homogenization noted in Table 3 is largely a function of the artifact discussed, the relationship between initial range and homogenization should be simply an elevated version of the straight-line curve predicted for the "Alone" condition—roughly equal homogenization at all ranges of initial discrepancy. If, on the other hand, social comparison processes are really at work in this condition, the relationship at issue should resemble that in the "Together Talk" condition. Clearly, though, subjects in this condition could not have as clear a picture of their fellow subjects' emotional states as would subjects in the "Together Talk" condition, and it would therefore be reasonable to expect that, if social comparison processes are at work, the plotted relationship between range and homogenization will be somewhat flatter in the "Together No-Talk" than in the "Together Talk" condition, i.e., somewhat greater homogenization at the extreme ranges, somewhat lower peak at the intermediate ranges.

Data on this relationship are presented in Figure 1. Along the abscissa are plotted the ranges of scores obtained in the experimental groups on the first administration of the "0 to 100 uneasiness" scale. The range obtained in each group is assigned to one of three classifications: "wide" initial range where the distance between the least and most anxious member of the group is between 80 and 100; "intermediate" initial ranges where this distance is between 55 and 79; and "narrow" initial ranges where this distance falls between 0 and 54. These particular cut-off points were chosen simply because they are the points at which one can come closest to assigning 25 percent of the total number of groups to the "wide" range category and 25 percent of the total number of groups to the "narrow" range category. Along the ordinate is plotted the mean index of homogenization for the groups in each of the categories. At 1.00 there has been no decrease in dispersion from initial to final measure. The closer the index to zero, the greater the decrease in dispersion of scores from first to final measure.

It can be seen immediately in Figure 1 that the curves for the "Alone" and "Together Talk" groups follow expectations closely. In the "Alone" condition, clearly there is no indication of relationship between initial range and degree of homogenization. All points on the "Alone" curve are quite close to 1.00—the point at which there is no change in dispersion. The "Together Talk" curve, on the

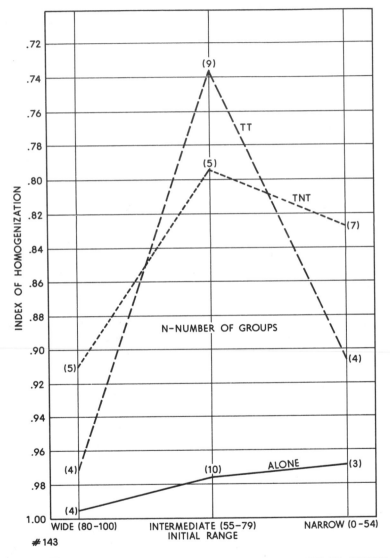

FIG. 1. The effects of initial range on homogenization of anxiety.

other hand, indicates a marked relationship between range and homogenization. For groups with both "wide" and "narrow" initial ranges, there is relatively little homogenization; "intermediate" range groups, on the other hand, markedly decrease dispersion from first to final measure of anxiety—precisely the pattern that the social comparison schema would lead us to expect. Neither wide- nor narrow-range groups on the "Together Talk" condition differ significantly from their counterparts in the "Alone" condition. "Together-Talk" intermediate-range groups are significantly greater than similar "Alone" groups at better than the .05 level of confidence by Median Test. "Together Talk" intermediate-range groups are significantly greater than "Together Talk" extreme-range groups at better than the .05 level of confidence by the same test.[3] The "Together No-Talk" curve does appear as a somewhat flattened version of the "Together Talk" curve, which might be taken as a tentative indication of the operation of comparison processes in this condition. However, the points on this curve are not significantly different from one another, and though it is engaging to speculate about

---

[3]Before concluding, on the basis of these data, that the tendency to cease comparing oneself with those who are extremely different is operating in the "Together Talk" condition of this experiment, one possibly confounding factor must be examined. Clearly, the wide-range groups will almost inevitably contain relatively more subjects who chose extreme positions than will the intermediate-range groups. It is conceivable that such subjects, who are initially either extremely worried or very calm, are simply less influencible than subjects whose initial reaction is between these extremes. Whether or not this is a factor can be simply determined by comparing the change patterns of such extreme subjects in wide- and intermediate-range groups. If the noninfluencibility of extreme subjects is the proper explanation there should be no difference between the two groups of subjects. If the tendency to cease comparison is the proper explanation, wide-range-extreme subjects should change less than intermediate-range-extreme subjects. The data are presented in the table below, where subjects in the "Together Talk" condition whose initial score on the "0 to 100" scale fell between 75 and 100 are considered extreme high-anxiety subjects and those whose initial score was between 0 and 25 are classified as extreme low-anxiety subjects.

	Together Talk Wide-Range Groups		Together Talk Intermediate-Range Groups	
	N	Gross change	N	Gross change
Extreme high Anx (75–100)	5	6.00	9	17.22
Extreme low Anx (0–25)	10	3.00	13	9.23

Clearly, there is considerably less change among the extremes of wide-range groups than among the extremes of intermediate-range groups. It may be concluded, then, that the difference in homogenization between wide- and intermediate-range "Together Talk" groups in Figure 1 does result from the operation of the "tendency to cease comparison with deviates" rather than from any artifactual effect of the presumed unchangeability of extreme subjects.

In the "Together No-Talk" condition the pattern of data is much the same, though the differences between extreme subjects in wide- and intermediate-range groups are somewhat smaller than in the "Together Talk" condition.

the possibility that social influence processes may be active even when subjects are limited to simple observation of one another, it is clear that such a hypothesis receives only tentative support within the present study.

Let us summarize this section. It has been hypothesized that the emotions, like the opinions and abilities, are evaluated by social comparison processes. The test of this hypothesis demands the demonstration that when discrepancies of emotional state exist among the members of a group, social influence and rejection processes are active. The decrease in discrepancy of anxiety states after a period of interaction in the "Together Talk" condition is evidence that social influence processes are operative. The failure to reduce discrepancy in wide-range groups is an indication of rejection.

Wrightsman's experiment, then, indicates that both the anxiety-reduction and self-evaluation explanations of the anxiety-affiliation relationship demonstrated in earlier experiments have good experimental support. Being with others is anxiety reducing for first-born subjects, precisely the subjects who, when anxious, choose to be with others. Being with others leads to strong manifestations of social influence and rejection, precisely the consequences demanded by the assumption of a need for evaluation of emotional states. There is good reason to believe, then, that the prime motivators of the choice of "Together" when anxious are needs for anxiety reduction and for self-evaluation. However, though we have fair confidence that both of these needs, independent of each other, have positive relationships with the affiliative tendency, it is clear that only an experiment which separately manipulates these two needs can definitively establish the point.

SATIATION AND SOCIAL COMPARISON PROCESSES

It is of course tempting to treat the results of the experiment just discussed as generalizable to all emotional states but, so far, our conclusions must be restricted to the state of anxiety and, more specifically still, to the breed of anxiety generated by physical fear. Is there evidence that social-comparison processes affect other states of emotion or feeling? A study conducted by Horwitz, Exline, Goldman, and Lee[4] yields evidence on the state of satiation or boredom. This experiment was designed to study the effects of a variety of

---

[4] M. Horwitz, R. Exline, M. Goldman, and F. Lee, "Motivational Effects of Alternative Decision-Making Processes in Groups, *Office of Naval Research Technical Report,* June, 1953.

group characteristics on the rate of satiation of group members working on a repetitive group task. Experimental groups in this study consisted of five subjects seated around a table, all facing a common work area. By a system of partitions the subjects were prevented from seeing one another. Each subject was provided with a stick, and the group task consisted of the assembly, using these sticks, of an exceedingly simple jigsaw puzzle. In the center of the work area was placed a simple outline drawing of a locomotive marked off in five sections. Five jigsaw pieces, cut to fit each of these sections, were placed around the drawing and the group's job was to fill in the drawing with these pieces. After the drawing was filled in the experimenter separated the pieces and the group repeated the task. This procedure continued for each group until it had completed at least forty trials of precisely the same task and had worked at least eighty minutes.

After each trial the subjects privately checked off a scale designed to measure satiation. For this measure they answered the question, "How do you feel about doing this particular task again?" by choosing one of six points ranging from "*a*. I feel at least *some interest* in repeating this task," to "*f*. I feel that repeating the task is *intensely distasteful* to me."

This was a six-condition experiment. In five of the conditions, the experimental groups were made up of strangers. In a sixth condition, experimental groups were made up of people who knew one another. The experiment was introduced to all groups with the instructions, "There must be absolutely no talking during the test." The groups of strangers obeyed these instructions to the letter and went about their task in complete silence. Among the groups of acquaintances, however, restraints against making noise were apparently somewhat lower and communication of a sort did take place in such groups. In no case did this involve more than rudimentary conversation. The subjects in such groups simply used occasional expletives, or groaned, sighed, and the like—in short, made just the sort of noises that effectively convey a mood or feeling. For our purposes, then, this experiment involves two sets of groups— one in which the subjects can neither see nor hear one another and have flatly no idea of how others are reacting to the situation; another in which subjects can hear, though not see, one another and in all likelihood, therefore, have a fair idea of how other members of the group are reacting. If it is correct that the feelings and emotions are evaluated by comparison with others, it should be anticipated that, as with anxiety, the degree of satiation within those groups where this rudimentary sort of communication takes place should be more homogeneous than in groups where there is no such communication. And the data indicate that this is the case. In those groups where communication took place, the within-groups variance for satiation scores is .92, with 31 degrees of freedom. In groups where there was no communication, within-groups variance on satiation is 1.56, with 146 degrees of freedom. The F value is 1.70, which is significant at better than the .05 level of confidence. It would certainly appear, then, that these subjects have evaluated their own feelings of fatigue, annoyance, and satiation by reference to the cues they receive from other group members. This interpretation is somewhat confounded, of course, by the fact that in this experiment degree of friendship and degree of communication varied simultaneously. It does seem a fairly safe bet, however, that communication is the crucial variable.

It should be noted, too, that, as with anxiety, this opportunity to get cues had no systematic effect on the degree of satiation beyond drawing the members of the group closer together in their feelings. Some of these communicating groups maintained a high degree of interest throughout the experiment, whereas others satiated very quickly. The mean level of satiation was similar for the two sets of groups.

For both the states of anxiety and satiation, then, there is good evidence that social-influence processes are operative and that the individual evaluates his own feelings by comparing himself with others. It should be noted that in both of these experiments, there were no externally imposed pressures to uniformity. There was no group goal, no reward for conformity, and no penalty for non-conformity. The subjects, in both experiments, made their judgments of their own emotional states in complete privacy. In short, there is every indication that the conformity evidenced in both studies is a manifestation of a genuine individual need for appraisal of a state of emotion or feeling.

PROPHECY FAILS AGAIN: A REPORT OF A FAILURE TO REPLICATE[*]

Jane Allyn Hardyck and Marcia Braden[1]

On July 4 of a recent year, a group of 135 men, women, and children vanished from their homes in a small southwestern town. Their homes were sealed; the windows were covered with newspapers; the cluster of houses was deserted. The only message they had left was a sign on the door of their church, reading "Gone for two weeks, camp meeting."

The neighbors of the group and the town officials soon discovered where the members of the Church of the True Word[2] had gone. In response to prophecies of a forthcoming nuclear disaster, the group had for many months been building and stocking underground fallout shelters, with as much secrecy as possible. On July 4, one of their prophets received a message, "The Egyptians are coming; get ye to the safe places," and they immediately obeyed what they believed to be a command from God. They were huddled in their shelters, awaiting the nuclear catastrophe. For 42 days and nights they remained there, in expectation of imminent disaster. While they stubbornly sat underground, the authors walked around the hot, dusty desert town piecing together the history of the group from interviews with townspeople and the few group members who, disillusioned, left the shelters.

The Church of the True Word is an evangelical Christian church

---
[*]Reprinted in its entirety from Jane Allyn Hardyck and Marcia Braden, "Prophecy Fails Again: A Report of a Failure to Replicate." *J. Abn. Soc. Psychol.*, Vol. 65, No. 2 (1962), pp. 136–41. Footnotes renumbered. Used by permission.

[1]This investigation was carried out during the tenure of a Predoctral Research Fellowship from the National Science Foundation to the first author and a Predoctoral Research Fellowship from the National Institute of Mental Health, United States Public Health Service, to the second author. The collection of data was undertaken in cooperation with the Studies in International Conflict and Integration, Stanford University, directed by Robert North. The authors would like to thank Larry Robertson, who helped in collecting the data, and Leon Festinger, who helped by his criticisms of many drafts of this paper.

[2]This is a fictitious name which, we believe, captures the flavor of the actual name of the group. All other names and places used in this paper have been similarly disguised.

associated with the Pentecostal movement. Its members believe in
the Bible as the literal word of God and accept as operating today
the gifts of the Holy Spirit delineated in First Corinthians of the
New Testament, Chapters 12 and 14. These gifts include speaking
and interpreting tongues, personal prophecy, and healing by faith.
The titular head of the group, a Mrs. Shepard, is their minister and
chief prophet, although important decisions are made only after
she has consulted with two of the group members, Peter Jameson
and David Blake, both of whom are also ordained ministers.

The "colony," as they call themselves, springs from two main
sources. Mrs. Shepard established a following about 5 years ago in
the small southwestern town, and soon began work on the present
church building. In this, she had the help of Jameson and Blake,
who at the time were missionaries to Central America from two
congregations in the Middle West. The second source of members
of the Church of the True Word was these midwestern churches.

Even in the early days of her ministry, Mrs. Shepard was preaching preparedness for nuclear attack, and almost 4 years ago a
prophecy was received in the Midwest to the effect that "in fewer
years than I have fingers on my right hand" there would be nuclear
devastation. The more recent history of the Church of the True
Word began with another prophecy. On November 23, 8 months
before the group finally went underground, a prophet in the Midwest received word that "you have 6 months to prepare." On receiving this message, Blake, Jameson, and various others packed up and
moved to the Southwest and about February began to build fallout
shelters and homes.

The shelters were built "through the inspiration of God," according to the specifications of Civil Defense, which is, for these people,
"the Noah's Ark of today." They were not designed as bomb shelters,
since the group believed that their town would receive only fallout
from a direct hit on Desert City, which lay 50 miles to the west.
There were probably five large shelters under houses and four
smaller ones dug in an open field nearby. The larger ones were quite
livable, although far from luxurious, as they lacked modern plumb-
ing and were rather badly ventilated. The shelters were stocked with
canned and dehydrated food, large cans of water, and other necessities, and were provided with generators for use when public power
failed.

For the group to make such careful and extensive preparations,
they must have had a rather clear and specific idea of what was to

happen. Indeed they did. From a particular interpretation of portions of the Book of Revelation, they believed that about one-third of the population of the earth would be wiped out by nuclear warfare and that injuries and sickness would be widespread among the survivors. The members of the Church of the True Word also expected that after the disaster they would receive special powers from God so that they might perform miracles of healing beyond what they were already able to do, and might be enabled to spread the gospel to all nations within the short space of about a year. It was the necessity of saving themselves for this purpose that dictated that they must keep their preparations secret. They feared that if the location and nature of their shelters were generally known, they would be unable to prevent others from breaking in at the time of the attack, thus creating a situation in which no one could survive.

From February until the "deadline" of May 23, many more families from the midwest congregations arrived to join in the preparations. There were also, of course, several families from the local community who were members of the church and who helped in the work. The shelters were not finished by May 23, and much apprehension arose among the members of the group. In an anxious flurry of preparations they waited until July 4, when they received the message, we believe through Mrs. Shepard, "The Egyptians are coming; get ye to the safe places." They then entered the shelters—29 families, about 135 men, women, and children.

Hypotheses to Be Tested

Our interest in the True Word group arose because of their apparent similarity to the "doomsday groups" discussed by Festinger, Riecken, and Schachter in *When Prophecy Fails*.[3] The historical accounts of such groups as well as an empirical study of a more recent group, the Lake City Group, suggest that the failure of the members to confirm their pessimistic predictions led them to increase in fervor of belief and in proselyting. Festinger et al. state five conditions that they feel must be met for this to occur:

1. A belief must be held with deep conviction and it must have some relevance to action, that is, to what the believer does or how he behaves.
2. The person holding the belief must have committed himself to it; that is, for the sake of his belief, he must have taken some important action that is difficult to undo. In general, the more important such actions

---

[3]L. Festinger, H. Riecken, and S. Schachter, *When Prophecy Fails* (Minneapolis: Univ. of Minnesota Press, 1956).

are, and the more difficult they are to undo, the greater is the individual's commitment to the belief.

3. The belief must be sufficiently specific and sufficiently concerned with the real world so that events may unequivocally refute the belief.

4. Such undeniable disconfirmatory evidence must occur and must be recognized by the individual holding the belief.

    The first two of these conditions specify the circumstances that will make the belief resistant to change. The third and fourth conditions together, on the other hand, point to factors that would exert powerful pressure on a believer to discard his belief.

5. The individual believer must have social support. It is unlikely that one isolated believer could withstand the kind of disconfirming evidence we have specified. If, however, the believer is a member of a group of convinced persons who can support one another, we would expect the belief to be maintained and the believers to attempt to proselyte or to persuade nonmembers that the belief is correct.[4]

These five conditions define a situation in which the believer has two sets of cognitions that clearly do not fit together. That is, he is experiencing a great deal of dissonance between the cognitions corresponding to his belief and the cognitions concerning the failure of the predicted event to occur. This situation, however, is one in which it is almost impossible for the individual to reduce his dissonance. He cannot give up his strongly held beliefs, and he cannot deny that the predicted event has failed to occur. He is also unable either to reduce the importance of his commitment to his beliefs or to make the disconfirmation irrelevant to them. Therefore, the believer who holds to his belief under these conditions has but one recourse if he is to reduce the dissonance; he must seek new information consonant with his beliefs. One of the best sources of new consonant cognitions is the knowledge that others' beliefs are the same. The authors suggest, then, that the need for new supporting cognitions will lead the believer to try to convince others of the validity of his beliefs.

Suitability of the True Word Group for a Test of the Hypothesis

Our purpose in learning about the history and beliefs of the True Word group was to determine whether the group met the conditions enumerated in *When Prophecy Fails* and thus would provide a test of the hypothesis under consideration. The first condition is that the group members must hold their belief with deep conviction and that the belief have some relevance to action. It is quite clear that the members held their general religious belief system with deep conviction. Many were originally ministers or missionaries

---

[4]*Ibid.*, p. 4.

actively engaged in Christian work, and most of the members to whom we spoke would refer to "gifts" they themselves or members of their families possessed. Also, as far as we were able to discover, Mrs. Shepard was respected by all of the congregation as a truly exceptional prophet. Thus, since the prophecy probably came from her and was loosely tied to their belief system, it seems clear that it would be very strongly believed by the majority of the congregation. The obvious fact that the group had acted on their belief by building and entering the shelters is the strongest evidence for their belief in the prophecy and also, of course, proof that the belief had relevance for action.

The second condition is that the person holding the belief must have committed himself to it by some action difficult to undo. For the Midwest contingent, the commitment was extreme. They had given up their jobs, had picked up and moved over a thousand miles, and had invested a great deal of time, effort, and money in the building and stocking of homes and shelters. Those from the local area had perhaps given up less, but in several cases they also had lost jobs and had invested considerable sums of money. The things that they have done they cannot undo; the money is spent and the jobs are lost. Most important, none of them can deny or take back the fact that he spent 42 days in hot, humid, crowded shelters and he did this because of his belief.

The third condition, that the belief must be sufficiently specific and sufficiently concerned with the real world so that events may unequivocally refute it, is also quite easy to document. At the time that the group went into the shelters, they believed that a nuclear attack was imminent, and that they would not come out of the shelters until that attack had occurred. That is, they expected to return to a world that had been devastated.

The fourth point, that "undeniable disconfirmatory evidence must occur and must be recognized by the individual holding the belief," is also clearly met. No nuclear attack occurred while the group was in the shelters, and they did not return to a devastated world. Thus, we must conclude that the True Word group suffered the unequivocal disconfirmation of a specific prediction.

The last condition that must be met in order that the True Word group may provide an adequate test of the hypothesis is that the individual believer have social support. This was so clearly the case that it hardly needs documentation. The members of the group had been living together as a separate, rather isolated community for

several months prior to July 4. Indeed, some of the members had
known each other for years and many were related by blood or marriage. During the time of the disconfirmation, social support was not
only present, it was unavoidable. There were as many as 35 people
in each shelter, and the shelters provided absolutely no privacy.
Furthermore, the shelters were organized in such a way that each
contained at least one very strongly convinced member who could
hold his group together, and all of the shelters were connected by
an intercom system so that the leaders could be consulted in case
any members should begin to weaken.

It can be concluded, then, that the five conditions enumerated
by Festinger et al. are met by the True Word group. Therefore, if
the theory as specified is valid, we should expect to observe an increase in fervor of belief, a greater openness to publicity, and strong
attempts to proselyte upon their emergence from their shelters.
This, of course, follows from the postulated need for the group
members to reduce their dissonance and their inability to do this
by any means other than by gaining new cognitions consonant with
their belief.

Behavior of the Group Following the Disconfirmation

In the very early morning of August 16, the 103 "faithful" who
had remained in the shelters for the full 42 days received the word
to come out. At about 9 A.M. they held a joyous reunion in the
church, led by their pastor, in which they were asked, "Did you
have victory?" In unison came the reply, "Yes, praise the Lord!!!"
Mrs. Shepard spoke of how their faith had not been shaken, "The
Lord has brought the people closer to Him, there is not division,
there's fellowship here and we are the holiness people." Many other
church members gave testimonies as to how their stay in the shelters had both strengthened their Christian fellowship and increased
their belief.

The information concerning the first meeting was obtained from
reporters who had been present. During the following week, the
authors were able to speak with almost all of the members of the
group, to attend their frequent church services, and to interview
many of the members, including the leaders, Jameson, Blake, and
Mrs. Shepard, quite intensively.

It is clear from our observations that the beliefs of the group remained intact. The group members did have a reinterpretation of

the purpose of their stay in the shelters that served as an explanation for the failure of the prediction. They had discovered by looking back over all of their messages that it had never been stated that an attack was imminent; they had simply misinterpreted God's purposes. Really, God had just been using them to warn a world that was asleep, while at the same time He was testing their faith. They passed the test and thus proved themselves even more worthy to be among God's elect. We further discovered that they all continued to believe that an attack would come soon. Thus, the group members should be suffering from dissonance; the reinterpretation may have lessened it somewhat, by giving them some reason for having sat so long in the shelters. But their prediction had been shown to be wrong, and they still believed; they should, then, seek publicity and attempt to proselyte.

This did not occur; one must look very hard to uncover even the slightest indication that the members of the Church of the True Word wished to find new converts to their beliefs. The prayer meeting on the morning of August 16 was a golden opportunity if the group wanted to seek new believers. The press was there en masse, including several reporters, cameramen, and TV representatives. One newsman, who had kept in close touch with the group from the beginning of their stay in the shelters, did report that the group was a little more friendly to the press than formerly. Blake asked the press to print certain passages from the scriptures in their reports, and these passages, which speak of widespread destruction, are clearly intended as a warning to the world. Also, Mrs Shepard, at this time and later, spoke favorably of all the free publicity they had gained for the Lord by the worldwide coverage of their activities. However, the group members were relatively indifferent to the attempts of Civil Defense officials to contact them and turned away curious tourists who asked to see their shelters. Furthermore, they made no immediate attempts to interest the townspeople in their church services. There is no indication from the behavior of the group when they first emerged or from our observations of them during the following week that they had any intentions of going out to seek new believers on a large scale.

DISCUSSION

The True Word group meets all of the criteria for a test of the theory as set forth in *When Prophecy Fails,* and yet their behavior following the disconfirmation does not conform to the expectations derived from that theory. Clearly, either the theory is wrong,[5] or it is incomplete in the sense that it specifies insufficiently the variables determining the predicted proselyting. We have two suggestions to make concerning differences between the True Word group and those previously studied that might have affected the differences in behavior that were observed.

The first difference that we wish to consider is that of the amount of social support present within the group. It is stated in *When Prophecy Fails* that one of the conditions necessary for proselyting to occur is the presence of social support for the believers. That is, a certain minimum amount of support is needed so that the individual believer may maintain his beliefs against the disconfirmation. But what might be the effect of additional amounts of social support? We would like to suggest that the more social support an individual receives above the minimum he needs to maintain his belief, the less need he will have to proselyte.

For this suggestion to be acceptable, it must be assumed, first, that there is some limit to the amount of support that is useful to an individual in his attempts to reduce his dissonance. For example, if only a few of your friends agree with a cherished belief of yours, you may be tempted to seek support by convincing others that you are right. On the other hand, if everyone with whom you associate agrees with you, you will feel very little need to go out and attempt to influence others in order to gain more support for your belief. Second, it must be assumed that a person will choose that means of reducing dissonance that is least likely to introduce new dissonance and most likely to reduce that which already exists. In the situation faced by the True Word group, and by other such groups, talking to other already convinced group members could not introduce new dissonance. In fact, interacting with others who had survived the same disconfirmation and who had emerged with their beliefs unshaken would be the best sort of support an individual could have. On the other hand, talking to the skeptical would be very likely to introduce new dissonance, since the person approached would probably reject one's attempts at influence and counter with arguments of his own. Thus, one would expect that, if at all possible, a person would choose to interact with those who agree with him rather than with the unbelievers.

---

[5]Leon Festinger, personal communication.

In a group such as the True Word group with strong social support and a strongly shared belief system, the believer can turn to any other member for confirmation of his beliefs. Following our two assumptions, then, a member of such a group would first choose to talk to other members in his attempts to reduce his dissonance. If in this way he is able to garner new cognitions consonant with his belief up to the limit that he can use, he will then feel no need to seek further support by proselyting. On the other hand, a believer who is a member of a group such as the Lake City group, in which there is less support and more disagreement with regard to the belief system, would be much less likely to encounter sufficient support from his fellows. Thus, he may well have to resort to the otherwise less preferred means of gaining new consonant cognitions, that of proselyting.

It is easy to document the fact that the Lake City group did not provide social support to a degree that even approached that provided by the True Word group. First of all, the Lake City group was not well under way until about 5 months prior to the predicted date of the catastrophe; on the other hand, many members of the True Word group had worked together for several years. Further, the Lake City group had never lived as a community separated from the rest of the world as did the True Word group. This close association present in the True Word group should, one would think, foster a degree of trust in and understanding of the other members that far exceeded that which developed in the Lake City group.

With regard to shared beliefs, there was often disagreement among the members of the Lake City group. For example, the messages received by the two primary leaders of the group often contradicted each other. In contrast, the members of the True Word group were unanimous in their support of Mrs. Shepard, as far as we were able to observe. There was one leader, and one coherent set of beliefs shared by all of the group members. In conclusion, the Lake City group seems to have been characterized by only a minimal degree of social support, and we are suggesting that this degree of support was far from sufficient to reduce the dissonance suffered by the members as a result of the disconfirmation. As a result, the members, in search of further support, felt the need to proselyte. In contrast, the True Word group was very close and had a strongly shared belief system. Thus, they may well have had as much support within the group as they could utilize to reduce their dissonance and consequently felt no need to proselyte.

An interesting, although almost anecdotal, further piece of support for this suggestion comes from a very short article written by a Dutch psychologist, Van Peype,[6] in a Dutch newspaper. He briefly visited a group called the "Communita," who had gathered together near the top of Mont Blanc in expectation of a flood that would destroy the world on July 14. They had existed as a group for over 4 years, and many of the members had lived in the lodge on Mont Blanc for several months, separated from the other people living in the area. They had one prophet, one coherent body of beliefs, and, as far as Van Peype reports, a feeling of community and fellowship. When their prediction was disconfirmed, the leader announced to the waiting reporters, "You should be happy that we made that error. Our faith does not waver . . . Amen."[7] He said no more to the assembled crowd and was reluctant to talk to Van Peype. The members had, then, not given up their belief and yet they showed no indications of a desire to proselyte. In the apparent degree of social support that was present, this group resembles the True Word group much more than it does the Lake City group, and their behavior following disconfirmation was essentially the same.

A second difference between the True Word group and the Lake City group that may have affected the amount of proselyting we observed lies in the amount of ridicule the groups received from the outside world. It would seem reasonable that if a group is receiving considerable ridicule from nonmembers, one way of reducing dissonance that would be apparent to them would be to convince these "unbelievers" that the group is right. If, however, the group is not receiving this sort of treatment from outsiders, this means of reducing dissonance would tend to be a great deal less salient to them. Furthermore, ridicule from others adds more dissonance to that which the group suffers from the disconfirmation. Thus, a very direct way of actually reducing part of the dissonance would be to eliminate the source of ridicule by converting the scoffers.

As far as we were able to determine, the True Word group received very little ridicule from townspeople and the press, considering the unusual step they had taken. The greatest amount of censure the group received seemed to come from other evangelical churches rather than from people in general. In talking to the local townspeople we often encountered statements such as "Yes, we

---

[6] W. F. Van Peype, Nu de Wereld op 14 Juli niet is vergaan, *Vrij Ned.*, July 30, 1960, p. 3.
   [7] *Ibid.*

knew they were building bomb shelters. We believe in doing that, too." The Civil Defense officials in the area even presented the group with an award for "the service which they have performed for the public." After the group had left the shelters, the Mayor of the town was quoted in the newspaper as saying, "I sincerely hope no one ridicules them for their beliefs." Newspaper accounts of the group were in general factual and did not make fun of the group.

The treatment the Lake City group received was very different.[8] Again, the news stories were generally factual and straightforward. But the headlines were cruel. In response to the announcement of the prediction, one paper headlined, "Tuesday—That Sinking Feeling," and another reported, "World Won't End, but Boy It Sure Will Shake". Columnists and editorial writers were equally unkind. Thus, since the Lake City group suffered more ridicule than did the True Word group, it might be supposed that it was easier for the Lake City group to see proselyting as an effective way of reducing the dissonance they had after the disconfirmation.

Evidence from the Mont Blanc group[9] gives somewhat equivocal support for this second suggestion. Van Peype reported that the Communita was very well thought of by the people in the town near their lodge, and was never ridiculed by them. However, they did receive some ridicule at the hands of reporters.

In conclusion, the True Word group, who had suffered a major disconfirmation of an important prediction, held to their beliefs and yet did not proselyte for them. This fact is in clear contradiction to expectation derived from the theory set forth in *When Prophecy Fails*. However, since dissonance theory has received considerable support in laboratory situations, it seems unlikely that it is completely wrong. Thus, we have assumed that the specification of the conditions that must obtain in the disconfirmation situation, in order that the predicted proselyting might occur, was insufficient. The two suggestions we have made for further conditions are that the group provide only minimal social support for its members and that the group receive ridicule from the outside world. It is, of course, impossible to know from the study of one group whether either of these has any relevance to proselyting. We can only say that there were clear differences on both these factors between the Lake City and True Word groups. We would like to suggest, then,

---

[8]Festinger *et al, op. cit.*, p. 137.
[9]W. F. Van Peype, personal communication.

that these two factors be considered and kept in mind by those investigating similar "doomsday groups" in the future.

SUMMARY

On July 4, 1960, a group of 135 men, women, and children began a 42-day stay in underground shelters in response to a prophecy of widespread nuclear disaster. Since their situation bore marked similarities to that of the group studied in *When Prophecy Fails*, their reactions to the disconfirmation of their prediction were observed in order to test the theory set forth in that book. Although the group members clung to their belief in the face of disconfirmation, and even seemed to increase in fervor, they did not attempt to proselyte for their belief. This result is contrary to expectations derived from the observations and the theory presented by Festinger et al.[10] Two variables, the degree of social support available within the group and the amount of ridicule the group received, are suggested as possibly having effected this difference in behavior.

---

[10]*Op. cit.*

PART III

Personal Change through

Interpersonal Relationships

A. ORGANIZATION OF THIS ESSAY

In our previous two essays we have considered interpersonal emotions and the process of identity formation and reality testing. Interpersonal relationships also serve the function of inducing or facilitating change in one or both parties through a process of influence. The interpersonal events which occur in socialization, education, role training, persuasion, seduction, consultation, therapy, and the like will be our focus in the present essay.

Almost any change in behavior, beliefs, attitudes, and values is mediated by interpersonal relationships of one kind or another. The child learns the mores and values of his society from parents and parent-surrogates; pupils learn from teachers; patients learn from therapists; salesmen influence their customers' buying behavior and product attitudes; friends and lovers induce subtle changes in each other; seductive persons influence the behavior and self-image of those prone to seduction. Some of the changes which result from interpersonal relationships are considered desirable by both parties and sanctioned by society; some are desirable but not sanctioned; some are desirable to only one party; and some are not desired by either the participants in the relationship or by society.

As we confront the bewildering array of types of change which result from interpersonal relationships, we face a number of issues which must be clarified and which will serve as the major foci for the organization of this essay. The questions we will try to deal with are:

333

1. Can the *types* of change processes be classified into some meaningful framework?
2. Can the *process* of change be conceptualized in terms of a model which will have meaning for the different types of change identified?
3. Can one begin to develop a theory of interpersonal influence by identifying some *mechanisms* which occur within the broader process of change?

We will attempt to develop tentative answers to these questions in terms of the following general scheme. For the first question we have used a frame of reference which starts not with the individual but with society. Thus, from a societal point of view, there are two basic dimensions which prove useful in identifying different types of change or influence: (1) the degree to which the process is *planned* by the individual or social group; and (2) the degree to which the process is *institutionalized.* By institutionalized influence we mean influence which results from *stable recognized patterns of interaction sanctioned by society* rather than accidental or unstable encounters. The four types of change or influence which result are shown in Figure 1 at the beginning of the next section.

For question *two*, the problem of the process of change, we have used a frame of reference which is anchored in a time dimension. Change is a process which occurs over time and must, therefore, be conceptualized in terms of *phases* or *stages.* We have found Lewin's conceptualization of the change process—a stage of *unfreezing,* a stage of *changing,* and a stage of *refreezing*—a convenient starting point, and have elaborated some mechanisms within these stages.

For question *three*, we have used a heterogeneous, eclectic point of view which reflects several theoretical strands. The symbolic interactionist point of view highlights the kinds of interpersonal forces which make people stable. Unless such forces are altered, no personal change can occur. The process assumes that man's stability derives from the confirmations he receives from his network of *significant others.* In analyzing the mechanisms by which *changes* occur, we will rely more heavily on psychoanalytic and cognitive models of learning. In analyzing the stage of *refreezing,* we find ourselves once again leaning on the symbolic interactionist point of view.

The Problem of Terminology

A central issue which we must confront is the problem of what kinds of terms to choose when discussing interpersonal change processes. In using the words *change* or *influence* rather than *growth* or *learning,* we have attempted to buttress our desire to be morally neutral about the process by choosing terms which are as nonevaluative as possible. Though they are awkward, we will adopt the terms *change agent* and *change target* when referring to the parties in the relationships. When referring to what is changed or influenced, we will use primarily two terms—*behavior* and *attitudes*. *Behavior* refers to *overt* acts which may or may not reflect covert mental processes or feelings. *Attitudes* cover the whole range of *covert* responses from beliefs and values on one extreme, to feelings, impulses, and motives at the other extreme.

Two Other Issues

The first issue concerns the question of whether to include in our conceptual scheme problems of influence through the mass media of communication as in propaganda, advertising, or educational television. Because such influence is clearly a one-way process flowing from an impersonal source to a passive audience, we have chosen not to treat it here. The mass media do not involve *inter*-personal dynamics as central mechanisms of change.

A second issue concerns the problem of the level of abstraction or generality to seek in any preliminary theoretical structuring of an area of human interaction. Do we seek the abstract generality of a social learning theory like Miller and Dollard's,[1] or do we settle for the descriptive uniqueness of a novel like Hulme's *The Nun's Story*?[2] Both deal with the problem of how people change in response to or in concert with other people. But, where Miller and Dollard seek generality through aggregating many processes under one very abstract mechanism, the principle of reinforcement, Hulme seeks understanding by fully describing the nuances of each instance of influence which she could identify in the process of becoming a nun. Our position would approximate Merton's[3] in seeking the interim solution of a "theory of the middle level," recognizing that in this quest, we risk losing both generality and intuitive understanding.

B. BASIC TYPES OF CHANGE PROCESSES

Figure 1 shows our classification of types of change processes in terms of whether the process is planned or unplanned, and in terms

---

[1]N. E. Miller and J. Dollard, *Social Learning and Limitation* (New Haven: Yale Univ. Press, 1941).

[2]K. Hulme, *The Nun's Story* (Boston: Little, Brown & Co., 1956).

[3]R. Merton, *Social Theory and Social Structure* (Glencoe, Ill.: Free Press, 1949).

	Institutionalized	*Not Institutionalized*
Planned.................	Formal socialization	Persuasion
	Education	Selling
	Formal role training	Seduction
	Institutional therapy	Therapy
	Rehabilitation	Coaching
	Brainwashing	Consultation
		Human relations training
Unplanned..............	Unintended consequence of the above process	Emergent change

FIG. 1. CLASSIFICATION OF TYPES OF CHANGE PROCESS.

of whether it occurs through an institutionalized mechanism or not.

1. *Planned institutionalized* influence is exemplified in the socialization of the child, education, institutionalized rehabilitation and therapy, formal role training in organizations or professional training institutions like academies or medical schools, and brainwashing or other attempts to re-educate through formal institutional mechanisms. Society designates certain official positions, the occupants of which perform change agent roles—parents, teachers, therapists, indoctrinators. The targets of influence—children, students, criminals, or patients—are also designated through official procedures or institutions.

The content or area in which influence is supposed to occur is circumscribed: children have to learn the basic culture and values of the society in which they live; students have to learn a designated curriculum; criminals have to learn certain social values and approved behavior patterns; and patients have to learn the behavior patterns, motives, attitudes, and values, defined as "normal" or "healthy" in the society in which they live. The nature of the change in the target person is generally defined as *basic* and is expected to be stable; it concerns the fundamental beliefs and values of the society. The influence is generally expected to flow in one direction only—from agent to target.[4]

2. *Unplanned institutionalized* influence is change which results through formal institutional mechanisms of influence but which is unintended and often undesired. In a way, each of the institutionalized forms of influence have their planned and unplanned out-

---

[4] Those occasional cases in which children, criminals, or patients influence parents, teachers, or therapists provide the kind of dramatic exceptions which highlight the degree to which we tend to take the unidirectional flow of influence for granted in the settings of home, school, prison, or hospital.

comes. Thus, in the process of socialization, the child learns not only the parents' overt values and attitudes but also often acquires their conflicts and antisocial impulses. Parents sometimes communicate their fears and repressed impulses in the very attempt to teach their child not to have those same fears and impulses. In the same way, teachers, therapists, and bosses communicate attitudes which they seek to hide, through behavior inconsistent with their official position. Some of the more tragic aspects of socialization and role training result when the change agent discovers that he has been more successful in imparting undesired behavior and attitudes than those desired ones which his official position required him to impart.

The disintegrative forces within any society, organization, or group are exposed in the unintended consequences of socialization or role training. Lack of integration manifests itself when change agents disagree among themselves on what is to be taught or when they carry within themselves the personal counterpart of the cultural conflict. Perhaps it is the necessity to minimize such conflict which causes institutions to put so much emphasis on the proper selection of change agents. Change agents such as priests, teachers, and therapists must be minimally conflicted and highly congruent with the values of that institution. They must minimize unplanned uninstitutionalized outcomes [5]

3. *Planned uninstitutionalized* influence occurs when one participant in an interpersonal relationship decides (for whatever reason) to influence another participant or to induce some change in him. Examples of this kind of process fall into two general categories:

a) Those where the change target is assumed to have some initial, conscious resistance to the change, as in persuasion, selling, or seduction; and

b) Those where the change target is considered to be a willing accomplice to the change, as in informal role training, coaching, or consultation.[6]

In either of the above cases, the change agent usually assumes his role voluntarily. He may or may not operate with formal, official sanctions to influence others. The status of change target is also

---

[5] The fact that society has relatively less control over who becomes a parent introduces some interesting problems. Adolescent delinquency or schizophrenia can both be viewed as unintended features of the socialization process because of lack of certain qualifications in the parents. On the other hand, Israeli experiments with the kibbutz illustrate an attempt by society to control socialization more closely.

[6] The change target is, of course, often *unconsciously* resistant to the change induction.

accepted voluntarily; in the former case, as a result of being put into that position by the activities of the change agent; in the latter case, as a result of his own initiative.

The nature of the change may or may not be as basic as that defined by planned institutionalized influence processes, but, generally, we associate this type of influence with the more surface and less permanent aspects of the change target's personality. The agent of change in this type of process has fewer formal rewards and punishments available with which to control the target. Hence, the agent is more vulnerable to counterinfluence from the target if the latter chooses to define the situation as one in which he will change only if the agent also changes (though not necessarily in the same area). This type of influence is therefore more likely to be reciprocal than is institutionalized influence.[7]

4. *Unplanned uninstitutionalized* influence or *emergent change* is a spontaneous outcome of the relationship and may involve one or both parties in the relationship. It is often associated with relationships formed primarily for reasons *other* than influence, i.e., influence is not a pivotal function of the relationship. Thus, lovers and friends induce a variety of changes in each other; the members of a work or athletic team influence each other in areas unrelated to their immediate work or play situation; and fleeting contacts between people in spontaneous situations often produce marked changes in one or both of them.

The statuses of change agent and change target are difficult, if not impossible, to identify because a mutual influence often occurs with the result that both people simultaneously occupy both statuses. The change may involve anything from relatively trivial behavioral accommodations to major reorientations of values.

C. THE PROCESS AND MECHANISMS OF CHANGE OR INFLUENCE

The conceptual scheme shown in Figure 2 was developed to encompass the kinds of changes in beliefs, attitudes, and values which we regard as fairly "central" or "deep"; changes which occur during

---

[7]Certain cases, like the practice of private psychotherapy, are difficult to categorize in terms of our scheme. Society has institutionalized the role of the doctor and has created for the psychiatrist the mandate to change people who are defined as patients. But, this very process of definition is highly fluid and unplanned. Similarly, there are a variety of change agents who have social sanction but who operate outside institutional structures without detailed planning either on their part or on the part of the change target. In our society, uncles, big brothers, advisers, leaders, and charismatic personalities fall into this borderland between uninstitutionalized and institutionalized change.

Stage 1. *Unfreezing:* creating motivation to change
  Mechanisms: *a*) Lack of confirmation or disconfirmation
                b) Induction of guilt-anxiety
                c) Creation of psychological safety by reduction of threat or removal of barriers

Stage 2. *Changing:* developing new responses based on new information
  Mechanisms: *a*) Cognitive redefinition through
                    (1) Identification: information from a single source
                    (2) Scanning: information from multiple sources

Stage 3. *Refreezing:* stabilizing and integrating the changes
  Mechanisms: *a*) Integrating new responses into personality
                b) Integrating new responses into significant ongoing relationships through reconfirmation

FIG. 2. THE PROCESS OF INFLUENCE AND THE MECHANISMS UNDERLYING EACH STAGE.

socialization, therapy, and other processes involving the person's self or identity. The scheme also draws attention to a much neglected problem, that of having to unlearn something before something new can be learned. Most of the kinds of changes we are concerned with involve attitudes or behaviors which are integrated around the self, where change implies the giving up of something to which the person has previously become committed and which he values.

Any change in behavior or attitudes of this sort tends to be emotionally resisted because even the possibility of change implies that previous behavior and attitudes were somehow wrong or inadequate, a conclusion which the change target would be motivated to reject. If change is to occur, therefore, it must be preceded by an alteration of the present stable equilibrium which supports the present behavior and attitudes. It is this step, difficult to pin down precisely, which we believe Lewin correctly saw as akin to "unfreezing"—making something solid into a fluid state. Any viable conceptual scheme of the influence process must begin with the process of unfreezing and thereby take account of the inherent threat which change represents. For any change to occur, the defenses which tend to be aroused in the change target must be made less operative, circumvented, or used directly as change levers.

Once the change target's present equilibrium has been upset, once he has become motivated to change, he will seek information relevant to his dilemma. That is, he will seek cues as to the kind of changes to make in his behavior or attitudes which will re-establish a comfortable equilibrium for him. Such information may come from personal or impersonal sources, from a single other person or an array of others, from a single communication or a prolonged search. It is this process, the seeking out, processing, and utilization of information for the purpose of achieving new perceptions, attitudes, and behaviors, which we have called "changing."

There remains the problem of whether the new behavior and attitudes fit well with the person's other behavior and attitudes, and whether they will be acceptable to his significant others. The process of integrating new responses into the ongoing personality and into key emotional relationships leads ultimately to changes which may be considered to be stable. If the new responses do not fit or are unacceptable to important others, a new process of unfreezing is initiated and a new cycle of influence is thereby set up. *Stable* change thus implies a reintegration or a stage of "refreezing," to continue with Lewin's terminology. Just as unfreezing is necessary for change to begin, refreezing is necessary for change to endure.

Let us next examine some of the key mechanisms which can be identified in each stage of the influence process.

1. Mechanisms of Unfreezing

Lack of Confirmation or Disconfirmation. The assumption which underlies a conceptual scheme such as the one proposed is that the change target's significant behavior, beliefs, attitudes, and values are organized around and supported by his self-image. It is further assumed that the person presents himself differently in different social situations. Therefore, it is his "operating self-image" which is relevant in any given situation.[8] This operating self-image does not exist in isolation but is usually integrated with the person's definition of the situation and his image of the other people in the situation. For example, when a young man enters a classroom and adopts the appropriate self-image of "student," this image is integrated with his view of the larger situation as a school in which certain kinds of learning are supposed to take place, and with his image of others who are defined as teachers and fellow students.

Because of the interdependence of self-image, definition of the situation, and image of others in the situation, the process of unfreezing can begin by a failure of confirmation or actual disconfir-

---

[8]The articles by Goffman, pages 226–49 and pages 377–91 are excellent analyses of the process of constructing "operating self-images."

mation in any one of the three aspects of the total situation.[9] The change target can be confronted with the information: (1) that his self-image is out of line with what others and the situation will grant him or be able to sustain; (2) that his definition of the situation is out of line with "reality" as defined by others in the situation; (3) that his image of the others is out of line with their image of themselves or of each other; and (4) one or more of the above in combination.

For example, the student entering the classroom may have seen himself as a passive listener only to discover suddenly that the teacher has called upon him; he may have defined the classroom as primarily a place to relax and meet girls, but discover that the course is, in fact, "hard" and that the instructor defines the class-room as a place for active participation by students; he may have perceived the instructor as a *laissez-faire* type of "good fellow," only to discover that the instructor sees himself as a tough taskmaster determined to make his classroom into a real learning environment. Each of these types of information can be thought of as *disconfirmatory* of some assumption which the student had made about himself, the situation, and/or the others in the situation.

By contrast, *lack of confirmation* occurs when relevant information is lacking. Thus, if the student placed high value on himself as a ladies' man and defined classrooms as places to meet coeds, he would experience lack of confirmation if he discovered that there were no girls among his fellow students. Another example might be the case of two students who initially reinforce in each other a self-image of indifference to learning and engage in horseplay during class meetings. If the teachers asks them to sit far apart, and if little opportunity to interact outside of class exists, one could say that these aspects of their self-image would subsequently be lacking in confirmation. In a situation where aspects of the self fail to be confirmed, one may predict that a *gradual* atrophy or unlearning of those aspects will occur.[10] In a situation where aspects of the self are

---

[9]In the fairly common situation where information conflicts, where both confirming and disconfirming cues are available, the person probably tends to pay attention only to the confirming cues. As long as an confirmation occurs, therefore, there are no real unfreezing forces present.

[10]The best examples of lack of confirmation occurred in Communist controlled POW camps in which prisoners were systematically segregated from each other and their social structure undermined to such a degree that mutual mistrust led to virtually no meaningful communication. See E. H. Schein, "The Chinese Indoctrination Program for Prisoners of War," *Psychiatry*, Vol. 19 (1959), pp. 149–72, and the

(Continued on next page.)

actually disconfirmed, the person confronts a more immediate disequilibrium which requires some immediate change or new learning.

The Induction of Guilt Anxiety. The induction of guilt-anxiety refers to the process wherein the person reacts to lack of confirmation or disconfirmation, not by rejecting the information or its source, but by feeling some sense of inadequacy or failure in himself. The sense of inadequacy may (1) be felt in reference to a failure in living up to some ideal self-image; (2) result from a feeling of disappointing others whose reactions are valued; or (3) result from a failure to honor some obligation that has been assumed. Such feelings may be summarized by the concept of "guilt-anxiety." Change will occur in the attempt to reduce or, more commonly, to *avoid* guilt anxiety.[11]

Creation of Psychological Safety by Reduction of Threat or Removal of Barriers. Unfreezing can also occur through the reduction of threat or the removal of barriers to change. In these instances, one must assume that the change target already has some motive or desire to change but experiences a conflict which prevents the actual change from occurring. Either the change is inherently anxiety provoking because it brings with it the unknown, or else it is perceived by the person to have consequences which he is unwilling or unable to bear. The change agent may in these instances (1) try to reassure the change target; or (2) try to help him bear the anxiety attendant upon change; or (3) attempt to show the target that the outcome is more palatable than he may have assumed.

Looking at the three unfreezing mechanisms together, we can say that a change or influence process can only be started when there is some *optimum balance* of disconfirmation, guilt anxiety, and psychological safety. It is the achievement of this balance which makes the job of change agent so difficult and, at the same time, so creative.

If disconfirmation and/or guilt anxiety are too high, the change target will either leave the situation or, if this is not possible, will become defensive and more rigidly cling to his present equilibrium.

paper by Schein in this section (pages 406–26). For a more extensive discussion of Communist indoctrination methods, see E. H. Schein with I. Schneier and C. H. Barker, *Coercive Persuasion* (New York: W. W. Norton, 1961), and R. J. Lifton, "'Thought Reform' of Western Civilians in Chinese Communist Prisons," *Psychiatry*, Vol. 19 (1956), pp. 173–95.

[11]See Schein, Schneier, and Barker in this part for a further discussion of guilt.

He will deny the validity of, or fail to perceive, disconfirming cues, and will repress feelings of guilt anxiety. If psychological safety is also high, the target might risk being less defensive, but it is difficult to create conditions where disconfirmation and safety are both very high.

If psychological safety is low, even minimal disconfirmations will appear as threats, thus reducing the likelihood that the person will pay attention to them. On the other hand, if psychological safety is high, conditions may be set up where either small disconfirmations in the present situation start a change process, or where *remembered disconfirmation from past experiences* serves to start the process of change. Thus, when a person enters a very supportive therapeutic relationship, he may find that he can begin to explore disconfirmatory experiences which happened long ago but which for the first time he can allow himself to plumb the real meaning of. In other words, it is not always necessary for the disconfirmation to occur in the psychological present. All of us have accumulated a history of disconfirmations which however never led to change because there was insufficient psychological safety to permit us to really pay attention to the cues. Once we are in a supportive safe relationship, these early cues can lead to significant change.

Examples of the Unfreezing Process

To illustrate these ideas, let us consider some examples from each of the basic types of change cited above.

1. *Institutionalized* influence, both planned and unplanned, typically operates through routinized, often institutionalized, methods of *disconfirmation*. The child, the criminal, and the sick person are systematically punished for responses out of line with expected cultural norms. Deviant behavior is pointed out and sanctions are brought to bear if it continues.

Institutions devoted to producing a change in self-image such as rehabilitation centers, schools, military academies, and mental hospitals usually begin their influence process by dramatic disconfirmations which Goffman has called "mortifications of the self."[12] Thus, the entrant may be deprived of his clothes, his name, his personal possessions, his hair, and his status, all of which communicates to him, in as clear a fashion as possible, that his old

---

[12]E. Goffman, "On the Characteristics of Total Institutions," *Proceedings of the Symposium on Preventive and Social Psychiatry* (Washington, D.C.: Walter Reed Army Institute of Research, 1957).

identity will be minimally valued in the new setting. Even the *voluntary* entrant into the institution may find that the change demanded of him is more than he bargained for, thus requiring him to unfreeze further before successful influence can occur. Stories of officer training procedures in a tough academy or in an Officers Candidate School and descriptions of the religious novitiate abound with examples of this type of unfreezing.[13]

Guilt anxiety is induced when (1) the change target perceives himself as having failed to live up to the image which society expects of him as conveyed either implicitly or explicitly by his parents, teachers, and significant others or (2) when he feels he has disappointed change agents who have invested time and effort in changing him. The unfulfilled obligation theme is reflected in the parental message that children *owe* certain kinds of behavior to their parents because of the heavy investment the parents have made in the children. Other kinds of change agents, such as therapists, also use this process. By investing a great deal of time, effort, and emotional energy in their change targets, they may succeed in arousing a need to change in the target who sees this as a form of repayment for the efforts invested in him.

The best examples of *threat or barrier reduction* may be found in the educational efforts which view certain kinds of limited performance in children not as instances of limited capacity, but as instances of learning blocks. Only when such blocks are removed is the child able to operate at full capacity. Many forms of rehabilitation and therapy operate on the assumption that one cannot *induce* motives toward change, but can attempt to locate and unblock such motives in patients and delinquents. It is our own assumption that both kinds of influence operate—that which takes advantage of motives already present in the person, and that which initiates the process by inducing motives through lack of confirmation or through actual disconfirmation.

2. In *planned uninstitutionalized* forms of influence, we find the process of disconfirmation somewhat less organized but no less potent. Goffman in his essay "On Cooling the Mark Out" (pages 377–91), provides an excellent example. A person invests in a get-rich-quick scheme, thinking of himself as a sharp operator, only to discover that not only has he failed to become rich but also has been defrauded by confidence men. The sudden discovery that what

---

[13]For an excellent example see Hulme, *op. cit.*

we claim to be and have committed ourself to is thoroughly discredited by others and external events serves to operate as a powerful force toward some new self-definition.

The major difference between the institutionalized and uninstitutionalized processes lies in the degree to which the potential change target can evade the situation in which unfreezing and changing is likely to occur. In most institutionalized change situations, both agent and target accept the fact that some change in the target is expected. In uninstitutionalized situations, by contrast, the influence agent may initially confront a potential target who will resist the role of target and refuse to define the situation as one in which influence is legitimate.

The salesman must first convince the person to see himself as a *potential* customer. Only then can he try to sell the particular product. The consultant often finds himself in a situation where the person most in need of change is the one least likely to recognize this need. The consultation process may then involve a long period of unfreezing in which the major goal is to help the client define the situation as one in which he can accept help for himself. Only then does the question shift to *what kind* of change is relevant for the client. But, even then, the potential customer or client can terminate the relationship at any time and thus evade any further influence attempts.

The agent of uninstitutionalized influence can not make use of coercive power or some of the more basic rewards and punishments which are available to parents, teachers, and doctors. As a result, he must rely more heavily on the manipulation of guilt anxiety or on unblocking already present motives to change by showing the potential target that he is not living up to some ideal which he himself has stated or that his ideals have some flaw in them. Both processes presuppose that the influence agent has somehow captured the attention of the target and is able to present himself in a believable and convincing manner (see pages 355-61 and Adelson's paper, pages 491-503 for a further discussion of this point).

Having captured the potential customer's attention, the salesman can (1) try to show him how buying a certain product is essential to the upholding of a self-image which the salesman presumes or knows that the customer holds; (2) try to build an ideal self-image for him which can be achieved primarily through purchase of the product; or (3) try to reduce whatever anxiety or barrier the customer is assumed to have about the purchase (e.g., "You can buy it on the installment plan," or "It will only cost you pennies a week"). Dramatic instances of failure to influence may result when the change agent incorrectly diagnoses the nature of the target's anxieties or barriers.

The consultant similarly tries to influence his client by (1) pointing the way toward a desired state; (2) demonstrating that this state can only be achieved through certain changes which the consultant advocates; and (3) helping the client to overcome barriers to these changes. The coach uses the trainee's desire for some ideal performance as a lever for influence, though sometimes he also functions as the person who defines what the ideal should be. An excellent analysis of this process is given in Strauss's essay on coaching a person to prepare him for promotion or some other change in status (see pages 370–77). The ability of the coach to be reassuring and to deal with barriers, without compromising performance standards, may be one of the important characteristics which differentiates the good from the poor coach.

A strategy which the change agent may employ to unfreeze the target is to elicit, either by persuasion, seduction, or outright trickery, some behavior which is inconsistent with the image the person is trying to uphold or achieve. This type of disconfirmation produces immediate embarrassment and guilt, and thus serves to initiate the influence process. In the sales situation, this process would be exemplified by the seduction of the steadfast "noncustomer" into trying out some product. Once he has agreed to a trial, he has implicitly given up his self-image as a "noncustomer." He has opened the door to further sales efforts as well as to guilt feelings which may be based either on his sense of failure to live up to his "noncustomer" image or on his reluctance to disappoint the salesman who has now invested more heavily in him.

The consultant often does not have to elicit behavior inconsistent with the client's self-image. Such behavior may already be present, but outside of the client's awareness. The consultant's problem then becomes one of how to point out the inconsistency so as to produce sufficient guilt to induce change without producing so much anxiety as to create defensiveness and thus block change.

3. In the case of *emergent change,* the influence process also begins by lack of confirmation, disconfirmation, the induction of guilt anxiety, and the reduction of threat. However, the interpersonal messages which initiate the process are more spontaneous and may not be sent with the explicit aim of influencing the other party.

Friends or lovers, in their desire to maximize mutual gratification in their relationship, will tend to be highly sensitive to disconfirmatory messages or lack of confirmation. Such sensitivity may result from the fact that mutual confirmation is the basis for defining the closeness of the relationship in the first place. That is, the growth of intimacy can be conceived of as a series of successive experiments by the parties to the relationship. As each private area of the self is tentatively exposed, the response of the other party is carefully calibrated so as to determine the amount of acceptance or confirmation it implies. As given areas are confirmed, i.e., as the person feels more and more "accepted," he may be motivated to experiment with ever more private areas.

However, in any relationship, certain areas will, in fact, not be acceptable to the other party, thus necessitating either some change in one or both parties, or an agreement to avoid that area in the relationship. The relationship of friends or lovers is therefore characterized by a constant tension between the process of mutual influence and mutual acceptance. Depending on the actual personalities which the partners bring with them, there will be some areas in which mutual acceptance is high. No change will be required in either party because of an initial harmony of personalities and roles. There will be some areas where the presented self of one partner (A) is more central to him than whatever disconfirmatory feelings or reactions are aroused in the other partner (B). In this case, B will change. He will withhold his reactions and gradually try to unlearn them. Finally, there will be some areas where the centrality of the disconfirmatory reactions in B is greater than the centrality of A's presented part of himself. In this case, A will attempt to change that part of himself so as not to arouse the painful reaction in B on future occasions.

Much of the emotional work of a close relationship is the complex dialogue which this difficult calculus of feelings makes necessary. Each partner must obtain valid information about the relative cost of changes in himself and changes in the other in order to make those changes which seem mutually desirable by properly balancing disconfirmation, reassurance, and help.

From the point of view of the psychologist, a further complexity derives from the fact that many factors influence how a given person will react to information about himself, and how he will decide how central some part of himself is relative to some part of his partner. As Cheever's brilliant story "The Scarlet Moving

Van" illustrates, the person who feels more strongly about something and who is able to present himself as totally sincere may induce change in another person even if his own behavior is "sick," "antisocial," and ultimately destructive to the change target (see pages 461–72). The successful persuader may well be the person who can convince others that it would cost him more to change than it would cost them to accommodate.

4. In summary, we have argued that any interpersonal change or influence presupposes a process of unfreezing which in turn consists of several other processes which occur singly or in combination. These are: (1) a process of *disconfirmation* or *lack of confirmation* of some part of the change target's self; (2) the *induction of guilt anxiety;* and/or (3) the creation of psychological safety by *reduction of threat or removal of barriers to change* if some change motive is already present in the target person.

The process of unfreezing has been discussed in considerable detail because it is this stage of the influence process which is usually given least attention. Indeed, in the traditional social psychological literature on attitude change, the process is hardly considered at all. The present theoretical formulation makes unfreezing a critical and necessary step in any change process. Without unfreezing, no change will occur, no matter how much effort is put into selling, persuading, coercing, rewarding, or punishing. Or to put it another way, the reason why so many change efforts run into resistance or outright failure is usually directly traceable to their not providing for an effective unfreezing process before attempting a change induction.

2. Mechanisms of Changing

Cognitive Redefinition. The problem of learning a *new* response or changing an attitude can be thought of as a problem of seeking out *reliable* and *valid* information from a plethora of sources which may or may not be credible to the target. In making this assertion, we are limiting the learning or change situation to those situations which are governed by *social reality* as contrasted with *physical reality;*[14] that is, we are only considering situations in which validity is *consensually* judged in terms of the beliefs and attitudes of others.

How does the change target choose and make up his mind from the welter of sources available? In the typical, stable social situation,

---

[14] L. Festinger, "Informal Social Communication," *Psychological Review,* Vol. 57 (1950), pp. 271–82.

the person pays attention to those sources of information (other people) who confirm his present behavior and attitudes. If others fail to provide confirmation or actually disconfirm present attitudes, yet the person must continue to interact with them (e.g., because the job demands it), we have a typical unfreezing situation with respect to those attitudes. The person knows something is wrong and that some kind of change is demanded of him, but he does not automatically know what is wrong or how to correct the situation.

In order to determine what is wrong or how to change, the person must first re-examine certain assumptions or beliefs he has about himself, others, and his definition of the situation. He must then decide if these assumptions are unwarranted or inconsistent with feelings and evaluations which the others in the situation hold about themselves, him, and the situation. *The first step in the change process, then, is to develop alternate assumptions and beliefs through a process of cognitive redefinition of the situation.*

This process involves (1) *new definitions* of terms in the semantic sense, (2) a *broadening of perceptions* or expanded consciousness which changes the frame of reference from which objects are judged, and/or (3) *new standards of evaluation and judgment.* The new attitudes and behavior which are the eventual outcome of the influence process result from this intermediate step of cognitive re-definition.

From this perspective, the process of unfreezing can be viewed as *becoming open* to certain kinds of information which are actually or potentially available in the environment. The process of changing is the *actual assimilation* of new information resulting in cognitive redefinition and new personal constructs.[15] These, in turn form the basis for new attitudes and new behavior.[16]

In making cognitive redefinition pivotal to the change process, we

---

[15]We are using constructs here in the sense that G. A. Kelly, *The Psychology of Personal Constructs* [New York: Norton, 1955], defined them, as the beliefs, assumptions, and evaluations a person has about some object in his social world.

[16]The best examples of this process were provided to us by the Chinese Communists (see Schein's analysis in this part, pp. 406–26). The prisoner changed his attitudes only after a prolonged process of unfreezing, the end result of which was a readiness to pay attention to the cues which cell mates were providing all along. Once he was paying attention to this category of information, the prisoner discovered that his meanings for words such as "crime" were different from theirs, and his standards of judgment based on his frame of reference were different from their standards because of their different frame of reference. Once he had redefined his own semantics and attempted to view the world from the cell-mates' frame of reference by applying their standards, he could accept himself as a guilty criminal and make a sincere confession.

have clearly allied ourselves with Gestalt theories of learning and have rejected reinforcement theories of learning. We would like to point out, however, that the reinforcement principle is very much relevant to the process of unfreezing and refreezing. The process of influence *begins* with the failure to obtain certain social reinforcements (lack of confirmation or disconfirmation); the process of influence *ends* with the reinforcement (confirmation) of new attitudes and behavior. The reinforcement principle cannot conveniently explain the actual mechanisms by which new assumptions, beliefs, or constructs develop and in turn lead to new attitudes and behaviors. We reject the notion of blind trial and error learning in the realm of social reality, favoring instead a position which makes the assimilation of information from the social environment the central process. The person does experiment in the process of change, but each experiment is based on some new definition of himself, others, and the situation and has, therefore, already been preceded by some cognitive redefinition.

The question arises whether this mechanism of change is always conscious or not. The answer is clearly negative. We have dramatic examples of cognitive redefinition in the realm of physical perceptions which occur entirely without awareness. There is no reason to doubt the existence of a similar process in the realm of social reality. The best examples come from psychophysical studies of judgments of weight or brightness. The entire frame of reference and pattern of judgments of the same stimuli can be altered simply by introducing an achoring stimulus at either extreme of the scale.[17] The subject does not realize that his judgments have changed, yet clearly, cognitive redefinition has taken place. In the realm of social perception and rumor transmission, we have similar effects. Once certain key stimuli are introduced as anchors (e.g., identifying a certain person in the story as a Negro), the scale of judgment of other stimuli shifts, though the person may be completely unaware of the process.[18]

Let us turn now to the next problem, that of the *source of information* which the person utilizes in redefining his cognitions about himself, others, and his situation. At one extreme, we have the acquisition of new information through a single source via some

---

[17] H. Helson, "Adaptation-Level as a Basis for a Quantitative Theory of Frames of Reference," *Psychological Review*, Vol. 55 (1948), pp. 297–313.

[18] G. W. Allport and L. Postman, *The Psychology of Rumor* (New York: Holt, 1947).

process of *identification.* The cues to which the person responds are those that come from a model to whom the person has chosen to relate himself emotionally. At the other extreme, we have the acquisition of new information through *scanning* a multiple array of sources, which may vary in salience and credibility but which do not elicit the kind of emotional focusing implied by identification. The sources are usually other people, but they need to be physically present to exert an influence. Their information may have just as much potency in written or broadcasted form.

We have labeled these two extreme forms of information acquisition by the terms *identification* and *scanning,* recognizing that there are many forms, like imitation, which fall in between. Let us now examine each of these processes in greater detail.[19]

Cognitive Redefinition through Identification. We can distinguish two basically different kinds of identification which have major consequences for the kind of influence or change produced in a change target. We have labeled these as *Type I* or *defensive* identification and *Type II* or *positive* identification. The conditions for, psychological processes of, and outcomes of these two types are shown in Figure 3.[20]

Looking first at the *conditions* for identification, we note that *defensive identification* tends to occur in settings which the target has entered involuntarily and from which he cannot escape. He usually experiences a sense of helplessness, relative impotence, fear, and threat. The relationship to the change agent is an imbalanced one in that the agent has most of the power. The agent usually occupies a formal position supported by institutionalized sanctions. The target's role is to change or learn and not to ask too many questions. The prototype of this relationship is the child *vis-à-vis* the powerful parent or the concentration camp prisoner *vis-à-vis* his captor.

---

[19]This analysis has been influenced by Kelman's excellent work on mechanisms of attitude change (H. C. Kelman, "Compliance, Identification, and Internalization: Three Processes of Attitude Change" *Conflict Resolution,* Vol. 2 [1958], pp. 51–60). We have not used his concepts of *compliance, identification,* and *internalization* because of our emphasis on deeper levels of change than those he deals with in his experiments. Kelman's concepts have greatly aided, however, in achieving some conceptual clarity in this area.

[20]The analysis of identification follows closely Slater's analysis of personal and positional identification. Our analysis, however, deals more with adult processes whereas his focuses on childhood socialization. For an excellent analysis see P. E. Slater, "Toward a Dualistic Theory of Identification" *Merrill-Palmer Quarterly,* Behavior and Development, Vol. 7, No. 2 (1961), pp. 113–26.

Positive identification, by contrast, tends to occur in situations which the target has entered voluntarily and from which he feels free to leave. He experiences a sense of autonomy and feels he can make choices. Instead of fear and threat *vis-à-vis* the change agent,

	Type I *Defensive Identification*	*Type II* *Positive Identification*
Conditions for *the Process*	Target is captive in the change situation	Target is free to leave situation
	Target role nonvoluntarily acquired	Target takes role voluntarily
	Agent in formal change agent position	Agent does not necessarily occupy formal role
	Target feels helpless, impotent, fearful, and threatened	Target experiences autonomy, sense of power, and choice
	Target must change	Target experiences trust and faith in agent
		Target can terminate change process
Psychological *Processes* *Involved*	Agent is primary source of unfreezing	Agent is usually not the source of unfreezing
	Target becomes position oriented to acquire the agent's perceived power	Target becomes person oriented because agent's power is seen to reside in his personality, not his position
	Target has limited and distorted view of agent, and lacks empathy for agent	Agent will be chosen on the basis of trust, clarity, and potency
	Target tends to imitate limited portions of agent's behavior	Target sees richness and complexity of agent as a person
		Target tends to assimilate what he learns from the model
Outcomes	New behavior in target is stilted, ritualized, restrictive, and narrowing	New behavior in target is enlarging, differentiated, spontaneous, and enabling of further growth
	New behavior is more likely to be acceptable to the influencing institution	New behavior is personally more meaningful but may be less acceptable to influencing institution

FIG. 3. ANALYSIS OF TWO TYPES OF IDENTIFICATION.

he experiences trust and faith. The power relationship is less tilted and is generally not supported by formal positions or institutional sanctions, though they may be present, as in the case of the psychotherapist. The prototype of this relationship is the mutual identification of husband and wife or close friends.

In terms of the *psychological processes* involved in the two types of identification, *defensive identification* generally implies a relationship in which the change agent operates as the primary source of unfreezing (i.e., he provides the bulk of the disconfirming cues). The target responds to this situation by becoming preoccupied with the change agent's position or status which is perceived to be the primary source of the change agent's power. This preoccupation with the position, in turn, implies a limited and often distorted view of the identification model. The change target tends to pay attention only to the power-relevant cues, tends to have little or no empathy for the person actually occupying the position, and tends to imitate blindly and often unconsciously only certain limited portions of the model's behavior. Or, to put it another way, if existing attitudes and parts of the target's self are chronically and consistently disconfirmed in a coercive way, one solution for the target is to abandon them completely and to substitute those attitudes and values perceived to be a property of the powerful disconfirmer. One of the best descriptions of the dynamics of this process is to be found in Moloney's article on psychic self-abandonment (pages 391–405).

Positive identification, by contrast, tends to be *person*—rather than *position*—oriented. The potential model is rarely the source of unfreezing and hence is less threatening. The model's power or salience is perceived to lie in some personal attributes rather than in some formal position. Because the change target feels free to leave the situation, he will use the criteria of trust and clarity to choose a model which, in turn, will lead to a fuller richer view of the personality of the model. He will tend to have empathy for the model and genuinely to assimilate the new information obtained from seeing the world through the model's eyes rather than directly imitating his behavior. Thus the target's new behavior and attitudes may not actually resemble the model's too closely. The whole process of identification will be more spontaneous, differentiated, and will enable further growth, rather than be compulsive and limiting.

Looking now at the *outcome,* we see that *defensive identification* leads to a more restricted, ritualized, and stilted set of responses and attitudes. On the other hand, *positive identification* leads to an enlarged, more differentiated, and fluid set of responses and attitudes. There is a greater likelihood of the latter process leading to psychological growth than is true of the former. However, the likelihood that the changes will be acceptable to the institution which has initiated the change process may be greater if defensive identification has taken place.

In both types of identification, the basic mechanism of change is the utilization of interpersonal cues which come from a change agent with whom the target identifies himself. These cues serve as the basis for redefining the cognitions the target holds about himself, others, and the situations in which he finds himself. But, it is obvious that a great deal of change occurs through processes other than these two types of identification. Even in the most coercive institutions, defensive identification may account for only a small portion of the total change in the target. To gain a more balanced picture of change mechanisms, we must look at the other end of the information acquisition scale, to the process we have called *scanning*.

Cognitive Redefinition through Scanning. The process of *scanning* can best be differentiated from the process of *identification* by the degree to which the change target or learner focuses on multiple models as contrasted with a single model in his social environment. Scanning thus involves a "cafeteria" approach to the utilization of the interpersonal information, and the absence of strong emotional relationships between the change target and his sources of relevant information. At the extreme, *scanning* implies attention to the *content* of the message regardless of the person, whereas *identification* implies attention to the *person* regardless of the content. In both cases, other people tend to be the primary source of information, but in scanning, others become salient only in terms of their perceived relevance or expertness in solving the particular problem which is bothering the change target.

The contrast between *scanning* and *identification* can best be exemplified in a group engaged in group therapy or in human relations training. Let us assume that each member of the group is unfrozen with respect to some areas of himself and is seeking information which will permit him to redefine his situation so as to reach a more comfortable equilibrium. An example of *defensive identification* would be the case of the group member who, because of his great fear of the authority of the therapist or staff member in the group, attempts to change by mimicking and imitating what he perceives to be the staff member's behavior and attitudes. An example of *positive identification* would be the case of the group member who establishes a close emotional relationship with another group member or the staff member, and attempts to view his own problems from the perspective of this other person. An example of *scanning* would be the case of the group member who looks to any source in the group for reactions which bear upon the particular problem he perceives, and attempts to integrate *all* the reactions he obtains. To reiterate, when a person scans, he relates himself primarily to the information he receives, not to the particular source from which the information comes.[21]

How does scanning compare with identification in the change outcome? In the case of scanning, the target may have a more difficult time locating reliable and useful information, but the solution he eventually finds is likely to fit better into his personality because of his power to accept or reject information voluntarily. If the change goal is personal growth, the change agent should attempt to produce a setting conducive to scanning or positive identification, and avoid a setting conducive to defensive identification. If the change goal is the acceptance of a particular set of behaviors and attitudes, the change agent should attempt to produce a setting conducive to positive identification and provide the target with a good representative of the point of view to be learned. To achieve the latter change goal, defensive identification would be next best and scanning would appear to be least likely to succeed.

A Digression: Attributes of Potential Positive Identification Models

It is our assumption that scanning is the primary process by which people change, and that it would always occur in the absence of certain salient, threatening, or seductive people in the social environment. Once certain people become salient, identification becomes more probable. We would further assume that role relationships which are institutionalized, thus making certain people salient through their position, tend to elicit primarily a defensive type of identification. Parents, teachers, and bosses are good examples of such roles. An intriguing question is, in the absence of such preordained role relationships, what factors make people salient as potential identification models, particularly for positive identification?

---

[21]Scanning could involve non-interactive processes such as reading, observing the reactions of others, conscious attempts at self-analysis and reorganization of own thoughts, listening to advice, and other similar processes. What limits such non-interactive processes as a basis for attitude and behavior change, however, is that the information obtained often turns out to be irrelevant or useless to the problems the target is working on. More useful information is likely to come from the individuals with whom the target is interacting in that he can at least infer their reactions and their way of looking at things.

The following discussion outlines two typologies which appear to be relevant to this problem. They concern the kinds of attributes which make people more or less likely to be chosen as positive identification models.

Typology A: Attributes Which Recreate Family Relationships. In any given interpersonal situation, the relative age, status, experience, and formal position of the potential model *vis-à-vis* the change target will determine whether the relationship will tend to be structured in terms of a parent-child, older sibling-child, or peer group relationship. Potential models can therefore be thought of as surrogates of parents, older sibling, or peers and their attributes can be analyzed in terms of the likelihood that they will represent one or another of such types for the change target. For purposes of this discussion, we will label such potential models as:

1. *Father* figures
2. *Big brother* figures
3. *Peer* figures
4. *Transitional types,* i.e., from peer to big brother and big brother to father.

The likelihood that a given person in the change target's environment will be perceived and treated as a father, big brother, peer, or person in transition will depend on that person's actual formal status relative to the target, his degree of perceived similarity to such figures from the target's earlier life, and his own presentation of himself (conscious or unconscious) as a father, big brother, or peer.

The type of emotional relationship which is recreated has implications for the trustworthiness, clarity, and actual content of what can be transmitted to the change target. Specifically, we would hypothesize that, other things being equal, peer figures are more likely to be trusted than big brothers, who in turn are more likely to be trusted than fathers. We would also hypothesize that peer figures are more understandable and clearer than big brothers, who are, in turn, more understandable and clearer than father figures. Therefore, the likelihood of positive identification is greatest with peer figures and least with father figures.

These hypotheses are based on two underlying theoretical notions. One is that the more powerful we perceive a potential model to be and the more dependent we are upon him, the less likely we are to trust him, in the sense of perceiving his goals and motives to be similar to our own. The second notion is that the more similarity we perceive between a potential model's experiences and our own, the more likely we are to be able to understand him and trust him. In the paradigm of child-parent relationships, the child is less likely to trust and understand his father than his brother because the father is perceived to be powerful, independent, and impossible to influence. The child sees the father as living in a different world and as having had experiences which are perceived to be so dissimilar to his own that he cannot help but question whether the father can understand him and therefore whether he can be trusted.

In stating these hypotheses we are speaking probabilistically. There are, of course, many situations where father figures do elicit trust and do serve as clear models. There are equally as many situations where the competition between brothers or peers destroys trust, however clear the brother model may be. Consequently, big brothers and peers may elicit *defensive* identification, but generally speaking fathers would tend to do so more often. It is likewise true that fathers may elicit *positive* identification, but big brothers and peers would tend to do so more often.

The kinds of influences which can be and generally are exerted by peers and big brothers often lead to behavior, attitudes, and values in the change target which run counter to those desired by the formal change institutions such as the family or school. Thus, while peer culture is a powerful instrument of influence, its values often run counter to those of the society in which the peer culture exists, setting the "parental" and peer culture into conflict with each other. *If* positive identification with parent figures can be achieved, the change target can learn the key norms, values, and behavior patterns of the society or organization to which he belongs. The dilemma of socialization, therefore, is how to balance the greater power of potentially countercultural change agents against the more functional learning to be obtained from change agents who have less chance of becoming influential.

Some Applications of Typology A. The relevance of this typology to the process of socialization is obvious. Somewhat less obvious is the fact that we tend to recreate these kinds of relationships in adult change or influence situations. An understanding of the change outcomes of such situations may then depend upon our ability to understand correctly the nature of the relationship which exists between change agent and target. For example, we rarely analyze the ubiquitous superior-subordinate relationship of modern organizational life in terms of whether the superior functions essentially as a father, big brother, or peer. Yet, we may not be able to understand why some superiors are able to influence the values of their subordinates more than others unless we stop to consider the role of such relationships.

Many business organizations, for example, have found that apprenticing a new member to an older, senior, high-ranking individual in the firm results in relatively little constructive learning in the new man. On the other hand, a productive and influential relationship results when the new man is assigned to a person only slightly older and one or two levels higher. Similarly, it is probably not accidental that so many induction programs, whether in military or civilian organizations, build in a "buddy" or "big brother" system. The function of these systems is to communicate the *informal* culture of the organization to the inductee, a task which would be difficult for the immediate superior to fulfill because of the likelihood that he would be viewed as a father figure and, therefore, as a symbol of only *formal* organizational values and norms.

The role of peer group influence can be seen clearly in prisons and certain mental hospitals where the inmates or patients band together to form a culture of their own in order to resist the formal authority of the institution. As new members join the organization, they learn the peer culture far more rapidly than the official value system. In industry, the counterpart of this phenomenon is "restriction of output," where such restriction is based on peer group norms of a "fair day's work for a fair day's pay." Once such norms have become established, incentive systems based on individual performance are relatively powerless to combat peer group pressures. Because the peer group relationship is such a powerful one, it has great potential for the transmission of organizational norms and values. The problem, from the point of view of the change agent, is how to insure the *congruence between peer group norms and organizational values.* Induction programs, such as those conducted by the Marines or by certain corporations which involve the peer group in "around the clock" organizational activities and which function primarily in terms of *group* incentives, appear to be able to achieve this goal. Perhaps the most notable industrial example is the Scanlon Plan, where even in unionized companies, workers and management organize into teams to fulfill the common aim of improving total organization performance.[22]

A few comments must be made on the role of the person in trans-

---

[22]F. G. Lesieur, *The Scanlon Plan* (New York: Wiley, 1958).

ition, because this type of person is potentially the most powerful model of all. The person in transition still belongs to the peer group, but his movement out of the group implies that he is embracing some values other than those of the group. If the group trusts him enough, and if it seems clear that these new values are being rewarded by the organization and are rewarding to the transitional person, it is possible that the entire group will change with him in the direction of these new values.[23]

In industry, there is a clear dictum that one way to get ahead is to learn to be like those who are already on the move. Many social service organizations established for the purpose of rehabilitating others, such as Alcoholics Anonymous, use former "patients" as the key change agents in the process of influencing new patients. Perhaps the clearest example of this type of influence comes from Chinese Communist coercive persuasion attempts. Prisoners who were already partly re-educated were assigned to the same cell as the lone newcomer to the prison and proved to be powerful agents of influence (see Schein, pages 406–26).

The power of the person in transition depends very much on whether he is perceived to be "still one of *us*" or is perceived to "have gone over to them," particularly in those instances where the peer group is defensively arrayed against the authority. Thus, in the prison, the trusty's influence over inmates is negligible because he has gone too far; he has defected. In the treatment of juvenile delinquent gangs, some therapeutic gains may be achieved if the leader or some respected member of the gang can be induced to accept the psychiatrist. But if this person accepts therapeutic goals to too great an extent, the others may handle the situation by rejecting him or reducing his status rather than allowing themselves to be influenced by him.

Typology B: Attributes Which Reflect Personal Qualities. The second typology is built on the personal qualities of the potential model and the manner in which the potential model presents himself to change targets. We are concerned here with the kinds of qualities which are referred to as *charisma*, and with the kinds of people who seem to inspire, be magnetic, and have a "powerful personality." These qualities may be stable personality characteristics, as in the case of the dedicated leader who trades on his sin-

---

[23]The dynamics of this process are complicated because alongside the trust and faith may exist feelings of jealousy and having been betrayed. The whole problem of sibling rivalry versus learning from a sibling requires further analysis.

cerity, conviction, and zeal; or they may be skills learned for the purpose of managing interpersonal relationships, as in the case of the skilled salesman, persuader, or seducer.

Adelson (see pages 491–503) has adapted a typology of primitive healers or witch doctors in his discussion of the kinds of teacher-student relationships which occur in classrooms. The categories he describes can be usefully applied to any potential identification model or change agent. Thus, the change agent can present himself to the change target as a shamam, magician, naturalist, mystic healer, or priest.

The *shaman* communicates to the target a sense of personal power, conviction, autonomy, faith-in-self, and narcissism. He demands allegiance and acceptance of his personal influence on the basis of his power and faith in himself. He stimulates the fatal fascination which others have for the narcissist.

The *magician,* by contrast, purports to produce changes in the target through the manipulation of secret rites and materials to which he has sole access. He elicits trust on the basis of the actual miracles he is able to produce through his magic.

The *naturalist,* too, claims power on the basis of some knowledge he possesses, rather than on some innate personality trait. He differs from the magician in that his knowledge is scientifically verifiable and not secret. His function is to translate natural principles into practical considerations. While presenting a façade of indifference to the change target, he nevertheless is able to communicate that anyone who does not take advantage of the scientific knowledge offered is a fool.

The *mystic healer* functions as a catalyst of the change process. He communicates the assumption that the potential for change is already present in the target and offers the needed help to get the process started. In a sense, he demands change because of his investments in and altruistic concern for the target.

The *priest* presents himself as a gatekeeper, a person who has the official power to control entry into some desired group or desired status. Because he is invested with power from a high source, he is able to specify what the target must learn to achieve membership or status in the desired profession, group, or organization.

Adelson makes an analogy between these types and different kinds of college teachers. Equally instructive might be a consideration of psychotherapists in these terms—the powerful personality (shaman) who achieves results through molding patients in his own image; the magician who may use hypnosis, electroshock, and other devices as "tricks" to impress his patients; the naturalist who uses a method such as psychoanalysis because he believes that if the method is followed correctly, the patient will be cured regardless of the particular personality of the therapist; the mystic who relies heavily on his concern and regard for the patient as the primary lever of influence and change; and the priest who dispassionately lays out the requirements for entering the community of the "healthy."

If scanning, positive identification, and defensive identification depend upon the salience of the potential model and the types of feelings he arouses in the target, we can state the following hypotheses. The naturalist is most likely to arouse scanning because he minimizes his own salience. He encourages the target to seek data wherever he can. The priest and magician are most likely to arouse defensive identification because of their power position relative to the target. The mystic healer is most likely to arouse positive identification because of his nonthreatening, altruistic concern for the target. The shaman is most likely to arouse some kind of identification because of his salient position in any relationship. Whether or not the identification will take a positive or negative form will depend on the shaman's particular approach, i.e., the degree of trust or fear he arouses in the target.

Examples of the Changing Mechanisms

1. Most *institutionalized* influence processes operate through defensive or positive identification and leave little room for scanning. The change target is not expected to discover his own cultural solutions to problems but is expected to benefit from the experience of his elders. If he cannot use symbolic models as guides (those ideal characters he hears about from his parents and teachers or those he reads about), he can always resort to identification with those models who happen to be physically available in the environment.

2. *Planned uninstitutionalized* influence is more difficult to characterize. If we are dealing with situations which involve primarily behavior change, as in the salesman-customer relationship, scanning is not apt to be prevalent, but whatever identification does take place is likely to be only with symbolic models. That is, the salesman may find that his best appeal is to discover who his customer's

important identification model is and to link his product with that model (as most advertising attempts to do). For many reasons, the salesman himself is not likely to become a model.

The consultant often finds himself in a situation where, having unfrozen the target, he would like him to engage in scanning to find a solution which best fits his (the target's) needs. The target, however, may be too uncomfortable to search for a solution, preferring instead to seek out the nearest available identification model for emulation. Under some conditions, the consultant may be an adequate model and thus facilitate the influence process; but, under other conditions, this process may produce an uncomfortable situation where the consultant is unable to come up with the ready solution expected by the target, resulting in a weakening of his position as an agent of effective unfreezing. All of us have witnessed cases where consultants were dismissed psychologically on the grounds that they could not handle the client's situation any better themselves. All of us have heard of therapists who were dismissed on the ground that they had "worse" problems than some of their patients or were "unable to bring up their own children."

The change target evidently is very disappointed if he discovers that the change agent is not an adequate positive identification model. Once he has become unfrozen, the target often sees identification as the easiest, even if it is not always the healthiest, influence mechanism. One reason why so many members of the "helping professions" emphasize that the greatest part of their job is to help the client recognize what his problem is, may be the recognition, on their part, that they play a more important role in unfreezing the client than they are able to or want to play in the actual induction of change. At any rate, this remains an important area for further study and conceptual analysis.

3. In the case of *emergent change*, we are least likely to get defensive identification and most likely to get positive identification. Scanning appears to be less probable because friends and lovers often serve as ideal identification models for each other. One may expect scanning to occur, however, in the case where disconfirmation is so severe that the relationship itself is severed. Unless the disconfirmed party can retrospectively discount the disconfirmation, he remains in an unfrozen condition without an immediately relevant identification model. In this instance, he may seek new attitudes and self-perceptions in a wider social network by a systematic search for relevant information about himself.

This example raises the whole issue of whether or not a separation of the unfreezing and changing phases should be built into an effective change strategy for maximum personal growth. The agent of unfreezing inevitably becomes salient in the relationship, yet he may be a poor model. His dilemma is how to keep the change process going without becoming too influential himself as an identification model.

3. Mechanisms of Refreezing

Personal and Interpersonal Reintegration. Once the target has made a change or been influenced, there still remains the problem of how well the new response fits in with other parts of the personality and whether or not it will be accepted and confirmed by his significant others. One can cite many examples from training programs or psychotherapy of changes which satisfied the trainee or patient but which were rejected by his friends, relatives, and co-workers. One can also find examples where, particularly through a process of identification, a person acquired beliefs, attitudes, and values which he later discovered did not fit well with other parts of himself. For any change to become a stable part of the person, it must, at some level, become integrated with other parts of himself and be acceptable to those whose opinions and reactions he values.

In situations of *planned institutionalized* influence, such as socialization and education, refreezing forces are automatically built into the situation, since the responses which the change target is expected to learn are those which the society or group which is doing the influencing defines as basic to its purposes. Thus, any successful change is automatically rewarded by the social environment as well as by the change agent. To the extent that the areas of learning or influence are defined as basic, the person is expected to accommodate other parts of himself to them. In the case of adult socialization, if the new values and attitudes really do not fit, the person has only one alternative—to give up membership in the group or society into which he is being socialized (unless, of course, he can tolerate the dissonance or incongruity).

Refreezing forces are also potentially built into *emergent change* situations. The change agent and/or identification model is usually also a significant other who can confirm whatever changes are induced. It is also possible, however, that the changes which a person makes in response to one significant other may give rise to a disconfirmatory response in other relevant people, thus creating further problems for the change target. We often see this exemplified in cases where one member of a family comes under the influence of a doctor, confidant, or other change agent outside the family and begins to change in a direction which threatens the family and is thus rejected by it. This dilemma is brilliantly depicted in Cheever's story (pages 461–72) of what happens when a potent but unconventional change agent enters a community.

As long as communication channels remain open, the changes resulting from a relationship of lovers or friends are likely to be easily integrated into the personality of both members and into the relationship. There are, however, dramatic instances where changes made by one party produce a greater negative reaction than the original behavior which initiated the change process. A husband gives cues to his wife that her knowledge of politics and world affairs leaves something to be desired. She responds not only by becoming knowledgeable, but by actively participating in political groups with the result that she has little time left for the activities that she and her husband had previously valued. Or, to take another example, a wife disconfirms certain patterns of masculine aggression in her husband. He responds by becoming overly passive and overly solicitous (which she discovers she likes less than the aggression). If the relationship is secure enough, it will allow several cycles of unfreezing, changing, new unfreezing, new changing, etc., until the new behavior is mutually satisfactory and can become refrozen. But, problems can obviously arise when a change is satisfactory to the person making it but unsatisfactory to significant others. In such instances, an unanticipated outcome of the change process may be that the relationship itself is gradually undermined.

Planned uninstitutionalized influence is least predictable with respect to refreezing because the change agent who is involved in the unfreezing and changing stages is often unrelated to the significant others who must refreeze the change. An excellent example is the evangelist crusades, such as those of Billy Graham, where a high percentage of the people who are converted during the services give up the religion within a matter of days or weeks *unless they are immediately integrated into a local church in their own community.*

Industrial training programs in human relations often produce changes which may disappear and even arouse an adverse reaction in the trainee if his fellow workers disconfirm the new attitudes and behavior learned during training.[24] A salesman can obtain a

---

[24]E. A. Fleishman, "Leadership Climate, Human Relations Training and Supervisory Behavior." *Personnel Psychology,* Vol. 6 (1953), pp. 205–22.

promise of a purchase from a potential customer only to have the order turned down later because the person's family "talked him out of it."

If the change agent is really concerned about the direction and permanence of change, he must worry not only about providing identification models or other information which will communicate the desired direction of change, but must also make provisions for the adequate refreezing of those changes which do occur. What this means, in practice, is that the change agent must spend some of his time working on the significant others of the change target in order to get them ready for and convinced of the desirability of the change which is being induced in the target. Thus, the consultant may spend a great deal of his time training the client's associates and his organization, even though the client himself is the prime change target. The therapist often discovers that though his role as change agent is adequately institutionalized, the changes he is able to produce do not receive institutionalized support. Thus, the family of a schizophrenic will provide treatment for the patient, but will be unprepared to reinforce and confirm the minor changes which initial treatment may make possible. The therapist, then, is often forced to work with the family and teach them to refreeze the changes which he has induced.

It should, of course, be noted that the mechanism by which the change is induced in the first place, has consequences for the ease or difficulty of refreezing. To the extent that scanning leads to self-selected solutions, it produces changes which are automatically integrated into the person's total personality. From the outset, such solutions have more stability and may, therefore, be more desirable in situations where the change agent has little control over the reactions of significant others. The therapist or consultant attempts to induce changes which fit the person's own needs in the hope that such changes will have a chance of surviving whatever negative reactions they may arouse in others.

Changes produced by positive identification, on the other hand, derive their stability from the stability of the relationship between the target and the model. If the model reinforces the changes and continues to be available to the target, the changes can be long lasting and stable. However, they may not necessarily be integrated into other parts of the target's self, and they may not be accepted by people other than the model.

The problem for the change agent, then, is to assess whether or not the changes which might be induced by identification, will, in fact, fit the person's needs and be reinforced by others. For example, if the consultant observes that his client tends to emulate him and identify with him, he must decide whether to encourage or discourage this process in terms of the above criterion. Similarly, the coach or therapist must decide how much identification to encourage. Of course, if the influence models are also the significant others with whom the target will have a continuous, long-run relationship, then positive identification is a highly functional mechanism of change, and one which will lead readily to refreezing. Thus, when we can, we put change targets into groups in which all the members set a correct example so that identification with any one of them will produce desired changes which will be reinforced.

SUMMARY AND CONCLUSIONS

An attempt has been made in this essay to identify some important dimensions of influence or change induced by interpersonal relationships. We have not dealt with all possible cases of influence or change, but rather have tried to focus on the kinds of changes which are generally associated with interpersonal relationships, namely changes in beliefs, attitudes, and values. The kind of conceptual scheme or model which has been presented is primarily geared toward attitudinal learning and relearning, and contributes little to an understanding of short-run behavioral compliance or reactions and impulses which arise in momentary encounters between people.

The conceptual scheme is organized around the notion that change or influence must be thought of as three separate though overlapping processes—unfreezing, changing, and refreezing. *Unfreezing* involves several basic mechanisms: (1) disconfirmation or lack of confirmation; (2) the induction of guilt anxiety; and (3) the removal of threat or barriers to change. *Changing* can occur through one of two basic mechanisms—identification or scanning. Both are mediated by a process of cognitive redefinition which makes the ultimate attitudinal change possible. *Refreezing* involves the integration of any new responses (attitudes) into the rest of the person's personality and into his significant ongoing relationships.

Several conclusions can be derived from an examination of the change process in terms of this model. *First,* it is apparent that the conceptual definition of *change agent* depends on the phase of the change process under discussion. Some persons may function as dis-

confirmers, others as inducers of change motives, and others as re-
movers of barriers. Whatever their function, they all facilitate unfreezing. They may not necessarily serve as identification models or
make the decisions as to what kinds of models will be available
and whether identification or scanning should be encouraged, insofar as any control over the change mechanism can be exerted.
Furthermore, the unfreezers and changers are not necessarily the
refreezers. Because each phase of the change process is different
from the other phases, it is difficult to pinpoint a single set of attributes for the effective change agent which will be suitable for all
cases. We have tried to show that the attributes of the effective un-
freezer are not the same as those of the effective changer, which in
turn, are not the same as those of the effective refreezer.

Second, it should be apparent that a stable change of attitudes or
values results from a particular *combination* of several sets of circumstances, *all of which have to be present.* Change is not possible
if there is no motivation for change and the induction of such motivation is often a complex process; no change is possible if the person
cannot locate solutions by scanning his social field or by finding
identification models; and change will not persist unless it is integrated into the personality and into all relationships in which the
target is involved. To define influence as just one of these phases
is an oversimplification which can only result in conceptual confusion.

Third, within the total range of interpersonal change situations
we have selected out four types which have different goals, different
outcomes, and involve different combinations of unfreezing, changing, and refreezing mechanisms. These types were labeled *planned*
and *unplanned institutionalized influence,* as exemplified by formal
and informal socialization, education, and rehabilitation; *planned
uninstitutionalized influence,* as exemplified by persuasion, consultation, and coaching; and *emergent change,* as exemplified by those
changes which are the unintended by-products of the relationship
of lovers, friends, and co-workers. One of the advantages of our
conceptual scheme is that it enables us to think about the similarities
and differences between these types of change situations.

Fourth, in thinking about actual mechanisms of change, it is important to differentiate two types of identification, one resulting
from the change target's need to defend himself against coercive
forces from which he cannot escape, and the other based on the
target's recognition that the attitudes and responses of certain avail-

able models in the environment could offer solutions to the problems he experiences as a result of having been unfrozen. Certain personal characteristics of potential influence models are associated with the latter kind of identification. Two typologies of models were presented—one based on the kind of family situation which the relationship recreates (whether the model is seen as a father, big brother, peer, or person in transition), and one based upon an analysis of primitive healers which deals with the more personal attributes of the change agent. Certain hypotheses were stated about the relative likelihood of identification with the different types of models and the kind of influence each of these types could exert in a relationship.

Finally, the process of refreezing was analyzed. Depending on the goals of the change effort and the means available to the change agent, it makes a considerable difference for the change outcome whether the situation is set up to be one which encourages identification or encourages scanning. We also pointed out the increasing importance of the change agent as an agent of refreezing through his work with the target's "back home" situation in an effort to insure that induced change will be reinforced.

In conclusion, we would like to underscore our conviction that interpersonal influence is an extremely complex process which has not as yet yielded to definitive theoretical analysis. Whether we take reinforcement theory or Gestalt theory from the psychology of learning, or balance theory from the psychology of attitude change, or some theory of growth and change derived from clinical work with patients, we will continue to find examples and processes which somehow are not adequately dealt with by these models. Our strategy has been to face the complexity directly and tolerate some of the ambiguity which a more complex conceptual scheme inevitability brings with it. We eventually hope to deal with this problem by developing an adequate "theory of the middle level" which neither oversimplifies the problem for the sake of elegance, nor overcomplicates it for the sake of clinical richness.

NOTES ON THE READINGS

In selecting readings to illustrate aspects of interpersonal influence and emergent change, we have attempted to avoid articles which are either very well known or which attempt to treat interpersonal relations in terms of oversimplified models. Wherever possible, we have gotten our materials from recent literature.

The first group of articles deals with planned and unplanned institutionalized influence such as socialization, role training, and political re-education. The Strauss article deals with socialization processes of the sort found in movement through an organization during the process of one's career. Goffman then explores some of the more intricate dynamics of role redefinition by focusing on a particular kind of role problem—adaptation to failure. These articles deal with adult socialization in the normal pursuit of one's occupation and career.

The next three articles illustrate the dynamics of adult socialization in the political realm, i.e., what happens when someone sets out to deliberately change the political beliefs and behavior of a captive group. Moloney explores the relationship between prisoner and interrogator. The next two papers deal with Chinese Communist approaches and focus us more heavily on total milieu control and the manipulation of peer-group forces. These papers should be studied, not only for their informational content about Communist methods of influencing people, but, more importantly, for the perspective they provide us on our own influence institutions. As a number of analysts have pointed out, there are more than casual similarities between Communist coercive persuasion and the kinds of influence which occur in schools, hospitals, prisons, and other "total institutions" in our society.

Our readings turn next to less institutionalized forms of influence. Perhaps the best examples of this type of influence come from therapeutic or educational settings. Frank,[25] for example, has written brilliantly on how therapy can be viewed as essentially a process of persuasion which bears many similarities to other kinds of persuasion. Rather than try to illustrate this aspect with our readings, we have attempted to locate material which illustrates the more common everyday version of seduction and emergent change. Leary provides a model and a set of prescriptions which is particularly timely today in view of the increasing problem which the taking of drugs poses for our society. We neither endorse nor deny Leary's position, but feel the reader should be entitled to Leary's own view of "how to change behavior." Lytle, Cheever, and Wodehouse provide three examples of emergent change from three different kinds of life situations—a fraternity, a suburban community, and a resort setting. The readings close with the provocative statement by Adelson on the different kinds of models which one can find among teachers and the influence process which is implied by each model.

---

[25]J. D. Frank, "The Dynamics of the Psychotherapeutic Relationship," *Psychiatry*, Vol. 22 (1959), pp. 17–39.

REGULARIZED STATUS-PASSAGE*

Anselm Strauss

The lives of men and women can—theoretically at least—be traced as a series of passages of status. Insofar as this is so, we most heartily agree with Erikson's striking statement that a sense of identity "is never gained nor maintained once and for all. Like a good conscience, it is constantly lost and regained. . . ."[1]

COACHING

When passages of status are more or less well regulated, those who have gone through the recognized steps stand ready, as I have said, to guide and advise their successors. This guidance is essential, for even regulated passage is perhaps more hazardous than my account has indicated.

In the well known novel, *The Late George Apley*, J. B. Marquand[2] portrays the well-ordered life of George as it follows the traditional Bostonian upper class pattern of growing up and growing old. As a young man, George is in danger of being drawn off the track when he becomes fond of an Irish girl far below him in social position. He is brought to heel through family pressure and by being shown how this incident "really" fits into his entire expected life cycle. Natural as it is for him to dally with such a girl, the "escapade" is not to be treated as a serious venture. The great danger of such an escapade is that through it some George Apley—if not this one—will be drawn off expected paths and lost to family and social class. However, the counsel of elders is requisite to status passages for reasons other than hazard, since all the future steps are clear only to those who have traversed them. Certain aspects of what lies over the horizon are blurred to the candidate, no matter how

---

*Reprinted with permission of the publisher from *Mirrors and Masks: the Search for Identity* by Anselm Strauss, pp. 109–18. Copyright 1959 by The Free Press, a Corporation.

[1] Erik H. Erikson, "Identity and Totality: Psychoanalytic Observations on the Problem of Youth," *Human Development Bulletin* (Fifth Annual Symposium, Committee on Human Development of the University of Chicago, 1954), p. 57.

[2] John P. Marquand, *The Late George Apley* (New York: Random House, 1936), chap. 8, "The Interlude," pp. 84–92.

clear may be his general path. This forces his predecessors not only to counsel and guide him, but to prepare and coach him beforehand. Coaching is an integral part of teaching the inexperienced— of any age.

Once we see this function of "the coach," we are prepared to discuss coaching quite apart from regularized status steps, and within wider contexts than athletics or professional drama. A coaching relationship exists if someone seeks to move someone else along a series of steps, when those step are not entirely institutionalized and invariant, and when the learner is not entirely clear about their sequences (although the coach is). The football coach attempting to turn out a good half-back, Iago seeking to induce Othello along the path of jealousy, the piano teacher trying to make a concert pianist out of a young man, the revivalist trying to work his audience into a frenzy of conversion, the psychiatrist carefully maneuvering his patient back to better psychological integration, and the confidence man manipulating his victim through sequential steps of involvement in an illicit deal: all are instances of coaching relationships, albeit each has different aspects. In each instance there is a man who has yielded himself (whether he knows it or not) to a teacher who guides him along at least partly obscure channels. Since every field in which such teaching goes on has its own prescriptions and rules of thumb, my discussion of coaching quite obviously must be very general, and will be pointed particularly toward those changes of identity that take place during coaching.

The general features of the coaching relationship flow from the learner's need for guidance as he moves along, step by step. He needs guidance not merely because in the conventional sense he needs someone to teach him skills, but because some very surprising things are happening to him that require explanation. The coach stands ready to interpret his responses, which may otherwise only have the status of ambiguous signs. If you look at something as nonpsychological as learning a physical skill, perhaps you can see the point more easily. The learner leans upon the coach's expert advice, for instance, whether a given muscular movement is going to lead forward, or down a false path; and without the coach he may not even notice his own movement. The coach literally calls attention to new responses: "Look, this is the first time you have managed to do this." Likewise, the coach explains away responses, saying "pay no attention" for what is happening either should be regarded as of no importance or as something that happens only "at this stage." The next steps are pointed out ("Don't worry, wait, this will happen"). In sum: because the sequences of steps are in some measure obscure, and because one's own responses become something out of the ordinary, someone must stand prepared to predict, indicate, and explain the signs.

But the tutor generally assigns himself a far more active role than I have suggested. He does not merely wait for the student to develop new responses; he throws him into situations so as to elicit certain responses from him. This provides an opportunity to indicate, interpret, and predict. Understandably, this involves the coach in a certain kind of duplicity upon occasion (as when a fencing teacher allows his pupil to hit him for the first time); the coach's position also requires that he may have to function like a playwright, arranging episodes, setting scenes, getting supporting characters to act in a certain way. Of course the pupil, by virtue of his acquisition of new skills or new perspectives, can be counted upon to engage other persons in new interactions. Like the infant who upon learning his first words encounters his parents differently, the learner's recently gained skills will throw him into novel situations. Some outcomes will be gratifying, but of course others can be terrifying or at least frightening. The coach utilizes both kinds of outcomes to retain control, occasionally even allowing him his head so as to be able to say—"I told you so, now then you see. . . ." The point is that the untutored can not see until he has tried for himself, just as generally he cannot visualize much of the proper path before hand.

In malevolent kinds of coaching—as in seduction, or in conning by confidence men—the relationship is one of trapper and victim. However, in almost all coaching there appears to be a strong element of inducement, temptation, and behind-the-scenes action. The con man baits, tempts, induces; but so does, although in less obvious ways, the art teacher, the basketball coach, or the psychiatrist. Abstractly stated, the coach not only works on current desires to get action directed along given paths, but seeks to create new desires and aims. He seeks to create a new identity for the pupil— or the victim—and to do this involves him in a variety of canny maneuvers.

In general, we should be struck by the importance of timing in all coaching. Because the pupil is being guided in his moves— muscularly, psychologically, socially—the coach is preoccupied with teaching him certain things at correct places and times. To begin with, the coach may be rejected if he forces too fast a pace, especially at the outset. The pupil may lose face or become frightened or otherwise distressed. In psychiatric coaching the patient may go elsewhere for help or, if the relationship is involuntary as when he is committed to a mental hospital, simply withdraw psychologically. On the other hand, the pupil (whether a patient, victim, or convert) may be lost to his mentor if the latter moves too slowly— lost through boredom, shattering of faith, or other reasons. Of course, the teacher may call attention to his superior experience and wisdom, as well as draw upon the resources of trust placed in him by the other, in order to set the pace; but he does so always at some risk. This risk is unavoidable and can only be minimized by shrewd tactics. The coach has to know when to force his man over a hurdle, and when to let him sidle up to it; when to schedule definite moves, and when to allow a period of relative free play. The coach must skillfully balance between two poles: he must not pressure the student by his own impatience; yet he must force movement at those junctures when the fellow appears ready but reluctant to move, is in fact really "there" but does not realize it.

Crucial tactics in this delicately balanced process are the prescription, the schedule, the challenge, the trial, and the accusation. Prescriptions for action are sometimes called "routines" or "exercises" or "lessons"; they are traditional step-by-step progressions that prepare the way for further movement. When the coaching relationship is well-institutionalized, such routine practices become a very visible and sometimes hampering part of the coaching profession. The schedule is also an integral aspect of the coaching process; notions arise of how fast or how slowly the pupil should move, and at what points he should move slower or faster. There is at least an implicit set of norms governing how quickly he should progress through certain stages. Recently, a psychologist has suggested to a group of psychiatrists how a standardized set of norms might be used to measure the progress of their patients. In the coaching relationship, a considerable potential strain exists because the coach must control his own impulses to standardize schedules too greatly.

Challenges or dares are also an invariant aspect of coaching. Since a person is being asked to relinquish old modes of doing and seeing, he is in effect being asked to do and say and even think things that look risky or dangerous. I recently heard a psychiatrist say to a patient, "It is now time to do. . . .You may fail but you are likely not to; it is a risk worth taking." Of course, there are clever and institutionalized ways of cushioning failure, but the important thing is that the person by meeting the challenge receives an indication of how far he has progressed. His overcoming of a challenge provides a marker, a milestone of his development.

Essential also to coaching is the accusation, hurled or insinuated. The coach will conceive of his pupil on occasion as backsliding, as giving in to old habits, old temptations, and therefore must be frankly reprimanded. The pupil will also be accused of loss of faith or trust: "How can you benefit from what I have to teach you if do not trust me now." From the learner's perspective, the coach may be neglecting his job, ruining one's talents, breaking faith, even engaging in betrayal. Accusations both block the process of learning and are vitally important for those reconciliations that mark turning points on the road forward.

I have mentioned the elements of risk and trust involved in the coaching relationship, although they loom as more obvious in some kinds of relationships than in others. The novice airplane pilot literally puts his life at the disposal of his instructor. In seduction or in confidence games the secret motivations that are involved highlight the risk and danger. Even in such mundane pursuits as piano and voice teaching or training for track meets, the pupil's potential level of performance may be greatly endangered by improper counsel. Insofar as the coaching process also leads to great changes of identity—as in G. B. Shaw's apocryphal drama *Pygmalion*—you, as a pupil, are in large measure ceding an unknown destiny to a mentor who presumably knows where he is taking you. A special danger is that the relationship may be broken off midstream, before "the treatment" is completed, with potential danger to both but particularly to the learner. One of the great and inevitable risks of coaching is precisely that the coach may die, or move away, leaving the student vulnerable in various ways: because he is in a stage of self-imputed personal helplessness, or standing upon the brink of a learning crisis, or not yet properly out of love with the coach ("transference"), or in the midst of meeting a great challenge. But a comparable risk is that the student has the final responsibility of judging when the coaching relationship is genuinely harmful to himself or to his "potential." There is a point beyond which he must not, like Cinderella, stay. The coach may have poor judgment. It is not impossible even that he evinces faulty judgment because he loves or hates his pupil too much; although he may be actually malevolent or merely indifferent. The learner always has an obligation to himself of assessing when he is being harmed and when he is being helped, even in those very traditional situations where the coach is supposed supremely knowledgable.

The reverse side of great risk and danger is trust and faith. To this should be added what the psychoanalysts call "identification"; that is, a very close modeling of self after the other, or after certain of his aspects. The coach is not only a partial model ("do as I do"), but in certain stages may become almost a total model ("be as I am" or "wish to be what I am"). The tutor, of course, may consciously utilize this desire or propensity. On the other hand, in many types of coaching, particularly after the earlier stages of learning, mere imitation is not sufficient for progress.

Let us now consider more explicitly the shifts of identity brought about through coaching, as against the mere acquisition of skill. One cannot, of course, discuss risk, trust, identification, duplicity, challenge, and merely talk of the acquisition of skill. In some coaching, the person may be taken as a *tabula rasa,* as if he had no previous commitments of the kind the coach is now about to build; the task is simply to build upon unimpeded ground. More often this is not a realistic stance for the coach to take. The learner has something to unlearn, to cope with, and this will enter the trajectory of his learning early and often stay with him until very late. This is perhaps another way of saying that the coach must challenge old modes of doing, seeing, and thinking, as well as point out new modes. When the learning and re-learning is extreme—and I shall consider a variety of this in the next section—there must be massive and frontal attack upon identities. In less drastic kinds of change, through the agency of coaches, a man is requested also to turn his back upon his past, to discount previous accomplishments, to divest himself of earlier prides, to disidentify himself with old practices, old allies, and even old loves.

One may sometimes observe during the initial sessions of a new coaching relationship how the participants gingerly hold back from much involvement until they are "sure." This is especially true of the student, but the teacher also may have provisos. Traditionally, the early phases may be coached in terms of "make-believe" or "not for keeps"; and institutionally they may take the form of not yet counting the score or recording the performance. All this, in a sense, represents a trial period; one is involved, but without much commitment to his own performance, and can retreat with honor and dignity. It is as if there were a kind of moratorium, during which effort is great but during which both sides ceremonially ignore negative performances. Of course, such a moratorium and such make-believe run all through the coaching process, perhaps particularly during the new phases in cycles of learning, when the person is particularly sensitive to criticism and must be encouraged and must encourage himself to chance certain endeavors. You can see this procedure operating in reverse when young art students are so jealous of their paintings, so serious about their performances, that they bridle when the teacher lays a brush upon their work.

In his fondest moments, the coach may believe that he has total control over the progress of his pupil. But the very character of coaching is likely to set into motion unpredictable changes of identity. The best model for visualizing this learning is not as a steady progression through a series of stages, mostly known to the coach, but rather to imagine a tree with many branches and twigs. The pupil moves along certain branches until he reaches alternatives, and the coach stands ready to guide or channel his movement until the next set of alternatives arises. But the best pupils, like the best children, get out from under the control and the vision of the best teachers, and the best teachers are pleased that this is so. At the outer limits of learning, the stages can no longer be as standardized as at the beginning; and the pupil discovers his own style, whether we are talking of religious conversion, musical composition, or anything else. For the coach, too, the process may be open-ended; he too may end with a different identity. This mutual change may be, as Nelson Foote has suggested, "a winning pattern for each,"[3] but unfortunately it may also be mutually destructive or end happily for one but not for the other.

Something should now be added to counteract the notion that coaching is merely a two-way relationship between a coach and a coached person, for many if not most coaching processes occur in organization or institutional context. Thus the teacher hands on pupils to higher or more famous teachers, saying "I can teach you no more, you are now beyond me—or at least it is said that you are beyond me." Although I shall not develop the point, you ought to recognize that the organizational framework within which the coaching goes on vitally affects the process and outcome of coaching. In some organizational contexts the coach may move his stu-

---

[3]Nelson Foote, "Concept and Method in the Study of Human Development," mimeographed manuscript of paper delivered at an Oklahoma conference in Social Psychology.

dents too quickly (for his own frame, or to get them sponsored jobs), or his coaching may become standardized (because of great numbers of pupils, or because of the excessively strict requirements of the organization) or he may handle his pupils far too impersonally (because of personal tensions engendered by his position, or because of rewards placed upon other activities associated with his position). He may bind his students too closely to himself for their rapid or maximum development (because of his own anxieties created again by his position); or he may fail to sustain proper trust of himself (because close relationships among age ranks are frowned upon in the organization). Since coaching is thus linked with social structure and with the positions and careers of both the coaches and the coached, one can scarcely speak of process as divorced from structure. My discussion of process has been exceedingly general and its details must be spelled out in relation to particular structures and worlds. This is a task for meticulous and thoughtful research.

ON COOLING THE MARK OUT: SOME ASPECTS OF ADAPTATION TO FAILURE*

Erving Goffman

In cases of criminal fraud, victims find they must suddenly adapt themselves to the loss of sources of security and status which they had taken for granted. A consideration of this adaptation to loss can lead us to an understanding of some relations in our society between involvements and the selves that are involved.

In the argot of the criminal world, the term "mark" refers to any individual who is a victim or prospective victim of certain forms of planned illegal exploitation. The mark is the sucker—the person who is taken in. An instance of the operation of any particular racket,

*Excerpted from Erving Goffman "On Cooling the Mark Out," reprinted by special permission of The William Alanson White Psychiatric Foundation, Inc., *Psychiatry*, Vol. 15, No. 4 (Nov., 1952), pp. 451–63. Copyright 1952 by The William Alanson White Psychiatric Foundation, Inc.

taken through the full cycle of its steps or phases, is sometimes called a play. The persons who operate the racket and "take" the mark are occasionally called operators.

The confidence game—the con, as its practitioners call it—is a way of obtaining money under false pretenses by the exercise of fraud and deceit. The con differs from politer forms of financial deceit in important ways. The con is practiced on private persons by talented actors who methodically and regularly build up informal social relationships just for the purpose of abusing them; white-collar crime is practiced on organizations by persons who learn to abuse positions of trust which they once filled faithfully. The one exploits poise; the other, position. Further, a con man is someone who accepts a social role in the underworld community; he is part of a brotherhood whose members make no pretense to one another of being "legit." A white-collar criminal, on the other hand, has no colleagues, although he may have an associate with whom he plans his crime and a wife to whom he confesses it.

The con is said to be a good racket in the United States only because most Americans are willing, nay eager, to make easy money, and will engage in action that is less than legal in order to do so. The typical play has typical phases. The potential sucker is first spotted, and one member of the working team (called the outside man, steerer, or roper) arranges to make social contact with him. The confidence of the mark is won, and he is given an opportunity to invest his money in a gambling venture which he understands to have been fixed in his favor. The venture, of course, is fixed, but not in his favor. The mark is permitted to win some money and then persuaded to invest more. There is an "accident" or "mistake," and the mark loses his total investment. The operators then depart in a ceremony that is called the blowoff or sting. They leave the mark but take his money. The mark is expected to go on his way, a little wiser and a lot poorer.

Sometimes, however, a mark is not quite prepared to accept his loss as a gain in experience and to say and do nothing about his venture. He may feel moved to complain to the police or to chase after the operators. In the terminology of the trade, the mark may squawk, beef, or come through. From the operators' point of view, this kind of behavior is bad for business. It gives the members of the mob a bad reputation with such police as have not yet been fixed and with marks who have not yet been taken. In order to avoid this adverse publicity, an additional phase is sometimes added at the end of the play. It is called cooling the mark out. After the blowoff has occurred, one of the operators stays with the mark and makes an effort to keep the anger of the mark within manageable and sensible proportions. The operator stays behind his team-mates in the capacity of what might be called a cooler and exercises upon the mark the art of consolation. An attempt is made to define the situation for the mark in a way that makes it easy for him to accept the inevitable and quietly go home. The mark is given instruction in the philosophy of taking a loss.

When we call to mind the image of a mark who has just been separated from his money, we sometimes attempt to account for the greatness of his anger by the greatness of his financial loss. This is a narrow view. In many cases, especially in America, the mark's image of himself is built up on the belief that he is a pretty shrewd person when it comes to making deals and that he is not the sort of person who is taken in by anything. The mark's readiness to participate in a sure thing is based on more than avarice; it is based on a feeling that he will now be able to prove to himself that he is the sort of person who can "turn a fast buck." For many, this capacity for high finance comes near to being a sign of masculinity and a test of fulfilling the male role.

It is well known that persons protect themselves with all kinds of rationalizations when they have a buried image of themselves which the facts of their status do not support. A person may tell himself many things: that he has not been given a fair chance, that he is not really interested in becoming something else; that the time for showing his mettle has not yet come; that the usual means of realizing his desires are personally or morally distasteful, or require too much dull effort. By means of such defenses, a person saves himself from committing a cardinal social sin—the sin of defining oneself in terms of a status while lacking the qualifications which an incumbent of that status is supposed to possess.

A mark's participation in a play, and his investment in it, clearly commit him in his own eyes to the proposition that he is a smart man. The process by which he comes to believe that he cannot lose is also the process by which he drops the defenses and compensations that previously protected him from defeats. When the blowoff comes, the mark finds that he has no defense for not being a shrewd man. He has defined himself as a shrewd man and must face the fact that he is only another easy mark. He has defined himself as possessing a certain set of qualities and then proven to himself that he is miserably lacking in them. This is a process of self-destruction of the self. It is no wonder that the mark needs to be cooled out and that it is good business policy for one of the operators to stay with the mark in order to talk him into a point of view from which it is possible to accept a loss.

In essence, then, the cooler has the job of handling persons who have been caught out on a limb—persons whose expectations and self-conceptions have been built up and then shattered. The mark is a person who has compromised himself, in his own eyes if not in the eyes of others.

Although the term, mark, is commonly applied to a person who is given shortlived expectations by operators who have intentionally misrepresented the facts, a less restricted definition is desirable in analyzing the larger social scene. An expectation may finally prove false, even though it has been possible to sustain it for a long time and even though the operators acted in good faith. So, too, the disappointment of reasonable expectations, as well as misguided ones, creates a need for consolation. Persons who participate in what is recognized as a confidence game are found in only a few social settings, but persons who have to be cooled out are found in many. Cooling the mark out is one theme in a very basic social story.

For purposes of analysis, one may think of an individual in reference to the values or attributes of a socially recognized character which he possesses. Psychologists speak of a value as a personal involvement. Sociologists speak of a value as a status, role, or relationship. In either case, the character of the value that is possessed is taken in a certain way as the character of the person who possesses it. An alteration in the kinds of attributes possessed brings an alteration to the selfconception of the person who possesses them.

The process by which someone acquires a value is the process by which he surrenders the claim he had to what he was and commits himself to the conception of self which the new value requires or allows him to have. It is the process that persons who fall in love or take dope call getting hooked. After a person is hooked, he must go through another process by which his new involvement finds its proper place, in space and time, relative to the other calls, demands, and commitments that he has upon himself. At this point certain other persons suddenly begin to play an important part in the individual's story; they impinge upon him by virtue of the relationship they happen to have to the value in which he has become involved. This is not the place to consider the general kinds of impingement that are institutionalized in our society and the general social relationships that arise: the personal relationship, the professional relationship, and the business relationship. Here we are concerned only with the end of the story, the way in which a person becomes disengaged from one of his involvements.

In our society, the story of a person's involvement can end in one of three general ways. According to one type of ending, he may withdrawn from one of his involvements or roles in order to acquire a sequentially related one that is considered better. This is the case when a youth becomes a man, when a student becomes a practitioner, or when a man from the ranks is given a commission.

Of course, the person who must change his self at any one of these points of promotion may have profound misgivings. He may feel disloyal to the way of life that must be left behind and to the persons who do not leave it with him. His new role may require action that seems insincere, dishonest, or unfriendly. This he may experience as a loss in moral cleanliness. His new role may require him to forgo the kinds of risk-taking and exertion that he previously enjoyed, and yet his new role may not provide the kind of heroic and exalted action that he expected to find in it.[1] This he may experience as a loss in moral strength.

There is no doubt that certain kinds of role success require certain kinds of moral failure. It may therefore be necessary, in a sense, to cool the dubious neophyte in rather than out. He may have to be convinced that his doubts are a matter of sentimentality. The adult social view will be impressed upon him. He will be required to understand that a promotional change in status is voluntary, desirable, and natural, and that loss of one's role in these circumstances is the ultimate test of having fulfilled it properly.

It has been suggested that a person may leave a role under circumstances that reflect favorably upon the way in which he performed it. In theory, at least, a related possibility must be considered. A person may leave a role and at the same time leave behind him the standards by which such roles are judged. The new thing that he becomes may be so different from the thing he was that criteria such as success or failure cannot be easily applied to the change which has occurred. He becomes lost to others that he may

---

[1]Mr. Hughes has lectured on this kind of disappointment, and one of his students has undertaken a special study of it. See Miriam Wagenschein, " 'Reality Shock': A Study of Beginning School Teachers," M.A. thesis, Dept. of Sociology, Univ. of Chicago, 1950.

find himself; he is of the twice-born. In our society, perhaps the most obvious example of this kind of termination occurs when a woman voluntarily gives up a prestigeful profession in order to become a wife and a mother. It is to be noted that this illustrates an institutionalized movement; those who make it do not make news. In America most other examples of this kind of termination are more a matter of talk than of occurrence. For example, one of the culture heroes of our dinner-table mythology is the man who walks out on an established calling in order to write or paint or live in the country. In other societies, the kind of abdication being considered here seems to have played a more important role. In medieval China, for instance, anchoritic withdrawal apparently gave to persons of quite different station a way of retreating from the occupational struggle while managing the retreat in an orderly, face-saving fashion.[2]

Two basic ways in which a person can lose a role have been considered; he can be promoted out of it or abdicate from it. There is, of course, a third basic ending to the status story. A person may be involuntarily deprived of his position or involvement and made in return something that is considered a lesser thing to be. It is mainly in this third ending to a person's role that occasions arise for cooling him out. It is here that one deals in the full sense with the problem of persons' losing their roles.

Involuntary loss seems itself to be of two kinds. First, a person may lose a status in such a way that the loss is not taken as a reflection upon the loser. The loss of a loved one, either because of an accident that could not have been prevented or because of a disease that could not have been halted, is a case in point. Occupational retirement because of old age is another. Of course, the loss will inevitably alter the conception the loser has of himself and the conception others have of him, but the alteration itself will not be treated as a symbol of the fate he deserves to receive. No insult is added to injury. It may be necessary, nonetheless, to pacify the loser and resign him to his loss. The loser who is not held responsible for his loss may even find himself taking the mystical view that all involvements are part of a wider con game, for the more one takes pleasure in a particular role the more one must suffer when it is time to leave it. He may find little comfort in the fact that the play has provided him with an illusion that has lasted a lifetime.

---

[2]See, for example, Max Weber, *The Religion of China* (H. H. Gerth, tr.); Glencoe, Ill., Free Press, 1951; p. 178.

He may find little comfort in the fact that the operators had not meant to deceive him.

Secondly, a person may be involuntarily deprived of a role under circumstances which reflect unfavorably on his capacity for it. The lost role may be one that he had already acquired or one that he had openly committed himself to preparing for. In either case the loss is more than a matter of ceasing to act in a given capacity; it is ultimate proof of an incapacity. And in many cases it is even more than this. The moment of failure often catches a person acting as one who feels that he is an appropriate sort of a person for the role in question. Assumption becomes presumption, and failure becomes fraud. To loss of substance is thereby added loss of face. Of the many themes that can occur in the natural history of an involvement, this seems to be the most melancholy. Here it will be quite essential and quite difficult to cool the mark out. I shall be particularly concerned with this second kind of loss—the kind that involves humiliation.

It should be noted, parenthetically, that one circle of persons may define a particular loss as the kind that casts no reflection on the loser, and that a different circle of persons may treat the same loss as a symbol of what the loser deserves. One must also note that there is a tendency today to shift certain losses of status from the category of those that reflect upon the loser to the category of those that do not. When persons lose their jobs, their courage, or their minds, we tend more and more to take a clinical or naturalistic view of the loss and a nonmoral view of their failure. We want to define a person as something that is not destroyed by the destruction of one of his selves. This benevolent attitude is in line with the effort today to publicize the view that occupational retirement is not the end of all active capacities but the beginning of new and different ones.

A consideration of consolation as a social process leads to four general problems having to do with the self in society. First, where in modern life does one find persons conducting themselves as though they were entitled to the rights of a particular status and then having to face up to the fact that they do not possess the qualification for the status? In other words, at what points in the structures of our social life are persons likely to compromise themselves or find themselves compromised? When is it likely that a person will have to disengage himself or become disengaged from one of his involvements? Secondly, what are the typical ways in which

persons who find themselves in this difficult position can be cooled
out; how can they be made to accept the great injury that has
been done to their image of themselves, regroup their defenses,
and carry on without raising a squawk? Thirdly, what, in general,
can happen when a person refuses to be cooled out, that is, when
he refuses to be pacified by the cooler? Fourthly, what arrangements
are made by operators and marks to avoid entirely the process of
consolation?

In all personal-service organizations customers or clients sometimes make complaints. A customer may feel that he has been given
service in a way that is unacceptable to him—a way that he interprets as an offense to the conception he has of who and what he is.
The management therefore has the problem of cooling the mark out.
Frequently this function is allotted to specialists within the organization. In restaurants of some size, for example, one of the crucial
functions of the hostess is to pacify customers whose self-conceptions have been injured by waitresses or by the food. In large stores
the complaint department and the floorwalker perform a similar
function.

One may note that a service organization does not operate in an
anonymous world, as does a con mob, and is therefore strongly
obliged to make some effort to cool the mark out. An institution,
after all, cannot take it on the lam; it must pacify its marks.

One may also note that coolers in service organizations tend to
view their own activity in a light that softens the harsher details
of the situation. The cooler protects himself from feelings of guilt
by arguing that the customer is not really in need of the service he
expected to receive, that bad service is not really deprivational, and
that beefs and complaints are a sign of bile, not a sign of injury.
In a similar way, the con man protects himself from remorseful images of bankrupt marks by arguing that the mark is a fool and not
a full-fledged person, possessing an inclination towards illegal gain
but not the decency to admit it or the capacity to succeed at it.

In organizations patterned after a bureaucratic model, it is customary for personnel to expect rewards of a specified kind upon fulfilling requirements of a specified nature. Personnel come to define their career line in terms of a sequence of legitimate expectations and to base their self-conceptions on the assumption that in
due course they will be what the institution allows persons to become. Sometimes, however, a member of an organization may fulfill some of the requirements for a particular status, especially

the requirements concerning technical proficiency and seniority, but not other requirements, especially the less codified ones having to do with the proper handling of social relationships at work. It must fall to someone to break the bad news to the victim; someone must tell him that he has been fired, or that he has failed his examinations, or that he has been by-passed in promotion. And after the blowoff, someone has to cool the mark out. The necessity of disappointing the expectations that a person has taken for granted may be infrequent in some organizations, but in others, such as training institutions, it occurs all the time. The process of personnel selection requires that many trainees be called but that few be chosen.

When one turns from places of work to other scenes in our social life, one finds that each has its own occasions for cooling the mark out. During informal social intercourse it is well understood that an effort on the part of one person (ego) to decrease his social distance from another person (alter) must be graciously accepted by alter or, if rejected, rejected tactfully so that the initiator of the move can save his social face. This rule is codified in books on etiquette and is followed in actual behavior. A friendly movement in the direction of alter is a movement outward on a limb; ego communicates his belief that he has defined himself as worthy of alter's society, while at the same time he places alter in the strategic position of being able to discredit this conception.

The problem of cooling persons out in informal social intercourse is seen most clearly, perhaps, in courting situations and in what might be called de-courting situations. A proposal of marriage in our society tends to be a way in which a man sums up his social attributes and suggests to a woman that hers are not so much better as to preclude a merger or partnership in these matters. Refusal on the part of the woman, or refusal on the part of the man to propose when he is clearly in a position to do so, is a serious reflection on the rejected suitor. Courtship is a way not only of presenting oneself to alter for approval but also of saying that the opinion of alter in this matter is the opinion one is most concerned with. Refusing a proposal, or refusing to propose, is therefore a difficult operation. The mark must be carefully cooled out. The act of breaking a date or of refusing one, and the task of discouraging a "steady" can also be seen in this light, although in these cases great delicacy and tact may not be required, since the mark may not be deeply involved or openly committed. Just as it is harder to refuse a proposal than to refuse a date, so it is more difficult to

reject a spouse than to reject a suitor. The process of de-courting
by which one person in a marriage maneuvers the other into accepting a divorce without fuss or undue rancor requires extreme finesse
in the art of cooling the mark out.

In all of these cases where a person constructs a conception of
himself which cannot be sustained, there is a possibility that he has
not invested that which is most important to him in the soon-to-be-
denied status. In the current idiom, there is a possibility that
when he is hit, he will not be hit where he really lives. There is a
set of cases, however, where the blowoff cannot help but strike a
vital spot; these cases arise, of course, when a person must be dis-
suaded from life itself. The man with a fatal sickness or fatal
injury, the criminal with a death sentence, the soldier with a hopeless objective—these persons must be persuaded to accept quietly
the loss of life itself, the loss of all one's earthly involvements. Here,
certainly, it will be difficult to cool the mark out. It is a reflection
on the conceptions men have—as cooler and mark—that it is possible
to do so.

I have mentioned a few of the areas of social life where it becomes necessary, upon occasion, to cool a mark out. Attention may
now be directed to some of the common ways in which individuals
are cooled out in all of these areas of life.

For the mark, cooling represents a process of adjustment to an
impossible situation—a situation arising from having defined himself in a way which the social facts come to contradict. The mark
must therefore be supplied with a new set of apologies for himself,
a new framework in which to see himself and judge himself. A
process of redefining the self along defensible lines must be instigated and carried along; since the mark himself is frequently in too
weakened a condition to do this, the cooler must initially do it for
him.

One general way of handling the problem of cooling the mark out
is to give the task to someone whose status relative to the mark
will serve to ease the situation in some way. In formal organizations, frequently, someone who is two or three levels above the
mark in line of command will do the hatchet work, on the assumption that words of consolation and redirection will have a greater
power to convince if they come from high places. There also seems
to be a feeling that persons of high status are better able to withstand the moral danger of having hate directed at them. Incidentally, persons protected by high office do not like to face this issue,

and frequently attempt to define themselves as merely the agents of the deed and not the source of it. In some cases, on the other hand, the task of cooling the mark out is given to a friend and peer of the mark, on the assumption that such a person will know best how to hit upon a suitable rationalization for the mark and will know best how to control the mark should the need for this arise. In some cases, as in those pertaining to death, the role of cooler is given to doctors or priests. Doctors must frequently help a family, and the member who is leaving it, to manage the leave-taking with tact and a minimum of emotional fuss.[3] A priest must not so much save a soul as create one that is consistent with what is about to become of it.

A second general solution to the problem of cooling the mark out consists of offering him a status which differs from the one he has lost or failed to gain but which provides at least a something or a somebody for him to become. Usually the alternative presented to the mark is a compromise of some kind, providing him with some of the trappings of his lost status as well as with some of its spirit. A lover may be asked to become a friend; a student of medicine may be asked to switch to the study of dentistry;[4] a boxer may become a trainer; a dying person may be asked to broaden and empty his worldly loves so as to embrace the All-Father that is about to receive him. Sometimes the mark is allowed to retain his status but is required to fulfill it in a different environment: the honest policeman is transferred to a lonely beat; the too zealous priest is encouraged to enter a monastery; an unsatisfactory plant manager is shipped off to another branch. Sometimes the mark is "kicked upstairs" and given a courtesy status such as "Vice President." In the game for social roles, transfer up, down, or away may all be consolation prizes.

A related way of handling the mark is to offer him another chance to qualify for the role at which he has failed. After his fall from grace, he is allowed to retrace his steps and try again. Officer selection programs in the army, for example, often provide for possibilities of this kind. In general, it seems that third and fourth chances are seldom given to marks, and that second chances, while often given, are seldom taken. Failure at a role removes a person

---

[3]This role of the doctor has been stressed by W. L. Warner in his lectures at the University of Chicago on symbolic roles in "Yankee City."

[4]In his seminars, Mr. Hughes has used the term "second-choice" professions to refer to cases of this kind.

from the company of those who have succeeded, but it does not bring him back—in spirit, anyway—to the society of those who have not tried or are in the process of trying. The person who has failed in a role is a constant source of embarrassment, for none of the standard patterns of treatment is quite applicable to him. Instead of taking a second chance he usually goes away to another place where his past does not bring confusion to his present.

Another standard method of cooling the mark out—one which is frequently employed in conjunction with other methods—is to allow the mark to explode, to break down, to cause a scene, to give full vent to his reactions and feelings, to "blow his top." If this release of emotions does not find a target, then it at least serves a cathartic function. If it does find a target, as in "telling off the boss," it gives the mark a last-minute chance to re-erect his defenses and prove to himself and others that he had not really cared about the status all along. When a blow-up of this kind occurs, friends of the mark or psychotherapists are frequently brought in. Friends are willing to take responsibility for the mark because their relationship to him is not limited to the role he has failed in. This, incidentally, provides one of the less obvious reasons why the cooler in a con mob must cultivate the friendship of the mark; friendship provides the cooler with an acceptable reason for staying around while the mark is cooled out. Psychotherapists, on the other hand, are willing to take responsibility for the mark because it is their business to offer a relationship to those who have failed in a relationship to others.

It has been suggested that a mark may be cooled out by allowing him, under suitable guidance, to give full vent to his initial shock. Thus the manager of a commercial organization may listen with patience and understanding to the complaints of a customer, knowing that the full expression of a complaint is likely to weaken it. This possibility lies behind the role of a whole series of buffers in our society—janitors, restaurant hostesses, grievance committees, floorwalkers, and so on—who listen in silence, with apparent sympathy, until the mark has simmered down. Similarly, in the case of criminal trials, the defending lawyer may find it profitable to allow the public to simmer down before he brings his client to court.

A related procedure for cooling the mark out is found in what is called stalling. The feelings of the mark are not brought to a head because he is given no target at which to direct them. The operator may manage to avoid the presence of the mark or may convince the mark that there is still a slight chance that the loss has not really occurred. When the mark is stalled, he is given a chance to become familiar with the new conception of self he will have to accept before he is absolutely sure that he will have to accept it.

As another cooling procedure, there is the possibility that the operator and the mark may enter into a tacit understanding according to which the mark agrees to act as if he were leaving of his own accord, and the operator agrees to preserve the illusion that this was the case. It is a form of bribery. In this way the mark may fail in his own eyes but prevent others from discovering the failure. The mark gives up his role but saves his face. This, after all, is one of the reasons why persons who are fleeced by con men are often willing to remain silent about their adventure. The same strategy is at work in the romantic custom of allowing a guilty officer to take his own life in a private way before it is taken from him publicly, and in the less romantic custom of allowing a person to resign for delicate reasons instead of firing him for indelicate ones.

Bribery is, of course, a form of exchange. In this case, the mark guarantees to leave quickly and quietly, and in exchange is allowed to leave under a cloud of his own choosing. A more important variation on the same theme is found in the practice of financial compensation. A man can say to himself and others that he is happy to retire from his job and say this with more conviction if he is able to point to a comfortable pension. In this sense, pensions are automatic devices for providing consolation. So, too, a person who has been injured because of another's criminal or marital neglect can compensate for the loss by means of a court settlement.

I have suggested some general ways in which the mark is cooled out. The question now arises: what happens if the mark refuses to be cooled out? What are the possible lines of action he can take if he refuses to be cooled? Attempts to answer these questions will show more clearly why, in general, the operator is so anxious to pacify the mark.

It has been suggested that a mark may be cooled by allowing him to blow his top. If the blow-up is too drastic or prolonged, however, difficulties may arise. We say that the mark becomes "disturbed mentally" or "personally disorganized." Instead of merely telling his boss off, the mark may go so far as to commit criminal violence against him. Instead of merely blaming himself for failure, the mark may inflict great punishment upon himself by attempting suicide, or by acting so as to make it necessary for him to be cooled out in other areas of his social life.

Sustained personal disorganization is one way in which a mark can refuse to cool out. Another standard way is for the individual to raise a squawk, that is, to make a formal complaint to higher authorities obliged to take notice of such matters. The con mob worries lest the mark appeal to the police. The plant manager must make sure that the disgruntled department head does not carry a formal complaint to the general manager or, worse still, to the Board of Directors. The teacher worries lest the child's parent complain to the principal. Similarly, a woman who communicates her evaluation of self by accepting a proposal of marriage can sometimes protect her exposed position—should the necessity of doing so arise—by threatening her disaffected fiancé with a breach-of-promise suit. So, also, a woman who is de-courting her husband must fear lest he contest the divorce or sue her lover for alienation of affection. In much the same way, a customer who is angered by a salesperson can refuse to be mollified by the floorwalker and demand to see the manager. It is interesting to note that associations dedicated to the rights and the honor of minority groups may sometimes encourage a mark to register a formal squawk; politically it may be more advantageous to provide a test case than to allow the mark to be cooled out.

Another line of action which a mark who refuses to be cooled can pursue is that of turning "sour." The term derives from the argot of industry but the behavior it refers to occurs everywhere. The mark outwardly accepts his loss but withdraws all enthusiasm, good will, and vitality from whatever role he is allowed to maintain. He complies with the formal requirements of the role that is left him, but he withdraws his spirit and identification from it. When an employee turns sour, the interests of the organization suffer; every executive, therefore, has the problem of "sweetening" his workers. They must not come to feel that they are slowly being cooled out. This is one of the functions of granting periodic advancements in salary and status, of schemes such as profit-sharing, or of giving the "employee" at home an anniversary present. A similar view can be taken of the problem that a government faces in times of crisis when it must maintain the enthusiastic support of the nation's disadvantaged minorities, for whole groupings of the population can feel they are being cooled out and react by turning sour.

Finally, there is the possibility that the mark may, in a manner of speaking, go into business for himself. He can try to gather about him the persons and facilities required to establish a status similar to the one he has lost, albeit in relation to a different set of persons. This way of refusing to be cooled is often rehearsed in phantasies of the "I'll show them" kind, but sometimes it is actually realized in practice. The rejected marriage partner may make a better remarriage. A social stratum that has lost its status may decide to create its own social system. A leader who fails in a political party may establish his own splinter group.

All these ways in which a mark can refuse to be cooled out have consequences for other persons. There is, of course, a kind of refusal that has little consequence for others. Marks of all kinds may develop explanations and excuses to account in a creditable way for their loss. It is, perhaps, in this region of phantasy that the defeated self makes its last stand.

PSYCHIC SELF-ABANDON AND EXTORTION OF CONFESSIONS*

James Clark Moloney

Abraham Kardiner[1] some years ago reiterated the concept of "bound cathexes" as representing mastery (e.g., oral mastery). "Bound energy," he said, "has somatic connections which are fixed, and the qualities associated with each are specific and not freely interchangeable. Its functions are executive. . . . It can be directed toward the outer world or against the ego itself." In my opinion, energy not only is bound in the ego structure but also in the battle-line established to preserve the ego from being overcome by the superego. It is along this battle-line that armed neutrality exists.

Even during the helpless dependency of infancy the individual can sense whether his mother is compulsive, perfectionistic, and dominating—or permissive, warm, and relaxed. Recent studies in child development indicate that somewhere in his fibre he knows

*Reprinted in its entirety from James Clark Moloney, "Psychic Self-Abandon and Extortion of Confessions," *International Journal of Psycho-Analysis*, Vol. 36 (1955), pp. 53–60. Used by permission.
[1]A. Kardiner, "The Bio-Analysis of the Epileptic Reaction," *Psychoanal. Quarterly*, Vol. 1 (1932), pp. 455–56.

whether his mother requires unconditional obedience and submissiveness. Many individuals who have been dominated by their
mothers actually are afraid to accede to any request of the mother-
patterned superego even if the request is legitimate, reasonable,
and intelligent—lest by giving in even a little they be tricked into
meeting *all* of the demands of their superegos, and thereby become merely the superegos' carbon copies or "stooges." Out of their
fear they develop rebellious attitudes toward the superego and toward the mother, establishing intrapsychically an armed neutrality
between the self-system and the mother-system.

The paralysis of armed neutrality engendered in infancy may remain with an individual into adulthood. To maintain an apparent
adjustment to the world around him, such an individual must
constantly battle within himself, his self-strivings perpetually entrenched in opposition to the mother-inspired demands of his superego: entrenched, yet always seeking to gain an inch against the
"enemy." But if the individual finally relaxes in his inner struggle,
if he gives up trying to maintain this armed neutrality between his
self- and mother-systems, then he may experience a theophany—
a blinding flash of "inspiration" which seems to light the way toward
resolution of his inner conflicts. He readjusts his whole psychic
focus and surrenders his self-strivings, his own internal rhythms.

A theological concept closely associated with theophany is *kenosis,* defined by Webster as "Christ's action of emptying himself on
becoming man, humbling himself even to suffering death." Webster
refers to *Philippians* ii: 7 (Revised Version), which says Christ
"emptied himself, taking the form of a servant, being made in the
likeness of man." The *Abington Bible Commentary*[2] interprets this
passage as meaning that Christ "divested himself of divine glory
which he had when in the form of God. . . ."

Whatever its theological significance, psychologically speaking the
process of kenosis is one experienced by many men; but there seems
to me to be another meaning than the one attributed to it by
theologians. Rather than kenosis being an emptying from the God
(authoritarian) system into the self-system, I conceive it as being
exactly the opposite: the memorial self-system empties into the memorial authoritarian-system, creating a psychic self-abandon. God
does not, I feel, become man, but through the experiencing of God
in theophany and related occurrences man becomes God or, through

[2]F. C. Eisler, Edwin Lewis, and David G. Downey (eds.), *Abington Bible
Commentary* (Nashville: Abington Cokesbury Press, 1929).

experiencing an inspiration, becomes God-*like* in the sense of becoming able to comprehend or achieve what was formerly felt to be difficult or impossible. It is the sudden release of bound energy noted earlier which constitutes the sense of emptying, and the flashes of inspirational light.

Albert Stunkard[3] described a facet of the training of Zen Buddhist priests in which a type of theophany, or sudden enlightenment, known to the Zen followers as *satori*, is experimentally induced in each novitiate. Every Zen novice works under a master (a Zen priest), whose more or less constant presence during the training period is indispensable. The Zen master provides the novice with an insoluble problem called a *koan*, such as: A sound is made by the clapping of two hands. What sound is made by the clapping of one hand?

The novice applies himself to meditation on the *koan*, spending hours, days, weeks, sometimes months, while the master checks his progress or lack thereof. Finally, the novice becomes exhausted and gives himself up to a sense of utter defeat. But when he reaches this state, suddenly he experiences a flash of enlightenment, a "solution" to his problem. Stunkard[4] quotes one subject's account: "As I walked along I became aware that I was the same as the trees at which I was looking. It was not that I had ceased to be myself—but I had become the trees as well."

The experimentally induced theophany of the *satori* contains all the prerequisities for spontaneous theophany: sustained effort, subsequent exhaustion and/or relaxation of concentration, and, finally, sudden insight, inspiration, or solution. These are also the ingredients of creative inspiration and the "inspirational" experiences of psychotics.

Boisen[5], quoting from Hutchinson, said:

The scientist, the artist, the practical thinker—the profession makes little difference—has before him a problem involving some explicit production or decision in life situations: For months or years, it may be, this problem remains unsolved, this creative intention unfulfilled. Attempts at solution have ended only in bafflement. But suddenly, usually in a moment when the work has been abandoned temporarily, or when the attention is absorbed by irrelevant matters, comes an unpredicted *insight* into the solution. As if "inspired," "given," ideas arise which constitute a real integration of previously accumulated experience—an answer, a brilliant hypothesis, a useful "hunch," forming,

---

[3] Albert Stunkard, "Some Interpersonal Aspects of an Oriental Religion," *Psychiatry* Vol. 14 (1951), pp. 419–31.

[4] *Ibid.*

[5] Anton Boisen, "Onset in Acute Schizophrenia," *Psychiatry*, Vol. 10 (1947), p. 164.

it seems, a short cut to artistic or scientific advance. . . . Thus the pattern of insightful thinking . . . involves a period of preparation, a period of renunciation or recession, a period or moment of insight, and a period of verification, elaboration, or evaluation. The process of creative thinking is the cycle of these stages in multiple and ever-changing emphasis.

Joad[6] says in his discussion of the *Psychology of the Creative Process:*

Modern psychological theory supports the Platonic account of the aesthetic process, more particularly in respect of its recognition of two distinct stages, the first a stage of sustained intellectual effort, the second an ensuing flash of intuitive apprehension, which are very similar to those affirmed in the *Symposium* and the *Republic.* A brief account of modern psychological work on the subject may serve a useful purpose in developing the Platonic view.

In a well-known work, *The Art of Thought,* Professor Graham Wallas summarized the information which modern psychology has obtained with regard to the processes involved in the birth of new ideas in the world of thought and original inspiration in that of art. His summary goes beyond that of Plato's account in that it distinguishes *four* stages in the process which leads to the making of a new generalization, the discovery of a new formula, the devising of a new invention or the conception of a new work of art. The first is that of Preparation, during which a particular problem is investigated in all directions; the second, that of Incubation, during which no conscious thinking is done in connection with the problem or work of art with which the creative thinker or artist is concerned; the third, consisting of the "happy idea," together with psychological events accompanying that appearance, is called Illumination; and the fourth, embodying the working out and application of the idea in thought or the execution of the work of art, Verification.

Particular stress is laid upon the importance of Preparation as a preliminary to Illumination. Professor Wallas speaks of the many men of genius who have done their best work after a period of idleness. But the period of idleness must itself be preceded by a spell of hard thinking, during which the intellect is working at full pressure. To adopt the language of modern psychology, we may say that consciousness during the Preparation stage propounds a problem, collects the relevant data and explores different avenues for a possible solution. A period of rest ensues during which the problem and relevant data are transferred to the unconscious. That the unconscious may work effectively consciousness must, so far as possible, be unoccupied. The solution is worked out by the unconscious, and appears in due course in consciousness as the "happy idea" of the scientist and the inspiration of the artist.

The conclusion bears out Plato's hint in the *Symposium.* Wallas like Plato stresses the fact that the "happy idea" which succeeds the period of hard thinking is of an entirely different order from the thinking itself. It outruns the thinking, and, although it is led up to, is far from being necessitated by it. The mind, in other words, makes a definite jump, and it is for this reason that in the sphere of science a subsequent process of "Vertification" is necessary.

Boisen adds that the schizophrenic has in common with the normally creative thinker a "period of preparation or frustration, the

---

[6]C. E. M. Joad, *Guide to Philosophy* (New York: Random House, 1936), pp. 329–30.

unpredicted insight which comes as 'inspired' or 'given,' carrying authority because of the way in which it comes and producing a mood of exaltation and a sense of finality. In both there is the period of elaboration and criticism represented in the flood of new ideas and a consequent strain upon the critical faculties. What is not so clear is the period of 'renunciation' or 'recession.'" Elsewhere, Boisen[7] elaborates: "The origins of both Quakerism and Christianity can be found in the experience of individuals. In both cases they were men who were convinced that they had tapped anew the sources of spiritual power and were commissioned as spokesmen for a Greater-than-themselves."

The artificial induction of a theophany by means of the *koan* bears considerable similarity to the experience of Ignatius Loyola, though his theophany was unplanned and unexpected. The Zen theophanies, as we have seen, are induced almost as if they were laboratory experiments in psychology. Loyola, on the other hand, already in bad physical shape from a wounded leg, accidentally exhausted himself emotionally through intensive contemplation of Christian philosophy. When he ceased his contemplation and relaxed, he immediately experienced a vision of the Virgin Mary. When the Zen novice cannot achieve the solution of his *koan* by arduous, concentrated application of intellect, he too relaxes his efforts and some form of theophany immediately results.

When a phantom authoritarian and self-system reside together in the same mind, in some instances and combinations, their coexistence operates as an "influencing machine"[8] that produces strange and far-reaching results. It is evident on penetrating to the deepest level of the dynamics involved, that whatever the surface picture, in every instance of theophany, kenosis, psychosis, or inspiration, the individual achieves or attempts to achieve security through becoming a carbon-copy of his superego. If he does not dispute the master, the person becomes a part of the whole, a component part of the master's plan, and hence gains the master's power and protection. The unequivocal obedience and obsequiousness of every Japanese citizen to the emperor is a comparable phenomenon. The "peace-at-any-price" attitude, or return to the superego, which occurs in theophany and the like is analogous to the original "to-

---

[7]Anton Boisen, "The Development of Validation in Religious Faith," *Psychiatry*, Vol. 14 (1951), p. 459.

[8]Victor Tausk, "On the Origin of the 'Influencing Machine' in Schizophrenia, *The Psychoanalytic Reader*, Robert Fliess (ed.) (London: Hogarth Press, 1950).

getherness" with the mother. This corresponds with the "elation concept" of Lewin.[9]

The foregoing evidence bears a disturbing relationship to what has become in modern Communist intelligence circles the routine technique for extracting information or "confessions" from captives. One may reasonably assume that the now familiar interrogation methods, which are virtually identical whether applied in Russia, China, Spain, Hungary, or Czechoslovakia, were developed by the Russians and taught to their Communist puppets in other nations. Certainly the Russians, with their profound knowledge of psychology, and their Communist pupils in other lands seem deliberately and calculatingly to exploit "religious" experience in a manner reminiscent of the Zen Buddhists. The difference in application of the method is one of degree only, the Zen training lacking the overtones of cruelty and fear associated with the Communist questioning methods. There is also somewhat less emotional and physical stress involved in the Buddhist *satori*.

I must, however, emphasize that there is no great uniformity in the response of their victims. I postulate that the differences in the length of time it takes for the Communist to reduce various victims to the point of confession, as well as the individual's choice of escape from the Communist menace *before* capture, or suicide or escape *after* capture (or unsuccessful attempts at either) is the result of acquired subconscious differences in the psychological make-up of the various individuals. Jan Masaryk, for example, may have elected suicide because of a well-developed self-system and a clear understanding of reality. He may well have understood that martyrdom resulting from submission to interrogation and imprisonment could have value neither to his countrymen nor to himself. One-time Czech President Benes may have escaped from the range of the Communists because he, too, was unwilling to surrender self to authority and because, realistically, he knew that he could better serve his people as a free man rather than as a prisoner of the Communists. I have a strong feeling that even if Benes and Masaryk had been put through the type of interrogation to which Cardinal Mindszenty submitted, they might never have "confessed."

While it is difficult to support these postulations about the Masaryks and Beneses, we have Mindszenty's own statements[10] to

---

[9]Bertram Lewin, The *Psychoanalysis of Elation* (New York: W. W. Norton, 1950).
[10]Charles Donahue, *Face of the Heavenly Mother* (New York: Philosophical Library, 1952).

illustrate his predisposition to surrender to authority. That he did not, for example, differentiate his own mother from the Catholic Church, which symbolizes the Virgin Mother with Christ as the resident of her womb, nor any of these from his homeland, can be established from the prefatory statement in his book: "If this book should make these three stars—Mother, Church, Homeland—shine more brightly, we should be very happy." He also shows clearly the strong domination of the superego in his life: "God himself could raise the mother no higher, give her no greater glory, than that He Himself, who has called the worlds into being, who commands the winds and waves, who holds the primeval mountains in His hand—than that this almighty God should descend to a woman's womb and become her child; and she, His mother."

There can be no doubt that Mindszenty's preoccupation with the concept of becoming secure and powerful through the surrender of self to the greatest power of them all—his God idea—predisposed him to the response elicited in his experience with the Communist intelligence. For him the surrender of self-system to authoritarian-system was natural, as was the very principle of martyrdom.

In October, 1952, I was able to obtain further confirmation of my beliefs regarding the psycho-dynamics of the Communist interrogation methods. Acting on my behalf, a trained social worker personally interviewed Robert Vogeler, the American business man who fell into the hands of the Communists in Hungary.

The worker had prepared questions, but Mr. Vogeler, without prompting beyond the query, "Did you actually sign what the Communists call a 'confession'?" presented the information out of his own strong convictions and careful analysis of the interrogation procedures as he had experienced them.

He described the entire procedure—which with relatively few exceptions, was limited to mental or psychological torture—as a "conditioning process." First he was subjected to isolation for several days, after which he actually welcomed being summoned before his inquisitors. The association began on a level of friendly conversation. The questioners pointed out that they had also suffered at the hands of the people Vogeler represented—the capitalists. They implied sympathetically that he was now in the same position in which they had been—a political prisoner. Soon, however, their initially friendly conversation turned towards efforts both to indoctrinate and to trap him.

To accelerate the process of breaking him down, Vogeler was

constantly plied with stimulants. Cigarettes and coffee were routine, and he is convinced, from the extreme lightheadedness which the coffee induced, followed by a marked let-down, that a drug similar to amphetamine was added to the beverage much of the time. The first questioning continued for seventy hours without cessation except for brief interludes in which the chief examiners left the room. Each time he became drowsy and unclear they gave him more coffee. At all times during the questioning and in his cell bright lights shone in his eyes.

After seventy hours of interrogation Vogeler was placed in solitary confinement for about ten days. The only clothing left him was his trousers and shoes. The cell was cold and wet and equipped only with a steel bunk with slats and pillow of wood, lacking mattress or covers. His only method of gauging time during this period was the arrival once daily of a single slice of bread and some water passed through the window in his cell door. In adjacent cells he could hear heavy thuds, screams, and groans, sounds highly suggestive that other prisoners were being beaten. Mr. Vogeler said that the sounds seemed genuine, but he felt that they may have been faked for his benefit, adding more unknown fears to his uncertainty.

When the Communists saw that Vogeler was beginning to wear out, they presented him with a vicious accusation. It was apparent that they expected him to react negatively, but his refusal to agree to a preposterous statement brought a resumption of the questioning. In time, twenty such accusations were made, each less preposterous than the last, which he failed to sign.

Mr. Vogeler emphasized that the entire imprisonment and interrogation had been like a carefully rehearsed play, full of dramatic techniques and stage-effects. The cell door would be opened suddenly and then, as if discovering he was in the wrong place, the guard who had opened it would as suddenly retreat, always slamming the door hard behind him. There was much whispering—seldom loud talk, but persistent, almost constant whispering—which he described as far more disturbing than loud voices might have been. He was led to his questioners after sudden, rude awakenings at irregularly spaced hours. First for four hours, later for ten hours or more, a round of interrogations was punctuated by brief periods of "rest" in solitary confinement. He was told that he hadn't cooperated and that he would be held until he did. Witnesses, some of whom he knew, were introduced to testify against him and try to move him to agree to the accusations. Most of them had been terribly tortured. Many had had their nails pulled from their fingers. Others had had their feet beaten—a "favorite" form of Communist torture, he said, because it is agonizing but rarely fatal, hence often productive of confession.

Another ten days or so were passed without questioning, again in solitary confinement, before Vogeler again was presented with the accusations. Many of these were in his own words, more or less distorted by being taken out of context. Finally, after sixty days, he was at the end of his tether and wrote a "confession" which he consciously phrased as extravagantly as possible, hoping that its very ridiculousness might transmit a message indicating his desperate position. However, the Communists objected to this form of admission and a few days later they gave him a prepared list of twenty-three basic questions, with the desired answers bluepenciled. After the "subject" had memorized the marked answers, he was "permitted" to recite them at a trial and affix his signature to his "confession."

Throughout seventeen months of imprisonment Vogeler prayed a great deal and spent long intervals reviewing his life, trying to discover what he might have done to have gotten himself into his present situation. He worried a great deal about the welfare of his wife and two sons in Vienna, and even feared for the safety of his German-born father in America. Vogeler was convinced that a human being could not survive such treatment as he was undergoing without support from a higher source: under such circumstances prayer seemed a logical resort. His father was Lutheran and his mother had been a Catholic, but they had given him free rein in religious affiliation, and he had been confirmed an Episcopalian. Although never profoundly religious, he had always attended Church more or less regularly and tried to live as a good Christian.

Mr. Vogeler had attended Annapolis Naval Academy and served as a naval officer, facts which the Communists knew. Accordingly, throughout the questionings every possible means had been used to make him feel traitorous to his country. They succeeded well in this effort, for constantly he had been assailed by a sense of guilt and repeatedly asked himself, "Am I *really* a traitor? *Did* I say something to betray my country?"

Summarizing, Vogeler believed that the Communists seek some weakness in each subject's character—some fancied slight he had suffered in his life. With him the Communists stressed the fact that he had been *used* by a big corporation, sent to Hungary to exploit the workers, to endanger his own life and to fall into his present situation. They had said that the capitalist system had *abandoned* him and that inquiries about him had not been made by the United States.

In discussing possible psychological predisposition to confession under the circumstances to which he had been subjected, Cardinal Mindszenty was mentioned. It was pointed out that Mindszenty had a well-developed maternal orientation, both in reference to his own mother and in the religious extension—the holy mother, the Church. Vogeler agreed and remarked that this may well have accounted for the fact that the Cardinal had "confessed" after only forty days, while with less rigid religious orientation he had held out half as long again. He agreed that Jan Masaryk was undoubtedly of a different type from either of them.

The interview with Robert Vogeler presents clear evidence of the type of superego structure with which we are concerned. Several points should be emphasized. First, Vogeler's father was German, a nationality group which puts great store by authoritarianism, especially of the father. However benevolent this authoritarianism may be in actual application, it includes a generally clear tendency to defer to the male parents as the final authority in all family matters, particularly in the disciplining of children. The father in this instance was a member of a Christian sect noted for rigidity and rather extreme deference to a still higher authority, God. One may suppose that Vogeler's French mother may have been capable of greater flexibility and freer emotional activity than the father, which may well have contributed to her son's generally adequate emotional adjustment. Yet, his mother, too, belonged to a highly authoritarian religious group. It is interesting that both parents permitted their son to elect his own religious faith; and interesting that he did not depart far, choosing one also distinguished by clearly defined ritual and routine accession to the higher authority of God, Jesus Christ, and the Holy Ghost.

It is not surprising that Vogeler identified himself with the naval service, again an authoritarian milieu, both in obtaining an education and in pursuing for a while a peacetime naval career. The patriotism he developed to a considerable degree is but an extension of the superego involvement which must surely have resulted from the earlier familial and religious atmosphere.

The worker noted that Vogeler seemed to relate himself easily and directly toward another person and that he displayed considerable relaxation. She detected no lingering nervousness which might have carried over from his traumatic experience.

Mr. Vogeler mentioned his self-questioning of whether any of his acts might have led to his becoming a victim of Communist persecution. It is clear that he felt there were certain prescribed ways of life for him, and the feeling implied is that at some point in his life he accidentally or unconsciously might have surrendered to self, rather than acceding as usual to authoritarian demands. The statements regarding conviction of support from a higher power than his own self-preservation mechanisms and the resorting to invocation of that support through prayer demonstrate again his habitual reliance upon superego forces, especially in times of stress.

I feel these statements in no wise differ from what Mr. Vogeler himself believes. He said he had been susceptible to guilt-feelings insinuated by the Communists and pointed out that his patriotic and religious orientation encouraged the guilt-feelings. Perhaps most significant is his own expressed recognition of a difference only in degree between himself and Mindszenty. Moreover, it was he who called attention to the parallels and variations in the Communist methods and urged that I familiarize myself with the story of El Campesino[11] and with Edward Hunter's *Brain Washing in Red China*.[12]

Though the interpretations may be to some extent conjectural, such an accusation cannot be made with reference to the methodology of the Communists. Vogeler and other sources all show that the Communists have employed, as do the Zen Buddhists, the technique of inducing exhaustion after a prolonged period of unrelenting application of intellect to a problem. Vogeler was kept at the highest possible pitch through application of stimulants, lights, noise, and general badgering until he had reached a state of being completely exhausted, emotionally and physically. Then he was allowed to relax. At this point, and not before, he *gave up*. While for him an actual theophany did not occur, certainly the equivalent is evident in his memorizing and mouthing specious answers to specious questions. One cannot imagine more than a small portion

---

[11]Valentin Gonzalez and Julian Gorkin, *El Campesino: Life and Death in Soviet Russia* (New York: Putnam, 1952).

[12]Edward Hunter, *Brain Washing in Red China* (New York: Vanguard Press, 1951).

of his normal intellect and reasoning power remaining at the time of his trial.

By obeying the Communists' orders to memorize, recite, and sign the confession, Vogeler was merely acceding to the only authority which any longer seemed real to him, a parasitic superego, as Sperling[13] has described it. The authority of his captors for the moment served as the stern father, God, or military commander. To accede to them under such circumstances was identical with acceding to parents, priest or other authority in normal life situations. This is not to say that he transferred his allegiance and became imbued with Communist philosophy. Instead, he achieved a psychic transfer of the control of his self-system from the authoritarian superego-systems which had formerly governed it to this new power which now prevented his self-determinism.

Consider Vogeler's situation in the light of what occurred with St. Paul: Saul had previously surrended his self-system to the authoritarian-system represented by Jehovah and the dogma of Judaism. When his theophany occurred, Saul resolved his inner conflict, not by defeating the authoritarian or superego-system, not by thrusting his self-system into control, but by substituting a new superego-system for the old, i.e., Christianity for Judaism.

American intelligence officers have marked the amazing willingness of Japanese prisoners in World War II to answer honestly and without hesitation any and all questions put to them by their captors. Some Americans have believed such behaviour to be the result of lack of preparation of Japanese soldiers for the eventuality of capture. On the contrary, it is a striking example of the ready accession to the demands of anyone in authority which is inculcated in every Japanese from early infancy onward—yet another example of the St. Paul-Vogeler type of psychic *transfer* from one superego-figure to another.

Valentin Gonzalez's[14] account of his experiences under NKVD interrogation and imprisonment at the notorious Lubianka Prison makes it clear that he, El Campesino of the Spanish Civil War, was of a very different stamp from Mindszenty and Vogeler. Not only was he endowed with a sturdy physique and toughened by hardships over a period of years before he fell into the hands of the NKVD for the second time, but by his own words he was self-

---

[13]Otto E. Sperling, "The Interpretation of the Trauma as a Command," *Psychoanal. Quarterly,* Vol. 19 (1950), pp. 352–70.
[14]*Op. cit.*

respecting and self-sufficient in the extreme. Of the natives of his home province of Estremadura in Spain he wrote: "They had pride and a fierce belief in human dignity." Like Vogeler and the rest, his period of conditioning was marked by his captors' efforts at exhausting him, and again there were the lights and other artifices for increasing strain and fatigue.

A very interesting device employed by Gonzalez's tormentors was the rigid rule that he and his cell-mates sit stiffly on their bunks holding a book, with their eyes riveted on the eye of a guard who watched them continuously through a peephole in the cell door. It is easy to conceive the eye as representing to those prisoners whose self-systems were not well developed the very personification of their superegos. Gonzalez reported: "We saw . . . the eye of the guard, unceasingly fixed on us. Did we really see the eye? . . . It did not matter. The main thing was that we thought the eye was there and believed that we saw it."

When El Campesino consistently refused to acquiesce in Communist demands that he confess, they subjected him to various physical tortures. Commenting on his several experiences with the "freezing bath"—jets of ice-water striking the naked victim from all directions—he said:

How did I hold out when it would have been more normal and human to break down? I do not know. I think that the hard life I had always led made me exceptionally tough. Also, in my case the interrogators were defeated by their own tactics. By depriving me of sleep for such a long time they turned me into an unreasoning brute who acted from the obscure dictates of instinct [self-system]. But before I had reached this state, and while I was still capable of thought, I had fixed my mind stubbornly on not signing anything. Later, when I could only act by blind instinct, that mental command had become a part of instinct itself. I was incapable of changing my mind, for it functioned no longer . . . [The Russians] had not counted with the fact that I was not a Russian, with all that capacity for renunciation and submission, with that lack of individual pride and self-esteem, which seem inbred in them.

From this it is apparent that Gonzalez was equipped with a sturdy ego-structure and was not easily intimidated by authoritarian superego figures.

Gonzalez points out that not all foreigners are able to hold out as well or as long as he did. His description of the giving-up process strikingly parallels the connotations of Webster's definition of kenosis and many descriptions of religious experiences: "There comes a moment when the prisoner feels that he is caught like a fly in a spider's web, his vital substance being sucked away until he is nothing but an empty shell." This, of course, is an expression in lay terms of the emptying of the self-system into the superego-system.

While holding out against the Russians led only to worse conditions and longer imprisonment, Gonzalez gave further evidence of his firm ego-development: "My stubborn resistance did only one thing for me: it sent me to my fate with the knowledge that I had not bowed down before those unjust judges." Note that he never regarded his inquisitors as in any real sense authorities or in any way superior to himself except in the sense that they were numerous enough, and their walls strong enough, to hold him.

On one occasion El Campesino deliberately feigned complete obedience to the Iranian Communists. He spoke the Party language, chanted their phrases. He did this consciously to secure some advantage and improve his chances of escape. It was almost as if he had heeded the advice of old Lao-Tze to Confucius:

> Shrewd and clever people are always near to death, for they love to criticize and pass judgment on others. Those who know a great deal about practical affairs, and do things on a large scale, endanger their persons, for by their actions and their knowledge they reveal the mistakes of mankind. He who is only the son of another has nothing for himself, for he owes all to his father; he who is only the official of another has nothing for himself, for he owes all to his superior.[15]

Summary

Kenosis, theophany, *satori, samadhi,* certain types of delusional psychoses, the categorical positive transference in psychoanalysis, "confession" under Communist interrogation . . . all of these experiences or states of mind, and quite possibly all religious experience— all represent a surrender of the self to a "superior" power in the face of surroundings which are seemingly or actually hostile.

Preceding such experiences as these a psychological predisposition must have developed as a result of an originally unfavourable relationship with an authoritarian parent (generally speaking, the mother), fortified through the years by comparable experiences with other authoritarian forces. The individual, struggling to establish his own independent identity, struggling psychically to devour the breasts of his perfidious mother, finally reaches a point of emotional exhaustion. Then, "like one that wraps the drapery of his couch about him, and lies down to pleasant dreams"[16] he ceases his resistance and falls into a swoon. With this final surrender he delivers

---

[15]Carl Crow, *The Story of Confuscius: Master Kung* (New York: Tudor Publ. Co., 1937).

[16]William Cullen Bryant, *Thanatopsis.*

himself, amidst flashing lights and thundering sound, to the devouring breast of his paranoid mother (the Cosmic Mother).

In this vein, that is in the vein of surrendering to a parasitic inner power, Otto Sperling assembled a wealth of evidence for "The Interpretation of the Trauma as a Command."[17] He pointed out that "The onset of psychoneurosis in soldiers during training was often correctly regarded as a measure of their predisposition to psychoneurosis. . . ." Just as the "confession" response to Communist tactics is a measure of predisposition to accept a spurious superego.

Sperling reported that "in psychoanalysis of soldiers the traumata of war were sometimes . . . found to be unconsciously felt as commands from the enemy which something within them was ready to obey. . . . Psychoanalysis showed that American soldiers were deeply influenced by enemy propaganda. . . . The commonest unconscious fantasies of enemy commands that emerged in analysis were: the command to die, to hate one's country, to make oneself useless for the war effort, to yield to one's anxiety, to adopt the enemy and his ideologies."

Sperling said, "enemy propaganda, or the soldier's interpretation of what the enemy wants him to do, can become in some instances established as a kind of parasitic superego." I believe this "parasitic superego" is an overlay on a superego already conditioned and built into the personality through early contacts with the mother. It seems inescapable that groups of individuals predisposed to develop psychoneuroses from the traumata of war, especially enemy propaganda, would to a great extent be the same groups predisposed to react positively in response to the techniques employed by the Communists to obtain false confessions. Perhaps as a note of warning, the very likely possibility should be expressed that in psychoanalysis continued reiteration of erroneous interpretations would at a time of intense emotional stress produce a theophany of a type which would be predetermined by the calculated interpretations.

---

[17]*Op. cit.*

BRAINWASHING*

Edgar H. Schein

"Brainwashing" is a colloquial term which has been used in reference to the systematic efforts of the Chinese Communists (and by implication the Soviets) to persuade nonbelievers to accept Communist allegiance, commands, and/or doctrine by coercive means. More generally, the term has been applied to any technique designed to manipulate human thought or action against the desire, will, or knowledge of the individual. The word "brainwashing" derives from the Chinese phrase *Hsi Nao*[1] and is most appropriately used in reference to Chinese Communist "thought reform" or "ideological remolding" *(Szu Hsing Kao Tsao)*, a program of political indoctrination based on the conception that people who have not been educated in a Communist society have, by definition, incorrect bourgeois attitudes and beliefs, and must therefore be re-educated before they can take their place in a Communist society.[2]

Because of the close connections between Chinese and Soviet Communism and because of the importance which Soviet psychology seems to attach to the works of Pavlov,[3] the assumption has frequently been made that brainwashing is a highly refined adaptation of Pavlovian psychology. From this assumption and the image of scientific mental destruction which it stimulates has come the

---

*Much of the material in this paper is presented in greater detail in *Coercive Persuasion* (New York: W. W. Norton & Co., 1961). I wish to thank Inge Schneier and Curtis Barker who were my collaborators in preparing that volume and who therefore contributed importantly to this paper. This material was prepared for the 1961 *World Affairs Yearbook* and appears there in slightly condensed form.

[1] E. Hunter, *Brainwashing in Red China* (New York: Vanguard Press, 1951).

[2] R. J. Lifton " 'Thought Reform' of Western Civilians in Chinese Communist Prisons," *Psychiatry*, Vol. 19 (1956), pp. 173–95.

[3] There is some evidence that Pavlov was especially revered during Stalin's later years because of Stalin's personal desires to advance Pavlovian psychology, but that following Stalin's death there has been a steady decline of interest in Pavlov among Soviet psychologists. However, they often find it expedient to translate work which has only remote connections to Pavlovian psychology into Pavlovian terminology or to preface their work with praise of Pavlov, thus giving the impression of a steady monolithic growth of Pavlovianism. See R. C. Tucker, "Stalin and the Uses of Psychology," *World Politics*, Vol. 8 (1956), pp. 455–83; and A. Mintz, "Recent Developments in Psychology in the USSR," *Annu. Rev. Psychol.*, 1958, Palo Alto, Calif.

conception that brainwashing is a highly dangerous and possibly irresistible weapon against the mind of man.

Studies of Chinese Communist and Soviet methods of confession extraction and indoctrination have shown that they do have some common roots in the secret police methods of the pre-Communist autocracies in both countries and that both are heavily influenced by basic principles of Party organization, but also that they diverge in important respects from each other, and that the common connections to Pavlovian psychology are very doubtful.[4] Where the Soviets have put emphasis on confession extraction to justify public trials prior to eliminating the victim, the Chinese have from the beginning emphasized the role of confession extraction as only one step in the rehabilitation and reform of the prisoner; where the Soviets have traditionally isolated the prisoner and undermined his resistance by depriving him of any social contact, the crux of the Chinese approach has been to immerse the prisoner in a small group of other prisoners who are as, or more, advanced in their reform than he; where Soviet methods have suggested scientific and Machiavellian approaches to interrogation and confession extraction, the Chinese methods have suggested the image of a zealous enthusiastic mass movement sweeping converts into its ranks by virtue of its intrinsic message and have placed reliance on practical knowledge of interpersonal manipulation.

THOUGHT REFORM IN COMMUNIST CHINA

Chinese Communist attempts to reform their enemies—to cure the disease and save the man—were developed initially in response to the weak power position in which the Chinese Communist Party (CCP) found itself. The need to rely on peasants in building the movement, the need to recruit manpower from Kuomintang (KMT) defectors or prisoners of war, the scattering of forces which was necessitated by the guerilla strategy during the civil war, the opportunity to give political tutelage to uneducated masses over which the CCP had control early in its history, and the requirements of coalition government and united front strategy, all demanded a heavy reliance on persuasion rather than coercion, and resulted in the development of a cadre well versed in the details of Communist

---

[4]See L. E. Hinkle and H. G. Wolff, "Communist Interrogation and Indoctrination of 'Enemies of the State,'" *A.M.A. Arch. Neurol. Psychiat.*, Vol. 76 (1956), pp. 115–74; R. J. Lifton, *op. cit.*; R. A. Bauer, "Brainwashing: Psychology or Demonology?" *J. Soc. Issues*, Vol. 13 (1957), pp. 41–47; E. H. Schein, "Brainwashing and Totalitarianization in Modern Society," *World Politics*, Vol. 11 (1959), pp. 430–41.

ideology and well practiced in the arts of combining persuasion with whatever coercion the power position of the CCP warranted.

Many of the practical methods of persuasion developed were clearly evidenced in the Party Reform movement of the 1940's in which the CCP found itself, instead of physically purging its deviants, engaged in a large-scale effort to revitalize itself ideologically and to lay down Central Party policy to its scattered forces. These methods included (1) the encouragement of grievances against any and all non-Communist groups or ideas combined with a strong emphasis on highly acceptable positive ideals (e.g., get rid of corrupt landlords to help reconstruct China); (2) heavy reliance on group discussion in an atmosphere demanding of each member a complete exposure of his thought and feeling to the scrutiny and analysis of others; (3) the use of mutual and self-criticism to denigrate and destroy all emotional ties with the past; (4) the teaching of Communist doctrine in a group setting in which the group became a vehicle for the thinking through of ideological material to initially stated conclusions, and in which it was each member's responsibility to find the meaning of the theoretical material for his own concrete case; (5) an unmistakable threat of expulsion from the Party for anyone not willing to re-educate himself.

What is distinctive in this approach is the sophistication of the CCP in the use of social and interpersonal forces in the service of creating a situation in which persuasion was likely to be successful. Given that the individual could be coerced into exposing himself to the kinds of group forces described briefly above, it was highly likely that he would come to accept firmly the premises and attitudes which the leaders espoused.

Following the takeover, the CCP approach to organizing and controlling the large Chinese population was to rely on a complex mixture of coercion and persuasion. The leadership's willingness to use terror and coercion was clearly evidenced in the brutality associated with the Land Reform program, in the revival of the *pao chia* system of mutual surveillance, and in the forced conscription or arrest of masses of people who were unwilling to co-operate with the new government. At the same time, a tremendous amount of energy was devoted to propagandizing, educating, indoctrinating, and attempting to convert the Chinese people. The fiction has been constantly maintained that virtually everything the Chinese people are forced to do is done voluntarily and enthusiastically.[5]

[5] A. D. Barnett (ed.), *The United States and the Far East* (New York: Columbia University Press, 1956).

To support its attempts to indoctrinate the people, the CCP has made all mass media of communication an extension of the Party propaganda apparatus, and has supplemented this apparatus with an elaborate oral agitation network designed to mobilize the support of the large number of illiterates. Such widespread campaigns as "Land Reform" (1950), "Resist America, Aid Korea" (1950), "Three-Anti" (anticorruption, antiwaste, and antibureaucratism in government and Party) (1952), and "Ideological Remolding" (1952, 1957, and 1958) have served to mobilize the Chinese population behind the government and have futher facilitated indoctrination. Ideological remolding or thought reform was implemented throughout China through the use of groups devoted to self-criticism, accusation, "grievance telling," discussion, and study. Such groups were usually led by party cadre who reported to higher authorities on the progress of members of the group.

Study groups averaging in size from 10 to 12 were organized in every village, school, factory, prison, and farm, to "rationalize" material presented through reading or lecture and to make it possible for each member to think through how the theoretical point might apply to his own case. "Discussion within the group is often prolonged and intense. Members can and in fact are expected to raise doubts about the official 'correct' view on any subject; but when this happens all other members are expected to argue in favour of the official line. The final objective is mutual agreement and unanimous support of the official line."[6]

Accusation meetings were usually held in neighborhoods, villages, farms, or co-operatives for the purpose of mobilizing grievances against the KMT, landlords, feudalism, and most of all, American imperialism. By having individuals tell their life history and by suitably timing their own accusations, skilled activists could build up emotions in the group to fever pitch which sometimes resulted directly in the trial and perhaps execution of a "cruel landlord" or "corrupt official."

Criticism and self-criticism was often conducted as part of the study group. Everyone in the group was expected to write out a detailed autobiography (the illiterates could always find scribes to whom to dictate their life story) as a basis for pin-pointing sources of reactionary tendencies in his past and as preparations for revealing his "innermost" thoughts to the group. When the life histories were discussed critically in the group, the cadre or activist skillfully

---

[6]*Ibid.*, p. 127.

blended together political ideology with moralistic principles. Thus, to be a good Communist in the end was tantamount to being unselfish, modest, considerate, willing to take responsibility and so on, each defined, of course, in terms of the person's relationship to the government. To be unselfish, for example, meant to be willing to pay ever higher taxes to the government.

In meetings like these it was usually impossible to hide true feelings under the scrutiny of other group members who were competing with each other in the amount of "help" they could give in uncovering *basic* feelings and attitudes. The growing intimacy of members made it easier for them to see through rationalizations and other defenses, which forced each member into a genuine reappraisal of his own past and heightened the likelihood that he would discover positive features in an ideology which he knew he must accept anyway.

A more intensive form of thought reform was in evidence in the Revolutionary Universities which served as training grounds for cadres.[7] Promising young people would be recruited by methods ranging from elaborate promises of bright futures to virtual forced conscription and put through intensive indoctrination programs of several months' duration. Again a heavy emphasis was given to self-examination and confession in the context of small group discussion, with the aim of producing a genuine severance of all emotional ties to the past and a rebuilding of the student's self-image in terms of the new Communist society. As in other kinds of *rites de passage,* the student ratified his growing new identity by acts such as public denunciation of his father.

For those "students" who proved themselves to be recalcitrant or who needed a more "fundamental" kind of re-education, as well as for professionals, intellectuals, and party members whose occupations might make their class-consciousness too parochial, there was "reform through labor." Though reform through labor was rationalized as the best way quickly to acquire the proletariat point of view, it seems generally to have been perceived as punishment and to have been viewed as little more than slave labor to be avoided at all costs.

For those individuals (whether Chinese or foreigner) who were

---

[7]W. E. Gourlay, *The Chinese Communist Cadre: Key to Political Control* (Cambridge: Harvard University Russian Research Center, 1952); and R. J. Lifton, "Thought Reform of Chinese Intellectuals: A Psychiatric Evaluation," *J. Soc. Issues,* Vol. 13 (1957), pp. 5–20.

accused of, or suspected of, counterrevolutionary activity there were many kinds of prisons. However, it is noteworthy that the thought reform movement also permeated the prison, resulting in the assumption that the inmates should and could be reformed.

RESULTS

The *avowed* purpose of thought reform was to create a "new man" whose basic character and attitudes would be ideally fitted for the Communist society of the future. For the different target groups who became involved in thought reform this usually meant the adoption of certain specific attitudes as well as an underlying set of Communist premises—the peasant had to adopt "correct" attitudes about having his land collectivized, the businessman about having the government expropriate him, the bourgeois reactionary about having to give up his emotional ties to parents, friends, and sometimes spouses, if the latter were considered to be political liabilities. The political prisoner was expected to undergo a more fundamental re-evaluation of his past life and to recognize how various of his activities had been harmful to "the people."

The major *implicit* purposes of thought reform appeared to be the creation of obedient citizens and cadres, and the conversion of an entrenched bureaucracy and intelligentsia into an arm of the Communist state. In a sense, thought reform was an elaborate initiation rite which everyone who wished to acquire any status in the new Communist society had to undergo.

The success of the regime in fulfilling its purposes is difficult to evaluate. The visible effect of thought reform in combination with the coercive apparatus upon which it rests had been the creation of massive conformity in all sectors of Chinese society. Almost every visitor to Communist China has been struck by the degree to which all citizens look alike, speak alike, and act alike.[8] It has also been observed that the disciplined efforts of masses of the population have led to a number of tangible accomplishments—increased productivity in some areas of the economy, military success in Korea, and the eradication of certain vices ("there are no more beggars on the streets of Peking").

There is little doubt that the ascetic, moralistic, and idealistic tone of the message of thought reform has had a strong impact on a serious younger generation bent upon bringing the "New China"

---

[8]R. Guillain, *600 Million Chinese* (New York: Criterion Books, 1957).

into the front ranks of world powers. On the other hand, there are a number of indications that thought reform has not gone deep in influencing attitudes—the burst of criticism which followed Mao's *Let 100 Flowers Bloom* speech, the reports of defectors that group discussion, study, criticism, and self-criticism are engaged in only superficially, and the high number of unreconstructed critics in the political prisons (as estimated by Western repatriates). The safest conclusion is that the effects have been different on different parts of Chinese society and have varied with the skill and sophistication of the cadres responsible for it.

THE INVOLVEMENT OF WESTERN PRISONERS

Westerners became involved with Chinese Communist thought reform in two ways: several hundred European and American professionals, businessmen, and missionaries were arrested on the mainland and subjected to reform in prison, and several thousand United Nations prisoners of war (POW's) encountered a somewhat milder version in the POW camps of North Korea. The arrests on the mainland probably occurred for a number of reasons—to break spy rings which the Communists believed to be operating, to facilitate propaganda operations by discrediting Western efforts in China, to expropriate the properties of Westerners, to collect hostages for political negotiations, and to assert Asian superiority over a group to which the Chinese had felt inferior for so long. It is quite unlikely that any of the arrests occurred in order to subject the prisoner to thought reform; rather the reform was a regular part of prison procedure and had to involve all prisoners. In the case of the POW's also one gets the feeling that thought reform was incidental rather than basic, with the basic purpose being the exploitation of the POW for a variety of propaganda objectives.

TREATMENT OF WESTERN CIVILIANS IN PRISONS

The treatment of civilians in prison varied widely depending upon the location of the prison, the political climate, and the nature of the alleged crime.[9] The most refined thought reform was in evidence in the Peking prison from where came most of the cases of alleged successful brainwashing. The changes in the beliefs, attitudes, and values which the prison regimen produced (which in some cases

---

[9]Schein, *op. cit.* (1961).

were substantial and lasting) can only be accounted for by a consideration of all the pressures which the total experience generated, even though some of these pressures were incidental to the thought reform program as such.

The initial attitude of the prisoner was important. If he had seen only the good side of Communism, as exhibited in the admirable takeover operation in cities like Peking, he was more likely to accept the "lenient policy" and thus become favorably disposed towards Chinese Communist penal methods. If he had seen the brutal side of Communism as in the Land Reform movement, he was usually predisposed to believe nothing the Communists said and to resist any impulse to be favorably disposed toward them.

Arrest usually followed a period of surveillance and resulted in the prisoner's either being detained in his own house or being taken to some form of prison. He was usually not told the charges against him, yet it was made clear to him that he was considered to be guilty from the moment of arrest on. Once arrested he was expected to come to understand the following version of his predicament: he was in prison because the government considered him a criminal; his crime was obvious to everyone but to him; his first task was to understand the nature of his crime and in this task the authorities and fellow prisoners would do all they could to help him; through analysis of his past behavior he would be shown and would discover how the ultimate consequences of his actions had been harmful to the Chinese people. Once he saw his guilt, he was expected to confess, repent, and reform the undesirable thoughts, attitudes, feelings, and actions which had led to his crimes in the first place.

From the Communist point of view guilt was judged "objectively," which meant that anything which ultimately could have harmed the Chinese people was a crime even if unintended or not acted upon. Thus a prisoner might be considered guilty because of his associations, his alleged intentions, his incorrect thoughts or attitudes, and most importantly, his incorrect social origins. If he was other than proletarian by birth he was considered to have acquired incorrect points of view and attitudes throughout his life which eventually would result in harmful action toward the common people.

From the prisoner's point of view his arrest was unjustified, the accusations of guilt in the initial confrontation with judge or interrogator ridiculous, and the statements about leniency to those who confess meaningless. Only as the full force of the prison regimen made itself felt on him did he come to be able to appreciate intellectually and emotionally what was wanted of him.

The manner in which the prisoner came to be influenced to accept the Communist's definition of his guilt can best be described by distinguishing two broad phases—(1) a process of "unfreezing," in which the prisoner's physical resistance, social and emotional supports, self-image and sense of integrity, and basic values and personality were undermined, thereby creating a state of "readiness" to be influenced; and (2) a process of "changing," in which the prisoner discovered how the adoption of "the people's standpoint" and a reevaluation of himself from this perspective would provide him with a solution to the problems created by the prison pressures. The degree of permanence of the changes in attitude which had occurred would depend on the degree to which these were subsequently integrated with other values and attitudes the prisoner held and were supported by others back home.

Unfreezing

The prisoner's physical strength was undermined by the general inadequacy of the diet, loss of sleep due to intermittent and continuous interrogation, illnesses, lack of exercise, excessive cold or heat in combination with inappropriate clothing, prolonged standing or squatting during interrogation or as a punishment for infraction of the prison regulations, excessive pain from the wearing of manacles behind the back and ankle chains (which were put on as punishment if the authorities felt that the prisoner was not genuinely trying to reform himself), cuffing and beating by cell mates, and innumerable other events in the prison regimen.

The prisoner's social and emotional supports were undermined by his being completely cut off from any communication with the outside (no incoming or outgoing mail was permitted, and no non-Communist newspapers, etc., were available), by the prohibition of any close emotional relationship with another prisoner except in the context of reform, by the introduction of testimonials of various sorts in the form of confessions by others whom the prisoner respected or simply by surrounding the prisoner with cell mates who were enthusiastic about reforming themselves and who condemned all the values to which he adhered.

The prisoner's image of himself and his sense of integrity or inviolability were undermined primarily by the humiliation, revilement, and brutalization he suffered at the hands of his cell mates in the process of "struggle." Most prisoners were put into a cell containing several Chinese prisoners who were further along in reforming themselves and who saw it as their primary duty to "help" their most backward member to see the truth about himself in order that the whole cell might advance. Each such cell had a leader who was in close contact with the authorities for purposes of reporting on the cell's progress and getting advice on how to handle the Western member. In this setting the cell mates found ways of putting extreme pressure on their unreformed member, particularly since he was often completely dependent upon them for help in feeding himself, eliminating, etc. (especially if he were manacled).

The only thing which would satisfy the cell mates was a sincere confession, but since the prisoner could not guess initially what this meant or what he was to confess, he brought down the full wrath of the others upon his head. They believed in his guilt and felt that only his stubbornness and reactionary tendencies could account for his refusal to confess. The only valid identity granted to him was that of guilty criminal; any attempt to be anything else—a doctor, a missionary, an innocent victim of circumstances—was condemned violently. The fact that this pressure was applied twenty-four hours a day for weeks or months on end must have made it especially potent; there was no private time and no opportunity for retreat.

Other facets of the environment undermined the prisoner's self-image. The prisoner was identified only by number, his every action during the day was carefully prescribed—when to eat, when to go to the toilet, when to wash, etc. The time allotted to these activities was usually far too short to allow for their satisfactory completion (e.g., two minutes for running out to the toilet, eliminating, and returning at a given time of day); he was prohibited from making any decisions—every act had to be preceded by permission from the guard or co-ordinated carefully with the cell mates (e.g., since sleeping quarters were crowded, prisoners slept huddled together and all had to shift position in unison on an agreed-upon signal); judges and interrogators made a convincing argument that the prisoner could not hope to be released and ever be anything again unless he confessed and repented; the prisoner was often seduced into behavior violating his own self-image, such as making attempts at false confessions or denouncing loved ones. The whole prison atmosphere was completely demeaning.

Some of these same factors also tended to undermine the prisoner's more fundamental values and personality defenses. His state of complete dependency often aroused childhood conflicts and stimulated unconscious guilt; the cell mates constantly rejected and demeaned the prisoner's values, or if these were strong ethical principles, as in the case of priests, showed in many little ways how the person had in his past or was in his present behavior failing to live up to the very values he professed (e.g., pointing out that most missions employed Chinese in "demeaning" jobs such as cooks or houseboys, or that the priest's behavior in the cell was often selfishly motivated).

Guilt was also aroused by the recognition on the part of prisoners that their own middle class values did indeed lead them to subtle prejudices against the working classes and that these prejudices had shown up in their attitudes toward the Chinese prior to imprisonment (e.g., preference for living in fancy quarters, social contacts mostly with the embassy set, etc.). At the same time the values which the Communists professed are so universally valid as to have been unassailable—unselfishness, working for the greater good of humanity, peace, etc.—yet are so difficult to uphold in an absolute sense that the prisoner was constantly having his failures pointed out to him (e.g., taking up too much room while sleeping was considered evidence of selfishness reflecting bad bourgeois attitudes).

Change in Attitudes and Self-Image

The constant threats of death or permanent nonrepatriation led to anxiety and despair which was difficult to cope with. But even more difficult for the prisoner was his increasing recognition that his cell mates really took the lenient policy of the government seriously and were making a genuine attempt to reform themselves. As the cell mates came to be seen as real people rather than merely agents of the prison authorities, the prisoner felt increasingly guilty for his hostility toward them and increasingly committed to trying to understand their point of view. Because his own beliefs, values, and attitudes had been undermined, and because he found himself in an insoluble situation, he became increasingly disposed to trying to find a solution through forming relationships with others who seemed to have found a solution. As his identification with one or more cell mates grew, he came increasingly to understand the basic premises underlying "the people's standpoint," and how he might be perceived to be guilty from this standpoint.

Because the prison experiences had elicited a variety of guilt feelings already, it became possible for the prisoner to attach his guilt feelings increasingly to the crimes which he began to see in his own past behavior, and thus to begin a process of "sincere" confession. He could see that his innocent letters about his trip through a farm area could be giving valuable economic information to the American enemy, that his discussions with people in embassies concerning the morale of students could be used in psychological warfare against the Communists, that his hobnobbing with the embassy set was giving aid and comfort to reactionary forces, or that his failure to join the Communists could be construed as hostility toward them. Once this process of self re-evaluation began, the prisoner received all kinds of help and support from the cell mates and once again was able to enter into meaningful emotional relationships with others. His terrible social-emotional isolation was at an end and his role as repentant sinner was given increasing support.

The key elements in this process were (1) the identifications which formed with cell mates, thus making it possible for the prisoner to begin to understand the point of view from which he was judged guilty, and (2) the re-evaluation of actual behavior engaged in, which occurred when he applied the scale of values embodied in "the people's standpoint" to his own behavior. The prisoner was not expected to manufacture a false confession, but was expected to see that his actual behavior had in fact been criminal from the Communist point of view.

The intensive self-analysis which accompanied this process often led the prisoner to recognize genuine faults in his own character and as this happened his reform took on a personal as well as political meaning. Some of the prisoners had come to China uncertain of their basic identity and value systems and found in the prison experience an opportunity to arrive at some genuine resolutions of long standing conflicts or to become completely committed to *some* value system.

The group cell as an agent of influence was crucial for several reasons: (1) enforced close contact with others made it likely that strong guilt, anxiety and hostility would be aroused which, in turn, would increase the probability of identification with a cell mate (either as a defense against deeper conflicts or as a solution to the identity crisis which the cell had created); (2) the presence of several others heightened the probability of there being at least one among them who would "see through" and expose any defensive maneuver the prisoner might attempt; (3) the probability was height-

ened that there would be at least one other cell mate with whom
the prisoner could identify because of similar personality or background; (4) once the prisoner began to identify with a cell mate,
the group provided many models of how the prisoner was expected
to behave and could provide rapid "feed-back" in terms of rewarding or punishing his behavior; and (5) the sheer fact of a unanimous group arrayed against the prisoner provided a force which was
very difficult to resist psychologically.[10]

Study, Interrogation, and Trial

The events described thus far were supplemented by study sessions, criticism and self-criticism meetings, and autobiography writing, but these activities did not have genuine impact on the Western prisoner until he had begun the more fundamental self re-evaluation described above. If the prisoner was beginning to adopt new
attitudes toward himself and others, these activities would be useful in providing rationalizations and a broader conception of what
Communism meant, as well as acquainting the prisoner increasingly
with Communist semantics.

Throughout his imprisonment, the prisoner was periodically confronted with interrogation sessions and with discussions of his case
in the presence of one or more judges. The prisoner's relationship
to these authorities was not dissimilar to the heretic's relationships
to the inquisitor of the Middle Ages in that the case could only be
settled when the prisoner had made a suitable confession, "suitable"
being defined by the personal judgment of the authorities, not by
law. Psychologically meaningful relationships also grew up with
interrogators but not as frequently as with cell mates. Interrogation
more often than not was one of the stresses which tended to unfreeze the prisoner and make him increasingly search for a solution
to his dilemma.

Once the prisoner began to adopt "the people's standpoint" and
to apply this yardstick to his own behavior, he began to be able to
confess in a manner which satisfied the authorities. After varying
lengths of time, during which he might write and rewrite his confession a half dozen times or more, he would be brought to trial and
usually sentenced to imprisonment for a period roughly approximating the length of time he had already spent in prison, to be followed

---

[10]S. E. Asch, "Effects of Group Pressure upon the Modification and Distortion
of Judgments," *Groups, Leadership, and Men,* Harold Guetzkow (ed.) (Pittsburgh:
Carnegie Press, 1951).

by expulsion from China. The confession, then, usually served as the criterion of the degree of reform, though the authorities also had available to them the reports of the cell chief on the progress which a given prisoner was making. The release of Western prisoners was sometimes dictated more by international negotiations than by degree of reform or the adequacy of the confession. Many prisoners were released who apparently never made a damaging confession, and some were released who made confessions but who obviously did not adopt "the people's standpoint" (as evidenced by their repudiation of the confession following their release by the Communists). Finally, a number of Western prisoners have been given longer sentences which they are still serving.

RESULTS

The description of coercive persuasion given above applies only to a small number of Western prisoners (the number is difficult to estimate for obvious reasons but is perhaps no larger than 50, taking Americans and Europeans together). The majority of Westerners who were imprisoned either encountered inefficient prisons or were not considered important enough to be reformed. Many of them encountered reform in a superficial fashion—study sessions and criticisms performed as a necessary daily ritual rather than an important psychological activity. Many were never placed into group cells of more reformed prisoners, but were either kept in solitary confinement or placed with other "reactionary" prisoners with whom they were forbidden to communicate in any way whatsoever. Successful brainwashing, in the sense of the repatriate espousing Communist attitudes and reiterating his crimes following release from Communist China, was a rare outcome. Genuine attitude change could only occur if there were already a predisposition in the prisoner and if he encountered a highly effective prison regimen built around the use of the group cell.

Those Americans who exhibited Communist influence at the time of their release into Hongkong have had varied histories since their release. Several of them have re-evaluated their experiences once again after their return home and have ended up wondering how they could ever have believed what they professed to believe toward the end of their imprisonment. Several others have vacillated between sympathy for the Communist position and sympathy for the Western position and are continuing to search for some resolution to their value and attitude conflicts; several have had genuine personality changes built around ethical principles which Communism shares with other value systems, and these individuals have continued to believe that they were guilty of the crimes to which they confessed, that they were indeed treated leniently by the Communists, that the Communist position on matters of basic ethics and values is correct, and that they must continue to live by these principles even if they encounter hostility in the United States. Some have used thought reform as a basis for general personal reform and are grateful to the Chinese for providing this opportunity.

TREATMENT OF PRISONERS OF WAR IN KOREA

The problem which confronted the West with the POW's was not so much their ideological conversion, of which there was virtually none, but rather a variety of collaborative behaviors (such as making radio broadcasts praising the CCP, signing "peace" petitions, asking others to co-operate with the enemy, serving on "peace" committees, making germ warfare confessions, and so on) which the Communists used skillfully to embarrass the United States in particular during the Korean episode.

The American POW was completely unprepared for the political exploitation to which he was subjected, and many of his responses to the Chinese efforts are to be explained primarily by this lack of preparation. Shortly after the UN's entry into Korea the primary expectation on the part of the troops was that capture would result in being tortured, abandoned, or killed by the North Koreans. Subsequent studies of atrocities in Korea substantiated these rumors in that most of the brutal treatment of the POW was the result of North Korean handling."[11]

If a man was captured by the Chinese, however, he found instead of harshness and brutality a friendly welcome, an outstretched hand, and a greeting in broken English of "Welcome," "Congratulations, you have been liberated," or "You have now joined the Fighters for Peace." Because many of the men were unclear about their mission in Korea and resented fighting on foreign soil against an unfamiliar enemy, they were initially receptive to any mention of peace. The Chinese then typically gathered groups of prisoners together at collection points and further explained the "lenient policy": POW's were not viewed as enemy troops, but as misguided, uneducated, or unawakened people who had been "tricked into

[11]U.S. Army, *Extract of Interim Historical Report*, Korea War Crimes Division, 1953.

fighting for an evil capitalist society," and who could be brought to see the truth about the Korean war and the basic validity of Communist peace efforts.

Most of the men were captured during the winter of 1950–51. The first months of captivity were a tough struggle for survival, because of the marginal diet for Western soldiers, the high rate of illness, which was inadequately treated, lack of medical care for the wounded, and extensive exposure to the elements. This combination of circumstances resulted in more than 40 per cent of the POW's dying within the first six months of captivity. Psychologically, this was a most difficult time for the POW because the marginal conditions stimulated competition for the scarce resources available, morale was low anyway because of the uncertain future which capture by an Oriental enemy signaled, and the Chinese repeatedly protested that the inadequate supplies of food and medicine resulted from UN bombing of supply lines, not from their own deliberate policy or callousness. They were always highly solicitous and sympathetic, which robbed the prisoners of the opportunity to band together around their common hatred of the enemy. The fact that there were among the large number of prisoners some who from the outset were willing to take advantage of others or to curry the favor of the Chinese created an additional morale problem which the Chinese exacerbated by offering more and better food and medicine to those prisoners who showed a willingness to cooperate with them.

The men were marched north and housed in various kinds of temporary compounds during this winter and were moved into more permanent POW compounds along the banks of the Yalu during the spring of 1951. Shelter, food supplies, medical care, and clothing improved sharply with the settling into the permanent compounds, but psychological pressures did not cease because of the manner in which the Chinese organized and operated the camps.

Deliberate Disorganization of POW's in Permanent Camps

The most significant feature of Chinese prison camp control was the systematic destruction of the POW formal and informal group structure which in the end resulted in widespread mutual mistrust among the men, and the necessity for each man to withdraw increasingly into a shell even though he was in the midst of others.

The authority structure of the POW group was destroyed first by segregating all officers and later all noncommissioned officers, thus leaving the mass of prisoners without formal authority of any kind. The prisoners were organized into squads, platoons, and companies, but only the squads were permitted to be commanded by prisoners, and the appointed squad leaders were usually the lowest ranking enlisted men or prisoners who were willing to co-operate with the Chinese. While the ranks were still together the highest ranking officers in a group would sometimes be given the alternative of signing a peace petition and ordering their troops to sign or having their group punished severely. Attempts by these officers to work out compromises which would satisfy the Chinese yet would increase the chances of the survival of their men would often appear to lower ranking officers like collaboration. They would then either overtly or covertly fail to obey orders, thus destroying the chain of command and, in effect, throwing the troops on their own resources.

The informal social structure of the POW group was undermined by a variety of techniques: (1) the Chinese prohibited any form of organized activity not sponsored by themselves, including religious services and recreational activities; (2) emergent leaders were usually discouraged and segregated; (3) extensive use of spies and POW informers made possible close surveillance of all informal activities and the Chinese frequently let POW's know that even their most private conversations and plans were known, thus creating mutual mistrust since no one could be sure that his best friends were not informers; (4) the conduct of interrogations weakened social-emotional ties still further by the frequent presentation to a man of confessions or military information written out by a fellow prisoner; what he usually did not know was that the fellow prisoner had not provided the information voluntarily, but had perhaps agreed to copy it out of some manuals which the Chinese showed him they already possessed; written information of this sort was often widely publicized in camp newspapers to create the impression that collaboration was the rule rather than the exception; (5) the confessions of germ warfare which were coerced from a number of Air Force officers and enlisted men were exploited by forcing several of them to go to the POW camps to give lectures on how they had used germ warfare, usually creating a big impression on the listeners.

As in the case of the civilian prisoner, bonds to loved ones and to the home country were severed by the prohibition of any contact with the outside. Only pro-Communist literature was available in the prison camp libraries; mail was delivered to a prisoner only if it contained bad news or was completely innocuous; if a man inquired about his mail he was usually told that none had arrived, which he was told must mean that his loved ones had abandoned him.

Most of the POW's were forced to write autobiographies and to discuss details of their personal histories during lengthy interrogations. It would be pointed out to a man how any misfortune or difficulty he reported must be the product of the political system under which he grew up, a message which found a responsive chord in the drifters and malcontents and in those prisoners whose enlistment in the Army had, in the first place, been motivated by their failure to achieve any other kind of satisfactory occupational career.

Criticism and self-criticism could not be introduced directly into POW groups without it becoming a mere mockery of what was intended, but it was used effectively to embarrass individual POW's and thereby to weaken the morale of the whole group. For example, most men were required to sign lengthy camp rules shortly after their arrival at a permanent compound. Months later a man might be hauled to the camp commandant's office and accused of a serious crime like expectorating at a forbidden place. He then would be told that to avoid serious punishment he must make a public confession and self-criticism in front of his company or squad. Though the man usually managed to introduce enough idiom into such a procedure to ridicule it, the impact on other POW's of seeing a fellow prisoner humiliate himself was still considerable.

Rewards, Threats, and Punishments

Rewards and punishments were consistently manipulated to elicit collaborative behavior. Any tendency on the part of a POW to be co-operative with the Chinese was rewarded with increased food rations or luxury items like fresh fruit or cigarettes; any stiffening of resistance was punished with a decrease in food, medicine, or camp privileges, and, if resistance was chronic, led to segregation in special compounds for "reactionaries" in which hard labor was the typical activity. Threats of death or nonrepatriation, occasionally backed by mock executions or severe physical punishment, effectively curbed any violent resistance efforts. The memory of the horrors of the first six months kept alive the knowledge that the Communists were more than willing to let men die or kill them if it suited their purpose.

Prizes of food would be given for essays to be published in the camp newspapers. The winning essay, of course, would invariably be the one which was most pro-Communist. Perhaps the most important award for co-operation with the enemy was the status of "progressive," symbolized by being given a peace dove to wear in the lapel, which made it possible for the POW once again to enter into meaningful social relationships with others and to obtain a whole range of special privileges such as freedom of movement. For POW's who had not enjoyed any status in the society from which they came, such a status could be very meaningful even though based on co-operation with the enemy.

Lectures and Group Discussion

To present the Communist point of view and to provide the POW's with suitable reasons for why they should co-operate with the Chinese, the political sections of the Red Army units presented daily lectures to be followed by group discussions of the conclusions presented in the lecture. Attendance at both functions was mandatory and the group discussions were monitored by cadres or by "progressives." The content of the lectures was usually crude propaganda around topics like "Who Really Started the Korean War?" and was so full of blatant inaccuracies as to vitiate whatever appeal it might have had (e.g., the statement by the lecturer that "we know that in America very few of you own your own cars"). Certain specific themes like the plea for "peace" inevitably had appeal, however, and POW's found themselves supporting peace activities like signing petitions, inserting peace propaganda into their letters home (they were delivered only if such propaganda were inserted), and serving on peace committees which were formed in each camp.

RESULTS

The most important result was the social disorganization of the POW group which resulted in the bulk of the men withdrawing into an emotional shell and adapting as best they could by co-operating with the Chinese as much as they had to in order to survive, but trying to avoid giving any aid to their propaganda efforts. An important corollary result was the impairment of judgment which resulted from the social-emotional isolation. If a POW could not comfortably discuss his daily affairs with others, seek advice, or consider the consequences of actions he was contemplating, he was cut off from the most important source of validation available to man—the opinions, beliefs, and knowledge of others. Consequently much collaborative behavior occurred because of poor judgment or foresight. The POW's often were unaware how skilled the Communists were in using propaganda and were equally unaware how their behavior might be construed as disloyal. The important point, however, is that collaborative behavior was usually *not* motivated by disloyalty or opportunism, but rather was the complex resultant of attempts to survive in an environment where standards for behavior were extremely difficult to discern.

The extent of this psychological withdrawal showed up clearly in studies of the repatriates. In their observable behavior and on psychological tests they showed marked emotional constriction, inability and unwillingness to get involved with others, and even some impairment of intellectual functioning. It took a period of weeks or months in some cases for the men once again to feel comfortable in close emotional relationships with others.[12]

The Communists were highly successful in managing the prison camps with a minimum of guards. The isolation of the camps, the ready identifiability of Westerners among the North Koreans, the social disorganization of the POW group, and the fact that the armistice talks were going on from early 1951, all militated against extensive escape activities. Numerous escapes were attempted, but in most cases the men were recovered after a fairly short time. On the other hand, the very small percentage of men who were to any degree swayed by the ideological message of the Communists must be considered a dramatic failure of their indoctrination program.

BRAINWASHING: THE VERDICT

The outstanding conclusion one comes away with from a study of these events is that the methods of brainwashing are not diabolical, new, or irresistible. Rather, the Chinese have drawn on their

---

[12]H. D. Strassman, Margaret B. Thaler, and E. H. Schein, "A Prisoner of War Syndrome: Apathy as a Reaction to Severe Stress," *Amer. J. Psychiat.*, Vol. 112 (1956), pp. 998–1003; E. H. Schein, "The Chinese Indoctrination Program for Prisoners of War," *Psychiatry*, Vol. 19 (1956), pp. 149–72; E. H. Schein, W. F. Hill, H. L. Williams, and A. Lubin, "Distinguishing Characteristics of Collaborators and Resisters among American Prisoners of War," *J. Abnorm. Soc. Psychol.*, Vol. 55 (1957), pp. 197–201; Margaret T. Singer and E. H. Schein, "Projective Test Responses of Prisoners of War Following Repatriation," *Psychiatry*, Vol. 21 (1958), pp. 375–85; E. H. Schein, W. E. Cooley, and M. T. Singer, *A Psychological Followup of Former Prisoners of War of the Chinese Communists* (Cambridge, Mass.: Massachusetts Institute of Technology, Part I, 1960, Part II, 1962).

cultural sensitivity to the nuances of interpersonal relationships to put together some highly effective but well-known techniques of indoctrination. Their sophistication about the importance of the small group as a mediator of opinions and attitudes has led to some highly effective techniques of destroying group solidarity, as in the case of the POW's, and of using groups as a mechanism of changing attitudes, as in the political prisons.

THE SPECIAL ROLE OF GUILT IN COERCIVE PERSUASION*
E. H. Schein, I. Schneier, and C. H. Barker

One of the primary motives which leads the prisoner to begin a process of change (to begin to allow himself to be influenced) is *guilt,* which he comes to experience in various forms in the prison environment. This experience of guilt results from a combination of external pressures and internal predispositions. From the point of view of the interrogator or judge, criminal guilt is assumed once the prisoner has been arrested, but there are several different bases for such guilt. From the point of view of the prisoner there are a number of predispositions which lead to psychologically distinct types of guilt, though they may not be experienced as different. The purpose of this chapter is to explore these distinctions and thereby to show how the captor's presentation of the nature of guilt begins to unfreeze the prisoner by stimulating in him a sense of guilt, and how the type of guilt which he feels is related to the final outcome of the influence process.

THE CAPTOR'S VIEW OF GUILT

Once arrested, the prisoner must come to understand the following version of his predicament: he is in prison because the government considers him a criminal; his crime is obvious to everyone but to him; his first task is to understand the nature of his crime, and in this task the government will do its best to help him. Analysis of

---

*Reprinted from Schein, E. H. with Schneier, I. and Barker, C. H., *Coercive Persuasion* (New York: Norton, 1961), pp. 140–56.

his past will show him how he has been guilty, how the ultimate consequences of his acts have been harmful to the Chinese people. If he is honest with himself he will discover his guilt more rapidly and proceed easily to what is expected of the criminal: admission of guilt by confession, subsequent repentance, and reform of the undesirable thoughts, attitudes, feelings, and actions.

From the moment of his arrival in prison the prisoner has urged upon him the rationale of the Chinese authorities by his interrogator, judge, and, most important, his cell mates. He may attempt to defend himself against the accusations of guilt by denying criminal acts or intents, by laughing at their absurdity, or simply by failing to take them seriously, but the total prison regimen as outlined in the previous chapters may convince him that his own concepts of guilt and innocence are incorrect or at least are not shared by the other prisoners or the authorities.

The bases for being judged guilty which he must come to appreciate are the following:

1. *Guilt by Association.* The prisoner is guilty if he has associated with any others who are themselves guilty, even if he has not committed any acts "harmful to the Chinese people," or exhibited any intent to do so, or been aware of his association with other guilty parties.[1]

2. *Guilt by Intention.* The prisoner is guilty if he exhibits motives which could and probably eventually would lead to actions which would harm the Chinese people; thus the prisoner is at least a potential criminal who must be made to feel his guilt and be punished as social prophylaxis.

3. *Guilt for Incorrect Attitudes.* The prisoner is guilty if he takes a negative attitude toward the Party or the government or questions any of their decisions, because such an attitude undermines the effectiveness of the "people's representatives" in their programs to help the people; questioning his own guilt or asserting his innocence can be, of course, a further instance of such a negative attitude, thereby proving the government's correctness in the first instance.

4. *Guilt for Incorrect Thoughts.* The prisoner is guilty if he exhibits thought patterns which reflect bourgeois premises and if he fails to appreciate the validity of Communist premises, even if he does not exhibit intentions or attitudes which could be harmful

---

[1] Since the guilt of the "others" rests on bases similar to those discussed here, it can be seen that the attribution of guilt to anyone is possible.

to the people; it is assumed that wrong thoughts would eventually lead to harmful acts.

5. *Guilt for Having Knowledge.* The prisoner is guilty if he has knowledge about China which could in any conceivable way be used against the Chinese, no matter how vague or seemingly non-political it might be; if the prisoner is a foreigner such knowledge is particularly suspect because of the presumption that the only possible reason for his remaining in China after the takeover could be the gathering of "intelligence information"; thus activities such as research, casual questioning, and reading all become espionage.

6. *Guilt for Harmful Action.* The prisoner is guilty if he has committed acts which are harmful to the Chinese people, even if he does not recognize having committed them or does not recognize that they were harmful; seemingly innocuous acts can be defined as seriously harmful by the authorities, e.g., going to a party at a Western embassy is "establishing contact with spies" or actually "passing on information to Western agents"; looking something up in easily available volumes in the library for an attaché at a Western embassy (something he could easily have done himself) is "aiding in espionage activities," and so on.

7. *Guilt for Failure to Act.* The prisoner is guilty if he has *not* been active in his support of the Party and the government, if he has failed to show his own desire for the welfare of the people, if he has failed to give willingly his own possessions, time, and efforts in behalf of the Communist cause; to stand aside is to condone and support the old status quo.

8. *Guilt for Having a Characteristic Personal Fault or Faults.* The prisoner is judged guilty if he shows in his behavior in prison some fault, shortcoming, or character defect from the point of view of the idealized image of the "new man"; for example, the prisoner is constantly being shown evidence of his own selfishness, lack of concern for others, class and/or racial prejudice, personal weakness, failure to live up to his own stated ideals, and so on; because the idealized "new man" is morally "perfect" from both a Communist and non-Communist point of view, it is likely that the kinds of faults for which the prisoner is criticized will be perceived by him as faults also.

9. *Guilt for Having Dangerous Social Origins.* The prisoner is guilty if he was born into a bourgeois family, if his friends and/or relatives are capitalists, if he was educated under a capitalist system, or if he associated with others of dangerous social origins; it is

assumed that various of the consequences described above—incorrect attitudes and thoughts, failure to support the Communist cause, characteristic personal faults, are all due to such social origins; hence incorrect social origins are a primary and incontestable basis for guilt. What makes matters worse for the prisoner is that he cannot deny these origins, they are a matter of fact; he can only deny their effects which is not likely to be convincing.

As one reviews these bases of guilt, one sees that they overlap to a considerable extent and are linked by the underlying assumption that *all situations must be judged by their "objective" results, by their ultimate consequences.* Thoughts, attitudes, intentions, personal characteristics, and even accidents of birth and status must be judged by what they *could* lead to, not by the actual actions they have led to in the past. Thus the person may be guilty without knowing it, and it is the prison's primary task to make the prisoner conscious of his guilt as the prelude to reform. This logic carried to its extreme makes the primary basis of guilt simply the objective fact of having been arrested; arrest is the just consequence of guilt and the presumptive evidence of it.[2]

In general, the agents of influence (judge, interrogator, cell mate) presume the guilt of their subject(s). They believe the subject would never have been arrested if he were not considered a threat to the "people." They may not know the precise reason for the subject's guilt nor which grounds are justifiably applicable to him. They may not even be convinced that the grounds on which they are arguing are justified. Nonetheless they are able to be persuasive because of their "obvious" sincerity in working for the welfare of the people and in their belief that if the subject had not been guilty of something he would not have been arrested. Mistakes are considered unlikely and, in any case, must be made in favor of the system since it defines itself to be in a state of combat.

The frequent allegation that the interrogators, judges, and cell mates are Machiavellian in their tactics is probably based on the prisoner's perception that the agent is willing to manipulate the nature of the accusation to suit the subject's particular vulnerability. Thus the judge may sincerely believe that in some general fashion the prisoner is guilty of harming the people but may not believe the specific charges that he is making against the prisoner. Under the

---

[2]It is an interesting psychological fact that even some prisoners who thought they were arrested unjustly, who saw themselves as innocent, were convinced of the guilt of everyone else in the prison.

pressure of his job he may end up trying to convince the subject of his guilt rather than trying to ascertain whether he is guilty; and he may be willing in this process to make accusation after accusation until some are found which the subject seems to find difficult to refute. In the end the judge will most likely accept any honest confession drawn from the subject's general sense of guilt, and he will no longer attempt to ascertain facts relevant to the matters confessed to even if some of the confessed facts are incongruous or absurd. If the judge senses, however, that the confession is dishonest, in the sense of being merely an attempt by the prisoner to please him, he will probably be genuinely outraged and continue his efforts to find some basis for guilt which will elicit from the prisoner a genuine confession.

THE PRISONER'S EXPERIENCE OF GUILT

We shall assume at the outset that all socialized people experience a substantial amount of guilt when their behavior, desires, or feelings conflict with the dictates of the moral code or value system they have adopted or when they have not fulfilled some of the expectations held by themselves or by others. Because of their personal history and/or culture some people have stronger drives or make stronger moral demands on themselves than others; they therefore experience sharper conflicts and are consequently more guilt-prone than others.

Feelings of guilt are stimulated in the prison situation, both intentionally and inadvertently, by the exacerbation of old conflicts or the creation of new ones. For example, the prison regimen, whether handcuffs and ankle chains are used or not, makes the adult as dependent as a child and arouses some of the childhood conflicts, particularly around problems of authority. Or weakly held values are strengthened by continual emphasis until they begin to conflict with other values, as in the case of the priest for whom the value of unselfishness was sharpened to such a degree that it began to conflict with all efforts on his part to express any self-interest in the service of survival.

The prisoner can come to accept guilt on any one or more of the bases argued "logically" by the agents because he does begin to experience guilt in some form. This guilt may be felt primarily as guilt-anxiety, in which case the feeling is present but no psychological basis for it is perceived by the prisoner; or it may be consciously perceived to be related to one or more of the following areas of psychological functioning:

1. *Social Guilt.* A recognition on the part of the prisoner that much of what he has had in life has not been earned but has been given to him by accident of birth; thus for a middle-class person to have prejudices against the members of the lower class arouses guilt when he discovers that, in a sense, he has not earned but merely been given his middle-class status.

2. *Ego or Identity Guilt.* A recognition on the part of the prisoner that he has failed to live up to his image of himself.

3. *Persona Guilt.* The feeling of guilt which comes from wearing a mask, from the discovery or recognition of having deliberately or involuntarily deceived another person about oneself, for example, by playing the role of a guilty person while holding reservations.

4. *Loyalty Guilt.* A recognition on the part of the prisoner that he has failed in his service to a group with which he is strongly identified or has violated its norms or defiled its image by behaving in a manner not consistent with what is expected of members of that group.

5. *Situational Guilt.* Guilt which is aroused by the magnification on the part of others of minor infractions or petty acts which normally do not run counter to the prisoner's basic values or self-image, particularly when they are perceived to have been stimulated by great stress; feelings of guilt in reference to such acts imply that the prisoner has already accepted some of the norms and standards of evaluation of the cellmates and authorities.

These types of guilt are not logically discrete but are important to distinguish if one is to understand some of the psychological processes which characterized the influence process in our subjects. In the remainder of this chapter we shall attempt to illustrate each of these types of guilt by quoting or paraphrasing some of the statements made by our subjects concerning their prison experience.

Social Guilt

"Basically, I guess I always felt superior to the Negro. I didn't realize it before, but when I looked back on it from the prison situation, I could see it clearly."

"I realized that I had never done anything for society."

"What I came for [to China] was not so much to study, but to have a good time with the embassy set. To go to parties, and to make my dollar count in a country where help and housing was cheap."

"About ten years ago I was full of ideas of social climbing. I wanted to do some outstanding work so that I might acquire a distinguished social position. I wished to be above other people."

"We've always lived entirely for ourselves—not for others."

These paraphrased statements, taken from recent interviews, illustrates most directly what we mean by social guilt. The Communists tried to convince their prisoners that they had actually "harmed the people," or intended harm to them, or had at some time in their lives, as members of a more privileged class, intentionally or unconsciously taken advantage of others, because of inferior "class" status. The struggle meetings, both group criticism and self-criticism sessions, were designed to recall instances of such guilty behavior.

In his recollections, one American repatriate mentions how all foreigners living in China had at least subconscious feelings of superiority to the Oriental. He cites instances where even the unpretentious missionary family from which he came felt itself superior and, despite its low standard of living (lower than that of other foreigners), exploited the Chinese. Today he describes with pleasure, but also with considerable guilt, the gay, luxurious life of the foreign students, the parties, the hobnobbing with the intellectual, social, and political elite of the city.

Even one of the least guilt-prone of our subjects eventually became vulnerable to a sense of social guilt. For two years he had been in prison resisting influence, although making certain behavioral concessions. He recounts how, no matter what the agents tried, he continued to feel no guilt until a general personality crisis was precipitated which led him to "recognize" and accept social guilt.

As I continued my analysis I realized even more how my egotism had slowly developed to where I was incapable of seeing anything which was not to my advantage and where I was oblivious to the plight of others. I remembered how . . . I had looked with revulsion on the poverty around us when I arrived in China. One morning in November, 1948, we had stepped out of the gate of a friend's house where we had spent the night, to find a man stretched out dead on the doorstep, obviously starved to death. It was a shock to both of us and had brought an ugly note into a bright morning. Reflecting on my attitude that day, I realized now that the little sympathy I had felt for the man had been more overshadowed by annoyance over my day being spoiled in such a way. My attitude toward the Korean War had shown the same brutal disregard for the lives of others on a much larger scale.

This subject did not accept "social" guilt before this crisis, not only because he was not particularly guilt-prone but also because he had come from an underdog family, whose sufferings during the depression had made a deep impression on him. As his self-analysis continued, he was led to see the "selfishness" flaw in his character, and thus became ready to accept "social" guilt.

Though never a spy in our terms, he said:

Not wanting to harm others was no excuse at all, since a person totally blinded by his own self-interest is incapable of thinking of others, to begin with. If I had not been so blind, I would have been able to see long ago the fallacy in my supposition that my espionage activities had been of service to my country.

Having one's innermost self brought out and dissected under the glaring light of self-criticism was a shattering experience, but the resulting recognition of myself made me determined to overcome the weaknesses in my character which had been the cause of those former mistakes. Thus began the struggle with myself which was to last throughout the rest of my stay in prison and, indeed, goes on even today.

The creation and exploitation of social guilt were possible with almost every prisoner who had already been successfully weakened by other means, even if he was not initially guilt-prone. One reason, among others, is that some evidence of having felt superior can always be dug out and turned into such guilt. The intellectual is vulnerable to accusations such as "you don't mix with the common man; you don't even speak his language." The missionaries who went to China to bring Christianity to the people sometimes lived better than the masses "for whom they were supposed to be an example." If this argument was not convincing, it was pointed out to the missionary that he undoubtedly felt some superiority over the un-Christianized heathens.

Thus to have had a feeling of social guilt and to have acknowledged it was to accept some version of this argument: if I have shown a lack of social awareness and have taken no global social responsibility; if I have been prejudiced toward a minority group; if I have felt superior toward anyone because of class origin, in fact felt superior *at all;* if I have been so concerned with my own life as to be unaware of the interests of others or have been too concerned with my own status and ambitions to do things for others, I have been guilty of "a crime against the people."

Ego or Identity Guilt

". . . Once you have made a false confession you lose heart and self-confidence. If they get you to make another confession, then that lowers resistance even more."

The interviewer asked him, "Why did you make a false confession?"

He said, "Because I thought I would get out if I gave them what they wanted; I thought I would try it." (Apparently the first time he actually tried this was about four months after his imprisonment.)

The interviewer asked what he had confessed to, and he didn't want to tell but later in the conversation it came up. His lie was that he named some sort of organization, which he had made up, for which he had worked. Then he discovered that they had lied to him by telling him that if he made a confession he would get out; and then they didn't release him once they had gotten it. From that time on he decided he was not going to make a false confession.

But because he had once made a false confession he began to lose faith in himself. "Why had I given in, why had I lied?" he asked himself. . . . "There is something *degrading* about lying about yourself."

Because this confession undermined this man's self-image of being special, different, even heroic, it drastically lowered his self-esteem. It undermined his self-esteem not only because he had lied but also because he had been unable to resist. Each time he was forced to give in again (he confessed and retracted three or four times), his guilt increased. As his guilt increased, his self-esteem was lowered and his ability to resist making false confessions and believing them became increasingly undermined.

In his explanation of ego guilt he repeated, perhaps without realizing it, the theme: If only I had been what *I thought I was* I would have been able to resist. After having fought so hard and long to resist, and then having given in because he just wanted the pressure to stop, he could not face the idea that he was so weak as to give in, that he could be willing to lie "just" to relieve the discomfort. Perhaps he began to believe in his own guilt, as argued by the agent, because it was more bearable to believe that he really was a spy and had confessed justifiably than to believe that he was making false confessions about himself just to relieve the unceasing pressures of the agent. It was this man who said on release in Hong Kong:

I knew in the first place that I was guilty. In order to gain self-respect, one has to confess.

Ego or identity guilt is thus produced by eliciting from the prisoner behavior which is inconsistent with his self-image, by degrading him and/or provoking him into degrading behavior. One priest's attempt to resist such pressure is indicated in the following statement:

As soon as the door opens we file off quickly to the washing-room at the end of the corridor. With only six or seven places there, we have to wait for our turn. Soap may not be used. You just dip your towel in the trough and pass it over your face and hands. There's a time allowance of two minutes and no more for all the fifteen of us, since twenty eight other cells on this floor have to get through their ablutions in the course of the hour. We come and go back to our cell with the bowed heads of sentenced criminals, though no one has been condemned. The Communist technique sets much store on the outward sign. By subjecting the body to the posture of guilt, the spirit is moulded and brought into a responsiveness indistinguishable from that of domestic animals. That's what's wanted of everyone in the Communist regime. But why does my good friend, Number 1052, bend down lower than the rest, and outdo all by the exaggerated abjection of his posture? It hurts me every time I see this. The line I have adopted is "submissively nonconformist." I keep my eyes cast down like a nun, so that it's impossible to accuse me of breaking the rules by looking about. But I simply won't bow my head. Yet, apart from an occasional "telling-off," I have been left alone in my obstinacy.[3]

The use of handcuffs and ankle chains as punishment for refusal to confess of course insures degradation and dependency and thereby strongly heightens the probability of ego guilt. The provocation of behavior inconsistent with a man's image of himself is also made easier by the fact that in the intimacy of cell life it is not difficult for cell mates to discover those points on which a fellow prisoner is vulnerable.

One of our subjects after a long period of resistance started to make "concessions" in the form of confessions but he did not believe in any of the behavior he had confessed to, i.e., did not feel he had committed any crimes by his own standards. The close relationships which developed in the group cell and the constant argument and harangue from the interrogator led gradually to an intellectual acceptance of the Chinese Communist semantics and to some identification with cell mates, expressed most clearly in his calling his cell "a sort of home." The cell mates were the first Chinese that the subject felt he had ever known intimately.

Identification with his cell mates made it easier for this man to accept the validity of their definitions of crime. Gradually the acceptance of their definitions led to a habit of conceptualizing his activities and thoughts in terms of them. Finally he came to accept the point of view that he had been guilty of espionage, but then discovered in a newspaper article that repatriated POW's from Korea who had allegedly been brainwashed had been sent to Valley Forge "mental hospital," and concluded that if he stuck to his confession of espionage he would spend the rest of his days following release in an American mental hospital. To avoid this future possibility he decided to rewrite his confession in such a way as to make it seem harmless from an American point of view, and then settled down to await its acceptance by the authorities. After he had waited two months he was called before the investigating judge, at which time he offered to rewrite the confession again in the hope of finding a compromise version which would both be acceptable to the Chinese and get him off the hook with the United States. He was met with "cold hostility" and an order to get back to his cell and was most upset by the loathing and disgust in the voice of the judge. He

[3]A. Bonnichon, "Cell 23—Shanghai," *The Month* (1955), p. 4.

suddenly felt he had been caught red-handed; until then no one and no experience had presented him with direct "proof" of his flaws.

The feeling of having been dishonest with the Chinese made the subject wonder about the core of his character, whether he had any principles at all, and led to a determination to find the causes for his developing the way he had "or he would never have confidence in himself again." For this subject the crisis was precipitated by his acceptance of certain standards of honesty and sincerity *defined by the Chinese cell mates,* and it is these standards he had failed to live up to in his own eyes, in contrast to the first subject mentioned in this section to whom the false confession meant something entirely different. The subject was guilty because his motives for rewriting his confession were selfish, regardless of the truth or falsity of its contents, and because he was acting selfishly he was failing to live up to a self-image of helping "the people." This conflict at the surface must have made contact with a deeper conflict and must have elicited guilt which was attached to impulses and deeds stemming from his earlier life. We cannot guess what these were, but it is clear that the prisoner was able to use the crisis provoked in the prison situation to re-examine more fundamental aspects of his character and to "reform" some of them.

In conclusion, ego or identity guilt, if it was elicited by the imprisonment experience, could range from being relatively superficial to being quite deep and could be the basis for other guilt feelings such as social guilt. To the extent that basic identity components in the prisoner became involved in the intrapsychic conflict the experience of thought reform could lead to fundamental personality or character change.

Persona or Face-to-Face Guilt

"Isolation would have been heaven in that prison. . . . I dreaded it when the others would come [back to the cell] . . . because I knew I would have no peace. . . . Don't mention the word 'help' to me. I never want to hear that again. I had to watch myself, because they would jump on everything I said. But I couldn't avoid saying something, because I just couldn't sit back and withdraw. I'm just that way."

"I'd prepare some answer hours in advance so that I could use [it] if they asked me what I was thinking . . . and I'd feel guilty when I didn't reveal my true opinion, but used a phoney one to make them stop. . . . I'd feel miserable when, after really having made a sincere effort, they didn't believe me. . . . Of course everyone else was *playing a game* of accusations and self-criticism. . . . It was just because everyone was forced to do it. . . . I knew people were forced to play roles. . . . Still I'd feel guilty about playing my roles."

"You could never tell who was play-acting and who wasn't and you couldn't make any kind of a judgment. You didn't have any kind of a relationship with anyone . . . They were not speaking to *you*, they were speaking to *the confessed you* [the masked "you"]. . . . There was no one we could trust. And you always thought someone was going to inform. But there was one person— a cell mate—with whom I once talked . . . we spoke one night when everyone was asleep and he said to me. 'This is the first time I felt that someone didn't speak to me in a role.' He said, 'I am innocent, should I try to make up a crime, do you think it would be a good strategy if I confessed to something, then they will think I have confessed and they will let me go?" Then I answered him frankly and I said, "You must not make any kind of false confession. You must stick to the truth; otherwise you are going to get all confused.' "

This was the only honest conversation and the only private conversation he ever had with anyone in his three and one half years in prison.

Persona or face-to-face guilt is the feeling of guilt which comes from wearing a mask, or from deliberately playing a role which one is aware is not congruent with the self; in short, which comes from deceiving others about oneself. In prison, persona guilt most often resulted when the prisoner, in order to reduce the continued pressure to reform, deliberately began to act as if he were someone he was not, or pretended to opinions which were not his own. In the model reform prison specializing in group struggle meetings, all prisoners were forced initially to wear verbal masks.

This face-to-face deception was more bearable to some than to others. One subject to whom close personal relationships, even with the resented cell mates, were crucial, saw in this type of guilt one of the major stresses of imprisonment. Another subject refers merely to the "embarrassment" of having to manufacture beliefs he did not have. A third subject was hardly affected by this type of deception because he approached human relationships primarily on an intellectual plane: people to him were not really individuals but personified abstractions with whom one relates through ideas (words). In the prison situation, with all his companions hidden behind masks, he was doubly removed from them. Their verbal masks obliterated any clue to their true selves; they were not real people with whom one could have any relationships. Given this definition of the situation and relationships, this prisoner was quite impervious to the group struggle meetings and to cell mate pressures since the screaming, kicking, spitting, and verbal assault came from "ciphers," not real people.

Thus susceptibility to persona or face-to-face guilt depended on the meaning which deception had for the person, how significant others were for him as persons to be concerned about, and how important it was for the person to obtain confirmation of his "real" self from the others in the prison environment.

Loyalty Guilt

For an instant, as he stood there, looking out over the street from a window high in Loukawei Prison, there came to him without warning so great a desire to get out of prison that he almost cried out. It would be simple, really. All he had to do was say the word. One single word in answer to one single question and this whole dreadful nightmare existence would come to an end, so that he could walk down a street and be able to turn whichever way he wanted at the corner.

And then there arose in his mind the faces and names of people whom he knew and loved: priests and laymen who had calmly put their lives and freedom on the line, students who had with wide open eyes taken the deliberate step of depriving themselves of a career and the possibility of a decent livelihood, women who had stood dry-eyed and proud as their men, their sons, their brothers, had been marched off to jail, to slave labor camps, to the firing squad. He saw his Chinese fellow Jesuits boldly speaking out against the Red tyranny, knowing that when they went, they would not come back without breaking. "If I do come out, and say anything different from what I have said before and am saying now, have nothing to do with me. . . ."

Shaken and almost sick at the thought of how close he had come to betraying himself and his friends, Father Phillips turned away from the window and moved back toward the door.[4]

Loyalty guilt resulted from behavior, thoughts, or feelings which the prisoner felt to be a violation of the norms of important reference or membership groups or which would sully the image which others held of that group. Thus a priest felt guilty if he committed any actions which were unpriestlike, Marine POW's in Korea felt guilty if they committed un-Marinelike acts, imprisoned Communist sympathizers felt guilty if they were accused of harming rather than helping the people, cell members felt guilty if they violated the norms of the prison cell (assuming they had become identified with it) by refusing to reform themselves. Just as the prison situation could provoke behavior inconsistent with the person's image of himself, so it could provoke behavior inconsistent with his group membership (for example, provoking a priest into a fist fight over some cell privileges). Clearly loyalty guilt and ego guilt overlap to the extent that the person's image of himself to a large extent reflects his perceptions of group membership and identification. A distinction between the two is useful, however, because the subjects themselves distinguished quite sharply between the feelings which resulted from violation of self-image and those which resulted from letting down important others. Perhaps loyalty guilt can be thought of as ego guilt plus something more—a sense of failure in someone else's eyes as well as one's own.

[4]K. Becker, *I Met a Traveler: The triumph of Father Phillips* (New York: Farrar, Strauss and Cudahy, 1958).

Situational Guilt

All our subjects made some reference to their commission of "petty" acts which their cell mates would catch and exaggerate into an indication of a great bourgeois flaw. From every prison come stories of "great crimes" by Western prisoners—occasional slightly uneven distribution of food or blankets, petty stealing or cheating, accidental use of another's soap, inadvertent selfishness, and so on. This behavior was identified as serious signs of old bourgeois immorality which warranted the moral outrage and sharp attack of the entire cell group. A man who turned a little too far out of "his space" during sleep was told that he did not do so accidentally but because he was selfish. Any "error," even if it did not remotely involve a serious breach of major values, was not overlooked. It was caught, dwelt on, and exaggerated. Thus, no matter how much he tried to get along, the prisoner was likely to find himself being accused of one thing or another all day and night long. The entire prison environment was characterized by constant accusation, making it highly likely that some form of guilt would be stimulated even in the prisoner who was initially not very guilt-prone.

CONCLUSIONS

Regardless of its psychological basis, once guilt was felt the subject became more prone to accepting one or more of the many arguments of the agent concerning his *objective* guilt. The prisoner's subsequent willingness to confess then resulted from his need to attach his feelings of guilt to behavior or thoughts which the authorities sanctioned as crimes, not from having been "broken." In the case of social, persona, or situational guilt his subjectively felt shortcoming coincided with the objectively defined crimes; in the case of ego or loyalty guilt the subject may have been influenced because it was easier for him to accept psychologically the objective crimes he was accused of, and the belief system which defined these as crimes, than to face the weakness in himself which allowed the guilt-provoking behavior to occur in the first place. In the case of guilt-anxiety where the psychological conflict itself was unconscious, the same mechanism may of course have applied, in that the prisoner may have accepted objectively defined crimes and attached his guilt to them to prevent his unconscious conflicts from becoming conscious.[5]

[5] J. A. M. Meerloo, *The Rape of the Mind* (Cleveland: World Publishing Co., 1956).

We have treated the topic of guilt as an unfreezing force in some detail because it was undoubtedly one of the central forces motivating the prisoner to change. We wish to reiterate, however, that guilt was not the only force acting on the prisoner tending to unfreeze him; other forces could also start an influence process. On the other hand, the degree of susceptibilty to guilt varied sharply from prisoner to prisoner, and many prisoners had effective defenses against guilt which tended to prevent guilt feelings from precipitating major behavior and/or belief changes. Not all prisoners who experienced guilt were unfrozen by it and subsequently influenced. Many of them, like Father Phillips, quoted at the beginning of the section on loyalty guilt, used the small quantity of guilt which the *thought* of giving in stimuated as a defense against actually giving in. Others defended themselves by the usual mechanisms of repression, denial, rationalization, etc., at the psychological level, and by logical argument, or simple refusal to listen at the level of interaction with the agents.

HOW TO CHANGE BEHAVIOR*

Timothy Leary

It is my plan to talk to you tonight about methods of effecting change—change in man's behavior and change in man's consciousness.

Behavior and Consciousness. Please note the paired distinction. Behavior and Consciousness. Up until recently, I considered myself a behavioral scientist and limited the scope of my work to overt and measurable behavior. In so doing I was quite in the *Zeitgeist* of modern psychology. Studying the subject matter which our American predecessors defined some fifty years ago. Behavior. Routinely following the group rules they laid down. Scrupulously avoiding that which is most important to the subject: his consciousness. Concentrating, instead, on what is most important to us who seek to

*Timothy Leary, "How to Change Behavior" (lecture delivered at the International Congress of Applied Psychology, 14th Session, Copenhagen: August 18, 1961) in *Clinical Psychology*, (ed.) G. S. Nielsen, Vol. 4, Proceedings (Copenhagen: Munksgaard, 1962), pp. 50–68. (Reprinted with slight revision and expanded footnotes—IFIF, Reprints Division, Cambridge 38, Mass.)

observe, measure, manipulate, control and predict—the subject's overt behavior.

This decision to turn our backs on consciousness is, of course, typically Western and very much in tune with the experimental, objective bent of Western science. Professor Huston Smith of the Massachusetts Institute of Technology has pointed out some basic differences between the Western approach and the philosophies of China and India. Differences which have some importance for the applied psychologist concerned with behavior change. Professor Smith reminds us that our Western culture has stressed measurement and control of objects, whereas China has historically emphasized the rules of the social encounter, and Indian philosophy the development and expansion of human consciousness. Tonight I speak to you from a point midway between the western and eastern hemispheres of the cortex, presenting a theory and method which is Chinese in that behavior is seen as an intricate social game; Indian in its recognition of consciousness and the need to develop a more cosmic awareness; and finally Western in its concern to do good measurably well.

I plan to present, first, some thoughts on behavior change, then some new conceptions of consciousness and its alteration, and finally some data from recent research in these areas.

BEHAVIOR AND ITS CHANGE

Except for reflexes and instinctual reactions and random muscular movements (which fall into the province of physiology), all behavior is learned.

Behavior is therefore artifactual and culturally determined. Behavior sequences might usefully be considered as game sequences.

The use of the word "game" in this sweeping context is likely to be misunderstood. The listener may think I refer to "play" as opposed to the stern, real-life, serious activities of man. But, as you shall see, I consider the latter as "game."

At this point you are asking for and you deserve a definition. What do I mean by game? A game is a learned cultural sequence characterized by six factors:

1. *Roles:* A game assigns roles to the human beings involved.
2. *Rules:* A game sets up a set of rules which hold only during the game sequence.
3. *Goals:* Every game has its goal or purpose. The goals of baseball are to score more runs than the opponents. The goals of the game of psychology are more complex and less explicit, but they exist.

4. *Rituals:* Each game has its conventional behavior pattern not related to the goals or rules, but yet quite necessary to comfort and continuance.
5. *Language:* Each game has its jargon, unrelated to the rules and goals and yet necessary to learn and use.
6. *Values:* Each game has its standards of excellence or goodness.

Baseball and basketball have clearly definable roles, rules, rituals, goals, languages and values. Psychology, religion, politics are games, too: learned, cultural sequences with clearly definable roles, rules, rituals, goals, jargons, values. They are less explicitly formulated than the so-called sports and therein, dear friends, lies the pity. For this simple reason millions have died, and we may die tomorrow.

The behavior which psychiatrists label as disease entities can be considered as games, too. Dr. Thomas Szasz, the distinguished psychoanalyst-philosopher, in his book, *The Myth of Mental Illness,* suggests that "hysteria" is the name we give to a certain doctor-patient game involving deceitful helplessness. The "bluff" in poker is a similar deceitful but perfectly legitimate game device. Psychiatry, according to this model, is a behavior-change game.

Far from being frivolous, many so-called "play-games" are superior in their behavioral science and in their behavior-change techniques to the "not-called games" such as psychiatry and psychology.

In terms of the epistemology and scientific method employed, the "game" of American baseball is superior to any of the so-called behavioral sciences. Baseball officials have classified and they reliably record molecular behavior sequences (the strike, the hit, the doubleplay, etc.). Their compiled records are converted into indices most relevant for summarizing and predicting behavior (RBI, runs batted in; ERA, earned run average, etc.). Baseball employs well-trained raters to judge those rare events which are not obviously and easily coded. Their raters are called umpires.

When we move from behavior science to behavior-change, we see that baseball experts have devised another remarkable set of techniques for bringing about the results which they and their subjects look for: coaching. Baseball men understand the necessity for sharing time and space with their learners, for setting up role models, for feedback of relevant information to the learner, for endless practice of the desired behavior. And most important of all, baseball scientists understand the basic, cosmic lesson of percentage: that the greatest player gets, on the average, one hit in three tries; the winning team loses at least one game in three; and no team can lead the league every year, neither Rome, nor Athens, nor London, nor Moscow, nor Washington. Those who wish to measure, summarize, predict, and change human behavior could do worse than model themselves after this so-called "game."

All behavior involves learned games. But only that rare Westerner we call "mystic," or who has had a visionary experience of some sort, sees clearly the game structure of behavior. Most of the rest of us spend our time struggling with roles and rules and goals and concepts of games which are implicit and confusedly not seen as games. Trying to apply the roles and rules and rituals of one game to other games.

Worst of all is the not-knowing that it is a game. Baseball is a clean and successful game because it is seen as a game. You can shift positions. You know the game is limited in space and in time. You know how you are doing. You sign your contract. You renew your contract. You can quit. Start a new game.

Cultural stability is maintained by keeping the members of any cultural group from seeing that the Roles, Rules, Goals, Rituals, Language, and Values are game structures. The family game is treated by most cultures as far more than a game, with its implicit contracts, limited in time and space. The nationality game. It is treason not to play. The racial game. The religious game. And that most treacherous and tragic game of all, the game of individuality. The ego game. The Timothy Leary game. Ridiculous how we confuse this game, overplay it. Our own mystics and the Eastern philosophers have been warning us about this danger for centuries.

Cultural institutions encourage the delusion that the games of life are inevitable givens involving natural laws of behavior. These fixed delusions tend to rigidify behavior patterns. This rigidity, as Professor Osgood pointed out in his significant opening address to the Copenhagen Congress, now threatens the very survival of the human species itself.[1]

So now we come to behavior change. The currently popular method of behavior change is called psychotherapy. A medical game. A curing of the psyche. Psychotherapy interprets confusion and inefficiency in game-playing as illness. We call it sickness and attempt to cure it employing the medical game. Consider the football player who doesn't know the rules. Perhaps he picks up the ball and runs off the field. He is punished for not playing the game correctly. He feels badly. Shall we pronounce him sick and call the doctor?

[1]C. E. Osgood, "Towards International Behavior Appropriate to a Nuclear Age," in *Psychology and International Affairs,* Proceedings of the XIV International Congress of Applied Psychology (Copenhagen: Munksgaard, 1962), Vol. 1, pp. 109–32.

The failure to understand the game nature of behavior leads to confusion and eventually to helplessness. Helplessness. Let's look at this word for a moment. It's a big concept in understanding science, technology, rehabilitation and, for that matter, the working of the mind itself.

The basic aim of physical science is to reduce human helplessness in the face of the physical environment. Physical science has other goals, of course. To understand, explain, control, measure, predict. But certainly these are ends rather than means. Why explain? Why predict? To lessen fearful ignorance. The technologies which have grown up around the physical sciences, engineering, medicine, also take as their goal the reducing of human helplessness.

Do they not stem from the same survival motive? And the social technologies—psychiatry, social work, applied psychology. Is not their goal the reduction of confusion and the increase in human freedom?

Judged by these criteria the game of Western science has not been a glorious success. Our helplessness in the face of physical disease has certainly diminished. Our control over natural forces has given us a sense of mastery. We live longer and healthier lives. Good.

We have created a game model—the subject-object model—which allows us, on the one hand, to dominate "objects" but which has created a world full of human objects. Most of what we do in the name of science results in more and greater human helplessness.

The science game creates wonder drugs whose action is not understood by the user. And worse yet we turn over these drugs to those who play the doctor-game, the medical game—whose roles, rules, rituals, language, goals and values place the patient into a passive object-status.

The science game, the healing game, the knowledge game are magnificent human structures. They are our proudest game accomplishments. But they are great only as long as they are seen as game. When they go beyond this point, the trouble begins. Claims to a non-game reality status. The emergency of experts, professionals, priests, status-favored authorities. Claims to power and control and priority. Look at the A.E.C. Look at the A.M.A. And watch out! At this point you will find that games which began with the goal of decreasing human helplessness end up increasing it.

Human beings inhabiting those areas of the globe which the geographic game calls East are, for the most part, well aware of the foregoing issues. It's hard for Westerners to back away and see the artifactual game structures. We are so close to our games. We have been born into them. And we are born into a philosophic system which glorifies hierarchical expertise on the one hand and helplessness on the other. Monotheism, the Judaic-Christian tradition. Monotheism, that game started by a few persecuted outcasts (game losers) in the mid-eastern desert: the subject-object game. The false duality game, the manipulating, predicting, controlling game. Monotheism breeding helplessness.

Now. Let's apply this general discussion of helplessness and the behavior game to the issue of behavior change. In spite of our apparent executive control over nature we have had small success in developing behavior-change games. Indeed most of our attempts to change behavior increase human helplessness, lessen human freedom and thereby exaggerate the problem we set out to solve. Our behavior-change games invariably set up structures which give more power to the few and less power to the many. Invidious role models. Doctor-patient. Professor-student. Inequitable rules involving secrecy and control. The one-upmanship language we call jargon.

When people come to us and ask us to change their behavior, why can't we do it? Why can't we teach them to see the game structure of human society? The problem seems simple enough. Why can't we find out what games they are caught up in? Find out what games they want to commit themselves to. Make them explicit. Help them discover the rules of the game. The roles. The rituals. The goals. The concepts. Expose them to models of successful gameplaying. Encourage them to practice. Feed back objective appraisals of their performance. Care for them and their game struggles. How do you care for them? You share time and space with them. Nothing else can substitute. We have little else to offer. If we don't, they'll learn the games of those who do share time and space. If they're prisoners, then who will teach them behavior games? Who shares the most time and space with prisoners? That's right, the other prisoners, older criminals and younger criminals. So who influences behavior in what direction? And who shares the most amount of time and space with prisoners? That's right, the prison guards who in most American prisons teach them how to play the role of robber in the game of "cops and robbers." And we professional middle-class experts? How much time and space do we share with the prisoners? An hour a week on the medical ward?

O.K. It sounds simple enough, doesn't it? Just show people that their social identity and their entire cultural commitment is a game. They aren't aware of it. Sure, just tell them.

Yes, you smile when I say this. It's not quite that easy, is it? Here's the rub. Few people, a very few people (and we Westerners call them mystics) are willing and able to admit that the game is game. Most of our people become upset and even angry when the game is identified. The game of "I-and-all-I-stand-for."

At this point when you hear the word "mystic," you may be uneasily wondering if you are going to be subjected to a vague metaphysical discourse on general principles. Perhaps you will be surprised to hear me suggest the hypothesis that the most effective approach to the "practical" games of life is that of applied mysticism. Identify the game structure of the event. Make sure that you do not apply the rules and concepts of other games to this situation. Move directly to solve the problem, avoiding abstractions and irrelevant rituals. A mystic Martian or a person from a different culture might be an excellent consultant for a behavioral problem. They might be able to cut through irrelevant game-rules to what is most relevant to survival and peace of mind.

How can we make the point? How can we learn the lesson? How can we Westerners come to see that our own consciousness is infinitely greater than our little egos and the ego games into which we are so blindly caught up? That the universe within our skulls is infinitely more than the flimsy game-world which our words and minds create?

Put in a sentence—the task is to see that the mind is a tiny fragment of the brain-body complex. It is the game-playing fragment—a useful and entertaining tool but quite irrelevant to survival and indeed usually antagonistic to well-being.

The process of getting beyond the game structure, beyond the subject-object commitments, the dualities—this process is called the mystic experience. The visionary experience is the non-game, meta-game experience. Change in behavior can occur with dramatic spontaneity once the game structure of behavior is seen. The visionary experience is the key to behavior change.

CONSCIOUSNESS AND ITS CHANGE

How do we obtain the visionary state?

There are many methods for expanding consciousness beyond the game limits. Mr. Aldous Huxley this afternoon presented a scholarly history of the same classic and modern methods. Margaret Mead, the American anthropologist, has suggested several cross-cultural

methods. Have a psychotic episode. (This is to say, just stop playing the social game for a while and they'll call you insane, but you
may learn the great lesson.) Or expose yourself to some great trauma
that shatters the gamesmanship out of you. Birth by ordeal is a well
documented phenomenon. The concentration camp experience has
done this for some of our wisest men. Physical traumas can do it.
Electric shock. Extreme fatigue. Live in another and very different
culture for a year where your roles and rituals and language just
don't mean a thing. Or separate yourself from the game-pressure
by institutional withdrawal. Live for a while in a monastic cell. Or
marry a Russian. Sensory deprivation does it. Sensory deprivation
cuts through the game.

Certain forms of sensory stimulation alter consciousness beyond
games. The sexual orgasm is certainly the most frequently and natural, although so brief and so built into interpersonal courtship
games that it has lost much of its mystical meaning in the West. We
have recently learned from W. Grey Walter[2] and William Burroughs
about photostimulation as a means of consciousness alteration. Concentrated attention to a stroboscope or flicker apparatus can produce visionary experiences.

The most efficient way to cut through the game structure of Western life is the use of drugs. Consciousness-expanding drugs. From
here on I shall use the abbreviation CE to refer to consciousness-
expanding substances such as LSD, mescaline, psilocybin.

Now the reaction of the Western world to consciousness-expanding drugs is extremely interesting. We tend to apply our familiar
game roles, rituals, goals, rules, concepts to the non-game experience produced by these substances. Those of you who have not had
the shattering exposure to such old and worshipped plants as peyote
and the sacred mushroom and cannabis, or such startling newcomers
as psilocybin[3] and lysergic acid, will wonder at this point about the
nature of these experiences. What do these substances do? The
neuro-physiological answer—the answer from outside—to this question is not yet ready. The answer from the inside (from the awareness of the subject) can be cast in countless metaphors. Let's try
a physiological analogy. Let's assume that the cortex, the seat of

---

[2] W. Grey Walter, *The Living Brain* (N.Y.: W. W. Norton, 1953), p. 311. ("The
Norton Library," No. N 153, paperback, 1963.)

[3] Psilocybin is a synthetic of the active ingredients of the "sacred mushroom" of
Mexico. The divinatory mushroom was introduced to Western culture by Professor
Roger Heim of Paris and R. Gordon Wasson of New York and synthesized by Dr. A.
Hofmann of the Sandoz Laboratory in Basel, Switzerland, who is also known through
his work on lysergic acid. We are grateful to Sandoz, Ltd., for providing the research
materials used in these studies.

consciousness, is a millionfold network of neurons. A fantastic computing machine. Cultural learning has imposed a few, pitifully small programs on the cortex. These programs may activate perhaps one-tenth or one-hundredth of the potential neural connections. All the learned games of life can be seen as programs which select, censor, alert and thus drastically limit the available cortical response. (Mr. Aldous Huxley's reducing valves.)

The CE (i.e., consciousness-expanding) drugs unplug these narrow programs. They unplug the ego, the game-machinery, and the mind (that cluster of game-concepts). And with the ego and mind unplugged, what is left? Not the "id"; no dark, evil impulses. These alleged negative "forces" are, of course, part of the game, being simply anti-rules. What is left is something that Western culture knows little about. The open brain. The uncensored cortex, alert and open to a broad sweep. Huxley and Dr. Barron have told you in their own words what is left, and there is no need to add my lumbering prose.

There is need, however, to ask another question. Why is this ecstatic, brain-opening experience so strange and horrid to Western culture? Why have our ancestors and our colleagues tended to ignore and even to oppose the visionary experience? Mr. R. Gordon Wasson, banker, mycologist, anthropologist, gentleman-scholar-turned-mystic, has traced the persecution of the divine and divinatory mushroom back through the millennia.[4] Why the irrational fear so often aroused by research on CE drugs even to this day? Perhaps because our Western world is commited to over-playing the objective, external behavior game.

In particular we over-value the mind—that flimsy collection of learned words and verbal connections; the mind, that system of paranoid delusions with the learned self as center. And we eschew the non-mind, non-game intuitive insight-outlook which is the key to the religious experience, to the love experience.

We seem to oppose any process which puts our current games onto the long evolutionary timetable. This is a natural opposition and a healthy one. It is the greatest game of "the game" versus the "non-game." Behavior versus consciousness. The universal brain-body versus the cultural mind. The ego versus the species. A dialogue old and holy, like the dialogue of sea against land.

But this old game should be made explicit if it is to be fun. Unfortunately the West has no concepts for thinking and talking about

---

[4]Valentina Pavlovna Wasson and R. Gordon Wasson, *Mushrooms, Russia and History* (2 vols.; N.Y.: Pantheon Books, 1957), p. 435. (Out of print.)

this basic dialogue. There is no ritual for mystical experience, for the mindless vision. What should provoke intense and cheerful competition too often evokes suspicion, anger, impatience. What can be holy and intensely educational in the action of CE drugs on the cortex finds no ritual for application. This is to me one of the greatest challenges of our times.

The non-game visionary experiences are, I submit, the key to behavior change. Drug-induced *satori*. In three hours under the right circumstances the cortex can be cleared. The games that frustrate and torment can be seen in the cosmic dimension. But the West has no ritual, no game to handle the CE drug experience. In the absence of relevant rituals we can only impose our familiar games. The politics of the nervous system. The mind controlling the brain. Physicians seek to impose their game of control and prescription. The bohemians naturally strive to impose their games of back-alley secrecy. The police, the third member of the happy, symbiotic drug-triangle, naturally move in to control and prosecute.

Clearly we need new rituals, new goals, new rules, new concepts to apply and use these precious substances for man's welfare. To give the brain back to the species.

A group of investigators in the U.S. and Europe are now at work building up new games for the visionary experience. Trying to develop new roles, rules, rituals, concepts and values. While these will, of course, vary from group to group the goal remains constant—expansion of consciousness, freedom of the brain from the mind, freedom of the cortex for those centers—reticular (?) diencephalic (?) prefrontal (?)—which control, alert, censor and select what the cortex attends to. The work has hardly begun. This much is clear. The theory of the new game will be simple and basic. Space and time will be among the few variables required. Human equality will be a central principle, for the mystic experience tells us that the game differences between men are infinitely small compared with the age-old species similarities.

In our research endeavors we have developed eleven egalitarian principles based on the game nature of the human contract. Equality in determining role, rule, ritual, goal, language, commitment. Equality in the explicit contractual definition of the real, the good, the true, the logical.

Equality of the right to speak and to have access to relevant information. Any contract between men should be explicit about any temporary suspension of these equalities.

This past year at the Center for Research in Personality, Harvard

University, two research projects have attempted to put these egalitarian principles into operation. The first of these is a naturalistic study of drug-induced visions and the games which Americans impose on these new experiences. The second is a systematic study of the effects of consciousness-expanding drugs in a rehabilitation program. I hope that a description of these two projects will illustrate and clarify the preceding discussion.[5]

A NATURALISTIC STUDY OF PSILOCYBIN

The purpose of this study was to determine the effects of psilocybin when administered in a naturalistic, supportive setting; to observe the rituals and language imposed by Americans on an experience quite alien to their culture. One hundred and sixty-seven subjects were given the mushrooms; 43 female and 124 male. Of these, 26 were internationally distinguished intellectuals, scholars, artists; 10 were medical doctors; 73 were professional intellectuals, 21 were non-professional normals, 27 were drug addicts (psychological or physical), and 10 were inmates in a state prison.

The eleven principles for the human contract led to the following operations:

1. Participants alternated roles of observer and subject, i.e., the researchers took the drug with the subjects. The humanizing effect of this procedure cannot be over-estimated. Among other things, the subject-object issue is clearly settled.
2. Participants were given all available information about the drug. An atmosphere of mystery and secret experimentation was avoided.
3. Participants were given control of their own dosage. A maximum dosage was determined by the research team, and this maximum number of tablets was given to the subject, and he was free to dose himself at the rate and amount desired.
4. A comfortable, homelike environment was employed. The sterile impersonality of the laboratory was avoided.

---

[5]The Director of the Center for Research in Personality, Professor David C. Mc-Clelland, has provided these two projects with advice, support, and has labored to interpret our work to the non-visionary world. All American psychologists are indebted to Professor Henry A. Murray for his pioneer explorations into the human condition. From his neighborly presence, friendly interest and deep understanding of man's potentialities we have benefited. Dr. Frank Barron and Dr. Richard Alpert have been co-investigators in the mushroom research. Dr. W. Madison Presnell has lent psychiatric experience, administrative enthusiasm and clinical wisdom. George Litwin, James Ciarlo, Gunther Weil, Ralph Metzner, Ralph Schwitzgebel and Jonathan Shay have played important roles in charting the new realms of consciousness. Edward Travers, John Molinski, James Maloney, Frank Rafferty, Rodney Harrington, Henry Kinney, and Donald Levine have made significant contributions to the Concord project. Mr. George Litwin and his staff have taken responsibility for the computer analysis of the questionnaire data. Mrs. Pearl Chan, research administrator, has made things run.

5. Subjects were allowed to bring a relative or friend. No subject took the drug in a group where he was a stranger.

Three sets of data were obtained; questionnaires covering the reactions; written reports and tape recordings; observations by the research team.

While the results of this study are too extensive to summarize at this point, a few major conclusions can be stated: The psilocybin experience is pleasant and educational. Seventy-three per cent of our subjects reported the experience as "very pleasant" or ecstatic; ninety-five per cent thought the experience had changed their lives for the better.

Three out of four subjects reported happy and insightful reactions. When we recall that the drug was given only once under informal circumstances with no attempt to be therapeutic or problem-oriented, these data stimulate thoughts about the healing-educational possibilities of psilocybin. But how do these changes come about?

The most common reaction reported is the sudden perception of the effect of abstractions, rituals, learned game routines. Ecstatic pleasure at being temporarily freed from these limitations. A game-free honesty. Set and suggestive context account for ninety-nine per cent of the specific response to the drug. Thus you cannot sensibly talk about the effects of psilocybin. It's always the set and suggestive context triggered off by the drug. A fascinating tension between these two factors—set and context—inevitably develops. If both are positive and holy, then a shatteringly sacred experience results. If both are negative, then a hellish encounter ensues. There is, of course, the tendency for people to impose their familiar games onto the psilocybin experience. The more rigidly committed to the game, the stronger this tendency. If the drug-giving person is secure, flexible, supportive, then the experience is almost guranteed to be pleasant and therapeutic. Intensely deep communication occurs. Deep insights of a personal, social, and philosophic nature take place.

THE USE OF PSILOCYBIN IN A REHABILITATION PROGRAM

For many people, one or two psilocybin experiences can accomplish the goals of a long and successful psychotherapy. A deep understanding and game-free collaboration between participants plus insight. But what then? People vary tremendously in their readiness to move forward from this point. Many of the 167 subjects in our naturalistic study were able to exploit the close, honest relationship and the insight. They were already involved in rewarding games to which they could return with renewed vision and energy.

But many of our subjects came through the psilocybin experience with the knowledge that they were involved in non-rewarding games, caught in routines which they disliked. Some realized that they had no games they wanted to play. The "therapeutic" effect of the experience did not last for these subjects. Expanded consciousness narrowed back. They were left with pleasant memories of their visionary journey and nothing more.

After insight come the deeper questions as to the meaning of life. What games to play? Behavior change must follow change in consciousness.

Our research group is now committed to a series of investigations which seek to develop methods for perpetuating the positive effects of the psilocybin experience. Methods for helping the subject select and learn new games which give meaning to life.

The first of these projects concerned itself with the rehabilitation of inmates in a state prison. In helping prisoners we have of course found that the prisoners have rehabilitated us—changed our notions about crime, punishment, taught us about their games, made us see the limitations of our middle-class conceptions, expanded our consciousness and given deeper meaning to our lives.

Ten volunteer prisoners. A maximum security prison. The recidivism rate is 80 per cent. Eight of the ten would be expected back in prison a year after release. In baseball terms, eighty per cent is the error percentage our team attempted to lower.

After three orientation meetings with the prisoners the drug was given. I was the first one to take the drug in that bare hospital room behind barred windows. Three inmates joined me. Two psychologists and the other inmates served as observers—taking the drug three hours later. The psilocybin session was followed by three discussions. Then another drug session. Then more discussions. At this point the inmates have taken the drug an average of four times. There has been not one moment of friction or tension in some forty hours of egoless interaction. Pre-post testing has demonstrated marked changes on both objective and projective instruments. Dramatic decreases in hostility, cynicism, depression, schizoid ideation. Definite increases in optimism, planfulness, flexibility, tolerance, sociability.

The group has become a workshop for planning future games. Some prisoners are being trained to take over the function of research assistants. They are performing the tasks of a vocational guidance clinic—preparing occupational brochures for inmates about to be released, making plans to act as rehabilitation workers after their release, and to organize a half-way house for ex-convicts. Other prisoners are using their time to prepare for the games to which they will return—the family game, their old job.

The psilocybin experience made these men aware of the stereo-typed games in which they had been involved, the game of "cops and robbers," the game of being a tough guy, the game of outwitting the law, the game of resentful cynicism. "My whole life came tumbling down, and I was sitting happily in the rubble." But insight is the beginning, and the more demanding task is to help these men choose new games, help them learn the rules, the roles, the concepts, the rituals of the new game. Practical, collaborative reality-education. Of course, this phase of our work requires help from others. But the helpers get helped. The businessmen who help our inmates get jobs are invited into a new and exciting game which gives more meaning to their lives.

Our work progresses slowly and against strong opposition. Our new game of allowing criminals to take over responsibility and authority and prestige as experts on "crime and rehabilitation" brings us into game competition with the professional middle class. Anger and anxiety is aroused. Society has always produced and needed a criminal class. When criminals drop their roles and begin to play a different game, incredulous panic can ensue. Can society play its game without some men acting the part of criminals? If criminals are no longer criminals, where do the rest of us stand? The game of rehabilitator and client (i.e., a professional and a criminal) is being threatened. People are upset when their games are changed.

But our new game has begun. The game statistic for measuring success is clear-cut. Eighty per cent of convicts return to prison. Next season will reveal how well we have played our game.

SUMMARY

Let me summarize. We have been concerned with change in behavior and change in consciousness. It is considerably easier to change behavior if you understand the learned-game nature of behavior. This sort of insight can be brought about by the administration of conscious-expanding drugs, of which psilocybin is the most effective. But insight must be followed by behavior change. In the "rehabilitation game" we have been developing, the role of the helper is three-fold. He provides a serious, supportive context for the CE experience; sets up an atmosphere in which insight can quickly occur. He then joins with the subject in an all-out collaborative process of selecting and mastering new games. He keeps accurate records of his activities and those of his subjects so that the success of his game performance can be objectively appraised by his fellow men.

A final word of clarification. Those of us who talk and write about the games of life are invariably misunderstood. We are seen as frivolous or cynical anarchists tearing down the social structure. This is an unfortunate misapprehension. Actually, only those who see culture as a game, only those who take this evolutionary point of view, can appreciate and treasure the exquisitely complex magnificence of what human beings do and have done. To see it all as "serious, taken-for-granted reality" is to miss the point; is to derogate with bland passivity the greatness of the games we learn.

Those of us who play the game of "applied mysticism" respect and support good gamesmanship. You pick out your game. You learn the rules, rituals, concepts. You play fairly and cleanly. You don't confuse your games with other games. You do not impose your game rituals on others' games. You win today's game with humility. You lose tomorrow's game with dignity. Anger and anxiety are irrelevant because you see your small game in the context of the great evolutionary game which no one can win and no one can lose.

A NARRATIVE*

Dennis H. Lytle

Dave Spoffard will serve as an excellent example of a fraternity man for a typical four-year college experience. Dave was an outstanding student in high school, where he had graduated third in his class of seventy-six. In addition to his scholastic achievements, he had won a varsity letter in track, was president of the local chapter of a national scholastic honorary, and was voted most likely to succeed in his graduating class. He also had been awarded an MIT scholarship for one half of his freshman year's tuition.

*"A Narrative" reprinted in its entirety from an unpublished Bachelor's thesis by Dennis H. Lytle, "The Scholastic Problem in M.I.T. Fraternities," Massachusetts Institute of Technology, 1959. Used by permission.

Partially in response to the encouragement of an excellent general science instructor, Dave had developed technical interests early in his high school career. Even though he was not sure of the particular branch in which he was interested, Dave was convinced that engineering was the occupation that he wanted to pursue.

Dave knew only one person in Boston when he arrived for Rush Week, Jim Crosby. Jim was a senior, a member of a fraternity, and had traveled some 50 miles from his home during the summer to see Dave and his parents. It was largely because of Jim that Dave had decided to come to Rush Week. Dave and his parents had previously decided that a fraternity might not be the best thing for him, but Jim had maintained that this was based on experience with the fraternities of that area. He had assured them that fraternities at MIT were entirely different. He pointed out that fraternity costs were actually cheaper than the costs of dormitory living, and insisted that fraternities encouraged better scholarship by their freshmen than did the dormitories, both by having a minimum average for initiation and by providing upper-classmen tutors in freshman subjects.

Dave and his parents were favorably impressed by Jim, and so they decided that there would be no harm in Dave attending Rush Week, just to get a closer look at the fraternities. Both he and his parents thought that it might be best for Dave to spend some time in the dormitories before coming to a decision between the two, but the final decision was left up to Dave when he arrived at MIT.

Jim met Dave when his train came in and suggested that Dave use his fraternity house as a base of operations during Rush Week, explaining how convenient this would be, since he would be so much closer to the fraternities. The usual procedure was for the freshmen to stay in the dormitories, but they were located on the opposite side of the Charles River from the majority of the fraternities.

Dave saw eleven different fraternities during Rush Week. Everywhere he went he was treated like a king. He found several houses that he liked very much, but none of the others made him feel quite as much at home as Jim's fraternity. The thought of investigating the dormitories was very much present in his mind, but after talking to several men who had lived in the dormitories before pledging, he decided that the fraternities were definitely for him. From this point he did not take long to decide that, of the fraternities, Jim's was the place he wanted to spend his college days. Dave

pledged on the last day of Rush Week, and the members of Jim's
fraternity were so enthusiastic in their celebration that Dave was
overwhelmed, and he was even surer that he had made the correct
decision.

There was quite a party at the house that night, and the next
morning, which was the start of Freshman Week-end, there were
only a couple of brothers in addition to the new pledges at breakfast. Quite a few of the brothers went away during Freshman Week-
end, and the pledges stuck pretty much to themselves. Dave heard
several of the new pledges remark that there certainly was a let-
down after Rush Week, and he actually heard one say that he wasn't
sure that he had pledged the right house. The pledges had more
of a feeling of belonging, however, when the brothers returned for
the opening of school.

The first pledge meeting was held the second Wednesday after
school started. The Pledgemaster informed them that the meetings
would be held each Wednesday thereafter, and that quizzes would
be given each week on the material that had been assigned for
study. In addition, the pledges had to carry five nickels at all times
to give change to the brothers, to keep the soft drink machine filled
at all times, to answer the phone and doorbell on one ring, and to
keep the house scrapbook up to date. Each freshman was also required to spend Saturday afternoons working on the physical house.

When the Pledgemaster had finished, another brother, who was
introduced as the Scholastic Chairman, spoke for a few minutes
about the academic work that the freshmen were expected to do.
He explained that they were required to get a minimum term rating
of 2.5 to be eligible for initiation.

Later in the same week, a sophomore encouraged Dave to try to
be elected to the Freshman Council, which was made up of two
representatives from each freshman section. The sophomore explained that this was the place to meet the future leaders of the
class, and that it would not take up any more time than the individual desired since there were so many members. Dave ran and was
elected section leader from his section. The freshman council met
every Friday afternoon for a couple of hours. Dave did not take part
in any of the special committees, but he did attend most of the meetings to be able to represent his section.

When the winter track season started in November, Dave decided
to try out for the team, especially since he found out that freshman
sports could be used to fulfill the required athletic participation.

When his midterm grades were released, they were not as good as he had anticipated, but he was confident that he could improve them before the end of the term by spending a little more time on his studies. He figured out how much time he was spending on the various activities in which he was participating, and discovered that in addition to the time he spent in classes and preparation, he was spending an average of eight hours a week on pledge duties, eight hours a week on track, and two hours a week with the Freshman Council. In addition, there were only two Saturday nights in the term that he had not had a date. He decided that studying on Saturday evenings would be the only way that he would be able to improve his academic work and continue the activities in which he was participating.

Soon after he had started his program of Saturday evening study, several brothers mentioned that they noticed his new practice, and they strongly recommended that he reconsider. They maintained that a person cannot keep up the "grind" all the time without some relaxation and socializing on the week-ends. The brothers that spoke to Dave all had above average grades, and since they had more experience than he had, Dave thought that perhaps he had been a little too strict on himself, and decided to date a little more. Pretty soon, he was back in the habit of dating every Saturday night.

When the end of the first term was over, Dave was disappointed when his grades arrived. He had made B's in Chemistry and Engineering Drawing, C's in Calculus and Humanities, and a D in Physics, giving him a 3.1 term rating out of 5.0. He immediately resolved that this was not the quality of work with which he would be satisfied, and he was determined to perform better next term. He wrote this fact to his parents, whom he knew were disappointed. They replied that they were indeed disappointed, but that they were confident that he would do better the next term since he set his mind to it.

His plans for starting the second term off right were foiled by the fraternity's pre-initiation week activities which took the entire first week of school. The pledges had to perform many tasks, some of a constructive nature, like painting at a children's home, while others were not so constructive, like putting on skits for the benefit of the brothers. There were activities planned for all night every night, so the only sleep that the group got was during the day when they were away from the fraternity house. Following this week, the entire pledge class was initiated, and they all agreed that initiation was worth the trouble they had gone through. Shortly after initiation, the president of the fraternity called a special meeting of the new brothers and briefed them on the duties that they had as freshmen. They still had to tend the coke machine, answer phones during the evening, and spend Saturday afternoons working for the house. There was some grumbling in the group, but the majority realized that the work had to be done by someone, and it was most convenient to fulfill your obligation while you were still a freshman.

The next week, the same sophomore that had spoken to Dave about the Freshman Council suggested that Dave run for Class Secretary. The sophomore explained that the prestige connected with this office would be of great benefit to both Dave and the fraternity, and that people who have potential to be elected to such offices have somewhat of an obligation to the fraternity to try. Dave, even though he was not sure that he was interested, made a genuine effort. He spent much time preparing campaign material and visiting with members of the class. Unfortunately, a member of the Freshman Council who had been much more active on the council, and who had made a wider circle of friends was elected by a narrow margin.

Dave was still competing with the track team, and in addition, was spending about an hour a week working on the undergraduate Public Relations Committee. He decided to work on the PRC when he realized that he would no longer have the Freshman Council the following year.

The second term passed even more rapidly than the first, and when Dave's grades arrived at home during the summer, he found that his marks were a little lower than the previous term, because he had only gotten a C in the Drawing course, and all the other grades were the same.

During the summer, he spent some time considering the course that he would be going into the following term. After much thought and talk with his parents, he decided that he did not want to spend the rest of his life as an engineer, and thought that the best course of study for him would be the course in Industrial Management, where he would have relative freedom to choose an elective program that would give him as much of an engineering background as he needed.

He returned to MIT in early September for Work Week, which precedes Rush Week for the fraternities. As the term began, Dave once again was determined to make this the term that he was going to demonstrate that he had what it took to do well at MIT.

At the first house meeting of the new year, Dave was elected Assistant House Manager. This office required that Dave spend about every other Saturday afternoon helping supervise the freshmen in their work. Dave was still working with the PRC, and was attempting to make the Varsity track team. He was determined not to let these activities interfere with his high academic aspirations, however. He spent all of his spare time in the library studying, and would go to the library several nights a week to be able to work better. He disciplined himself very strictly, and was very seldom in "bull sessions," nor did he take "coffee breaks" in the middle of the evenings as did many of the men in the fraternity.

It soon became evident that some of the members of the fraternity did not appreciate the enthusiasm that Dave exhibited for his studies, however. He overheard one person referring to him as a "studying machine," while another said that it didn't seem that Dave valued the company of his fraternity brothers any more. These comments were disturbing to Dave, for though most of the people that he heard making such statements had better grades than he had, they did not approve of the emphasis that he was putting on improving his studies. Dave found that he spent considerable time with a book in his hand, but with his thoughts centered on the disapproval he was receiving. Gradually his afternoons in the library became less frequent, and he found that a little coffee in the middle of the evening helped him relax better during the remainder of the night.

Even though Dave thought that he was putting in as much time on his school work as those around him, his grades remained below average. He slowly became more depressed, and at one time was seriously considering transferring to another school. Maybe he wasn't cut out to be even this much of an engineer. After talking to his faculty advisor, he decided to stay at least until the remainder of that term and come to a final decision during the vacation between terms.

Dave's fraternity brothers were very much opposed to his transferring, and pointed out that men in the lower half of their class at MIT got better jobs than graduates from most other colleges. They were sure that Dave would be robbing himself of a good education if he transferred. Dave considered these points, and since he was not really doing poorly, he concluded that staying was the best thing for him to do.

When the second term began, Dave found that the pre-initiation week was as much a drain on his time as a brother as it was when he was a pledge. During the term that followed, Dave was still on the track team even though he did not make a letter for the indoor season. He was elected secretary of the Public Relations Committee, and was spending about two hours a week in that capacity.

As the track season progressed, and Dave did not seem to be improving much over his high school performance, he began to spend a little less time practicing, and found that the intramural sports were about as much fun, and you could compete in a greater variety of fields without as much time spent in practice. He continued his varsity competition, however, since he still needed the spring's points to complete his athletic obligation.

At the beginning of his junior year, he was elected Social Chairman. During the term that followed, he spent much time developing what was acclaimed as the best social season that the fraternity has seen in some while. When the time for winter track arrived, he decided against participating, having completed the required athletic participation. He continued to be a big supporter of the fraternity intramural teams, however. His grades during this term fell to the lowest point in his college career. He thought that he should buckle down a little more next term.

The second term of his junior year, Dave was nominated to be chairman of the PRC. This was somewhat of a surprise to him, because he had not been doing nearly as much work as some of the other members. He was elected by a narrow margin, so this activity took considerably more time than it had in the past. His second term grades were an improvement over the first term's grades, so both he and his parents were happier.

Dave began interviewing for jobs early in his senior year. Most of the men that he spoke to were very nice, and were interested in his plans, but at the end of the first term all the replies that he had received were polite, but definite, rejections. During the second term of his senior year, Dave and two other seniors rented an apartment near the fraternity house. They thought that such an atmosphere would be much more conducive to studying, and they were all writing theses. It was very convenient, but none of the group got any more done than they had in the fraternity house.

Dave became a little concerned about his thesis toward the end of the term, and at one time was afraid that he was not going to complete it. He was able to finish one day late, however, even though he was not really happy with the job that he had done.

During the last few weeks of school he received a letter from a

company that he had visited offering him a position in their technical sales department. Even though he had previously pictured himself in a position that required more technical and analytical ability,
Dave had heard many people say that sales was a growing field, so
he accepted this job, and joined the company three weeks after
he graduated.

As Dave started to work, he looked back on his college days. He
was very happy that he had not become so involved in his studies
that he missed all the social opportunities that were available at
MIT. He was sure that the activities in which he had participated
were going to be a genuine asset in his job, and this was especially
true of the experiences contributed by fraternity life.

THE SCARLET MOVING VAN*

John Cheever

Good-by to the mortal boredom of distributing a skinny chicken
to a family of seven and all the other rites of the hill towns. I don't
mean the real hill towns—Assisi or Perugia or Saracinesco, perched
on a three-thousand-foot crag, with walls the dispiriting gray of shirt
cardboards and mustard lichen blooming on the crooked roofs. The
land, in fact, was flat, the houses frame. This was in the eastern
United States, and the kind of place where most of us live. It was
the unincorporated township of B————, with a population of perhaps two hundred married couples, all of them with dogs and children, and many of them with servants; it resembled a hill town only
in a manner of speaking, in that the ailing, the disheartened, and
the poor could not ascend the steep moral path that formed its
natural defense, and the moment any of the inhabitants became in-
fected with unhappiness or discontent, they sensed the hopelessness
of existing on such a high spiritual altitude, and went to live in the
plain. Life was unprecedentedly comfortable and tranquil. B————
was exclusively for the felicitous. The housewives kissed their husbands tenderly in the morning and passionately at nightfall. In

---

*Reprinted in its entirety. John Cheever, "The Scarlet Moving Van," *The New
Yorker*, March 21, 1959, pp. 44–50. Reprinted by permission; © 1959 *The New
Yorker Magazine*, Inc.

nearly every house there were love, graciousness, and high hopes. The schools were excellent, the roads were smooth, the drains and other services were ideal, and one spring evening at dusk an immense scarlet moving van with gold lettering on its sides came up the street and stopped in front of the Marple house, which had been empty then for three months.

The gilt and scarlet of the van, bright even in the twilight, was an inspired attempt to disguise the true sorrowfulness of wandering. "We Carry Loads and Part Loads to All Far-Distant Places," said the gold letters on the sides, and this legend had the effect of a distant train whistle. Martha Folkestone, who lived next door, watched through a window as the portables of her new neighbors were carried across the porch. "That looks like real Chippendale," she said, "although it's hard to tell in this light. They have two children. They seem like nice people. Oh, I wish there was something I could bring them to make them feel at home. Do you think they'd like flowers? I suppose we could ask them for a drink. Do you think they'd like a drink? Would you want to go over and ask them if they'd like a drink?"

Later, when the furniture was all indoors and the van had gone, Charlie Folkestone crossed the lawn between the two houses and introduced himself to Peaches and Gee-Gee. This is what he saw. Peaches was peaches—blond and warm, with a low-cut dress and a luminous front. Gee-Gee had been a handsome man, and perhaps still was, although his yellow curls were thin. His face seemed both angelic and menacing. He had never (Charlie learned later) been a boxer, but his eyes were slightly squinted and his square, handsome forehead had the conformation of layers of scar tissue. You might have said that his look was thoughtful until you realized that he was not a thoughtful man. It was the earnest and contained look of those who are a little hard of hearing or a little stupid.

They would be delighted to have a drink. They would be right over. Peaches wanted to put on some lipstick and say good night to the children, and then they would be right over. They came right over, and what seemed to be an unusually pleasant evening began. The Folkestones had been worried about who their new neighbors would be, and to find a couple as sympathetic as Gee-Gee and Peaches made them very high-spirited. Like everyone else, they loved to express an opinion about their neighbors, and Gee-Gee and Peaches were, naturally, interested. It was the beginning of a friendship, and the Folkestones overlooked their usual concern with time and sobriety. It got late—it was past midnight—and Charlie did not notice how much whiskey was being poured or that Gee-Gee seemed to be getting drunk. Gee-Gee became very quiet—he dropped out of the conversation—and then he suddenly interrupted Martha in a flat, unpleasant drawl.

"God, but you're stuffy people," he said.

"Oh, no, Gee-Gee!" Peaches said. "Not on our first night!"

"You've had too much to drink, Gee-Gee," Charlie said.

"Like hell I have," said Gee-Gee. He bent over and began to unlace his shoes. "I haven't had half enough."

"Please, Gee-Gee, please," Peaches said.

"I have to teach them, honey," Gee-Gee said. "They've got to learn."

Then he stood up and, with the cunning and dexterity of a drunk, got out of most of his clothing before anyone could stop him.

"Get out of here," Charlie said.

"The pleasure's all mine, neighbor," said Gee-Gee. He kicked over a hammered-brass umbrella stand on his way out the door.

"Oh, I'm frightfully sorry!" Peaches said. "I feel terribly about this!"

"Don't worry, my dear," Martha said. "He's probably very tired, and we've all had too much to drink."

"Oh, no," Peaches said. "It always happens. Everywhere. We've moved eight times in the last eight years, and there's never been anyone to say good-by to us. Not a soul. Oh, he was a beautiful man when I first knew him! You never saw anyone so fine and strong and generous. They called him the Greek God at college. That's why he's called Gee-Gee. He was All-America twice, but he was never a money player—he always played straight out of his heart. Everybody loved him. Now it's all gone, but I tell myself that I once had the love of a good man. I don't think many women have known that kind of love. Oh, I wish he'd come back. I wish he'd be the way he was. The night before last, when we were packing up the dishes in the old house, he got drunk and I slapped him in the face, and I shouted at him, 'Come back! Come back! Come back to me, Gee-Gee!' But he didn't listen. He didn't hear me. He doesn't hear anyone any more—not even the voices of his children. I ask myself every day what I've done to be punished so cruelly."

"I'm sorry, my dear!" Martha said.

"You won't be around to say good-by when we go," Peaches said. "We'll last a year. You wait and see. Some people have tender farewell parties, but even the garbage man in the last place was glad to see us go." With a grace and resignation that transcended the ruined evening, she began to gather up the clothing that her husband had scattered on the rug. "Each time we move, I think that the change will be good for him," she said. "When we got here tonight, it all looked so pretty and quiet that I though he might change. Well, you don't have to ask us again. You know what it's like."

A few days or perhaps a week later, Charlie saw Gee-Gee on the station platform in the morning and saw how completely personable his neighbor was when he was sober. B——— was not an easy place to conquer, but Gee-Gee seemed already to have won the affectionate respect of his neighbors. Charlie could see, as he watched him standing in the sun among the other commuters, that he would be asked to join everything. Gee-Gee greeted Charlie heartily, and there was no trace of the ugliness he had shown that night. Indeed, it was impossible to believe that this charming and handsome man had been so offensive. In the morning light, and surrounded by new friends, he seemed to challenge the memory. He seemed almost able to transfer the blame onto Charlie.

Arrangements for the social initiation of the new couple were unusually rapid and elaborate, and began with a dinner party at the Watermans'. Charlie was already at the party when Gee-Gee and Peaches came in, and they came in like royalty. Arm in arm, radiant and beautiful, they seemed, at the moment of their entrance, to make the evening. It was a large party, and Charlie hardly saw them until they went in to dinner. He sat close to Peaches, but Gee-Gee was at the other end of the table. They were halfway through dessert when Gee-Gee's flat and unpleasant drawl sounded, like a parade command, over the general conversation.

"What a God-damned bunch of stuffed shirts!" he said. "Let's put a little vitality into the conversation, shall we?" He sprang onto the center of the table and began to sing a dirty song and dance a jig. Women screamed. Dishes were upset and broken. Dresses were ruined. Peaches pled to her wayward husband. The effect of this outrageous performance was to empty the dining room of everyone but Gee-Gee and Charlie.

"Get down off there, Gee-Gee," Charlie said.

"I have to teach them," Gee-Gee said. "I've got to teach them."

"You're not teaching anybody anything but the fact that you're a rotten drunk."

"They've got to learn," Gee-Gee said. "I've got to teach them."

He got down off the table, breaking a few more dishes, and wandered out into the kitchen, where he embraced the cook, and then went on out into the night.

One might have thought that this was warning enough to a worldly community, but unusual amounts of forgiveness were extended to Gee-Gee. One liked him, and there was always the chance that he might not misbehave. There was always his charming figure in the morning light to confound his enemies, but it began to seem more and more like a lure that would let him into houses where he could break the crockery. Forgiveness was not what he wanted, and if he seemed to have failed at offending the sensibilities of his hostess he would increase and complicate his outrageousness. No one had ever seen anything like it. He undressed at the Bikers'. At the Levys' he drop-kicked a bowl of soft cheese onto the ceiling. He danced the Highland fling in his underpants, set fire to wastebaskets, and swung on the Townsends' chandelier—that famous chandelier. Inside of six weeks, there was not a house in B——— where he was welcome.

The Folkestones still saw him, of course—saw him in his garden in the evening and talked to him across the hedge. Charlie was greatly troubled at the spectacle of someone falling so swiftly from grace, and he would have liked to help. He and Martha talked with Peaches, but Peaches was without hope. She did not understand what had happened to her Adonis, and that was as far as her intelligence took her. Now and then some innocent stranger from the next town or perhaps some newcomer would be taken with Gee-Gee and ask him to dinner. The performance was always the same, the dishes were always broken. The Folkestones were neighbors—there was this ancient bond—and Charlie may have thought that he could save the man. When Gee-Gee and Peaches quarreled, sometimes she telephoned Charlie and asked his protection. He went there one summer evening after she had telephoned. The quarrel was over; Peaches was reading a comic book in the living room, and Gee-Gee was sitting at the dining-room table with a drink in his hand. Charlie stood over his friend.

"Gee-Gee."

"Yes."

"Will you go on the wagon?"

"No."

"Will you go on the wagon if I go on the wagon?"

"No."

"Will you go to a psychiatrist?"

"Why? I know myself. I only have to play it out."

"Will you go to a psychiatrist if I go with you?"

"No."

"Will you do anything to help yourself?"

"I have to teach them." Then he threw back his head and sobbed, "Oh, Jesus. . . ."

Charlie turned away. It seemed, at that instant, that Gee-Gee had heard, from some wilderness of his own, the noise of a distant horn that prophesied the manner and the hour of his death. There seemed to be some tremendous validity to the drunken man. Folkestone felt an upheaval in his spirit. He felt he understood the drunken man's message; he had always sensed it. It was at the bottom of their friendship. Gee-Gee was an advocate for the lame, the diseased, the poor, for those who through no fault of their own live out their lives in misery and pain. To the happy and the wellborn and the rich he had this to say—that for all their affection, their comforts, and their privileges, they would not be spared the pangs of anger and lust and the agonies of death. He only meant for them to be prepared for the blow when the blow fell. But was it not possible to accept this truth without having him dance a jig in your living room? He spoke from some vision of the suffering in life, but was it necessary to suffer oneself in order to accept his message? It seemed so.

"Gee-Gee?" Charlie asked.

"Yes."

"*What* are you trying to teach them?"

"You'll never know. You're too God-damned stuffy."

They didn't even last a year. In November, someone made them a decent offer for the house and they sold it. The gold-and-scarlet moving van returned, and they crossed the state line, into the town of Y——, where they bought another house. The Folkestones were glad to see them go. A well-behaved young couple took their place, and everything was as it had been. They were seldom remembered. But through a string of friends Charlie learned, the following winter, that Gee-Gee had broken his hip playing football a day or two before Christmas. This fact, for some reason, remained with him, and one Sunday afternoon when he had nothing much better to do he got Gee-Gee's telephone number from Information and called his old neighbor to say that he was coming over for a drink. Gee-Gee roared with enthusiasm and gave Charlie directions for getting to the house.

It was a long drive, and halfway there Charlie wondered why he had undertaken it. Y—— was several cuts below B———. The house was in a development, and the builder had not stopped at mere ugliness; he had constructed a community that looked, with its rectilinear windows, like a penal colony. The streets were named after universities—Princeton Street, Yale Street, Rutgers Street and so forth. Only a few of the houses had been sold, and Gee-Gee's house was surrounded by empty dwellings. Charlie rang the bell and heard Gee-Gee shouting for him to come in. The house was a mess, and as he was taking his coat off, Gee-Gee came slowly down the hall half-riding in a child's wagon, which he propelled by pushing a crutch. His right hip and leg were encased in a massive cast.

"Where's Peaches?" Charlie asked.

"She's in Nassau. She and the children went to Nassau for Christmas."

"And left you alone?"

"I wanted them to go. I made them go. Nothing can be done for me. I get along all right on this wagon. When I'm hungry, I make a sandwich. I wanted them to go. I made them go. Peaches needed a vacation, and I like being alone. Come on into the living room and make me a drink. I can't get the ice trays out—that's about the only thing I can't do. I can shave and get into bed and so forth, but I can't get the ice trays out."

Charlie got some ice. He was glad to have something to do. The image of Gee-Gee in his wagon had shocked him, and he felt a terrifying stillness over the place. Out of the kitchen window he could see row upon row of ugly, empty houses. He felt as if some hideous melodrama were approaching its climax. But in the living room Gee-Gee was his most charming, and his smile and his voice gave the afternoon a momentary equilibrium. Charlie asked if Gee-Gee couldn't get a nurse to stay with him. Couldn't someone be found to stay with him? Couldn't he at least rent a wheelchair? Gee-Gee laughed away all these suggestions. He was contented. Peaches had written him from Nassau. They were having a marvelous time.

Charlie believed that Gee-Gee had made them go. It was this detail, above everything else, that gave the situation its horror. Peaches would have liked, naturally enough, to go to Nassau, but she never would have insisted. She was much too innocent to have any envious dreams of travel. Gee-Gee would have insisted that she go; he would have made the trip so tempting that she could not, in her innocence, resist it. Did he wish to be left alone, drunken and crippled, in an isolated house? Did he need to feel abused? It seemed so. The disorder of the house and the image of his wife and children running, running, running on some coral beach seemed like a successful contrivance—a kind of triumph.

Gee-Gee lit a cigarette and, forgetting about it, lit another, and fumbled so clumsily with the matches that Charlie saw that he might easily burn to death. Hoisting himself from the wagon into a chair, he nearly fell, and, if he were alone and fell, he could easily die of hunger and thirst on his own rug. But there might be some drunken cunning in his clumsiness, his playing with fire. He smiled slyly when he saw the look on Charlie's face. "Don't worry about me," he said "I'll be all right. I have my guardian angel."

"That's what everybody thinks," Charlie said.

"Oh, but I have."

Outside, it had begun to snow. The winter sky was overcast, and it would soon be dark. Charlie said that he had to go. "Sit down," Gee-Gee said. "Sit down and have another drink." Charlie's conscience held him there a few moments longer. How could he openly abandon a friend—a neighbor, at least—to the peril of death? But he had no choice; his family was waiting and he had to go. "Don't worry about me," Gee-Gee said when Charlie was putting on his coat. "I have my angel."

It was later than Charlie had realized. The snow was heavy now, and he had a two-hour drive, on winding back roads. There was a little rise going out of Y——, and the new snow was so slick that he had trouble making the hill. There were steeper hills ahead of him. Only one of his windshield wipers worked, and the snow quickly covered the glass and left him with one small aperture onto the world. The snow sped into the headlights at a dizzying rate, and at one place where the road was narrow the car slid off onto the shoulder and he had to race the motor for ten minutes in order to get back onto the hard surface. It was a lonely stretch there— miles from any house—and he would have had a sloppy walk in his loafers. The car skidded and weaved up every hill, and it seemed that he reached the top by the thinnest margin of luck.

After driving for two hours, he was still far from home. The snow was so deep that guiding the car was like the trickiest kind of navigation. It took him three hours to get back, and he was tired when he drove into the darkness and peace of his own garage— tired and infinitely grateful. Martha and the children had eaten their supper, and she wanted to go over to the Lissoms' and discuss some school-board business. He told her that the driving was bad, and since it was such a short distance, she decided to walk. He lit a fire and made a drink, and the children sat at the table with him while he ate his supper. After supper on Sunday nights, the Folkestones played, or tried to play, trios. Charlie played the clarinet, his daughter played the piano, and his older son had a tenor recorder. The baby wandered around underfoot. This Sunday night they played simple arrangements of eighteenth-century music in the pleasantest family atmosphere—complimenting themselves when they squeezed through a difficult passage, and extending into the music what was best in their relationship. They were playing a Vivaldi sonata when the telephone rang. Charlie knew immediately who it was.

"Charlie, Charlie," Gee-Gee said. "Jesus. I'm in hot water. Right after you left I fell out of the God-damned wagon. It took me two hours to get to the telephone. You've got to get over. There's nobody else. You're my only friend. You've got to get over here. Charlie? You hear me?"

It must have been the strangeness of the look on Charlie's face that made the baby scream. The little girl picked him up in her arms, and stared, as did the other boy, at their father. They seemed to know the whole picture, every detail of it, and they looked at him calmly, as if they were expecting him to make some decision that had nothing to do with the continuing of a pleasant evening in a snowbound house—but a decision that would have a profound effect on their knowledge of him and on their final happiness. Their looks were, he thought, clear and appealing, and whatever he did would be final.

"You hear me, Charlie? You hear me?" Gee-Gee asked. "It took me damned near two hours to crawl over to the telephone. You've got to help me. No one else will come."

Charlie hung up. Gee-Gee must have heard the sound of his breathing and the baby crying, but Charlie had said nothing. He gave no explanation to the children, and they asked for none. They knew. His daughter went back to the piano, and when the telephone rang again and he did not answer it, no one questioned the ringing of the phone. They seemed happy and relieved when it stopped ringing, and they played Vivaldi until nine o'clock, when he sent them up to bed.

He made a drink to diminish the feeling that some emotional explosion had taken place, that some violence had shaken the air. He did not know what he had done or how to cope with his conscience. He would tell Martha about it when she came in, he thought. That would be a step toward comprehension. But when she returned he said nothing. He was afraid that if she brought her intelligence to the problem it would only confirm his guilt. "But why didn't you telephone me at the Lissoms'?" she might have asked. "I could have come home and you could have gone over." She was too compassionate a woman to accept passively, as he was doing, the thought of a friend, a neighbor, lying in agony. She went on upstairs. He poured some whiskey into his glass. If he had called the Lissoms', if she had returned to care for the children and left him free to help Gee-Gee, would he have been able to make the return trip in the heavy snow? He could have put on chains, but where were the chains? Were they in the car or in the cellar? He didn't know. He hadn't used them that year. But perhaps by now the roads would have been plowed. Perhaps the storm was over. This last, distressing possibility made him feel sick. Had the sky betrayed him? He switched on the outside light and went hesitantly, unwillingly, toward the window.

The clean snow gave off an ingratiating sparkle, and the beam of light shone into empty and peaceful air. The snow must have stopped a few minutes after he had entered the house. But how could he have known? How could he be expected to take into consideration the caprices of the weather? And what about that look the children had given him—so stern, so clear, so like a declaration that his place at that hour was with them, and not with the succoring of drunkards who had forfeited the chance to be taken seriously?

Then the image of Gee-Gee returned, crushing in its misery, and he remembered Peaches standing in the hallway at the Watermans' calling, "Come back! Come back!" She was calling back the youth that Charlie had never known, but it was easy to imagine what Gee-Gee must have been—fair, high-spirited, generous, and strong—and why had it all come to ruin? *Come back! Come back!* She seemed to call after the sweetness of a summer's day—roses in bloom and all the doors and windows open on the garden. It was all there in her voice; it was like the illusion of an abandoned house in the last rays of the sun. A large place, falling to pieces, haunted for children and a headache for the police and fire departments, but, seeing it with its windows blazing in the sunset, one thinks that they have all come back. Cook is in the kitchen rolling pastry. The smell of chicken rises up the back stairs. The front rooms are ready for the children and their many friends. A coal fire burns in the grate. Then as the light goes off the windows, the true ugliness of the place scowls into the dusk with redoubled force, as, when the notes of that long-ago summer left Peaches' voice, one saw the finality and confusion of despair in her innocent face. *Come back! Come back!* He poured himself some more whiskey, and as he raised the glass to his mouth he heard the wind change and saw—the outside light was still on—the snow begin to spin down again, with the vindictive swirl of a blizzard. The road was impassable; he could not have made the trip. The change in the weather had given him sweet absolution, and he watched the snow with a smile of love, but he stayed up until three in the morning with the bottle.

He was red-eyed and shaken the next morning, and ducked out of his office at eleven and drank two Martinis. He had two more before lunch and another at four and two on the train, and came reeling home for supper. The clinical details of heavy drinking are familiar to all of us; it is only the human picture that concerns us here, Martha was finally driven to speak to him. She spoke most gently.

"You're drinking too much darling," she said. "You've been drinking too much for three weeks."

"My drinking," he said, "is my own God-damned business. You mind your business and I'll mind mine."

It got worse and worse, and she had to do something She finally went to their rector—a good-looking young bachelor who practiced both psychology and liturgy—for advice. He listened sympathetically. "I stopped at the rectory this afternoon," she said when she got home that night, "and I talked with Father Hemming. He wonders why you haven't been in church, and he wants to talk to you. He's such a good-looking man," she added, trying to make what she had just said sound less like a planned speech, "that I wonder why he's never married." Charlie—drunk, as usual—went to the telephone and called the rectory. "Look, Father," he said. "My wife tells me that you've been entertaining her in the afternoons. Well, I don't like it. You keep your hands off my wife. You hear me? That damned black suit you wear doesn't cut any ice with me. You keep your hands off my wife or I'll bust your pretty little nose."

In the end, he lost his job, and they had to move, and began their wanderings, like Gee-Gee and Peaches, in the scarlet-and-gold van.

And what happened to Gee-Gee—what ever became of him? That

boozy guardian angel, her hair disheveled and the strings of her harp broken, still seemed to hover over where he lay. After telephoning Charlie that night, he telephoned the fire department. They were there in eight minutes flat, with bells ringing and sirens blowing. They got him into bed, made him a fresh drink, and one of the firemen, who had nothing better to do, stayed on until Peaches got back from Nassau. They had a fine time, eating all the steaks in the deep freeze and drinking a quart of bourbon every day. Gee-Gee could walk by the time Peaches and the children got back, and he took up that disorderly life for which he seemed so much better equipped than his neighbor, but they had to move at the end of the year, and, like the Folkestones, vanished from the hill towns.

ROMANCE AT DROITGATE SPA*
P. G. *Wodehouse*

It has been rightly said—and it is a fact on which we pride ourselves—that in the bar parlor of the Angler's Rest, distinctions of class are unknown. Double Best Ports hobnob on terms of the easiest affability with humble Ginger Ales, and I myself have heard a Draught Beer in a Pewter call a Half Bottle of Champagne "old chap" and be addressed in his turn as "old fellow." Once inside that enchanted room, we are all brothers, all equals, from the highest to the lowest.

It was with distress and embarrassment, therefore, that we had watched the Plain Vichy snubbing the friendly overtures of a meek little Milk and Soda, high-hatting him so coldly and persistently that in the end he gave it up and slunk out. Soon afterwards the Vichy also left, explaining that his doctor had warned him not to be out of bed after 10 o'clock at night, and as the door closed behind him we settled down to discuss the unfortunate affair. The Small Bass who had introduced the two men to one another scratched his head ruefully.

"I can't understand it," he said. "I thought they'd have got on so well together. Twin souls, I thought they'd have been."

---

*Reprinted from P. G. Wodehouse, *Crime Wave at Blandings*. By permission of P. G. Wodehouse and Herbert Jenkins, Ltd.

Mr. Mulliner stirred his hot scotch and lemon.

"What made you think that?"

"Well, they've both just had operations, and they both like talking about them."

"Ah," said Mr. Mulliner, "but what you are forgetting is that while one has been operated on for duodenal ulcer, the other has merely had his tonsils removed."

"What difference would that make?"

"Every difference. There is no sphere of life in which class consciousness is so rampant as among invalids. The ancient Spartans, I believe, were a little standoffish towards their Helots, but not so standoffish as the man who has been out in Switzerland taking insulin for his diabetes towards the man who is simply undergoing treatment from the village doctor for an ingrowing toenail. This is particularly so, of course, in those places where invalids collect in gangs—Bournemouth, for example, or Buxton, or Droitgate Spa. In such resorts the atmosphere is almost unbelievably clique-y. The old aristocracy, the topnotchers with maladies that get written up in the medical journals, keep themselves to themselves pretty rigidly, I can assure you, and have a very short way with the smaller fry."

Mention of Droitgate Spa (said Mr. Mulliner, having ordered a second hot scotch and lemon) recalls to my mind the romance of my distant connection, Frederick Fitch-Fitch, whose uncle, Major General Sir Aylmer Bastable, lived there. It was at Droitgate Spa that the story had its setting, and I have always thought it one that throws a very interesting light on conditions in the class of the community of which we have been speaking.

Frederick at that time was a young man of pleasing manners and exterior who supported life on a small private income, the capital of which was held in trust for him by his uncle, Sir Aylmer; and it was his great desire to induce the other to release this capital so that he could go into the antique business.

For that was where Frederick's heart was. He wanted to buy a half interest in some good Olde Shoppe in the Bond Street neighborhood and start selling walnut tables and things. So every once in a while he would journey down to Droitgate Spa and plead for the stuff, but every time he did so he went away with his dreams shattered. For circumstances had unfortunately so ordered themselves as to make this uncle of his a warped, soured uncle.

Major General Sir Aylmer Bastable, you see, had had an un-

pleasant shock on coming to settle in Droitgate Spa. The head of a
fine old family and the possessor of a distinguished military record,
he had expected upon his arrival to be received with open arms by
the best people and welcomed immediately into the inner set. But
when it was discovered that all he had wrong with him was the
gout in the right foot, he found himself cold-shouldered by the men
who mattered and thrust back on the society of the asthma patients
and the fellows with slight liver trouble.

This naturally soured his disposition a good deal, and his ill
humor reacted upon his nephew. Every time Freddie came asking
for capital to invest in antique shoppes, he found his uncle smarting
from a snub from some swell whom the doctors had twice given up
for dead, and so in no mood to part.

And then one day a more serious issue forced itself onto the
agenda paper. At a charity matinée Freddie for the first time set eyes
on Annabel Purvis. She was the assistant of The Great Boloni, a
conjurer who had been engaged to perform at the entertainment,
her duties being to skip downstage from time to time, hand him a
bowl of goldfish, beam at the audience, do a sort of dance step, and
skip back again. And with such winsome grace did she do this that
Freddie fell in love at first sight.

It is not necessary for me to describe in detail how my distant
connection contrived to make the girl's acquaintance, nor need I
take you step by step through his courtship. Suffice it to say that
during the cheese and celery course of a luncheon *à deux* some few
weeks later Freddie proposed and was accepted. So now it became
even more imperative than before that he induce his uncle to release
his capital.

It was with a certain uneasiness that he traveled down to Droitgate Spa, for he was fully alive to the fact that the interview might
prove a disagreeable one. However, his great love bore him on, and
he made the journey and was shown into the room where the old
man sat nursing a gouty foot.

"Hullo-ullo-ullo, Uncle!" he cried, for it was always his policy on
these occasions to be buoyant till thrown out. "Good morning, good
morning, good morning."

"Gaw!" said Sir Aylmer, with a sort of long, shuddering sigh. "It's
you, is it?"

And he muttered something which Freddie did not quite catch,
though he was able to detect the words "last straw."

"Well," he went on, "what do you want?"

"Oh, I just looked in," said Freddie. "How's everything?"

"Rotten," replied Sir Aylmer. "I've just lost my nurse."

"Dead?"

"Worse. Married. The clothheaded girl has gone off and got spliced to one of the *canaille*—a chap who's never even had so much as athlete's foot. She must be crazy."

"Still, one sees her point of view."

"No, one doesn't."

"I mean," said Freddie, who felt strongly on this subject, "it's love that makes the world go round."

"It isn't anything of the kind," said Sir Aylmer. Like so many fine old soldiers, he was inclined to be a little literal-minded. "I never heard such dashed silly nonsense in my life. What makes the world go round is . . . Well, I've forgotten at the moment, but it certainly isn't love. How the deuce could it?"

"Oh, right ho. I see what you mean," said Freddie. "But put it another way. Love conquers all. Love's all right, take it from me."

The old man looked at him sharply.

"Are you in love?"

"Madly."

"Of all the young cuckoos! And I suppose you've come to ask for money to get married on?"

"Not at all. I just dropped round to see how you were. Still, as the subject has happened to crop up—."

Sir Aylmer brooded for a moment, snorting in an undertone.

"Who's the girl?" he demanded.

Freddie coughed, and fumbled with his collar. The crux of the situation, he realized, had now been reached. He had feared from the first that this was where the good old snag might conceivably sidle into the picture. For his Annabel was of humble station, and he knew how rigid were his relative's views on the importance of birth. No bigger snob ever swallowed a salicylate pill.

"Well, as a matter of fact," he said, "she's a conjurer's stooge."

"A *what?*"

"A conjurer's assistant, don't you know. I saw her first at a charity matinée. She was abetting a bloke called The Great Boloni."

"In what sense, abetting?"

"Well, she stood there upstage, don't you know, and every now and then she would skip downstage, hand this chap a bowl of gold-fish or something, beam at the audience, do a sort of dance step and skip back again. You know the kind of thing."

A dark frown had come into Sir Aylmer's face.

"I do," he said grimly. "So! My only nephew has been ensnared by a bally, beaming goldfish-hander! Ha!"

"I wouldn't call it ensnared exactly," said Freddie deferentially.

"I would," said Sir Aylmer. "Get out of here."

"Right." said Freddie, and caught the 2:35 express back to London. And it was during the journey that an idea flashed upon him.

The last of the Fitch-Fitches was not a great student of literature, but he occasionally dipped into a magazine; and everybody who has ever dipped into a magazine has read a story about a hardhearted old man who won't accept the hero's girl at any price, so what do they do but plant her on him without telling him who she is and, by Jove, he falls under her spell completely and then they tear off their whiskers and there they are. There was a story of this nature in the magazine which Freddie had purchased at the newsstand at Droitgate Spa station, and, as he read it, he remembered what his uncle had told him about his nurse handing in her portfolio.

By the time the train checked in at Paddington, his plans were fully formed.

"Listen," he said to Annabel Purvis, who had met him at the terminus, and Annabel said, "What?"

"Listen," said Freddie, and Annabel again said "What?"

"Listen," said Freddie, clasping her arm tenderly and steering her off in the direction of the refreshment room, where it was his intention to have a quick one. "To a certain extent I am compelled to admit that my expedition has been a washout . . ."

Annabel caught her breath sharply.

"No blessing?"

"No blessing."

"And no money?"

"No money. The old boy ran entirely true to stable form. He listened to what I had to say, snorted in an unpleasant manner and threw me out. The old routine. But what I'm working round to is that the skies are still bright and the bluebird on the job. I have a scheme. Could you be a nurse?"

"I used to nurse my Uncle Joe."

"Then you shall nurse my uncle Aylmer. The present incumbent, he tells me, has just tuned out, and he needs a successor. I will phone him that I am despatching immediately a red-hot nurse whom he will find just the same as Mother makes, and you shall go down to Droitgate Spa and ingratiate yourself."

"But how?"

"Why, cluster round him. Smooth his pillow. Bring him cooling drinks. Coo to him, and give him the old oil. Tell him you are of gentle birth, if that's the expression I want. And when the time is ripe, when you have twined yourself about his heart and he looks upon you as a daughter shoot me a wire, and I'll come down and fall in love with you and he will give us his consent, blessing and the stuff. I guarantee this plan. It works."

So Annabel went to Droitgate Spa, and about three weeks later a telegram arrived for Freddie, running as follows:

HAVE INGRATIATED SELF   COME AT ONCE   LOVE AND KISSES ANNABEL

Within an hour of its arrival, Freddie was on his way to Podagra Lodge, his uncle's residence.

He found Sir Aylmer in his study. Annabel was sitting by his side, reading aloud to him from a recently published monograph on certain obscure ailments of the medulla oblongata. For the old man, though a mere gout patient, had pathetic aspirations towards higher things. There was a cooling drink on the table, and as Freddie entered the girl paused in her reading to smooth her employer's pillow.

"Gaw!" said Sir Aylmer. "You again?"

"Here I am," said Freddie.

"Well, by an extraordinary chance, I'm glad to see you. Leave us for a moment, Miss Purvis. I wish to speak to my nephew here, such as he is, on a serious and private matter. Did you notice that girl?" he said, as the door closed.

"I did, indeed."

"Pretty."

"An eyeful."

"And as good," said Sir Aylmer, "as she is beautiful. You should see her smooth pillows. And what a cooling drink she mixes! Excellent family, too, I understand. Her father is a colonel. Or, rather, was. He's dead."

"Ah well, all flesh is as grass."

"No, it isn't. It's nothing of the kind. The two things are entirely different. I've seen flesh and I've seen grass. No resemblance whatever. However, that is not the point at issue. What I wanted to say was that if you were not a damned fool, that's the sort of girl you would be in love with."

"I am."

"A damned fool?"

"No. In love with that girl."

"What! You have fallen in love with Miss Purvis? Already?"

"I have."

"Well, that's the quickest thing I ever saw. What about your beaming goldfish?"

"Oh, that's all over. A mere passing boyish fancy."

Sir Aylmer took a deep swig at his cooling drink, and regarded him in silence for a moment.

"Well," he said at length, breathing heavily, "if that's the airy, casual way in which you treat life's most sacred emotions, the sooner you are safely married and settled down, the better. If you're allowed to run around loose much longer, indulging those boyish fancies of yours, I foresee the breach-of-promise case of the century. However, I'm not saying I'm not relieved. I am relieved. I suppose she wore tights, this goldfish girl?"

"Pink."

"Disgusting. Thank God it's all over. Very good, then. You are free, I understand, to have a pop at Miss Purvis. Do you propose to do so?"

"I do."

"Excellent. You get that sweet, refined, most-suitable-in-all-respects girl to marry you, and I'll hand over that money of yours, every penny of it."

"I will start at once."

"Heaven speed your wooing," said Sir Aylmer.

And 10 minutes later Freddie was able to inform his uncle that his whirlwind courtship had been successful, and Sir Aylmer said that when he had asked heaven to speed his wooing he had had no notion that it would speed it to quite that extent. He congratulated Freddie warmly and said he hoped that he appreciated his good fortune, and Freddie said he certainly did, because his love was like a red, red rose, and Sir Aylmer said, No, she wasn't, and when Freddie added that he was walking on air, Sir Aylmer said he couldn't be, the thing was physically impossible.

However, he gave his blessing and promised to release Freddie's capital as soon as the necessary papers were drawn up, and Freddie went back to London to see his lawyer about this.

His mood, as the train sped through the quiet countryside, was one of perfect tranquillity and happiness. It seemed to him that his troubles were now definitely ended. He looked down the vista of the years and saw nothing but joy and sunshine. If somebody had told Frederick Fitch-Fitch at that moment that even now a V-shaped depression was coming along which would shortly blacken the skies and lower the general temperature to freezing point, he would not have believed him.

Nor when, two days later, as he sat in his club, he was informed that a Mr. Rackstraw was waiting to see him in the small smoking room, did he have an inkling that here was the V-shaped depression in person. His heart was still light as he went down the passage, wondering idly, for the name was unfamiliar to him, who this Mr. Rackstraw might be. He entered the room, and found there a tall, thin man with pointed black moustaches who was pacing up and down, nervously taking rabbits out of his top hat as he walked.

"Mr. Rackstraw?"

His visitor spun round, dropping a rabbit. He gazed at Freddie piercingly. He had bright, glittering, sinister eyes.

"That is my name. Mortimer Rackstraw."

Freddie's mind had flown back to the charity matinée at which he had first seen Annabel, and he recognized the fellow now.

"The Great Boloni, surely?"

"I call myself that professionally. So you are Mr. Fitch? So *you* are Mr. Fitch? Ha! Fiend!"

"Eh?"

"I am not mistaken? You are Frederick Fitch?"

"Frederick Fitch-Fitch."

"I beg your pardon. In that case, I should have said 'Fiend! Fiend!' "

He produced a pack of cards and asked Freddie to take one—any one—and memorize it and put it back. Freddie did so absently. He was considerably fogged. He could make nothing of all this.

"How do you mean—Fiend-Fiend?" he asked.

The other sneered unpleasantly.

"Cad!" he said, twirling his moustache.

"Cad?" said Freddie, mystified.

"Yes sir. Cad. You have stolen the girl I love."

"I don't understand."

"Then you must be a perfect ass. It's quite simple, isn't it? I can't put it any plainer, can I? I say you have stolen . . . Well, look here," said Mortimer Rackstraw. "Suppose this top hat is me. This rabbit," he went on, producing it from the lining, "is the girl I love. You come along and, presto, the rabbit vanishes."

"It's up your sleeve."

"It is not up my sleeve. And if it wcrc, if I had a thousand sleeves and rabbits up every one of them, that would not alter the fact that you have treacherously robbed me of Annabel Purvis."

Freddie began to see daylight. He was able to appreciate the other's emotion.

"So you love Annabel too?"

"I do."

"I don't wonder. Nice girl, what? I see, I see. You worshipped her in secret, never telling your love . . ."

"I did tell my love. We were engaged."

"Engaged?"

"Certainly. And this morning I get a letter from her saying that it's all off, because she has changed her mind and is going to marry you. She has thrown me over."

"Oh, ah? Well, I'm frightfully sorry—deepest sympathy, and all that—but I don't see what's to be done about it, what?"

"I do. There still remains—revenge."

"Oh, I say, dash it! You aren't going to be stuffy about it?"

"I am going to be stuffy about it. For the moment you triumph. But do not imagine that this is the end. You have not heard the last of me. Not by any means. You may have stolen the woman I love with your underhanded chicanery, but I'll fix you."

"How?"

"Never mind how. You will find out how quite soon enough. A nasty jolt you're going to get, my good friend, and almost immediately. As sure," said Mortimer Rackstraw, illustrating by drawing one from Freddie's back hair, "as eggs are eggs. I wish you a very good afternoon."

He took up his top hat, which in his emotion he had allowed to fall to the ground, brushed it on his coat sleeve, extracted from it a cage of lovebirds and strode out.

A moment later he returned, bowed a few times to right and left and was gone again.

To say that Freddie did not feel a little uneasy as the result of this scene would be untrue. There had been something in the confident manner in which the other had spoken of revenging himself that he had not at all liked. The words had had a sinister ring, and all through the rest of the day he pondered thoughtfully, wondering what a man so trained in the art of having things up his sleeve might have up it now. It was in meditative mood that he dined, and only on the following morning did his equanimity return to him.

Able, now that he had slept on it, to review the disturbing conversation in its proper perspective, he came to the conclusion that the fellow's threats had been mere bluff. What, after all, he asked himself, could this conjurer do? It was not as if they had been living in the Middle Ages, when chaps of that sort used to put spells on you and change you into things.

No, he decided, it was mere bluff, and with his complacency completely restored had just lighted a cigarettee and fallen to dreaming of the girl he loved, when a telegram was brought to him.

It ran as follows:

COME AT ONCE   ALL LOST   RUIN STARES FACE   LOVE AND KISSES   ANNABEL.

Half an hour later, he was in the train, speeding towards Droitgate Spa.

It had been Freddie's intention, on entering the train, to devote the journey to earnest meditation. But, as always happens when one wishes to concentrate and brood during a railway journey, he found himself closeted with a talkative fellow traveler.

The one who interrupted Freddie's thoughts was a flabby, puffy man of middle age, wearing a red waistcoat, brown shoes, a morning coat and a bowler hat. With such a Grade A bounder, even had his mind been at rest, Freddie would have little in common, and he sat chafing while the prismatic fellow prattled on. Nearly an hour passed before he was freed from the infliction of the other's conversation, but eventually the man's head began to nod, and presently he was snoring and Freddie was able to give himself up to his reverie.

His thoughts became less and less agreeable as the train rolled on. And what rendered his mental distress so particularly acute was the lack of informative detail in Annabel's telegram. It seemed to him to offer so wide a field for uncomfortable speculation.

"All lost," for instance. A man could do a lot of thinking about a phrase like that. And "Ruin stares face." Why, he asked himself, did ruin stare face? While commending Annabel's thriftiness in keeping the thing down to twelve words, he could not help wishing that she could have brought herself to spring another twopence and be more lucid.

But of one thing he felt certain. All this had something to do with his recent visitor. Behind that mystic telegram he seemed to see the hand of Mortimer Rackstraw, that hand whose quickness deceived the eye, and he knew that in lightly dismissing the other as a negligible force he had been too sanguine.

By the time he reached Podagra Lodge, the nervous strain had become almost intolerable. As he rang the bell, he was quivering like some jelly set before a diet patient, and the sight of Annabel's face as she opened the door did nothing to alleviate his perturbation. The girl was obviously all of a twitter.

"Oh, Freddie!" she cried. "The worst has happened."

Freddie gulped.

"Rackstraw?"

"Yes," said Annabel. "But how did you know about him?"

"He came to see me, bubbling over a good deal with veiled menaces and what not," explained Freddie. He frowned and eyed her closely. "Why didn't you tell me you had been engaged to that bird?"

"I didn't think you would be interested. It was just a passing girlish fancy."

"You're sure? You didn't really love this blighted prestidigitator?"

"No, no. I was dazzled for a while, as any girl might have been, when he sawed me in half, but then you came along and I saw that I had been mistaken and that you were the only man in the world for me."

"Good egg," said Freddie, relieved.

He kissed her fondly and, as he did so, there came to his ears the sound of rhythmic hammering from somewhere below.

"What's that?" he asked.

Annabel wrung her hands.

"It's Mortimer!"

"Is he here?"

"Yes. He arrived on the one-fifteen. I locked him in the cellar."

"Why?"

"To stop him going to the Pump Room."

"Why shouldn't he go to the Pump Room?"

"Because Sir Aylmer has gone there to listen to the band and they must not meet. If they do, we are lost. Mortimer has hatched a fearful plot."

Freddie's heart seemed to buckle under within him. He had tried to be optimistic, but all along he had known that Mortimer Rackstraw would hatch some fearful plot. He could have put his shirt on it. A born hatcher.

"What plot?"

Annabel wrung her hands again.

"He means to introduce Sir Aylmer to my uncle Joe. He wired to him to come to Droitgate Spa. He had arranged to meet him at the Pump Room, and then he was going to introduce him to Sir Aylmer."

Freddie was a little fogged. It did not seem to him much of a plot.

"Now that I can never be his, all he wants is to make himself unpleasant and prevent our marriage. And he knows that Sir Aylmer will never consent to your marrying me if he finds out that I have an uncle like Uncle Joe."

Freddie ceased to be fogged. He saw the whole devilish scheme now—a scheme worthy of the subtle brain that could put the ace of spades back in the pack, shuffle, cut three times, and then produce it from the inside of a lemon.

"Is he so frightful?" he quavered.

"Look," said Annabel simply. She took a photograph from her bosom and extended it towards him with a trembling hand. "That is Uncle Joe, taken in the masonic regalia of a Grand Exalted Periwinkle of the Mystic Order of Whelks."

Freddie glanced at the photograph and started back with a hoarse cry. Annabel nodded sadly.

"Yes," she said. "That is how he takes most people. The only faint hope I have is that he won't have been able to come. But if he has —"

"He has," cried Freddie, who had been fighting for breath. "We traveled down in the train together."

"What!"

"Yes. He must be waiting at the Pump Room now."

"And at any moment Mortimer will break his way out of the cellar. The door is not strong. What shall we do?"

"There is only one thing to do. I have all the papers . . ."

"You have no time to read now."

"The legal papers, the ones my uncle has to sign in order to release my money. There is just a chance that if I rush to the Pump Room I may get him to put his name on the dotted line before the worst happens."

"Then rush," cried Annabel.

"I will," said Freddie.

He kissed her quickly, grabbed his hat, and was off the mark like a jack rabbit.

A man who is endeavoring to lower the record for the distance between Podagra Lodge, which is in Arterio-Sclerosis Avenue, and the Droitgate Spa Pump Room has little leisure for thinking, but Freddie managed to put in a certain amount as his feet skimmed the pavement. And the trend of his thought was such as to give renewed vigor to his legs. He could scarcely have moved more rapidly if he had been a character in a two-reel film with the police after him.

And there was need for speed. Beyond a question, Annabel had been right when she had said that Sir Aylmer would never consent to their union if he found out that she had an uncle like her Uncle Joe. Uncle Joe would get right in amongst him. Let them but meet, and nothing was more certain than that the haughty old man would veto the proposed nuptials.

A final burst of speed took him panting up the Pump Room steps and into the rotunda where all that was best and most refined in Droitgate Spa was accustomed to assemble of an afternoon and listen to the band. He saw Sir Aylmer in a distant seat and hurried towards him.

"Gaw!" said Sir Aylmer. "You?"

Freddie could only nod.

"Well, stop puffing like that and sit down," said Sir Aylmer. "They're just going to play 'Poet and Peasant.'"

Freddie recovered his breath.

"Uncle——" he began. But it was too late. Even as he spoke, there was a crash of brass and Sir Aylmer's face assumed that reverent, doughlike expression of attention so familiar in the rotundas of cure resorts.

"Sh," he said.

Of all the uncounted millions who in their time have listened to bands playing "Poet and Peasant," few can ever have listened with such a restless impatience as did Frederick Fitch-Fitch on this occasion. Time was flying. Every second was precious. At any moment disaster might befall. And the band went on playing as if it had taken on a life job. It seemed to him an eternity before the final oom-pom-pa.

"Uncle," he cried, as the echoes died away.

"Sh," said Sir Aylmer testily, and Freddie, with a dull despair, perceived that they were going to get an encore.

Of all the far-flung myriads who year in and year out have listened to bands playing the "Overture" to *Raymond,* few can ever have chafed as did Frederick Fitch-Fitch now. This suspense was unmanning him, this delay was torture. He took the papers and a fountain pen from his pocket and toyed with them nervously. He wondered dully as he sat there how the opera *Raymond* had ever managed to get itself performed, if the "Overture" was as long as this. They must have rushed it through in the last five minutes of the evening as the audience groped for its hats and wraps.

But there is an end to all things, even to the "Overture" from *Raymond.* Just as the weariest river winds somewhere safe to sea, so does this "Overture" eventually finish. And when it did, when the last notes faded into silence and the conductor stood bowing and smiling with that cool assumption, common to all conductors, that it is they and not the perspiring orchestra who have been doing the work, he started again.

"Uncle," he said, "may I trouble you for a moment . . . These papers."

Sir Aylmer cocked an eye at the documents.

"What papers are those?"

"The ones you have to sign, releasing my capital."

"Oh, those," said Sir Aylmer genially. The music had plainly mellowed him. "Of course, yes. Certainly, certainly. Give me . . ."

He broke off, and Freddie saw that he was looking at a distinguished, silvery-haired man with thin, refined features, who was sauntering by.

"Afternoon, Rumbelow," he said.

There was an unmistakable note of obsequiousness in Sir Aylmer's voice. His face had become pink, and he was shuffling his feet and twiddling his fingers. The man to whom he had spoken paused and looked down. Seeing who it was that had accosted him, he raised a silvery eyebrow. His manner was undisguisedly supercilious.

"Ah, Bastable," he said distantly.

A duller man than Sir Aylmer Bastable could not have failed to detect the cold hauteur in his voice. Freddie saw the flush on his uncle's face deepen. Sir Aylmer mumbled something about hoping that the distinguished-looking man was feeling better today.

"Worse," replied the other curtly. "Much worse. The doctors are baffled. Mine is a very complicated case." He paused for a moment, and his delicately chiseled lip curled in a sneer. "And how is the gout, Bastable? Gout! Ha, ha!"

Without waiting for a reply, he passed on and joined a group that stood chatting close by. Sir Aylmer choked down a mortified oath.

"Snob!" he muttered. "Thinks he's everybody just because he's got telangiecstasis. I don't see what's so wonderful about having telangiecstasis. Anybody could have . . . What on earth are you doing? What the devil's all this you're waving under my nose? Papers? Papers? I don't want any papers. Take them away, sir!"

And before Freddie could burst into the impassioned plea which trembled on his lips, a commotion in the doorway distracted his attention. His heart missed a beat, and he sat there, frozen.

On the threshhold stood Mortimer Rackstraw. He was making some enquiry of an attendant, and Freddie could guess only too well what that enquiry was. Mortimer Rackstraw was asking which of those present was Major General Sir Aylmer Bastable. Attached to arm, obviously pleading with him and appealing to his better self, Annabel Purvis gazed up into his face with tear-filled eyes.

A moment later, the conjurer strode up, still towing the girl. He halted before Sir Aylmer and threw Annabel aside like a soiled glove. His face was cold and hard and remorseless. With one hand he was juggling mechanically with two billiard balls and a bouquet of roses.

"Sir Aylmer Bastable?"

"Yes."

"I forbid the banns."

"What banns?"

"Their banns," said Mortimer Rackstraw, removing from his lips the hand with which he had been coldly curling his moustache and jerking it in the direction of Annabel and Freddie, who stood clasped in each other's arms, waiting for they knew not what.

"They're not up yet," said Annabel.

The conjurer seemed a little taken aback.

"Oh?" he said. "Well, when they are, I forbid them. And so will you, Sir Aylmer, when you hear all."

Sir Aylmer puffed.

"Who is this tight bounder?" he asked irritably.

Mortimer Rackstraw shook his head and took the two of clubs from it.

"A bounder, maybe," he said, "but not tight. I have come here, Sir Aylmer, in a spirit of altruism to warn you that if you allow your nephew to marry this girl the grand old name of Bastable will be mud."

Sir Aylmer started.

"Mud?"

"Mud. She comes from the very dregs of society."

"I don't," cried Annabel.

"Of course she doesn't," cried Freddie.

"Certainly she does not," assented Sir Aylmer warmly. "She told me herself that her father was a colonel."

Mortimer Rackstraw uttered a short, sneering laugh and took an egg from his left elbow.

"She did, eh? Did she add that he was a colonel in the Salvation Army?"

"What!"

"And that before he saw the light he was a Silver Ring bookie, known to all the heads as Rat-Faced Rupert, the Bermondsey Twister?"

"Good God!"

Sir Aylmer turned to the girl with an awful frown.

"Is this true?"

"Of course it's true," said Mortimer Rackstraw. "And if you want further proof of her unfitness to be your nephew's bride, just take a look at her Uncle Joe, who is now entering left-center."

And Freddie, listless now and without hope, saw that his companion of the train was advancing towards them. He heard Sir Aylmer gasp and was aware that Annabel had stiffened in his arms. He was not surprised. The sun, filtering through the glass of the rotunda, lit up the man's flabby puffiness, his morning coat, his red waistcoat and his brown shoes, and rarely, if ever, thought Freddie, could the sun of Droitgate Spa have shone on a more ghastly outsider.

There was nothing, however, in the newcomer's demeanor to suggest that he felt himself out of place in these refined surroundings. His manner had an easy self-confidence. He sauntered up and without *gêne* slapped the conjurer on the back and patted Annabel on the shoulder.

" 'Ullo, Mort. 'Ullo, Annie, my dear."

Sir Aylmer, who had blinked, staggered and finally recovered himself, spoke in a voice of thunder.

"You, sir! Is this true?"

"What's that, old cock?"

"Are you this girl's uncle?"

"That's right."

"Gaw!" said Sir Aylmer.

He would have spoken further, but at this point the band burst into "Pomp and Circumstance" and conversation was temporarily suspended. When it became possible once more for the human voice to make itself heard, it was Annabel's Uncle Joe who took the floor. He had recognized Freddie.

"Why, I've met you," he said. "We traveled down in the train together. Who's this young feller, Annie, that's huggin' and squeezin' you?"

"He is the man I am going to marry," said Annabel.

"He is not the man you are going to marry," said Sir Aylmer.

"Yes, I am the man she is going to marry," said Freddie.

"No, you're not the man she is going to marry," said Mortimer Rackstraw.

Annabel's Uncle Joe seemed puzzled. He appeared not to know what to make of this conflict of opinion.

"Well, settle it among yourselves," he said genially. "All I know is that whoever does marry you, Annie, is going to get a good wife."

"That's me," said Freddie.

"No, it isn't," said Sir Aylmer.

"Yes, it is," said Annabel.

"No, it's not," said Mortimer Rackstraw.

"Because I'm sure no man," proceeded Uncle Joe, "ever had a better niece. I've never forgotten the way you used to come and smooth my pillow and bring me cooling drinks when I was in the hospital."

There was the sound of a sharp intake of breath. Sir Aylmer, who was saying, "It isn't, it isn't, it isn't," had broken off abruptly.

"Hospital?" he said. "Were you ever in a hospital?"

Mr. Boffin laughed indulgently.

"Was I ever in a hospital! That's a good 'un. That would make the boys on the medical council giggle. Ask them at St. Luke's if Joe Boffin was ever in a hospital. Ask them at St. Christopher's. Why, I've spent most of my life in hospitals. Started as a child with Congenital Pyloric Hypertrophy of the Stomach and never looked back."

Sir Aylmer was trembling violently. A look of awe had come into his face, the look which a small boy wears when he sees a heavyweight champion of the world.

"Did you say your name was Joe Boffin?"

"That's right."

"Not *the* Joe Boffin. Not the man there was that interview with in the Christmas number of the *Lancet?*"

"That's me."

Sir Aylmer started forward impulsively.

"May I shake your hand?"

"Put it there."

"I am proud to meet you, Mr. Boffin. I am one of your greatest admirers."

"Nice of you to say so, ol' man."

"Your career has been an inspiration to me. Is it really true that you have Thrombosis of the Heart *and* Vesicular Emphysema of the Lungs?"

"That's right."

"And that your temperature once went up to 107.5?"

"Twice. When I had Hyperpyrexia."

Sir Aylmer sighed.

"The best I've ever done is 102.2."

Joe Boffin patted him on the back.

"Well, that's not bad," he said. "Not bad at all."

"Excuse me," said a well-bred voice.

It was the distinguished-looking man with the silvery hair who had approached them, the man Sir Aylmer had addressed as Rumbelow. His manner was diffident. Behind him stood an eager group, staring and twiddling their fingers.

"Excuse me, my dear Bastable, for intruding on a private conversation, but I fancied . . . and my friends fancied . . ."

"We all fancied," said the group.

"That we overheard the name Boffin. Can it be, sir, that you are Mr. *Joseph* Boffin?"

"That's right."

"Boffin of St. Luke's?"

"That's right."

The silvery-haired man seemed overcome by a sudden shyness. He giggled nervously.

"Then may we say—my friends and I—how much . . . We felt we would just like . . . Unwarrantable intrusion, of course, but we are all such great admirers . . . I suppose you have to go through a good deal of this sort of thing, Mr. Boffin . . . people coming up to you, I mean, and . . . perfect strangers, I mean to say . . ."

"Quite all right, old man, quite all right. Always glad to meet the fans."

"Then may I introduce myself? I am Lord Rumbelow. These are my friends, the Duke of Mull, the Marquis of Peckham, Lord Percy . . ."

" 'Ow are you, 'ow are you? Come and join us, boys. My niece, Miss Purvis."

"Charmed."

"The young chap she's going to marry."

"How do you do?"

"And his uncle, Sir Aylmer Bastable."

All heads were turned towards the Major General. Lord Rumbelow spoke in an awed voice.

"Is this really so, Bastable? Your nephew is actually going to marry Mr. Boffin's niece? I congratulate you, my dear fellow. A most signal honor." A touch of embarrassment came into his manner. He coughed. "We were just talking about you, oddly enough, Bastable, my friends and I. Saying what a pity it was that we saw so little of you. And we were wondering—it was the Duke's suggestion—if you would care to become a member of a little club we have—quite a small affair—rather exclusive, we like to feel—the Twelve Jolly Stretcher Cases. . . ."

"My dear Rumbelow!"

"We have felt for a long time that our company was incomplete without you. So you will join us? Capital, capital! Perhaps you will look in there tonight? Mr. Boffin, of course," he went on deprecatingly, "would, I am afraid, hardly condescend to allow himself to be entertained by so humble a little circle. Otherwise——"

Joe Boffin slapped him affably on the back.

"My dear feller, I'd be delighted. There's nothing stuck up about me."

"Well, really! I hardly know what to say . . ."

"We can't all be Joe Boffins. That's the way I look at it."

"The true democratic spirit."

"Why, I was best man at a chap's wedding last week, and all he'd got was emotional dermatitis."

"Amazing! Then you and Sir Aylmer will be with us tonight? Delightful. We can give you a bottle of lung tonic which I think you will appreciate. We pride ourselves on our cellar."

A babble of happy chatter had broken out, almost drowning the band, which was now playing the "Overture" to *William Tell*, and Mr. Boffin, opening his waistcoat, was showing the Duke of Mull the scar left by his first operation. Sir Aylmer, watching them with a throbbing heart, was dizzily aware of a fountain pen being thrust into his hand.

"Eh?" he said. "What? What's this? What, what?"

"The papers," said Freddie. "The merry old documents in the case. You sign here, where my thumb is."

"Eh? What? Eh? Ah yes, to be sure, Yes, yes, yes," said Sir Aylmer, absently affixing his signature.

"Thank you, Uncle, a thousand——"

"Quite, quite. But don't bother me now, my boy. Busy. Got a lot to talk about to these friends of mine. Take the girl away and give her a sulfur water."

And, brushing aside Mortimer Rackstraw, who was offering him a pack of cards, he joined the group about Joe Boffin. Freddie clasped Annabel in a fond embrace. Mortimer Rackstraw stood glaring for a moment, twisting his moustache. Then he took the flags of all nations from Annabel's back hair and with a despairing gesture strode from the room.

THE TEACHER AS A MODEL*

Joseph Adelson

Discussions of the Good Teacher are likely to leave us more uplifted than enlightened. The descriptions we read generally amount to little more than an assemblage of virtues; we miss in them a sense of the complexity and ambiguity that we know to characterize the teacher's work. Here are some paradoxes to help us get going: a teacher may be a good teacher yet not serve as a model to any of his students; he may inspire his students and yet fail to influence them; he may influence them without inspiring them; he may be a model for them and yet not be an effective teacher; and so on. To say all of this is to make the point—an obvious one but generally overlooked in the more solemn and global discussions of the Teacher—that charisma, competence and influence do not necessarily go hand in hand. A great many college teachers, perhaps most of them, are "good" teachers—good in the sense that they are conscientious and devoted, that they are lucid, articulate and fairminded lecturers, and that more often than not they succeed in illuminating the subject matter. Their students learn from them, often learn very much; yet these teachers ultimately do not make much of a difference in their students' lives beyond the learning they impart. At another extreme we have those rare teachers who stir and enchant their students, and yet who may be spectacularly

*Excerpted from Joseph Adelson, "The Teacher as a Model," reprinted from *The American Scholar*, Vol. 30, No. 3 (Summer, 1961), pp. 383–406. Copyright © 1961 by the United Chapters of Phi Beta Kappa. By permission of the publishers.

inept in teaching subject matter. I think now of a former colleague
of mine, in some ways a truly great man, who is so ebullient, erratic
and distractable, so easily carried away by the rocketing course of
his thought, that his students—even the bright ones—just sit there,
benumbed, bewildered and finally enthralled. They know themselves to be close to a Presence and are willing to suffer incoherence
to join vicariously in that demonic enthusiasm.

What we must do, plainly, is to recognize the pluralism in teaching—the many styles of influence, the many modes of connection
that bind student and teacher to each other. Teaching styles are
so diverse that they can be categorized in a great many different
ways. The grouping I want to try out was suggested by the yet unpublished work of Merrill Jackson, an anthropologist who has been
doing a cross-cultural study of the healer's role. He has isolated five
distinct modes of healing: shamanism, magic, religion, mysticism
and naturalism. Here is an abbreviated description of these types:
the shaman heals through the use of personal power, using craft,
charm and cunning; the magician heals through his knowledge of
arcane and complex rules, and his ability to follow ritual precisely;
the priest claims no personal power, but achieves his healing capacity as an agent or vessel of an omnipotent authority; the mystic
healer relies on insight, vision and wisdom, through which he cures
the sick soul; the naturalist (the present-day physician) is impersonal, empirical, task-oriented.

You may be struck, as I was, by the reflection that these separate
modes of healing in some sense persist to this day. While the present-day type of medicine is naturalistic (and in fact it is a common
complaint that medical specialists are *too* impersonal, and do not
give enough attention to the patient as a human being), we nevertheless find that the physician's relation to the patient is often patterned on an older style. Thus we have those physicians who follow
the shamanistic mode, in that they implicitly define healing as a
struggle between disease on the one hand and their own cunning
and power on the other; or those for whom medicine involves a
ritualistic following of rules; or those who claim no personal charisma, but define themselves to the patient as humble servants of
a Godhead, in this case Modern Medical Science. This typology
may be a useful one for treating other forms of interaction, such as
those that obtain between teacher and student. For example, those
teachers who define themselves primarily as experts in subject-
matter are roughly equivalent to naturalistic healers, in that the

relationship to the client is in both cases impersonal and task-oriented. In any case, it is worth trying; I want to use Jackson's schema to consider in detail three types of teachers.

The Teacher as Shaman. Here the teacher's orientation is narcissistic. The public manner does not matter; this type of teacher is not necessarily vain or exhibitionistic; he may in fact appear to be withdrawn, diffident, even humble. Essentially however he keeps the audience's attention focused on himself. He invites us to observe the personality in its encounter with the subject matter. He stresses charm, skill, *mana,* in the self's entanglement with ideas. When this orientation is combined with unusual gifts, we have a *charismatic* teacher, one of those outstanding and memorable personalities who seem more than life-size. The charismatic teacher is marked by power, energy and commitment: by power we mean sheer intellectual strength or uncommon perceptiveness and originality; by energy we mean an unusual force or vivacity of personality; and by commitment a deep absorption in the self and its work. Generally, all of these qualities are present to some degree: energy without power turns out to be mere flamboyance; power without energy or commitment is likely to be bloodless, arid, enervating.

This tells us only part of the story. In that group of teachers whom we term narcissistic we find considerable variation in the degree of impact on the student. In some cases the narcissistic teacher's impression on us is strong but transient; he moves us, but the spell does not survive the moment. We admire him as we admire a great performer, in his presence we dream of doing as well ourselves. But when the occasion is past we return to our mundane selves, out of the spell, unchanged, uninfluenced. In other instances, we may find the teacher's narcissism at the least distasteful and at times repelling. Something in it warns us to keep our distance, to remain wary and uncommitted.

What makes the difference? I am not sure that we know, but I think we will understand it better when we know more about variations in narcissism. There is a narcissism that makes a hidden plea to the audience; it cries out: "Look how wonderful I am! Admire me! Love me!" There is also a narcissism that is vindictive and vengeful; it says: "I love myself. Who needs you?" In either case the audience, or at least a good share of it, seems to sense the infantile source and quality of the teacher's narcissism, senses the petulance or anxiety that informs the teacher's manner, and keeps itself from becoming involved.

There is another and rarer form of narcissism that affects us quite differently from these. It is directed neither toward nor against the audience; it is autonomous, internally fed, sustaining itself beyond the observer's response to it. The best description of its appeal remains Freud's:

> It seems very evident that one person's narcissism has a great attraction for those others who have renounced part of their own narcissism and are seeking after object-love; the charm of a child lies to a great extent in his narcissism, his self-sufficiency and inaccessibility, just as does the charm of certain animals which seem not to concern themselves about us, such as cats and the large beasts of prey. . . . It is as if we envied them their power of retaining a blissful state of mind—an unassailable libido-position which we ourselves have since abandoned.

It is this form of narcissism—ingenuous, autonomous—that, when it is joined to other qualities, makes the teacher memorable. This orientation invites us to identification, to share in its bounty, to seek its protection and care or to join its omnipotence. Yet teachers of this kind are most problematic. They tempt us into regressions. We may come to feel them to be too exalted to serve as models for us. Or we may feel defeated by them before we begin, thinking that anything we achieve will be only second-rate, that we can never grow up enough to equal them.

The Teacher as Priest. The priestly healer claims his power not through personal endowment, but through his office; he is the agent of an omnipotent authority. Do we have a parallel to this in teaching? I would say it is the teacher who stresses not his personal virtues, but his membership in a powerful or admirable collectivity, for example, physics, psychoanalysis, classical scholarship. The narcissistic teacher to some degree stands apart from his discipline and seems to say: "I am valuable in myself." The priestly teacher says: "I am valuable for what I belong to. I represent and personify a collective identity."

It is difficult to generalize about this mode of teaching, since the teacher's behavior toward the student varies so much with the nature of the collectivity. It is one thing when the collectivity is coterminous with a subject-matter, and another when it is an enclosed or beleaguered sect within a discipline (for example, the various "schools" within sociology and psychology). Collectivities differ in their openness, their degree of organization, their status vis-à-vis other groups. Some are easy to enter, while others are closed; some are loose and informal, bound by common interest and camaraderie, and others are stratified and formal; some are marginal in status,

while others are secure, entrenched elites. Other differences involve the teacher's status in the collectivity: the undergraduate
teacher may proselytize, seeking recruits among the promising students; the graduate-professional school teacher will first indoctrinate, then examine and finally ordain the recruit.

To illustrate the teacher's activity in the priestly mode, I will
refer to the more enclosed and differentiated collectivities. We generally find the following elements: *Continuity.* The collectivity defines itself along a temporal dimension. It has a version of the past
and a vision of the future. In the past there were Great Ancestors
whose qualities and trials established the collective identity. There
is a program for the immediate future as well as a prophecy of
the distant future. One of the teacher's tasks is to help the student absorb the sense of the collective past and accept the common
blueprint for the future. *Hierarchy.* Generally (although not always) the collectivity is stratified in prestige and authority. The
teacher's personal authority depends in some part on his position
on the ladder of authority. While the teacher is superordinate to
the student, he in turn is subordinate to more elevated figures. The
student internalizes the group's system of hierarchy, and learns
that he is beholden not only to his teacher but to other members
of the hierarchy. One of the distinctive features of this mode of
teaching is that both teacher and student may share a common
model or group of models, either exalted contemporaries or Great
Ancestors. *Election.* When the group is an elite, when membership
in it is desirable and hard to achieve, we generally will find that
emphasis is placed on discipline, the enduring of trials and self-
transformation. The educational process is in some degree an extended rite of passage; the teacher's role is to prepare the student
for the trials he will endure, and to administer the tests that will
initiate him. *Mission.* The collectivity often offers a utopian view
of the future (especially when it is powerless and competitive) as
well as a program for achieving dominance and instituting reforms.
In these cases, the teacher's work is informed by missionary zeal;
the student is expected to absorb the group's sense of mission and
in turn to recruit and socialize others once he himself has achieved
office.

There is no question of the potency of the priestly mode of teaching. It achieves its effectiveness for a great many different reasons.
Teacher and student are generally in a close relationship to each
other. The student is encouraged to model his *activity* after the

teacher's, very much as in those charming experiments on imprint-
ing, where the baby duck follows the decoy. We also find a good
deal of close coaching, both of behavior and ideology. In most
cases the teaching is both positive and negative—that is, the student is trained not only to develop new behaviors, but also is required to eliminate competing or discordant responses. Generally
the student is given an unambiguous ideal of character and behavior
(he may be allowed, as part of the strategy of training, to feel uncertain whether he is meeting this ideal, but the ideal itself is usually clear cut enough). In some instances the collectivity offers
an encompassing doctrine, and the student is exhorted to re-inter-
pret his experiences in the vocabulary of the doctrine; and when
this is not the case, the training itself demands so complete a commitment of time and energy that the student's ideational world
narrows to include only the collectivity and its concerns. The
teacher customarily enjoys a great deal of power in relation to the
student, which reinforces the latter's dependency. The student's tie
to the collectivity is further reinforced by his close association with
peers—rivals, fellow-aspirants, fellow-sufferers—who share his trials,
sustain him in moments of doubt, restore his flagging spirits and
keep alive his competitive drive. Finally, this mode of teaching is
effective because it offers to the student a stake in a collective,
utopian purpose, and also a promise of such tangible rewards as
power, position, money, intellectual exclusiveness.

Less obviously, but quite as important, the collectivity makes its
appeal to the student in helping him to resolve internal confusions.
His participation allows a distinct identity choice; it supports that
choice by collective approval; it reduces intellectual and moral
ambiguity. A great many advantages also accrue to the collectivity;
over the short run, at least, it is helped in achieving its aims by its
capacity to recruit a cadre of devoted, disciplined believers. (The
history of my own field, psychology, has been decisively influenced
by the ability of certain schools to select and organize students in
the "priestly" framework, an ability that has very little to do with
intellectual merit.) But we also must recognize that this mode of
education possesses some deadly disadvantages, both to the student
and the group. The student purchases direction, force and clarity,
but does so by sacrificing some share of his own development; in
some important ways he is no longer his own man. For the collectivity the danger is in a loss of flexibility and innovation. (We have
a perfect example in the history of the psychoanalytic movement.

Through the 1930's it was, in its policies of recruitment and training, the most cosmopolitan of groups, a circumstance that produced an extraordinary boldness and vivacity of thought. Since its capture by American psychiatry it has developed a priestly mode of education, the result being a severe loss in intellectual scope and energy. It has now settled into its own Alexandrian age, repeating itself endlessly, living off its intellectual capital, affluent yet flatulent, an ironic example of the failure of success.)

The dominance of this mode of teaching in the graduate and professional schools, while regrettable, is probably inevitable. It is more disturbing to note its steady encroachment in undergraduate education. For many college teachers the introductory courses have less value in themselves than as a net in which to trap the bright undergraduate, while the advanced courses increasingly serve only to screen and socialize students for what the faculty deems "the great good place"—namely, the graduate school. Furthermore, academic counseling at the freshman and sophomore level frequently produces a guerilla warfare between disciplines, each seeking to capture the promising talents for itself, and without too much regard for the student's needs and interests. If matters are not worse than they already are, it is not because the disciplines have any genuine concern for the undergraduate or for liberal ideals of education, but because the leviathans have managed to neutralize each other's demands. Even so, the pressure of required courses and prerequisites serves to force the student into premature career commitment, while the onerous demands on his time (especially in the laboratory sciences, but also and increasingly in other fields) keep him from trying anything else.

The Teacher as Mystic Healer. The mystic healer finds the source of illness in the patient's personality. He rids his patient of disease by helping him to correct an inner flaw or to realize a hidden strength. The analogy here—perhaps it is a remote one—is to the teacher I will term *altruistic.* He concentrates neither on himself, nor the subject-matter, nor the discipline, but on the student, saying: "I will help you become what you are." We may recall Michelangelo's approach to sculpture: looking at the raw block of marble, he tried to uncover the statue within it. So does the altruistic teacher regard his unformed student; this type of teacher keeps his own achievement and personality secondary; he works to help the student find what is best and most essential within himself.

At this point we are uncomfortably close to the rhetoric of the college brochure. This is what the colleges tell us they do; and yet we know how very rarely we find altruistic teaching. Why is it so rare? For one thing, it is a model-less approach to teaching; the teacher points neither to himself nor to some immediately visible figure, but chooses to work with his students' potential and toward an intrinsically abstract or remote ideal. For another, this mode of teaching demands great acumen, great sensitivity—the ability to vary one's attack according to the phase of teaching and to the student—now lenient, now stern, now encouraging, now critical.

But the reason that the altruistic mode is so rarely successful lies deeper than these. The mode is selfless; it demands that the teacher set aside, for the moment at least, his own desires and concerns to devote himself without hidden ambivalence to the needs of another. In short, the teacher's altruism must be genuine; and altruism, as we know, is a fragile and unsteady trait, all too frequently reactive, born out of its opposite. If the teacher's selflessness is false, expedient or mechanical, if it comes out of a failure in self-esteem, or if it gives way to an underlying envy—and, in the nature of things, these are real and every-present possibilities—then the teaching at best will not come off and at the worst may end in damaging the student.

Some years ago I taught at an excellent progressive college that, quite unwittingly, induced some of its younger faculty to opt for a pseudo-altruistic mode of teaching. The college was committed to the ideal of student self-realization, and this was not, I should say, the usual pious cant, but a conscious, deliberate aim that showed itself in day-to-day planning and policy. In pursuit of this ideal, the college authorities stressed altruistic teaching; it was held that talent, productivity and eminence were of only secondary importance in the hiring and firing of faculty, that teaching talent *per se* was primary. Here things went seriously awry; for a variety of reasons, the college managed to attract an astonishing proportion of charismatic teachers—either men of established reputation, or ambitious and talented young men on the way up, but in either case men of great vitality, self-confidence and self-absorption. The presence of these teachers produced a star system: the students, quite naturally, adored them; and they gave the college its distinctive tone—febrile, impassioned.

When a young teacher was hired by the college it was quite natural for him to gravitate to the charismatic mode of teaching. But sometimes it did not work out for him—he did not have, or felt that he did not have, the necessary resources of talent, drive and "personality." If he wanted to survive at the college (or so he believed) he had to carve out a niche for himself, or even better, make himself indispensable. He had to find a new style, and he was likely to choose altruism, whether or not it really suited him. He played the role of the teacher who had given up his own ambitions to put himself at the service of youth. In some cases, I suspect, this role was chosen coolly and cynically, the teacher reasoning, quite correctly, that the college authorities would find it embarrassing to fire someone who was so true a believer in the college's ideology; in other cases the teacher adopted this role gradually and without deliberation, waking up one morning, so to speak, to discover that this had been his métier all along.

Expedient altruism very rarely came off, either for the teacher or his students. The latter sometimes showed an uncanny, although largely, unconscious, sensitivity in these matters—they could sense that the pseudo-altruist was somehow not quite the real thing. They might deem him "nice," "friendly" and "very helpful," but they said so in a forced or lukewarm way that often concealed a polite disdain. The teacher's manner was often so artificial and oversolicitous that students, I think, were made uneasy by it, feeling that they did not really merit all that elaborate concern. This type of teacher tended to attract the marginal and unmotivated students, primarily because he was reputed to be soft. The more serious students continued to prefer the charismatic teacher, however difficult and demanding he might occasionally be; and this was so, I think, not only because of his greater gifts, but also because they would cleave only to someone who showed them that he loved himself.

Expedient altruism produced most of the time a kind of dead-level mediocrity in teaching; students were not much influenced, but neither were they damaged. It was a very different matter when this mode was chosen not as a survival technique but to perform some obscure personal restitution, when the teacher loved his students to avoid hating them, helped them to avoid harming them. As I suggested before, this equilibrium is ordinarily too delicate to sustain, and in fact I know of no examples where the students of the reactively altruistic teacher did not in some way suffer from a breakthrough of envy or sadism on the teacher's part. I remember one man, widely known to be lovable, who was warm and encouraging to his students and who, when their backs were turned, would write the most damning letters of recommendation for them. In another more spectacular instance a particularly sanctimonious advocate of good teaching was fired when his own major students petitioned the college to do so. It turned out that he had the habit of helping his students by being "sincerely frank" with them, expositing their "weak points" at great length and in excruciating detail, and so managing to wound and humiliate them deeply.

This last anecdote reminds us of what might otherwise escape our attention, that the teacher may sometimes serve as a negative or *anti-model*. Here student uses teacher as a lodestar, from which he sails away as rapidly as he can, seeming to say: Whatever he is, I will not be; whatever he is for, I will be against. Teachers who exercise this power of revulsion are, in their own way, charismatic types; indeed, the teacher who is charismatically positive for some will be negative for others. He breeds disciples or enemies; few remain unmoved. If we follow a student's development closely enough we generally discover both positive and negative models; the decision to be or become like someone goes hand in hand with a negative choice of identity and ideal.

An even more important topic on the negative side of modeling concerns the teacher whose value changes—the *disappointing* model. I would not have thought this to be so important—it does not come up in casual conversations on modeling; but close interviewing frequently brings to light examples of disappointments in the model.

Let me suggest why this may be so. It may be trite and facile to say so, but we are led again to the importance of the Oedipal motif, especially where we find a close relationship between teacher and student. These apprenticeships tend to be colored by the student's earlier tie to the father; they repeat or complete the Oedipal interaction. For most of us—and for some of us acutely—one outcome of the Oedipal situation was our coming to feel disappointed by the father. When we were very young, we thought him to be grand and omnipotent; then we learned better, and for some this was a galling discovery. In these cases the close tie to an esteemed teacher has the meaning of a second chance, an opportunity to relive and master that early disenchantment. The attempt to cure disappointment, however, generally leads to its repetition. The student must keep up the fiction of his teacher's perfection; any flaw, any failing in the teacher, must be denied out of existence. It is too hard a position to maintain, and sooner or later the discovery of some defect in the now idealized teacher will send the student into a state of acute disappointment.

When the student uses his relation to the teacher in this repetitive way, he is especially vulnerable to any failure in the teacher's work or character. In the main, students are not so vulnerable; they learn to be realistic about their teachers, enough so that they are spared any strong sense of disappointment. Indeed, they manage it so well that we are likely to remain unaware that it *is* a problem, that even the "normal" student undergoes at some time some crisis, however minor, concerning the clay feet of an intellectual idol. I remember a poignant moment when talking to a young man who was telling me of his admiration for a brilliant teacher. After working for this man for some time, it dawned on him that the teacher was in some respects petty, petulant and vain. At first, he told me, he had a hard time reconciling these traits with the man's great intellectual gifts; but then he was able to recognize that the two really had nothing to do with each other. What was poignant—painful in fact—was that the student told me this in a strained, bluff, overly hearty manner that spoke tellingly of the struggle it had been to accept it.

The student's responses to disappointment depend not only on his susceptibility but also on the type of flaw he discovers in the teacher. It makes a difference whether or not the failing is *role-relevant*. It puts a greater strain on the student when the model's fault involves role performance than when it is unrelated to how the teacher does his work. In the latter instance the student can more easily compartmentalize his view of the teacher.

Probably the most difficult type of failure for the student to accept is a moral one. By "moral" I do not mean, primarily, the teacher's living up to conventional standards in pleasure-seeking; rather I mean such qualities as integrity, fairness, ethical sensitivity, courage. The student is not overly demoralized to discover that his model's ego qualities are not quite what he thought or hoped they were, that his teacher is not as intelligent, penetrating or perceptive as he first appeared to be. It is, indeed, part of the student's maturation that he learn to tolerate this fact, just as the child in growing up learns to give up his belief that the parents are omnicompetent. But a moral failure is not so easily accepted and, if it is serious enough in nature, is likely to be a disheartening or even a shattering experience. When we think of the teacher as a model, we think naturally of the teacher as an ego ideal—an avatar of virtue—and take for granted, and thus ignore, the superego aspects. Yet some teachers influence us primarily because they embody the moral ideals of the role, or because they represent the unpleasant necessities of work, duty or intellectual honesty. Edward Tolman played such a role for graduate students (and faculty too, I image) at Berkeley; many of us were not deeply influenced by him intellectually, but all of us were profoundly touched by his integrity and humility. And Freud has told us how, many years later, he could still recall an incident of his student days when, arriving late to work, he was "overwhelmed by the terrible gaze of his [Brucke's] eyes." Most of us do our work in the silent presence of some such gaze, terrible or (nowadays) merely reproachful.

The teacher's life is as filled with moral tension and ambiguity as any other, but the moral dimension is most visibly operative in areas that do not affect the student (such as departmental politics); consequently, moral issues do not ordinarily become problematic in the teacher-student relationship. But when they do, we become intensely aware of their tacit importance. I know of only one clear-cut occurrence of this kind: a group of students in one of the sciences discovered that their teacher—ordinarily full of pieties about the holy obligations of the scientist—was not entirely responsible in his handling of evidence; he was not guilty of outright fabrication but of cutting, fitting and suppressing data to fit the needs of the study. Not all of the students were distraught by his discovery—here again vulnerability varies—but some were entirely demoralized and in one case a student (who had been sitting on the fence) decided to give up research altogether and choose an applied career.

Those of us who were at the University of California during the loyalty oath troubles had a unique opportunity to observe how the moral qualities of our teachers, ordinarily taken for granted and so overlooked, could assume overweening importance in a moment of moral crisis. It was an uncanny time for us: with one part of ourselves we lived in the routine of things, concerned with courses, prelims, dissertations; and all the while our inner, central attention was elsewhere, held in a fretful preoccupation with the morality play in which our teachers were involved. We wondered how things would turn out, of course, but beyond and deeper than that the intimate, compelling question was whether our models would behave honorably. Most of them did not, although for a time we kept ourselves from recognizing this, largely by allying ourselves psychically with the very few who acted heroically while ignoring the very many who did not. It taught us, on the one hand, that moral courage is possible and, on the other, that it is uncommon. All in all, it was a quick and unpleasant education. Perhaps it is just as well for all of us, teachers and students alike, that serious moral examination occurs so rarely.

PART IV

The Instrumental Relationship

Introduction

In this part we should like to consider a type of relationship which is central to our lives—the instrumental or work relationship. While it is true that man does not live by bread alone, it is equally true that bread (or some other product) is vital to his life; and often that bread is obtained through a process of interaction with other people.[1] An "instrumental relationship" may be defined as any relationship of two or more persons which has as its ultimate function the performance of a task.

The main portion of this essay will be concerned with some of the issues relevant to the *work* relationship. In the closing part, a special case will be considered: that of the "creative relationship," where the desired output is some sort of new, innovative product such as a creative solution to a problem or an artistic work.

Background

Until recently, most of the attention to man's work was centered on its more technical and formalistic aspects. Problems of the work setting, the proper rules structure, the nature of the technical operations required, etc., received the major focus of attention. In other words, work was generally conceived as being something which an isolated individual or single person performed. Only recently has there been a shift of emphasis toward recognition of the fact that work itself involves a relationship between people.

We may mark the Hawthorne Studies of Elton Mayo and his asso-

---

[1] In this context, we are considering work to be an end in itself, not just a sublimation of other needs or a diversion of aggressive or hostile impulses.

ciates[2] as the beginning of a shift of interest toward the interpersonal aspects of the work process and a movement toward adding more flesh to man's skeletal conception of task interaction. From these studies to the present there has been a continual increase in the amount of research effort and interest directed toward this area, especially toward such phenomena as group norms and their growth, problems in communication between individuals and groups,[3] and resistances to change in work and interaction routines.[4]

The Basis for Instrumental Relationships

We now turn to a simple but fundamental question, the answer to which should provide us with a clearer image of our topic: why is an instrumental *relationship* necessary, desirable, useful, or practicable in a given task situation? There seem to be several rather basic answers to this question.

1. For a number of reasons, one person may not be able to do the work alone. There may be too much to do, too much time pressure, or some other constraint; so help from another person is needed to complete the task. Or there may be a set of complementary skills required for completion, such as in certain kinds of problem-solving situations which require members to have varied bits of knowledge or different skills. Or, there may be too many activities required simultaneously to permit their performance by one individual, even if he does have the requisite abilities. Too much to do, too little time, too many skills required, too many things to do at once. These factors may be summarized as follows: Man needs the help of others when his activities or instrumental goals become so large or com-

[2]F. J. Roethlisberger and W. J. Dickson, *Management and the Worker* (Cambridge: Harvard University Press, 1939).

[3]A. Bavelas, "Communication Patterns in Task-Oriented Groups," D. Lerner and H. D. Lasswell (eds.), *The Policy Sciences* (Stanford, Calif.: Stanford University Press, 1951), pp. 193–202; also H. Guetzkow and H. A. Simon, "The Impact of Certain Communication Nets upon Organization and Performance in Task-Oriented Groups," *Management Science*, Vol. 1 (1955), pp. 233–50.

[4]L. Coch and J. R. P. French, "Overcoming Resistance to Change," *Human Relations*, Vol. 1 (1947), pp. 512–32.

Much of the research and thinking done on the work process today may also be considered under the new field of "organization theory." For extensive bibliographies specifically related to this field, see C. Argyris, *Personality and Organization* (New York: Harper Bros., 1957); P. Blau and W. R. Scott, *Formal Organizations: A Comparative Approach* (San Francisco: Chandler Pub. Co., 1962); J. G. March and H. A. Simon, *Organizations* (New York: John Wiley & Sons, 1958). For collections of articles, see M. Haire (ed.), *Modern Organization Theory* (New York: John Wiley & Sons, 1959), and J. G. March (ed.), *Handbook of Organizations* (Chicago: Rand McNally, Inc., 1963), and James D. Thompson (ed.), *Approaches to Organizational Design* (Pittsburgh: University of Pittsburgh Press, 1966).

plex that they prohibit his obtaining them by himself. This is clearly one major source of human work organizations, and of most other organizations that have some sort of output as a goal.

2. Those who perform a service for others generally must enter into a relationship with the recipient of the service, even though that relationship may be quite "fleeting" and only minimally co-operative.[5]

3. The relationship may be of value as an end in itself—it may simply be more satisfying to work with others than to work alone.[6] There appear to be wide individual variations in the degree of importance placed on satisfaction of relational needs.[7] As Rosenberg[8] found, some people hold as one of their major criteria for choice of work the opportunity to perform their work in relationships with others, while others expressed little or no specific interest in this aspect of different occupations.

4. A work relationship may also be formed in order to reduce competition which, if continued, could be harmful to both parties. When two newsboys on the same corner decide to work together at rush hour, with one handing out papers and the other collecting money, this decision may come in part from a belief that together they will sell more than they would separately. It may also be motivated by anxiety stemming from each's fear that he may be completely driven out of business by the other. The actual danger of this happening may be real or fantasied, but the force toward getting together can act in either case.

5. The example just cited implies an ultimately co-operative relationship. The relationship may also be formed *in order to compete*. This is evidently the case with Lee and Yang, the Nobel Prize winning physicists,[9] who help to keep their interest high by racing each other to different kinds of solutions. Even in this type of competitive relationship, however, there is an implicit agreement to co-operate in the competition.[10]

---

[5]See the articles by Davis and Becker in this part.

[6]See Roy, "Banana Time," in this part.

[7]For a systematic measuring of these needs see William Schutz, *FIRO–B: A Three-Dimensional Theory of Interpersonal Behavior* (New York: Rinehart, 1958).

[8]M. Rosenberg, *Occupations and Values* (Glencoe, Ill.: The Free Press, 1957).

[9]"Profiles, A Question of Parity," *New Yorker Magazine* (May 12, 1962), pp. 49–104.

[10]The mere fact of remaining together in the relationship may not *always* indicate an agreement to co-operate. There may be other forces keeping the parties together. An interesting case of this is the small-group experimental setting where the subjects' decisions to participate in the experiment create a commitment to remain in the group even though the task demands continued competition.

6. Finally, an instrumental relationship may result when the distribution of power between the partners is so uneven that one can control the other and keep him in the relationship for the controller's own ends. The prototype of this is, of course, the master-slave relationship, which has lost its importance in the United States but still exists in some other cultures.

To summarize, we have presented six bases for the formation of an instrumental relationship: (1) to *break down* a task that is too large, complex, etc., to be performed alone; (2) to have someone for whom to perform a *service;* (3) for the satisfaction of *interacting* with another person; to either (4) *avoid* the costs or (5) *gain* the benefits of *competition;* and (6) because one who holds *power* over another wishes to accomplish certain goals through the other. Two final comments are needed to clarify this list. First, a specific relationship may be initiated for any one or for a *mixture* of these reasons. Second, a relationship may be formed for one reason but become important for other reasons as it changes over time.

Types of Instrumental Relationships

Having considered the reasons for the formation of instrumental relationships, let us move on to the question of how we might *classify* relationships. Two basic dimensions will be used here to illustrate how we can make distinctions.[11] Both dimensions relate to the personal orientation of the parties in the relationship. The first dimension is concerned with the trust orientation of the parties toward each other. For simplicity, the two alternatives will be called *friendly* and *antagonistic*. In the friendly orientation, the dominant assumptions people hold toward each other are positive. On the whole, person A trusts the other person, B, and does not fear that B will strive to fulfill some vested interest of his own at A's expense. Conversely, in the antagonistic orientation there is a negative set and a sense of mistrust—that A must be on his toes lest B use an opening to some personal advantage that A considers inappropriate and harmful to himself.

The second dimension is concerned with whether ends to be obtained in the relationship will be joint or individual. The two possibilities here are a *co-operative* orientation, where the effort of each member is seen as collaborative and useful to the other, and a *com-*

---

[11]These are, of course, only two out of many different dimensions that might be used to develop typologies of instrumental relationships.

petitive orientation, where attainment of goals by one member is seen as a threat to the goal attainment of the other.[12]

These two dimensions, then, provide us with four logical types of instrumental relationship: *(a)* friendly co-operation; *(b)* antagonistic competition; *(c)* friendly competition; *(d)* antagonistic co-operation. Each of these will be briefly described in turn.

a) Friendly Co-operation. In this type of instrumental relationship the general orientation of the parties is one of generally positive feelings toward one other and help is given and received in the process of moving toward what is usually a common goal. One example of this type might be two mechanical engineers trying to solve a heat transfer problem.

b) Antagonistic Competition. This is the opposite of friendly co-operation and might be considered by many not to be a relationship at all. We consider it to be such by using "relationship" to mean that one person's actions must be recognized and responded to by the other, and vice versa. In this type, the personal orientations of the participants are generally negative, including disrespect, mistrust, and often hostility. The individual efforts are not seen as contributing toward any common end. An interesting example of this type is the relationship between a dance musician and his audience, where the competition is for a curious mixture of power, self-esteem, enjoyment, and artistic taste.[13]

c) Friendly Competition. This is a mixed case, where the parties have a basically positive personal orientation toward one another, even though at some level they are using their individual efforts to compete with one another. An example already cited earlier is quite appropriate here: the case of Lee and Yang, who race each other to problem solutions. Another would be professional golfers opposing each other in a tournament where they are essentially competing for a prize and often still feel quite close and trusting

---

[12]This dimension is basically the same as Deutsch's orientation variable which hinges on what he calls "promotive interdependence" in co-operative situations. "'Promotive interdependence' specifies a condition in which individuals are so linked together that there is a positive correlation between their goal attainments." M. Deutsch, "Cooperation and Trust: Some Theoretical Notes," *Nebraska Symposium on Motivation*, 1962, (Lincoln: University of Nebraska Press), pp. 275–319.

[13]See Becker's article in this part. Becker also raises the question of *which* relationship is chosen for analysis of instrumental activities like services—the relationship between performer and client, or the one between performer and colleagues. It would appear that in most cases of antagonistic-competitive performer-client relationships the performer also had simultaneously a more supportive relationship with his own colleagues.

toward one another, playing under an elaborate system of courtesies and other norms. That this is the case is illustrated by the exceptions (the very stir they cause proves the point), such as the recent (1967) antagonism between Gary Player and Gay Brewer in a British tournament. They had slipped into an Antagonistic-Competition mode.

d) *Antagonistic Co-operation.*[14] This is the other mixed case, where there is a negative personal orientation of the parties toward each other, even though there also exists ostensibly an orientation of co-operation or pooling of efforts in pursuit of a group goal. A good example of this type of relationship is that of a student discussion group trying to arrive at solutions to cases. In some of these groups, the participants co-operate in a generally polite manner, but they are actually holding back their best ideas for individual use at a later date.[15]

Figure 1 presents these basic dimensions. Once again it should be noted that instrumental relationships do not necessarily occur in these "pure" types. Any given relationship may have elements of any or all of these types in it, in varying strengths.

ORIENTATION TO CONTRIBUTIONS

		Co-operative	Competitive
ORIENTATION TO OTHER PARTY	*Friendly*	(a) Friendly Co-operation	(c) Friendly Competition
	Antagonistic	(d) Antagonistic Co-operation	(b) Antagonistic Competition

FIG. 1. TYPES OF INSTRUMENTAL RELATIONSHIPS

By way of illustrating the possible implication of this typology, we may consider the six bases of a work relationship presented above and ask whether relationships formed for different reasons would tend to be found in specific cells of Figure 1.

1. Relationship formed to reduce complexity. We would expect the majority of these relationships to be found in cell (a), Friendly

---

[14]This term was originally suggested by David Riesman.

[15]Robert Ardrey provides a fascinating chapter describing the antagonistic-co-operative orientation in certain groups of animals and men—the society of inward antagonism which he calls "the noyau." In fact, these groups reverse the axes of our typology and are really "co-operatively antagonistic," where the antagonism is the output and they need one another to continue the process. See Robert Ardrey, *The Territorial Imperative,* (New York: Atheneum, 1966), Chap. v.

Co-operation, since they are generally formed voluntarily to accomplish some sort of joint goal that cannot be obtained singly. There will also be some cases of *(d)* Antagonistic Co-operation, as when the task demands that people work together who would ordinarily not choose to associate; and cases of *(c)* Friendly Competition, as in the Yang-Lee case noted above, where the participants compete within a limited framework while agreeing to pool their output in the end.

2. Service relationship. This may fall into any one of the four cells, depending on the nature of the roles involved. Important here would be such elements as the expectations of each party for the other and the type and length of contact between the parties.[16]

3. Relationship formed for interaction. This relationship would generally fall in cell *(a)*, Friendly Co-operation, and secondarily in cell *(c)*, Friendly Competition. The very nature of its formation indicates that when it ceased to have a friendly and trusting orientation it would not satisfy its original function and would tend to break down.

4. Relationship to avoid competition. This type will by definition fall into the two co-operative cells. It may result in Friendly Co-operation, but there is also a good chance for an orientation of Antagonistic-Co-operation, especially if feelings of mistrust, hostility, and the like that were built up during the competitive phase were not adequately worked through when the switch was made from competition to co-operation.

5. Relationship to gain effects of competition. The predominant orientation here would be cell *(c)*, Friendly Competition, especially since there has usually been a Friendly Co-operative orientation prior to the decision to compete. If the orientation changed over time to an antagonistic one, we could assume that the basis for the relationship had also changed.

6. Relationship formed because of power one holds over another. This would result in a generally antagonistic orientation, in cells *(d)* or *(b)*. This orientation is caused on the one hand by the controller's feelings that he *must* use his power to obtain desired performance from the controlled person and therefore he cannot trust the controlled to do it on his own, and on the other hand by the controlled's feelings of hostility for being controlled and his feelings that he cannot trust the controller's interests to be the same as his

---

[16]See Davis' article in this part for an example of a service relationship which is characterized by a mix of antagonistic co-operation and competition.

own. This relationship is probably most often found to be a *mixture* of Antagonistic Co-operation and Competition, as in the case of a chain-gang convict who both produces some sort of work and sabotages his foreman by explicitly following some directive which he knows from his experience to be incorrect.

Problems in the Relationship and Their Solution

Now that we have considered formation of the instrumental relationship and one possible typology, let us move on to the kinds of problems that must be solved if the relationship is to continue once it has been formed.

Our basic assumption, following several different authors,[17] is that there are two fundamental problem areas which must be dealt with in an instrumental relationship: *(a)* problems concerning the *task* involved and operations for its performance, and *(b)* problems concerning the *maintenance* of the relationship or control of its "socioemotional" state.[18] In making this assumption we are also more generally asserting that a system has two needs, both of which must be met to some minimum degree and balanced with each other if the system is to continue. Members must therefore enact roles during the life of the group which carry out these functions or meet these needs.[19]

Task issues, generally, are concerned with how to proceed in performing the task—what goals are to be set for the relationship; how influence and control are to be distributed for decison making; which strategies, division of labor, and the like are to be used; what actual operations are to be used and how they will be carried out;

---

[17]The "Task" and "Socioemotional" distinction has been closely associated with Bales and his associates; these are similar to the leadership functions of "initiating structure" and "consideration" associated with the Ohio State studies. See E. A. Fleishman, "Leadership Climate, Human Relations Training, and Supervisory Behavior," *Personnel Psychology,* Vol. 6 (1953), pp. 205–22, and A. W. Halpin and B. J. Winer, "A Factorial Study of the Leader Behavior Descriptions," in R. M. Stogdill and W. M. Coons (eds.) *Leader Behavior: Its Description and Measurement,* Bureau of Business Research Monog. 88 (Columbus: Ohio State University, 1957). This section is also influenced by the formulations of the National Training Laboratories concerning task and maintenance functions in a group. See L. P. Bradford, J. R. Gibb, and K. D. Benne, *T-Group Theory and Laboratory Method* (New York: John Wiley & Sons, 1964).

[18]Another way of making the division would be (1) technical or content aspects of the job itself; (2) the area of structure—division of labor, who does which parts of (1); (3) the socioemotional problems listed as *(b)* above. However, for simplification of the considerations which follow, our purposes are best served by combining (1) and (2) under the general heading of task problems.

[19]For an enumeration of the forms which these roles may take, see K. D. Benne and P. Sheats, "Functional Roles of Group Members," *Journal of Social Issues,* Vol. 4 (1948), pp. 41–60.

and feedback on past performance. Note that these task areas are more relevant for shared communication in some types of instrumental relationships than they are in others. For instance, they would be of prime consideration in most relationships formed specifically to get help in doing a certain job. On the other hand, for a relationship that was formed for the relational value itself, task problems may at times be suppressed to a great extent. Intermediate between these two would be the service relationship, which would have certain task areas defined as being the responsibiltiy of the service person and *not* appropriate for sharing with the client.

Maintenance issues, on the other hand, are oriented more specifically toward the relationship itself and its continuance; that is, these issues most often have to do with tensions that result from either just being together or from trying to do a task. They can be characterized by such questions as: How close or distant are the partners with each other, and how do they want to be? How do members *feel* about each other? How shall hostility and other *disruptive feelings* be handled in the relationship? What effect will *transference* phenomena (reacting to the partner in terms of people in earlier relationships) have on the relationship? How will *evaluations* of one another be handled?[20]

For each of these two sets of problems the basic process for solution is one of *information transaction* between the parties. The basic idea is that task and maintenance functions are accomplished through a *feedback* process where information is exchanged concerning the state of the task, the relationship, or the individuals involved.[21] This exchange serves both to change these states and to trigger other kinds of action which change the system. For instance, if one partner in a relationship tells the other that he dislikes having to do all the detail work, this might then create a situation where the *distribution* of work may be rearranged to be more satisfactory to both parties or more realistic in terms of abilities. Task performance might improve as a result of this process. Then information must be exchanged again, and the general process is repeated.[22]

These transactions may be verbal, such as the sharing of ideas or

[20]For a view of this area which is not limited to the instrumental relationship, see the essay on "Emotional Modalities" which introduces Part I of this volume. See also Henry C. Smith, *Sensitivity to People* (New York: McGraw-Hill, 1966).

[21]For a fuller description of this feedback process and one author's view of the effect that it can have on an instrumental relationship, see Argyris' article in this part.

[22]Related to this feedback process, but more general, is the function of *reality testing* which may be performed by these information transactions between parties to a relationship. See the essay which introduces Part V of this volume.

personal feelings at a particular moment, or they may be nonverbal, such as actual physical action that is taken. The transactions may also be *intended,* as when one party to the relationship tells the other that they might be able to accomplish more if they divided up the work, or they may be unintended, as when the same statement about work division is made and the listener gets two other messages that the sender is unaware he is transmitting—*(a)* that the sender does not trust the listener in certain work areas and *(b)* that he does not feel that he can discuss it openly with the listener, for whatever reasons.

Relationship between Task and Maintenance Problems

There are many ways in which task operations affect maintenance of the relationship. *First,* decisions and arrangements concerning the power distribution may strongly affect both parties if *(a)* the one with less power feels hostile toward the one with more power, or *(b)* if either has less commitment because of the unequal distribution, or *(c)* if it is equally distributed and one party feels ambivalent about this because of his previous relationships, which have all been unbalanced.[23] *Second,* decisions, ideas, plans, etc., and the process by which they are produced will affect the participants' evaluations of one another, and these impressions will affect each one's feelings about the other and his own feelings about the perception of himself in the situation.[24]

Third, just general interaction and contact in performance of a task may tend to increase the participant's feelings for one another as a result of a continuing increase in information held about each other.[25] *Fourth,* the giving or receiving of help on a particular task may affect one's sense of self-esteem, the status that one confers on the other, and one's desire to continue in the relationship.[26] *Fi-*

---

[23]It should be pointed out here that although the question of power and influence distribution is not emphasized in this essay, it is a major concern of many writers who have developed normative theories of organization. See such writers as Argyris, *op. cit.;* R. Likert, *New Patterns of Management* (New York: McGraw-Hill Book Co., Inc., 1961), and *The Human Organization* (New York: McGraw-Hill, 1967), D. McGregor, *The Human Side of Enterprise* (New York: McGraw-Hill Book Co., Inc., 1960), and the synthesizing article by W. G. Bennis, "Leadership Theory and Administrative Behavior: The Problem of Authority," *Administrative Science Quarterly,* Vol. 4 (1959), pp. 260–301.

[24]For a broader perspective on this view, see the classics by C. H. Cooley, *Human Nature and the Social Order* (New York: Scribner, 1902), and G. H. Mead, *Mind, Self and Society* (Chicago: University of Chicago Press, 1935).

[25]G. C. Homans, *The Human Group* (New York: Harcourt, Brace & Co., 1950).

[26]See Homans' article in this part.

nally, the general trustworthiness which one exhibits in working on the task may have a strong effect on the other's perception of him as trustworthy in other areas of the relationship.[27]

There may be points where task and maintenance considerations come into conflict. It may be necessary because of time limitations to overemphasize completion of the task, even to the detriment of the relationship itself. This is especially likely if the relationship must meet some external standard such as showing a profit.[28] Or it may be necessary to discuss maintenance in order to break out of a situation which has become locked on one task element which will remain unproductive, as when an argument over appropriate meeting times must be considered in terms of the influence or control each party is exerting before a final decision can be made. In this case a maintenance problem is blocking progress and must be dealt with, even if it is an apparent digression from work on the schedule.

In the other direction, as well as helping loosen a persistent problem situation, discussion of the relationship may drive out all task considerations and contribute to anxiety-motivated flight from the task at hand.[29] This would be exemplified by the case of a partnership that spent all its time talking, for instance, about the effects the partners had on one another, thereby preventing them from making any decisions or producing anything. The motive here would generally be an avoidance of the possibility of making mistakes or failing in some task situation.[30]

Implied but not explicitly stated above is the notion that the conflict between task and maintenance may be reduced by a higher-order maintenance element: a commitment or climate in the relationship which allows a free and open interchange about the *state* of a relationship and how the task and maintenance functions themselves are being performed. This climate allows the relationship and

---

[27]For an experimental analysis of trust as a variable in the relationship, see M. Deutsch, *op. cit.*

[28]There is a trap here, however. The relationship may be ignored in order to meet some external standard in the short run, and the resulting deterioration in the state of the relationship may then cause failure of task performance in the long run. See Likert's (*op. cit*) analysis of the differences in how this problem is handled by effective and ineffective leaders of work groups.

[29]M. S. Olmstead, "Orientation and Role in the Small Group," *American Sociological Review,* Vol. 19 (Dec., 1954), pp. 741–51.

[30]Although exclusive focus on maintenance may also be motivated by a general hunger for closer, more involving relationships than are characteristic of our society today, this hunger would account for part of the rapid growth in T-group activity since its inception in 1947. See Bradford, Gibb, and Benne, *op. cit.*

its parties to learn from their experience and grow toward more effective attainment of their goals since this type of information transaction determines in part the effectiveness of transactions in both of the basic problem areas.[31]

Dealing with Task and Maintenance Problems in the Different Types of Relationships

In this concluding section on work relationships, we would like to make some predictions about tendencies toward effective information sharing about task and maintenance issues in the four types of relationships described above. These tendencies would be a factor in whether the relationship would be productive and/or would continue.

a) Friendly Co-operation. The tendency here would be toward being able to deal with both task and maintenance issues as they are appropriate. The friendly (high trust) orientation would promote the taking of risk as far as raising tawdry or difficult issues is concerned,[32] and the co-operative orientation would provide a basic motivation—wanting to do better as a team—which could be related in the partner's minds to a striving and sharing together (about the task) rather than separately.

b) Antagonistic Competition. In this case, the tendency would be toward low willingness to deal with both maintenance and task issues. The low trust level would make risk taking more difficult, and the open competition would orient the persons toward not dealing with task issues, since any information shared might help the other and consequently hurt one's self. Information that is shared is often calculated to mislead or distort, thus pushing the two persons (or groups, or nations) farther apart.[33]

c) Friendly Competition. In this instance, the basically positive orientation toward one another would promote dealing with maintenance issues. However, talking about the task would be more questionable, since the competitive situation again implies that information sharing might mean a lost advantage. Individuals would probably experience some conflict over how to proceed on the task and would be drawn toward seeking out "safe" moments when the task can be talked about without hurting one's own position—such as

---

[31]This implication may be seen as moving toward normative theory and away from description. See again the essay on "Towards Better Interpersonal Relationships" which introduces Part V of this volume.

[32]See Argyris' article in this part.

[33]See Blake's article on intergroup competition in this part.

professional football players on opposing teams discussing crucial plays *after* the game or at the *end* of a season. The competitive element makes it hard for them to change what they are doing *in process.*

d) *Antagonistic Co-operation.* In this other mixed case, dealing with maintenance would tend to be low owing to negative feelings and mistrust (poor climate for risk taking), and dealing with the task would probably be moderate. There is a pull toward task discussions because of the partners' interdependence, but this pull could "run down" over time as untended maintenance problems build up. Motivation toward the task goal could become less potent than desires to get out of the relationship or to protect one's self from the other person. Unsatisfactory superior-subordinate relationships often fit this pattern.

By way of summarizing these predictions, we should note one striking pattern: There is a clear trend toward "the rich get richer and the poor get poorer."[34] In Friendly Co-operation, where tensions and difficulties would tend to be lower than the other three, the tendencies are toward freer discussion of both task and maintenance. Conversely, in Antagonistic Co-operation, for instance, a good deal of tension is generated by the process of working together, and the situation is loaded against dealing with it, thus allowing the problems to build, making it still more difficult to share information and so on.

From this view, we can see why in recent years a good deal of interest has been generated in the process of helping a relationship through a third party (consultant, counselor, etc.).[35] An "outsider" can often observe patterns and can communicate information that is too risky for the partners to raise. This sharing may provide them with a view of reality that they can use to break out of their downward spiral.

THE CREATIVE RELATIONSHIP

Let us now consider a special case—that of the *creative* relationship. By a creative relationship we mean a relationship whose main expected product is some new, unusual, original combination of

---

[34]This point was clarified through a discussion with Tim Hall.

[35]See R. Beckhard, "The Confrontation Meeting," *Harvard Business Review,* Vol. 45, No. 2 (March–April 1967); R. R. Blake, Jane S. Morgan, and R. L. Sloma, "The Union-Management Intergroup Laboratory," *Journal of Applied Behavioral Science,* Vol. 1, No. 1 (Spring 1965); F. I. Steele, "Consultants and Detectives," *Journal of Applied Behavioral Science,* in press.

elements that is found to be useful by some group at some time.[36] The output can involve music, drama, painting, sculpture, and other visual art forms; architectural products combining form and function; ingenious solutions to business-related problems; new experiences in an affective relationship; new solutions to pressing problems of international co-operation and interaction;[37] advances in scientific knowledge, theory, organizations of concepts, and so on.

From this list it can be seen that this "type" of relationship really cuts across many of the categories found in this book and may exist simultaneously in any of them at a given time. The reason for its inclusion in this section is that there is a *product* of some sort involved. It is, however, the *creative* aspect of this product that is of importance at this point. At the same time we do not mean to deny the fact that the instrumental aspects of a relationship may have a marked effect on the creative output of the relationship. This effect is interestingly demonstrated in an article by Becker,[38] who analyzes the role of the professional dance musician. In it he illustrates vividly the tensions of dance musicians, who resent the fact that they are forced to satisfy the requirements of an instrumental relationship with their audience because the audience response determines the economic criterion of success or failure. The musicians feel that the need to satisfy an audience prevents development of a creative relationship with that audience and severely handicaps them in their efforts to be creative, spontaneous artists with expressional integrity.

Background

By and large the interpersonal aspects of creativity have been neglected in social science[39] and even in the humanities. Even for those who have been students of this area, the issue that has preoccupied most of them has been group versus individual problem solving, with no clear-cut evidence emerging that would be of general application to different kinds of groups and situations.[40]

This same formulation of the issue has pervaded areas other than

[36]M. I. Stein, "Creativity and Culture," *Journal of Psychology*, Vol. 36 (1953), pp. 311–22.

[37]See Blake's article in this part.

[38]Included in this part.

[39]For an illustration of the scope of work in the general area of creativity, see the bibliographic collection by M. I. Stein and S. J. Heinze, *Creativity and the Individual* (Chicago: Graduate School of Business, University of Chicago, and Glencoe, Ill.: The Free Press, 1960).

[40]I. Lorge, D. Fox, J. Davitz, and M. Brenner, "A Survey of Studies Contrasting the Quality of Group Performance and Individual Performance," *Psych. Bulletin*, Vol. 55, No. 5 (1958), p. 337.

the academic. The technique of "brainstorming" grew up in the American business world as an effort to stimulate creativity, especially in the pursuit of advertising themes. Then Taylor and his associates did their well-known experiment on brainstorming versus individual idea-production. Some real doubt was cast upon the efficacy of the group-creation process with the finding that *ad hoc* groups of individuals whose ideas were pooled *after the fact* did better than the real groups whose members interacted with one another.[41]

In general, this result confirms the belief of those whose basic orientation toward creativity is that it must be an individual phenomenon. For example, C. P. Snow, in summing up his point of view on science and its values in *The Search,* has Fane say, with regard to the proposed concept of a *team* to do the research in a new institute, that "I'm inclined to think we want more individuals in research, not less. . . I don't believe very much in these teams of yours for solving problems . . . and even if I did, I think I'd prefer that a few things in life were left to the individual man."[42]

With a few exceptions, psychoanalysts have also tended to ignore the interpersonal aspects of creativity. Ernest Schachtel is one of the exceptions, but he, too, emphasizes the inhibitory side of interpersonal relations. He illuminates quite effectively what he feels are the interpersonal sources of man's blocks to experiencing in actual terms that which happens to and around him.[43] His thesis is that as people grow and are socialized into the ways of their society, they begin to experience phenomena in terms of the categories which they are taught. Subsequently they do not necessarily experience phenomena in ways which are most appropriate for the reality itself. Schachtel sees this socialization as a source of stereotyped or rigidly structured cognitions denying the experiential process. This leads to an attenuation of fresh ideas, phenomena, and concepts available to man.

His most striking point is a description of how people experience events in categories or terms which they anticipate will best serve to describe the event or experience to others and not in terms which are most appropriate for themselves in the actual situation.

Even when Schachtel mentions the relationship with the psycho-

---

[41]D. W. Taylor, P. C. Berry, and C. H. Block, "Does Group Participation When Using Brainstorming Facilitate or Inhibit Creative Thinking?" *Administrative Science Quarterly,* Vol. 3 (1958), pp. 23–47.

[42]C. P. Snow, *The Search* (New York: Charles Scribner's Sons, 1958), p. 226.

[43]E. G. Schachtel, "On Memory and Childhood Amnesia," in P. Mullahy (ed.), *A Study of Interpersonal Relations* (New York: Hermitage Press, 1949).

analyst as one way to break down certain of the systematized sche-
mata that have been built up by people to view their world, he
merely mentions it in passing but does not deal with the actual aspects of the relationship that might help in this process.

In a recent *New Yorker* profile[44] the reporter wrote about Yang
and Lee, the two Nobel Prize winning physicists who have produced some very fine results while working as a team. Yet in the
process no investigation was made into the elements of factors which
made this relationship a creative one. The author's only note on the
relationship itself was that it was "unusual" for two physicists to
work closely together and to produce results such as theirs. Wilson's
article on the Strayhorn-Ellington relationship (in this book) is
better in this regard, but still a far cry from an in-depth analysis
of what really makes the difference in a relationship such as theirs.

One gets the general feeling is each of these examples, as in many
others that could be presented, that creativity is viewed as being of
necessity an individual process, and therefore a relationship has no
relevance to it; or if it does, it is one of inhibition only. An essay by
Murphy[45] is one counter to this orientation, although in very general terms. It is his thesis that not only is a relationship not necessarily antithetical to the creative process, but that it may be vital
to creativity, given the nature of our rapidly changing society. From
this he concludes that man's real task may be to deal with the reality
of the existence of interpersonal relationships rather than to reject
or deny that they have any part in the creative process.

Henry Murray, in an article entitled "Unprecedented Evolutions,"[46] also calls for a new look at the possibilities for creative relationships, especially with respect to the kinds of international
problems which threaten the very continuation of life itself on this
planet. It is his view that the solutions to these kinds of problems
may in fact be the result of creative "synthesism" or combination of
diverse points of view in relationships.

What Is the Creative Process Itself?

For the moment, let us consider one model of the creative process,
that presented by Murray.[47] He distinguishes what he considers to

---

[44]*New Yorker Magazine, op. cit.*

[45]Gardner Murphy, "Creativeness in Our Own Era," *Human Potentialities* (New
York: Basic Books, Inc., 1958), Chap. x.

[46]Henry Murray, "Unprecedented Evolutions," *Daedalus,* Vol. 90, No. 3 (1961).

[47]H. Murray, "Vicissitudes of Creativity," In H. H. Anderson (ed.), *Creativity and
Its Cultivation,* Interdisciplinary Symposia of Creativity, Michigan State University,
1957–58 (New York: Harper & Bros., 1959), pp. 110–18.

be the four necessary conditions for creativity: *(a)* the circulation of combinable entities; *(b)* permeable boundaries between categories, spheres of interest, the conscious and the unconscious, etc.; *(c)* periodic decompositions—de-differentiations and disintegrations (or re-examinations of what has already been done—and discarding if necessary); and *(d)* favorable conditions for new combinations.

In general, the process seems to be that of "mixing it up," or of having as wide as possible a conception on the part of those involved of the alternatives available or potentially available, plus favorable conditions for becoming aware of new "paths" even after having traveled part way down one that originally appeared to be fruitful.

Effects of Interpersonal Relationships on the Creative Process

The kinds of processes that we have described above as being most relevant to creativity include experimentation, innovation, regeneration, risk taking, starting over, questioning of assumptions, relief from anxiety, etc. What is the relationship between these processes and interpersonal phenomena? In general, most of these processes would seem to vary with the strength of *perceived threat* in different situations. More specifically, creative processes would be undermined in situations where anxiety is aroused concerning loss of one's status, inclusion in the relationship, or basic self-worth and sense of self-esteem. When these kinds of threats are perceived, then internally or externally produced alternatives (relating to a particular problem *or* to a more general style of operation) are reduced, often with no awareness on the part of the individual that this limiting has taken place.[48]

For the relationship to facilitate creativity, therefore, a climate must be created which reduces perceived threat and makes creativity the norm.[49] However, when creativity becomes the only acceptable product, new anxiety will be generated in the participants over their relative status or sense of self-worth if they are not able to be creative 100 per cent of the time. This new anxiety may again limit alternatives. To avoid this new anxiety the relationship must develop a climate of mutual support and reduced competitiveness.

Thus, the two necessary elements of a creative relationship appear to be *(a)* appropriate norms toward creativity and innovation *plus (b)* a shared feeling of acceptance of the individual as an indi-

---

[48]See Schachtel's discussion of "childhood amnesia," *op. cit.*

[49]See W. J. J. Gordon, *Synectics: the Development of Creative Capacity* (New York: Harper & Bros., 1961).

vidual in the relationship.[50] This acceptance should include a will-ingness to allow and help him to be himself in the relationship, to grow as a result of it, and to make the most of his experiences as they occur for him. There is good evidence that for most creative peo-ple, such as Darwin or Freud, there was a small but strong reference group supporting them, even in the face of much larger opposition from the total society.

These are not the only variables relevant to a creative relation-ship. The interpersonal competence of the individual members may allow a broader spectrum of thought and action to come into play in combination than either member had by himself. Individual dif-ferences are also important in determining the extent to which this kind of climate effectively releases these potential abilities. An indi-vidual who is immobilized by the mere presence of others, regardless of the immediate atmosphere that his partner attempts to foster, may be quite inappropriate for collaborative creative endeavors, and should be recognized as such. This does not rule out the possibility of the relationship serving as a change environment in which such an individual can express himself more freely, thereby allowing a more creative output, which in turn may further free him from former inhibitions. The question of how this circular process can be initiated is beyond the scope of this paper, but satisfactions coming from relating *per se* early in the relationship may be a crucial element here.

THE READINGS

The readings that follow in this part illustrate both this paper's concepts and many others. Homans provides us with a general framework for relational transactions and their development over time in the work setting. Roy presents a participant-observation study of the manner in which the relational aspects of a work setting may act to offset some of the negative effects of very boring, repeti-tive tasks, and Davis' article demonstrates alienation arising from structural features of the service being performed.

Blake's paper confronts the major problem area of intergroup relations, considering both sources of difficulty and strategies for improving relations between groups. Argyris presents his general ideas concerning the manner in which interpersonal values and re-sultant behavioral styles may influence the task-performance aspects

---

[50]C. Rogers, "The Characteristics of a Helping Relationship," *On Becoming a Per-son* (Boston: Houghton-Mifflin, 1961).

of interaction in an organizational setting. Potter's chapter on "Businessmanship" is in the tradition of his general thesis that all life is a competition—that "he who is not one-up is one-down." His humor helps us to see how often we create relational patterns day to day that look suspiciously like we agree with this assumption. Gibb's paper provides a systematic discussion of interpersonal climates that lead toward open or defensive communication about self and task.

In the area of the creative relationship Becker, dealing with both a service and a creative relationship, shows the alienation of the dance musician from his audience because of value conflicts. Parloff and Handlon report an experiment on a specific block to creativity in problem-solving relationships: the tendency to throw away possible solutions too soon. Finally, Wilson's article from *The New York Times* highlights the singularly productive creative relationship between composer-pianist-band leader Duke Ellington and his collaborator, the late Billy Strayhorn.

SOCIAL BEHAVIOR AS EXCHANGE*

George C. Homans

THE PROBLEMS OF SMALL-GROUP RESEARCH

This essay will hope to honor the memory of Georg Simmel in two different ways. So far as it pretends to be suggestive rather than conclusive, its tone will be Simmel's; and its subject, too, will be one of his. Because Simmel, in essays such as those on sociabilty, games, coquetry, and conversation, was an analyst of elementary social behavior, we call him an ancestor of what is known today as small-group research. For what we are really studying in small groups is elementary social behavior: what happens when two or three persons are in a position to influence one another, the sort of thing of which those massive structures called "classes," "firms," "communities," and "societies" must ultimately be composed.

As I survey small-group research today, I feel that, apart from

*Reprinted in its entirety from George C. Homans, "Social Behavior as Exchange," *American Journal of Sociology*, Vol. 63, No. 6 (May, 1958), pp. 597–606. The University of Chicago Press, used by permission.

just keeping on with it, three sorts of things need to be done. The first is to show the relation between the results of experimental work done under laboratory conditions and the results of *quasi*-anthropological field research on what those of us who do it are pleased to call "real-life" groups in industry and elsewhere. If the experimental work has anything to do with real life—and I am persuaded that it has everything to do—its propositions cannot be inconsistent with those discovered through the field work. But the consistency has not yet been demonstrated in any systematic way.

The second job is to pull together in some set of general propositions the actual results, from the laboratory and from the field, of work on small groups—propositions that at least sum up, to an approximation, what happens in elementary social behavior, even though we may not be able to explain why the propositions should take the form they do. A great amount of work has been done, and more appears every day, but what it all amounts to in the shape of a set of propositions from which, under specified conditions, many of the observational results might be derived, is not at all clear—and yet to state such a set is the first aim of science.

The third job is to begin to show how the propositions that empirically hold good in small groups may be derived from some set of still more general propositions. "Still more general" means only that empirical propositions other than ours may also be derived from the set. This derivation would constitute the explanatory stage in the science of elementary social behavior, for explanation *is* derivation.[1] (I myself suspect that the more general set will turn out to contain the propositions of behavioral psychology. I hold myself to be an "ultimtae psychological reductionist," but I cannot know that I am right so long as the reduction has not been carried out.)

I have come to think that all three of these jobs would be furthered by our adopting the view that interaction between persons is an exchange of goods, material and non-material. This is one of the oldest theories of social behavior, and one that we still use every day to interpret our own behavior, as when we say, "I found so-and-so rewarding"; or "I got a great deal out of him"; or, even, "Talking with him took a great deal out of me." But, perhaps just because it is so obvious, this view has been much neglected by social scientists. So far as I know, the only theoretical work that makes explicit use of it is Marcel Mauss's *Essai sur le don,* published in

---

[1] See R. B. Braithwaite, *Scientific Explanation* (Cambridge: Cambridge University Press, 1953).

1925, which is ancient as social science goes.[2] It may be that the tradition of neglect is now changing and that, for instance, the psychologists who interpret behavior in terms of transactions may be coming back to something of the sort I have in mind.[3]

An incidental advantage of an exchange theory is that it might bring sociology closer to economics—that science of man most advanced, most capable of application, and, intellectually, most isolated. Economics studies exchange carried out under special circumstances and with a most useful built-in numerical measure of value. What are the laws of the general phenomenon of which economic behavior is one class?

In what follows I shall suggest some reasons for the usefulness of a theory of social behavior as exchange and suggest the nature of the propositions such a theory might contain.

AN EXCHANGE PARADIGM

I start with the link to behavioral psychology and the kind of statement it makes about the behavior of an experimental animal such as the pigeon.[4] As a pigeon explores its cage in the laboratory it happens to peck a target, whereupon the psychologist feeds it corn. The evidence is that it will peck the target again; it has learned the behavior, or, as my friend Skinner says, the behavior has been reinforced, and the pigeon has undergone *operant conditioning*. This kind of psychologist is not interested in how the behavior was learned: "learning theory" is a poor name for this field. Instead, he is interested in what determines changes in the rate of emission of learned behavior, whether pecks at a target or something else.

The more hungry the pigeon, the less corn or other food it has gotten in the recent past, the more often it will peck. By the same token, if the behavior is often reinforced, if the pigeon is given much corn every time it pecks, the rate of emission will fall off as the pigeon gets *satiated*. If, on the other hand, the behavior is not reinforced at all, then, too, its rate of emission will tend to fall off, though a long time may pass before it stops altogether, before it is *extinguished*. In the emission of many kinds of behavior the pigeon incurs *aversive stimulation*, or what I shall call "cost" for short, and this, too, will lead in time to a decrease in the emis-

[2] Translated by I. Cunnison as *The Gift* (Glencoe, Ill.: Free Press, 1954).

[3] In social anthropology D. L. Oliver is working along these lines, and I owe much to him. See also T. M. Newcomb, "The Prediction of Interpersonal Attraction," *American Psychologist*, XI (1956), 575–86.

[4] B. F. Skinner, *Science and Human Behavior* (New York: Macmillan Co., 1953).

sion rate. Fatigue is an example of a "cost." Extinction, satiation, and cost, by decreasing the rate of emission of a particular kind of behavior, render more probable the emission of some other kind of behavior, including doing nothing. I shall only add that even a hard-boiled psychologist puts "emotional" behavior, as well as such things as pecking, among the unconditioned responses that may be reinforced in operant conditioning. As a statement of the propositions of behavioral psychology, the foregoing is, of course, inadequate for any purpose except my present one.

We may look on the pigeon as engaged in an exchange—pecks for corn—with the psychologist, but let us not dwell upon that, for the behavior of the pigeon hardly determines the behavior of the psychologist at all. Let us turn to a situation where the exchange is real, that is, where the determination is mutual. Suppose we are dealing with two men. Each is emitting behavior reinforced to some degree by the behavior of the other. How it was in the past that each learned the behavior he emits and how he learned to find the other's behavior reinforcing we are not concerned with. It is enough that each does find the other's behavior reinforcing, and I shall call the reinforcers—the equivalent of the pigeon's corn—*values,* for this, I think, is what we mean by this term. As he emits behavior, each man may incur costs, and each man has more than one course of behavior open to him.

This seems to me the paradigm of elementary social behavior, and the problem of the elementary sociologist is to state propositions relating the variations in the values and costs of each man to his frequency distribution of behavior among alternatives, where the values (in the mathematical sense) taken by these variables for one man determine in part their values for the other.[5]

I see no reason to believe that the propositions of behavioral psychology do not apply to this situation, though the complexity of their implications in the concrete case may be great indeed. In particular, we must suppose that, with men as with pigeons, an increase in extinction, satiation, or aversive stimulation of any one kind of behavior will increase the probability of emission of some other kind. The problem is not, as it is often stated, merely what a man's values are, what he has learned in the past to find reinforcing, but how much of any one value his behavior is getting him now. The

---

[5]*Ibid.,* pp. 297–329. The discussion of "double contingency" by T. Parsons and E. A. Shils could easily lead to a similar paradigm (see *Toward a General Theory of Action* [Cambridge, Mass.: Harvard University Press, 1951], pp. 14–16).

more he gets, the less valuable any further unit of that value is to him, and the less often he will emit behavior reinforced by it.

THE INFLUENCE PROCESS

We do not, I think, possess the kind of studies of two-person inter-action that would either bear out these propositions or fail to do so. But we do have studies of larger numbers of persons that suggest that they may apply, notably the studies by Festinger, Schachter, Back, and their associates on the dynamics of influence. One of the variables they work with they call *cohesiveness*, defined as anything that attracts people to take part in a group. Cohesiveness is a value variable; it refers to the degree of reinforcement people find in the activities of the group. Festinger and his colleagues consider two kinds of reinforcing activity: the symbolic behavior we call "so-cial approval" (sentiment), and activity valuable in other ways, such as doing something interesting.

The other variable they work with they call *communication* and others call *interaction*. This is a frequency variable; it is a measure of the frequency of emission of valuable and costly verbal behavior. We must bear in mind that, in general, in one kind of variable is a function of the other.

Festinger and his co-workers show that the more cohesive a group is, that is, the more valuable the sentiment or activity the members exchange with one another, the greater the average frequency of interaction of the members.[6] With men, as with pigeons, the greater the reinforcement, the more often is the reinforced behavior emit-ted. The more cohesive a group, too, the greater the change that members can produce in the behavior of other members in the direc-tion of rendering these activities more valuable.[7] That is, the more valuable the activities that members get, the more valuable those that they must give. For if a person is emitting behavior of a certain kind, and other people do not find it particularly rewarding, these others will suffer their own production of sentiment and activity, in time, to fall off. But perhaps the first person has found their sentiment and activity rewarding, and, if he is to keep on getting them, he must make his own behavior more valuable to the others.

[6]K. W. Back, "The Exertion of Influence through Social Communication," in L. Festinger, K. Back, S. Schachter, H. H. Kelley, and J. Thibaut (eds.), *Theory and Experiment in Social Communication* (Ann Arbor: Research Center for Dynamics, University of Michigan, 1950), pp. 21–36.
[7]S. Schachter, N. Ellerston, D. McBride, and D. Gregory, "An Experimental Study of Cohesiveness and Productivity," *Human Relations*, IV (1951), pp. 229–38.

In short, the propositions of behavioral psychology imply a tendency toward a certain proportionality between the value to others of the behavior a man gives them and the value to him of the behavior they give him.[8]

Schachter also studied the behavior of members of a group toward two kinds of other members, "conformers" and "deviates."[9] I assume that conformers are people whose activity the other members find valuable. For conformity is behavior that coincides to a degree with some group standard or norm, and the only meaning I can assign to *norm* is "a verbal description of behavior that many members find it valuable for the actual behavior of themselves and others to conform to." By the same token, a deviate is a member whose behavior is not particularly valuable. Now Schachter shows that, as the members of a group come to see another member as a deviate, their interaction with him—communication addressed to getting him to change his behavior—goes up, the faster the more cohesive the group. The members need not talk to the other conformers so much; they are relatively satiated by the conformers' behavior: they have gotten what they want out of them. But if the deviate, by failing to change his behavior, fails to reinforce the members, they start to withhold social approval from him: the deviate gets low sociometric choice at the end of the experiment. And in the most cohesive groups—those Schachter calls "high cohesive-relevant"—interaction with the deviate also falls off in the end and is lowest among those members that rejected him most strongly, as if they had given him up as a bad job. But how plonking can we get? These findings are utterly in line with everyday experience.

PRACTICAL EQUILIBRIUM

At the beginning of this paper I suggested that one of the tasks of small-group research was to show the relation between the results of experimental work done under laboratory conditions and the results of field research on real-life small groups. Now the latter often appear to be in practical equilibrium, and by this I mean nothing fancy. I do not mean that all real-life groups are in equilibrium. I certainly do not mean that all groups must tend to equilibrium. I do not mean that groups have built-in antidotes to change: there is no homeostasis here. I do not mean that we

---

[8]Skinner, *op. cit.*, p. 100.

[9]Schachter, "Deviation, Rejection, and Communication," *Journal of Abnormal and Social Psychology*, XLVI (1951), pp. 190–207.

assume equilibrium. I mean only that we sometimes *observe* it, that for the time we are with a group—and it is often short—there is no great change in the values of the variables we choose to measure. If, for instance, person A is interacting with B more than with C both at the beginning and at the end of the study, then at least by this crude measure the group is in equilibrium.

Many of the Festinger-Schachter studies are experimental, and their propositions about the process of influence seem to me to imply the kind of proposition that empirically holds good of real-life groups in practical equilibruim. For instance, Festinger *et al.* find that, the more cohesive a group is, the greater the change that members can produce in the behavior of other members. If the influence is exerted in the direction of conformity to group norms, then, when the process of influence has accomplished all the change of which it is capable, the proposition should hold good that, the more cohesive a group is, the larger the number of members that conform to its norms. And it does hold good.[10]

Again, Schachter found, in the experiment I summarized above, that in the most cohesive groups and at the end, when the effort to influence the deviate had failed, members interacted little with the deviate and gave him little in the way of sociometric choice. Now two of the propositions that hold good most often of real-life groups in practical equilibrium are precisely that the more closely a member's activity conforms to the norms the more interaction he receives from other members and the more liking choices he gets from them too. From these main propositions a number of others may be derived that also hold good.[11]

Yet we must ever remember that the truth of the proposition linking conformity to liking may on occasion be masked by the truth of other propositions. If, for instance, the man that conforms to the norms most closely also exerts some authority over the group, this may render liking for him somewhat less than it might otherwise have been.[12]

Be that as it may, I suggest that the laboratory experiments on

---

[10]L. Festinger, S. Schachter, and K. Back, *Social Pressures in Informal Groups* (New York: Harper & Bros., 1950), pp. 72–100.

[11]For propositions holding good of groups in practical equilibrium see G. C. Homans, *The Human Group* (New York: Harcourt, Brace & Co., 1950), and H. W. Riecken and G. C. Homans, "Psychological Aspects of Social Structure," in G. Lindzey (ed.), *Handbook of Social Psychology* (Cambridge, Mass.: Addison-Wesley Publishing Co., 1954), II, pp. 786–832.

[12]See Homans, *op. cit.*, pp. 244–48, and R. F. Bales, "The Equilibrium Problem in Small Groups," in A. P. Hare, E. F. Borgatta, and R. F. Bales (eds.) *Small Groups* (New York: A. A. Knopf, 1953), pp. 450–56.

influence imply propositions about the behavior of members of small groups, when the process of influence has worked itself out, that are identical with propositions that hold good of real-life groups in equilibrium. This is hardly surprising if all we mean by equilibrium is that all the change of which the system is, under present conditions, capable has been effected, so that no further change occurs. Nor would this be the first time that statics has turned out to be a special case of dynamics.

PROFIT AND SOCIAL CONTROL

Though I have treated equilibrium as an observed fact, it is a fact that cries for explanation. I shall not, as structural-functional sociologists do, use an assumed equilibrium as a means of explaining, or trying to explain, why the other features of a social system should be what they are. Rather, I shall take practical equilibrium as something that is itself to be explained by the other features of the system.

If every member of a group emits at the end of, and during, a period of time much the same kinds of behavior and in much the same frequencies as he did at the beginning, the group is for that period in equilibrium. Let us then ask why any one member's behavior should persist. Suppose he is emitting behavior of value A_1. Why does he not let his behavior get worse (less valuable or reinforcing to the others) until it stands at $A_1-\triangle A$? True, the sentiments expressed by others toward him are apt to decline in value (become less reinforcing to him), so that what he gets from them may be $S_1-\triangle S$. But it is conceivable that, since most activity carries cost, a decline in the value of what he emits will mean a reduction in cost to him that more than offsets his losses in sentiment. Where, then, does he stabilize his behavior? This is the problem of social control.[13]

Mankind has always assumed that a person stabilizes his behavior, at least in the short run, at the point where he is doing the best he can for himself under the circumstances, though his best may not be a "rational" best, and what he can do may not be at all easy to specify, except that he is not apt to think like one of the theoretical antagonists in the *Theory of Games*. Before a sociologist rejects this answer out of hand for its horrid profit-seeking implications, he will do well to ask himself if he can offer any other answer

---

[13]Homans, *op. cit.*, pp. 281–301.

to the question posed. I think he will find that he cannot. Yet experiments designed to test the truth of the answer are extraordinarily rare.

I shall review one that seems to me to provide a little support for the theory, though it was not meant to do so. The experiment is reported by H. B. Gerard, a member of the Festinger-Schachter team, under the title "The Anchorage of Opinions in Face-to-Face groups."[14] The experimenter formed artificial groups whose members met to discuss a case in industrial relations and to express their opinions about its probable outcome. The groups were of two kinds: high-attraction groups, whose members were told that they would like one another very much, and low-attraction groups, whose members were told that they would not find one another particularly likable.

TABLE 1

PERCENTAGE OF SUBJECTS CHANGING TOWARD SOMEONE IN THE GROUP

	Agreement	Mild Disagreement	Strong Disagreement
High attraction............	0	12	44
Low attraction............	0	15	9

TABLE 2

PERCENTAGE OF SUBJECTS CHANGING TOWARD THE PAID PARTICIPANT

	Agreement	Mild Disagreement	Strong Disagreement
High attraction............	7	13	25
Low attraction............	20	38	8

At a later time the experimenter called the members in separately, asked them again to express their opinions on the outcome of the case, and counted the number that had changed their opinions to bring them into accord with those of other members of their groups. At the same time, a paid participant entered into a further discussion of the case with each member, always taking, on the probable outcome of the case, a position opposed to that taken by the bulk of the other members of the group to which the person belonged. The experimenter counted the number of persons shifting toward the opinion of the paid participant.

The experiment had many interesting results, from which I choose only those summed up in Tables 1 and 2. The three differ-

---

[14]*Human Relations*, VII (1954), pp. 313–25.

ent agreement classes are made up of people who, at the original sessions, expressed different degrees of agreement with the opinions of other members of their groups. And the figure 44, for instance, means that, of all members of high-attraction groups whose initial opinions were strongly in disagreement with those of other members, 44 per cent shifted their opinion later toward that of others.

In these results the experimenter seems to have been interested only in the differences in the sums of the rows, which show that there is more shifting toward the group, and less shifting toward the paid participant, in the high-attraction than in the low-attraction condition. This is in line with a proposition suggested earlier. If you think that the members of a group can give you much—in this case, liking—you are apt to give them much—in this case, a change to an opinion in accordance with their views—or you will not get the liking. And, by the same token, if the group can give you little of value, you will not be ready to give it much of value. Indeed, you may change your opinion so as to depart from agreement even further, to move, that is, toward the view held by the paid participant.

So far so good, but, when I first scanned these tables, I was less struck by the difference between them than by their similarity. The same classes of people in both tables showed much the same relative propensities to change their opinions, no matter whether the change was toward the group or toward the paid participant. We see, for instance, that those who change least are the high-attraction, agreement people and the low-attraction, strong-disagreement ones. And those who change most are the high-attraction, strong-disagreement people and the low-attraction, mild-disagreement ones.

How am I to interpret these particular results? Since the experimenter did not discuss them, I am free to offer my own explanation. The behavior emitted by the subjects is opinion and changes in opinion. For this behavior they have learned to expect two possible kinds of reinforcement. Agreement with the group gets the subject favorable sentiment (acceptance) from it, and the experiment was designed to give this reinforcement a higher value in the high-attraction condition than in the low-attraction one. The second kind of possible reinforcement is what I shall call the "maintenance of one's personal integrity," which a subject gets by sticking to his own opinion in the face of disagreement with the group. The experimenter does not mention this reward, but I cannot make sense of the results without something much like it. In different degrees for different subjects, depending on their initial positions, these rewards are in competition with one another: they are alternatives. They are not absolutely scarce goods, but some persons cannot get both at once.

Since the rewards are alternatives, let me introduce a familiar assumption from economics—that the cost of a particular course of action is the equivalent of the foregone value of an alternative[15]—and then add the definition: Profit = Reward − Cost.

Now consider the persons in the corresponding cells of the two tables. The behavior of the high-attraction, agreement people gets them much in the way of acceptance by the group, and for it they must give up little in the way of personal integrity, for their views are from the start in accord with those of the group. Their profit is high, and they are not prone to change their behavior. The low-attraction, strong-disagreement people are getting much in integrity, and they are not giving up for it much in valuable acceptance, for they are members of low-attraction groups. Reward less cost is high for them, too, and they change little. The high-attraction, strong-disagreement people are getting much in the way of integrity, but their costs in doing so are high, too, for they are in high-attraction groups and thus foregoing much valuable acceptance by the group. Their profit is low, and they are very apt to change, either toward the group or toward the paid participant, from whom they think, perhaps, they will get some acceptance while maintaining some integrity. The low-attraction, mild-disagreement people do not get much in the way of integrity, for they are only in mild disagreement with the group, but neither are they giving up much in acceptance, for they are members of low-attraction groups. Their rewards are low; their costs are low too, and their profit—the difference between the two—is also low. In their low profit they resemble the high-attraction, strong-disagreement people, and, like them, they are prone to change their opinions, in this case, more toward the paid participant. The subjects in the other two cells, who had medium profits, display medium propensities to change.

If we define profit as reward less cost, and if cost is value foregone, I suggest that we have here some evidence for the proposition that change in behavior is greatest when perceived profit is least.

---

[15]G. J. Stigler, *The Theory of Price* (rev. ed.; New York: Macmillan Co., 1952), p. 99.

This constitutes no direct demonstration that change in behavior is least when profit is greatest, but if, whenever a man's behavior brought him a balance of reward and cost, he changed his behavior away from what got him, under the circumstances, the less profit, there might well come a time when his behavior would not change further. That is, his behavior would be stabilized, at least for the time being. And, so far as this were true for every member of a group, the group would have a social organization in equilibrium.

I do not say that a member would stabilize his behavior at the point of greatest conceivable profit to himself, because his profit is partly at the mercy of the behavior of others. It is a commonplace that the short-run pursuit of profit by several persons often lands them in positions where all are worse off than they might conceivably be. I do not say that the paths of behavioral change in which a member pursues his profit under the condition that others are pursuing theirs too are easy to describe or predict; and we can readily conceive that in jockeying for position they might never arrive at any equilibrium at all.

DISTRIBUTIVE JUSTICE

Yet practical equilibrium is often observed, and thus some further condition may make its attainment, under some circumstances, more probable than would the individual pursuit of profit left to itself. I can offer evidence for this further condition only in the behavior of subgroups and not in that of individuals. Suppose that there are two subgroups, working close together in a factory, the job of one being somewhat different from that of the other. And suppose that the members of the first complain and say: "We are getting the same pay as they are. We ought to get just a couple of dollars a week more to show that our work is more responsible." When you ask them what they mean by "more responsible," they say that, if they do their work wrong, more damage can result, and so they are under more pressure to take care.[16] Something like this is a common feature of industrial behavior. It is at the heart of disputes not over absolute wages but over wage differentials—indeed, at the heart of disputes over rewards other than wages.

In what kind of proposition may we express observations like these? We may say that wages and responsibility give status in

[16]G. C. Homans, "Status among Clerical Workers," *Human Organization,* XII (1953), pp. 5–10.

the group, in the sense that a man who takes high responsibility and gets high wages is admired, other things equal. Then, if the members of one group score higher on responsibility than do the members of another, there is a felt need on the part of the first to score higher on pay too. There is a pressure, which shows itself in complaints, to bring the *status factors,* as I have called them, into line with one another. If they are in line, a condition of *status congruence* is said to exist. In this condition the workers may find their jobs dull or irksome, but they will not complain about the relative position of groups.

But there may be a more illuminating way of looking at the matter. In my example I have considered only responsibility and pay, but these may be enough, for they represent the two kinds of thing that come into the problem. Pay is clearly a reward; responsibility may be looked on, less clearly, as a cost. It means constraint and worry—or peace of mind foregone. Then the proposition about status congruence becomes this: If the costs of the members of one group are higher than those of another, distributive justice requires that their rewards should be higher too. But the thing works both ways: If the rewards are higher, the costs should be higher too. This last is the theory of *noblesse oblige,* which we all subscribe to, though we all laugh at it, perhaps because the *noblesse* often fails to *oblige.* To put the matter in terms of profit: though the rewards and costs of two persons or the members of two groups may be different, yet the profits of the two the excess of reward over cost should tend to equality. And more than "should." The less-advantaged group will at least try to attain greater equality, as, in the example I have used, the first group tried to increase its profit by increasing its pay.

I have talked of distributive justice. Clearly, this is not the only condition determining the actual distribution of rewards and costs. At the same time, never tell me that notions of justice are not a strong influence on behavior, though we sociologists often neglect them. Distributive justice may be one of the conditions of group equilibrium.

EXCHANGE AND SOCIAL STRUCTURE

I shall end by reviewing almost the only study I am aware of that begins to show in detail how a stable and differentiated social structure in a real-life group might arise out of a process of exchange between members. This is Peter Blau's description of the behavior of sixteen agents in a federal law-enforcement agency.[17]

The agents had the duty of investigating firms and preparing reports on the firms' compliance with the law. Since the reports might lead to legal action against the firms, the agents had to prepare them carefully, in the proper form, and take strict account of the many regulations that might apply. The agents were often in doubt what they should do, and then they were supposed to take the question to their supervisor. This they were reluctant to do, for they naturally believed that thus confessing to him their inability to solve a problem would reflect on their competence, affect the official ratings he made of their work, and so hurt their chances for promotion. So agents often asked other agents for help and advice, and, though this was nominally forbidden, the supervisor usually let it pass.

Blau ascertained the ratings the supervisor made of the agents, and he also asked the agents to rate one another. The two opinions agreed closely. Fewer agents were regarded as highly competent than were regarded as of middle or low competence; competence, or the ability to solve technical problems, was a fairly scarce good. One or two of the more competent agents would not give help and advice when asked, and so received few interactions and little liking. A man that will not exchange, that will not give you what he has when you need it, will not get from you the only thing you are, in this case, able to give him in return, your regard.

But most of the more competent agents were willing to give help, and of them Blau says:

> A consultation can be considered an exchange of values: both participants gain something, and both have to pay a price. The questioning agent is enabled to perform better than he could otherwise have done, without exposing his difficulties to his supervisor. By asking for advice, he implicitly pays his respect to the superior proficiency of his colleague. This acknowledgment of inferiority is the cost of receiving assistance. The consultant gains prestige, in return for which he is willing to devote some time to the consultation and permit it to disrupt his own work. The following remark of an agent illustrates this: "I like giving advice. It's flattering, I suppose, if you feel that others come to you for advice."[18]

Blau goes on to say: "All agents like being consulted, but the value of any one of very many consultations became deflated for

[17]Peter M. Blau, *The Dynamics of Bureaucracy* (Chicago: University of Chicago Press, 1955), pp. 99–116.
[18]*Ibid.*, p. 108.

experts, and the price they paid in frequent interruptions became inflated."[19] This implies that, the more prestige an agent received, the less was the increment of value of that prestige; the more advice an agent gave, the greater was the increment of cost of that advice, the cost lying precisely in the foregone value of time to do his own work. Blau suggests that something of the same sort was true of an agent who went to a more competent colleague for advice: the more often he went, the more costly to him, in feelings of inferiority, became any further request. "The repeated admission of his inability to solve his own problems . . . undermined the self-confidence of the worker and his standing in the group."[20]

The result was that the less competent agents went to the more competent ones for help less often than they might have done if the costs of repeated admissions of inferiority had been less high and that, while many agents sought out the few highly competent ones, no single agent sought out the latter much. Had they done so (to look at the exchange from the other side), the costs to the highly competent in interruptions to their own work would have become exorbitant. Yet the need of the less competent for help was still not fully satisfied. Under these circumstances they tended to turn for help to agents more nearly like themselves in competence. Though the help they got was not the most valuable, it was of a kind they could themselves return on occasion. With such agents they could exchange help and liking, without the exchange becoming on either side too great a confession of inferiority.

The highly competent agents tended to enter into exchanges, that is, to interact with many others. But, in the more equal exchanges I have just spoken of, less competent agents tended to pair off as partners. That is, they interacted with a smaller number of people, but interacted often with these few. I think I could show why pair relations in these more equal exchanges would be more economical for an agent than a wider distribution of favors. But perhaps I have gone far enough. The final pattern of this social structure was one in which a small number of highly competent agents exchanged advice for prestige with a large number of others less competent and in which the less competent agents exchanged, in pairs and in trios, both help and liking on more nearly equal terms.

Blau shows, then, that a social structure in equilibrium might be the result of a process of exchanging behavior rewarding and costly

---

[19]*Ibid.*, p. 108.
[20]*Ibid.*, p. 109.

in different degrees, in which the increment of reward and cost varied with the frequency of the behavior, that is, with the frequency of interaction. Note that the behavior of the agents seems also to have satisfied my second condition of equilibrium: The more competent agents took more responsibility for the work, either their own or others', than did the less competent ones, but they also got more for it in the way of prestige. I suspect that the same kind of explanation could be given for the structure of many "informal" groups.

SUMMARY

The current job of theory in small-group research is to make the connection between experimental and real-life studies, to consolidate the propositions that empirically hold good in the two fields, and to show how these propositions might be derived from a still more general set. One way of doing this job would be to revive and make more rigorous the oldest of theories of social behavior —social behavior as exchange.

Some of the statements of such a theory might be the following. Social behavior is an exchange of goods, material goods but also non-material ones, such as the symbols of approval or prestige. Persons that give much to others try to get much from them, and persons that get much from others are under pressure to give much to them. This process of influence tends to work out at equilibrium to a balance in the exchanges. For a person engaged in exchange, what he gives may be a cost to him, just as what he gets may be a reward, and his behavior changes less as profit, that is, reward less cost, tends to a maximum. Not only does he seek a maximum for himself, but he tries to see to it that no one in his group makes more profit than he does. The cost and the value of what he gives and of what he gets vary with the quantity of what he gives and gets. It is surprising how familiar these propositions are; it is surprising, too, how propositions about the dynamics of exchange can begin to generate the static thing we call "group structure" and, in so doing, generate also some of the propositions about group structure that students of real-life groups have stated.

In our unguarded moments we sociologists find words like "reward" and "cost" slipping into what we say. Human nature will break in upon even our most elaborate theories. But we seldom let it have its way with us and follow up systematically what these words imply.[21] Of all our many "approaches" to social behavior, the one that sees it as an economy is the most neglected, and yet it is the one we use every moment of our lives—except when we write sociology.

"BANANA TIME"—JOB SATISFACTION AND INFORMAL INTERACTION*

Donald F. Roy

This paper undertakes description and exploratory analysis of the social interaction which took place within a small work group of factory machine operatives during a two-month period of participant observation. The factual and ideational materials which it presents lie at an intersection of two lines of research interest and should, in their dual bearing, contribute to both. Since the operatives were engaged in work which involved the repetition of very simple operations over an extra-long workday, six days a week, they were faced with the problem of dealing with a formidable "beast of monotony." Revelation of how the group utilized its resources to combat that "beast" should merit the attention of those who are seeking solution to the practical problem of job satisfaction, or employee morale. It should also provide insights for those who are trying to penetrate the mysteries of the small group.

Convergence of these two lines of interest is, of course, no new thing. Among the host of writers and researchers who have suggested connections between "group" and "joy in work" are Walker and Guest, observers of social interaction on the automobile assembly line.[1] They quote assembly-line workers as saying, "We have a lot of fun and talk all the time,"[2] and, "If it weren't for the talking and fooling, you'd go nuts."[3]

---

[21]*The White-Collar Job* (Ann Arbor: Survey Research Center, University of Michigan, 1953), pp. 115–27.

*Excerpted from Donald F. Roy, "Banana Time," *Human Organization,* Vol. 18, No. 4 (Winter, 1959–60), pp. 158–168. Used by permission.

[1]Charles R. Walker and Robert H. Guest, *The Man on the Assembly Line,* Harvard University Press, Cambridge, 1952.

[2]*Ibid.,* p. 77.

[3]*Ibid.,* p. 68.

My account of how one group of machine operators kept from "going nuts" in a situation of monotonous work activity attempts to lay bare the tissues of interaction which made up the content of their adjustment. The talking, fun, and fooling which provided solution to the elemental problem of "psychological survival" will be described according to their embodiment in intra-group relations. In addition, an unusual opportunity for close observation of behavior involved in the maintenance of group equilibrium was afforded by the fortuitous introduction of a "natural experiment." My unwitting injection of explosive materials into the stream of interaction resulted in sudden, but temporary, loss of group interaction.

My fellow operatives and I spent our long days of simple, repetitive work in relative isolation from other employees of the factory. Our line of machines was sealed off from other work areas of the plant by the four walls of the clicking room. The one door of this room was usually closed. Even when it was kept open, during periods of hot weather, the consequences were not social; it opened on an uninhabited storage room of the shipping department. Not even the sounds of work activity going on elsewhere in the factory carried to this isolated work place. There were occasional contacts with "outside" employees, usually on matters connected with the work; but, with the exception of the daily calls of one fellow who came to pick up finished materials for the next step in processing, such visits were sporadic and infrequent.

Moreover, face-to-face contact with members of the managerial hierarchy were few and far between. No one bearing the title of foreman ever came around. The only company official who showed himself more than once during the two-month observation period was the plant superintendent. Evidently overloaded with supervisory duties and production problems which kept him busy elsewhere, he managed to pay his respects every week or two. His visits were in the nature of short, businesslike, but friendly exchanges. Otherwise he confined his observable communications with the group to occasional utilization of a public address system. During the two-month period, the company president and the chief chemist paid one friendly call apiece. One man, who may or may not have been of managerial status, was seen on various occasions lurking about in a manner which excited suspicion. Although no observable consequences accrued from the peculiar visitations of this silent fellow, it was assumed that he was some sort of efficiency expert, and he was referred to as "The Snooper."

As far as our work group was concerned, this was truly a situation of laissez-faire management. There was no interference from staff experts, no hounding by time-study engineers or personnel men hot on the scent of efficiency or good human relations. Nor were there any signs of industrial democracy in the form of safety, recreational, or production committees. There was an international union, and there was a highly publicized union-management cooperation program; but actual interactional processes of cooperation were carried on somewhere beyond my range of observation and without participation of members of my work group. Futhermore, these union-management get-togethers had no determinable connection with the problem of "toughing out" a twelve-hour day at monotonous work.

Our work group was thus not only abandoned to its own resources for creating job satisfaction, but left without that basic reservoir of ill-will toward management which can sometimes be counted on to stimulate the development of interesting activities to occupy hand and brain. Lacking was the challenge of intergroup conflict, that perennial source of creative experience to fill the otherwise empty hours of meaningless work routine.[4]

The clicking machines were housed in a room approximately thirty by twenty-four feet. They were four in number, set in a row, and so arranged along one wall that the busy operator could, merely by raising his head from his work, freshen his reveries with a glance through one of three large barred windows. To the rear of one of the end machines sat a long cutting table; here the operators cut up rolls of plastic materials into small sheets manageable for further processing at the clickers. Behind the machine at the opposite end of the line sat another table which was intermittently the work station of a female employee who performed sundry scissors operations of a more intricate nature on raincoat parts. Boxed in on all sides by shelves and stocks of materials, this latter locus of work appeared a cell within a cell.

The clickers were of the genus punching machines; of mechanical construction similar to that of the better-known punch presses, their leading features were hammer and block. The hammer, or punching head, was approximately eight inches by twelve inches at its flat striking surface. The descent upon the block was initially forced

---

[4]Donald F. Roy, "Work Satisfaction and Social Reward in Quota Achievement: An Analysis of Piecework Incentive," *American Sociological Review,* Vol. XVIII (October, 1953), 507–14.

by the operator, who exerted pressure on a handle attached to the side of the hammer head. A few inches of travel downward established electrical connection for a sharp, power-driven blow. The hammer also traveled, by manual guidance, in a horizontal plane to and from, and in an arc around, the central column of the machine. Thus the operator, up to the point of establishing electrical connections for the sudden and irrevocable downward thrust, had flexibility in maneuvering his instrument over the larger surface of the block. The latter, approximately twenty-four inches wide, eighteen inches deep, and ten inches thick, was made, like a butcher's block, of inlaid hardwood; it was set in the machine at a convenient waist height. On it the operator placed his materials, one sheet at a time if leather, stacks of sheets if plastic, to be cut with steel dies of assorted sizes and shapes. The particular die in use would be moved, by hand, from spot to spot over the materials each time a cut was made; less frequently, materials would be shifted on the block as the operator saw need for such adjustment.

Introduction to the new job, with its relatively simple machine skills and work routines, was accomplished with what proved to be, in my experience, an all-time minimum of job training. The clicking machine assigned to me was situated at one end of the row. Here the superintendent and one of the operators gave a few brief demonstrations, accompanied by bits of advice which included a warning to keep hands clear of the descending hammer. After a short practice period, at the end of which the superintendent expressed satisfaction with progress and potentialities, I was left to develop my learning curve with no other supervision than that afforded by members of the work group. Further advice and assistance did come, from time to time, from my fellow operatives, sometimes upon request, sometimes unsolicited.

THE WORK GROUP

Absorbed at first in three related goals of improving my clicking skill, increasing my rate of output, and keeping my left hand unclicked, I paid little attention to my fellow operatives save to observe that they were friendly, middle-aged, foreign-born, full of advice, and very talkative. Their names, according to the way they addressed each other, were George, Ike, and Sammy.[5] George, a stocky fellow in his late fifties, operated the machine at the opposite end of the line; he, I later discovered, had emigrated in early youth

---

[5]All names used are fictitious.

from a country in Southeastern Europe. Ike, stationed at George's left, was tall, slender, in his early fifties, and Jewish; he had come from Eastern Europe in his youth. Sammy, number three man in the line, and my neighbor, was heavy set, in his late fifties, and Jewish; he had escaped from a country in Eastern Europe just before Hitler's legions had moved in. All three men had been downwardly mobile as to occupation in recent years. George and Sammy had been proprietors of small businesses; the former had been "wiped out" when his uninsured establishment burned down; the latter had been entrepreneuring on a small scale before he left all behind him to flee the Germans. According to his account, Ike had left a highly skilled trade which he had practiced for years in Chicago.

I discovered also that the clicker line represented a ranking system in descending order from George to myself. George not only had top seniority for the group, but functioned as a sort of leadman. His superior status was marked in the fact that he received five cents more per hour than the other clickermen, put in the longest workday, made daily contact, outside the workroom, with the superintendent on work matters which concerned the entire line, and communicated to the rest of us the directives which he received. The narrow margin of superordination was seen in the fact that directives were always relayed in the superintendent's name; they were on the order of, "You'd better let that go now, and get on the green. Joe says they're running low on the fifth floor," or, "Joe says he wants two boxes of the 3-die today." The narrow margin was also seen in the fact that the superintendent would communicate directly with his operatives over the public address system; and, on occasion, Ike or Sammy would leave the workroom to confer with him for decisions or advice in regard to work orders.

Ike was next to George in seniority, then Sammy. I was, of course, low man on the totem pole. Other indices to status differentiation lay in informal interaction, to be described later.

With one exception, job status tended to be matched by length of workday. George worked a thirteen-hour day, from 7 A.M. to 8:30 P.M. Ike worked eleven hours, from 7 A.M. to 6:30 P.M.; occasionally he worked until 7 or 7:30 for an eleven and a half- or a twelve-hour day. Sammy put in a nine-hour day, from 8 A.M. to 5:30 P.M. My twelve hours spanned from 8 A.M. to 8:30 P.M. We had a half hour for lunch, from 12 to 12:30.

The female who worked at the secluded table behind George's

machine put in a regular plant-wide eight-hour shift from 8 to 4:30. Two women held this job during the period of my employment; Mable was succeeded by Baby. Both were Negroes, and in their late twenties.

A fifth clicker operator, an Arabian *emigré* called Boo, worked a night shift by himself. He usually arrived about 7 P.M. to take over Ike's machine.

THE WORK

It was evident to me, before my first workday drew to a weary close, that my clicking career was going to be a grim process of fighting the clock, the particular timepiece in this situation being an old-fashioned alarm clock which ticked away on a shelf near George's machine. I had struggled through many dreary rounds with the minutes and hours during the various phases of my industrial experience, but never had I been confronted with such a dismal combination of working conditions as the extra-long workday, the infinitesimal cerebral excitation, and the extreme limitation of physical movement. The contrast with a recent stint in the California oil fields was striking. This was no eight-hour day of racing hither and yon over desert and foothills with a rollicking crew of "roustabouts" on a variety of repair missions at oil wells, pipelines, and storage tanks. Here there were no afternoon dallyings to search the sands for horned toads, tarantulas, and rattlesnakes, or to climb old wooden derricks for raven's nests, with an eye out, of course, for the telltale streak of dust in the distance which gave ample warning of the approach of the boss. This was standing all day in one spot beside three old codgers in a dingy room looking out through barred windows at the bare walls of a brick warehouse, leg movements largely restricted to the shifting of body weight from one foot to the other, hand and arm movements confined, for the most part, to a simple repetitive sequence of place the die, ——— punch the clicker, ——— place the die, —— punch the clicker, and intellectual activity reduced to computing the hours to quitting time. It is true that from time to time a fresh stack of sheets would have to be substituted for the clicked-out old one; but the stack would have been prepared by someone else, and the exchange would be only a minute or two in the making. Now and then a box of finished work would have to be moved back out of the way, and an empty box brought up; but the moving back and the bringing up involved only a step or two. And there was the half hour for lunch, and occasional trips to the lavatory or the drinking fountain to break up the day into digestible parts. But after each momentary respite, hammer and die were moving again: click, ——— move die, ——— click, ——— move die.

Before the end of the first day, Monotony was joined by his twin brother, Fatigue. I got tired. My legs ached, and my feet hurt. Early in the afternoon I discovered a tall stool and moved it up to my machine to "take the load off my feet." But the superintendent dropped in to see how I was "doing" and promptly informed me that "we don't sit down on this job." My reverie toyed with the idea of quitting the job and looking for other work.

The next day was the same: the monotony of the work, the tired legs and sore feet and thoughts of quitting.

THE GAME OF WORK

In discussing the factory operative's struggle to "cling to the remnants of joy in work," Henri de Man makes the general observations that "it is psychologically impossible to deprive any kind of work of all its positive emotional elements," that the worker will find *some* meaning in any activity assigned to him, a "certain scope for initiative which can satisfy after a fashion the instinct for play and the creative impulse," that "even in the Taylor system there is found luxury of self-determination."[6] De Man cites the case of one worker who wrapped 13,000 incandescent bulbs a day; she found her outlet for creative impulse, her self-determination, her meaning in work by varying her wrapping movements a little from time to time.[7]

So did I search for *some* meaning in my continuous mincing of plastic sheets into small ovals, fingers, and trapezoids. The richness of possibility for creative expression previously discovered in my experience with the "Taylor system"[8] did not reveal itself here. There was no piecework, so no piecework game. There was no conflict with management, so no war game. But, like the light bulb wrapper, I did find a "certain scope for initiative," and out of this slight freedom to vary activity, I developed a game of work.

The game developed was quite simple, so elementary, in fact, that its playing was reminiscent of rainy-day preoccupations in child-

---

[6]Henri de Man, *The Psychology of Socialism,* Henry Holt and Company, New York, 1927, pp. 80–81.

[7]*Ibid.,* p. 81.

[8]Roy, *op. cit.*

hood, when attention could be centered by the hour on colored bits of things of assorted sizes and shapes. But this adult activity was not mere pottering and piddling; what it lacked in the earlier imaginative content, it made up for in clean-cut structure. Fundamentally involved were: *(a)* variation in color of the materials cut, *(b)* variation in shapes of the dies used, and *(c)* a process called "scraping the block." The basic procedure which ordered the particular combination of components employed could be stated in the form: "As soon as I do so many of these, I'll get to do those." If, for example, production scheduled for the day featured small, rectangular strips in three colors, the game might go: "As soon as I finish a thousand of the green ones, I'll click some brown ones." And, with success in attaining the objective of working with brown materials, a new goal of "I'll get to do the white ones" might be set. Or the new goal might involve switching dies.

Scraping the block made the game more interesting by adding to the number of possible variations in its playing; and, what was perhaps more important, provided the only substantial reward, save for going to the lavatory or getting a drink of water, on days when work with one die and one color of material was scheduled. As a physical operation, scraping the block was fairly simple; it involved application of a coarse file to the upper surface of the block to remove roughness and unevenness resulting from the wear and tear of die penetration. But, as part of the intellectual and emotional content of the game of work, it could be in itself a source of variation in activity. The upper left-hand corner of the block could be chewed up in the clicking of 1,000 white trapezoid pieces, then scraped. Next, the upper right-hand corner, and so on until the entire block had been worked over. Then, on the next round of scraping by quadrants, there was the possibility of a change of color or die to green trapezoid or white oval pieces.

Thus the game of work might be described as a continuous sequence of short-range production goals with achievement rewards in the form of activity change. The superiority of this relatively complex and self-determined system over the technically simple and outside-controlled job satisfaction injections experienced by Milner at the beginner's table in a shop of the feather industry should be immediately apparent:

Twice a day our work was completely changed to break the monotony. First Jennie would give us feathers of a brilliant green, then bright orange or a light blue or black. The "ohs" and "ahs" that came from the girls at each change was proof enough that this was an effective way of breaking the monotony of the tedious work.[9]

But a hasty conclusion that I was having lots of fun playing my clicking game should be avoided. These games were not as interesting in the experiencing as they might seem to be from the telling. Emotional tone of the activity was low, and intellectual currents weak. Such rewards as scraping the block or "getting to do the blue ones" were not very exciting, and the stretches of repetitive movement involved in achieving them were long enough to permit lapses into obsessive reverie. Henri de Man speaks of "clinging to the remnants of joy in work," and this situation represented just that. How tenacious the clinging was, how long I could have "stuck it out" with my remnants, was never determined. Before the first week was out this adjustment to the work situation was complicated by other developments. The game of work continued, but in a different context. Its influence became decidedly subordinated to, if not completely overshadowed by, another source of job satisfaction.

INFORMAL SOCIAL ACTIVITY OF THE WORK GROUP: TIMES AND THEMES

The change came about when I began to take serious note of the social activity going on around me; my attentiveness to this activity came with growing involvement in it. What I heard at first, before I started to listen, was a stream of disconnected bits of communication which did not make much sense. Foreign accents were strong and referents were not joined to coherent contexts of meaning. It was just "jabbering." What I saw at first, before I began to observe, was occasional flurries of horseplay so simple and unvarying in pattern and so childish in quality that they made no strong bid for attention. For example, Ike would regularly switch off the power at Sammy's machine whenever Sammy made a trip to the lavatory or the drinking fountain. Correlatively, Sammy invariably fell victim to the plot by making an attempt to operate his clicking hammer after returning to the shop. And, as the simple pattern went, this blind stumbling into the trap was always followed by indignation and reproach from Sammy, smirking satisfaction from Ike, and mild paternal scolding from George. My interest in this procedure was at first confined to wondering when

<hr/>

[9]Lucille Milner, *Education of An American Liberal,* Horizon Press, New York, 1954, p. 97.

Ike would weary of his tedious joke or when Sammy would learn to check his power switch before trying the hammer.

But, as I began to pay closer attention, as I began to develop familiarity with the communication system, the disconnected became connected, the nonsense made sense, the obscure became clear, and the silly actually funny. And, as the content of the interaction took on more and more meaning, the interaction began to reveal structure. There were "times" and "themes," and roles to serve their enaction. The interaction had subtleties, and I began to savor and appreciate them. I started to record what hitherto had seemed unimportant.

Times

This emerging awareness of structure and meaning included recognition that the long day's grind was broken by interruptions of a kind other than the formally instituted or idiosyncratically developed disjunctions in work routine previously described. These additional interruptions appeared in daily repetition in an ordered series of informal interactions. They were, in part, but only in part and in very rough comparison, similar to those common fractures of the production process known as the coffee break, the coke break, and the cigarette break. Their distinction lay in frequency of occurrence and in brevity. As phases of the daily series, they occurred almost hourly, and so short were they in duration that they disrupted work activity only slightly. Their significance lay not so much in their function as rest pauses, although it cannot be denied that physical refreshment was involved. Nor did their chief importance lie in the accentuation of progress points in the passage of time, although they could perform that function far more strikingly than the hour hand on the dull face of George's alarm clock. If the daily series of interruptions be likened to a clock, then the comparison might best be made with a special kind of cuckoo clock, one with a cuckoo which can provide variation in its announcements and can create such an interest in them that the intervening minutes become filled with intellectual content. The major significance of the interactional interruptions lay in such a carryover of interest. The physical interplay which momentarily halted work activity would initiate verbal exchanges and thought processes to occupy group members until the next interruption. The group interactions thus not only marked off the time; they gave it content and hurried it along.

Most of the breaks in the daily series were designated as "times" in the parlance of the clicker operators, and they featured the consumption of food or drink of one sort or another. There was coffee time, peach time, banana time, fish time, coke time, and, of course, lunch time. Other interruptions, which formed part of the series but were not verbally recognized as times, were window time, pickup time, and the staggered quitting times of Sammy and Ike. These latter unnamed times did not involve the partaking of refreshments.

My attention was first drawn to this times business during my first week of employment when I was encouraged to join in the sharing of two peaches. It was Sammy who provided the peaches; he drew them from his lunch box after making the announcement, "Peach time!" On this first occasion I refused the proffered fruit, but thereafter regularly consumed my half peach. Sammy continued to provide the peaches and to make the "Peach time!" announcement, although there were days when Ike would remind him that it was peach time, urging him to hurry up with the mid-morning snack. Ike invariably complained about the quality of the fruit, and his complaints fed the fires of continued banter between peach donor and critical recipient. I did find the fruit a bit on the scrubby side but felt, before I achieved insight into the function of peach time, that Ike was showing poor manners by looking a gift horse in the mouth. I wondered why Sammy continued to share his peaches with such an ingrate.

Banana time followed peach time by approximately an hour. Sammy again provided the refreshments, namely, one banana. There was, however, no four-way sharing of Sammy's banana. Ike would gulp it down by himself after surreptitiously extracting it from Sammy's lunch box, kept on a shelf behind Sammy's work station. Each morning, after making the snatch, Ike would call out, "Banana time!" and proceed to down his prize while Sammy made futile protests and denunciations. George would join in with mild remonstrances, sometimes scolding Sammy for making so much fuss. The banana was one which Sammy brought for his own consumption at lunch time; he never did get to eat his banana, but kept bringing one for his lunch. At first this daily theft startled and amazed me. Then I grew to look forward to the daily seizure and the verbal interaction which followed.

Window time came next. It followed banana time as a regular consequence of Ike's castigation by the indignant Sammy. After "taking" repeated references to himself as a person badly lacking in morality and character, Ike would "finally" retaliate by opening the window which faced Sammy's machine, to let the "cold air" blow in on Sammy. The slandering which would, in its echolalic repetition, wear down Ike's patience and forbearance usually took the form of the invidious comparison: "George is a good daddy! Ike is a bad man! A very bad man!" Opening the window would take a little time to accomplish and would involve a great deal of verbal interplay between Ike and Sammy, both before and after the event. Ike would threaten, make feints toward the window, then finally open it. Sammy would protest, argue, and make claims that the air blowing in on him would give him a cold; he would eventually have to leave his machine to close the window. Sometimes the weather was slightly chilly, and the draft from the window unpleasant; but cool or hot, windy or still, window time arrived each day. (I assume that it was originally a cold season development.) George's part in this interplay, in spite of the "good daddy" laudations, was to encourage Ike in his window work. He would stress the tonic values of fresh air and chide Sammy for his unappreciativeness.

Following window time came lunch time, a formally designated half-hour for the midday repast and rest break. At this time, informal interaction would feature exchanges between Ike and George. The former would start eating his lunch a few minutes before noon, and the latter, in his role as straw boss, would censure him for malobservance of the rules. Ike's off-beat luncheon usually involved a previous tampering with George's alarm clock. Ike would set the clock ahead a few minutes in order to maintain his eating schedule without detection, and George would discover these small daylight saving changes.

The first "time" interruption of the day I did not share. It occurred soon after I arrived on the job, at eight o'clock. George and Ike would share a small pot of coffee brewed on George's hot plate.

Pickup time, fish time, and coke time came in the afternoon. I name it pickup time to represent the official visit of the man who made daily calls to cart away boxes of clicked materials. The arrival of the pickup man, a Negro, was always a noisy one, like the arrival of a daily passenger train in an isolated small town. Interaction attained a quick peak of intensity to crowd into a few minutes all communications, necessary and otherwise. Exchanges invariably included loud depreciations by the pickup man of the amount of work accomplished in the clicking department during the preceding twenty-four hours. Such scoffing would be on the order of "Is that all you've got done? What do you boys do all day?" These devaluations would be countered with allusions to the "soft job" enjoyed by the pickup man. During the course of the exchanges news items would be dropped, some of serious import, such as reports of accomplished or impending layoffs in the various plants of the company, or of gains or losses in orders for company products. Most of the news items, however, involved bits of information on plant employees told in a light vein. Information relayed by the clicker operators was usually told about each other, mainly in the form of summaries of the most recent kidding sequences. Some of this material was repetitive, carried over from day to day. Sammy would be the butt of most of this newscasting, although he would make occasional counter-reports on Ike and George. An invariable part of the interactional content of pickup time was Ike's introduction of the pickup man to George. "Meet Mr. Papeatis!" Ike would say in mock solemnity and dignity. Each day the pickup man "met" Mr. Papeatis, to the obvious irritation of the latter. Another pickup time invariably would bring Baby (or Mable) into the interaction. George would always issue the loud warning to the pickup man: "Now I want you to stay away from Baby! She's Henry's girl!" Henry was a burly Negro with a booming bass voice who made infrequent trips to the clicking room with lift-truck loads of materials. He was reputedly quite a ladies' man among the colored population of the factory. George's warning to "Stay away from Baby!" was issued to every Negro who entered the shop. Baby's only part in this was to laugh at the horseplay.

About mid-afternoon came fish time, George and Ike would stop work for a few minutes to consume some sort of pickled fish which Ike provided. Neither Sammy nor I partook of this nourishment, nor were we invited. For this omission I was grateful; the fish, brought in a newspaper and with head and tail intact, produced a reverse effect on my appetite. George and Ike seemed to share a great liking for fish. Each Friday night, as a regular ritual, they would enjoy a fish dinner together at a nearby restaurant. On these nights Ike would work until 8:30 and leave the plant with George.

Coke time came late in the afternoon, and was an occasion for total participation. The four of us took turns in buying the drinks and in making the trip for them to a fourth floor vending machine. Through George's manipulation of the situation, it eventually became my daily chore to go after the cokes; the straw boss had noted that I made a much faster trip to the fourth floor and back than Sammy or Ike.

Sammy left the plant at 5:30, and Ike ordinarily retired from the scene an hour and a half later. These quitting times were not marked by any distinctive interaction save the one regular exchange between Sammy and George over the former's "early washup." Sammy's tendency was to crowd his washing up toward five o'clock, and it was George's concern to keep it from further creeping advance. After Ike's departure came Boo's arrival. Boo's was a striking personality productive of a change in topics of conversation to fill in the last hour of the long workday.

Themes

To put flesh, so to speak, on this interactional frame of "times," my work group had developed various "themes" of verbal interplay which had become standardized in their repetition. These topics of conversation ranged in quality from an extreme of nonsensical chatter to another extreme of serious discourse. Unlike the times, these themes flowed one into the other in no particular sequence of predictability. Serious conversation could suddenly melt into horseplay, and vice versa. In the middle of a serious discussion on the high cost of living, Ike might drop a weight behind the easily startled Sammy, or hit him over the head with a dusty paper sack. Interaction would immediately drop to a low comedy exchange of slaps, threats, guffaws, and disapprobations which would invariably include a ten-minute echolalia of "Ike is a bad man, a very bad man! George is a good daddy, a very fine man!" Or, on the other hand, a stream of such invidious comparisons as followed a surreptitious switching-off of Sammy's machine by the playful Ike might merge suddenly into a discussion of the pros and cons of saving for one's funeral.

"Kidding themes" were usually started by George or Ike, and Sammy was usually the butt of the joke. Sometimes Ike would have to "take it," seldom George. One favorite kidding theme involved Sammy's alleged receipt of $100 a month from his son. The points stressed were that Sammy did not have to work long hours, or did not have to work at all, because he had a son to support him. George would always point out that he sent money to his daughter; she did not send money to him. Sammy received occasional calls from his wife, and his claim that these calls were requests to shop for groceries on the way home were greeted with feigned disbelief. Sammy was ribbed for being closely watched, bossed, and henpecked by his wife, and the expression "Are you man or mouse?" became an echolalic utterance, used both in and out of the original context.

Ike, who shared his machine and the work scheduled for it with Boo, the night operator, came in for constant invidious comparison on the subject of output. The socially isolated Boo, who chose work rather than sleep on his lonely night shift, kept up a high level of performance, and George never tired of pointing this out to Ike. It so happened that Boo, an Arabian Moslem from Palestine, had no use for Jews in general; and Ike, who was Jewish, had no use for Boo in particular. Whenever George would extol Boo's previous night's production, Ike would try to turn the conversation into a general discussion on the need for educating the Arabs. George, never permitting the development of serious discussion on this topic, would repeat a smirking warning, "You watch out for Boo! He's got a long knife!"

The "poom poom" theme was one that caused no sting. It would come up several times a day to be enjoyed as unbarbed fun by the three older clicker operators. Ike was usually the one to raise the question, "How many times you go poom poom last night?" The person questioned usually replied with claims of being "too old for poom poom." If this theme did develop a goat, it was I. When it was pointed out that I was a younger man, this provided further grist for the poom poom mill. I soon grew weary of this poom poom business, so dear to the hearts of the three old satyrs, and, knowing where the conversation would inevitably lead, winced whenever Ike brought up the subject.

I grew almost as sick of a kidding theme which developed from some personal information contributed during a serious conversation on property ownership and high taxes. I dropped a few remarks about two acres of land which I owned in one of the western states, and from then on I had to listen to questions, advice, and general nonsensical comment in regard to "Danelly's farm."[10] This "farm" soon became stocked with horses, cows, pigs, chickens, ducks, and the various and sundry domesticated beasts so tunefully listed in "Old McDonald Had a Farm." George was a persistent offender with this theme. Where the others seemed to be mainly interested

---

[10]This spelling is the closest I can come to the appellation given me in George's broken English and adopted by other members of the group.

in statistics on livestock, crops, etc., George's teasing centered on
a generous offering to help with the household chores while I
worked in the fields. He would drone on, *ad nauseam*, "when I come
to visit you, you will never have to worry about the housework,
Danelly. I'll stay around the house when you go out to dig the
potatoes and milk the cows, I'll stay in and peel potatoes and help
your wife do the dishes." Danelly always found it difficult to change
the subject on George, once the latter started to bear down on the
farm theme.

Another kidding theme which developed out of serious discussion
could be labelled "helping Danelly find a cheaper apartment." It
became known to the group that Danelly had a pending housing
problem, that he would need new quarters for his family when the
permanent resident of his temporary summer dwelling returned
from a vacation. This information engendered at first a great deal of
sympathetic concern and, of course, advice on apartment hunting.
Development into a kidding theme was immediately related to previous exchanges between Ike and George on the quality of their
respective dwelling areas. Ike lived in "Lawndale," and George
dwelt in the "Woodlawn" area. The new pattern featured the reading aloud of bogus "apartment for rent" ads in newspapers which
were brought into the shop. Studying his paper at lunchtime, George
would call out, "Here's an apartment for you, Danelly! Five rooms,
stove heat, $20 a month, Lawndale Avenue!" Later, Ike would read
from his paper, "Here's one! Six rooms, stove heat, dirt floor, $18.50
a month! At 55th and Woodlawn." Bantering would then go on in
regard to the quality of housing or population in the two areas.
The search for an apartment for Danelly was not successful.

Serious themes included the relating of major misfortunes suffered in the past by group members. George referred again and
again to the loss, by fire, of his business establishment. Ike's chief
complaints centered around a chronically ill wife who had undergone various operations and periods of hospital care. Ike spoke with
discouragement of the expenses attendant upon hiring a house-
keeper for himself and his children; he referred with disappointment and disgust to a teen-age son, an inept lad who "couldn't even
fix his own lunch. He couldn't even make himself a sandwich!"
Sammy's reminiscences centered on the loss of a flourishing business
when he had to flee Europe ahead of Nazi invasion.

But all serious topics were not tales of woe. One favorite serious
theme which was optimistic in tone could be called either "Danelly's future" or "getting Danelly a better job." It was known that

I had been attending "college," the magic door to opportunity, although my specific course of study remained somewhat obscure. Suggestions poured forth on good lines of work to get into, and these suggestions were backed with accounts of friends, and friends of friends, who had made good via the academic route. My answer to the expected question, "Why are you working here?" always stressed the "lots of overtime" feature, and this explanation seemed to suffice for short-range goals.

There was one theme of especially solemn import, the "professor theme." This theme might also be termed "George's daughter's marriage theme"; for the recent marriage of George's only child was inextricably bound up with George's connection with higher learning. The daughter had married the son of a professor who instructed in one of the local colleges. This professor theme was not in the strictest sense a conversation piece; when the subject came up George did all the talking. The two Jewish operatives remained silent as they listened with deep respect, if not actual awe, to George's accounts of the Big Wedding which, including the wedding pictures entailed an expense of $1,000. It was monologue, but there was listening, there was communication, the sacred communication of a temple, when George told of going for Sunday afternoon walks on the Midway with the professor, or of joining the professor for a Sunday dinner. Whenever he spoke of the professor, his daughter, the wedding, or even the new son-in-law, who remained for the most part in the background, a sort of incidental like the wedding cake, George was complete master of the interaction. His manner, in speaking to the rank-and-file of clicker operators, was indeed that of master deigning to notice his underlings. I came to the conclusion that it was the professor connection, not the straw-boss-ship or the extra nickel an hour, which provided the fount of George's superior status in the group.

If the professor theme may be regarded as the cream of verbal interaction, the "chatter themes" should be classed as the dregs. The chatter themes were hardly themes at all; perhaps they should be labelled "verbal states," or "oral autisms." Some were of doubtful status as communication; they were like the howl or cry of an animal responding to its own physiological state. They were exclamations, ejaculations, snatches of song or doggerel, talkings-to-oneself, mutterings. Their classification as themes would rest on their repetitive character. They were echolalic utterances, repeated over and over. An already mentioned example would be Sammy's repetition of "George is a good daddy, a very fine man! Ike is a bad man, a very bad man!" Also, Sammy's repetition of "Don't bother me! Can't you see I'm busy? I'm a very busy man!" for ten minutes after Ike had dropped a weight behind him would fit the classification. Ike would shout "Mamariba!" at intervals between repetition of bits of verse such as:

> Mama on the bed,
> Papa on the floor,
> Baby in the crib
> Says giver some more!

Sometimes the three operators would pick up one of these simple chatterings in a sort of chorus. "Are you man or mouse? I ask you, are you man or mouse?" was a favorite of this type.

So initial discouragement with the meagerness of social interaction I now recognized as due to lack of observation. The interaction was there, in constant flow. It captured attention and held interest to make the long day pass. The twelve hours of "click, ——— move die, ——— click, ——— move die" became as easy to endure as eight hours of varied activity in the old fields or eight hours of playing the piecework game in a machine shop. The "beast of boredom" was gentled to the harmlessness of a kitten.

THE CABDRIVER AND HIS FARE: FACETS OF FLEETING RELATIONSHIP*

Fred Davis[1]

Even in an urban and highly secularized society such as ours, most service relationships, be they between a professional and his client or a menial and his patron, are characterized by certain constraints on too crass a rendering and consuming of the service.[2] That

---

*Reprinted in its entirety from Fred Davis, "The Cabdriver and His Fare: Facets of a Fleeting Relationship," *American Journal of Sociology*, Vol. 65, No. 2 (Sept., 1959), pp. 158–65. Used by permission of The University of Chicago Press.

[1]This articles is based largely on notes and observations made by me over a six-month period in 1948 when I worked as a cabdriver for one of the larger taxicab firms in Chicago. I am greatly indebted to Erving Goffman, Everett C. Hughes, and Howard S. Becker for their comments and criticisms.

[2]Talcott Parsons, *The Social System* (Glencoe, Ill.: Free Press, 1951), pp. 48–56.

is to say, in the transaction, numerous interests besides that of simply effecting an economic exchange are customarily attended to and dealt with. The moral reputation of the parties,[3] their respective social standing, and the skill and art with which the service is performed[4] are but a few of the non-instrumental values which are usually incorporated into the whole act.

Tenuous though such constraints may become at times, particularly in large cities where anonymous roles, only segmentally related, occur in great profusion, it is at once evident that for them to exist at all something approximating a community must be present. Practitioners and clients must be sufficiently in communication for any untoward behavior to stand a reasonable chance of becoming known, remarked upon, remembered, and, in extreme cases, made public. And, whereas the exercise of sanctions does not necessarily depend on a community network[5] that is closely integrated (or one in which there is a total identity of values and interests), it does depend on there being some continuity and stability in the relationships that make up the network, so that, at minimum, participants may in the natural course of events be able to identify actions and actors to one another.[6]

It is mainly, though not wholly, from this vantage point that big-city cabdriving as an occupation is here discussed, particularly the relationship between cabdriver and fare and its consequences for the occupational culture.[7] Approximating in certain respects a provincial's caricature of the broad arc of social relations in the metropolis, this relationship affords an extreme instance of the weakening and attenuation of many of the constraints customary in other client-and-patron-oriented services in our society. As such, its analysis can perhaps point up by implication certain of the rarely con-

[3]Erving Goffman, *The Presentation of Self in Everyday Life* (Edinburgh: University of Edinburgh Social Science Research Centre, 1956), pp. 160–62.

[4]Everett C. Hughes, *Men and Their Work* (Glencoe, Ill.: Free Press, 1958), pp. 88–101.

[5]Because it better delineates the boundaries and linkages of informal sanctioning groups found in large cities, the term "network" is used here to qualify the more global concept of "community." See Elizabeth Bott, *Family and Social Network* (London: Tavistock, 1957), pp. 58–61.

[6]Robert K. Merton, "The Role Set: Problems in Sociological Theory," *British Journal of Sociology*, VIII, No. 2 (June, 1957), 114.

[7]Parallel studies of this aspect of occupational culture are: Hughes, *op. cit.*, pp. 42–55; Howard S. Becker, "The Professional Dance Musician and His Audience," *American Journal of Sociology*, LVII (September, 1951), 136–44; Ray Gold, "Janitor versus Tenants: A Status-Income Dilemma," *American Journal of Sociology*, LVII (March, 1951), 486–93.

sidered preconditions for practitioner-client relations found in other, more firmly structured, services and professions.

In a large city like Chicago the hiring of a cab by a passenger may be conceived of in much the same way as the random collision of particles in an atomic field. True, there are some sectors of the field in which particles come into more frequent collision than others, for example, downtown, at railroad depots, and at the larger neighborhood shopping centers. But this kind of differential activity within the field as a whole provides little basis for predicting the coupling of any two specific particles.

To a much more pronounced degree than is the case in other client-and-patron-oriented services, the occupation of cabdriver provides its practitioners with few, if any, regularities by which to come upon, build up, and maintain a steady clientele. The doctor has his patients, the schoolteacher her pupils, the janitor his tenants, the waitress her regular diners; and in each case server and served remain generally in some continuing or renewable relationship. By contrast, the cabdriver's day consists of a long series of brief contacts with unrelated persons of whom he has no foreknowledge, just as they have none of him, and whom he is not likely to encounter again.

Furthermore, by virtue of the differential spatial, social, and organizational arrangements of the community, it is also likely that the clients of these other practitioners will, in some manner at least, know one another and be related to one another in ways that often transcend the simple circumstance of sharing the same services: they may also be friends, kin, neighbors, or colleagues. For this reason the clientele of most practitioners is something more than an aggregate of discrete individuals; it is, as well, a rudimentary social universe and forum to which the practitioner must address himself in other than purely individual terms.[8]

The cabdriver, by comparison, has no such clientele. He has no fixed business address, and his contacts with passengers are highly random and singular. To a striking degree he is a practitioner without reputation because those who ride in his cab do not comprise, except perhaps in the most abstract sense, anything approximating a social group. They neither know nor come into contact with one another in other walks of life, and, even if by chance some do, they are unaware of their ever having shared the services of the same

---

[8]Merton, *op. cit.*, pp. 110–12.

anonymous cabdriver. Even were the driver deliberately to set out to build up a small nucleus of steady and favored passengers, the time-space logistics of his job would quickly bring such a scheme to naught. Unable to plot his location in advance or to distribute time according to a schedule, he depends on remaining open to all comers wherever he finds himself. Much more so than other classes of service personnel, cabdrivers are both the fortuitous victims and the beneficiaries of random and highly impersonal market contingencies.

This set of circumstances—fleeting, one-time contact with a heterogeneous aggregate of clients, unknown to one another—exerts an interesting influence on the role of cabdriver.

Unable, either directly through choice or indirectly through location, to select clients, the cabdriver is deprived of even minimal controls. His trade therefore exposes him to a variety of hazards and exigencies which few others, excepting policemen, encounter as frequently; for example: stick-ups, belligerent drunks, women in labor, psychopaths, counterfeiters, and fare-jumpers. Unlike the policeman's however, his control over them is more fragile.

Nor, incidentally, is the cabdriver's social status or level of occupational skill of much help in inducing constraint in fares. Patently, his status is low, in large part precisely because, unlike the professional and other practitioners commanding prestige, he can hardly be distinguished from his clients in task-relevant competence. Not only is the operation of a motor car a widely possessed skill, but a large portion of fares have, for example, a very good idea of the best routes to their destination, the rules and practices of the road, and the charges for a trip. Though they are rarely as adept or sophisticated in these matters as the cabdriver, the discrepancy is so small that many think they know the driver's job as well as he does. Periodically, a cabdriver will boldly challenge a difficult and critical passenger to take over the wheel himself. Others, wishing to impress on the fare that theirs is a real service requiring special talent and skill, will resort to darting nimbly in and out of traffic, making neatly executed U-turns and leaping smartly ahead of other cars when the traffic light changes.

Goffman[9] speaks of a category of persons who in some social encounters are treated as if they were not present, whereas in fact they may be indispensable for sustaining the performance. He terms these

---

[9] Goffman, *op. cit.*, p. 95.

"non-persons" and gives as an example a servant at a social gathering. Although cabdrivers are not consistently approached in this way by fares, it happens often enough for it to become a significant theme of their work. Examples are legion. Maresca[10] tells of the chorus girl who made a complete change from street clothing into stage costume as he drove her to her theater. More prosaic instances include the man and wife who, managing to suppress their anger while on the street, launch into a bitter quarrel the moment they are inside the cab; or the well-groomed young couple who after a few minutes roll over on the back seat to begin petting; or the businessman who loudly discusses details of a questionable business deal. Here the driver is expected to, and usually does, act as if he were merely an extension of the automobile he operates. In actuality, of course, he is acutely aware of what goes on in his cab, and, although his being treated as a non-person implies a degraded status, it also affords him a splendid vantage point from which to witness a rich variety of human schemes and entanglements.

The fleeting nature of the cabdriver's contact with the passenger at the same time also makes for his being approached as someone to whom intimacies can be revealed and opinions forthrightly expressed with little fear of rebuttal, retaliation, or disparagement. And though this status as an accessible person is the product of little more than the turning inside-out of his non-person status—which situation implies neither equality nor respect for his opinion—it nevertheless does afford him glimpses of the private lives of individuals which few in our society, apart from psychiatrists and clergy, are privileged to note as often or in such great variety. It is probably not a mistaken everyday generalization that big-city cabdrivers, on their part, feel less compunction about discussing their own private lives, asking probing questions, and "sounding off" on a great many topics and issues than do others who regularly meet the public, but less fleetingly.[11]

In cabdriving, therefore, propriety, deference, and "face" are, in the nature of the case, weaker than is the case in most other service

---

[10]James V. Maresca, *My Flag Is Down* (New York: E. P. Dutton & Co., 1945). Essentially the same incident is related by an unidentified cabdriver on the documentary recording of Tony Schwartz, *The New York Taxi Driver* (Columbia Records, ML 5309, 1959).

[11]Cf. Schwartz, *op. cit.* In fact, these characteristic qualities, with a work-adapted, bitter-sweet admixture of cynicism and sentimentality, comprise the core of the personality widely imputed to cabdrivers by the riding public. Cf. Hughes, *op. cit.*, pp. 23–41.

relationships. This absence contributes to a heightened preoccupation with and focusing on the purely instrumental aspect of the relationship which for the driver is the payment he receives for his services. This perhaps would be less blatantly the case were it not for the gratuity or tip. For the non-cab-driving company driver, the sum collected in tips amounts roughly to 40 per cent of his earnings. Considering, for example, that in Chicago in the late forties a hard-working cabdriver, who worked for ten hours a day, six days a week, would on the average take home approximately seventy-five dollars a week including tips, the importance of tipping can readily be appreciated. For the family man who drives, tips usually represent the difference between a subsistence and a living wage. Also, tips are, apart from taxes, money "in the clear," in that the driver does not have to divide them with the company as he does his metered collections.[12] Sum for sum, therefore, tips represent greater gain for him than do metered charges.

It would probably be incorrect to hold that pecuniary considerations are the sole ones involved in the cabdriver's attitude toward the tip. Yet in such tip-sensitive occupations as cabdriving, waitering, and bellhopping to suggest[13] that the tip's primary significance is its symbolic value as a token of affection or appreciation for a service well performed would be even wider of the mark. Vindictive caricatures abound among cabdrivers, as they do among waiters, waitresses, and bellhops, of the "polite gentleman" or "kind lady" who with profuse thanks and flawless grace departs from the scene having "stiffed" (failed to tip) them. In occupations where the tip constitutes so large a fraction of the person's earnings, the cash nexus, while admittedly not the only basis upon which patrons are judged, is so important as to relegate other considerations to a secondary place. Will the fare tip or will he "stiff?" How much will he tip? The answers remain in nearly every instance problematic to the end. Not only is there no sure way of predicting the outcome, but in a culture where the practice of tipping is neither as widespread nor as standardized as in many Continental countries, for example, the driver cannot in many cases even make a guess.

No regular scheme of work can easily tolerate so high a degree of ambiguity and uncertainty in a key contingency. Invariably, at-

---

[12] In Chicago in 1948 the company driver's share of the metered sum was 42½ per cent. Since that time the proportion has been increased slightly.

[13] Cf. William F. Whyte, *Human Relations in the Restaurant Industry* (New York: McGraw-Hill Book Co., 1948), p. 100.

tempts are made to fashion ways and means of greater predictability and control; or, failing that, of devising formulas and imagery to bring order and reason in otherwise inscrutable and capricious events. In the course of a long history a rich body of stereotypes, beliefs, and practices[14] has grown up whose function is that of reducing uncertainty, increasing calculability, and providing coherent explanations.

A basic dichotomy running through the cabdriver's concept of his client world is of regular cab users and of non-cab users, the latter referred to as "jerks," "slobs," "yokels," "public transportation types," and a host of other derogatory terms. The former class, though viewed as quite heterogeneous within itself, includes all who customarily choose cabs in preference to other forms of local transportation, are conversant with the cab-passenger role, and, most of all, accept, if only begrudgingly, the practice of tipping. By comparison, the class of non-cab users includes that vast aggregate of persons who resort to cabs only in emergencies or on special occasions, and are prone too often to view the hiring of a cab as simply a more expensive mode of transportation.

Take, for example, the familiar street scene following a sudden downpour or unexpected breakdown in bus service, when a group of individuals cluster about a bus stop, several of whom dart from the curb now and then in hope of hailing a cab. Such persons are almost by definition non-cab users or they would not be found at a bus stop in the rain; nor would they be keeping an eye out for a possible bus. A potential fare in this predicament is to the cabdriver a foul-weather friend, and drivers are on occasion known to hurtle by in spiteful glee, leaving the supplicant standing.

He who hires a cab only on special occasions, frequently to impress others or, perhaps, himself alone, is another familiar kind of non-cab user. Writing of his experiences as a London cabdriver, Hodge relates a by no means uncommon encounter:

> But tonight is different. Perhaps the Pools have come up for once. Anyhow, he's got money. He signals me with exaggerated casualness from the cinema entrance. . . . She steps in daintily, the perfect lady, particularly where she puts her feet. As soon as she's safely inside, he whispers the address . . . and adds, as one man of the world to another, "No hurry, driver." Then he dives in with such utter *savoire faire, comme il faut,* and what not, that he trips over the mat and lands face first on the back seat.[15]

---

[14]Cf. here and in the section to follow the pertinent remarks of Hughes on "guilty knowledge" developed by those in a service occupation with reference to their clientele. Hughes, *op. cit.,* pp. 81–82.

[15]Herbert Hodge, "I Drive a Taxi," *Fact,* No. 22 (January, 1939), pp. 28–29.

Perhaps the most obvious kind of non-user is the person who, after hailing a cab, will ask the driver some such question as, "How much will it cost to take me to 500 Elm Street?" By this simple inquiry this person stands revealed as one who takes a narrow view of cab travel and from whom not much, if anything, can be expected by way of tip. On the other hand, regular cab users demonstrate in a variety of ways that for them this is a customary and familiar mode of travel. The manner in which they hail a cab, when and how they announce their destination, the ease with which they enter and exit, how they sit—these, and more, though difficult to describe in precise detail, comprise the Gestalt.

There exists among drivers an extensive typology of cab users, the attributes imputed to each type having a certain predictive value, particularly as regards tipping. Some of the more common and sharply delineated types are:

The Sport. The cabdriver's image of this type combines in one person those attributes of character which he views as ideal. While the Sport's vocation may be any one of many, his status derives more from his extra-vocational activities, e.g., at the race track, prize fights, ball games, popular restaurants, and bars. He is the perennial "young man on the town." Gentlemanly without being aloof, interested without becoming familiar, he also is, of course, never petty. Most of all, his tips are generous, and even on very short rides he will seldom tip less than a quarter. A favorite success story among cabdrivers describes at length and in fine detail the handsome treatment accorded the driver on an all night tour with a Sport.[16]

The Blowhard. The Blowhard is a false Sport. While often wearing the outer mantle of the Sport, he lacks the real Sport's casualness, assured manners, and comfortable style. Given to loquaciousness, he boasts and indiscriminately fabricates tales of track winnings, sexual exploits, and the important people he knows. Often holding out the promise of much by way of tip, he seldom lives up to his words.

The Businessman. These are the staple of the cab trade, particularly for drivers who work by day. Not only are they the most frequently encountered; their habits and preferences are more uniform than those of any other type: the brisk efficiency with which they engage a cab, their purposefulness and disinclination to partake of small talk. Though not often big tippers, they are thought fair. Thus they serve as something of a standard by which the generosity or stinginess of others is judged.

The Lady Shopper. Although almost as numerous as businessmen, Lady Shoppers are not nearly as well thought of by cabdrivers. The stereotype middle-aged woman, fashionably though unattractively dressed, sitting some-

---

[16]As in the past, the Sport still serves as something of a hero figure in our culture, particularly among the working classes. A type midway between the Playboy and the Bohemian, his unique appeal rests perhaps on the ease and assurance with which he is pictured as moving between and among social strata, untainted by upper-class snobbishness, middle-class conventionality and lower-class vulgarity. In *The Great Gatsby,* Fitzgerald gives us a penetrative exposition of the myth of the Sport and its undoing at the hands of the class system.

what stiffly at the edge of her seat and wearing a fixed glare which bespeaks her conviction that she is being "taken for a ride." Her major delinquency, however, is undertipping; her preferred coin is a dime, no more or less, regardless of how long or arduous the trip. A forever repeated story is of the annoyed diver, who, after a grueling trip with a Lady Shopper, hands the coin back, telling her, "Lady, keep your lousy dime. You need it more than I do."[17]

Live Ones.[18] Live Ones are a special category of fare usually encountered by the cabdriver who works by night. They are, as a rule, out-of-town conventioneers or other revelers who tour about in small groups in search of licentious forms of entertainment: cabarets, burlesques, strip-tease bars, pick-up joints, etc. As often as not, they have already had a good deal to drink when the cabdriver meets them, and, being out-of-towners they frequently turn to him for recommendations on where to go. In the late forties an arrangement existed in Chicago whereby some of the more popular Near North Side and West Madison Street "clip joints" rewarded cabdrivers for "steering" Live Ones to their establishments. Some places paid fifty cents "a head"; others a dollar "for the load." As do the many others who regularly cater to Live Ones—e.g., waitresses, bartenders, female bar companions (B-girls), night-club hosts and hostesses, entertainers, prostitutes—cabdrivers often view them as fair game. And while their opportunities for pecuniary exploitation are fewer and more limited than those open, for example, to B-girls and night-club proprietors, many drivers feel less inhibited about padding charges and finagling extras from Live Ones than they do from other fares. Often extravagant in their tips because of high spirits and drink, Live Ones are also frequently careless and forget to tip altogether. Knowing that Live Ones are out to "blow their money" anyway, many drivers believe they are justified in seeing to it that they are not deprived of a small portion.

Although the cab culture's typology of fares stems in a large part from the attempt to order experience, reduce uncertainty, and further calculability of the tip, it is questionable of course as to how accurate or efficient it is. For, as has often been remarked, stereotypes and typologies have a way of imparting a symmetry and regularity to behavior which are, at best, only crudely approximated in reality. Too often it happens, for example, that a fare tabbed as a Sport turns out to be a Stiff (non-tipper), that a Blowhard matches his words with a generous tip, or that a Lady Shopper will give fifteen or even twenty cents. The persistence of the typology therefore has perhaps as much to do with the cabdriver's *a posteriori* reconstructions and rationalizations of fare behavior as it does with the typology's predictive efficiency.

To protect and insure themselves against an unfavorable out-

[17]The stereotype of women as poor tippers is widely shared by other tip-sensitive occupations. Cf. Frances Donovan, *The Woman Who Waits* (Boston: Badger, 1920).

[18]The term "Live Ones" is employed in a variety of pursuits as apparently diverse as retail selling, night-club entertainment, traveling fairs, and panhandling. Generally, it designates persons who are "easy touches," eager to succumb to the oftentimes semifraudulent proposals of the operator. Cf. W. Jack Peterson and Milton A. Maxwell, "The Skid Row Wino," *Social Problems*, V (Spring, 1958), 112.

come of tipping, many drivers will, depending upon circumstances, employ diverse tactics and stratagems (some more premeditated than others) to increase the amount of tip or to compensate for its loss should it not be forthcoming. Certain of these are listed below. It should be understood, however, that in the ordinary instance the driver makes no attempt to manipulate the fare, believing resignedly that in the long run such means bear too little fruit for the effort and risk.

Making Change. Depending on the tariff and the amount handed him, the driver can fumble about in his pockets for change, or make change in such denominations as often to embarrass a fare into giving a larger tip than he had intended. The efficacy of this tactic depends naturally on the determination and staying power of the fare, qualities which many fares are averse to demonstrate, particularly when it comes to small change.

The Hard-Luck Story. This is usually reserved for young persons and others who, for whatever reason, evidence an insecure posture vis-à-vis the driver. Typically, the hard-luck story consists of a catalogue of economic woes, e.g., long and hard hours of work, poor pay, insulting and unappreciative passengers, etc. In "confiding" these to the fare, the driver pretends to esteem him as an exceptionally sympathetic and intelligent person who, unlike "the others," can appreciate his circumstances and act accordingly. Most drivers, however, view the hard-luck story as an unsavory form of extortion, beneath their dignity. Furthermore, while it may work in some cases, its potential for alienating tips is probably as great as its success at extracting them.

Fictitious Charges. The resort to fictitious and fraudulent charges occurs most commonly in those cases in which the driver feels that he has good reason to believe that the fare will, either through malice or ignorance, not tip and when the fare impresses him as being enough of a non-cab user as not to know when improper charges are being levied. Once, when I complained to a veteran cabdriver about having been "stiffed" by a young couple, newly arrived in Chicago, to whom I had extended such extra services as carrying luggage and opening doors, I was told: "Wise up kid! When you pick up one of these yokels at the Dearborn Station carrying a lot of cheap straw luggage on him, you can bet ninety-nine times out of a hundred that he isn't going to tip you. Not that he's a mean guy or anything, but where he comes from, they never heard of tipping. What I do with a yokel like that is to take him to where he's going, show him what the fare is on the meter, and tell him that it costs fifteen cents extra for each piece of luggage. Now, he doesn't know that there's no charge for hand luggage, but that way I'm sure of getting my tip out of him."

The "Psychological" Approach. Possibly attributing more art to their trade than is the case, some drivers are of the opinion that a cab ride can be tailored to fit a passenger in much the same way as can a suit of clothes. One cabdriver, boasting of his success at getting tips, explained: "In this business you've got to use psychology. You've got to make the ride fit the person. Now, take a businessman. He's in a hurry to get someplace and he doesn't want a lot of bullshit and crapping around. With him you've got to keep moving. Do some fancy cutting in and out, give the cab a bit of a jerk when you take off from a light. Not reckless, mind you, but plenty of zip. He likes that.[19] With old

[19]Cf. Hodge, *op. cit.*, p. 17.

people, it's just the opposite. They're more afraid than anyone of getting hurt or killed in a cab. Take it easy with them. Creep along, open doors for them, help them in and out, be real folksy. Call them 'Sir' and 'Ma'am' and they'll soon be calling you 'young man.' They're suckers for this stuff, and they'll loosen up their pocketbooks a little bit."

In the last analysis, neither the driver's typology of fares nor his stratagems further to any marked degree his control of the tip. Paradoxically, were these routinely successful in achieving predictability and control, they would at the same time divest the act of tipping of its most distinguishing characteristics—of its uncertainty, variability, and of the element of revelation in its consummation. It is these—essentially the problematic in human intercourse[20]—which distinguish the tip from the fixed service charge. And though another form of remuneration might in the end provide the cabdriver with a better wage and a more secure livelihood, the abrogation of tipping would also lessen the intellectual play which uncertainty stimulates and without which cabdriving would be for many nothing more than unrelieved drudgery.

That the practice of tipping, however, expressly befits only certain kinds of service relationships and may under slightly altered circumstances easily degenerate into corruption or extortion is demonstrated, ironically enough, by the predicament of some cabdrivers themselves. To give an example: In the garage out of which I worked, nearly everyone connected with maintenance and assignment of cabs expected tips from drivers for performing many of the routine tasks associated with their jobs, such as filling a tank with gas, changing a tire, or adjusting a carburetor. Although they resented it, drivers had little recourse but to tip. Otherwise, they would acquire reputations as "stiffs" and "cheapskates," be kept waiting interminably for repairs, and find that faulty and careless work had been done on their vehicles. Particularly with the dispatcher did the perversion of the tipping system reach extortionate proportions. His power derived from the assignment of cabs; to protect themselves from being assigned "pots" (cabs that would break down in the middle of the day), drivers tipped him fifty cents at the beginning of every week. Since nearly every driver tipped the dispatcher and since there were more drivers than good cabs, a certain numbers of drivers would still be assigned "pots." Some, wishing to insure doubly against this would then raise the bribe to a dollar and a half a week, causing the others to follow suit in a vi-

---

[20]Cf. Donovan, *op. cit.*, p. 262.

cious spiral. If little else, this shows how the tip—as distinguished from the gift, honorarium, inducement, or bribe—depends for its expressive validity on there not being a too close, long sustained, or consequential relationship between the parties to a service transaction.

Among service relationships in our society, that between the big city cabdriver and his fare, due to the way in which they come into contact with each other, is especially subject to structural weakness.

The relationship is random, fleeting, unrenewable, and largely devoid of socially integrative features which in other client and patron oriented services help sustain a wider range of constraints and controls between the parties to the transaction. (Much the same might be said of such service occupations as waitress, bellhop and hotel doorman, the chief difference being, however, that these operate from a spatially fixed establishment, which in itself permits of greater identifiability, renewability, and hence constraint in one's relationship to them.) As a result, the tendency of the relationship is to gravitate sharply and in relatively overt fashion toward those few issues having to do with the basic instrumental terms of the exchange. The very fact of tipping, its economic centrality and the cab culture's preoccupation with mastering its many vagaries reflect in large part the regulative imbalance inherent in the relationship.

By inference, this analysis raises anew questions of how to account for the many more formidable and apparently more binding practitioner-client constraints found in other personal service fields, in particular the professions. To such matters as career socialization, colleague groups, socially legitimated skill monopolies, and professional secrecy there might be added a certain safe modicum of continuity, stability, and homogeneity of clientele.[21] For, given too great and random a circulation of clients among practitioners, as might occur for example under certain bureaucratic schemes for providing universal and comprehensive medical service, the danger is that informal social control networks would not come into being in the community, and, as in big-city cabdriving, relations between servers and served would become reputationless, anonymous, and narrowly calculative.

---

[21]William J. Goode, "Community within a Community: The Professions," *American Sociological Review*, XXII, No. 2 (April, 1957), 198–200, and Eliot Freidson, "Varieties of Professional Practice," draft version of unpublished paper, 1959.

PSYCHOLOGY AND THE CRISIS
OF STATESMANSHIP*

Robert R. Blake

Resolution of conflict between groups of people—whether between nations, between management and labor, the departments of a business or university, or between social agencies within a community setting—requires the exercise of statesmanship. Permanent resolutions may be brought about through a realistic approach to the source of conflict. Whatever the circumstances, however, attempts at resolutions involve people—people who talk, make judgments, and give commitments, usually under face-to-face conditions. In a word, solutions and resolutions involve psychological aspects. Statesmen are confronted with designing psychological structures that can contribute to the handling of differences. Occasionally statesmen are successful. Too frequently they fail.

Fundamental divisions between groupings of peoples confront us today. They affirm that the problem of statesmanship is crucial. On the international scene there rages a full-blown cold war. The first satellite appears in the sky and is described here as a "hunk of iron." Two weeks later the sputnik cocktail is available: one part of vodka and two of sour grape juice. Within social groupings segregation and integration constitute burning issues of the hour. Troops, not statesmanship, prevent the eruption of conflict. On the economic front, a fundamental breach separates labor and management on basic issues regarding the organization of work, even on ways toward bringing an end to the current recession. Bickering among military services goes on unabated. Religious differences split groups and generate the very rivalry and discord the precepts of religion are intended to diminish or obliterate. There seems no end. Some divisions produce constructive competitiveness and are healthy. Many are not. The result is unwanted and unnecessary friction that blocks more basic pursuits.

*Reprinted from *American Psychologist*, Vol. 4 (1959), pp. 87–94. This article was originally presented as the Presidential Address, Southwestern Psychological Association, 1958. Appreciation expressed to Muzafer Sherif and Jane Srygley Mouton for suggestions regarding this manuscript.

Secret negotiations in smoke-filled rooms, in palaces, or on yachts; slick operators pulling strings and making deals; and blind resistance with bland refusal to examine issues have not served too well in managing or relieving differences between groupings of peoples. Statesmanship in all fields is faltering. Without theory, statesmen lack clear-cut guides for planning and action. Yet principles of behavior are involved. Some have been identified through psychological research. The resurgence of statesmanship is contingent on the effective use of such knowledge. My purpose is to examine approaches for resolving differences between groups against the background of psychological theory and research. Research in this area is only in the early stages of development, but it does provide guide lines for clarifying the nature and the scope of the problems and for identifying solutions that may bring permanent reduction in intergroup conflicts.

APPROACHES TO THE MANAGEMENT OF INTERGROUP DISPUTES

When groups stand opposed, four ways of terminating the conflict are possible: (a) isolate the groups and eliminate contact between them; (b) unite them into one group, even if it means "cracking their heads together"; (c) join the contest, let the more powerful annihilate the weaker: "Right will prevail"; and (d) maintain the identity of each group and through functional relations seek resolution by interaction, discussion, and decision. Except for rare instances the first three: isolationism, enforced unification, and extinction all contain significant negative components more repugnant than the conflict they seek to relieve. They will not be commented upon further. The fourth way holds genuine promise. It seems so obvious. "When you have a difference, sit down and talk it through. If not that, tell it to a neutral person and let him decide." Yet the path that seeks resolution through interaction, discussion, and decision itself is permeated with subtle difficulties. Here is where true statesmanship enters, for to take cognizance of the psychological characteristics of various approaches is to increase the probability of successful resolution of intergroup conflict.

RESOLUTION OF DIFFERENCES THROUGH INTERACTION, DISCUSSION, AND DECISION

Six fundamental approaches to the reduction of intergroup tensions through interaction are: negotiations by group members, use of the "good offices" of an intermediary, exchange of persons, hand-

ing the conflict to judges, the use of special decision-making panels
to plot solutions that involve specific common goals, and intergroup
therapy. Each is examined below from the standpoint of research
evidence when available and, where not, from the point of view of
field experience and logical analysis. The goal is to provide a general
orientation to problems of intergroup relations.

Negotiations by Group Members

Negotiations by Representatives. Solutions are sought most commonly through negotiations carried on by representatives, either the
leaders themselves or persons specifically designated to negotiate.
The United Nations is an example on the international level. Within
universities and companies, members of departments are called together as committees where each participant is expected to represent his department in the resolution of matters that affect it. Bargaining teams in labor-management negotiations also are composed
in this way. A key for evaluating this approach is found in the fact
that the representative is a *member* of the group he represents. He
knows the problem from an ingroup point of view.

As background for evaluating the representational approach, consider the following. Two or more groups stand opposed on a critical issue. Each has a preferred solution which its members support.
Both solutions are publicly known in advance of negotiations. Representatives meet. Frequently the interaction develops into a win-
lose contest, with each representative maintaining his group's position while attempting to provoke the other representative to capitu-
late. The representative who exerts influence on the opposing representative and in doing so obtains their acceptance of his group's position may be accorded a "hero" reaction within his group for bringing it victory (Blake & Mouton, 1958). On the other hand, the representative who relinquishes his group's position, thus giving victory
to the opposition, often is treated as disloyal or as "traitorous" by
members of his own group. The representative who wins stands to
enjoy increased status within his group, and he senses it. The representative who capitulates loses prestige and is confronted with
possible ostracism. He knows that too (Roethlisberger, 1945). It is
probable that the more cohesive the group and the more basic the
issue in the life of the group, the more the "hero" or "traitor" reaction is magnified, since the hero has supported the group's position
and the traitor has deviated from it in a significant manner (Schachter, 1951).

"Deadlock" is one result of the traitor threat. If a representative cannot win, through deadlocking the issue he can avoid losing. Through deadlocking, a traitor reaction can be avoided, but representatives of both sides stand to suffer reduction in membership status relative to the increased power accompanying victory. Another alternative to defeat is "compromise": give as little as possible and get as much, or create the appearance that both sides have yielded some, but with neither suffering defeat. Unfortunately such compromises often may be mechanical and brittle, constituting artificial solutions rather than real resolutions.

When negotiations take a win-lose turn, as they often do if preferred positions constitute public standards announced in advance, then quest for resolution by representatives may be replete with obstacles. The core of the difficulty seems to be that representatives are "committed" people. From the standpoint of their own group membership they are not entirely "free" to act in accord with "fact," or even to engage in compromise, if to do so would be interpreted by group members as "defeat." To a degree the limitations noted here may be reduced when representatives are freed to negotiate without prior instructions. Even then, however, they may be "expected" to act in certain ways even though formal instructions have not been placed on them.

The critical limitation in seeking resolutions through representatives seems to be in the "conflict of interest" aspect. For the representative to suffer defeat may be for him to place his membership status in jeopardy, while by gaining victory he may enhance his membership position. In the negotiation situation though, logical considerations may require that the representative renounce his group's prior position in order to gain a valid resolution of the intergroup problem. Where there is conflict of interest, the situation is such that ingroup loyalty can overwhelm logic.

Negotiations through Summit Conference. When negotiations by representatives fail, the plea is heard: "If only the *leaders* would get together, that would do more good than any other one step that could be taken." Let us examine this one. It is tricky. On first glance it appears to be a most practical and concrete approach. If leaders cannot agree, who can?

Modern history shows that summit conferences on the international scene have resulted in something less than complete success to either side. One has only to recall Yalta, Potsdam, and Geneva within the recent past for examples. White House conferences on education, social welfare, and so on have fared little better. Repeated parlays by the Joint Chiefs of Staff have not resulted in satisfactory unification of military activity.

Leaders face the inherent limitations of any representative in negotiating. A further consideration in this approach is related to the source from which the leader's power is derived. To the degree he is an autocratic leader, with power to regulate followers through control of their physical, economic, or political systems, he also has power to negotiate and to commit. Why? The logic is that he can go against existing standards and norms within his group, still retain his power, and enforce the changes to which he has committed himself. Not so when leadership power is derived through an elective system. Evidence suggests that under elective conditions the leader may be even *less* free to negotiate than are other group members. It may be that the norms for leadership are more exacting and require greater responsibility than for others within the group (Harvey, 1953; Whyte, 1943). Then too, Kelley and Volkart (1952) have demonstrated an inverse correlation between evaluation by a person of his membership in a group and his susceptibility to communication on topics opposed to group norms. Also, O. J. Harvey (1952) has shown that middle and lower status group members have higher expectations for leaders than for other members and that the leader shares their expectations for his own performance. A leader, in other words, seems to be more subject to regulation by his own group than other members are. Efforts to change leaders, and other members as well, which would make them deviate from these norms will encounter strong resistances (Cartwright, 1951).

When prevailing leadership has failed to bring about resolution or when it has made no attempt in this direction, according to Pelz (1951) the result may be increased frustration of the group expectations and consequent loss of influence by the leader. Under these conditions the suggestion to "get new leaders" frequently is heard. Leaders do come and go, and often a new leader will try, by traditional means, to accomplish what predecessors have failed to attain. No less frequently does a new leader fail. He stands in the same or a similar relationship to accepted standards and norms within his group as did the old one. The Merei study (1949) suggests his difficulty. Strong leaders were brought into groups whose traditions and standards already had been formed. To exert leadership influence within the group, they had first to *accept* the very positions they sought to change. In other words the "fresh" approach soon dies under the impact of prevailing conditions. The rule seems to be that, rather than "a new broom sweeping clean," the "new look" is rapidly transformed into an old wheeze.

The Use of Intermediaries

An approach in some respects comparable with the use of representatives or with the search for resolution of intergroup conflict through formal leaders involves the intermediary. Intermediaries usually hold membership in neither of the contending groups, but are from an outside organization or a level in an organization higher than the groups which are in conflict. The intermediary is expected to pass between the groups and to aid in the reduction of conflict through identifying areas of agreement, clarifying areas of disagreement, and developing proposals designed to ease tensions which are acceptable to both sides in a controversy. The intermediary, in other words, supplies a critical link of communication. He can pierce the boundaries which otherwise constitute barriers to communication. Usually he acts without formal authority. His success is based primarily on the goodwill and confidence that his reputation and his status as one who belongs to neither group creates.

The intermediary role needs experimental evaluation before a critical appraisal of its advantages and limitations can be given. History contains examples of conspicuous successes and outstanding failures of this approach. From a logical point of view it does appear, however, to have the advantage of increasing communication between contending groups. It has the further advantage that final responsibility for resolution rests, not on the judgment of the intermediary, but on attitudes within the competing groups themselves. A major limitation is in the fact that many situations of intergroup conflict are such that there is no organization outside or above the groups which are in disagreement which can arrange the appointment and acceptance from both sides of an intermediary.

A further disadvantage is possibly of greater importance. Basic communication between groups is not necessarily improved through actions of an intermediary, since arrangements for intergroup communication are likely to remain the same after his departure or as they were before his services were employed. The result is that *conditions* similar to those responsible for the initial eruption of conflict may remain unchanged. In a sense the intermediary role is better suited to the relief of symptoms than to the correction of basic causes.

Exchange of Persons

An approach said to have implications for resolving intergroup differences in the long-term view involves exchange of persons across the boundaries of the competing groups. The idea is that exposure on a people-to-people basis for the purpose of getting to know others, their institutions, and cultural products can serve to increase understanding as a background for future co-operation. The appeal is that if people will but look and see with their own eyes they will penetrate their prejudices and stereotypes. Educational exchanges from student activities to the Fulbright fellowship program are examples in the academic field. Examples from business and industry include exchanges of industrial productivity teams between the United States and Europe as well as the pattern in business of rotating personnel from one position to another in the effort to develop managers who have a company orientation rather than a provincial, departmental point of view. There may be other advantages to this approach aside from its contribution to the resolution of intergroup differences, but that is the aspect being considered here.

Findings from a half-dozen experiments involving exchanges between political and racial groupings point to two general conclusions (Ram & Murphy, 1952; Saenger, 1953). One is that people-to-people interaction across groups may serve to make those whose attitudes initially are pro, more pro, and those who initially are anti, more anti. Rather than being subject to fundamental alteration it appears that attitudes and convictions which already are established undergo intensification, though there is some evidence that changes related to the specific conditions of interaction may appear.

A second generalization is based on the observation that social, political, and economic attitudes, rather than being determined solely on an individual personality basis, are significantly anchored in reference groups. If, through an exchange experience, an individual's attitudes shift in a direction away from those formerly held, on return to his group he is subject to confrontation from his peers for expressing attitudes contrary to those accepted by them. The Bennington study (Newcomb, 1943) is an outstanding early example of the extent to which individuals express attitudes which maintain congruency with attitudes anchored in their group memberships. French and Zajonc (1957) have carried the analysis of the problem further, presenting evidence which suggests that when an individual is faced with an intergroup norm conflict the attitudes expressed are those which are most congruent with situational factors. That is to say, an individual who is under exchange-of-persons conditions, and moves from one group to another, is more prone to express attitudes consistent with the views of the group in which he is located. Another consideration is that contact between groups does not always lead to a lessening of conflict. A study in the Near East shows that ingroups may be most hostile to those groups with which they come in closest contact (Dodd, 1935).

While exchange programs as approaches for resolving intergroup conflict leave much to be desired, two implications can be drawn. One is that those who initially are neutral are most susceptible to influence. Without pre-formed attitudes there is a real possibility that the increased exposure provided can result in a more objective appraisal of experiences. It is from an awareness of this consideration that the most intensive efforts by both sides in the cold war are concentrated on the so-called uncommitted people. The effort is to move them away from a neutral position on the argument of the "immorality of neutrality."

The other implication is that plans involving the exchanges of *groups* may create a favorable background for future intergroup resolution, where person-to-person programs fail. The reason is that, when individuals undergo new experiences *as a group*, attitudes anchored at the group level may themselves be subject to modification. Refusal by an individual to maintain altered attitudes then constitutes deviation from the group norms with consequent rejection confronting the individual who refuses to change (Schachter, 1951). Thus reinforcement of changed attitudes comes about through group membership.

The Use of "Judges"

Resolution of differences is sought through judges, persons trained to evaluate materials relevant to the issue under examination. Since judges hold membership in neither of the competing groups, they are not subject to the conflict of interest situation described above; therefore, they can be "fair." The Supreme Court and federal and state legal systems all are based on gaining resolution through the use of judges. Because of the judge's "outside" position, contestants are expected to accept the outcome as an impartial one.

Do they? The answer depends on where you sit. It is likely to be "Yes," if the decision favors your group; "No," if it goes against the position your group embraces. Listen to the following remarks from exploratory studies (Harvey, 1957; Human Relations Training Laboratory, 1958). They are reactions toward "neutral" judges from those defeated by his decision.

The judge is biased, unfair, and incompetent . . . he has no grasp of the problem . . . he does not possess the intelligence prerequisite to be fair and unbiased . . . he doesn't seem to know too much about the subject . . . he didn't take enough time.

In other words, when group members are committed to their position and a judge decides against it, either the group is wrong or the judge is wrong. In their initial reactions group members have *little* doubt as to which: it is the judge. Results from several sources suggest that the stronger the commitment of a group to its solution, the more relevant the problem to the life of the group, and the more cohesive the group, the greater the negative reactions to a judge whose decision defeats them. Even though obligated to accept the verdict, attitudes remain more or less consistent with convictions held prior to the rendering of the judgment.

When intergroup competition has been generated for study purposes under laboratory training conditions with resolution of the conflict placed in the hands of a judge, a delayed reaction of considerable importance has been noted among members within some defeated groups (Human Relations Training Laboratory, 1958). Though the initial reaction in the defeated group toward the judge is as noted above, "it's the judge who is at fault," a delayed reaction among some members is, "it's our group which is at fault." Such a reaction seems to arise among the members who were the least committed to the group's position before the issue was submitted. Rather than venting their frustrations from defeat on the judge, they discharge it by aggressive attacks on other group members. A consequence is that the group tends to "splinter," to loose its former degree of cohesion and to disrupt.

When the judge renders a verdict favoring a group's position, two things are evident. The judge is experienced as being fair and unbiased all right, because the judgment he proclaims "only proves that we were right in the first place." He is experienced as being a *good* judge because he sees the situation as members themselves see it. "If there was any doubt in our minds before, his ruling eliminated it. Now we know we're right." Resolutions thus attained may have administrative consequences, particularly if the judge's decision is reinforced by sanctions. To those who lose, the resolution retains an arbitrary, mechanical quality. Losers comply because the ground rules require it, but they remain unconvinced.

By comparison with a representative or a leader a judge is not gripped in the vise of a conflict-of-interest situation. Yet the judge is as suspect by those whose position he defeats as is the representative who goes against his group. The inherent difficulty is that the judge's decision may carry little force in comparison with the strength of the group's commitment to its position. The defeated frequently are not moved to alter their position.

Common Goals with Crisscross Panels

A situation favoring resolution is present when both of the opposing sides are confronted with a common goal which can only be reached through interdependent effort. This set of circumstances has confronted social agencies in raising operating budgets. Competing with one another was found to be less than successful, but when agencies came together and agreed on a superordinate goal which could only be reached through joint effort, greater success was achieved. Each group maintained its identity, and yet through embracing a common goal, the area of conflict was eliminated and one of co-operation was created. Another example of a new grouping designed to achieve a common goal is the proposed single agency to take the place of competing individual services in the development and coordination of approaches to outer space. Control of military uses of atomic energy and programs for world reduction of arms constitute goals at the international level which have been dreamt about but not yet realized. Companies that have introduced cost concern programs on a common goal basis have found this approach quite successful (Hood, 1957). Only recently, however, has experimental work been oriented toward a more systematic assessment of the approach.

In three highly ingenious studies Sherif, who originally formulated the problem discussed here, has explored a variety of ways of relieving differences between contending groups (Sherif, 1958; Sherif & Sherif, 1953, 1956). Groups were placed in competition on a win-lose basis. Unsuccessful in relieving the tensions thus produced were contacts between members, contacts between leaders, and preaching and coercion. More fruitful was the solution of competing groups joining together in order to defeat a third, outside group, but in this way the area of conflict was widened. The most appropriate way found was that of confronting contending groups with a common problem which could be resolved only through their joint efforts. Once a superordinate goal was accepted as a challenge by high status members of both sides then mutual efforts by individuals, with less regard for primary group affiliations, became more common. Contending groups started to pull together, and contacts between members turned to positive purposes instead of serving as occasions for accusations and mutual irritations.

Several conditions are necessary for employing the superordinate goal approach. Both sides must *desire* a genuine solution, and the mere presence of friction is not by any means indicative that they do. The absence of such requisite problem-solving motivation precludes the success of any approach. In addition there is a need for a single definition of the problem developed by both sides without a prior statement of preferred solutions. This way avoids commitments which are prone to become irreversible when one side appears to be losing, and strategies for dealing with the "loss of face" problem become unnecessary. Fundamental conditions for successful resolution are present when both of these considerations have been met.

A limitation in employing the superordinate goal approach is in the fact that all members of competing groups rarely are able to combine efforts toward attaining superordinate goals. There is need of a way for representatives to interact toward the attainment of superordinate goals which can provide freedom of action without the status reduction that occurs with going against one's own group's position.

There is a possibility which avoids difficulties encountered by other methods. Each side develops a list of nominees whom they consider qualified to represent them with respect to one particular source of friction. Next, from the list of nominees, members of both groups elect a decision-making panel through voting on representatives from *both* sides. The final panel contains members who represent their own group and yet who simultaneously represent the other group as well.

By the conditions of their selection, being jointly elected, representatives are more free to confront the problem, without facing the hero-traitor dynamic that arises from the usual unilateral group orientation. Why? The reason is that group members from both sides experience such representatives as oriented toward a "fair" solution. Even when they go against a prevailing standard of their group the action is experienced as more "legitimate" that when they do so as unilateral representatives. Furthermore, representatives themselves are motivated to examine issues from the frames of reference of both groups, rather than from that of their own group alone.

The crisscross panel is a way of approaching the resolution of intergroup disputes that is currently under experimental evaluation. The procedure constitutes but an extension of democratic methods to the solution of problems. Even now a modification of it is employed to settle labor-management disputes which have gone into deadlock. The method provides the possibility of progress toward reduction of intergroup conflict, whether the point of application involves disputes between nations, labor-management, government agencies, departments of a company organization, or between social agencies within a community.

Intergroup Therapy

A final possibility remains when other approaches fail. It is based on therapeutic conceptions that deal with problems of relationship. The *unit* of therapy, rather than being focused on the individual, the interpersonal level, or the group, is comprised of competing groups *in relationship* with one another. The rationale is that groups may hold perceptions and stereotypes of one another which are distorted, negative, or so hidden that they prevent functional relationships from arising between them. Only *after* basic problems of relationships have been eliminated is effective interaction possible. If the contending groups are so large as to eliminate the possibility of interchange among all members simultaneously, segments of groups may be employed, with the procedure repeated until fundamental sources of intergroup animosity have been neutralized.

One procedure of intergroup therapy is to bring contending groups together as *groups*. In private each discusses and seeks to agree on its perception and attitudes toward the other and its perceptions of itself as well. Then *representatives* of both groups talk together in the presence of other group members from both sides who are obligated to remain silent. During this phase representatives are responsible for accurate communication of the picture that each group has constructed of the other and of itself. They are free to ask questions for clarification of the other group's point of view, but ground rules prevent them from giving rationalizations, justifications, etc. The reason for using representatives is that communication remains more orderly and responsibility is increased for them to provide an accurate version of the situation. Members of both groups then discuss *in private* the way they are perceived by each other in order to develop understanding of the discrepancies between their own view of themselves and the description of them by the other side. Finally, again working through representatives, each helps the other to appreciate bases of differences, to correct *invalid* perceptions, and to consider alternative explanations of past behavior. Fundamental value conflicts not based on distortions also can be identified and examined; then suggestions can be developed for ways of working on problems which can result in solutions apart from basic value conflicts.

Intergroup therapy is relatively unexplored, although it has been tried with success in industrial settings on several occasions. Many problems, themselves subject to solution through the superordinate goal approach, cannot even be faced until deeper animosities *between* groups have been resolved or at least explored and neutralized. If emotion-laden negative attitudes and stereotypes are dealt with first, it becomes increasingly possible in a second phase to formulate and work toward the attainment of superordinate goals as described above.

Now to return to my thesis. Statesmanship is faltering. Many problems of tremendous import continue to be handled by statesmen on an intuitive basis—a paradox in a world where scientific method has advanced understanding so far. Approaches frequently are used which fail to recognize the psychological characteristics of people and the dilemmas confronting them when engaging in discussion intended to resolve intergroup disputes. What are some of the psychological characteristics of people that must be considered?

Take, for example, the situation of a typical representative. In negotiation he is faced with a fundamental conflict of interest. Stephen Decatur in 1816 said: "Our country! In her intercourse with foreign nations, may she always be in the right; but our country, right or wrong!" In this remark he was identifying the dilemma facing all representatives of groups which are in competition, whether leaders or other members. If to yield or to compromise means defeat, it exposes the responsible person to rejection and ostracism by his peers. To resist and gain victory can lead to his acclamation as a hero. The consequence is that representatives are motivated to win, or at least to avoid defeat, even though a realistic solution of an intergroup problem may be sacrificed in the process. An intermediary who holds membership in neither group may be employed to develop solutions acceptable to both groups. This approach, which has some positive merits, when it is possible to appoint an intermediary from some outside group, may be successful in resolving a specific problem but is likely to do little to effect resolution of basic cleavages between groups, since lines of communication supplied by the action of this intermediary are likely to be eliminated after his departure.

Resolution of conflict through the action of judges also suffers a critical limitation. Rendering a judgment which defeats a side does not convince the vanquished protagonists of the error of their ways. Further, the force to implement the verdict is not within the group, but must be added from the outside. Neither understanding, nor acceptance, nor commitment, but coercion is likely to be the force which prevents the extension of conflict. The limitations of this procedure frequently outweigh its possible merits for the simple reason that punitive action, or the threat of it, is basic to enforcement.

There is another way which seems more constructive. Acting with respect to common goals, representatives can be selected through a crisscross election method in such a way as to free them to confront the problem more squarely, rather than trying to "win" from a partisan point of view. When this is done, subscribing to the outcome is an obligation within *both* groups. It can occur through acceptance and commitment, without coercion. Concrete application should begin with problems of lesser significance at low levels in order to permit an assessment of the method and the development of skill in using it in specific situations. Then, with success, the procedure can be applied to more important problems at higher levels until issues of substance and significance are being dealt with in a constructive manner.

When an approach to resolution of intergroup problems through superordinate goals cannot be made because of negative, emotionally saturated perceptions, attitudes, and stereotypes, a possibility of solution still remains. Through insertion of a preliminary phase involving the concepts of intergroup therapy, conditions favoring problem solving may be created. If the approach "unblocks" intergroup relationships, then the actions required by superordinate goal considerations can be introduced.

Theory of behavior relating to individuals in group situations and relations between groups is basic to the enlightened practice of statemanship. It provides guidelines for planning and action. The outcome of the crisis of our times may well rest on whether or not statesmen can design situations for the resolution of intergroup disputes which are sound. Introduction of a psychological point of view may constitute a condition for survival.

REFERENCES

BLAKE, R. R. and MOUTON, JANE S. "Heroes and Traitors: Two Patterns of Representing Groups in a Competitive Situation," *International Journal of Sociometry* (1958), in press.

CARTWRIGHT, D. Achieving Change in People: Some Applications of Group Dynamics Theory," *Human Relations* Vol. 4 (1951), pp. 381–92.

DODD, S. C. "A Social Distance Test in the Near East," *American Journal of Sociology*, Vol. 41 (1935), pp. 194–204.

FRENCH, J. R. P., JR. and ZAJONC, R. B. "An Experimental Study of Cross-Cultural Norm Conflict," *Journal of Abnormal and Social Psychology* Vol. 54 (1957), pp. 218–24.

HARVEY, J. "Subjective Reactions to a Judge as a Function of His Verdict." Unpublished manuscript, University of Texas, 1957.

HARVEY, O. J. "An Experimental Approach to the Study of Status Relations in Informal Groups," *American Sociological Review*, Vol. 18 (1953), pp. 357–67.

HOOD, R. *Concern for Costs.* Ann Arbor: Survey Reseach Center, University of Michigan, 1957.

HUMAN RELATIONS TRAINING LABORATORY, *Proceedings.* Taos, N.M.: Human Relations Training Laboratory, 1958.

KELLEY, H. H. and VOLKART, E. H. "The Resistance to Change of Group-Anchored Attitudes," *American Sociological Review*, Vol. 17 (1952), pp. 453–65.

MEREI, F. "Group Leadership and Institutionalization," *Human Relations*, Vol. 2 (1949), pp. 23–39.

NEWCOMB, T. M. *Personality and Social Change.* New York: Dryden, 1943.

PELZ, D. C. "Leadership within a Hierarchical Organization," *Journal of Social Issues*, Vol. 7 (1951), pp. 49–55.

RAM, P. and MURPHY, G. C. "Recent Investigations of Hindu-Muslim Relations in India," *Human Organization*, Vol. 11 (1952), pp. 13–16.

ROETHLISBERGER, F. J. "The Foreman: Master and Victim of Double Talk," *Harvard Business Review*, Vol. 23 (1945), pp. 283–98.

SAENGER, G. *The Social Psychology of Prejudice.* New York: Harper, 1953.

SCHACHTER, S. "Deviation, Rejection, and Communication," *Journal of Abnormal and Social Psychology*, Vol. 46 (1951), pp. 190–207.

SHERIF, M. "Reduction of Intergroup Conflict," *American Journal of Sociology*, Vol. 53 (1958), pp. 349–56.

SHERIF, M. and SHERIF, CAROLYN W. *Groups in Harmony and Tension.* New York: Harpers, 1953.

SHERIF, M. and SHERIF, CAROLYN W. *An Outline of Social Psychology*, 2d ed. New York: Harpers, 1956.

WHYTE, W. F. *Street Corner Society.* Chicago: University of Chicago Press, 1943.

INTERPERSONAL COMPETENCE AND ORGANIZATIONAL EFFECTIVENESS*
Chris Argyris

In the previous chapter [not included in this volume] we concluded that organizations are developed from, and conceived according to the image of a particular strategy. Implicit in the strategy were certain assumptions about how individuals will behave effectively in an organization. These assumptions were found to be questionable in light of what is known about the nature of human beings.

The next step is to become more specific so hypotheses can be stated regarding the impact of these assumptions on the individuals and the organization.

Recently there has developed an increasing awareness of the relevance of values to understanding human behavior[1,2] and decision making in organization.[3] Let us define values as commands or directives to which individuals are committed.[4] We may then ask what are the commands or directives (or imperatives) implicit in the formal strategy used to create organizations. If we can discover these organizational commands or directives, we can hypothesize that to the extent the participants follow them, their behavior can be understood, predicted, and influenced by knowing these values.

As Margenau suggests, a command may define a value, but it requires a dedication to command if the value is to affect human behavior.[5] The major factor to be evaluated, therefore, is the degree of commitment or dedication to these values. The stronger the dedication, the greater the probability that the behavior can be under-

---

*Chris Argyris, "Interpersonal Competence and Organizational Effectiveness," chap. 2 cf. *Interpersonal Competence and Organizational Effectiveness* (Homewood, Ill.: Richard D. Irwin, Inc., 1962), pp. 38–54. Used by permission.

[1]Donald W. Taylor, "Toward an Information Processing Theory of Motivation," Marshall R. Jones (ed.), *Nebraska Symposium on Motivation* (Lincoln, Neb.: University of Nebraska Press, 1960), pp. 51–79.

[2]A. H. Maslow (ed.), *New Knowledge in Human Values* (New York: Harper & Bros., 1959).

[3]Herbert Simon, *Administrative Behavior* (New York: The Macmillan Co., 1957).

[4]Henry Margenau, "The Scientific Basis of Value Theory," *New Knowledge in Human Values*, pp. 42–43.

[5]*Ibid.*, p. 45.

stood independently of the particular personality of each participant. To test this hypothesis one must not only learn the organizational values, but one must ascertain the extent to which participants follow, and are dedicated to these values as determiners of
their behavior. (Indeed, we may find that it is easier for certain personality patterns to be dedicated to these values.[6] Important as this
hypothesis is for our theory, we are not going to attempt to test it at
this time.) In this study, we are going to ascertain the impact of a
specific set of organizational values upon the behavior of the participants on the organization.

We begin to develop a model by asking what would happen if
participants followed the organizational values. Once the consequences are spelled out, we can go to the empirical world to see if
the predicted consequences do exist when the participants adhere
to or are dedicated to the values.

THE VALUES IMPLICIT IN FORMAL ORGANIZATIONS

The basic values outlined in the previous chapter about effective
human relationships inherent in the formal organizational strategy
can be summarized as follows:

1. The important human relationships are those that are related to achieving the organization's objective. (Getting the job done.)
2. Effectiveness in human relationships increases as behavior is rational,
logical, and clearly communicated. Effectiveness decreases as emotionality increases.
3. Human relationships are most effectively influenced through direction,
coercion, and control as well as a set of rewards and penalties that serve to
emphasize the rational behavior and getting the job done.[7]

We may ask:

a) What would tend to happen to interpersonal competence and to interpersonal human relationships if these values are followed?
b) How do (the resulting) interpersonal relationships feed back to influence
   such rational activities as decision making, problem exploration, information transmission?
c) How do (the resulting) interpersonal relationships feed back to influence

---

[6]This is a hypothesis of men like Fromm, May, and men who worked on several
of the research projects stemming from the California studies on the authoritarian
personality.

[7]For other studies consonant with these conclusions see Douglas McGregor, *The
Human Side of Enterprise* (New York: McGraw-Hill Book Co., Inc., 1960); Robert
L. Katz, "Toward a More Effective Enterprise," *Harvard Business Review*, Vol. 38,
No. 5 (September-October, 1960), pp. 80–120; James March, and Herbert Simon,
Organizations (New York: John Wiley & Sons, Inc., 1959).

the norms of the organization toward or against such phenomena as dependence, conformity, interexecutive trust, and internal commitment?

d) How are such factors as organizational rigidity, flexibility, and climate influenced by all the factors above?

THE IMPACT OF THE FORMAL VALUES ON INTERPERSONAL COMPETENCE

To the extent that individuals dedicate themselves to the value of rationality and "getting the job done," they will tend to be aware of and emphasize the rational, intellective aspects of the interactions that exist in an organization and suppress the interpersonal and emotional aspects, especially those that do not seem to be relevant to achieving the task. For example, one frequently hears in organizations, "Let's keep feelings out of the discussion," or "Look here, our task today is to achieve objective *x* and not to get emotional."

As the interpersonal and emotional aspects of behavior become suppressed, we may hypothesize that an organizational norm will tend to arise that coerces individuals to hide their feelings. Their interpersonal difficulties will either be suppressed, or disguised and brought up as rational, technical, intellectual problems. In short, receiving or giving feedback about interpersonal relationships will tend to be suppressed.

Under these conditions we may hypothesize that the individuals will find it very difficult to develop competence in dealing with feelings and interpersonal relationships. In a world where the expression of feelings is not permitted, one may hypothesize the individuals will build personal and organizational defenses to help them suppress their own feelings or inhibit others in their attempts to express their feelings.[8] If feelings are suppressed, the tendency will be for the individual not to permit himself or others to *own* their feeling. For example, the individual may say about himself, "No, I didn't mean that," or "Let me start over again. I'm confusing the facts." Equally possible is for one individual to say to another, "No, you shouldn't feel that way," or "That's not effective executive behavior," or "Let's act like mature people and keep feelings out of this."

Another way to prevent individuals from violating the organizational values of rationality, and from embarrassing one another, is

---

[8]This is a common phenomenon in the opening sessions of T-groups. To tell the "truth" is usually interpreted to mean "Let's clobber one another," "tell each other our faults," "to put me on the table and open me up," and so on.

to block out, refuse to consider (consciously or unconsciously) ideas and values which, if explored, could expose suppressed feelings. Such a defensive reaction in the organization may eventually lead to a barrier of intellectual ideas as well as values. The participants will tend to limit themselves to those ideas and values that are not threatening, and so not violate organizational norms. The individuals in the organization will tend to decrease its capacity to be open to new ideas and values. As the degree of openness decreases, the capacity to experiment will tend to decrease, and the fear to take risks will tend to increase. As the fear to take risks increases, the probability of experimentation is decreased and the range or scope of openness is decreased, which decreases risks. We have a closed circuit that could be an important cause of the loss of vitality in an organization.[9]

To summarize, to the extent that participants are dedicated to the values implicit in the formal organization, they will tend to create a social system where the following will tend to *decrease* (see Figure 1):

1. Receiving and giving nonevaluative feedback.
2. Owning and permitting others to own their ideas, feelings, and values.
3. Openness to new ideas, feelings, and values.
4. Experimentation and risk taking with new ideas and values.

As any one of these decreases, it acts to decrease all the others and to increase the opposite states of affairs. In terms of our model (Figure 1) inputs (values) feed into a "black box" composed of highly interrelated variables, where an increase or decrease in any one can set off a chain of reactions that influence all the others.

As the above states of affairs continue, we may hypothesize the following "outputs":

1. Members of this system of relationships will *not* tend to be aware of their interpersonal impact upon others (they may be aware of their rational, intellectual impact).
2. The members of this system of relationships will not tend to solve interpersonal problems in such a way that they (or similar problems) will not tend to reoccur.

We may conclude that the organizational values, if followed, will tend to create a social system in which the members' interpersonal competence will tend to decrease (see Figure 1). (Up to this point we are not hypothesizing the impact upon rational, intellective com-

---

[9]For a recent student who emphasizes the importance of vitality see Marshall E. Dimock, *A Philosophy of Administration* (New York: Harper & Bros., 1957).

FIGURE 1

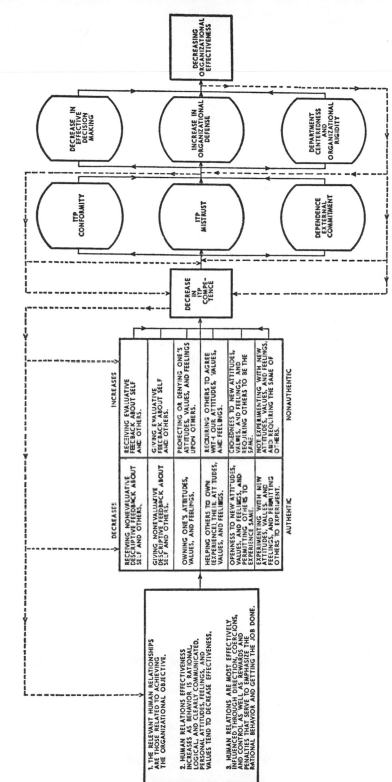

petence which presumably should not be so affected by these values.)

THE IMPACT UPON THE ORGANIZATION OF DECREASING INTERPERSONAL COMPETENCE

Let us continue our theoretical analysis with the following question: What may we hypothesize are some of the implications upon the organization of decreasing interpersonal competence?

If individuals are in social systems where they are unable to predict accurately their interpersonal impact upon others, and others' impact upon themselves, they may begin to feel confused. "Why are people behaving that way toward me?" "Why do they interpret me incorrectly?" Since such questions are not sanctioned in a rationally dominated system, much less answered, the confusion will tend to turn to frustration and feelings of failure regarding interpersonal relations. In an attempt to maintain their sense of esteem, the members may react by questioning the honesty and genuineness of the interpersonal behavior of their fellow workers. Simultaneously, they may place an even greater emphasis upon the rational, technical interactions, in which they are probably experiencing a greater degree of success. The increased emphasis upon rationality will act to suppress the feelings even more, which in turn will decrease the probability that the questions of confusion and the mistrust (of self and others) will be explored.

As interpersonal mistrust increases, and as the capacity (individual and organizational) to cope with this mistrust decreases, then the members may tend to adapt by "playing it safe." The predisposition will be to say those things that cannot be misunderstood and to discuss those issues for which there exist clear organizational values and sanctions. The desire "to say the right thing" should be especially strong toward one's superiors, toward one's peers with whom one is competing, and toward one's subordinates, who may be known to bypass their superiors. The result is that conformity begins to develop within an organization. Along with conformity, the interpersonal relationships will tend to be characterized by "conditional acceptance" (to use a Rogerian concept) where the members will tend to feel accepted if they behave in accordance with certain organizational specifications.

Another possible important force acting toward conformity is the predisposition of individuals to bring around them people whose self-concepts are congruent. There is a tendency to hire or upgrade individuals who manifest the accepted image of the system.[10] For example, Ward found that executives prefer subordinates who do not make trouble, are not argumentative, are somewhat retiring, meek, and even bashful to the more argumentative, impatient, rebellious types. This would be understandable in terms of our model, since the latter qualities would violate the norms of the executive systems and consequently require a degree of interpersonal competence that may not exist. In the same study Ward showed that another preferred pattern was for the subordinate to be systematic, orderly, precise, and accurate. These qualities are consonant with the "inputs of rationality."[11] Evidence consonant with Ward's findings was published by Freeman and Taylor. They found that while 100 top executives said that they looked for aggressive, energetic applicants, they personally wanted "tactful subordinates." The executives tended to attribute their own success to "brain and character," but they preferred "emotionally controlled and balanced" subordinates rather than overly bright or highly ethical ones.[12]

Basic to the formal strategy is power over and control of the subordinates by the superior. The power is especially related to the capacity to direct, reward, and penalize. If we now add the existence of mistrust and conformity to dependence, we may hypothesize that the members' commitment to the organization will tend to be external as far as interpersonal activities are concerned. By "external·commitment," I mean that the source of commitment to work for any given individual lies in the power, rewards, and penalties that some other individual may use to influence the first individual. Internal commitment exists when the motive for a particular behavior resides from within (for example, self-realization). A certain amount of internal commitment restricted to rational activities may be possible in this system, if the rational, intellective aspects of the job are consonant with the individual's abilities and expressed needs.

External commitment will tend to reinforce the conformity with, conditional acceptance of, and especially the dependence upon the leader. The subordinates will tend to look for cues from the leader

---

[10]E. J. McCormick and R. W. Middaugh, "The Development of a Tailor-Made Scoring for the How-Supervise? Test," *Personnel Psychology,* Vol. IX (1956), pp. 27–37.

[11]Lewis B. Ward, "Do You Want a Weak Subordinate?" *Harvard Business Review,* September-October, 1961, pp. 6–26.

[12]G. L. Freeman and E. K. Taylor, *How to Pick Leaders* (New York: Funk & Wagnalls Co., 1950).

and will be willing to be influenced and guided by him. In fact, they may develop great skill in inducing the leader to define the problems, the range of alternatives, and so on. The subordinates will tend to operate within limits that they know to be safe. As the dependence increases, the need for the subordinates to know where they "stand" will also tend to increase.[13]

Thus, interpersonal mistrust, conformity, conditional acceptance, external commitment, and dependence tend to be "outputs" of decreasing interpersonal competence. Each of these feeds back to reinforce itself. All, in turn, feed back upon interpersonal competence to decrease it further or to reinforce it at its existing level.

At some point (to be empirically determined) the consequences above will tend to feed back to influence the rational intellective competence of the executives. For example, in some of the situations to be discussed later we learned that executives (with mathematical and engineering background) dealing with highly technical issues developed strong emotional attachments to these issues. During discussions held to resolve technical rational issues, the emotional involvements tended to block understanding. Since the men did not tend to deal with emotions, their inhibiting effects were never explored. On the contrary, they were covered up by technical, rational arguments. Since these arguments were attempts by people to defend their self or attack others', there was a tendency for the rationality of the arguments to be weak. This in turn troubled the receiver of the argument, who tended to attack obvious rational flaws immediately. The attack tended to increase the degree of threat experienced by the first person, and he became even more defensive. Similar impacts upon rational decision making were also discovered in areas such as investment decisions, purchasing policies, quality control standards, product design, and marketing planning.

Similar problems tended to occur with decisions that involved human factors in an organization. They were not explored thoroughly, especially when the values and ideas to be explored were not tolerated by the system. Demotions, promotions, reprimands, discipline, and evaluation of ineffectiveness are but a few examples of such decisions. Finally, there were cases on record in which the

---

[13]I am perplexed as to how many writers "prove" the importance of "merit ratings" or "evaluation" programs by citing peoples' needs to know. These data may simply show how dependent the subordinates are and how well the programs are institutionalizing the dependence.

organization never explored a new product or a new manufacturing process because the "powers that be wouldn't hear of it."

Another crucial area of decision making that could be influenced by interpersonal incompetence would be the area of organizational change. For example, let us consider an organization that desires to go from a highly centralized to a decentralized structure. One may predict that executives operating under the conditions above will not tend to explore or take adequate account of the feelings that subordinates under decentralization would have regarding decentralization. The executives will tend to "sell" decentralization by using rational reasons, largely missing such subordinate's feelings as dependence, conformity, and fear of authority. The subordinates in turn will tend to suppress such feelings (assuming they are even aware of them) and communicate to their superiors that they understand the meaning of decentralization and that they agree with it. However, one would predict that if the superiors actually did decentralize and give the subordinates authority and responsibility, the latter will tend to seek ways to induce their superiors to make the decisons. The superiors, in turn, will tend to feel perplexed if not irritated. However, since the expression of such feelings is not sanctioned, they will tend to find indirect ways to express their disappointment and/or hold new meetings loaded with new rational reasons "selling" the importance of decentralization.

When executives perceive that their present leadership is not as effective as they wish it to be, one finds that they tend to take two courses of action. The first is to emphasize even more the values of the formal organizational structure. This means that they tend to place greater emphasis on the use of rationality, direction, control, rewards, and penalties. In practice this tends to mean that they begin to check on other people's work not only to see if it is done but also how it was accomplished. Another activity is to manage through detailed questioning about issues and problems that may exist at levels lower than the man being questioned but for which he is responsible. For example, asking a personnel vice-president the capacity of a parking lot in a plant away from the home office.

The result of such action on the part of the superior is to create a defensiveness in the subordinate. The subordinate now finds himself constantly checking on all details so he will not be "caught" by the superior. However, the activity of the organization is not carried forward with such behavior. The result is simply one of making the subordinates (and usually his subordinates) more defensive. Their response is to build up organizational defenses to protect themselves. For example, in one case where executives were managing by detail, the subordinates created the "JIC" file which stands for "just in case" some superior asks. This file was kept up to date by several lower-level managers who were full time and countless other people working part time. The JIC file is an organizational defense against threat experienced by individuals at various levels.

In short, one may hypothesize that organizational defenses may be developed in an organization to protect various individuals and groups.

These organizational defenses can be used to "needle" people. This tends to occur when the rational methods seem to fail. But since the use of feelings is deviant behavior and since the superior or subordinates do not have much experience in their use, the tendency may be to have feelings "overdetermined." By "overdetermined," I mean that feelings tend to be much stronger than the situation warrants. Their overdeterminedness is compounded by the fact that subordinates do not tend to be accustomed to dealing with feelings.

Executives may speak of "needling the boys," "once in a while, 'raising hell' to keep them on their toes," and so on. If these conditions continue, it is not long before the "hot" decisions of the organization are administered by using emotions. This is commonly known in industry as "management by crisis."

As management by crisis increases, the subordinate's defensive reaction to these crises will tend to increase. One way to protect himself is to make certain that his area of responsibility is administered competently and that no other peer executive "throws a dead cat into his yard." The subordinate's predisposition will tend to be centered toward the interests of his department. As the department centeredness increases, the interdepartmental rivalries will tend to increase. All these decrease the organization's flexibility for change as well as the co-operation among departments. This decrease, in turn, will tend to be adapted to by the top management by increasing their directives, which in turn begins to recentralize the organization.

The external commitment, conformity, interpersonal mistrust, ineffective decision making, management by crisis, and organizational rigidity will tend to feed back to reinforce each other and to decrease interpersonal competence (see Figure 1). Moreover, each will feed upon all the others to reinforce itself. We would conclude that under these conditions the tendency will be to increase the energy required to produce the same input, or some day it may even decrease the output, although the input remains constant. When this state of affairs occurs, the organization may be said to have begun to be ineffective.

This analysis may help us to understand some of the findings of Guetzkow and Gyr and March and his associates. Guetzkow and Gyr[14] found that groups in industry tend to postpone (withdraw from) complex problems. They prefer to play it safe and deal with the easier problems. In an interesting paper March concludes that rationality in an organization is qualified and constrained. Consequently, organizational decision-making behavior is primarily adaptive rather than rational. March mentions four critical activities that can constrain rationality, three of which would be predicted by our model. They are: (1) conflict among parties within the firm (intergroup competition in our terms), (2) avoidance of uncertainty, (3) searching "in the neighborhood" of the problem symptom current alternative, and (4) organizational learning.[15]

We have suggested that intergroup conflict is inherent in the pyramidal structure, managerial controls, directive leadership.[16] In this study we suggest that it is also inherent in the emphasis upon rationality and suppression of emotionality. If the above is valid, in a world where interpersonal mistrust, dependence, conformity, management by crisis, through detail, and fear are prevalent, then playing it safe and not getting hurt would be predictable. Under these conditions avoiding uncertainty, searching for solutions close to the problem, and looking primarily at the available alternatives would be adaptive. In other words, the conditions March accepts as independent variables or "givens," we view as dependent and changeable. It is hoped that this study (plus the already mentioned work by Blake and Shepard) will suggest that changes can be made in organizations so that at least the first three conditions can be modified. If we learn to modify them to a considerable degree, we

[14]H. Guetzkow and J. Gyr, "An Analysis of Conflict in Decision-Making Groups," *Human Relations*, Vol. VII (1954), pp. 367-82.

[15]James March, "Some Models of Organizational Decision Making," symposium at American Psychological Association, Sept. 5, 1961 (mimeographed, Carnegie Institute of Technology).

[16]Chris Argyris, *Personality and Organization*.

may even be able to change the degree to which, as well as the activities through which, an organization learns.

SOME FORCES INHIBITING ORGANIZATIONAL INEFFECTIVENESS

The reader may wonder if we mean to imply that when interpersonal competence is low, the organization is automatically doomed to failure. The answer is obviously "No."

First, in any organization a large proportion of the decision making is related to "getting the widgets out." There are many technical, professional decisions that must be made if an organization is to achieve its objective. The more the organization requires intellective rational competence, and the more it has such competence, the *less* the probability up to a point (to be empirically determined) that a low interpersonal competence will tend to have negative impact of great significance. However, as we shall show, there is a point at which interpersonal competence becomes so crucial that it can significantly affect the rational (as well as the interpersonal) activities of the organization. Competing organizations are able to obtain the finest minds and the best equipment that they need then. In a competitive world, the one that is able to support these resources with effective human relationships may well increase its opportunity for survival.

Another important consideration is that the above state of affairs is consonant with the formal organizational values about effective human relationships. Thus, although the consequences (decreasing interpersonal trust, competence; increasing management by crisis, and so on) may be unintended, and even not desired, they flow naturally from the kind of organizational world in which men are placed. The unintended consequences are, therefore, functional. They are necessary if the executives are to survive in a world of organizational stress. In other words the values about effective human relationships held by the executives, and implict in the formal organizational structure and managerial controls, lead to a stressful world where a subordinate is dependent upon a superior. To adapt to and operate within this dependence and stress, the subordinates adhere to the same values. The values will probably be maintained as long as their "maintenance cost" does not exceed the cost of their negative impact upon the executive system, the decision making, and the relationship throughout the entire organization.

A third moderating influence is the degree with which interpersonal feelings are openly discussed. One might hypothesize that in an organization feelings are never completely blocked. Our analysis above has been a theoretical one. We have purposely not considered the possibility that feelings may be discussed at times, even if they violate the organizational values. There are examples on record where executives describe a meeting as one in which "the lid blew off" or an interview situation where "we had it out." In studying a specific organization, the degree to which these meetings occur will be determined. If they occur frequently, we should find that (1) they are perceived as violating the organizational values and/or (2) the organization had, in addition to the values listed above, another set that sanctioned such behavior.

A fourth possibility is that after many years in such a system the members will tend to decrease their expectation that feelings are important and relevant in their everyday activities. Given such expectations, the "emotional apathy and noninvolvement" and the frustration of suppressed feelings will not tend to be as great. However, the organizational consequences of conformity, and so on, will still tend to arise.

Finally, although I know of no existing data, it may be that there are "threshold" points which prevent a system from increasing its interpersonal ineffectiveness indefinitely. Similarly there may exist threshold points which will tend to make it increasingly difficult to increase effectiveness indefinitely. One may also hypothesize that at some point and under certain conditions (at the moment unknown) the degree of effectiveness or ineffectiveness will not tend to increase or decrease but tend to remain constant. Any activity continuing in the direction of the dominant state of affairs (effectiveness or ineffectiveness) will only tend to reinforce these states of affairs.

A NOTE ON THE NATURE OF OUR PREDICTIONS

If one examines the model that we have presented, one will find that it contains certain assumptions about the behavior that it purports to understand. They are:

1. Some human behavior in organization can be understood as caused by individuals adhering or dedicating themselves to organizational values. The greater the commitment to the values, the less one needs to include personality factors to explain the behavior. For example, people with psychologically different personalities (as

measured by a test of one's choosing) would still tend to behave in the direction and manner specified by the model. Thus, our focus is on the study of *systems of behavior* which, once in operation, are independent of the particular individuals that composed them.

This does not mean that personality factors are completely irrelevant. The individuals must be capable of perceiving the values and becoming dedicated to them. The system would never be able to influence the behavior of the members, if the members were simply unable to recognize or have the values communicated to them. Nor could the system operate if one attempted to populate it with personality types who simply could not dedicate themselves to these values. One reason why the second condition tends to occur rarely in our society is that our schools, churches, recreational groups, and even some aspects of family life are also based upon formal organizational values. Thus, in our culture, individuals are prepared to live more or less in accordance with formal organization values.

2. The second assumption is that the system, with its inputs, outputs, and feedback processes, will tend to remain relatively stable. The stability occurs as the individuals act within the values of the system, thereby keeping out disturbing influences.

Change may be induced in this system through external pressures (that is, environment) or through the "seeding" of the system with enough individuals who are capable of, indeed need to behave in accordance with, other values and have the necessary power to do so.

3. Any change attempted in the outputs (for example, through new policies) designed to be superimposed upon the individuals will tend to be resisted. Changes that do not or are not permitted to influence the inputs (values) will tend to fail. One can make, for example, changes in organization structure policies require a decrease in interdepartmental conflicts, and so on. None of these changes will have lasting effects unless the inputs are appropriately influenced. The appropriate influence is in the direction of increasing interpersonal competence.

Although increasing interpersonal competence is a necessary first step, *it is not enough*. We may recall that the structure of the organization, its technology, job design, controls, incentive systems, and so on, are all based on the same set of values. Consequently these factors must eventually be modified or else one can negate the changes that may occur through an increase in interpersonal competence. To summarize, the basic changes will require a modification or addition to the present values. To effect changes, organiza-

tional, technological, and interpersonal factors will require alteration. The interpersonal factors, however, should come first, closely
followed by the others.[17]

BUSINESSMANSHIP*

S. Potter

THE PROBLEM

Yeovil's School of Businessmanship is not yet fully formed. It is a
strange fact, which we here state in all frankness and without criticism, that vast as are its resources, the business world has made
small contribution to our funds. "We invented Lifemanship before
you were born," said a bulk buyer of synthetic soup by-products to
me the other day, and this conveys the attitude of the whole business community. "Certainly," said his friend, who disposed of the
residue of the soup by-products, which he patented as compressed
fuel. "And didn't we invent the word Salesmanship?"

FIG. 1. Businessmanship basic.

"It's men like you we want."
Alternatively
"It's men like me you want."

"Yes, and Chairmanship too," said a heavy-jowled older man, who
bought up the remains of the residue of this soup by-product for
his firm, Natural Broths, Ltd.

---

[17]This assertion has implications for planning laboratories. For example, one would
not tend to focus on intergroup problems until interpersonal competence is adequate;
conversely, working *only* on interpersonal competence will not tend to be enough, if
the organization is characterized by built-in "win-lose" battles among departments.

And of course one must sympathize with this view. "Businessman-ship—Salesmanship—Lifemanship" . . . and yet. At any rate when the concrete request came for guidance, a request from the business quarter of New York City, we were glad to add this youngest of all our student courses to our schedule.

Lifemanship's Principle of Negative Selling

What is our approach? On the wall of Commercial Corner, in the East Wing of our college, there hangs a picture. It is taken from the wrapper of a popular American salesmanship manual. (Note to Illustrator: reproduce *picture only* on the cover of *Sizzlemanship* by Elmer Wheeler.) Look at the picture. On the left is a figure full of the confidence of the man who knows his job and knows it is well-done. The salesman. On the right is the prospective client, the "Prospect," his eagerness to buy only matched by his astonished admiration of this fine and courageous personality who is forcing him into a deal which his reason abhors. That is the implied inter-pretation.

There you have the business of business. But in businessmanship the roles must be reversed. The sitting figure on the *right* is the sales-man, trained by us in that bungling diffidence which alone can in-fuse confidence into the buyer and fill him with certainty that this feeble sap before him couldn't deceive a milk pudding.[1]

The No-Pen Approach

For our first simple lesson we demonstrate the basic gambit of the No-Pen Approach—easy phrase to remember. Childishly pri-mary, it yet embodies the Lifemanship's Principle of Negative Selling.

Lay businessmen when they are anxious—typical business prob-lem—to persuade a client to sign some document containing a clause which on closer inspection will be seen to the client's disadvantage

---

[1]This is the only picture in our business lecture room because it can be used to illustrate the right and wrong methods of salesmanship and anything else as well. E.g., I am sometimes asked is there a Lifeman's put-off for insurance salesman. Yes, there is, and this picture demonstrates it. In Method One, the "Prospect" (left) is countering the insurance salesman (right) by a sudden stream of praise for insur-ance policies in general and a suggestion, since the salesman earns his living by talk-ing, that he should insure either (*a*) his hard palate or (*b*) his right fist, essential in forceful speech and especially liable to accident. In Method Two, Prospect (right) is asking salesman (left) if he would mind continuing the conversation at home, take potluck with his aunts, and give a comic recitation to help entertain the displaced children of the Paper-cutters' Orphanage—"they're quite all right if you know how to handle them, and we ought to be back before 1 A.M."

sometimes do it like this. With the document on the desk, the dialogue is as follows:

LAY BUSINESSMAN: I think you'll find everything quite in order, Mr. Fortinbras.
FORTINBRAS: Oh yes, but what about the—
L.B. (*oiling in*): You did want us to keep mutually independent? Now, you sit here.
FORTINBRAS (*puzzled*): Something about "giving you right of transference"?
L.B.: That's right.
FORTINBRAS (*suspicious*): Yes, but—
L.B.: Now, if you just put your name where I penciled it in. I think you'll find my pen in working order . . . .

What is wrong? The untrained businessman is standing ready with gleaming fountain pen full of rich ink. He is hovering. He is amiable. Client is put on the defensive and ten to one he will begin to ask questions.

Study now the Lifemanship-trained businessman in the same position. Once more, the document is on the table, all ready for Mr. Fortinbras.

FIG. 2. MANAGING DIRECTOR'S DESK.

Wrong (left)   Right (right)

BUSINESS LIFEMAN: I think this is the thing you're supposed to sign.
MR. FORTINBRAS: I beg your pardon?
B.L.: Only for goodness' sake let's make sure. Must get my secretary to tidy my desk.
F. (*amused*). Well, here's my name, anyhow.
B.L.: Let's try and take it in. (*Reading very slowly.*) "Whereas the party hereinafter called the copyholders shall within the discretion of both signatories"—can't understand a word.
F. (*almost paternal already*): Let me. I'm used to this sort of jargon. "The parties assigned. . . ."
B.L.: Look. Wonderful, isn't it? (*They laugh.*)
F. (*taking charge*): That's right, and I'm supposed to sign there—paragraphs individually, aren't I?

B.L.: Oh? I mean *yes.* Awfully sorry, don't seem to have a pen (*rustles through papers.*) I'm most awfully sorry, I've got a new secretary. Josephine! Probably at coffee. Typical.

F.: It's all right, I've got a pen.

B.L. (*keen for the first time*): Oh, isn't that the new sort that writes on ice, or something? Marvelous little thing. Can I look at it? Sorry, after you.

"Sorry," because client is already in the act of signing the document. The client is helping. To make assurance doubly sure in this technique, it is no bad thing if businessman actually puts client's borrowed pen into his own pocket, after admiring it, as if by mistake. Client now leaves, not only having signed the paper but full of a queer sort of confidence. This signature technique was first perfected by Lumer Farr, and it is known as Lumer's Bumbling Approach.

This negative fountain-penmanship sets the note of our course. We teach students to remember that it is only men *below* the highest rank in any firm who take exact measurements of the carpet in their office room to make sure it is not narrower than Y's or less thick than Z's. But in Supreme Boss-ship we always teach plainness, simplicity, and downright ordinariness. No Yeovil-trained managing director ever dreams of being seen behind a desk clanking with telephones, loud speakers, soft speakers, buzzers, little flashing lights, and silver boxes overflowing with splendid cigarettes and engraved with the signatures of supposedly affectionate colleagues. No. Take Lumer Farr, Yeovil-trained Vice President (lifeword for Complete Boss) of International Packing Cases. "You'd never think," I have heard people say, "that Lumer Farr controlled three quarters of the crude teak export trade of Canada." Actually he didn't but why should anyone think he did?

Lumer likes to be called "The Guv'nor," but likes it to be thought that he likes to be called "Bert."[2] His nose is a thin beak, but his eyes and chin are faint and ghostly, neither commanding nor firm. He creeps about in a little black coat. His desk is a plain-deal table with nothing on it whatever. The only telephone in the room is an

---

[2]In the science of Christian-naming, Lumer is associated with Farr's Law of Mean Familiarity. This can be expressed by a curve, but is much clearer set down as follows:

The Guv'nor addresses:

Co-director Michael Yates as	Mike
Assistant director Michael Yates as	Michael
Sectional manager Michael Yates as	Mr. Yates
Sectional assistant Michael Yates as	Yates
Apprentice Michael Yates as	Michael
Night-watchman Michael Yates as	Mike

old-fashioned candlestick one in the corner with a winder. He gets up and answers it himself about twice during the morning. Guarding his room of course there are ranks and ranks of fashionable men and women dressed as secretaries, whose function it is to be extremely busy and to keep anybody except some ne'er-do-well nephew[3] from ringing up or speaking to Lumer. These rebuffs in which he has trained this group are delightfully contrasted with Lumer's occasional bemused and affable appearances at the doorway of his office when he may ask you himself to come in, and apologizes for the lack of courtesy with which you have been treated. Then he will fumble out a broken packet and offer you a twisted cigarette.

Lumer is always slipping out of the room and slipping into the room in a way which is supposed to be unnoticed but which in fact everybody is supposed to notice. When he gets out of a car or a plane or even coming out of the theater, he will slip quietly away, head down, as if he were avoiding a reporter. And quite late at night he will be seen, by arrangement, alone at this empty desk, on the plain-deal chair.

COMMITTEESHIP

I have enunciated a general principle. Let me now outline the work of one of our study circles, Committeeship.

It is axiomatic that Committeeship is the art of coming into a discussion without actually understanding a word of what anybody is talking about. But this entry can be made effective only if the speaker *decides what sort of person he, the speaker, is, and sticks to it.* The sort doesn't much matter; consistency is what counts, but the following committeeship types are especially recommended:

Type One, MULSIPRAT. The man who, pretty high and perhaps chairman, is yet rather muddled. At the same time he is never in a flap about his mistakes but says, "There I go again" or "There's another of my beauts."[4] This is endearing, and in fact the point of Mulsiprat is being adored by everybody. He may employ two special secretaries, one male and one female, whose exclusive difficult duty is to[5] obviously adore him.

---

[3]Lumer's "Ploy of the Ridiculously Soft Heart." He always says, "Suppose I'd better speak to the young scallywag." But he has never actually given him either help or money.

[4]The wording here and certain other ploys in this section were hacked out in committee with a dissatisfied group of low-ranking members of the editorial staff of *Fortune.*

[5]For our life-sponsored split infinitive, see our next publication, *Womanship,* 1954.

Type Two, GALEAD, is also rather mad. But this rather-madman-ship is of a totally different sort. Galead is manic, never cuts nails, has one shoelace undone, wears new jackets *with one button missing,* reveals faint tremor of the left hand, chain-smokes (dummy nicotine stains may be varnished onto the backs of the fingers). He sometimes adds to this a speech-disability sign—e.g., starting every remark with a long downward cadence whistle—it *(whistle)* "cures my stammer."

FIG. 3. DIAGRAM OF MAN IN THE STREET.

In committee he is the permanently "difficult" one: *"(Whistle)* Yes, but *how?"* Early in the meeting he finds himself in definite disagreement with the chairman and managing director on some minor issue, which makes it all the easier for him to be overwhelmingly on their side round about lunchtime.

FIG. 4. DIAGRAM OF MAN NOT IN THE STREET. (Drawn to
reduced scale.)

Type Three, LUDLOW, is the tremendously ordinary chap, valuable because he is in close touch with tremendously ordinary people and can, himself, talk tremendously ordinarily.[6] We can't do without Ludlow because he is the man in the street.

---

[6]Not to be confused with the man who talks tremendously ordinarily to children. See *Lifemanship,* Chap. 1.

Type Four, MAIDENHAIR, we draw special attention to because he represents a totally new type, of high value, as we believe, and something we are perhaps rather specially proud of because he has been developed entirely through Lifemanship-sponsored organizations. He is the man not in the street. Sometimes, he has taken a First in Classics, and is often therefore brilliant.

Type Five, TEMPESTRIAN, is not brilliant at all but sensible. He counters suggestions of brilliant Type Maidenhair by saying, "Yes, but don't let's forget the big picture. What, after all, are we trying to do?"

Type Six, CO-AX, is in a way wicked, or at any rate puts business first and says so. In the world of journalism, he is so hard-boiled about tender feelings that rival committeemen are thought to feel awe. His voice is thin and waxy. "What we want on this page here," he says, "is a picture of a displaced crippled sick orphan of exiled alien parents and plug it for all we're worth." One day we were discussing the insertion of a rather daring portrait of fairly pretty Paulette O. in our little mag. "Page three," Co-Ax said, hard-boiling. "We want sex on page three, nine inches by eight. Always assuming that we have a story about cruelty to animals on page seven." This always goes down particularly well with the shyer shareholders who may be fairly strong family men and churchwardens. "Co-Ax knows his job," they say afterwards, downing their small gin-and-limes in one.

Type Seven, HOSPITER, can be any of the foregoing, and yet none. He is the natural countercommitteeman, the underminer. It is not what he is, but what he says, that matters.

Hospiter Parlettes, many of them silent, are as follows:

A. When rival committeeman is speaking.
   1. Look sadly at boots (it is best to have actual boots).
   2. Doodle and continue to doodle with the faintest possible deepening of the corners of the mouth. Try to suggest that you see something irresistibly inappropriate or comic in what your rival is saying, but wild horses wouldn't make you spoil his little speech by mentioning it now. This delicate and highly expert little ploy was first described to me independently by H. Whyte and F. Anderson, and named by the latter the "Mona Lisa Ploy."
B. When rival committeeman has finished speaking, say:
   1. "Well, we sort of came to a decision about that, didn't we, after a fairly full discussion last week, a rather good discussion, I thought. I mean we agree."

Or alternatively say:

   2. "Well," (*pause and look hard at chairman as if only you two know*

this) "there are definite reasons why that is going to become im-
practicable fairly shortly, aren't there?"

Or say:

3. "Yes, but we have got to think of the effect on the ordinary nice
   people we meet in the street. They are not terribly brainy, but they
   are quite nice people really."

If rival makes obviously good, bold, and original point, counter
it by saying:

1. "Yes, I think that's a good idea—I wonder if we were right to discard
   it five years ago when there was all that row."

Or:

2. If you can only think of something conventional and commonplace
   as alternative, *make* your flat suggestion in an "Of course I'm completely mad" voice (*flairship*), and add "I know you'll think I'm
   making a fool of myself, but I think some of us are bound to make
   fools of ourselves before anything really happens, don't you?"

Or:

3. Simply say, "Yes, but that isn't really what we're discussing, is it?"

Regil and the Economics Ploy

Type Eight, REGIL,[7] is different from all the foregoing if only
because he knows, if possible, less about the subject under discussion, and the business of the committee generally, than anybody
else present. He is rather like Maidenhair, the First in Classics, except that the general impression is that Regil took a first in Economics.

Regil invariably creates an economics wicket by referring everything to the social or monetary sciences. He often speaks of "structured behavior" and uses the phrase "inner directed," frequently
mixing it, according to Whyte of Manhattan, with a colloquialism
("He's pretty much of an inner-directed guy.").

Regil, however, certainly comes into his best on his own subject,
economics—"the plonking science," as Matthew Arnold called it;
and it is generally agreed that almost any phrase from any chapter
of this extraordinary subject will meet any emergency, if the sentences are spelt out sufficiently slowly and clearly.

---

[7]These titles may have some religious or cosmographical significance, or they may
be the names of the first eight losers backed by us in the Yeovil Handicap, Spring,
1952.

Sometimes, of course, Regil, especially after a short snifter, enjoyed himself with a little wild incomprehensibility (Economics Approach A).

"If you want to influence the general liquidity situation of banks *and* public," he would say, pretending to expect a reply. "If you do," he would go on, "I think you're forgetting that the Bank of England's discretionary action on the cash basis took the shape of dealings in Treasury Bills, the market rate of discount on which could *and did* fluctuate."

Regil would firm up his voice a good deal on "did fluctuate." But he was always at his best I though on the more classical Economics Approach B (The Approach of Utter Obviousness).

This "stupefaction of the exhaustingly clear" (Watertower) was used by Regil at moments of some crisis. "I'm not going to tell you why most demand curves slope downward," he would begin, as a paralyzer. Then he would become clear, in that frightful way of his. "Unless something happens to change the state of demand," he would say, as if he was quoting, and incredibly enough he was, "more will be bought at any given price than at any higher price."

Another pause, before the next sentence, when his voice became so cuttingly audible it seemed to pass straight to the center of my head and shortcut the organs of comprehension completely: "Any rise in price WILL REDUCE THE VOLUME OF SALES."

Suddenly he was quiet again—for the homely instance:

"When a child enters a shop to buy a penworth of sourballs, *by the mere fact of asking for the sourballs it incurs a debt of one penny.* Look . . ."

I knew this "look" of Regil's. It was the prelude to a sort of Economics Oration, which we were all too hypnotized to interrupt:

"Look, and what do you see?"
Generally I saw the ashtray, steaming with unfinished cigarettes.
"You see the farm laborer in the fields, tending the cattle to be marketed. The factory workers controlling the machines, feeding them with raw materials which they *transform into manufactured produce.* The miner is extracting mineral deposits from the earth, the clerk is recording transations in the office, transport workers are moving persons and goods from one place to another. By cable and wireless, instructions are transmitted with amazing speed . . ."

And so it went on. The fact that most of us were always complaining of telephone delays, and that none of us had ever actually seen any of these things (except perhaps Rusper, the clerk) didn't stop Regil from having another of his recurrent successes, from flattening the committee into respectful silence, and from mounting, with one foot on "produce" and another on "goods," yet one more rung on Businessmanship's difficult ladder.

DEFENSIVE COMMUNICATION*
Jack R. Gibb

One way to understand communication is to view it as a people process rather than as a language process. If one is to make fundamental improvements in communication, he must make changes in interpersonal relationships. One possible type of alteration—and the one with which this paper is concerned—is that of reducing the degree of defensiveness.

Defensive behavior is defined as that behavior which occurs when an individual perceives threat or anticipates threat in the group. The person who behaves defensively, even though he also gives some attention to the common task, devotes an appreciable portion of his energy to defending himself. Besides talking about the topic, he thinks about how he appears to others, how he may be seen more favorably, how he may win, dominate, impress, or escape punishment, and/or how he may avoid or mitigate a perceived or an anticipated attack.

Such inner feelings and outward acts tend to create similarly defensive postures in others, and if unchecked, the ensuing circular response becomes increasingly destructive. Defensive behavior, in short, engenders defensive listening, and this in turn produces postural, facial, and verbal cues which raise the defense level of the original communicator.

Defense arousal prevents the listener from concentrating upon the message. Not only do defensive communicators send off multiple value, motive, and affect cues, but also defensive recipients distort what they receive. As a person becomes more and more defensive, he becomes less and less able to perceive accurately the motives, the values, and the emotions of the sender. My analyses of tape-recorded discussions revealed that increases in defensive behavior were cor-

*Reprinted by permission from *ETC: A Review of General Semantics,* Vol. XXII, No. 2; copyright 1965, by the International Society for General Semantics.

related positively with losses in efficiency in communication.[1] Specifically, distortions became greater when defensive states existed in the groups.

The converse, moreover, also is true. The more "supportive" or defense reductive the climate, the less the receiver reads into the communication distorted loadings which arise from projections of his own anxieties, motives, and concerns. As defenses are reduced, the receivers become better able to concentrate upon the structure, the content, and the cognitive meanings of the message.

In working over an eight-year period with recordings of discussions occurring in varied settings, I developed the six pairs of defensive and supportive categories presented in Table 1. Behavior which a listener perceives as possessing any of the characteristics listed in the left-hand column arouses defensiveness, whereas that which he interprets as having any of the qualities designated as supportive reduces defensive feelings. The degree to which these reactions occur depends upon the personal level of defensiveness and upon the general climate in the group at the time.[2]

TABLE 1

CATEGORIES OF BEHAVIOR CHARACTERISTIC OF SUPPORTIVE
AND DEFENSIVE CLIMATES IN SMALL GROUPS

Defensive Climates	*Supportive Climates*
1. Evaluation	1. Description
2. Control	2. Problem Orientation
3. Strategy	3. Spontaneity
4. Neutrality	4. Empathy
5. Superiority	5. Equality
6. Certainty	6. Provisionalism

Speech or other behavior which appears evaluative increases defensiveness. If by expression, manner of speech, tone of voice, or verbal content the sender seems to be evaluating or judging the listener, then the receiver goes on guard. Of course, other factors may inhibit the reaction. If the listener thought that the speaker regarded him as an equal and was being open and spontaneous, for example, the evaluativeness in a message would be neutralized and perhaps not even perceived. This same principle applies equally

[1] J. R. Gibb, "Defense Level and Influence Potential in Small Groups," in L. Petrullo and B. M. Bass (eds.), *Leadership and Interpersonal Behavior* (New York, 1961), pp. 66–81.

[2] J. R. Gibb, "Sociopsychological Processes of Group Instruction, in N. B. Henry (ed.), *The Dynamics of Instructional Groups* (Fifty-ninth Yearbook of the National Society for the Study of Education, Part II, 1960), pp. 115–135.

to the other five categories of potentially defense-producing climates. The six sets are interactive.

Because our attitudes toward other persons are frequently, and often necessarily, evaluative, expressions which the defensive person will regard as nonjudgmental are hard to frame. Even the simplest question usually conveys the answer that the sender wishes or implies the response that would fit into his value system. A mother, for example, immediately following an earth tremor that shook the house, sought for her small son with the question: "Bobby, where are you?" The timid and plaintive "Mommy, I didn't do it" indicated how Bobby's chronic mild defensiveness predisposed him to react with a projection of his own guilt and in the context of his chronic assumption that questions are full of accusation.

Anyone who has attempted to train professionals to use information-seeking speech with neutral effect appreciates how difficult it is to teach a person to say even the simple "Who did that?" without being seen as accusing. Speech is so frequently judgmental that there is a reality base for the defensive interpretations which are so common.

When insecure, group members are particularly likely to place blame, to see others as fitting into categories of good or bad, to make moral judgments of their colleagues, and to question the value, motive, and affect loadings of the speech which they hear. Since value loadings imply a judgment of others, a belief that the standards of the speaker differ from his own causes the listener to become defensive.

Descriptive speech, in contrast to that which is evaluative, tends to arouse a minimum of uneasiness. Speech acts which the listener perceives as genuine requests for information or as material with neutral loadings are descriptive. Specifically, presentations of feelings, events, perceptions, or processes which do not ask or imply that the receiver change behavior or attitude are minimally defense producing. The difficulty in avoiding overtone is illustrated by the problems of news reporters in writing stories about unions, Communists, Negroes, and religious activities without tipping off the "party" line of the newspaper. One can often tell from the opening words in a news article which side the newspaper's editorial policy favors.

Speech which is used to control the listener evokes resistance. In most of our social intercourse someone is trying to do something to someone else—to change an attitude, to influence behavior, or to restrict the field of activity. The degree to which attempts to control produce defensiveness depends upon the openness of the effort, for a suspicion that hidden motives exist heightens resistance. For this reason, attempts of nondirective therapists and progressive educators to refrain from imposing a set of values, a point of view, or a problem solution upon the receivers meet with many barriers. Since the norm is control, noncontrollers must earn the perceptions that their efforts have no hidden motives. A bombardment of persuasive "messages" in the fields of politics, education, special causes, advertising, religion, medicine, industrial relations, and guidance has bred cynical and paranoid responses in listeners.

Implicit in all attempts to alter another person is the assumption by the change agent that the person to be altered is inadequate. That the speaker secretly views the listener as ignorant, unable to make his own decisions, uninformed, immature, unwise, or possessed of wrong or inadequate attitudes is a subconscious perception which gives the latter a valid base for defensive reactions.

Methods of control are many and varied. Legalistic insistence on detail, restrictive regulations and policies, conformity norms, and all laws are among the methods. Gestures, facial expressions, other forms of nonverbal communication, and even such simple acts as holding a door open in a particular manner are means of imposing one's will upon another and hence are potential sources of resistance.

Problem orientation, on the other hand, is the antithesis of persuasion. When the sender communicates a desire to collaborate in defining a mutual problem and in seeking its solution, he tends to create the same problem orientation in the listener, and of greater importance, he implies that he has no predetermined solution, attitude, or method to impose. Such behavior is permissive in that it allows the receiver to set his own goals, make his own decisions, and evaluate his own progress—or to share with the sender in doing so. The exact methods of attaining permissiveness are not known, but they must involve a constellation of cues and they certainly go beyond mere verbal assurances that the communicator has no hidden desires to exercise control.

When the sender is perceived as engaged in a stratagem involving ambiguous and multiple motivations, the receiver becomes defensive. No one wishes to be a guinea pig, a role player, or an impressed actor, and no one likes to be the victim of some hidden motivation. That which is concealed also may appear larger than it really is, with the degree of defensiveness of the listener determining the perceived size of the suppressed element. The intense reaction of the reading audience to the material in the *Hidden Persuaders* indicates the prevalence of defensive reactions to multiple motivations behind strategy. Group members who are seen as "taking a role," as feigning emotion, as toying with their colleagues, as withholding information, or as having special sources of data are especially resented. One participant once complained that another was "using a listening technique" on him!

A large part of the adverse reaction to much of the so-called human relations training is a feeling against what are perceived as gimmicks and tricks to fool or to "involve" people, to make a person think he is making his own decision, or to make the listener feel that the sender is genuinely interested in him as a person. Particularly violent reactions occur when it appears that someone is trying to make a stratagem appear spontaneous. One person has reported a boss who incurred resentment by habitually using the gimmick of "spontaneously" looking at his watch and saying, "My gosh, look at the time—I must run to an appointment." The belief was that the boss would create less irritation by honestly asking to be excused.

Similarly, the deliberate assumption of guilelessness and natural simplicity is especially resented. Monitoring the tapes of feedback and evaluation sessions in training groups indicates the surprising extent to which members perceive the strategies of their colleagues. This perceptual clarity may be quite shocking to the strategist, who usually feels that he has cleverly hidden the motivational aura around the gimmick.

This aversion to deceit may account for one's resistance to politicians who are suspected of behind-the-scenes planning to get his vote, to psychologists whose listening apparently is motivated by more than the manifest or content-level interest in his behavior, or to the sophisticated, smooth, or clever person whose "oneupmanship" is marked with guile. In training groups the role-flexible person frequently is resented because his changes in behavior are perceived as strategic maneuvers.

In contrast, behavior which appears to be spontaneous and free of deception is defense reductive. If the communicator is seen as having a clean id, as having uncomplicated motivations, as being straightforward and honest, and as behaving spontaneously in response to the situation, he is likely to arouse minimal defense.

When neutrality in speech appears to the listener to indicate a lack of concern for his welfare, he becomes defensive. Group members usually desire to be perceived as valued persons, as individuals of special worth, and as objects of concern and affection. The clinical, detached, person-as-an-object-of-study attitude on the part of many psychologist-trainees is resented by group members. Speech with low affect that communicates little warmth or caring is in such contrast with the affect-laden speech in social situations that it sometimes communicates rejection.

Communication that conveys empathy for the feelings and respect for the worth of the listener, however, is particularly supportive and defense reductive. Reassurance results when a message indicates that the speaker identifies himself with the listener's problems, shares his feelings, and accepts his emotional reactions at face value. Abortive efforts to deny the legitimacy of the receiver's emotions by assuring the receiver that he need not feel badly, that he should not feel rejected, or that he is overly anxious, though often intended as support giving, may impress the listener as lack of acceptance. The combination of understanding and empathizing with the other person's emotions with no accompanying effort to change him apparently is supportive at a high level.

The importance of gestural behavioral cues in communicating empathy should be mentioned. Apparently spontaneous facial and bodily evidences of concern are often interpreted as especially valid evidence of deep-level acceptance.

When a person communicates to another that he feels superior in position, power, wealth, intellectual ability, physical characteristics, or other ways, he arouses defensiveness. Here, as with the other sources of disturbance, whatever arouses feelings of inadequacy causes the listener to center upon the affect loading of the statement rather than upon the cognitive elements. The receiver then reacts by not hearing the message, by forgetting it, by competing with the sender, or by becoming jealous of him.

The person who is perceived as feeling superior communicates that he is not willing to enter into a shared problem-solving relationship, that he probably does not desire feedback, that he does not require help, and/or that he will be likely to try to reduce the power, the status, or the worth of the receiver.

Many ways exist for creating the atmosphere that the sender feels himself equal to the listener. Defenses are reduced when one perceives the sender as being willing to enter into participative planning with mutual trust and respect. Differences in talent, ability, worth, appearance, status, and power often exist, but the low defense communicator seems to attach little importance to these distinctions.

The effects of dogmatism in producing defensiveness are well known. Those who seem to know the answers, to require no additional data, and to regard themselves as teachers rather than as co-workers tend to put others on guard. Moreover, in my experiment, listeners often perceived manifest expressions of certainty as connoting inward feelings of inferiority. They saw the dogmatic individual as needing to be right, as wanting to win an argument rather than solve a problem, and as seeing his ideas as truths to be defended. This kind of behavior often was associated with acts which others regarded as attempts to exercise control. People who were "right" seemed to have low tolerance for members who were "wrong"—that is, those who did not agree with the sender.

One reduces the defensiveness of the listener when he communicates that he is willing to experiment with his own behavior, attitudes, and ideas. The person who appears to be taking provisional attitudes, to be investigating issues rather than taking sides on them, to be problem solving rather than debating, and to be willing to experiment and explore tends to communicate that the listener may have some control over the shared quest or the investigation of the ideas. If a person is genuinely searching for information and data, he does not resent help or company along the way.

CONCLUSION

The implications of the above material for the parent, the teacher, the manager, the administrator, or the therapist are fairly obvious. Arousing defensiveness interferes with communication and thus makes it difficult—and sometimes impossible—for anyone to convey ideas clearly and to move effectively toward the solution of therapeutic, educational, or managerial problems.

CAREERS IN A DEVIANT
OCCUPATIONAL GROUP: THE
DANCE MUSICIAN*

Howard S. Becker

I have already discussed, particularly in considering the development of marihuana use, the *deviant career* (the development, that is, of patterns of deviant behavior). I would like now to consider the kinds of careers that develop among dance musicians, a group of "outsiders" that considers itself and is considered by others to be "different." But instead of concentrating on the genesis of deviant modes of behavior, I will ask what consequences for a person's occupational career stem from the fact that the occupational group within which he makes that career is a deviant one.

In using the concept of career to study the fate of the individual within occupational organizations, Hughes has defined it as "objectively . . . a series of statuses and clearly defined offices . . . typical sequences of position, achievement, responsibility, and even of adventure. . . . Subjectively, a career is the moving perspective in which the person sees his life as a whole and interprets the meaning of his various attributes, actions, and the things which happen to him."[1] Hall's discussion of the stages of the medical career focuses more specifically on the career as a series of adjustments to the "network of institutions, formal organizations, and informal relationships" in which the profession is practiced.[2]

The career lines characteristic of an occupation take their shape from the problems peculiar to that occupation. These, in turn, are a function of the occupation's position vis-a-vis other groups in

*Reprinted in its entirety, chap. 6, "Careers in a Deviant Occuptional Group: The Dance Musician" from Howard S. Becker, *Outsiders: Studies in the Sociology of Deviance* (Glencoe, Ill.: The Free Press, a Division of the Macmillan Co., N. Y., 1963), pp. 101-19. Used by permission.
    [1]Everett C. Hughes, "Institutional Office and the Person," *American Journal of Sociology,* XLIII (November, 1937), 409-10.
    [2]Oswald Hall, "The Stages of a Medical Career," *American Journal of Sociology,* LIII (March, 1948), 327.

the society. The major problems of musicians, as we have seen, revolve around maintaining freedom from control over artistic behavior. Control is exerted by the outsiders for whom musicians work, who ordinarily judge and react to the musician's performance on the basis of standards quite different from his. The antagonistic relationship between musicians and outsiders shapes the culture of the musician and likewise produces the major contingencies and crisis points in his career.

Studies of more conventional occupations such as medicine have shown that occupational success (as members of the occupation define it) depends on finding a position for oneself in that influential group or groups that controls rewards within the occupation, and that the actions and gestures of colleagues play a great part in deciding the outcome of any individual's career.[3] Musicians are no exception to this proposition, and I shall begin by considering their definitions of occupational success and the way the development of musical careers depends on successful integration into the organization of the music business.

There is more to the story of the musician's career, however. The problem of freedom from outside control creates certain additional career contingencies and adds certain complications to the structure of the occupation; I consider these next.

Finally, the musician's family (both the one he is born into and the one he creates by marrying) has a major effect on his career.[4] Parents and wives are typically not musicians and, as outsiders, often fail to understand the nature of the musician's attachment to his work. The misunderstandings and disagreements that arise often change the direction of a man's career and, in some cases, bring it to an end.

CLIQUES AND SUCCESS

The musician conceives of success as movement through a hierarchy of available jobs. Unlike the industrial or white-collar worker, he does not identify his career with one employer; he expects to

---

[3]See Everett C. Hughes, *French Canada in Transition* (Chicago: University of Chicago Press, 1943), pp. 52–53; and Melville Dalton, "Informal Factors in Career Achievement," *American Journal of Sociology*, LVI (March, 1951), 407–15, for discussions of the influence of the colleague group on careers in industrial organizations; and Hall, *op. cit.*, for a similar analysis of colleague influence in the medical profession. Hall's concept of the "inner fraternity" refers to that group which is so able to exert greatest influence.

[4]See the discussion in Howard S. Becker, "The Implications of Research on Occupational Careers for a Model of Household Decision-Making," in Nelson N. Foote,

change jobs frequently. An informally recognized ranking of these jobs—taking account of the income involved, the hours of work, and the degree of community recognition of achievement felt—constitutes the scale by which a musician measures his success according to the kind of job he usually holds.

At the bottom of this scale is the man who plays irregularly for small dances, wedding receptions, and similar affairs, and is lucky to make union wages. At the next level are those men who have steady jobs in "joints"—lower class taverns and night clubs, small "strip joints," etc.—where pay is low and community recognition lower. The next level is comprised of those men who have steady jobs with local bands in neighborhood ballrooms and small, "respectable" night clubs and cocktail lounges in better areas of the city. These jobs pay more than joint jobs and the man working them can expect to be recognized as successful in his community. Approximately equivalent to these are men who work in so-called "class B name" orchestras, the second rank of nationally known dance orchestras. The next level consists of men who work in "class A name" bands, and in local orchestras that play the best night clubs and hotels, large conventions, etc. Salaries are good, hours are easy, and the men can expect to be recognized as successful within and outside of the profession. The top positions in this scale are occupied by men who hold staff positions in radio and television stations and legitimate theaters. Salaries are high, hours short, and these jobs are recognized as the epitome of achievement in the local music world, and as jobs of high-ranking respectability by outsiders.

A network of informal, interlocking cliques allocates the jobs available at a given time. In securing work at any one level, or in moving up to jobs at a new level, one's position in the network is of great importance. Cliques are bound together by ties of mutual obligation, the members sponsoring each other for jobs, either hiring one another when they have the power or recommending one another to those who do the hiring for an orchestra. The recommendation is of great importance, since it is by this means that available individuals become known to those who hire; the person who is unknown will not be hired, and membership in cliques insures that

editor, *Household Decision Making* (New York: New York University Press, 1961), pp. 239–54; and Howard S. Becker and Anselm L. Strauss, "Careers, Personality, and Adult Socialization," *American Journal of Sociology*, LXII (November, 1956), 253–63.

one has many friends who will recommend one to the right people.

Clique membership thus provides the individual with steady employment. One man explained:

> See, it works like this. My right hand here, that's five musicians. My left hand, that's five more. Now one of these guys over here gets a job. He picks the men for it from just these guys in this group. Whenever one of them gets a job, naturally he hires this guy. So you see how it works. They never hire anybody that isn't in the clique. If one of them works, they all work.

The musician builds and cements these relationships by getting jobs for other men and so obligating them to return the favor:

> There were a couple of guys on this band that I've got good jobs for, and they've had them ever since. Like one of those trombone players. I got him on a good band. One of the trumpet players, too. . . . You know the way that works. A leader asks you for a man. If he likes the guy you give him, why every time he needs a man he'll ask you. That way you can get all your friends on.

Security comes from the number and quality of relationships so established. To have a career one must work; to enjoy the security of steady work one must have many "connections":

> You have to make connections like that all over town, until it gets so that when anybody wants a man they call you. Then you're never out of work.

A certain similarity to the informal organization of medical practice should be noted. Musicians cooperate by recommending each other for jobs in much the same way that members of the medical "inner fraternity" cooperate by furnishing each other with patients.[5] The two institutional complexes differ, however, in that medical practice (in all except the largest cities) tends to revolve around a few large hospitals which one, or a few, such fraternities can control. In music, the number of possible foci is much greater, with a correspondingly greater proliferation of organization and, consequently, there are more opportunities for the individual to establish the right connections for himself and a lessening of the power of any particular clique.

In addition to providing a measure of job security for their members, cliques also provide routes by which one can move up through the levels of jobs. In several cliques observed, membership was drawn from more than one level of the hierarchy; thus men of lower position were able to associate with men from a higher level. When a job becomes available higher in the scale, a man of the lower level may be sponsored by a higher-ranking man who recom-

---

[5]Hall, *op. cit.*, p. 332.

mends him, or hires him, and takes the responsibility for the quality of his performance. A radio staff musician described the process in these terms:

Now the other way to be a success is to have a lot of friends. You have to play good, but you have to have friends on different bands and when someone leaves a band, why they're plugging to get you on. It takes a long time to work yourself up that way. Like I've been 10 years getting the job I have now.

If the man so sponsored performs successfully he can build up more informal relationships at the new level and thus get more jobs at that level. Successful performance on the job is necessary if he is to establish himself fully at the new level, and sponsors exhibit a great deal of anxiety over the performance of their protégés. The multiple sponsorship described in this incident from my field notes illustrates this anxiety and its sources in the obligations of colleagues:

A friend of mine asked me if I was working that night. When I told him no, he led me over to another guy who, in turn, led me to an old fellow with a strong Italian accent. This man said, "You play piano, huh?" I said, "Yes." He said, "You play good, huh?" I said. "Yes." He said, "You play good? Read pretty good?" I said, "Not bad. What kind of a deal is this?" He said, "It's at a club here in the Loop. It's nine to four-thirty, pays two-fifty an hour. You're sure you can handle it?" I said, "Sure!" He touched my shoulder and said, "OK. I just have to ask you all these questions. I mean, I don't know you, I don't know how you play, I just have to ask, you see?" I said, "Sure." He said, "You know, I have to make sure, it's a spot downtown. Well, here. You call this number and tell them Mantuno told you to call Mantuno. See, I have to make sure you're gonna do good or else I'm gonna catch hell. Go on, call 'em now. Remember, Mantuno told you to call."

He gave me the number. I called and got the job. When I came out of the booth my friend who had originated the deal came up and said, "Everything all right? Did you get the job, huh?" I said, "Yeah, thanks an awful lot." He said, "That's all right. Listen, do a good job. I mean, if it's commercial, play commercial. What the hell! I mean, if you don't then it's my ass, you know. It isn't even only my ass, it's Tony's and that other guy's, it's about four different asses, you know."

In short, to get these top job positions requires both ability and the formation of informal relationships of mutual obligation with men who can sponsor one for the jobs. Without the necessary minimum of ability one cannot perform successfully at the new level, but this ability will command the appropriate kind of work only if a man has made the proper connections. For sponsors, as the above quotation indicates, the system operates to bring available men to the attention of those who have jobs to fill and to provide them with recruits who can be trusted to perform adequately.

The successful career may be viewed as a series of such steps, each one a sequence of sponsorship, successful performance, and the building up of relationships at each new level.

I have noted a similarity between the musician's career and careers in medicine and industry, shown in the fact that successful functioning and professional mobility are functions of the individual's relation to a network of informal organizations composed of his colleagues. I turn now to the variation in this typical social form created by the strong emphasis of musicians on maintaining their freedom to play without interference from nonmusicians, who are felt to lack understanding and appreciation of the musician's mysterious, artistic gifts. Since it is difficult (if not impossible) to attain this desired freedom, most men find it necessary to sacrifice the standards of their profession to some degree in order to meet the demands of audiences and of those who control employment opportunities. This creates another dimension of professional prestige, based on the degree to which one refuses to modify one's performance in deference to outside demands—from the one extreme of "playing what you feel" to the other of "playing what the people want to hear." The jazzman plays what he feels while the commercial musician caters to public taste; the commercial viewpoint is best summarized in a statement attributed to a very successful commercial musician: "I'll do anything for a dollar."

As I pointed out earlier, musicians feel that there is a conflict inherent in this situation, that one cannot please the audience and at the same time maintain one's artistic integrity. The following quotation, from an interview with a radio staff musician, illustrates the kind of pressures in the top jobs that produce such conflict:

> The big thing down at the studio is not to make any mistakes. You see, they don't care whether you play a thing well or not, as long as you play all the notes and don't make any mistakes. Of course, you care if it doesn't sound good, but they're not interested in that. . . . They don't care what you sound like when you go through that mike, all they care about is the commercial. I mean, you might have some personal pride about it, but they don't care. . . . That's what you have to do. Give him what you know he likes already.

The job with most prestige is thus one in which the musician must sacrifice his artistic independence and the concomitant prestige in professional terms. A very successful commercial musician paid deference to artistic independence while stressing its negative effect on career development:

> I know, you probably like to play jazz. Sure I understand. I used to be interested in jazz, but I found out that didn't pay, people didn't like jazz. They

like rumbas. After all, this is a business, ain't that right? You're in it to make a living or you're not, that's all. And if you want to make a living you can't throw jazz at the people all the time, they won't take it. So you have to play what they want, they're the ones that are paying the bills. I mean, don't get me wrong. Any guy that can make a living playing jazz, fine. But I'd like to see the guy that can do it. If you want to get anywhere you gotta be commercial.

Jazzmen, on the other hand, complain of the low position of the jobs available to them in terms of income and things other than artistic prestige.

Thus the cliques to which one must gain access if one is to achieve job success and security are made up of men who are definitely commercial in their orientation. The greatest rewards of the profession are controlled by men who have sacrificed some of the most basic professional standards, and one must make a similar sacrifice in order to have any chance of moving into the desirable positions:

See, if you play commercial like that, you can get in with these cliques that have all the good jobs and you can really do well. I've played some of the best jobs in town—the Q——— Club and places like that—and that's the way you have to do. Play that way and get in with these guys, then you never have to worry. You can count on making that gold every week and that's what counts.

Cliques made up of jazzmen offer their members nothing but the prestige of maintaining artistic integrity; commercial cliques offer security, mobility, income, and general social prestige.

This conflict is a major problem in the career of the individual musician, and the development of his career is contingent on his reaction to it. Although I gathered no data on the point, it seems reasonable to assume that most men enter music with a great respect for jazz and artistic freedom. At a certain point in the development of the career (which varies from individual to individual), the conflict becomes apparent and the musician realizes that it is impossible to achieve the kind of success he desires and maintain independence of musical performance. When the incompatibility of these goals becomes obvious, some sort of choice must be made, if only by default, thus determining the further course of his career.

One response to the dilemma is to avoid it, by leaving the profession. Unable to find a satisfactory resolution of the problem, the individual cuts his career off. The rationale of such a move is disclosed in the following statement by one who had made it:

It's better to take a job you know you're going to be dragged [depressed] with, where you expect to be dragged, than one in music, where it could be

great but isn't. Like you go into business, you don't know anything about it.
So you figure it's going to be a drag and you expect it. But music can be so
great that it's a big drag when it isn't. So it's better to have some other kind
of job that won't drag you that way.

We have seen the range of responses to this dilemma on the part
of those who remain in the profession. The jazzman ignores audience demands for artistic standards while the commercial musician
does the opposite, both feeling the pressure of these two forces.
My concern here will be to discuss the relation of these responses
to career fates.

The man who chooses to ignore commercial pressures finds himself effectively barred from moving up to jobs of greater prestige
and income, and from membership in those cliques which would
provide him with security and the opportunity for such mobility.
Few men are willing or able to take such an extreme position;
most compromise to some degree. The pattern of movement involved in this compromise is a common career phenomenon, well
known among musicians and assumed to be practically inevitable:

> I saw K——— E———. I said, "Get me a few jobbing dates, will you?" He
> said, imitating one of the "old guys,"[6] "Now son, when you get wise and
> commercial, I'll be able to help you out, but not now." In his normal voice
> he continued, "Why don't you get with it? Gosh, I'm leading the trend over to
> commercialism, I guess. I certainly have gone in for it in a big way, haven't I?"

At this crucial point in his career the individual finds it necessary
to make a radical change in his self-conception; he must learn to
think of himself in a new way, to regard himself as a different
kind of person:

> This commercial business has really gotten me, I guess. You know, even
> when I go on a job where you're supposed to blow jazz, where you can just
> let yourself go and play anything, I think about being commercial, about
> playing what the people out there might want to hear. I used to go on a
> job with the idea to play the best I could, that's all, just play the best I knew
> how. And now I go on a job and I just automatically think, "What will these
> people want to hear? Do they want to hear Kenton style, or like Dizzy Gillespie
> [jazz orchestras], or like Guy Lombardo [a commercial orchestra], or what?"
> I can't help thinking that to myself. They've really gotten it into me, I guess
> they've broken my spirit.

A more drastic change of self-conception related to this career
dilemma is found in this statement:

> I'll tell you, I've decided the only thing to do is really go commercial—
> play what the people want to hear. I think there's a good place for the guy

---

[6]"Old guys" was the term generally used by younger men to refer to the cliques
controlling the most desirable jobs.

that'll give them just what they want. The melody, that's all. No improvising, no technical stuff—just the plain melody. I'll tell you, why shouldn't I play that way? After all, let's quit kidding ourselves. Most of us aren't really musicians, we're just instrumentalists. I mean, I think of myself as something like a common laborer, you know. No sense trying to fool myself. Most of those guys are just instrumentalists, they're not real musicians at all, they should stop trying to kid themselves they are.

Making such a decision and undergoing such a change in self-conception open the way for movement into the upper levels of the job hierarchy and create the conditions in which complete success is possible, if one can follow up the opportunity by making and maintaining the proper connections.

One way of adjusting to the realities of the job without sacrificing self-respect is to adopt the orientation of the craftsman. The musician who does this no longer concerns himself with the *kind* of music he plays. Instead, he is interested only in whether it is played *correctly*, in whether he has the skills necessary to do the job the way it ought to be done. He finds his pride and self-respect in being able to "cut" any kind of music, in always giving an adequate performance.

The skills necessary to maintain this orientation vary with the setting in which the musician performs. The man who works in bars with small groups will pride himself on knowing hundreds (or even thousands) of songs and being able to play them in any key. The man who works with a big band will pride himself on his intonation and technical virtuosity. The man who works in a night club or radio studio boasts of his ability to read any kind of music accurately and precisely at sight. This kind of orientation, since it is likely to produce just what the employer wants and at a superior level of quality, is likely to lead to occupational success.

The craftsman orientation is easier to sustain in the major musical centers of the country: Chicago, New York, Los Angeles. In these cities, the volume of available work is great enough to support specialization, and a man can devote himself single-mindedly to improving one set of skills. One finds musicians of astounding virtuosity in these centers. In smaller cities, in contrast, there is not enough work of any one kind for a man to specialize, and musicians are called on to do a little of everything. Although the necessary skills overlap—intonation, for instance, is always important—every man has areas in which he is just barely competent. A trumpet player may play excellent jazz and do well on small jazz jobs but read poorly and do much less well when he works with a big band. It is difficult to maintain pride as a craftsman when one is continually faced with jobs for which he has only minimal skills.

To sum up, the emphasis of musicians on freedom from the interference inevitable in their work creates a new dimension of professional prestige which conflicts with the previously discussed job prestige in such a way that one cannot rank high in both. The greatest rewards are in the hands of those who have sacrificed their artistic independence, and who demand similar sacrifice from those they recruit for these higher positions. This creates a dilemma for the individual musician, and his response determines the future course of his career. Refusing to submit means that all hope of achieving jobs of high prestige and income must be abandoned, while giving in to commercial pressures opens the way to success for them. (Studies of other occupations might devote attention to those career contingencies which are, likewise, a function of the occupation's basic work problems vis-à-vis clients or customers.)

PARENTS AND WIVES

I have noted that musicians extend their desire for freedom from outside interference in their work to a generalized feeling that they should not be bound by the ordinary conventions of their society. The ethos of the profession fosters an admiration for spontaneous and individualistic behavior and a disregard for the rules of society in general. We may expect that members of an occupation with such an ethos will have problems of conflict when they come into close contact with that society. One point of contact is on the job, where the audience is the source of trouble. The effect of this area of problems on the career has been described above.

Another area of contact between profession and society is the family. Membership in families binds the musician to people who are squares, outsiders who abide by social conventions whose authority the musician does not acknowledge. Such relationships bear seeds of conflict which can break out with disastrous consequences for the career and/or the family tie. This section will spell out the nature of these conflicts and their effect on the career.

The individual's family has a great influence on his occupational choice through its power to sponsor and aid the neophyte in his chosen career. Hall, in his discussion of the early stages of the medical career, notes that:

> In most cases family or friends played a significant role by envisaging the career line and reinforcing the efforts of the recruit. They accomplished the

latter by giving encouragement, helping establish the appropriate routines, arranging the necessary privacy, discouraging anomalous behavior, and defining the day-to-day rewards.[7]

The musician's parents ordinarily do not aid the development of his career in this way. On the contrary, as one man observed, "My God, most guys have had a terrific hassle with their parents about going into the music business." The reason is clear: regardless of the social class from which he comes, it is usually obvious to the prospective musician's family that he is entering a profession which encourages his breaking with the conventional behavior patterns of his family's social milieu. Lower-class families seem to have been most distressed over the irregularity of musical employment, although there is evidence that some families encouraged such a career, seeing it as a possible mobility route. In the middle-class family, choice of dance music as an occupation is viewed as a movement into Bohemianism, involving a possible loss of prestige for both individual and family, and is vigorously opposed. Considerable pressure is applied to the person to give up his choice:

> You know, everybody thought it was pretty terrible when I decided to be a musician. . . . I remember I graduated from high school on a Thursday and left town on Monday for a job. Here my parents were arguing with me and all my relatives, too, they were really giving me a hard time. . . . This one uncle of mine came on so strong about how it wasn't a regular life and how could I ever get married and all that stuff.

The conflict has two typical effects on the career. First, the prospective musician may, in the face of family pressure, give up music as a profession. Such an adjustment is fairly common at an early stage of the career. On the other hand, the young musician may ignore his family's desires and continue his career, in which case he is often deprived of his family's support at an earlier age than would otherwise be the case and must begin to "go it alone," making his way without the family sponsorship and financial aid that might otherwise be forthcoming. In music, then, the career is ordinarily begun, if at all, without the family aid and encouragement typical of careers in many other occupations.

Once he has married and established his own family, the musician has entered a relationship in which the conventions of society are presented to him in an immediate and forceful way. As a husband he is expected by his wife, typically a non-musician, to be a com-

[7]Hall, *op. cit.*, p. 328. See also Becker, "The Implications of Research on Occupational Careers . . . ," *op. cit.*; and James W. Carper and Howard S. Becker, "Adjustments to Conflicting Expectations in the Development of Identification with an Occupation," *Social Forces*, 36 (October, 1957), 51–56.

panion and provider. In some occupations there is no conflict between the demands of work and of the family. In others there is conflict, but socially-sanctioned resolutions of it exist which are accepted by both partners as, for example, in medical practice. In deviant occupations, such as the music business, professional expectations do not mesh at all with lay expectations, with consequent difficulties for the musician.

Musicians feel that the imperatives of their work must take precedence over those of their families, and they act accordingly:

> Man, my wife's a great chick, but there's no way for us to stay together, not as long as I'm in the music business. No way, no way at all. When we first got married it was great. I was working in town, making good gold, everybody was happy. But when that job was through, I didn't have anything. Then I got an offer to go on the road. Well, hell, I needed the money, I took it. Sally said, "No, I want you here in town, with me." She'd sooner have had me go to work in a factory! Well, that's a bunch of crap. So I just left with the band. Hell, I like the business too much, I'm not gonna put it down for her or any woman.

Marriage is likely to turn into a continuing struggle over this issue; the outcome of the struggle determines whether the man's musical career will be cut short or will continue, as the following incident from my field notes illustrates:

> The boys down at the Z——— Club are trying to get Jay Marlowe to go back to work there full time. He's splitting the week with someone now. He's got a day job in the same office in which his wife works, doing bookkeeping or some minor clerical job. The boys are trying to talk him into quitting. Apparently his wife is bitterly opposed to this.
>
> Jay's been a musician all his life, as far as I know; probably the first time he ever had a day job. Gene, the drummer at the Z——— Club, said to me, "It's foolish for him to have a day job. How much can he make down there? Probably doesn't clear more than thirty, thirty-five a week. He makes that much in three nights here. Course, his wife wanted him to get out of the business. She didn't like the idea of all those late hours and the chicks that hang around bars, that kind of stuff. But after all, when a guy can do something and make more money, why should he take a sad job and work for peanuts? It don't make sense. Besides, why should he drag himself? He'd rather be playing and it's a drag to him to have that fucking day job, so why should he hold on to it?" Johnny, the saxophone player, said, "You know why, because his wife makes him hold on to it." Gene said, "He shouldn't let her boss him around like that. For Christ's sake, my old lady don't tell me what to do. He shouldn't put with that crap."
>
> They've started to do something about it. They've been inviting Jay to go out to the race track with them on week days and he's been skipping work to do so. Gene, after one of these occasions, said, "Boy was his wife mad! She doesn't want him to goof off and lose that job, and she knows what we're up to. She thinks we're bad influences. Well, I guess we are, from her way of thinking."
>
> [A few weeks later Marlowe quit his day job and returned to music.]

For other men who feel their family responsibilities more strongly the situation is not so simple. The economic insecurity of the music business makes it difficult to be a good provider, and may force the individual to leave the profession, one of the typical patterns of response to this situation:

No, I haven't been working too much. I think I'm going to get a God-damn day job. You know, when you're married it's a little different. Before it was different. I worked, I didn't work, all the same thing. If I needed money I'd borrow five from my mother. Now those bills just won't wait. When you're married you got to keep working or else you just can't make it.

Even if the career is not cut off in this fashion, the demands of marriage exert a very strong pressure that pushes the musician toward going commercial:

If you want to keep on working, you have to put with some crap once in a while. . . . I don't care. I've got a wife and I want to keep working. If some square comes up and asks me to play the "Beer Barrel Polka" I just smile and play it.

Marriage can thus speed the achievement of success by forcing a decision which affords, although it does not guarantee, the opportunity for movement into those cliques which, being commercially oriented, are best able to keep their members in steady work.

The family then, as an institution that demands that the musician behave conventionally, creates problems for him of conflicting pressures, loyalties and self-conceptions. His response to these problems has a decisive effect on the duration and direction of his career.

THE DUKE'S ALTER EGO*

John S. Wilson

The relationship between Billy Strayhorn and Duke Ellington, which lasted 28 fruitful years until Strayhorn's death at 51 on May 31, was unique in the jazz world, and would have been unusual in any creative field. During all these years Strayhorn was Ellington's chief arranger, associate composer and musical alter ego to such an extent that neither man, in retrospect, could be sure who wrote

---

*Reprinted from *The New York Times* (July, 1967).

what part of anything they had worked on together. It was a role that called for self-effacement without denial of self.

The self-effacement, so far as public presentation was concerned, seemed admirably suited to Strayhorn's taste. As for self-denial, this simply did not come up. Strayhorn's musical self was, to a great extent, so in tune with Ellington's that the two men thought creatively in an almost identical manner.

Strayhorn once recalled an occasion when the Duke phoned him in the early hours of the morning, after finishing a night's performance somewhere, and ordered "three or four minutes in D flat" as part of a suite that Ellington had been commissioned to write.

With no further clue, Strayhorn produced the required three or four minutes and was startled to find, when the whole suite was run through by the Ellington orchestra for the first time, that his contribution was a development of a theme that Ellington had written into an earlier section of the piece.

He "Broke the Code"

But Strayhorn was more than a mere reflection of Ellington. He was, as Ellington said, the man who "broke the Ellington code"— a reference to the numerous unsuccessful attempts to write in the Ellington manner before Strayhorn appeared on the scene. Yet there was also a distinctive and positive strain in his work that was Strayhorn's own creative style. It was best exemplified in the wry romanticism of "Lush Life," a Strayhorn song which, unlike all his other well-known works, was not popularized by Duke Ellington's band (the late Nat "King" Cole gave the definitive performance of it).

This aspect of Strayhorn's writing became part of the over-all Ellington coloration, for it brought out the full power of one facet of the performing style of Johnny Hodges, Ellington's brilliant alto saxophonist. Hodges was moving toward an unusually lyrical manner of playing before Strayhorn joined the Ellington entourage in 1939, but when Strayhorn began providing him with tunes such as "Passion Flower" and "Day Dream," Hodges reached the complete realization of the style that has been his primary identification for the past quarter of a century.

The last long work on which Strayhorn collaborated with Ellington before his death was "The Far East Suite" (RCA Victor LPM 3782; LSP 3782), a series of musical impressions gathered during the Ellington band's 1963 tour for the State Department to India, Iran, Iraq, Syria, Afghanistan, Turkey and Ceylon. The East that the band covered may seem more Near and Middle than Far but, relatively speaking, that is neither here nor there so far as the music of Ellington and Strayhorn is concerned.

It is all distinctively Ellington, even including two pieces that appear to stem primarily from Strayhorn. One is "Bluebird of Delhi," which is based, according to Ellington, on a lick that a bird kept singing to Strayhorn in his hotel room. The other is a showcase for the Hodges-cum-Strayhorn style, "Isfahan." In neither case is one overtly conscious of Strayhorn as a separate composing identity. His style had, by this time, become so much a part of the over-all Ellington style that almost everything attributed to Ellington in the past two decades or more reflects to some extent the personality of Billy Strayhorn.

"The Far East Suite," as a whole, is one of Ellington's more colorful long works. The exotic backgrounds are a somewhat more legitimate variation of the pseudo-Eastern exotica that Juan Tizol used to contribute to the Ellington book ("Caravan," "Pyramid"), designed to feature the various Ellington soloists.

Hodges, in addition to his lush "Isfahan," shows the opposite side of his attack in his lean and gutty solo on "Blue Pepper." There is a showcase for Harry Carney's dark and elegant declamations on baritone saxophone, another for Lawrence Brown's trombone in fervent wail, and a piece called "Depk" which gives the whole Ellington ensemble a rare opportunity to display its pulsing sonority.

Yet none of the eight pieces that make up "The Far East Suite" has quite the verve of the distinctive character of an 11-minute addendum on the disk, "Ad Lib on Nippon," in which the Duke's piano forms a vital, vigorous core around which Jimmy Hamilton's clarinet, John Lamb's bass, and the full band swirl through a tremendously rhythmic and melodically colorful performance.

THE INFLUENCE OF CRITICALNESS
ON CREATIVE PROBLEM SOLVING
IN DYADS*

Morris B. Parloff and Joseph H. Handlon

On the happy assumption that creativity is not the exclusive property of the select few but is characteristic of the human condition, considerable effort has been made to define the psychological states in which most persons may utilize more of their inherent creative capacities. Although classical empiricists and rationalists have held that the expression of creativity is the direct product of logical reasoning, more recently philosophers and social scientists have challenged this position and have proposed instead that creativity may, in fact, require the temporary suspension of logic in order to permit freer play of fantasy and imagination. As a consequence, techniques for promoting the relaxation of critical judgment have been widely employed in the expectation that the number and quality of ideas occurring to the scientist and artist alike would thereby be increased. This paper reports an experimental test of the hypothesis that techniques for the reduction of critical judgment need not increase the "generation" of creative ideas but can achieve their results by increasing the subject's willingness to report more fully the ideas which he ordinarily tends to dismiss as unworthy.

Support for the proposition that the suspension of critical judgment may facilitate creative output is found in the subjective retrospective accounts by many recognized creative persons in the arts and sciences.[1] This view is also well represented in the formulations

*Reprinted from Psychiatry, Vol. 29 (1966), pp. 17–27.

The authors wish to express their gratitude to Dr. Donald F. Morrison for his guidance in the area of statistical analysis and to Miss Adrian Tinsley for her assistance in the collection and analysis of the data.

[1]See, for example, Brewster Ghiselin (ed.), *The Creative Process* (New York: Mentor Books, 1955); Sigmund Freud, "The Interpretation of Dreams," *Standard Edition of the Complete Psychological Works* 4 (1900) (London: Hogarth, 1953), pp. 102–103; Henri Poincaré, "Mathematical Creation," in James R. Newman (ed.), *The World of Mathematics,* (New York: Simon and Schuster, 1956), IV, 2048.

of psychoanalysts concerning the role of the unconscious and pre-conscious in creative thinking.

Recent extensions of psychoanalytic theory by Kris suggest that the temporary release from the constrictions of ego controls permits "regression in the service of the ego."[2] Such regressions from reality-oriented thinking to more primitive mechanisms of thought are alleged to characterize both the creative man and the psychotic. The creative man, however, retains the capacity to reassert conscious control and to evaluate his products. The suspension of ego controls is assumed to increase the likelihood that novel and effective ideas will be generated; moreover, the merit of the ideas generated will be recognized by their author, who may then pursue and perfect them. Some evidence that such a process may be operative in persons designated as creative is offered by the studies of Pine and Holt and of I. H. Cohen.[3]

Some of the avenues by which this desired state of release may be achieved are said to include (1) intensive psychotherapy;[4] (2) ingestion of consciousness-altering drugs, such as LSD-25, mescaline, psilocybin, and diethyltryptamine;[5] and (3) conscious efforts to reduce the exercise of critical judgment.[6] The first two techniques represent heroic efforts to alter states of consciousness; the third, which is most popularly represented by the inelegant term "brain-storming," appears to be the most direct and simple. This technique involves the training of individuals or groups engaged in joint problem solving to express freely all solutions which occur to them without attempting to evaluate either their own ideas or those of their fellow group members. To date there is no experimental evidence which compares the relative effectiveness of these three techniques in enhancing creativity. The proponents of brainstorming, however, have undertaken to demonstrate experimentally its usefulness in facilitating creative problem solving.

The research evidence in favor of brainstorming is equivocal. The

[2]Ernst Kris, *Psychoanalytic Explorations in Art* (New York: Internat. Univ. Press, 1952).

[3]Fred Pine and Robert R. Holt, "Creativity and Primary Process: A Study of Adaptive Regression," *J. Abnormal and Social Psychol.*, Vol. 61 (1960), pp. 370–79. Irwin H. Cohen, "Adaptive Regression and Creativity," paper read at Midwestern Psychological Association, Chicago, May, 1961.

[4]Lawrence S. Kubie, *Neurotic Distortion of the Creative Process* (Lawrence, Kans.: University of Kans. Press, 1958).

[5]Abram Hoffer and Humphrey Osmond, *The Chemical Basis of Clinical Psychiatry* (Springfield, Ill.: Charles C Thomas, 1960).

[6]Alex F. Osborn, *Applied Imagination* (rev. ed.; New York: Scribner's, 1957).

experiments reported by the investigators at the Creative Education Foundation consistently favor subjects functioning under the reduced critical judgment instructions.[7] Investigators in other settings appear to be less successful.[8]

In this study we did not attempt to reconcile these conflicting findings or to evaluate the possible influences of the many variables in which these studies differ. Instead, our investigation was concerned with identifying some of the processes which might be affected by the technique of suspended judgment. It is generally assumed that the suspension of critical judgment operates to decrease inhibiting or interfering forces and thereby permits the generation of a greater number of creative ideas. However, the studies which purport to find a positive relationship between a reduction of critical judgment and an increased number of good solutions to problems do not constitute conclusive evidence that the effect is due to the increased "generation" of good quality ideas. Similar results might be produced if the reduction of critical judgment enabled the individual to report ideas already available to him which he would ordinarily reject as trivial or worthless. Such ideas may be valued far more by a judge than by the person reporting them. Studies of creative thinking in which a criterion product is involved usually confound the variables of the subject's capacity to *generate* responses and his willingness to *report* them. Our study is aimed at determining whether the changes in "creativity" can be explained in terms of alterations in the "availability" of responses or in terms of shifts in the subject's standards for selecting a solution from his available alternatives.

We know of no method for assessing the availability of ideas independent of their expression. Presumably ideas which the subject is willing to express have passed some subjective criterion. The rigor-

---

[7]Arnold Meadow and Sidney J. Parnes, "Evaluation of Training in Creative Problem Solving," *J. Applied Psychol.*, Vol. 43 (1959), pp. 189–94. Sidney J. Parnes and Arnold Meadow, "Effects of 'Brainstorming' Instructions on Creative Problem Solving by Trained and Untrained Subjects," *J. Educ. Psychol.*, Vol. 50 (1959), pp. 171–76. Arnold Meadow, Sidney J. Parnes, and Hayne Reese, "Influences of Brainstorming Instructions and Problem Sequence on a Creative Problem Solving Test," *J. Applied Psychol.*, Vol. 43 (1959), pp. 413–16. Sidney J. Parnes and Arnold Meadow, "Evaluation of Persistence of Effects Produced by a Creative Problem-Solving Course," *Psychol. Reports*, Vol. 7 (1960), pp. 357–61. Sidney J. Parnes, "Effects of Extended Effort in Creative Problem Solving," *J. Educ. Psychol.*, Vol. 52 (1961), pp. 117–22.

[8]Ray Hyman, "On Suspending Judgment while Producing Ideas," paper read at Eastern Psychological Association, New York, April, 1960. E. Paul Torrance, "Priming Creative Thinking in the Primary Grades," *Elem. School J.*, Vol. 62 (1961), pp. 34–41. Edith Weisskopf-Joelson and Stephen E. Thomas, "An Experimental Study of the Effectiveness of Brainstorming," *J. Applied Psychol.* Vol. 45 (1961), pp. 45–49.

ousness of the conscious censoring of ideas depends in large part on the anticipated response of the audience. The censorship involved in the free discussion of tentative ideas with a friend may be less stringent than the standards imposed on ideas which are to be submitted in writing to unknown judges for their evaluation. We reasoned, therefore, that the conversational interchange between two members of a problem-solving team would provide a more complete account of their ideation than would the written list of ideas they finally submitted. In the studies conducted by the Creative Education Foundation, the judgments of the number and quality of responses were based on written solutions. We undertook, therefore, to analyze the number and quality of solutions expressed orally by our subjects as an index of "availability of ideas." These findings were compared with those based on the final team solutions submitted in writing to the examiners.

In addition to controlling the mode of response—spoken or written —the research design involved the manipulation of (1) the standards of subjects (low-critical instructions requested them to suspend critical judgment and high-critical instructions requested them to maximize critical judgment); (2) the degree of mutual congeniality of the dyad members—that is, congenial *v.* uncongenial dyads; and (3) types of problems, real *v.* unreal. Factors such as intelligence of subjects, their initial problem solving ability, order of problems, and conditions of instructions were experimentally controlled.

The basic thesis to be tested is that the usual techniques of eliciting states of reduced or increased critical judgment do not differentially affect the generation of "good" ideas but affect instead the completeness with which ideas are reported. Under the high-critical condition fewer good ideas may be reported than under the low-critical set, for in the absence of a clear-cut standard by which the subject can evaluate his ideas, he may consider some of his "good" ideas poor and fail to report them.

This view led to the prediction that if the data in our study were limited to written solutions, as is the case in most studies of brainstorming, then the results would be consistent with those reported by Parnes and Meadow (1959) and by Meadow, Parnes, and Reese.[9] If, however, the data permitted the analysis of the total pool of ideas from which the subjects selected the ideas to be written, then the number of good ideas produced under high-critical and

---

[9]See footnote 7.

under low-critical instructions would no longer be found to differ.

These predictions are summarized in the following two hypotheses:

Hypothesis I. Dyads under the low-critical instructions will *commit to writing* more solutions and more "good" solutions than will those under high-critical instructions.

Hypothesis II. Dyads under the low-critical instructions will not *generate* more "good" solutions than will dyads under high-critical instructions.

As has been demonstrated by students of small-group interaction[10] and particularly of group problem solving,[11] the feelings of group members toward each other play a considerable role in determining the nature of the group's success. It was assumed, therefore, that the congeniality of the group would interact with problem-solving instructions so that the mutually congenial dyads under low-critical instructions would verbalize and submit in writing a higher quantity and quality of ideas than would dyads composed of mutually uncongenial persons. The nature of the problems was also varied on the assumption that "unreal" problems may be more conducive to the establishment of the low-critical condition than "real" problems.

METHOD

The Subjects

The subjects were 24 females, age 18 to 24 years, selected from a pretest sample of 26. The majority were college students who during the summer had come to live as volunteer controls on the wards of a large research hospital, the Clinical Center of the National Institutes of Health, Bethesda, Maryland. During their 12-week stay, they lived in a setting similar to that of a college dormitory. They served as subjects for a variety of experiments and held various part-time jobs.

After the subjects had lived together for at least six weeks, they were asked to fill out sociometric rankings. Sociometric rankings

---

[10]David Cohen, John W. Whitmyre, and Wilmer H. Funk, "Effect of Group Cohesiveness and Training upon Creative Thinking," *J. Applied Psychol.*, Vol. 44 (1960), pp. 319–22.

[11]Harold H. Kelley and John W. Thibaut, "Experimental Studies of Group Problem Solving and Process," in Gardner Lindzey (ed.) *Handbook of Social Psychology*, II (Cambridge, Mass.: Addison-Wesley, 1954). William C. Schutz, *FIRO: A Three-Dimensional Theory of Interpersonal Behavior* (New York: Rinehart, 1958). Rudolf H. Moss and Joseph C. Speisman, "Group Compatibility and Productivity," *J. Abnormal and Social Psychol.*, Vol. 65 (1962), pp. 190–96.

were taken in two groups of 13 members each, from two different wards. Each girl was asked to rank all the other girls in her group along five dimensions: (1) Who would be most useful in helping you draft a set of practical recommendations regarding some general social problem? (2) In whom are you most likely to confide? (3) Whom do you respect the most? (4) Who likes you the best? (5) Whose opinion about you is most important to you? Since these sociometric ratings were included in a routine psychological testing procedure administered to all volunteers, there is no reason to believe that the subjects connected them with the subsequent experiment.

Twelve dyads were selected for the subsequent problem-solving procedures, six mutually congenial and six mutually uncongenial. Since the pairings were based on rankings, no assessment can be made of the absolute level of congeniality in any dyad. The possible scores ranged from 10 for highest mutual choices to 120 for highest mutual rejection. The actual range obtained was from 18 to 120. The congenial group included scores from 18 to 30; the uncongenial group ranged from 90 to 120.

Dyads composing the congenial group averaged approximately 13.5 years of education; dyads included in the uncongenial group averaged approximately 13.9 years of schooling. This difference is not significant.

The subjects' intelligence was estimated by employing four subtests from the Wechsler Adult Intelligence Scale: Information, Vocabulary, Block Design, and Picture Arrangement. The mean estimated full IQ score of the subjects in the congenial dyads was 118.4 and of those in the uncongenial dyads, 118.3, a nonsignificant difference. Although the congenial dyads tended to show a greater homogeneity of IQ's between members of each pair than did uncongenial dyads, the difference in variance between the congenial and uncongenial dyads was not significant.

When the subjects first met as a group for introduction to the procedure, an attempt was made to motivate them by informing them that studies conducted at an unnamed university had recently found males to be more creative than females. The examiner suggested that these findings might be in error because of the nature of the problems employed, which tended to favor males. In order to check this hypothesis, the current experiment was being undertaken with problems which would be equivalent for both sexes.

The Problems

The six problems used were of an open-ended variety in that there was no single correct solution for any problem. Three were classified as "real" problems which might be encountered in everyday life: How can we solve the teacher shortage? How can a shy girl go about meeting a boy she regularly sees on a bus? How can foreign tourists be encouraged to visit the United States? The remaining three problems were classified as "unreal," referring to events that were highly unlikely: What would the consequences be of having an extra thumb on each hand? What would the probable results be of a mutation that would increase rate of physical maturation but not mental maturation? What would be the advantages and disadvantages of having the power to read minds regardless of the distance?

The experiment began with individual work on these problems. Each subject was given the set of problems and was told to work on each problem individually for 10 minutes, writing as many solutions as occurred to her during that period. Upon completion of the test session, the subjects were requested not to discuss with each other the problems presented until told to do so. As far as could be determined, this "security" request was strictly adhered to.

Within a five-day period following the individual testing, the various dyads were assembled. Under high-critical or low-critical conditions, each dyad was required to work further on the problems that had been presented to the subjects during the individual problem-solving session. For training purposes, all the dyads worked together first on the Teacher and Thumb problems under neutral instructions of "Work together in any way which seems most comfortable for you." Throughout all of the dyad procedures, before the members of any team worked together on a problem, each member was given two minutes to work on the problem again individually. The answer sheet upon which each subject had previously written her individual solutions was returned to her with the instructions that new solutions were to be added to her list. This procedure was followed to ensure that the dyad members working together subsequently as a team on the same problems would be required to collaborate in producing ideas novel to them. In all instances, individual subjects "ran dry" of new ideas during this two-minute period.

Under all conditions—neutral, high-critical, and low-critical instructions—the subjects were asked to work together to produce new ideas—that is, ideas which neither had reported during the individual testing on the same problems. Each idea which the team *mutually agreed* was new and appropriate was to be entered by one of the team members (selected by the dyad) on a team recording sheet provided. They were also told that tape recordings of their collaborative efforts would be made in order that individual as well as team scores could be derived by the examiners. Microphones were clearly visible in the testing room. After each problem was presented, the examiner ostentatiously set a large timer for 10 minutes and left the room. The subjects were then observed through a one-way vision screen and their conversation monitored. The examiner returned to the examination room immediately after each 10-minute time period.

After working on two problems under neutral instructions, each dyad worked on the remaining four problems under high-critical or low-critical instructions, depending upon the order dictated by the experimental design. The experimental conditions were designed to duplicate the order of presentation of problems under high-critical and low-critical instructions for the congenial and uncongenial dyads.[12] The design required that each team work on two problems under high-critical instructions and two problems under low-critical instructions. The Tourist, Bus, Growth, and ESP problems were presented comparably under the low-critical and high-critical instructions.

The directions used for the subjects when working under the low-critical conditions were essentially the same as those used for brainstorming, stressing the avoidance of criticism and urging them to give their imaginations free rein. After the directions were presented, the technique was illustrated by the playing of a tape recording on which two staff members role-played a low-critical dyadic session, attempting to develop ideas for a new breakfast food.

The directions used for the subjects under the high-critical conditions stressed the advantages of doing one's best and urged them to analyze and scrutinize carefully each idea in order to select only

---

[12]However, because of the fact that congenial dyad 5 worked on only real problems and congenial dyad 6 worked on only unreal problems under the high- and low-critical instructions, it was necessary to collapse the data from these dyads during the statistical analysis and treat them as a single team in order to deal with the problem of missing observations. Data from dyads 11 and 12 of the uncongenial group were treated in the same manner for the same reason. One of the effects of this procedure was to reduce the within degrees of freedom to 8.

the "good" ideas. Another demonstration tape recording was played
to exemplify the high-critical interaction in attempting to develop
ideas for a new breakfast food.

After two problems had been completed under a given condition,
the dyad members were individually administered a questionnaire
covering the following: the satisfactions of the subject regarding her
own performance and her partner's performance, the feeling of
being helped or hindered by the partner, speculations about the
dyad's performance in contrast to that of other teams, and confidence about future improvement as a team.

The Solutions

Dyad solutions were obtained from two sources: (1) transcrip-
tions of complete tape recordings of the dyads' conversations during
the time in which they worked on each problem; and (2) reports
submitted in writing by each dyad. The transcripts permitted the
determination of the number and quality of all the solutions *expressed*—that is, those generated; the solutions submitted by each
team represented the ideas which the dyads were mutually willing
to *write* and to offer the examiner as the product of their collaborative work.

All solutions were first screened for novelty. Team solutions were
regarded as novel if the idea had not been submitted by either member of a dyad during the individual testing period. Each solution
generated (written or unwritten) by a dyad was transcribed onto
an individual coded card and screened by the examiners.[13] They
compared these ideas with the solutions submitted by the members
of the same dyad during the individual testing; all ideas determined
to be redundant for a given team were eliminated from the study.
Novel ideas were submitted to two judges who assessed their quality
without knowing the source of the solution. The criterion of quality
was derived from the work of Taylor and his co-authors in evaluating
solutions to similar problems.[14] The criteria for judging the solutions
to "real" problems (Tourist and Bus) included (1) *effectiveness,* or
how well the proposed solution solves the problem; (2) *feasibility,*
or how readily the means suggested for the solution are available;

---

[13]All "solutions," written and unwritten, were reviewed in order to identify each
nonredundant idea. The per cent of complete agreement between two pairs of judges
in identifying nonredundant ideas was 86 for "written solutions" and 79 for "unwritten solutions."

[14]Donald W. Taylor, Paul C. Berry, and Clifford Block, "Does Group Participation
When Using Brainstorming Facilitate or Inhibit Creative Thinking?," *Technical Report No. 1,* Contract Nonr 60920; (New Haven, Conn.: Yale Univ., November, 1957).

and (3) *clarity,* or how clearly the solution is spelled out. In the judging process, effectiveness was most heavily weighted.

For the "unreal" problems (Growth and ESP), the criteria included (1) *significance,* or how important the suggested consequence is; (2) *probability,* or how likely it is that the suggested consequence will occur; and (3) *clarity,* or how clearly the suggested consequence is spelled out. For these problems, the greatest weight was given to significance.

The judges were instructed to classify all solutions as good, indifferent, or poor. The judges first worked independently, then met to reconcile differences and to arrive at the consensus rating which is used in all calculations. In order to determine the reliability of the ratings, the same procedure was repeated by the two judges approximately eight months after the initial judgments had been made, and a second consensus rating was determined for each solution. The judges revealed complete test-retest agreement in 81 percent of the ratings of the 611 solutions, partial test-retest agreement in 18 percent, and complete disagreement in only 1 per cent.

RESULTS

A major portion of the data obtained has been studied by an analysis of variance technique devised by Greenhouse and Geisser for quantitative, noncategorical profile data.[15] This method assumes

TABLE 1

ANALYSIS OF VARIANCE MODEL

Source of Variation	Degrees of Freedom	Error Terms
(A) Problems	1	(H)
(B) Criticalness	1	(I)
(C) Congeniality	1	(D)
(D) Dyads within groups	8	—
(E) Problems × Criticalness	1	(K)
(F) Problems × Congeniality	1	(H)
(G) Criticalness × Congeniality	1	(I)
(H) Problems × Dyads	8	—
(I) Criticalness × Dyads	8	—
(J) Problems × Criticalness × Congeniality	1	(K)
(K) Problems × Criticalness × Dyads	8	
Total	39	

that the variables have multinormal distributions with an arbitrary variance-covariance matrix. The model for the five analyses of variance reported in this study can be seen in Table 1. Only sources

[15]Samuel W. Greenhouse and Seymour Geisser, "On Methods in the Analysis of Profile Data," *Psychometrika,* Vol. 24 (1959), pp. 95–112.

of variance found to be significant by a conservative *F* test will be presented.

Hypothesis I predicted that a greater total number of ideas and a greater number of "good" ideas would be written down under the low-critical conditions. A summary of the 272 written team solutions, organized to assess the influence of criticalness, congeniality, and type of problem, is presented in Table 2. Using the analysis of variance technique just described, it was found that significantly more written solutions were obtained under low-critical conditions than under high-critical conditions ($p<.001$). No other main effects or any interactions were statistically significant.

TABLE 2

TOTAL WRITTEN SOLUTIONS

Congeni-ality	High-Critical Condition*			Low-Critical Condition			Total		
	Real Problem	Unreal Problem	Total	Real Problem	Unreal Problem	Total	Real Problem	Unreal Problem	Total
High....	10	13	23	66	51	117	76	64	140
Low....	11	8	19	54	59	113	65	67	132
Total...	21	21	42	120	110	230	141	131	272

*Source of variance, criticalness; $F = 44.93$, p ($df = 1,8$) $<.001$.

The written team solutions judged to be "good" are summarized in Table 3. Again, only the variable of criticalness is significant ($p<.01$), with the low-critical situation producing more "good" solutions than the high-critical. Thus, Hypothesis I is supported by the data. These findings appear to be consistent with the brainstorming hypothesis that low-critical conditions produce more solutions and also more "good" solutions than do high-critical conditions.

TABLE 3

TOTAL WRITTEN "GOOD" SOLUTIONS

Congeni-ality	High-Critical Condition*			Low-Critical Condition			Total		
	Real Problem	Unreal Problem	Total	Real Problem	Unreal Problem	Total	Real Problem	Unreal Problem	Total
High....	5	8	13	15	11	26	20	19	39
Low....	6	2	8	10	11	21	16	13	29
Total...	11	10	21	25	22	47	36	32	68

*Source of variance, criticalness; $F = 13.41$, p ($df = 1,8$) $<.01$.

Influence of Criticalness on Problem Solving in Dyads   639

Hypothesis II predicted that if the analyses were based on the total number of ideas generated—that is, verbalized by the dyads—in contrast to written solutions, the number of "good" solutions would not differ for the low-critical v. high-critical conditions. When the data analyses were based on the transcripts of the tape-recorded sessions rather than on the written reports submitted by the dyads, it was found that the total number of solutions increased from 272 to 611. Under the high-critical condition, 234 solutions were identified, of which 192 had been omitted from the team reports; under the low-critical condition, 377 solutions were found, of which 147 had been unreported. The difference between 234 and 377 solutions is statistically significant at less than the .005 level ($F = 23.53$, $df = 1,8$).

TABLE 4

TOTAL GENERATED (WRITTEN AND UNWRITTEN) "GOOD" SOLUTIONS

Congeni-ality	High-Critical Condition			Low-Critical Condition			Total		
	Real Problem	Unreal Problem	Total	Real Problem	Unreal Problem	Total	Real Problem*	Unreal Problem	Total
High....	15	31	46	17	22	39	32	53	85
Low....	16	26	42	10	24	34	26	50	76
Total...	31	57	88	27	46	73	58	103	161

*Source of variance, problem type; $F = 13.32$, p ($df = 1,8$) <.01.

The total number of "good" ideas identified from the tape recording increased from the 68 reported in writing to 161. An analysis of the 161 "good" solutions verbalized is presented in Table 4. As predicted, there was no significant difference in the number of "good" solutions verbalized under the high-critical and low-critical conditions. However, in contrast to the usual brainstorming expectations, subjects functioning under the high-critical conditions tended to produce somewhat *more* "good" solutions than did those under the low-critical conditions. Further, there were significantly more "good" solutions verbalized for the unreal problems than for the real problems ($p<.01$). There were, however, no significant main effects due to congeniality, nor were there any significant interactions.

An analysis of the solutions which were verbalized by the dyads but *not* reported in writing is presented in Table 5. It reveals that more ideas were omitted for unreal than for real problems ($p<.01$).

Further, as may be seen in Table 6, more "good" ideas remain *un-reported* for unreal than for real problems ($p<.01$). Again, congeniality did not contribute significantly to the variance, and there were no significant interactions among the variables.

TABLE 5

TOTAL UNWRITTEN SOLUTIONS

Congeni-ality	High-Critical Condition			Low-Critical Condition			Total		
	Real Problem	Unreal Problem	Total	Real Problem	Unreal Problem	Total	Real Problem*	Unreal Problem	Total
High....	40	58	98	35	52	87	75	110	185
Low....	38	56	94	15	45	60	53	101	154
Total...	78	114	192	50	97	147	128	211	339

*Source of variance, problem type; $F = 11.80$, p ($df = 1,8$) $<.01$.

The thesis that increasing the number of ideas produced by subjects will also increase the number of "good" ideas is not supported by these findings. Although the dyads functioning under the low-critical condition produced significantly more ideas than under the high-critical condition (377 and 234, respectively), the actual number of good ideas produced was not significantly different (73 and 88, respectively).

TABLE 6

UNWRITTEN "GOOD" SOLUTIONS

Congeni-ality	High-Critical Condition*			Low-Critical Condition			Total		
	Real Problem	Unreal Problem	Total	Real Problem	Unreal Problem	Total	Real Problem†	Unreal Problem	Total
High....	10	23	33	2	11	13	12	34	46
Low....	10	24	34	0	13	13	10	37	47
Total...	20	47	67	2	24	26	22	71	93

*Source of variance, criticalness; $F = 7.96$, p ($df = 1,8$) $<.025$.
†Source of variance, problem type; $F = 13.89$, p ($df = 1,8$) $<.01$.

In brief, the influence of high-critical *v.* low-critical conditions upon the quality of solutions appears to differ markedly depending upon whether the data are restricted to the responses submitted in writing by the subjects or include the total number of responses *verbalized* during the dyad interaction. Of the 88 "good" responses voiced by the dyads under high-critical conditions, 67 (76 per cent) were not subsequently written. Under low-critical conditions, 73 "good" responses were verbalized, but only 26 (36 per cent) remained unwritten. These findings indicate that low-critical conditions did not enhance the production of "good' ideas but did increase the probability of their being reported.

The nonsignificant effect of the variable of congeniality upon the production of solutions is paralleled to some extent by data from the individual questionnaires administered after each dyad experience. There was no significant difference between the congenial and uncongenial groups in their ratings of satisfaction with partners during high-critical or low-critical conditions. However, there is evidence that the members of congenial dyads experienced each other more favorably than did the members of the uncongenial dyads. Members of congenial dyads expressed a higher appreciation of their partners' help during their initial collaboration (under *neutral* conditions) than did the members of uncongenial groups ($p<.02$). In addition, the mean rating of partners made by members of congenial dyads was without exception higher, although not significantly, following neutral, high-critical, and low-critical conditions, than that by members of the uncongenial dyads on each of the five questionnaire items. This finding is significant at the .01 level of confidence as determined by a sign test.

DISCUSSION

The suspension of critical judgment has been presumed to facilitate the formation of, or increase the access to, new and effective ideas. Our findings suggest, however, that the suspension of critical judgment may simply lower the subjects' standards for reporting ideas without substantially increasing their repertoire of "good" ideas. An analysis of the recorded verbalizations revealed that under the high-critical condition good ideas were frequently dismissed as inconsequential or inappropriate by one or the other teammate. Frequently ideas were put forth in so tentative a manner that the recorder made no effort to report them, apparently on the assumption that they were not worthy of serious consideration.

Obviously, this study is not an adequate test of the efficacy of any prolonged brainstorming training technique.[16] Although our instruc-

[16]Any proponent of such a training technique must take into account the question of whether the individual is being trained to be "creative" or trained to alter his standards to conform more closely with those of the judges. One major problem bedevilling research in the area of creative problem solving is the establishment of

(Continued on next page.)

tions for the low-critical condition were based on the brainstorming instructions, no attempt was made to include other aspects of the brainstorming techniques, such as training in analysis of problems, preparatory interval, specified size of groups, and length of sessions.

A further restriction in interpreting the different results based on written and "unwritten" solutions is that failure of the subject to write down an expressed idea may have been due not only to conscious rejection of that idea but also to forgetting. Although such memory losses may be interpreted as reflections of the operation of "standards," the fact remains that to the degree that forgetting was a factor, it tended to affect differentially the quantity of written rather than spoken solutions.

The differential influence of "real" and "unreal" problems on the number of "good" solutions which were generated but remained unwritten has relevance to the importance of the role of standards. During the postexperiment interviews, the subjects frequently complained that evaluating responses was more difficult for unreal problems than for real problems. Presumably, greater disagreement among the members of the dyads regarding standards for evaluating responses to unreal problems resulted in the disproportionate omission of "good" team solutions to unreal problems, particularly under the high-critical conditions.

The definition of novelty used in this study is somewhat at variance with the criterion of uniqueness that is commonly found in the literature.[17] The frequency with which a solution was proposed by the other dyads did not affect its categorization as novel with respect to a specific team. The requirement that a novel solution must have been new to the dyad was invoked in order to differentiate between responses readily available to individual group members and those arising in the group situation. Lorge and Solomon have pointed out that if the group includes one individual who can solve the prob-

---

meaningful criteria for evaluating the quality of the solutions. Thus far the concern of most investigators has been with establishing interjudge reliability. However, a further stumbling block in experimental work in this area is the possible lack of congruence between the subjects' evaluation of their productions and the judges' evaluation. To the degree that this congruence is overtly or covertly improved by training of the subject, the subject will appear more "creative." Before the available experimental efforts can be interpreted as having demonstrated that an individual's capacity to produce novel and effective solutions is increased by simple techniques designed to reduce self-criticalness, the issue of communality of standards must be squarely faced.

[17]Irving Maltzman, Seymore Simon, David Raskin, and Leonard Licht, "Experimental Studies in the Training of Originality," *Psychol. Monogr.*, Vol. 74, No. 6 (1960), (Whole No. 493).

lem, then the group gets credit for the solution even if the others cannot solve it; hence, it is not a true test of group functioning.[18] It is necessary to determine the ability of the individuals to cope with the problem by themselves in order to evaluate the effect of the group *per se*. Thus we attempted to exhaust the individual's response repertoire before the pairs were asked to resume working on the same problem.

The finding that dyad congeniality produced no significant principal or interaction effects upon *productivity* raises the question of whether the designation of the congenial and uncongenial dyads was in fact valid. The sociometric data provided rankings rather than ratings and therefore the designation of congenial and uncongenial was made on relative rather than absolute scores. If the cohesiveness of the total group in absolute terms was either high or low, a very narrow range of congeniality may have been represented. The rank scores may not reflect appreciably less cohesiveness in the uncongenial dyads than in the congenial dyads. Further, it may be argued that the dimensions used to obtain sociometric rankings had little predictive value for the congenial *v.* uncongenial dyads, since the questions had little relevance to the problem-solving tasks involved. Nevertheless, despite a lack of effect upon the number and quality of solutions produced, congeniality seemed to have had some influence upon the perception of the partner's activity as reflected in the questionnaire data.

The finding that the proportion of "good" ideas generated does not vary directly with the total number of ideas generated is consistent with the report of Hyman.[19] A "good" idea is, by definition, a statistically rare phenomenon for the subject. In contrast, an almost infinite number of inadequate and irrelevant ideas may be generated by instructions which emphasize sheer quantity of solutions independent of quality or apparent relevance.

To what degree was the condition of suspension of critical judgment actually achieved in this study? The decision to use subjects who were relatively untrained in the technique may have limited the degree to which they were able to relax critical judgment. It was decided to take this risk because the other alternatives had even more serious drawbacks. If both subjects and controls were highly

---

[18]Irving Lorge and Herbert Solomon, "Individual Performance and Group Performance in Problem Solving Related to Group Size and Previous Exposure to the Problem," *J. Psychol.*, Vol. 48 (July 1959), pp. 107–14.

[19]Ray Hyman, "On Prior Information and Creativity," *Psychol. Reports*, Vol. 9 (1961), pp. 151–61.

trained, then requiring them to function under the condition of high criticalness would involve their role-playing, a condition which they had presumably overcome. This would merely test inhibition rather than demonstrate facilitation due to low criticalness. The alternative of comparing untrained and trained groups would also pose difficulties of interpretation, for any differences could be due principally to the fact that the trained subjects showed a greater willingness than the untrained to verbalize and to write out solutions available to them. The effect due to increased willingness to express these ideas orally or in writing would be confounded with the variable of increased repertoire of ideas.

Despite unanswered questions regarding the degree to which the subjects were in fact able to relax critical judgment, it is clear that the low-critical and high-critical conditions were sufficiently established in this study to produce significant differences in the number of "good" responses which were selected for reporting from those already verbalized.

Most investigators concerned with the creative process tend to limit their research to variables which are presumed to influence the conception of ideas. The creative process may be viewed as including a variety of steps, of which the formulation of ideas is but one. The individual must recognize the idea and value its potential sufficiently to elaborate, test, and report it. Having a good idea is a necessary but not sufficient condition for effective problem solving. The results of this study suggest that effective creativity may be increased by providing conditions in which a person feels freer to report more of his thoughts. It may be useful to investigate procedures whereby the individual can learn not only to suspend critical judgment but also to consider the possible implications and values of the ideas which do occur to him. One important characteristic of the creative person appears to be his assumption that he is capable of achieving good ideas. This requires a measure of self-esteem and confidence in his abilities to function effectively, at least in the area of the problem.

We believe it important, therefore, to investigate further techniques which will improve the individual's self-confidence. The experience of problem solving under conditions of low criticalness is potentially useful in providing the subject with the opportunity to learn that he is capable of producing ideas valued by competent judges. Such repeated experiences may assist him to develop a greater regard for his own capacities, and this may enable him to be freer to utilize them. If the subject's own estimate of his capacity to solve certain problems is increased, he may be more willing to persist in a task and explore avenues of association without prematurely dismissing them as unfruitful.

This study has attempted to differentiate between two psychological processes which may appear to enhance the creativity of individuals functioning under conditions of reduced or suspended critical judgment. The results do not support the current view that the effects of lowered critical judgment are achieved by means of stimulating the *generation* of a greater number of creative ideas. Instead, the process appears to involve the lowering of evaluative standards, thereby permitting the subjects to report ideas which they would otherwise tend to dismiss. The findings indicate that people may regularly generate many good ideas which they reject and therefore fail to exploit. The principal effect of reduced criticalness in this study appears to be due to the technique of shifting the judging task from the subject to an external judge, rather than actually changing the generative capacity of the subject.

PART V

Towards Better

Interpersonal Relationships

This is our pad
we all have a ball here
we don't have much bread but
bread is really not very important
when you have good relationships

From Suzuki Beane

Social scientists, more often than not, are reluctant to expose their own value-systems. To make matters worse, the idea of a "good" *relationship* is slightly foreign, even distasteful, to many students of human behavior who can regard only individual skin boundaries as "real." We will have to forego both of these biases in what follows.

Until now we have either consciously avoided or only vaguely implied two important aspects of interpersonal relationships. The first has to do with the word "better" in our title; "better" implies improvement, and improvement implies a desired state, that is, a "good" state . So we will be dealing here with the normative side of interpersonal relationships, with notions about "good and bad," "healthy and sick." We aim to make explicit the values that govern our own choices and styles of interpersonal relationships.

Secondly, if we can envision a good relationship, then we have to ask: what kinds of personal competencies and what kinds of environmental conditions are conducive to the development and maintenance of these relationships?

In short this essay and the readings that follow are concerned with (1) a vision of ideal interpersonal relations, and (2) the most effective way to reach that state. Let us start with the normative question: what is a *good* relationship?

I. NORMATIVE ASPECTS OF INTERPERSONAL RELATIONSHIPS

1. A Framework for Evaluating Interpersonal Relationships

Can we establish a single criterion of goodness or badness which would be relevant for all interpersonal relationships? Consider the following: customer-salesman, psychiatrist-patient, husband-wife, manager-foreman, guard-inmate, lover-mistress, nurse-doctor. Or take the following kinds of relationships: puppy love, friendship, a crush, an affair; rivals, enemies, boyfriends, fraternity brothers, colleagues, cousins, siblings; or conditions like enforced, contractual, clandestine, accidental, "stuffy," informal, creative, chronic, stable. Or take the following settings: bureaucracy, fraternity, family, board of education, classroom. Does goodness mean the same thing for all of these? Obviously not.

We have to ask: "good for what?" As a starting analytic point let us say that all interpersonal relationships are oriented toward some *primary goal,* that is, some goal or function whose presence is necessary for the relationship to exist and whose absence would seriously undermine it. For example, if two friends stop satisfying each others' affiliative needs, the relationship would end. If two research collaborators can no longer do good research together, they will drift to more productive partners or work on their own. When the pupil can no longer learn from the teacher or the teacher thinks he can no longer impart new knowledge, the relationship will draw to a close. Thus, the *raison d'être* of the relationship, the salient reason for its formation, serves as a framework for evaluation.

On this basis we can characterize four distinct types of relationships: *Type A:* a relationship formed for the purpose of fulfilling *itself,* such as love, marriage, friendship. The main transaction in the relationship is "feelings" and for that reason we will refer to Type A as *expressive-emotional.*[1]

A *Type B* relationship exists in order to establish "reality," but of two distinct kinds. The content of the interpersonal transaction for one kind of Type B (1) is information about the "self" or about

---

[1]Essentially, this book is organized around the four types of relationships. For example, the "expressive-emotional" is treated in Part I, etc.

the relationship. This could include interpersonal "feedback" or reflected appraisals. The content of the interpersonal transaction for the other kind of Type B (2) encompasses information about the environment or a "definition of the situation." The former kind (1) exists in order to understand the relationship and the "self;" the latter (2) exists in order to comprehend social realities. An example of (1) might be a pair of friends who help each other find their identity. The other (2) can often be observed in social groups, say a fraternity, where the norms of the group establish certain social realities: e.g. "what courses or professors are best," "what kind of girls are the best 'dates,'" etc. In either case (1) or (2) we refer to Type B as *confirmatory*.[2]

A *Type C* relationship is formed for the purpose of *change* or *influence*. Thus one or both parties to the relationship come together to create a change in each other or the relationship. The change may entail anything from acquiring new behaviors to attitude change. The main transaction between the change-agent and change-target is information about the desired state to be achieved and feedback on how the target is doing. Examples of change are psychiatrist-patient, teacher-student, parent-child, etc.[3]

A *Type D* relationship is formed in order to achieve some goal or task: a conductor and his violin section or a foreman and his workers or collaborators on a research project are all examples of Type D. We will call this type, *instrumental*; the main coin of interpersonal exchange is information *about the task*.[4]

Before continuing our analysis, we should mention that these four types can rarely, if ever, be observed in "pure" form; the purpose of a relationship cannot be so simple or monolithic. A couple, for example, may marry not only for the relationship itself (Type A) but for some instrumental purpose as well (Type D). We know of two anthropologists whose marriage was based on "love" and the need to work together. And we know of many co-workers, engaged in instrumental activities who permit—even desire—the relationship itself to take priority over the task. Conversely, there are partners in business, often brothers, whose relationship has become increasingly contractual rather than familial. And Type B, confirmatory relationships are, of course, a category of the more general

---

[2] See the essay introducing Part II for a complete treatment of these types of relationships.

[3] See the essay introducing Part III for a complete treatment of these types of relationships.

[4] See the essay introducing Part IV for a detailed treatment of Type D.

Primary Function of Interpersonal Relationship: / Defining Characteristics	(1) The Content of the Interpersonal Transaction	(2) Criteria for Good Relationships	(3) Outcomes of Good Relationships	(4) Outcomes of Bad Relationships
Type A: Emotional-Expressive	Feelings	Mutual satisfaction	"Solidarity"	Alienation Ambivalence Hostility
Type B: Confirmatory	Information about self: 1) Interpersonal feedback; reflected appraisals	1) Confirmation	1) Integrated identity Self-actualization	1) Disconfirmation
	Information about environment: 2) Definitions of the situation	2) Consensus	— Consensus about Reality — 2) Cognitive mastery	2) Anomie
Type C: Change-Influence	Information about desired goal and progress toward achieving goal	Desired change	Growth Termination Internalization	Resistance Interminable dependence
Type D: Instrumental	Information about task	Productivity Creativity	Competence Output	Inadequate Low output

FIG. 1. MULTIPLE CRITERIA FRAMEWORK FOR EVALUATING INTERPERSONAL RELATIONSHIPS.

types, particularly Type C, change relationships. In any case, we have never seen a purely "confirmatory" relationship. So we are not dealing with mutually exclusive types, but with overlapping categories with multiple functions. Despite this qualification, we do want to stress for analytical purposes that every relationship is formed—indeed, is caused—in order to realize one primary function.

Now we are in a better position to answer the question raised earlier on: what is a good relationship? Let us now turn to Figure 1. This diagram shows the four types of relationships ordered down the vertical axis. In column (1) we have listed the content of the interpersonal transactions. In column (2) we have listed the various criteria for a good relationship. This is based on our main assertion, only implied until now, that a relationship is considered good to the extent that it fulfills its primary function. Thus, to determine whether a Type A relationship is good, we have to estimate if it is mutually *satisfying* to the participants; that is: do they have the desired relationship? For Type B there are two kinds of criteria depending on whether or not the exchange concerns the establishing of an interpersonal or self reality or whether or not the relationship was used to apprehend external reality. If (1), then we observe confirmation, some agreement about the relationship. If (2), then we observe consensus, some agreement about the definition of the situation. For Type C the desired change is the main criterion; for Type D, productivity (or creativity) is the key. *Satisfaction, confirmation* (and *consensus*), *desired change,* and *productivity* are the terms which can be applied to the goodness of a relationship, depending upon its unique function.

2. Outcomes of Good and Bad Relationships

If the primary function of a relationship is fulfilled—what we have been calling a *good* relationship—we can expect a positive outcome; if not, then a negative one. What are the outcomes of good and bad relationships? Columns (3) and (4) list these.

A. For Type A, solidarity is the indicator of a good relationship, and *ambivalence, alienation,* or *chronic hostility* are the indicators of a bad relationship. Let us say a word or two more about "solidarity," a term which has had the recent misfortune of connoting "togetherness." What we have in mind is closer to Murray's Dionysian couple:

. . . engaged now and again in unpremeditated, serious yet playful, dramatic outbursts of feeling, wild imagination, and vehement interaction, in which one of them—sometimes Adam, sometimes Eve—gave vent to whatever was pressing for expression. Walpurgis was the name they gave to episodes of this insurgent nature . . . each of the two psyches, through numberless repetitions, discharged its residual as well as emergent and beneficient dispositions, until nearly every form of sexuality and nearly every possible complementation of dyadic roles had been dramatically enacted . . . and all within the compass of an ever mounting trust in the solidarity of their love, evidenced in the Walpurgis episodes by an apparently limitless mutual tolerance of novelty and emotional extravagance.[5]

In our view, then, solidarity encompasses a wide range of complex emotions as well as the capacity for the individuals to risk the confrontation of their emotional vicissitudes; at the same time they must remain together despite and because of their own anxieties and appetites.

B. It might be useful to state with greater clarity than before the two classes of relationships we are grouping in Type B. Both have to do with comprehending reality, one an *interpersonal* reality that develops from the interactions between the participants and serves to define the boundaries of self-hood and of the interpersonal relationship. The "self" is born in the communicative acts and, according to this symbolic-interactionist position, "we begin to see each other as others see us" and begin to "take the role of the other." Thus, the formation, definition, and evaluation of the self emerge from the successive interactions we have with significant others.[6]

The other class of Type B has to do with apprehending some element in the environment, an item "x," let us say, for which we require interpersonal support in order to "understand" it. This is identical to Festinger's idea concerning the attainment of "social reality."[7] He asserts that opinions, attitudes, and beliefs—as differentiated from physical realities, which could be proved or disproved by physical means—need anchorage in a socially valued group. Thus, one powerful motive for people to come together in interpersonal relationships is to "make sense," to order, to develop cognitive mastery over the outside world. As Festinger says: "An opinion, a belief, an attitude is correct, valid, and proper to the extent that it is anchored in a group of people with similar beliefs, opinions, and attitudes."[8]

---

[5]H. A. Murray, "Vicissitudes of Creativity," in H. H. Anderson (ed.), *Creativity and Its Cultivation,* Interdisciplinary Symposia on Creativity, Michigan State University, 1957–58 (New York: Harper & Bros., 1959), pp. 110–18.

[6]For a recent discussion stemming from this tradition of Mead and Cooley see H. D. Duncan, *Communication and Social Order* (New York: Bedminister Press, 1962).

[7]L. Festinger, "Informal Social Communication," *Psychological Review,* Vol. 57 (1950), pp. 271–82.

[8]*Ibid.,* p. 273.

To this extent we are all "conformists;" that is, all of us need interpersonal evidence to attain cognitive control over our environments.

Let us come back now to the possible outcomes of good and bad Type B relationships. If we consider the interpersonal class, (1), then in a good relationship, an integrated "personal identity" or self-actualization and self-enhancement would emerge as well as a realistic relationship; in the external (2) case, cognitive mastery over some salient aspect of the environment would emerge. In either case *the outcomes of goodness in Type B is the consensus and confirmation regarding the perception of reality.*

This increased perception of reality that comes about through consensus or confirmation—regardless of its *validity*—has a tremendous liberating effect leading to a self-expansiveness and self-acceptance in (1) and a high degree of morale and confidence in (2).

A bad Type B (1) would consist of chronic refutation and dissonance and therefore probably not last. Farber[9] writes movingly of his experience with a patient who refused to confirm him (Farber)—by simply not getting "well;" that is, by not acting like a patient should. We have all experienced and witnessed situations like this where a group or person has denied self or role confirmation to another, consciously or not: students who won't learn, children who won't obey, audiences who won't approve, followers who won't be influenced, and friends who won't share or confirm our delusions about self, and in fact, stubbornly transmit cues counter to our own self-image.[10]

A bad Type B (2) exists when the parties to a relationship cannot agree on or make sense about external realities. It is most graphically described in the works of Kafka where even the reader gets fooled into thinking that the Kafkaesque world *is* more eerie and ambiguous than "real life." The fact of the matter is that the *world* is no more or less complicated but *people* cannot arrive at any agreement about it. So it is a world without "norms," without clear-cut references—evolved out of a shared frame of reference—necessary to establish consensus about "reality." The ability to predict future events, the need to reduce uncertainty—all these matters we call

[9] L. Farber, "Therapeutic Despair," *Psychiatry*, Vol. 21 (Feb., 1958), pp. 7–20.

[10] Recently, some evidence has been gathered which shows the effects of role confirmation and refutation on a group of nurses. (J. E. Berkowitz and N. H. Berkowitz, "Nursing Education and Role Conception," *Nursing Research*, Vol. 9 [1960], "briefs".) It was felt that the patients who responded to treatment were confirming the nurses' role and those patients who did not respond to treatment were refuting the nurses' role. The hypothesis, supported by the data, was: patients who were disconfirmers would not be liked or treated as well by the nursing staff as those patients who were role-confirmers.

"cognitive mastery"—are essential for man's security. It is one of the main reasons (and costs) for interpersonal relationships, for without it, relationships devolve into *anomie*, a disoriented, ambiguous, uncertain world.

There is a special case of a bad outcome for a Type B that bears some attention. Imagine a situation where two or more people come together and confirm their own relationship but seriously distort some aspect of "social reality." Let us take an example from literature. In Thomas Mann's story, "The Blood of the Walsungs,"[11] the twin brother and sister seriously misperceive (but agree on) the outside world and withdraw further and further into the nest of their own distortions. The fact that they hold a unique and different view from most people tends to further intensify their alienation, for the only support they can find is restricted. This form of social withdrawal has been observed, for example, among apocalyptic messianic groups.[12]

This distortion of and rejection by the outside world—always linked with libidinal contraction and intensification—leads to a state of affairs Slater calls "social regression."[13]

The tandem alcoholism of the married couple in the movie, "Days of Wine and Roses," as well as the bizarre and autistic games played by George and Martha in Albee's play, *Who's Afraid of Virginia Woolf?*[14] are both good examples of this phenomenon. Sometimes this type of relationship resembles "solidarity," like the Walpurgis experiences reported above, but they are always different by nature. "Social regression" flourishes only in a social vacuum and when there is a powerful motive to distort external reality. Solidarity can last only if there is some realistic connection with the outside world.

C. A Type C relationship is defined by its pivotal concern with the acquisition or modification of behavior or attiudes, as imparted by a change-agent (A) to some change target (B). It is true that changes occur in the other types of relationship discussed, but only spontaneously and adventitiously. Type C encompasses primarily the class of change-inductions that are planned; for example, it

---

[11]T. Mann, *Stories of Three Decades* (New York: Knopf, 1936), pp. 279–319.

[12]L. Festinger, H. W. Riecken, Jr., and S. Schachter, *When Prophecy Fails* (Minneapolis: University of Minnesota, 1956); also J. A. Hardyck and M. Braden, "Prophecy Fails Again: A Report of a Failure to Replicate," *J. of Abn. Soc. Psychol.*, Vol. 65 (1962), pp. 136–41.

[13]P. Slater, "On Social Regression," *American Soc. Review*, Vol. 28 (1963), pp. 339–64.

[14]E. Albee, *Who's Afraid of Virginia Woolf?* (New York: Atheneum, 1963).

would include primarily relationships resulting in changes due to formal course work (teacher-student or work partner in "lab"), and only incidentally the informal or unplanned kinds of relationships such as those which occur in "bull-session" groups. Type C covers a wide range of relationships, from parent-child to psychiatrist-patient, from coach-pupil to warden-inmate.[15]

In addition to this emphasis on change, growth, and learning, an analysis of Type C further reveals two unique characteristics. First, these relationships are almost always oriented toward termination (graduation, parole, or death). An "interminable" psychoanalysis is considered deplorable, while an "interminable" marriage is considered honorable. Secondly, Type C reveals a special kind of relationship between the change-agent (A) and the target (B) which we refer to as "tilted." In other words we expect A to influence B, to "give to" B, to teach B more—than the other way around. As a rule students learn from teachers, patients from psychiatrists, pupils from coaches.[16] Thus the interpersonal exchange is slanted and less reciprocal, by definition, than other types. With these preliminary considerations out of the way, let us turn to the indicators of a good and bad Type C relationship.

A good Type C leads to three distinct, but related, outcomes. First, there is consensus between A and B that the desired growth or change or influence has been attained. Second, the relationship has reached a state wherein its continuation, while possibly helpful, will not lead to significant advances. It must end. Third, the client must have internalized the learning process, such that the process of learning begun in the relationship can continue. Thus *growth, termination,* and *internalization* are the indicators of a good Type C relationship.

The reverse of these criteria serve to signify badness. Dissatisfaction with B's rate of progress on the part of either A or B is a common indicator. The frequently heard remark: "I must change my teacher-therapist-coach-trainer; we're not getting anywhere" is an example. Second, the relationship cannot be extended indefinitely.

---

[15]The reader is referred back to the essay introducing Part III where change relationships are treated in detail.

[16]We have omitted those exceptional, but highly interesting, cases where B can influence A more than A can influence B. More often than not, these are perverse, given our definition of Type C. Teachers may indeed learn from students, but this is different from exploitation and "stealing ideas." Analysts may "use" counter-transference productively for the patient's ultimate health, but this is different from cashing in on stock tips or sexual exploitation. See Cheever (p. 461, this volume) for a literary treatment of an interesting exception to the rule.

That is, there must be some point at which the hoped-for changes will occur. Without this explicit termination point, both A and B can possibly get trapped in a false dream where the original and primary purpose of the relationship gets sidetracked.[17] Third, the target must be able to use what he has learned in an autonomous fashion; that is, without undue dependence on the change-agent. Patients who are forever returning to their therapists are not "cured"; acting students who suffer immobilizing stage fright unless their coach is watching from the wings are not "trained." We do not mean to imply that in a good Type C relationship the client has nothing more to learn and never returns for further training; we do mean that the client is relatively free of dependence and has learned how to continue the process on his own.

D. Instrumental relationships, Type D, are formed in order to produce or create: a song, an idea, a car, a formula, a dress. It encompasses the range of relationships involved in those activities which function in order to produce a "good or service."[18] It is ordinarily what people "do for a living"; it is certainly what most people do to earn enough for other types of relationships. As the need for interdependence and collaboration increases—that is to say: as specialization increases—this form of relationship will grow in importance and will call for more searching examination. It may be already the most ubiquitous form of interpersonal relationship in an industrialized society such as ours.

These are two main indicators of a good instrumental relationship; *competence* and *output.* The latter is objectively measured, usually in the form of a productivity rate: stories sold *per* year, pages typed *per* day, articles published *per* year, bolts attached *per* minute, profits earned *per* quarter, etc. Because of the relative ease of

---

[17]What often happens in these cases is that both partners in the relationship shift consciously or unconsciously to another type of relationship; the ski-instructor who marries his student, for example, is a switch from C to A. We will return to this point later.

[18]Unaccounted for here are those instrumental relationships we associate with the service industries, such as some customer-salesman relationships, cabbie-passenger, receptionist-customer. We have ignored this class of relationships for two reasons. First because this type of relationship rarely involves more than a brief encounter in a transient setting. Second because there is a peculiar lack of reciprocity. The waitress is instrumentally involved with the diner, but he is not involved instrumentally with her—and typically he has only a "service" relationship to her. This is a difficult class of problems for our analytic scheme to handle. Temporary relationships, such as games, vacation trips, etc., are examined brilliantly in a recent essay by M. Miles, "On Temporary Systems," manuscript (New York: Columbia University, 1963); see also A. R. Anderson and O. K. Moore, *Autotelic Folk-Models* (New Haven: Sociology Department, Yale University, 1959).

measuring output, instrumental relationships are often easier to judge as good or bad.

Less objective than output, but equally important from our point of view, is the way participants engaged in an instrumental relationship manage their work. Decision making, problem solving, co-ordination, quality of collaboration, energy expenditure: these are some of the elements in the complex factor we refer to as *competence*.[19]

A bad instrumental relationship exists, then, if either competence or output is unsatisfactory relative to certain norms. One would expect that these two factors would be positively correlated, but there is inadequate evidence to make this assertion.[20]

3. Aberrations, Anomalies, and Confusions in Interpersonal Relationships

Before going on to section two of this essay, where we will discuss the personal and environmental conditions for attaining good interpersonal relations, it might be useful to pause briefly to pursue some suggestive leads which the foregoing analysis provides. These have to do with those relationships which seem "special" or irregular, relationships which capture the imagination, which attract the public eye, which fascinate.[21] Often they are puffed-up beyond all recognition by the popular press; at times they seem bizarre and/or perverse. In any case, they seem to be the stuff of romance, tragedy, farce and dreams—of fiction and plays rather than "real life." In fact, we will suggest that they represent a class of problems, latent in all interpersonal relationships: *problems arising out of (a) transformations, (b) conflicts and ambiguities, and (c) deceit regarding the goal of the relationship.* Our multiple criteria framework

---

[19]Time and space considerations do not allow for a complete discussion of these issues. They go far beyond the purposes of this essay. The so-called "criterion problem" has perplexed industrial psychologists and students of organizational behavior for some time and we do not aim to settle any issues with this inadequate discussion. For a fuller statement, see W. G. Bennis "Towards a 'Truly' Scientific Management: The Concept of Organization Health," *General Systems Yearbook* (Ann Arbor: Mental Health Research Institute, 1962).

[20]C. Argyris, *Interpersonal Competence and Organizational Effectiveness* (Homewood, Ill.: Irwin-Dorsey Press, 1962); R. Likert, *New Patterns of Management* (New York: McGraw-Hill Book Co., Inc., 1961).

[21]Again, we are constrained by our lack of concepts for a relationship. We can talk of a charismatic person; how about a charismatic "interperson"? or bizarre "interperson"? Don't married couples and types of relationships have "character" at least as much as a person does? Don't couples have a "presentation of a unit" as much as an individual has a "presentation of self"? A primitive start on such a language was made by Shepard and Bennis ("A Theory of Training by Group Methods," *Human Relations,* Vol. 9 [1956], pp. 403–44). Much more needs to be done.

(Figure 1) can provide the necessary analytic framework for this analysis.

a) Collusive Transformations.   In the musical comedy, "How to Succeed in Business without Really Trying," a chorus of secretaries cry out in shock and anger at one of their number who, on the verge of marrying her boss, decides to break the engagement. Their disappointment, and the audience's, is clear: the girl is about to destroy their constant dream, a cherished image they all hold and which partly keeps them at work. This fascination for secretaries who marry bosses, teachers who marry students, actresses who marry their leading men, analysts who marry their patients, we usually think of as "romantic" or morbid, depending on our orientation. In fact, it represents a joint decision—not necessarily conscious— where a relationship shifts from one modality to another. We call this "collusive transformation."

One of the most interesting examples of this can be seen in Shaw's "Pygmalion." Henry Higgins and Eliza Doolittle enter into a Type C relationship in order to alter her manners and "character," but end up with an incipient Type A relationship. Every bit of drama and comedy is derived from this shift: whether or not Eliza will return to Higgins, how Colonel Pickering, Mr. Doolittle, and Higgins' mother perceive the relationship,[22] how the Type A emphasis becomes more pivotal without awareness on the part of Eliza or Higgins, etc. Another interesting example of the same shift (Type C to Type A) can be seen in the Rodgers and Hammerstein musical, "The King and I." The tension and drama of the play evolved from a collusive shift from a change (Type C) to an expressive-emotional (Type A) relationship. Romance, according to our analysis, can always be reduced to a collusive transformation, shifting from any type, to Type A.

An interesting example of another style of collusive transformation (Type A to B) can be seen in the play and movie, "Tea and Sympathy." A friendly relationship develops between the wife of an instructor and his student. The student becomes increasingly morose concerning doubts about his masculinity. The wife of the instructor, toward the end of the drama, decides to shift her relationship with the boy in order to *confirm* his manhood. The play ends as she removes her blouse in preparation for the rites of passage.

Other styles of collusive transformations can be observed, though

---

[22]For a discussion of class or hierarchy as a determining feature in interpersonal relationships, see Duncan, *op. cit.*

possibly with less frequency than the shift to Type A. A Type A to any other type is perhaps the rarest, though Danny Kaye and Sylvia Fine, his ex-wife, still collaborate on his musical numbers (going from A to D).

b) Conflict or Unclarity. There is a class of relationships which can end only in one of two ways, depending upon one's orientation: if one is observing, then absurdity; if one is participating, then despair. It must end because the relationship is construed and entered into for different reasons. Turgenev's "A Month in the Country," provides an example. A young tutor falls madly in love with the mother of his charges—because she is a "lady." She in turn loves him because his love rejuvenates her. To the audience this is the absurd love of age and youth.

A more striking example comes from the recent novella, *One Hundred Dollar Misunderstanding.*[23] A young college boy—middle-class and pompous—propositions and goes to bed with a fourteen year-old Negro prostitute. He refuses to pay her her one hundred dollar fee because he naïvely thinks she went to bed with him because she "found him attractive." The entire book is based on this misperception of the relationship.

One other case, also from recent fiction, comes from James Baldwin's *Another Country.*[24] A young man enters into a relationship with a married woman in order to asert or confront his masculinity (Type B), she gets involved for love (Type A). The relationship was constructed on conflicting purposes and shortly dissolved. Baldwin writes: "But it was only love which could accomplish the miracle of making a life bearable—only love, and love itself mostly failed; and he had never loved her. He had used her to find out something about himself. And even this was not true. He had used her in the hope of avoiding a confrontation with himself. . . ."[25]

c) Deceit. The Negro prostitute in the example above was not dissembling; she was not "conning" the boy like a B-girl at the bar of some café who insinuates unimaginable sexual adventures awaiting the "unsuspecting" victim if he only continues to buy her more *ersatz* whiskey. The girl made it perfectly clear to the boy that she was a "pro" and that she was interested in him only as a client.[26]

---

[23]R. Gover, *One Hundred Dollar Misunderstanding* (New York: Grove Press, 1961).

[24]J. Baldwin, *Another Country* (New York: Dell, 1963).

[25]*Ibid.,* p. 340.

[26]It's difficult to know who's dissembling to whom in such cases, and for what reasons. It's perfectly obvious, in most situations, that these B-girls are using sex as

(Continued on next page)

660   INTERPERSONAL DYNAMICS

But in the case of the B-girl or the con-man or in any relationship of an exploitative kind, the relationship is jointly and publicly formed for one reason, but privately formed for another reason by one of the parties to the relationship: the teacher who makes "friends" with the ninth grade girl because she was told that the youngster is a "problem"; the opportunistic starlet who manages to "fall in love" with every director; the young executive who marries the boss's daughter for power; the psychologist who asks the college sophomore to do some work but in fact is using him as an experimental subject; and so on. All of these are basically exploitative, the basis of the "con-game."

If we sharpen our focus on the exploitative relationship, we will be able to make some interesting distinctions. As we conceive it, this relationship is always characterized by its *double meaning* to one, and only one, participant. So we are not talking about *joint mystification* where both parties enter into it for a professed reason, while each conceals a more basic, identical one. Comedy movies of the 1930's were made of this stuff: Girl meets Boy in fancy hotel on the Riviera; each pretends gigantic wealth and amorous interest in the other; each intends to use the other instrumentally. The movies usually end, after successively hilarious misunderstandings, in a collusive (and explosive) transformation to Type A.

We are not talking about *unconscious exploitation,* either of a collusive nature where both parties are involved in it or where only one participant is unconsciously involved. The boss's daughter marries the young executive because she unconsciously wants her father replaced; the man marries the daughter because he also unconsciously wants the father replaced. They are "in love," but under false pretenses; i.e., unconsciously for other reasons.

Finally, exploitative relationships must be distinguished from *conscious collusion,* wherein A and B come together for a professed type of relationship which both know to be other than their real

---

a come-on, as an inducement. It is perfectly obvious to the reader in *One Hundred Dollar Misunderstanding* that the girl is a prostitute. It is hard to believe that the "mark" is oblivious to these cues or that he is unconscious of them. Most likely, he simply doesn't tell himself what is really going on because this doesn't conform to his self-image, at least his *ideal* self-image. It's a bit like cheating at solitaire; one knows one is acting not altogether "proper" but at the same time, one doesn't have to admit it fully. We discussed this in reference to self-rating inventories or personality tests in the essay introducing Part I. The point is worth stating again. Most people don't cheat on tests and they rarely "try" even if they know they are the only ones who will see the results. But they do play "against themselves," that is dissemble slightly—not fully—in order to "come out the way you want to."

purpose. A middle-aged woman goes to a dance-instructor for the expressed purpose of learning new dance steps. In fact, the woman knows she continues her lessons for other reasons, of an expressive-emotional kind, while he continues to see her for instrumental, not change, reasons. They both know that the other knows his or her reasons for their relationship. Thus, it continues, each of them satisfying a different pivotal goal than the other.

There are other classes of irregularities and anomalies which our approach cannot account for and others that it can. We hope we have demonstrated, however, that if we focus attention on the primary function of a relationship and relate this to transformation, clarity, conflict, and deceit, it is possible to illuminate some relationships which we ordinarily consider bizarre or perverse, or at least, "irregular."

Before turning to section two, let us summarize our approach and propose some conclusions. Our approach to the normative issues —of good and bad—is a *functional* one. If a relationship satisfies its functions, then it is good; if not, then it is bad. Inasmuch as there are *four* primary functions for relationships, our approach has been based on *multiple criteria*. Evidence is adduced for goodness (or health) by certain outcomes presented in Figure 1. Irregularities and anomalies can be derived by analyzing confusions, transformations, conflicts, and deceit with regard to primary functions.

The final point we want to make, by way of conclusion, has to do with the outcomes of goodness we presented in Figure 1: solidarity, confirmation and reality, growth, and competence. They cannot be, nor should they be, restricted so neatly to their "own" type of relationship as portrayed. An instrumental relationship, devoid of change or solidarity, would be arid. A change relationship, devoid of competence or confirmation, would become stagnant. And so on. *All* of the outcomes must be involved, to some degree, in all relationships.

Figure 2 reveals the substance of the remainder of the essay. We start from the assumption that the fabric of our social environment and the personal competencies of the individuals involved determine the success of the interpersonal relationship. We hope to articulate these conditions in the most general way so that they encompass *any social milieu* where interpersonal dynamics occur.

All relationships exist in some social context—a group, an organization, a community, an institution. Whatever we call it—environment or society—it provides a texture within which our relationships are embedded and by which they are governed. To some degree the goodness and badness of interpersonal relationships are dependent on the conditions of the social setting. In any case, relationships do not exist in a vacuum. We intend now to explore the *social conditions* upon which our relationships are based. In Section B we shall examine the personal conditions that determine the quality of relationships.

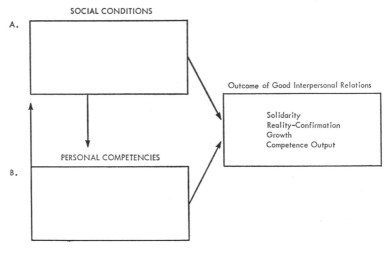

FIG. 2.

A. The Social Conditions

Our vision of a "social architecture" conducive to forming and maintaining good interpersonal relationships consists of three sets of "blueprints." One set has to do with (1) "system-characteristics," the social processes which govern behavior. The others are (2) values and (3) goals.

II. SOCIAL AND PERSONAL CONDITIONS OF GOOD INTERPERSONAL RELATIONS

1. *System Characteristics.* A system is simply a set of mutually dependent elements or parts in interaction. We propose that good interpersonal relationships can only occur in certain kinds of systems, specifically ones which have the following characteristics:

a) The System Should Be "Open." G. Allport has pieced together four criteria of open systems:

(1) There is intake and output of both matter and energy. (2) There is the achievement and maintenance of steady (homeostatic) states, so that the

intrusion of outer energy will not seriously disrupt internal form and order. (3) There is generally an increase of order over time, owing to an increase in complexity of and differentiation of parts. (4) Finally, at least at the human level, there is more than mere intake and output of matter and energy; *there is extensive transactional commerce with the environment.*[27]

The importance of the open system for us is its emphasis on the transactions between system and environment. A closed system, on the other hand, is defined as one which is isolated and self-contained: "Like a decaying bridge," Allport says, "it sinks into thermodynamic decay."[28]

Because an open system negotiates, merges, connects with its environments it contains a number of unique potentialities. Because it confronts unexpected stimuli, it can learn from external inputs; this allows for varied inputs and experiences, incongruities and surprises. These exogenous infusions, as well as providing productive energy and inputs, also work to challenge the system. If the system can "adapt" and cope with these external stresses, it can continually develop new patterns, possibilities and shapes—like a kaleidoscope with an infinite variety of designs. But these environmental transactions may also create insurmountable problems to the open system. New inputs may occur, for example, which are ignored by the system or inadequately managed. If the system fails to adjust to the environment it loses its integrity or it collapses and decays.[29]

The cost of closed and open systems should be clear. In one case, we have a system which *contacts* the environment. In the closed system case, there is practically no contact. Thus the closed system is adjustive, preservative, programed, but insulative. We are opting for the strains of the open system: adaptive, restorative, unprogramed, permeable, but stressful.

b) The Influence Structure Should Be Balanced and Characterized by Interdependence. When we talk of influence we shall be less abstract than we were in our discussion of an open system; for influence encompasses the ways in which people exert power and express subordination. In social systems this governs an important

---

[27]G. Allport, *Personality and Social Encounter* (Boston: Beacon Press, 1960), p. 43. Emphasis added.

[28]*Ibid.*, p. 42.

[29]There are many ways for an open system to regress or decay: through complacency, poor reality-testing, and internal strains which reduce external commerce. The "causal texture of the environment" is another crucial variable which F. E. Emery and E. L. Trist ("The Causal Texture of Organizational Environments," paper presented at the International Congress of Psychology, Washington, D.C., 1963) have recently analyzed.

part of the interactions. People are made to do things by fiat, order, and command; or by fear, intimidation, and coercion; or by persuasion, reward, and attraction. And people respond to these forces by surrender, rebellion, "apeing," consent, agreement, consensus, avoiding, denying, dissembling, complying, and obeying. Whatever system we observe, there is some structure of influence.

One of the main problems in most influence structures is *hierarchy:* a formal or informal arrangement whereby some person—a boss, teacher, a policeman—tells other people what to do. When the subordinates do what they are told and do it well, they are rewarded; when they do not do it or do it poorly, the rewards are withheld or punishment is applied. Our world view is partly based on this simple Law of Effect.[30] Party leaders, managers, teachers, parents, dictators, ministers all employ it.

Influence of this simple reward-and-punishment type is ubiquitous, tending more often than not to be dysfunctional. For example, one of its problems is that subordinates spend an awesome amount of time in an attempt to divine what they think the influencing agent, the authority, wants. Whether or not the subordinates guess correctly and act appropriately is problematical; what is not problematical is the fruitless complexity of the search. As one of our M.I.T. students put it recently: "We seem to spend about 75 per cent of our time solving the professor, and 25 per cent, the problem."[31]

Another problem with the traditional form of influence has to do with the assumptions bosses hold about subordinates. If one assumes that people are lazy, dumb, dishonest, passive, and simple hedonists —as the more traditional theories of hierarchial influence imply— then directive and coercive controls are probably necessary. Of course, the coercive controls produce the very behavior they assume, and thus we have a classic example of a self-fulfilling prophecy. An additional irony is that even people who are inadequate, passive, and inert rarely respond positively to unilateral subordination.

---

[30]The Law of Effect can be summarized by saying that people tend to repeat behaviors which are rewarded and stop behaviors which are punished: "Spare the rod and spoil the child."

[31]The reader must be warned of our oversimplified discussion of this issue. We are compressing, but not, we hope, distorting the problem. Some of these issues are treated in more detail in the essay introducing Part III of this volume. For a thorough treatment, see W. G. Bennis, "Leadership Theory and Administrative Behavior: The Problem of Authority," *Administrative Science Quarterly,* Vol. 4 (1959), pp. 259–301; and D. McGregor, *The Human Side of Enterprise* (New York: McGraw-Hill Book Co., Inc., 1960).

A number of behavioral scientists have been concerned with influence structures in a variety of settings: classroom, work place, research lab, family, office. Their recommendations are phrased in different ways but all point towards a more balanced and interdependent influence structure; from "informational-interdependent"[32] to "internalization";[33] from "Theory Y"[34] to "autotelic folk-models."[35] But the moral and practical impact is the same: influence is appropriate to the degree (1) that there is a collaborative—not authoritarian—relationship; (2) that people act on "credible" information; and (3) that self-determination plays a crucial role in the influence structure.

These three factors define what we mean by *interdependence*. The concept can be further elaborated and summarized this way: Influence, of an interdependent type, involves a joint effort toward reaching some mutually determined goal which requires complementary skills and information. This collaborative interaction evolves from the press of task demands and personnel resources, not from formal status, personal tyranny, or bureaucratic code. Interdependence involves an integration between authority and the subordinate —not freedom from either. Freedom and autonomy are limited only by credible information, task requirements, and self-impositions. Restrictions to freedom are certainly never due to extrinsic rewards in the social system we are envisaging, but only to internal rationalizations. Finally, interdependence does not imply "permissiveness" or "protectiveness"; such terms indicate only the shallow indulgencies of a pseudodemocratic system.

c) Decisions Should Be Made by Consensus. We can distinguish influence from decision making in an arbitrary fashion. The former was defined exclusively in terms of hierarchy, the power dimension. Decision making, on the other hand, encompasses two sets of activities: (1) procedures for conflict resolution and (2) procedures for choosing and evaluating alternatives. The criterion for these two activities can be briefly summarized as the *principle of consensus.*

Consensus is a *portmanteau* term which tends to mean all things to all people. To the "true-believer" consensus is democracy, if not truth. To the skeptic, it is an uninformed majority and a cowed

[32]O. J. Harvey, D. E. Hunt, and H. M. Schroder, *Conceptual Systems and Personality Organization* (New York: Wiley, 1961).

[33]H. C. Kelman, "Compliance, Identification, and Internalization; Three Processes of Attitude Change," *Journal of Conflict Resolution,* Vol. 2 (1958), pp. 51–60.

[34]McGregor, *op. cit.*

[35]Anderson and Moore, *op. cit.*

minority. To the innocent, it is a "unanimous vote." The problem is not only a conceptual one, though consensus *is* a protean and elastic idea. The fact is that it also bootlegs in an emotional and moral cargo, difficult to untangle from conceptual fuzziness.[36]

To us, consensus is a procedure for deciding among alternatives in interpersonal (or group) situations. This procedure must fulfill the following conditions: (1) It must include only those items which are salient to the membership and for which the membership has evidenced a distinctive competence. (2) If there is a conflict or difference, it must be resolved by valid and credible data, publicly shared and communicated; differences are never resolved by impersonal orders, rank, or personal vicissitudes. (3) If differences exist, they are always to be faced and dealt with, rather than avoided or denied. (4) There should be as much involvement and participation in the decision making process as salience and competence permits.

These are stringent criteria for consensus and only possible, perhaps, under unique conditions. But they are guidelines and may hold genuine promise.

d) The Communication Structure Should Maximize Clarity. Every system requires some mechanism for transmitting, receiving, and storing information. The ideal communication structure must function to maintain clarity, economy, and relevance. Three conditions should be realized for this: (1) Information must be transmitted in the most unambiguous fashion possible in order to insure cognitive clarity. (2) Information should be transmitted only to the relevant parts of the system. (3) Information must not be filtered or distorted because of status anxieties or threat to the organization.

This last point is probably the most crucial and vexing of the three. How does a system guarantee valid (undistorted) upward communication if the information may displease or contradict the boss or teacher? A story circulating about Samuel Goldwyn takes its humor from this theme. Apparently Goldwyn called his staff together and was reported to have said: "Now, look: I want each and

---

[36]It should be remembered that consensus *is* a moral as well as practical issue. The fact that we favor it morally (and ultimately for pragmatic reasons—under certain conditions) is not related to its empirical validation—which is problematical. There are many conditional qualifiers to be made for the effective operation of consensus or any kind of group decision making. The interested reader should consult Krech, Crutchfield, and Ballachey, *Individual in Society* (New York: McGraw-Hill Book Co., Inc., 1962), Chap. 13.

every one of you to tell me what's wrong with our operation here— even if it means losing your job!"[37]

And how does a system guarantee valid information and feedback from its environment when these threaten the system's existence? Emery and Trist[38] have observed such cases where organizations misperceive or ignore environmental cues. This leads inexorably to an organizational demise, either suicide or annihilation. Surely organizations, like individuals, have ways of distorting reality—or "selective inattention"—for who would dare to forecast doom, death, struggle, or any profound change when it's easier to deny, delay, or distort the truth?

e) The System Must Have Adequate Reality-Testing Mechanisms. These problems cannot be settled satisfactorily by providing only an adequate communication structure, whose main function is clarity and relevance. We need an additional mechanism, some way to guarantee adequate determinations of the internal state of the system as well as the boundaries relevant to the system and what is going on outside the boundaries. In short, every system requires some formal mechanism for establishing "truth" about its internal and external relationships and functioning. Most systems possess mechanisms that are either inadequate and convenient, or adequate and inconvenient. An example of the former is the (useless and illusory) bookkeeping statistics kept by some business firms. The latter can be seen when a system finds itself imperiled, too late to effect a "comeback." Emery and Trist, for example, tell of a case in which a canning company—going ahead in a major expansion— failed to recognize certain trends (frozen foods, Common Market, etc.) and continued to fail to recognize them until it was too late. "The managing director and indeed most of the other senior people were removed."[39]

What is most needed is some formal agency to ascertain and mea-

---

[37] A more serious example of this same phenomenon can be inferred from research by E. P. Torrance, "Some Consequences of Power Differences on Decision Making in Permanent and Temporary Three-Man Groups," *Research Studies, State College of Washington,* Vol. 22 (1954), pp. 130–40. Here we see how subordinates in the military not only censored the communication of the right answer when they had it, but also allowed the authority to answer incorrectly when they, the subordinates, knew the correct answer. What permits a situation to develop where subordinates let superiors make mistakes when they know better and for superiors to assume that they, and never subordinates, have the key to intelligent action?

[38] *Op. cit.*

[39] *Ibid.,* p. 4.

sure the relevant values connected with the system, not only for the present but for the changing future.

Open-system, interdependence, consensus, clarity, and *reality:* these are the idealized set of system characteristics we propose. There is a final one, only implied: that there be a "principle of appropriateness" which essentially determines the validity of the action. For example, it is not at all certain that interdependence and consensus is always appropriate. Some people and some situations, require different styles. Even "clarity" is not *always* desirable; sometimes a boss may have to employ "ambiguity" as a weapon or tool, and so on. We encourage these system-characteristics to be employed, but they should be used appropriately—not with a dogmatic or Utopian vengeance. Let us now turn to the second set of conditions of our social architecture.

2. *Values.* We will define values as those standards or directives upon which we base our decisions and to which we are committed. They are inherent in all systems for they govern to a great extent, the way people interact. They help to shape how "close" people get, how power and influence are enforced, how work gets accomplished, how truth is revealed, and so on. Values permit or preclude certain system characteristics; values stress and understress certain dimensions of institutional life. (If the system characteristics and the value system are discordant, one must be modified or the system will fragment.) Values make possible the "identity" of a system, the possibilities and limitations of its actions. It follows that values are important, not just "academic."[40]

In combing the literature and in examining our own superegos we have arrived at five values that affirm the system characteristics described in the previous section. The first is *openness* in interpersonal expression; to "speak what we feel, not what we ought to say." This openness implies the free expression of observations, feelings, ideas, associations, opinions, evaluations; free expression of thoughts and feelings *without,* however, threatening or limiting others. Obviously, there are precautions and choices which must be taken;[41] openness can be destructive, too. The important thing to register

---

[40]For a penetrating analysis of the role of value in institutions, see P. Selznick, *Leadership in Administration* (Evanston, Ill.: Row Peterson, 1957).

[41]Uninhibited expression of feelings may be as dysfunctional and as phony as the uninhibited suppression of them. There is no easy formula for the right balance. It depends on the legitimacy of feelings, and the personalities, skill, insights of the participants. See the papers by Argyris and Bennis in this part for points of view on this matter.

here, even with these qualifications, is that the system should encourage the expression of feelings, rather than their suppression.

Closely related to openness is the value of *experimentalism,* the willingness to expose new ideas and to translate ideas into action. Experimentalism implies risk taking, uncertainty, "sticking one's neck out," as distinguished from "playing it safe," conservatism, etc.

In order for openness and experimentalism to exist, another value must accompany them. We will call this *threat-reduction,* to signify values which can be characterized by a climate which allows mistakes readily, tolerates failures without retaliation or renunciation, encourages a sense of responsible risk taking without fear.

A number of writers have identified a similar, if not identical, value in discussions of the social conditions for learning or creativity: Rogers' "psychological safety"[42] or Lasswell's "warmly indulgent relation."[43] And Anderson and Moore[44] suggest that a good learning environment must be "cut off" from the more serious aspects of society's activities. They mean that a person should be allowed to make mistakes without dire consequences either to himself or society.

The fourth value we propose for our idealized system is *integration* or fusion between man's emotional needs and the system's rational goals. What is required is the understanding that man is not only head and hands, but also heart. The value system must encourage reciprocation between the emotions of the participants and the intellective press of the environment.[45]

The fifth and final value has to do with what we call a *spirit of inquiry,* or unflinching curiosity to look at the way things are, a boldness with which to look at the processes which govern the behavior of the system. This value provides the security for the preservation of all other values for it insures the continual scrutiny of so-called "givens," and questions the legitimacy of "received notions" and the hallowed, but hobbling, "past." This process of inquiry, turned inside and outside, what we are calling a "spirit of inquiry," provides the impulse for appropriate choices and adaptability.

---

[42]C. Rogers, "Toward a Theory of Creativity," in H. Anderson (ed.), *Creativity and Its Cultivation* (New York: Harper & Bros., 1959), pp. 69–82.

[43]H. Lasswell, "The Social Setting of Creativity," in *ibid.,* pp. 203–21.

[44]*Op. cit.*

[45]C. Argyris (*Personality and Organization* [New York: Harper & Bros., 1957]) and more recently H. Levinson ("Reciprocation: The Relationship between Man and Organization," invited address, American Psychological Association, Division of Industrial Psychology, 1963) have been examining this issue. The reader is referred to their works for a more thorough discussion.

3. *Characteristics of Goal.*   The final consideration in this analysis of the social conditions required for good interpersonal relations is the *goal.* We want to stress only one aspect here. The goal should be *intrinsically* rewarding and should contain its *own sources of motivation.* In other words, the goal should contain enough valence or reward for the individual so that exogenous rewards are unnecessary.[46]

Figure 3 summarizes the social conditions for good interpersonal relations. We should say, before going on, that our remarks on the

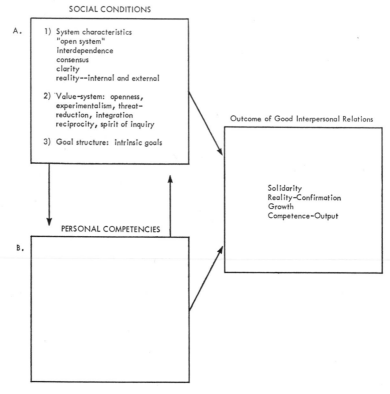

SOCIAL CONDITIONS

A.   1) System characteristics
     "open system"
     interdependence
     consensus
     clarity
     reality--internal and external

     2) Value-system: openness,
     experimentalism, threat-
     reduction, integration
     reciprocity, spirit of inquiry

     3) Goal structure: intrinsic goals

Outcome of Good Interpersonal Relations

Solidarity
Reality-Confirmation
Growth
Competence-Output

PERSONAL COMPETENCIES

B.

FIG. 3.

social architecture deserve more elaboration and qualification than we provide. Whatever unqualified exaggerations still exist can be blamed on the very nature of social Utopias.

B. The Personal Competencies

Assume that we are dealing with a population of mature adults reasonably motivated for interaction. What are the competencies

---

[46]McGregor, *op. cit.*

(or capacities) that would lead to good interpersonal relationships? We are biased toward those capacities that tend to deepen and widen the *emotional interchange* as well as *increase understanding:*

1. *Capacity to Receive and Send Information and Feelings Reliably.* This not only includes the ability to *listen* and *perceive* accurately and fully, but other qualities as well. For example, it includes *sensitivity,* meaning a lowered threshold or heightened alertness to salient interpersonal events; that is, an active and creative awareness, not simply a passive absorption.

2. *Capacity to Evoke the Expression of Feelings.* Most anybody can listen passively to someone; the kind of listening that makes a difference is where the other is unafraid to express a thought, a belief, a feeling ordinarily reserved for autistic reveries or denied to the self. Just as we *maintain* a certain threshold to human experience, we also communicate our threshold, and quite often "stop" or inhibit the other.[47]

3. *Capacity to Process Information and Feelings Reliably and Creatively.* This means that we can conceptualize and order our interpersonal experience, that we can abstract and play with various combinations of interpersonal exchanges and arrive at some diagnosis. Points one and two have to do with *sensitivity;* this point has to do with adequate *diagnosis.*

4. *Capacity to Implement a Course of Action.* A diagnosis may indicate a certain behavior; say the girl really requires more dominance or the boy needs to be included more but doesn't know how to ask for it. What is required are *action*-skills. Diagnostic sensitivity without remedial action may be no more disastrous than action without diagnosis, but it is often sadder. *Behavioral flexibility* plus diagnostic sensitivity raises the prospects for better interpersonal relations.

5. *Capacity to Learn in Each of the Above Areas.* It is far easier to talk of the *blocks* to learning—and "learning how to learn" in the interpersonal area—than to suggest some positive steps. Nevertheless, let us try. First, the individual must attempt to develop an attitude of "observant participation"; that is, a frame of mind that permits and encourages a constant analysis and interpretation of his interpersonal experiences. People simply do not learn from experience alone; it is experience observed, processed, analyzed, inter-

---

[47]An unexplored, but important, area for research is the role of the *listener* in interpersonal relations. There are "charismatic listeners" and "dull listeners"; there are listeners who evoke deep, meaningful human encounters and others who foreclose them. Why? We should know more about this.

preted, and verified that we learn from. This constant scrutiny of one's own and other's behavior causes some stiltedness at first[48] and may interfere with spontaneity, but gaining any new skill causes this initial uneasiness.

This constant review and reflection is difficult, for it asks the individual to consider data that may be not only "new" (i.e., unnoticed until now) but also contradictory to the way the person ordinarily likes to see himself. Socrates once said that "the unexamined life isn't worth living." Modern psychiatry would tell him that the examined life is no fun either.

In any case, learning is simply not possible without continual surveillance and appraisal. And this examination is not possible without the possibility of gaining validating (or disconfirming) data from one's personal environment.

How these capacities are developed; how individuals learn "empathy," or learn to "identify" or learn to listen and perceive more realistically; how individuals learn to make connections, to induce trust, to permit other people to understand them and vice-versa, to develop an observant-participating orientation; how human beings can become more sensitive: these are all questions that deserve better answers than we now have.

We are, almost all of us, equally in the dark on this issue. And society seems reluctant to consider or provide viable methods for satisfying the enormous curiosity about, and the will to enhance, interpersonal relations. Two roads, only, seem available. We have the "how-to-do" approach symbolized by the Sunday rotogravure personality test; on the other hand, we have a long-term bout with psychotherapy, where the person is defined as "ill."

Please do not misunderstand. Psychoanalysis is irreplaceable as a healing force in our society; even "do-it-yourself" personality tests may help to engender curiosity. But certainly a society such as ours which is placing increasing emphasis on interpersonal skills and knowledge requires more institutional avenues for fulfillment than these.[49]

---

[48]Exposure to almost anyone undergoing the early days of psychoanalysis or a human relations training laboratory, such as those conducted by the National Training Laboratory, is sufficient indication of a spastic, "overserious," rather mannered self-examination. To the outsider it is Theater of the Absurd. The insider sympathizes with what the outsider is missing.

[49]The National Training Laboratory in this country and Tavistock Institute in England have developed the methodology of "human relations training" to a genuinely professional level. We feel this is an encouraging sign and will be a development that will increase its momentum in and import on our society. We still await,

This book, alas, also fails to do more than scratch the surface. Learning about interpersonal relations by *reading* about them is almost a contradiction in terms. One learns by doing and examining. But even that last sentence is hollow for this is hard work.

Figure 4 represents the summary of our essay. It was our intention to derive a set of criteria to represent good interpersonal relations and to speculate on the social conditions and personal competencies which lead in that direction.

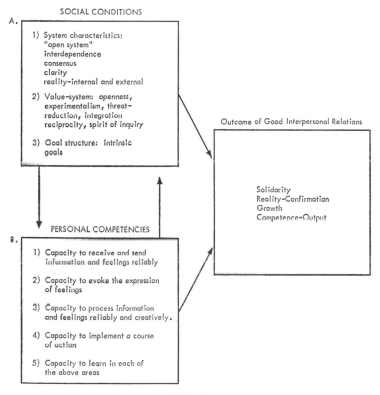

SOCIAL CONDITIONS

A.

1) System characteristics:
"open system"
interdependence
consensus
clarity
reality-internal and external

2) Value-system: openness, experimentalism, threat-reduction, integration reciprocity, spirit of inquiry

3) Goal structure: intrinsic goals

Outcome of Good Interpersonal Relations

Solidarity
Reality-Confirmation
Growth
Competence-Output

PERSONAL COMPETENCIES

B.

1) Capacity to receive and send information and feelings reliably

2) Capacity to evoke the expression of feelings

3) Capacity to process information and feelings reliably and creatively.

4) Capacity to implement a course of action

5) Capacity to learn in each of the above areas

FIG. 4.

The readings follow the outline employed in the essay. Section I deals with the goals and values of interpersonal relationships, the normative side. We have included in this section five papers, each covering a rather unique and important aspect of interpersonal relationships in a variety of settings: psychotherapy, educational

---

however, a sound statement on "positive mental health" that will legitimize the idea of *enhancement* as well as cure (E. H. Schein, and W. G. Bennis, *Personal and Organizational Change through Group Methods* [New York: Wiley, 1964]).

settings, and human relations training. The two articles by Carl Rogers develop some of his very personal and significant ideas and ideals regarding the proper learning environment. Bennis discusses the values of "laboratory training," where he stresses the "principle of appropriateness." Robert White and Abraham Maslow, in different ways, emphasize the personal and interpersonal evasions and responsibilities for maximizing healthy relationships.

Section II covers some of the personal competencies necessary to build good interpersonal relationships. The articles we selected tend to favor the interpersonal rather than the situational factors, though the latter were emphasized in the body of this essay. Ichheiser stresses the perceptual side of interpersonal behavior while Jourard and Argyris go into significant detail on the kinds of interpersonal skills necessary to build valid and lasting and deep interpersonal relationships.

SENSE OF INTERPERSONAL COMPETENCE: TWO CASE STUDIES AND SOME REFLECTIONS ON ORIGINS*

Robert W. White

Every interaction with another person can be said to have an aspect of competence. Acts directed toward another are intended, consciously or unconsciously, to have an effect of some kind, and the extent to which they produce this effect can be taken as the measure of competence. When interactions are casual, when we are merely "passing the time of day," the element of competence may be minimal, although even in such cases we are surprised if we produce no effect at all, not even an acknowledging grunt. When matters of importance are at stake, the aspect of competence is bound to be larger. If we are seeking help or offering it, trying to evoke love or giving it, warding off aggression or expressing it, resisting influence by others or trying to exert influence, the effectiveness of our behavior is a point of vital concern. In extreme cases interpersonal acts may have virtually no purpose beyond the testing or display of competence. This is true when dominance over others has become an autonomous end, when "throwing one's weight around" and taking command of situations is done simply for the joy of being effective—a joy that is undoubtedly all the greater when it counteracts a fear that one is not effective.

In the main, competence is not the most distinctive feature of interpersonal behavior, and its significance is sometimes overlooked. If the transaction involves an important need, our attention is drawn to the gratification or frustration of that need rather than to the background theme of effectiveness in dealing with people. Yet this background theme is always there, and we should always try to reckon with it. When a child wants to go to the circus but cannot persuade his parents to take him, he suffers a frustration of those urges that draw children to the circus—curiosity, excitement, adventure—and he may also be wounded by the revealed shortcoming of parental love, especially if it signifies that a sibling, taken to the circus the year before, is more warmly loved. But implicit in the whole situation is a setback to his sense of competence in dealing with his parents. He has failed to elicit their sympathetic interest in his heartfelt desires; he has failed to secure their cooperation in satisfying those desires. Along with his more direct frustrations, he has suffered a decrement of confidence in his ability to make himself effective in the human environment.

Competence means capacity, fitness, or ability. The competence of a living organism means its fitness or ability to carry on those transactions with the environment which result in its maintaining itself, growing, and flourishing. In the human case, effectiveness in dealing with the environment is achieved largely through learning. The child's attempts to remove his pains and gratify his needs, and especially his playful explorations and manipulations during the spare time between such crises, build up in him a knowledge of the effects he can have on his surroundings, as well as a knowledge of the effects they can have on him.[1] To describe it neurologically, competence is an achieved state of affairs in the nervous system which makes effective action possible; and it can be approximately

---

[1] These points are developed in detail in Robert W. White, "Motivation Reconsidered: The Concept of Competence," *Psychological Review,* Vol. 66 (1959), pp. 297–333.

measured in some of its aspects by tests of aptitude, intelligence, and achievement. The subjective side of this can be called sense of competence. We know that for various reasons one's sense of competence does not correspond exactly to actual competence as estimated by others, though it is always related to it. Abilities to deal with physical surroundings and to control one's body effectively are matters of no small importance to the child, but the central significance of the human environment confers a corresponding significance on the sense of interpersonal competence.[2]

In clinical work, sense of competence has been widely recognized in negative forms: feelings of helplessness, inhibition of initiative, the inferiority complex. The positive side has perhaps been poisoned for many of us by that hastily conceived dream figure of perfect mental health who has attained invulnerable self-confidence and serene self-esteem—obviously a conceited fool. But the extreme cases, real or fictional, should not draw attention away from sense of competence at the daily operating level. Our best insight comes from the ordinary phenomenon of confidence, which is an aspect of virtually every act. We can detect it by horse sense; that, at least, is what horses do when inexperienced riders are on their backs. A horse can apparently deduce from the first few physical contacts with the novice that the situation is right for a little fun along the bridle path or an unscheduled return to the stable. Similarly, though with less whimsical intent, a teacher making the acquaintance of a new class will notice how the children approach each activity. At the crafts table, for instance, she will see behavior ranging from picking things up quickly and using them firmly, through all grades of tentativeness and uncertainty, to hanging back or turning completely away. If the tools had horse sense, they could rate the confidence of the children who picked them up.

We can detect the influence of sense of competence in the judgments we are constantly making, often half-consciously, about what we can and cannot do. We can step across this puddle but not the next one; we can build rough shelves in the playroom but not a finished bookcase for the living room; we would be glad to paint and shift the scenery for the play but not to act or promote the sale of tickets; we undertake with relative equanimity to criticize a fault in

---

[2]The expression "interpersonal competence" has been used in a much more inclusive sense than the one intended here by Nelson N. Foote and Leonard S. Cottrell, *Identity and Interpersonal Competence* (Chicago: University of Chicago Press, 1955).

a subordinate but suffer no small anxiety when the boss calls a meeting to criticize long-range company policy. How do we know so well what we can and cannot do? Since in the beginning we could not do any of these things, even step across the smallest puddle, it is safe to say that we have learned it all through experience. Past actions, successful and unsuccessful, have taught us the ranges of our effectiveness. Sense of competence is the result of cumulative learning, and it is ever at work influencing the next thrust of behavior.

INTERPERSONAL INCOMPETENCE IN SCHIZOPHRENIA

The schizophrenic, we are repeatedly told, withdraws from reality. This phrase has performed miracles in obscuring our understanding of the schizophrenic disorder. For company-hungry Americans it is a wicked thing to withdraw, a sign of secret pride and an evil sense of superiority; and this judgment seems to be verified if the patient entertains grandiose fantasies of his own importance. The implication of the phrase is that the patient has a happy, secret place to which he can retire, a utopia of lovely fantasies which draw him like a magnet when the going gets rough in the responsible adult world. But surely this is the daydream of slightly weary responsible citizens rather than the experience of schizophrenic patients, whose jumbled world is often full of suffering and pain.

A small change in the formulation may, it seems to me, bring us closer to the psychological truth. The patient, let us say, gives up in his attempts to make himself effective in his human environment. He does so because he has always felt his influence upon it to be small and because even his modest hopes have been shattered by recent disappointments. One aspect of the disorder, in other words, is a chronic weakness in sense of interpersonal competence, which leads under stress to a surrender of effort in actuality and thus to a loss of control over dreamlike ideation. This is not, of course, the whole story of schizophrenia, which may have constitutional and biochemical aspects, as well as peculiarities in the direction and control of impulses; but I believe that it expresses correctly a significant aspect of the disorder. Even in the paradoxical case in which the patient fancies himself to have the power of Napoleon, his sense of actual interpersonal competence is often enough represented by a docile conformity to hospital routines.

It is often said that schizophrenic patients have strong latent dependent needs. To this we must add that they feel remarkably incompetent to obtain satisfaction of their needs. They may, like a borderline case beautifully described by Rickers-Ovsiankina and Riggs,[3] view the human environment as a mysterious puzzlebox to which they have not found the key; they may ask the therapist to tell them what he knows about the inscrutable business of handling people. They show their low expectations by breaking off the therapeutic relation if there is even a hint of indifference on the part of the therapist. They feel themselves to be at the mercy of what other people do to them, even to the point of entertaining delusions of hostile intent and of humanly inspired influencing machines. They see no way to set these things right.

Why do schizophrenics find the human environment so intractable? Clues are now coming in from the study of disorders very early in childhood. It is characteristic of autistic children that they do not interact with the human environment. Often they look around people rather than at them, and it is extremely difficult to draw them into games such as pat-a-cake or rolling a ball back and forth.[4] Kanner[5] and Ritvo and Provence[6] point out that in some cases this lack of interaction is specific to the human environment; with inanimate objects the child plays in relatively normal fashion. There are two possible reasons for this state of affairs: what Erikson has called a "lack of sending power in the child";[7] and what Kanner, Eisenberg, and others have described as cold, preoccupied, mechanical attitudes in the parents.[8] Whatever may be the relative influence of the two factors, the result is that the child does not experience his own effort as having any effect on the human environment; therefore, it draws his interest no more than furniture, over which he has no influence. If the human environment inspires anxiety, lack of interest may be frozen into an inhibition of interest.

These observations suggest that one of the factors contributing

---

[3]Maria A. Rickers-Ovsiankina and Margaret M. Riggs, "To Be or Not To Be: A Schizophrenic Personality," A. Burton and R. E. Harris (eds.) *Clinical Studies of Personality* (New York: Harper & Brothers, 1955), Chap. 4.

[4]Beata Rank, "Adaptation of the Psychoanalytic Technique for the Treatment of Young Children with Atypical Development," *American Journal of Orthopsychiatry*, Vol. 19 (1949), pp. 130–39.

[5]Leo Kanner, "Autistic Disturbances of Affective Contact," *The Nervous Child*, Vol. 2 (1943), pp. 217–50.

[6]Samuel Ritvo and Sally Provence, "Form Perception and Imitation in Some Autistic Children," *Psychoanalytic Study of the Child* (New York: International Universities Press, 1953), VIII, 155–61.

[7]Erik H. Erikson, *Childhood and Society* (New York: W. W. Norton, 1950).

[8]Leon Eisenberg, "The Fathers of Autistic Children," *American Journal of Orthopsychiatry*, Vol. 27 (1957), pp. 715–24.

to schizophrenia, with its fragile social confidence, is a bad start in eliciting response from the human environment. And they further suggest the more general formulation that *sense of interpersonal competence develops through effort and its efficacy in human interactions.* This provides us with a clue to the kinds of events that are likely to be important for development.

DEVELOPMENTAL CRISES OF INTERPERSONAL CONFIDENCE

Interaction with the human environment is a continuous process, but like any other form of development, it tends to have dramatic moments and critical peaks. It is misleading, I believe, to identify these peaks with Freud's stages of psychosexual development; the growth of competence is not captured by these affective crises, however important they may be.[9] I shall not undertake here a systematic sketch of development; let it suffice just to mention some of the situations that are likely to be critical.

One of these is the situation of play with the parents apart from the satisfying of bodily needs. Does the child show initiative, and do the parents respond with pleasure and interest, or do they find it a bit of a bore? Another is the situation created by the child's early steps toward independence, as when he undertakes to feed himself. Is he eager and persistent in these attempts? Do they meet maternal acquiescence, or do they produce irritation at the slow progress and messy spilling? The theme of independence continues through various stages, as manipulation and locomotion permit the child to explore larger and perhaps more dangerous spheres. Another crisis may occur over the expression of will through language. The often observed period of negativism, which we must now interpret interactively as probable negativism on both sides, comes when the child is first capable of issuing verbal commands and offering verbal defiance. How vigorously does he pursue these investigations and to what extent will his parents think it necessary to "break his will" and assert their own? Then there is the question of justice, which is often sharpest in disputes between siblings. Can the child plead his cause and be heard, or does he feel that nothing is effective, either because of favoritism or because of a blanket injunction against quarreling?

In all these situations the interaction is mainly between child and

---

[9]Robert W. White, "Competence and the Psychosexual Stages of Development," *Nebraska Symposium on Motivation* (Lincoln, Nebraska: University of Nebraska Press, 1960), pp. 97–141.

parents, but new crises occur when the child ventures into play with other children. Is he able to influence the course of interaction, dominate the play, and keep his toys; or does he have to follow unwillingly and lose a few of his possessions? Can he cut an effective figure in competitive activities and thus elicit the respect of his contemporaries? Can he become something of a persuasive force and exert a share of leadership in serious pursuits? These issues extend all the way into adolescence, when a further crisis may arise from the revitalized problem of confidence with the other sex. And, of course, the problems continue even later, as we have seen by pursuing our two subjects into their late twenties.

In 1938 Murray wrote as the opening words of *Explorations in Personality* "Man is today's great problem." If "today" is moved forward to 1963 the statement is only the more true. The study of lives must set for itself the goal of understanding development in all its significant aspects. If sense of interpersonal competence develops through effort and its efficacy in human interactions, we shall not fully understand today's great problem without uncovering this theme in the life history.

GOALS AND META-GOALS OF LABORATORY TRAINING*

Warren G. Bennis

By "laboratory training" I mean essentially those human relations training activities associated with the National Training Laboratories in this country and with Tavistock in England. Although there are variations in the training programs offered, they usually involve an attention to interpersonal, group, organizational, and change processes derived from psychological and psychiatric disciplines. T-groups, sensitivity or group dynamics training are often used as examples of the laboratory method insofar as they all at-

---

*Warren G. Bennis, "Goals and Meta-Goals of Laboratory Training," *Human Relations Training News*, National Training Laboratories, Washington, D.C., Vol. 6, No. 3 (Fall, 1962), pp. 1–4. Used by permission.

tempt to use *experienced behavior* of the group members to generate meaningful learning.[1]

I think there is general agreement about the goals of laboratory education. The "take-home" booklets, the promotional material, the opening lectures of laboratories generally reflect this consensus. And while there are some variations of the stated goals, depending on the staff and participant composition (e.g., Church Laboratory, School Administrator Laboratory, and so on), they usually include objectives such as these: *(a)* self-insight, or some variation of learning related to increased self-knowledge; *(b)* understanding the conditions which inhibit or facilitate effective group functioning; *(c)* understanding interpersonal operations in groups; and *(d)* developing skills for diagnosing individual, group, and organizational behavior.

But beyond these explicit goals, there rests another set of learnings which shall be referred to as "meta-goals" (or "values," if you would prefer). These meta-goals transcend and shape the articulated goals. They are "in the air" at every laboratory and undoubtedly guide staff decisions ranging from laboratory design to trainer interventions. More crucial is the realization that the meta-goals, if internalized, lead to a set of values which may run counter to the participant's sponsoring ("back-home") organization. I would like to suggest four privotal meta-goals for discussion; the hope being that, if reasonable, they can be integrated into future human relations training more explicitly.

1. Expanded Consciousness and Recognition of Choice

Extracting men in organizations from their day-to-day preoccupations and transplanting them into a culture where they are urged to observe and understand personality and group dynamics creates conditions where "givens" become choices—or at least create potentials for choice. Laboratory training—if anything—is a device which de-routinizes, which slows down for analysis, processes which are "taken for granted." It is a form of training which questions received notions and attempts to "unfreeze" role expectations (the Lewinian re-educational and change process of "unfreezing, restructuring, and refreezing"). The impulse for this cognitive restructuring comes

---

[1]See L. Bradford, J. Gibb, and K. Benne (eds.), *T-Group Theory and Laboratory Method* (New York: Wiley, 1964) and Edgar H. Schein and Warren G. Bennis, *Personal and Organizational Change through Group Methods* (New York: Wiley, 1965).

about primarily because the control mechanisms taken for granted in institutionalized behavior are decisively absent in a laboratory. I am referring to control mechanisms which serve to regulate behavior, such as mission, authority patterns, norms regulating intimacy and control, decision apparatus, communication, traditions, and precedents. The ambiguity of norms, of behavioral constraints, of anticipatory rewards, creates what Lewin referred to as a "primitivization" of behavior due to the regressive climate. And the happy necessity of this human existence, to paraphrase T. S. Eliot, is for men to find things out for themselves, i.e., to create order, clarify one's identity, establish norms and a sense of community. In fact, one can look at laboratory training as the formation of norms and structure which build a community—except that, unlike most communities, the constituent members are present at its birth.

There are many analogies to this process; psychotherapy, perhaps, is the most obvious. According to one of its proponents, Karl Menninger, a regressive situation is evoked whereby the patient is deliberately forced to re-experience situations which bind and immobilize present choices. The indoctrination and socialization practices of many institutions, particularly "total institutions" where attempts are made to reshape normative patterns, bear a close resemblance to this unfreezing process. The "insight culture" of mental hospitals,[2] the "coercive persuasion" and "thought control"[3] programs used in Korean P.O.W. camps, military indoctrination programs,[4] and even some management development programs[5] are all to some degree exemplars.

Laboratory training, then, realizes its meta-goal of "expanded consciousness and recognition of choice points" by way of a very complicated process: extracting participants from their day-to-day preoccupations, cultural insulation, and de-routinization. Parallel to and combined with this unfreezing process is an emphasis on awareness, sensitivity, and diagnosis, all of which encourage the participant to think about his behavior—most particularly to think about how he chooses to behave.

---

[2]Alfred Stanton and Morris S. Schwartz, *The Mental Hospital* (New York: Basic Books, 1954).

[3]Edgar H. Schein, *Coercive Persuasion* (New York: W. W. Norton, 1961).

[4]Sanford M. Dornbusch, "The Military Academy as an Assimilating Institution," *Social Forces,* May, 1955, pp. 316–21.

[5]Edgar H. Schein, "Management Development as a Process of Influence," *Industrial Management Review, M.I.T.,* May, 1961.

2. A "Spirit of Inquiry"

Closely related to the meta-goals of choice—and, in fact, only conceptually separable—is an attitude of inquiry associated with science. It is a complex of human behavior and adjustment that has been summed up as the "spirit of inquiry" and includes many elements. The first may be called the hypothetical spirit, the feeling for tentativeness and caution, the respect for probable error. Another is experimentalism, the willingness to expose ideas to empirical testing. The exigencies of the laboratory situation help to create this orientation. For the ambiguous and unstructured situation creates a need to define and organize the environment. In addition, the participants are prodded and rewarded by staff members to question old, and try new, behaviors; they are reinforced by concepts to probe, to look at realities unflinchingly, to ask "why."

Again this bears a kinship with the methodology—although *not,* notably, the symbolic interpretive system—of psychoanalysis. Nevitt Sanford has said in this connection (in an S.P.S.S.I. Presidential Address at an American Psychological Association meeting in August, 1958) that it appears ". . . most notably in Freud's psychoanalytic method of investigation and treatment. (This method is, in my view, Freud's greatest, and it will be his most lasting contribution. By the method, I mean the whole contractual arrangement according to which both therapist and patient become investigators, and both objects of careful observation and study; in which the therapist can ask the patient to face the truth because he, the therapist, is willing to try to face it in himself; in which investigation and treatment are inseparable aspects of the same humanistic enterprise.)"

In laboratory training all experienced behavior is a subject for questioning and analysis, limited only by the participants' threshold of tolerance to truth and new ideas.

Both meta-goals, the "spirit of inquiry" and the "recognition of choice," imply that curiosity about and making sense of human behavior are as legitimate and important (if not as "sanitary") as non-human phenomena. (I have always been perplexed and sometimes annoyed at observing the most gifted and curious natural scientists and engineers stop short of asking "why" when it touched on the human condition. Part of laboratory education, I suspect, is to expand the range of curiosity and experimental attitude to "people.")

3. Authenticity in Interpersonal Relations

An important imperative in laboratory training has to do with the relatively high valuation of feelings: their expression and their effects. The degree to which participants can communicate feelings and in turn evoke valid feelings from other members is regarded as an important criterion of group growth. One theory postulates that "group development involves the overcoming of obstacles to valid communication,"[6] i.e., where valid communication is defined as interpersonal communication free—as far as humanly possible—of distortion.

Authenticity, "leveling," and "expressing feelings" comprise an important part of the laboratory argot, all of which can be summed up in a passage from *King Lear:* "Speak what we feel, not what we ought to say."

This tendency toward authenticity should not be surprising when we consider that so much time and attention are devoted to the analysis of interpersonal behavior, to understanding the effects of a participant's behavior on other group members. Measurements of changes during these training programs, indeed, suggest personal growth resembling that seen in psychotherapy;[7] i.e., the participant, as he knows himself, will be much the same person as he is known to others.[8]

4. A Collaborative Conception of the Authority Relationship

Permeating the atmosphere of laboratory training is a concept of the authority relationship which differs substantially from the legalistic Weberian emphasis on legitimacy of position. The contractual elements are understressed, and the collaborative and interdependent elements are accentuated. In McGregor's writings we can identify the major elements in this conception of authority: *(a)* Management by objective, i.e., the requirements of the job are set by the situation (they need not be seen by either party as personal requirements established by the superior),[9] so that the au-

---

[6]Warren G. Bennis and Herbert A. Shepard, "A Theory of Group Development," *Human Relations* Vol. 4 (1956).

[7]Richard L. Burke and Warren G. Bennis, "Changes in Perception of Self and Others During Human Relations Training," *Human Relations* Vol. 2 (1961), pp. 165–82.

[8]Marie Jahoda, *Current Concepts of Positive Mental Health* (New York: Basic Books, 1958).

[9]Douglas M. McGregor, *The Human Side of Enterprise* (New York: McGraw-Hill, 1960).

thority relationship is viewed as a collaborative process where superior and subordinate attempt to develop ground rules for work and productivity; *(b)* the recognized interdependence between subordinates and superiors; *(c)* the belief that subordinates are capable of learning *self-control*, i.e., to internalize and exercise standards of performance congruent with organizational objectives without reliance on controls from exogenous sources.

Underlying this conception of authority is the "double reference" held toward superiors and subordinates based on person and role ingredients. For the subordinate and superior have to view each other as *role incumbents* with a significant power differential (even taking into account the interdependence) as well as *human beings* with strengths and weaknesses. Most theories of organization deny the personality elements of role and thereby fail to come to terms with the basic antagonism and tension between role and personality in organizational behavior.

How this conception of authority is internalized during laboratory training is beyond the scope of this paper; moreover, the process is not altogether clear. Readings and lectures cover the material somewhat, and identification with staff members undoubtedly contributes. But most important is the realization that *the teaching-learning process of laboratory training is a prototype of the collaborative conception of authority.* Putting it differently, we can say that learning is accomplished through the requirements of the situation and a joint, collaborative venture between the trainer and participants. Also, there is the belief that participants can exercise self-control in the learning process; i.e., the participant accepts influence on the basis of own evaluation rather than reliance on outside controls, such as rewards and punishments. Internalization, through credibility—rather than compliance, through exogenous controls—is the type of social influence employed in laboratory training.[10] It is precisely this form of influence which holds for the collaborative conception of authority we have been discussing.

These four meta-goals, then—expanded consciousness and recognition of choice, spirit of inquiry, authenticity in interpersonal relations, and a collaborative conception of authority—represent what I think to be the most important results gained from laboratory

---

[10]This formulation of social influence is taken from Herbert Kelman's "Processes of Opinion Change," *Public Opinion Quarterly* (Spring, 1961), reprinted in Warren G. Bennis, Kenneth D. Benne, and Robert Chin (ed.), *The Planning of Change* (New York: Holt, Rinehart, and Winston, 1961), pp. 509–17.

training. (Another important meta-goal not discussed here is the professionalization of the manager's role.)

It is interesting that critics of this approach regularly misconstrue or fail to understand these meta-learnings. Dubin, in an otherwise thoughtful analysis of this training, wonders whether it doesn't train managers to be "other-directed," or to become "permissive leaders."[11] From other sources, charges are made about "togetherness," brainwashing, and "group-thinking." It is not entirely the fault of the critics, for the writing in the field has generally stressed the purely "group dynamics" aspects while slighting the meta-goal emphasis presented here.

I think we trainers, too, have colluded in this misunderstanding from time to time. We become preoccupied with matters of "expressing feelings" or "shared leadership" or "manipulative behavior" or "giving feedback" or "democratic functioning," or with "people who talk too much vs. people who remain silent" or with "cohesive vs. fragmented groups," and so on. These are, of course, legitimate matters and should concern trainers. But they've gained a hegemony which I want to question.

For I care much less about a participant's learning that he talked too much and will, in the future, talk less, than I do about his recognizing that choice exists and that there are certain clear consequences of under- or over-participation. I care much less about producing a "cohesive" group than I do about members' understanding the "costs" and gains of cohesiveness, when it's appropriate and worth the cost and when it may not be. I care far less about developing shared leadership in the T Group than I do about the participants' recognizing that a choice exists among a wide array of leadership patterns. In short, I care far more about developing *choice and recognition of choice points than I do about change.* Change, I think, is the participants' privilege, but choice is something trainers must emphasize. (This goes right across the board. I will try doggedly to create valid conditions for "giving and receiving feedback," for example. I will doggedly insist that the members "experience" it so that they have a basis for choice. Then I will just as doggedly insist that a choice remain open, to continue or not, to modify or not.)

---

[11]Robert F. Dubin, "Psyche, Sensitivity, and Social Structure," in Tannenbaum, Weschler, and Massarik, *Leadership and Organization* (New York: McGraw-Hill, 1961), pp. 401–15.

Emphasizing the meta-goals has another importance with respect to organizational change. For they represent what the participant internalizes and transfers to his organization. "Everything the child learns in school he forgets," goes an old French maxim, "but the education remains." Similarly the meta-goals remain. These internalized learnings have profound implications for the individual and for the organization because they deeply affect and modify the value and motivational commitments which determine the individual's orientation to his role. I think we have to keep them explicitly in mind in our training and in our future designs.

GRADUATE EDUCATION IN PSYCHOLOGY: A PASSIONATE STATEMENT*

Carl R. Rogers

When we examine what we *do* in our programs of graduate education in psychology rather than what we *say*, the picture which emerges is a sorry one indeed. We operate on a set of fallacious and outmoded assumptions such as "The student can't be trusted"; "Evaluation is education"; "Method is science"; "Creative scientists develop from passive learners"; "Weeding out 85 per cent of our selected applicants is proof of high standards." The weight of research evidence and professional opinion is against these operative principles. If psychology took a hard clear look at its graduate training, it would, for the most part, throw it out and build on new and more adequate principles and hypotheses.

I wish in this article to express a strong and growing personal concern about the educational policies which are operative in most departments of psychology in their graduate training programs. Very briefly, the theme of my statement is that we are doing an unintelligent, ineffectual, and wasteful job of preparing psychologists, to the detriment of our discipline and society.

*Unpublished manuscript, 1965, Western Behavioral Science Institute, La Jolla, California.

My concern has its basis in the knowledge that the future of civilization may depend on finding the solutions to psychological problems. It is a truism that man has made great progress in solving many of the material problems of his existence but that he may well be defeated, and perhaps annihilated, by his failure to solve the *psychological* problems which face him—interpersonal, interracial, and international frictions, delinquency, the disturbances labeled "mental illness," the growing loss of a sense of purpose, and the inability to learn at a rate which will keep up with our expanding knowledge. Thus, the logic of our culture *demands* that the behavioral sciences play an increasingly important part in the foreseeable future of our society as it confronts these problems.

Obviously this situation constitutes a challenge to psychology and the other behavioral sciences. We should be selecting and training individuals for creative effectiveness in seeking out and discovering the significant new knowledge which is needed. Furthermore, since psychology, more than the other sciences, has access to the cumulating research knowledge regarding learning, creativity, and the development of autonomous persons, it would seem that our programs for the preparation of psychologists should be superior to programs in other fields.

Is this the case? I fear not. As Sigmund Koch has recently said of psychologists, "We are not known for our readiness to be in the wavefront of history." Granting that American psychologists have not been noted as pioneers, it seems to me unnecessary that in our graduate programs we should so frequently display timid or reactionary patterns which put us in the backwaters rather than the wavefront of history.

In recent years I have had opportunity to observe a number of psychology departments. I have gathered material from graduate students in widely divergent places. For me these observations and this material raise profound and disturbing questions about the general pattern of scientific and professional education in our discipline. When we examine what we *do*, rather than what we profess, in this area, the picture which emerges is, in my estimation, a sorry one. I am well aware that members of other sciences and professions often feel similarly critical of graduate education in their own areas. I am limiting my remarks to the field of psychology for two reasons. It is the only field in which I can speak from firsthand knowledge. It is also the science which should be leading the way in preparation of new members of its science and profession.

IMPLICIT ASSUMPTIONS

I believe that we may best consider our programs of graduate education by examining the implicit assumptions on which they appear to be based. I will present these assumptions as I see them and some of the evidence which challenges them. I trust the reader will think of these statements in relation to some departmental situation he knows and see to what extent they apply.

Implicit Assumption 1: The student cannot be trusted to pursue his own scientific and professional learning

This is an extremely pervasive assumption in the great majority of departments. One might suppose that the graduate student who has chosen to become a psychologist could be trusted to pursue that purpose, and that the function of the faculty would be to give help in fulfilling his aim of learning the material of his science and profession. Instead, it is almost uniformly true that the faculty attitude is one of mistrustful guidance. Work must be assigned; the completion of this work must be supervised; students must be continually guided and then evaluated. It is very rare indeed that the graduate student finds his program to be an experience in which he is *set free* to pursue the learnings which are of importance to himself.

Many years ago I endeavored to state the divergent views on this point:

> Many believe that the goals of graduate education can best be reached by requiring students to work through a carefully guided program in which the content to be required, the credits to be gained, and the courses to be taken are quite carefully and clearly defined. They believe that a carefully planned curriculum which sets forth the knowledge and skills to be acquired is perhaps our best method of achieving such a goal.
>
> Others believe that quite a different method is called for in achieving these goals. To them it seems that the best education, and particularly the best graduate education, is that which frees the student to pursue the knowledge, skills, attitudes, and experiences which seem to him related to his own goals of ultimate professional and scientific competence. To this second group this seems to be more in accord with what we know of the laws of learning and the principles of individual development and growth.

A graduate student discusses the same issue with more feeling. She says:

> The general attitude in higher education today is one of student *v.* faculty, rather than student *with* faculty. I wonder if this "opposing attitude" in education doesn't go back to the system of learning in the primary and elementary system. Here the student is asked to memorize rules rather than to understand intrinsically the basic concepts and reasons for these rules. One is "taken to"

learning by the hand, rather than "guided toward" knowledge by desire. Professors have learned this way, and the majority of them carry this "opposition learning" to the student. It is what they have experienced, and thus, it is what they transfer to the next fellow.

Later in her statement she gives an appealing view of the alternative possibility:

> In my mind, the two most basic, and at the same time, most general, qualities that should exist in learning, are freedom and responsibility. Freedom of time and freedom of thought, allowing students to relax and become "swept up" by a stimulating environment, to become involved, to be able to give to as well as take from. Responsibility should be felt and accepted by the student— a responsibility to himself and to his field—to learn, to be involved, to question what he does and thinks and what others do and think.

Her statement is strongly echoed by a distinguished group of nine psychologists who spent four weeks in formulating the principles by which graduate education in psychology might lead to more initiative for research and more significant research. They say:

> The attitudes, the independence of thought, and the willingness to persist in one's own interests and beliefs that characterize good research work are often the very traits that lead an individual to resist actively pressures toward conformity to a given pattern of study, toward mastery of given areas of knowledge, or toward acceptance of given ways of thinking. Consequently, the imposition of standardized patterns may often operate to exclude individuals with traits desirable for research (Education for Research in Psychology, 1959, p. 173).

Thus, there seems reason to believe that trusting the student would be a much sounder assumption than the present attitude of mistrust which has a definitely damaging effect upon self-confidence. MacKinnon, in studying creativity in architects, gives a list of the factors in the early life of these men which are highly associated with their present creativeness (as judged by their fellows). The first such background factor is "An extraordinary respect for the child and confidence in his ability to do what was appropriate" (1963, p. 20).

We might try extending such respect and confidence to our graduate students.

Implicit Assumption 2: Ability to pass examinations is the best criterion for student selection and for judging professional promise

The best candidate to be selected for training as a psychologist is one who has passed examinations in the past. The most promising graduate student is the one who best passes the examinations in this department.

This assumption, again implicit in the great majority of departments, leads to a heavy stress on the academic record and the grade-point average in the process of selecting graduate students. It also leads to the use of measures such as the Graduate Record Examination and the Miller Analogies Test, in the hope that they will predict "academic success," that is, the ability to pass courses similar to undergraduate courses. It also, of course, leads to the use of examinations as the primary criterion for assessing the promise of those students who have been selected for graduate work.

While it is clear that examination passing ability is a useful skill and has a place in professional training, it almost certainly emphasizes rote learning and mental agility rather than originality of thought and scientific curiosity, traits which in the long run are much more valuable. Guilford has pointed out that education

> . . . has emphasized abilities in the areas of convergent thinking and evaluation, often at the expense of development in the area of divergent thinking. We have attempted to teach students how to arrive at "correct" answers that our civilization has taught us are correct. This is convergent thinking . . . . Outside the arts we have generally discouraged the development of divergent thinking abilities, unintentionally but effectively (1957, p. 19).

Likewise, in terms of the research by Getzels and Jackson, it would appear that our present methods of selection and assessment tend to place value on what they term the high-IQ individual rather than the creative individual. It is useful to think of our usual assessment procedures in the light of their comments about these two types of student:

> It seems to us that the essence of the performance of our creative adolescents lay in their ability to produce new forms, to risk conjoining elements that are customarily thought of as independent and dissimilar, to "go off in new directions." The creative adolescent seemed to possess the ability to free himself from the usual, to "diverge" from the customary. He seemed to enjoy the risk and uncertainty of the unknown. In contrast, the high-IQ adolescent seemed to possess to a high degree the ability and the need to focus on the usual, to be "channeled and controlled" in the direction of the right answer—the customary. He appeared to shy away from the risk and uncertainty of the unknown and to seek out the safety and security of the known (1963, p. 172).

The effect of this second assumption is that students who are selected and valued as psychologists-to-be tend to excel in examination passing rather than in those qualities which would give them promise as independent discoverers of new knowledge.

Implicit Assumption 3: Evaluation is education; education is evaluation.

It is incredible the way this preposterous assumption has become completely imbedded in graduate education in the United States. Examinations have become the beginning and the end of education.

They are a way of life for the graduate student, and a more stultifying way of life could hardly be imagined. In one university the
graduate student in psychology is faced with these major evaluation
hurdles:

1. Examination in first foreign language
2. Examination in second foreign language
3. First six-hour qualifying examination
4. Second six-hour qualifying examination (both of these in the first
    graduate year)
5. Three-hour examination in methodology and statistics
6. Four-hour examination in a chosen major field of psychology
7. Two-hour examination in a minor field
8. Oral examination on Master's thesis
9. Committee evaluation of Ph.D. proposal
10. Committee evaluation of Ph.D. thesis
11. Oral examination on Ph.D. thesis

Since 10 to 50 percent of those taking any of these examinations
are failed on the first attempt, the actual number of examinations
taken is considerably greater than indicated above. Understandably,
the anxiety on the second attempt is considerably (sometimes un-
bearably) greater. Furthermore, these examinations are so spaced
out that during the four to seven years of his graduate work the student's main concern is with the next sword of Damocles which hangs
over his career. As if the above list were not enough, it should be
made clear that these major examinations are *in addition to* any
quizzes, midsemester, and final examinations given in his courses.

Obviously the student cannot possibly have the sense of fully independent freedom which is clearly at the base of creative professional work. Small wonder that a graduate student leaving this program wrote:

> I don't mind a certain amount of academic hazing of graduate students by
> the faculty. I know that they feel that they must "get tough." But at this
> university the point is never reached at which the student feels "The depart-
> ment is now behind me in my endeavor to get a degree."[1]

The way in which examinations stultify real learning is indicated
by a student from another university who writes:

> A lot of people are never sure when they write an exam what grade range
> they are in. The grade on the exam depends upon whether you have hit the

---

[1] It is important to note that all of the graduate students quoted in this paper are
doing highly creditable graduate work. One holds a National Science Foundation
Fellowship; others hold other national fellowships based on merit. One is known to
have a straight-A graduate record. None of the quotations are "gripes" from marginal
or failing students. For reasons of diplomacy, the authors of the quotations prefer
not to be identified.

point or points that the professor is looking for. In class you have to tune your mind into the wavelength of the instuctor. You would like to understand what he is getting at, but this is barred by trying to determine what he wants fed back on an exam (Clark, 1962, p. 42).

Another graduate student in still another university expresses something of the bitterness which this approach engenders:

One leaves the course knowing gobs of jargon and most of "the" answers. He has filled all the pages of his notebook with the professor's speeches, and on the final exam, he has hopefully given back to the professor most of the important facts and basic ideas. The professor looks for and expects a blind acceptance; he wants back what he gave you, not giving you the opportunity for digestion and reaction. There is little chance for synthesis. The student is requested to conform to the instructor's view, and no reward is given for creative thought and individual reaction to the material. The subject is presented as black and white, and one-dimensional. As I write this I feel frustrated. It is a feeling of bitterness, of rebellion—feeling all steamed up inside but without a hole in the kettle spout to let out some steam; it is a burning steam.

Frequently, for the major examinations, the student is given almost no clues as to what the examination will cover. It will simply be an examination in "general psychology" or "social psychology" or some other field. But since the student knows that the examination questions will be formulated by Professors X and Y, he does not waste his time concentrating on what for him is important in general or social psychology. He focuses instead on learning the interests and prejudices of the two professors. One student, commenting on this aspect, says:

One spends so much time trying to "second guess" what exam questions will be that he has no time to learn what he *wants* to learn.

Lest one feel that these are merely the rantings of callow graduate students, let me add one more quotation from a scientist looking back on some of his experience:

This coercion had such a deterring effect (upon me) that after I had passed the final examination, I found the consideration of any problem distasteful for me for an entire year.

This is a statment by Albert Einstein. It portrays very well the impact of an evaluative system upon a sensitive, inquiring, and creative mind. A less restrained statement comes from another mature scientist, Raymond Lyttleton, the noted Cambridge astronomer:

All real advances in knowledge come from people who are doing what they like to do. We all know the effect on children of compulsory spinach and compulsory rhubarb; it's the same with compulsory learning. They say, "It's spinach and to hell with it!" (1958, p. 68)

It is difficult to exaggerate the damage done to promising graduate students by this completely fallacious assumption that they learn by being threatened, time after time, with catastrophic failure. While I am sure most faculty members would deny that they hold to this assumption, their behavior shows all too clearly that this is the operational principle by which they work.

Implicit Assumption 4: Presentation equals learning: What is presented in the lecture is what the student learns

It scarcely seems possible that intelligent men could hold this assumption. Yet one has only to observe a hard-working, serious-minded committee of faculty members arguing over the topics to be included in a graduate survey course in psychology to realize that in their view of the course, what is "covered" (a marvelous term!) is what is learned.

Here is the reaction of a graduate student in the midst of taking such a carefully planned course:

> Worst of all, I think, is the fact that not many of the students feel that they are learning anything at all. They feel that it is just a continuation of the idiocy of undergraduate school, in which huge amounts of material are thrown at you and you are expected to regurgitate most of it on a test and then supposedly you have learned something. You may indeed have gained some separated facts about psychology, but none of them can be integrated in any coherent way.

The assumption that learning is equivalent to hearing a lecture is closely tied in with the preceding assumption that education is evaluation. They are both closely related to the next assumption.

Implicit Assumption 5: Knowledge is the accumulation of brick upon brick of content and information

One might think that psychology, of all the scientific disciplines, would be the least likely to hold this implicit assumption. It is psychologists who have shown that learning takes place primarily and significantly when it is directly related to the meaningful purposes and motives of the individual. Yet most graduate departments proceed upon the conviction that there are a series of fundamental building blocks in the science of psychology which must be mastered sequentially by the student, whether or not they fit in with his current interests.

Some of the best minds in psychology know differently. The Conference on Education for Research in Psychology, mentioned previously, makes these important observations:

A knowledge of facts of psychology is important for research. How much of this is to be imparted during graduate study, however, is not easy to determine. Much of the factual knowledge of the mature scientist has been accumulated during the course of his career and probably cannot be duplicated by explicit instruction. Moreover, substantive courses inevitably compete for the student's time with practical experience in the methods and art of research. For all these reasons, we urge caution against the overloading of an individual's graduate program with substantive courses, either as the result of department requirements or as the result of choice by the student (1959, p. 172).

In general, we question the assumption that the more formal preparation the individual has for research, the more productive and creative he will be in research. Specifically, we doubt that the more complete the individual's mastery of statistical and other tools, the more effective he will be in research; we doubt that the greater his scholarly knowledge of the literature, the more likely he will be to contribute to that knowledge; we doubt that the value of theory in research increases continuously as it becomes more formalized and detailed (1959, p. 170).

I believe it is pertinent to note that Harvard and a number of other leading medical schools have done away with the premed undergraduate major, a requirement based on the "brick by brick" philosophy. Harvard found that by the third year of medical school those without the premed major were doing slightly better in their grades than those with such a major, besides having greater breadth and greater promise.

Implicit Assumption 6: The truths of psychology are known

In some departments of my acquaintance this assumption of an orthodoxy of knowledge is quite evident. In other departments there is much more acceptance of divergence. To the extent that there is only one acceptable view, this seems most unfortunate in a developing science. One graduate student describes his experience thus:

"There is an orthodoxy here." (He then describes the ritual and dogma of his particular department in terms which might be identifying.) He goes on to say: ". . . Here, it seems, one speaks only in imitation of one's elders. The result is a 'new scholasticism'; stultifying repetition of the thoughts and prejudices of the faculty."

One related procedure, which struck me most forcefully in my first class session, is what I call "study-citing behavior," name-dropping about any member whatsoever of certain approved classes of research. It is behavior well calculated to gain the favor of the faculty; it serves the further end of eliminating any necessity for the citer having to think and is also effective in cutting off an opponent in argument. While appeal to research findings can have value if it does not itself become an authoritarianism, it is indicative of the closed-mindedness of the department that only certain brands of research have approved citing status . . . . One learns here rather quickly what is expected of him.

There is no point to belaboring this issue. Often faculty members talk critically about dogmatism, yet display an extreme degree of it in their behavior. Sometimes the orthodoxy is in regard to method, and it is the "truth methods" of scientific psychology that are regarded as immutable. In any event, where attitudes such as those described above exist in a department, the atmosphere is opposed to any true scientific endeavor. Only a pseudo-science can result.

Implicit Assumption 7: Method is science

Here is an assumption which I find particularly widespread in American psychology. A rigorous procedure is often considered (if one may judge by faculty behavior) as far more important than the ideas it is intended to investigate. A meticulous statistics and a sophisticated research design seem to carry more weight than significant observations of significant problems.

Here again, when prominent scientists in the field of psychology think together about graduate training, they resolutely reject such an assumption:

> Education for research must do more than develop competence in designing, executing, and interpreting experimental or other studies. Development of such competence is important, but much more important is the development of the individual's creativeness—his ability to discover new relations, to reformulate or systematize known facts, to devise new techniques and approaches to problems (Education for Research on Psychology, 1959, p. 170).

Implicit Assumption 8: Creative scientists develop from passive learners

A number of the preceding assumptions make it evident that many departments believe, operationally, that the student who absorbs and then gives back on examinations is the one on whom they are placing their bets for the future. Yet I know of no studies in the field which would support this assumption. Anne Roe (1963), from her extensive work in studying leading scientists, comes to the conclusion that some of the factors in our educational procedures which adversely affect students in their development as scientists are the following:

1. Insufficient valuation of problem-solving attitudes in the school.
2. The general tendency of teachers to sweeping devaluation of "wild" or "silly" ideas.
3. Restriction upon curiosity.

Similarly a broadly based study of several hundred colleges by Thistlethwaite (1963) shows that vigorous class discussions and flexibility of curriculum are significantly associated with the number of Ph.D.'s in the social sciences produced by these colleges, relative to enrollment. Interestingly enough these same elements are somewhat negatively associated with the production of Ph.D.'s in the natural sciences. Here is an issue worth further study.

MacKinnon, from his extensive work in the investigation of creativity, points up a fact which is too little considered. He says:

> . . . ledge, the second element in the word *knowledge,* means sport. Knowledge is the result of playing with what we know, that is, with our facts. A knowledgable person in science is not, as we are often wont to think, merely one who has an accumulation of facts, but rather one who has the capacity to have sport with what he knows, giving creative rein to his fancy in changing his world of phenomenal appearances into a world of scientific constructs (1963, p. 23).

I think I know what would happen, in most departments, to the graduate student who gave "creative rein to his fancy!"

Yet when students are *taught* to defer judgments about ideas and are encouraged in a permissive atmosphere simply to *produce* ideas no matter how unreasonable they may seem, they are found to produce a greater quantity and a higher quality of problem-solving ideas than a control group, as research by Parnes and Meadow (1963) has shown.

In my judgment, in our insecurity as a profession, we attach enormous importance to turning out "hard-headed" scientists and strongly punish any of the sensitive, speculative, sportive openness which is the essence of the real scientist. What departments of psychology of your acquaintance would value these qualities in their graduate students?

> 1. Students who are "unusually appreciative of the intuitive and nonrational elements of their nature; distinguished by their profound commitment to the search for esthetic and philosophic meaning in all experience" (Taylor and Barron, 1963, p. 386).
> 2. Students who exhibit "an openness to their own feelings and emotions, esthetic interests, and a sensitive awareness of self and others" (MacKinnon, 1963, p. 36).

Yet these statements are taken from summaries of the objective characteristics of outstanding young scientists and outstandingly creative professional men. They are, however, the type of personal qualities which many psychologists fear in themselves and in their students.

Implicit Assumption 9: "Weeding out" a majority of the students is a satisfactory method of producing scientists and clinicians

To me it seems a scandalous waste of manpower that of the carefully selected graduate students whom we take into our programs, only a small proportion ever obtain their degrees. It is indicative of the irresponsible attitude of our discipline that most departments have no idea what percentage of their students obtain a Ph.D. It appears that in fortunate departments perhaps one out of two students is successful. In some departments only one out of five, or even one out of seven of those who start actually obtain the degree. Usually this is regarded as evidence that the department maintains "high standards." I know of no other field of work in which such an attitude would be taken. Medicine has long ago recognized that when they select a talented group as medical students, the profession has an obligation to conserve this potentiality. Failure is seen as being as as much a reflection upon the medical school as upon the student. Industry, too, realizes that it must conserve talented manpower. But in psychology it is not so.

The shameful attrition rate referred to above occurs in part because students fail some of the numerous evaluative hurdles previously mentioned and are eliminated from the program or discouraged from continuing. But it also occurs in considerable part because students with an original turn of mind become disenchanted with the sterility of a program based on the assumptions outlined in these pages and leave for other fields. As I have watched this process it is my conviction that among the students who leave our psychology departments one would find both the least promising and the most promising of our potential future psychologists. Any system of continuous evaluation weeds out some of the less competent or less intelligent. Yet it also tends very definitely to eliminate the most unique and creative of our students who simply refuse to, as they say, "put up with all that Mickey Mouse."

All in all, it seems clear that most departments are quite satisfied with a weeding out process which wastes the vast majority (from 50 to 85 per cent) of the graduate students who have been so carefully selected. The thought that the profession has a responsibility to "grow psychologists" out of the talented individuals they select seems scarcely to have entered our thinking. In my opinion, every student who leaves a department should be considered as a possible failure on the part of the department, either in selection, in teaching, in faculty-student relationship, or in the provision of a stimulating professional and scientific climate. His leaving should be carefully considered from each of these angles, in order that deficiencies may be corrected. Industry endeavors to learn from its "exit interviews." Psychology might do likewise.

Implicit Assumption 10: Students are best regarded as manipulable objects, not as persons

Certainly in a number of departments the relationship between students and faculty is remote and impersonal. This seems to grow out of two causes. In the first place the current ultrabehavioristic philosophy which underlies today's psychology tends to see all individuals simply as machines, managed by reward and punishment. Hence students are dealt with on this same basis. Since students do not like to be treated as objects, the net effect is low morale. Students even tend to treat each other in the same fashion. In some departments where there is a very heavy stress on evaluation, Student A will not give help to Student B because any improvement in B's showing will automatically put A lower "on the curve." This seems to be a vicious sort of attitude for a professional person who will later be expected to be a part of a scientific or professional team.

There is another factor in this remoteness of faculty-student relationship. It is that it is almost impossible to be close to a student if one's primary relationship to him is that of a judge and evaluator. This is hinted at by a graduate student who describes the faculty-student relationship at his university:

I see . . . instructors hiding behind a mask of impersonal, "scientific" objectivity in order to avoid the risk involved in *personal* interpersonal relationships, and perhaps out of distaste for the evaluative task they have imposed upon themselves.

In some instances faculty members put the student in a real "double bind" situation by giving him a contradictory message. It is as if the faculty member said: "I welcome you to a warm and close interpersonal relationship—and when you come close I will clobber you with my evaluation." The analogy to the parents of schizophrenics is painfully clear.

Again, solid evidence exists to contradict this 10th assumption. Thistlethwaite, in a study referred to above, found that faculty "informality and warmth of student-faculty contacts" in the institution is significantly related to the rate of production of Ph.D.'s in the natural sciences, and also in the arts, humanities, and social sciences (1963). Psychology may be hurting its own future by its insistence that the individual is nothing more than a machine.

WHY THESE ASSUMPTIONS?

Why is it that departments cling to these behaviors and their underlying assumptions when even a casual study would expose their fallacies. Why is it that advancement and prestige in departments of psychology depends on adherence to these shaky assumptions? Why is it, for example, that a faculty member who fails half his students on an examination is likely to be regarded as a better, because more "tough-minded," instructor than his colleague who fails none? Why is it that the man who treats his students as persons, as human beings, as junior colleagues, is apt to be looked on with some suspicion by his fellows? How is it that the behaviors described have been so rewarding that they have become imbedded in American psychology, in spite of their fallacious base?

I can only speculate. No doubt one reason is that students, consciously or unconsciously, after 16 years of academic spoonfeeding, tend to demand more of the same. Another reason may be that original, curious, autonomous students, pursuing their own goals, are nearly always disturbing to have around. They challenge pet beliefs and fixed ways of doing things, and hence as faculty members we may tend to avoid producing them. Still another reason is that as research has become an end rather than a means, various results follow. Teaching is devalued, purity of research design becomes all important, students are a means of getting research done. There is little concern with the true nurture of young scientists. Most important of all, perhaps, is that the philosophical views of psychologists regarding education and the nature of man seem not to have caught up with the advances in their own field. These are only possibilities. The question needs a great deal more investigation. There must be a rational explanation for the stubborn way in which psychology departments cling to these outmoded ideas.

SOME ALTERNATIVE ASSUMPTIONS

I am well aware that not all of the teaching which goes on in graduate programs operates on the assumptions I have listed. One graduate student, after making a number of complaints, writes:

More rarely, I will leave a class feeling inspired, excited, and stimulated. Here is the rare professor who encourages freedom of thought. He does not yield to the pressures of having to see his students pass the "finish line," but realizes that there is no finish line. A questioning, thought-provoking atmosphere exists. The student has the opportunity to react openly and honestly and to lend his own creative thoughts to the subject. The professor does not want his students to take what he says for granted, but rather he encourages them to think about what he says: to think, to react, to question; to accept, to reject, to incorporate.

It is the good fortune of psychology to have a number of such teachers, operating on a very different set of hypotheses, whose open-minded venturesome honesty leads to scientific curiosity and excitement in their students.

Although the operational procedures in most of our graduate programs tend to be in line with the assumptions I have listed, it would not be too difficult to implement a vastly improved program, based upon sharply different principles. Many of the elements of such a program have already been spelled out in the report on Education for Research in Psychology, to which I have made several references.

To set forth in detail what would be involved in such a program would necessarily be the topic of another article. Yet it might be fruitful to suggest an alternative list of assumptions, hypotheses, principles upon which a more enlightened graduate education might be based. To state these principles without amplification is to present only the skeleton of such a development, but perhaps even in their brief form they might stimulate thought and discussion. I would suggest the following as useful:[2]

1. The objective of the graduate program in psychology is to develop psychologists who can make original, significant, and continuing contributions primarily to the science of psychology and also to the professional practice related to this science.

2. The selection of graduate students is best based on three criteria: originality, intelligence, independence of thought. More adequate methods of assessing the first and third are needed.

3. Other things being equal, the best background training for a psychologist is a broad education including the humanities, arts, and sciences.

4. Students have the potentiality of learning, developing, making sensible educational choices. This potentiality can be released by a suitable psychological climate whose principal ingredients are freedom and stimulation.

---

[2]In formulating this condensation of assumptions, I have drawn upon an unpublished statement by Richard E. Farson, whose assistance is gratefully acknowledged.

5. Significant learning takes place when the subject matter is seen by the student to have relevance for his own purposes and development.

6. Learning is facilitated when the student participates responsibly in the learning process, choosing directions, making his own contributions, living with the consequences of his choices.

7. The time of the faculty member is best spent in providing resources which stimulate the desire to learn rather than in planning a guided curriculum.

8. Much significant learning is through doing. Placing the student in direct experiential confrontation with research problems, clinical problems, ethical and philosophical problems, is one of the most effective modes of promoting learning.

9. Learning is most likely to occur in the students when the faculty member approaches the interaction as learner rather than teacher.

10. Creativity of thought is facilitated when self-criticism and self-evaluation are basic, and evaluation by others is relegated to a position of minimal importance.

11. A meaningful certification for the Ph.D. is based on the quality of the research completed by the graduate student, the quality of his professional work, and the quality of the other products of learning. This certification would best be made by representatives of psychology as a whole, rather than by the student's own faculty.

These assumptions would constitute a basis for a very different type of graduate education than now exists. A detailed plan for their implementation would best be worked out by a group interested in such an orientation.

A CONCLUDING REMARK

If the day comes when psychology wishes to make a thoughtful appraisal of its methods of professional preparation, it will, I believe, throw out most of its current assumptions and procedures. I have tried to indicate, however, that lying all about, in the research literature of psychology itself, are the facts and findings upon which we could build a graduate program of which we could be proud— a program productive of freely independent, openly curious psychologists, unafraid in their search for genuinely new and deeply significant approximations to the truth.

REFERENCES

CLARK, J. V. *Education for the Use of Behavioral Science.* Los Angeles: Institute of Industrial Relations, UCLA, 1962.

EDUCATION FOR RESEARCH IN PSYCHOLOGY. (Report of a seminar group sponsored by the Education and Training Board of the A.P.A.) *Amer. Psychologist,* Vol. 19 (1959), pp. 167–79.

GETZELS, J. W. and JACKSON, P. W. "The Highly Intelligent and the Creative Adolescent," in C. Taylor and F. Barron (eds.), *Scientific Creativity: It's Recognition and Development.* New York: John Wiley and Sons, 1963.

GUILFORD, J. P. "A Revised Structure of Intellect," *Reports from the Psychol. Lab.,* #19. Los Angeles: Univ. of Southern Calif., 1957.

LYTTLETON, RAYMOND, as quoted in *Time Magazine* (Dec. 22, 1958).

MACKINNON, D. W. "The Nature of Creativity," in *Creativity and College Teaching,* Proceedings of a conference held at the Univ. of Kentucky, *Bull. of the Bureau of School Service,* Vol. 35, No. 4 (1963).

PARNES, S. J. and MEADOW, A. "Development of Individual Creative Talent," in C. Taylor and F. Barron (eds.), *Scientific Creativity: It's Recognition and Development.* New York: John Wiley and Sons, 1963.

ROE, ANNE. "Personal Problems and Science," in C. Taylor and F. Barron (eds.), *Scientific Creativity: Its Recognition and Development.* New York: John Wiley and Sons, 1963.

TAYLOR, C. and BARRON, F. (eds.), *Scientific Creativity: It's Recognition and Development.* New York: John Wiley and Sons, 1963.

THISTLETHWAITE, D. "The College Environment as a Determinant of Research Potentiality," in C. Taylor and F. Barron (eds.), *Scientific Creativity: It's Recognition and Development.* New York: John Wiley and Sons, 1963.

THIS IS ME*

Carl R. Rogers

I would like to take you inside, to tell you some of the things I have learned from the thousands of hours I have spent working intimately with individuals in personal distress.

I would like to make it very plain that these are learnings which have significance for *me.* I do not know whether they would hold true for you. I have no desire to present them as a guide for anyone else. Yet I have found that when another person has been willing to tell me something of his inner directions this has been of value to me, if only in sharpening my realization that my directions

---

*Excerpted from "This is Me," *On Becoming a Person* (Boston: Houghton Miffin Co., 1961), pp. 15–27. Used by permission.

are different. So it is in that spirit that I offer the learnings which follow. In each case I believe they became a part of my actions and inner convictions long before I realized them consciously. They are certainly scattered learnings, and incomplete. I can only say that they are and have been very important to me. I continually learn and relearn them. I frequently fail to act in terms of them, but later I wish that I had. Frequently I fail to see a new situation as one in which some of these learnings might apply.

They are not fixed. They keep changing. Some seem to be acquiring a stronger emphasis, others are perhaps less important to me than at one time, but they are all, to me, significant.

I will introduce each learning with a phrase or sentence which gives something of its personal meaning. Then I will elaborate on it a bit. There is not much organization to what follows except that the first learnings have to do mostly with relationships to others. There follow some that fall in the realm of personal values and convictions.

I might start off these several statements of significant learnings with a negative item. *In my relationships with persons I have found that it does not help, in the long run, to act as though I were something that I am not.* It does not help to act calm and pleasant when actually I am angry and critical. It does not help to act as though I know the answers when I do not. It does not help to act as though I were a loving person if actually, at the moment, I am hostile. It does not help for me to act as though I were full of assurance, if actually I am frightened and unsure. Even on a very simple level I have found that this statement seems to hold. It does not help for me to act as though I were well when I feel ill.

What I am saying here, put in another way, is that I have not found it to be helpful or effective in my relationships with other people to try to maintain a façade, to act in one way on the surface when I am experiencing something quite different underneath. It does not, I believe, make me helpful in my attempts to build up constructive relationships with other individuals. I would want to make it clear that while I feel I have learned this to be true, I have by no means adequately profited from it. In fact, it seems to me that most of the mistakes I make in personal relationships, most of the times in which I fail to be of help to other individuals, can be accounted for in terms of the fact that I have, for some defensive reason, behaved in one way at a surface level, while in reality my feelings run in a contrary direction.

A second learning might be stated as follows—*I find I am more effective when I can listen acceptantly to myself, and can be myself.* I feel that over the years I have learned to become more adequate in listening to *myself* so that I know, somewhat more adequately than I used to, what I am feeling at any given moment—to be able to realize *I am* angry; or that I *do* feel rejecting toward this person; or that I feel very full of warmth and affection for this individual; or that I am bored and uninterested in what is going on; or that I am eager to understand this individual; or that I am anxious and fearful in my relationship to this person. All of these diverse attitudes are feelings which I think I can listen to in myself. One way of putting this is that I feel I have become more adequate in letting myself *be* what I *am*. It becomes easier for me to accept myself as a decidedly imperfect person, who by no means functions at all times in the way in which I would like to function.

This must seem to some like a very strange direction in which to move. It seems to me to have value because the curious paradox is that when I accept myself as I am, then I change. I believe that I have learned this from my clients as well as within my own experience—that we cannot change, we cannot move away from what we are, until we thoroughly *accept* what we are. Then change seems to come about almost unnoticed.

Another result which seems to grow out of being myself is that relationships then become real. Real relationships have an exciting way of being vital and meaningful. If I can accept the fact that I am annoyed at or bored by this client or this student, then I am also much more likely to be able to accept his feelings in response. I can also accept the changed experience and the changed feelings which are then likely to occur in me and in him. Real relationships tend to change rather than to remain static.

So I find it effective to let myself be what I am in my attitudes; to know when I have reached my limit of endurance or of tolerance, and to accept that as a fact; to know when I desire to mold or manipulate people, and to accept that as a fact in myself. I would like to be as acceptant of these feelings as of feelings of warmth, interest, permissiveness, kindness, understanding, which are also a very real part of me. It is when I do accept all these attitudes as a fact, as a part of me, that my relationship with the other person then becomes what it is, and is able to grow and change most readily.

I come now to a central learning which has had a great deal of significance for me. I can state this learning as follows: *I have found it of enormous value when I can permit myself to understand another person.* The way in which I have worded this statement may seem strange to you. Is it necessary to *permit* oneself to understand another? I think that it is. Our first reaction to most of the statements which we hear from other people is an immediate evaluation, or judgment, rather than an understanding of it. When someone expresses some feeling or attitude or belief, our tendency is, almost immediately, to feel "That's right"; or "That's stupid"; "That's abnormal"; "That's unreasonable"; "That's incorrect"; "That's not nice." Very rarely do we permit ourselves to *understand* precisely what the meaning of his statement is to him. I believe this is because understanding is risky. If I let myself really understand another person, I might be changed by that understanding. And we all fear change. So as I say, it is not an easy thing to permit oneself to understand an individual, to enter thoroughly and completely and empathically into his frame of reference. It is also a rare thing.

To understand is enriching in a double way. I find when I am working with clients in distress, that to understand the bizarre world of a psychotic individual, or to understand and sense the attitudes of a person who feels that life is too tragic to bear, or to understand a man who feels that he is a worthless and inferior individual—each of these understandings somehow enriches me. I learn from these experiences in ways that change me, that make me a different and, I think, a more responsive person. Even more important perhaps, is the fact that my understanding of these individuals permits them to change. It permits them to accept their own fears and bizarre thoughts and tragic feelings and discouragements, as well as their moments of courage and kindness and love and sensitivity. And it is their experience as well as mine that when someone fully understands those feelings, this enables them to accept those feelings in themselves. Then they find both the feelings and themselves changing. Whether it is understanding a woman who feels that very literally she has a hook in her head by which others lead her about, or understanding a man who feels that no one is as lonely, no one is as separated from others as he, I find these understandings to be of value to me. But also, and even more importantly, to be understood has a very positive value to these individuals.

There is another learning which has had importance for me. *I have found it enriching to open channels whereby others can communicate their feelings, their private perceptual worlds, to me.* Because understanding is rewarding, I would like to reduce the barriers between others and me so that they can, if they wish, reveal themselves more fully.

In the therapeutic relationship there are a number of ways by which I can make it easier for the client to communicate himself. I can by my own attitudes create a safety in the relationship which makes such communication more possible. A sensitiveness of understanding which sees him as he is to himself, and accepts him as having those perceptions and feelings, helps too.

But as a teacher also I have found that I am enriched when I can open channels through which others can share themselves with me. So I try, often not too successfully, to create a climate in the classroom where feelings can be expressed, where people can differ—with each other and with the instructor. I have also frequently asked for "reaction sheets" from students—in which they can express themselves individually and personally regarding the course. They can tell of the way it is or is not meeting their needs, they can express their feelings regarding the instructor, or can tell of the personal difficulties they are having in relation to the course. These reaction sheets have no relation whatsoever to their grade. Sometimes the same sessions of a course are experienced in diametrically opposite ways. One student says, "My feeling is one of indefinable revulsion with the tone of this class." Another, a foreign student, speaking of the same week of the same course says, "Our class follows the best, fruitful and scientific way of learning. But for people who have been taught for a long, long time, as we have, by the lecture type, authoritative method, this new procedure is ununderstandable. People like us are conditioned to hear the instructor, to keep passively our notes and memorize his reading assignments for the exams. There is no need to say that it takes long time for people to get rid of their habits regardless of whether or not their habits are sterile, infertile and barren." To open myself to these sharply different feelings has been a deeply rewarding thing.

I have found the same thing true in groups where I am the administrator, or perceived as the leader. I wish to reduce the need for fear or defensiveness, so that people can communicate their feelings freely. This has been most exciting, and has led me to a whole new view of what administration can be. But I cannot expand on that here.

There is another very important learning which has come to me in my counseling work. I can voice this learning very briefly. *I have found it highly rewarding when I can accept another person.*

I have found that truly to accept another person and his feelings is by no means an easy thing, any more than is understanding. Can I really permit another person to feel hostile toward me? Can I accept his anger as a real and legitimate part of himself? Can I accept him when he views life and its problems in a way quite different from mine? Can I accept him when he feels very positively toward me, admiring me and wanting to model himself after me? All this is involved in acceptance, and it does not come easy. I believe that it is an increasingly common pattern in our culture for each one of us to believe, "Every other person must feel and think and believe the same as I do." We find it very hard to permit our children or our parents or our spouses to feel differently than we do about particular issues or problems. We cannot permit our clients or our students to differ from us or to utilize their experience in their own individual ways. On a national scale, we cannot permit another nation to think or feel differently than we do. Yet it has come to seem to me that this separateness of individuals, the right of each individual to utilize his experience in his own way and to discover his own meanings in it,—this is one of the most priceless potentialities of life. Each person is an island unto himself, in a very real sense; and he can only build bridges to other islands if he is first of all willing to be himself and permitted to be himself. So I find that when I can accept another person, which means specifically accepting the feelings and attitudes and beliefs that he has as a real and vital part of him, then I am assisting him to become a person, and there seems to me great value in this.

The next learning I want to state may be difficult to communicate. It is this. *The more I am open to the realities in me and in the other person, the less do I find myself wishing to rush in to "fix things."* As I try to listen to myself and the experiencing going on in me, and the more I try to extend that same listening attitude to another person, the more respect I feel for the complex processes of life. So I become less and less inclined to hurry in to fix things, to set goals, to mold people, to manipulate and push them in the way that I would like them to go. I am much more content simply to be myself and to let another person be himself. I know very well that this must seem like a strange, almost an Oriental point of view. What is life for if we are not going to do things to people? What is life for if we are not going to mold them to our purposes? What is life for if we are not going to teach them the things that *we* think they should learn? What is life for if we are not going to make them think and feel as we do? How can anyone hold such an inactive point of view as the one I am expressing? I am sure that attitudes such as these must be a part of the reaction of many of you.

Yet the paradoxical aspect of my experience is that the more I am simply willing to be myself in all this complexity of life and the more I am willing to understand and accept the realities in myself and in the other person, the more change seems to be stirred up. It is a very paradoxical thing—that to the degree that each one of us is willing to be himself, then he finds not only himself changing, but he finds that other people to whom he relates are also changing. At least this is a very vivid part of my experience, and one of the deepest things I think I have learned in my personal and professional life.

Let me turn now to some other learnings which are less concerned with relationships, and have more to do with my own actions and values. The first of these is very brief. *I can trust my experience.*

One of the basic things which I was a long time in realizing, and which I am still learning, is that when an activity *feels* as though it is valuable or worth doing, it *is* worth doing. Put another way, I have learned that my total organismic sensing of a situation is more trustworthy than my intellect.

All of my professional life I have been going in directions which others thought were foolish, and about which I have had many doubts myself. But I have never regretted moving in directions which "felt right," even though I have often felt lonely or foolish at the time.

I have found that when I have trusted some inner non-intellectual sensing, I have discovered wisdom in the move. In fact, I have found that when I have followed one of these unconventional paths because it felt right or true, then in five or ten years many of my colleagues have joined me, and I no longer need to feel alone in it.

As I gradually come to trust my total reactions more deeply, I find that I can use them to guide my thinking. I have come to have more respect for those vague thoughts which occur in me from time to time, which *feel* as though they were significant. I am inclined to think that these unclear thoughts or hunches will lead me to important areas. I think of it as trusting the totality of my experience, which I have learned to suspect is wiser than my intellect. It is fallible I am sure, but I believe it to be less fallible than my conscious mind alone. My attitude is very well expressed by Max Weber the artist, when he says, "In carrying on my own humble creative effort, I depend greatly upon that which I do not yet know, and upon that which I have not yet done."

Very closely related to this learning is a corollary that, *evaluation by others is not a guide for me.* The judgments of others, while they are to be listened to, and taken into account for what they are, can never be a guide for me. This has been a hard thing to learn. I remember how shaken I was, in the early days, when a scholarly, thoughtful man who seemed to me a much more competent and knowledgeable psychologist than I, told me what a mistake I was making by getting interested in psychotherapy. It could never lead anywhere, and as a psychologist I would not even have the opportunity to practice it.

In later years it has sometimes jolted me a bit to learn that I am, in the eyes of some others, a fraud, a person practicing medicine without a license, the author of a very superficial and damaging sort of therapy, a power seeker, a mystic, etc. And I have been equally disturbed by equally extreme praise. But I have not been too much concerned because I have come to feel that only one person (at least in my lifetime, and perhaps ever) can know whether what I am doing is honest, thorough, open and sound, or false and defensive and unsound, and I am that person. I am happy to get all sorts of evidence regarding what I am doing and criticism (both friendly and hostile) and praise (both sincere and fawning) are a part of such evidence. But to weigh this evidence and to determine its meaning and usefulness is a task I cannot relinquish to anyone else.

In view of what I have been saying the next learning will probably not surprise you. *Experience is, for me, the highest authority.* The touchstone of validity is my own experience. No other person's ideas, and none of my own ideas, are as authoritative as my experience. It is to experience that I must return again and again, to discover a closer approximation to truth as it is in the process of becoming in me.

Neither the Bible nor the prophets—neither Freud nor research—neither the revelations of God nor man—can take precedence over my own direct experience.

My experience is the more authoritative as it becomes more primary, to use the semanticist's term. Thus the hierarchy of experience would be most authoritative at its lowest level. If I read a theory of psychotherapy, and if I formulate a theory of psychotherapy based on my work with clients, and if I also have a direct experience of psychotherapy with a client, then the degree of authority increases in the order in which I have listed these experiences.

My experience is not authoritative because it is infallible. It is the basis of authority because it can always be checked in new primary ways. In this way its frequent error or fallibility is always open to correction.

Now another personal learning. *I enjoy the discovering of order in experience.* It seems inevitable that I seek for the meaning or the orderliness or lawfulness in any large body of experience. It is this kind of curiosity, which I find it very satisfying to pursue, which has led me to each of the major formulations I have made. It led me to search for the orderliness in all the conglomeration of things clinicians did for children, and out of that came my book on *The Clinical Treatment of the Problem Child.* It let me to formulate the general principles which seemed to be operative in psychotherapy, and that has led to several books and many articles. It has led me into research to test the various types of lawfulness which I feel I have encountered in my experience. It has enticed me to construct theories to bring together the orderliness of that which has already been experienced and to project this order forward into new and unexplored realms where it may be further tested.

Thus I have come to see both scientific research and the process of theory construction as being aimed toward the inward ordering of significant experience. Research is the persistent disciplined effort to make sense and order out of the phenomena of subjective experience. It is justified because it is satisfying to perceive the world as having order, and because rewarding results often ensue when one understands the orderly relationships which appear in nature.

So I have come to recognize that the reason I devote myself to research, and to the building of theory, is to satisfy a need for perceiving order and meaning, a subjective need which exists in me. I have, at times, carried on research for other reasons—to satisfy others, to convince opponents and skeptics, to get ahead professionally, to gain prestige, and for other unsavory reasons. These errors in judgment and activity have only served to convince me more deeply that there is only one sound reason for pursuing scientific activities, and that is to satisfy a need for meaning which is in me.

Another learning which cost me much to recognize, can be stated in four words. *The facts are friendly.*

It has interested me a great deal that most psychotherapists, especially the psychoanalysts, have steadily refused to make any scientific investigation of their therapy, or to permit others to do this. I can understand this reaction because I have felt it. Especially in our early investigations I can well remember the anxiety of waiting to see how the findings came out. Suppose our hypotheses were *dis*proved! Suppose we were mistaken in our views! Suppose our opinions were not justified! At such times, as I look back, it seems to me that I regarded the facts as potential enemies, as possible bearers of disaster. I have perhaps been slow in coming to realize that the facts are *always* friendly. Every bit of evidence one can acquire, in any area, leads one that much closer to what is true. And being closer to the truth can never be a harmful or dangerous or unsatisfying thing. So while I still hate to readjust my thinking, still hate to give up old ways of perceiving and conceptualizing, yet at some deeper level I have, to a considerable degree, come to realize that these painful reorganizations are what is known as *learning*, and that though painful they always lead to a more satisfying, because somewhat more accurate, way of seeing life. Thus at the present time one of the most enticing areas for thought and speculation is an area where several of my pet ideas have *not* been upheld by the evidence. I feel if I can only puzzle my way through this problem that I will find a much more satisfying approximation to the truth. I feel sure the facts will be my friends.

Somewhere here I want to bring in a learning which has been most rewarding, because it makes me feel so deeply akin to others. I can word it this way. *What is most personal is most general.* There have been times when in talking with students or staff, or in my writing, I have expressed myself in ways so personal that I have felt I was expressing an attitude which it was probable no one else could understand, because it was so uniquely my own. Two written examples of this are the Preface to *Client-Centered Therapy* (regarded as most unsuitable by the publishers), and an article on "Persons or Science." In these instances I have almost invariably found that the very feeling which has seemed to me most private, most personal, and hence most incomprehensible by others, has turned out to be an expression for which there is a resonance in many other people. It has led me to believe that what is most personal and unique in each one of us is probably the very element which would, if it were shared or expressed, speak most deeply to others. This has helped me to understand artists and poets as people who have dared to express the unique in themselves.

There is one deep learning which is perhaps basic to all of the things I have said thus far. It has been forced upon me by more than twenty-five years of trying to be helpful to individuals in personal distress. It is simply this. *It has been my experience that persons have a basically positive direction.* In my deepest contacts with individuals in therapy, even those whose troubles are most disturbing, whose behavior has been most anti-social, whose feelings seem most abnormal, I find this to be true. When I can sensitively understand the feelings which they are expressing, when I am able to accept them as separate persons in their own right, then I find that they tend to move in certain directions. And what are these directions in which they tend to move? The words which I believe are most truly descriptive are words such as positive, constructive, moving toward self-actualization, growing toward maturity, growing toward socialization. I have come to feel that the more fully the individual is understood and accepted, the more he tends to drop the false fronts with which he has been meeting life, and the more he tends to move in a direction which is forward.

I would not want to be misunderstood on this. I do not have a Pollyanna view of human nature. I am quite aware that out of defensiveness and inner fear individuals can and do behave in ways which are incredibly cruel, horribly destructive, immature, regressive, anti-social, hurtful. Yet one of the most refreshing and invigorating parts of my experience is to work with such individuals and to discover the strongly positive directional tendencies which exist in them, as in all of us, at the deepest levels.

Let me bring this long list to a close with one final learning which can be stated very briefly. *Life, at its best, is a flowing, changing process in which nothing is fixed.* In my clients and in myself I find that when life is richest and most rewarding it is a flowing process. To experience this is both fascinating and a little frightening. I find I am at my best when I can let the flow of my experience carry me in a direction which appears to be forward, toward goals of which I am but dimly aware. In thus floating with the complex stream of my experiencing, and in trying to understand its ever-changing complexity, it should be evident that there are no fixed points. When I am thus able to be in process, it is clear that there can be no closed system of beliefs, no unchanging set of principles which I hold. Life is guided by a changing understanding of an interpretation of my experience. It is always in process of becoming.

I trust it is clear now why there is no philosophy or belief or set of principles which I could encourage or persuade others to have or hold. I can only try to live by *my* interpretation of the current meaning of *my* experience, and try to give others the permission and freedom to develop their own inward freedom and thus their own meaningful interpretation of their own experience.

If there is such a thing as truth, this free individual process of search should, I believe, converge toward it. And in a limited way, this is also what I seem to have experienced.

THE JONAH COMPLEX*

Abraham H. Maslow

In the time I have left I'd like to turn to one of the many reasons for what Angyal (1965) called the evasion of growth. Certainly everybody in this room would like to be better than he is. We have, all of us, an impulse to improve ourselves, an impulse toward

*This is excerpted from a paper which was presented at an Institute of Men symposium, Duquesne University, Nov. 18, 1966. Published in *Humanitas*, 1967.

actualizing more of our potentialities, toward self-actualization, or full humanness, or human fulfillment, or whatever term you like. Granted this for everybody here then, what holds us up? What blocks us?

One such defense against growth that I'd like to speak about specially—because it hasn't been noticed much—I shall call the Jonah Complex.[1]

In my own notes I had at first labeled this defense the "fear of one's own greatness" or the "evasion of one's destiny" or the "running away from one's own best talents." I had wanted to stress as bluntly and sharply as I could the non-Freudian point that we fear our best as well as our worst, even though in different ways. It is certainly possible for most of us to be greater than we are in actuality. We all have unused potentialities or not fully developed ones. It is certainly true that many of us evade our constitutionally suggested vocations (call, destiny, task in life, mission). Often we run away from the responsibilities dictated (or rather suggested) by nature, by fate, even sometimes by accident, just as Jonah tried—in vain—to run away from *his* fate.

We fear our highest possibilities (as well as our lowest ones). We are generally afraid to become that which we can glimpse in our most perfect moments, under the most perfect conditions, under conditions of greatest courage. We enjoy and even thrill to the god-like possibilities we see in ourselves in such peak moments. And yet we simultaneously shiver with weakness, awe, and fear before these very same possibilities.

I have found it easy enough to demonstrate this to my students simply by asking, "Which of you in this class hopes to write the great American novel, or to be a Senator, or Governor, or President? Who wants to be Secretary-General of the United Nations? Or a great composer? Who aspires to be a saint, like Schweitzer, perhaps? Who among you will be a great leader?" Generally everybody starts giggling, blushing, and squirming until I ask, "If not you, then who else?" Which, of course, is the truth. And in this same way, as I push my graduate students towards these higher levels of aspiration, I'll say, "What great book are you now secretly planning to write?" And then they often blush and stammer and push me off in some way. But why should I not ask that question? Who else will write the books on psychology except psychologists? So I can ask,

---

[1] This name was suggested by my friend, Professor Frank Manual, with whom I had discussed this puzzle.

"Do you not plan to be a psychologist?" "Well, yes." "Are you in training to be a mute or an inactive psychologist? What's the advantage of that? That's not a good path to self-actualization. No, you must want to be a first-class psychologist, meaning the best, the very best you are capable of becoming. If you deliberately plan to be less than you are capable of being, then I warn you that you'll be deeply unhappy for the rest of your life. You will be evading your own capacities, your own possibilities."

Not only are we ambivalent about our own highest possibilities, we are also in a perpetual and, I think, universal—perhaps even *necessary*—conflict and ambivalence over these same highest possibilities in other people, and in human nature in general. Certainly we love and admire good men, saints—honest, virtuous, clean men. But could anybody who has looked into the depths of human nature fail to be aware of our mixed and often hostile feelings toward saintly men? Or toward very beautiful women or men? Or toward great creators? Or toward our intellectual geniuses? It is not necessary to be a psychotherapist to see this phenomenon—let us call it "Countervaluing." Any reading of history will turn up plenty of examples, or perhaps even I could say that any such historical search might fail to turn up a single exception throughout the whole history of mankind. We surely love and admire all the persons who have incarnated the true, the good, the beautiful, the just, the perfect, the ultimately successful. And yet they also make us uneasy, anxious, confused, perhaps a little jealous or envious, a little inferior, clumsy. They usually make us lose our aplomb, our self-possession and self-regard. (Nietzsche is still our best teacher here.)

Here we have a first clue. My impression so far is that the greatest people, simply by their presence and by being what they are, make us feel aware of our lesser worth, whether or not they intend to. If this is an unconscious effect and we are not aware of why we feel stupid or ugly or inferior whenever such a person turns up, we are apt to respond with projection; i.e., we react as if he were *trying* to make us feel inferior, as if we were the target (L. Huxley, 1963). Hostility is then an understandable consequence. It looks to me so far as if conscious awareness tends to fend off this hostility. That is, if you are willing to attempt self-awareness and self-analysis of your *own* countervaluing—i.e., of your unconscious fear and hatred of true, good, beautiful, etc., people—you will very likely be less nasty to them. And I am willing also to extrapolate to the guess that if you can learn to love more purely the highest values in others, this might make you love these qualities in yourself in a less frightened way.

Allied to this dynamic is the awe before the highest, of which Rudolf Otto (1958) has given us the classical description. Putting this together with Eliade's insights (1961) into sacralization and desacralization, we become more aware of the universality of the fear of direct confrontation with a god or with the godlike. In some religions death is the inevitable consequence. Most preliterate societies also have places or objects that are taboo because they are too sacred and, therefore, *too dangerous*. In the last chapter of my *Psychology of Science* (1966) I have also given examples, mostly from science and medicine of desacralizing and resacralizing, and tried to explain the psychodynamics of these processes. Mostly it comes down to awe before the highest and best. (I want to stress that this awe is intrinsic, justified, *right*, suitable, rather than some sickness or failing to get "cured of.")

But here again my feeling is that this awe and fear need not be negative alone, something to make us flee or cower. These are also desirable and enjoyable feelings capable of bringing us even to the point of highest ecstasy and rapture. Conscious awareness, insight, and "working through," *à la* Freud, is the answer here too I think. This is the best path I know to the acceptance of our highest powers and whatever elements of greatness or goodness or wisdom or talent we may have concealed or evaded.

A helpful sidelight for me has come from trying to understand why peak experiences are ordinarily transient and brief (1962). The answer becomes clearer and clearer. *We are just not strong enough to endure more.* It is just too shaking and wearing. So often people in such ecstatic moments say, "It's too much" or "I can't stand it" or "I could die." And as I get the descriptions, I sometimes feel, Yes, they *could* die. Delirious happiness cannot be borne for long. Our organisms are just too weak for any large doses of greatness, just as they would be too weak to endure hour-long sexual orgasms, for example.

The word "peak experience" is more appropriate than I realized at first. The acute emotion must be climactic and momentary and it *must* give way to nonecstatic serenity, calmer happiness, and the intrinsic pleasures of clear, contemplative cognition of the highest goods. The climactic emotion can not endure, but B-Cognition *can* (Maslow, 1964, 1966).

Doesn't this help us to understand our Jonah Complex? It is partly a justified fear of being torn apart, of losing control, of being shattered and disintegrated, even of being killed by the experience. Great emotions after all can in *fact* overwhelm us. The fear of surrendering to such an experience, a fear which reminds us of all the parallel fears found in sexual frigidity, can be understood better I think through familiarity with the literature of psychodynamics and depth psychology, and of the psychophysiology and medical psychomatics of emotion.

There is still another psychological process that I have run across in my explorations of failure to actualize the self. This evasion of growth can also be set in motion by a fear of paranoia. Of course this has been said in more universal ways. Promethean and Faustian legends are found in practically any culture.[2] For instance, the Greeks called it the fear of *hubris*. It has been called "sinful pride," which is, of course, a permanent human problem. The person who says to himself, "Yes, I will be a great philosopher and I will rewrite Plato and do it better," must sooner or later be struck dumb by his grandiosity, his arrogance. And especially in his weaker moments, will say to himself, who? me? and think of it as a crazy fantasy or even fear it as a delusion. He compares his knowledge of his inner private self, with all its weakness, vacillation, and shortcomings, with the bright, shining, perfect, and faultless image he has of Plato. Then, of course, he'll feel presumptuous and grandiose. (What he doesn't realize is that Plato, introspecting, must have felt just the same way about himself but went ahead anyway, overriding his doubts about himself.)

For some people this evasion of one's own growth, setting low levels of aspiration, the fear of doing what one is capable of doing, voluntary self-crippling, pseudo-stupidity, mock humility is, in fact, defense against grandiosity, arrogance, sinful pride, hubris. There are people who cannot manage that graceful integration between the humility and the pride which is absolutely necessary for creative work. To invent or create you must have the "arrogance of creativeness" which so many investigators have noticed. But, of course, if you have *only* the arrogance without the humility, then you are in fact paranoid. You *must* be aware not only of the godlike possibilities within, but also of the existential human limitations. You must be able simultaneously to laugh at yourself and at all human pre-

---

[2]W. H. Sheldon's excellent book on this subject (*Psychology and the Promethean Will* [New York: Harper & Row, 1936]) is not quoted often enough on this subject, possibly because it came before we were quite ready to assimilate it.

tensions. If you can be amused by the worm trying to be a god (Wilson, 1959), then in fact you may be able to go on trying and being arrogant without fearing paranoia or bringing down upon yourself the evil eye. This is a good technique.

May I mention one more such technique that I saw at its best in Aldous Huxley, who was certainly a great man in the sense I've been discussing—one who was able to accept his talents and use them to the full. He managed it by perpetually marveling at how interesting and fascinating everything was, by wondering like a youngster at how miraculous things are, by saying frequently, "Extraordinary! Extraordinary!" He could look out at the world with wide eyes, with unabashed innocence, awe, and fascination, which is a kind of admission of smallness, a form of humility, and then proceed calmly and unafraid to the great tasks he set for himself.

Finally, may I refer you to a paper of mine (1963), relevant in itself but also as the first in a possible series. Its name, "The need to know and the fear of knowing," illustrates well what I want to say about *each* of the intrinsic or ultimate values that I've called Values of Being (B-Values). I am trying to say that these ultimate values, which I think are also the highest needs (or metaneeds, as I called them [1967]) fall, like all basic needs, into the basic Freudian schema of impulse *and* defense against that impulse. Thus it is certainly demonstrable that we need the truth and love it and seek it. And yet it is just as easy to demonstrate that we are also simultaneously *afraid* to know the truth. For instance, certain truths carry automatic responsibilities which may be anxiety producing. One way to evade the responsibility and the anxiety is simply to evade consciousness of the truth.

I predict that we will find a similar dialectic for each of the intrinsic Values of Being, and I have vaguely thought of doing a series of papers on, e.g., "The love of beauty and our uneasiness with it," "Our love of the good man and our irritation with him," "Our search for excellence and our tendency to destroy it," etc. Of course, these countervalues are stronger in neurotic people, but it looks to me as if all of us must make our peace with these mean impulses within ourselves. And my impression so far is that the best way to do this is to transmute envy, jealousy, *presentiment,* and nastiness into humble admiration, gratitude, appreciation, adoration, and even worship via conscious insight and working through (1960). This is the road to feeling small and weak and unworthy and *accepting* these feelings instead of needing to protect a spuriously high self-esteem by striking out (Horney, 1950).

And again I think it is obvious that understanding of this basic existential problem should help us to embrace the B-Values not only in others, but also in ourselves, thereby helping to resolve the Jonah Complex.

REFERENCES

ANGYAL, A. *Neurosis and Treatment: A Holistic Theory.* New York: Wiley, 1965.

ELIADE, M. *The Scared and the Profane.* New York: Harper & Row, 1961.

HORNEY, K. *Neurosis and Human Growth.* New York: W. W. Norton, 1950.

HUXLEY, L. *You Are Not the Target.* New York: Farras, Straus, 1963.

MASLOW, A. H. "Lessons from the Peak-Experiences," *Journal·of Humanistic Psychology,* Vol. 2 (1962), pp. 9–18.

———. "The Need to Know and the Fear of Knowing," *Journal of General Psychology,* Vol. 68 (1963), pp. 111–25.

———. *Religions, Values, and Peak-Experiences.* Columbus: Ohio State University Press, 1964.

———. *The Psychology of Science: A Reconnaissance.* New York: Harper & Row, 1966.

———. "The Biological Rooting of the Spiritual Life." *The Humanist,* 1967.

MASLOW, A. H., RAND, H., and NEWMAN, S. "Some Parallels between the Dominance and Sexual Behavior of Monkeys and the Fantasies of Patients in Psychotherapy," *Journal of Nervous & Mental Disease,* Vol. 131 (1960), pp. 202–12.

OTTO, R. *The Idea of the Holy.* New York: Oxford University Press, 1958.

SHELDON, W. H. *Psychology and the Promethean Will.* New York: Harper & Row, 1936.

WILSON, C., *The Stature of Man.* New York: Houghton Mifflin, 1959.

HEALTHY PERSONALITY AND SELF-DISCLOSURE*

Sidney M. Jourard

For a long time, health and well-being have been taken for granted as "givens," and disease has been viewed as the problem for man to solve. Today, however, increasing numbers of scientists have begun to adopt a reverse point of view: Disease and trouble

---

*Talk given November 20, 1958, at a meeting of the North Florida Section of the American Personnel and Guidance Association and published in *Mental Hygiene,* Vol. 43 (1959).

are coming to be viewed as the givens, and specification of positive health and its conditions as the important goal. Physical, mental, and social health are values representing restrictions on the total variance of being. The scientific problem here consists in arriving at a definition of health, determining its relevant dimensions, and then identifying the independent variables of which these are a function.

Scientists, however, are supposed to be hard-boiled, and they insist that phenomena, in order to be counted "real," must be public. Hence, many behavioral scientists ignore man's self, or soul, since it is essentially a private phenomenon. Others, however, are not so quick to allocate man's self to the limbo of the unimportant, and they insist that we cannot understand man and his lot until we take his self into account.

I probably fall into the camp of these investigators who want to explore health as a positive problem in its own right and who, further, take man's self seriously—as a reality to be explained and as a variable which produces consequences for weal or woe. In this chapter, I would like more fully to explore the connection between positive health and the disclosure of self. Let me commence with some sociological truisms.

Social systems require their members to play certain roles. Unless the roles are adequately played, the social systems will not produce the results for which they have been organized. This flat statement applies to social systems as simple as one developed by an engaged couple and to those as complex as a total nation among nations.

Societies have socialization "factories" and "mills"—families and schools—which serve the function of training people to play the age, sex, and occupational roles which they shall be obliged to play throughout their life in the social system. Broadly speaking, if a person plays his roles suitably, he can be regarded as a more or less normal personality. *Normal personalities, however, are not necessarily healthy personalities* (Jourard, 1958, pp. 16–18).

Healthy personalities are people who play their roles satisfactorily and at the same time derive personal satisfaction from role enactment; more, they keep growing and they maintain high-level physical wellness (Dunn, 1959). It is probable enough, speaking from the standpoint of a stable social system, for people to be normal personalities. But it is possible to be a normal personality and be absolutely miserable. We would count such a normal personality unhealthy. In fact, normality in some social systems—successful acculturation to them—reliably produces ulcers, piles, paranoia, or compulsiveness. We also have to regard as unhealthy those people who have never been able to enact the roles that legitimately can be expected from them.

Counselors, guidance workers, and psychotherapists are obliged to treat—with both patterns of unhealthy personality—those people who have been unable to learn their roles and those who play their roles quite well, but suffer the agonies of boredom, frustration, anxiety, or stultification. If our clients are to be helped, they must change, and change in *valued* directions. A change in a valued direction may arbitrarily be called growth. We have yet to give explicit statement to these valued directions for growth, though a beginning has been made (Fromm, 1947; Jahoda, 1958; Jourard, 1958; Maslow, 1954; Rogers, 1958). We who are professionally concerned with the happiness, growth, and well-being of our clients may be regarded as professional lovers, not unlike the Cyprian sisterhood. It would be fascinating to pursue this parallel further, but for the moment let us ask instead what this has to do with self-disclosure.

To answer this question, let's tune in on an imaginary interview between a client and his counselor. The client says, "I have never told this to a soul, doctor, but I can't stand my wife, my mother is a nag, my father is a bore, and my boss is an absolutely hateful and despicable tyrant. I have been carrying on an affair for the past 10 years with the lady next door, and at the same time I am a deacon in the church." The counselor says, showing great understanding and empathy, "Mm-humm!"

If we listened for a long enough period of time, we would find that the client talks and talks about himself to this highly sympathetic and empathic listener. At some later time, the client may eventually say, "Gosh, you have helped me a lot. I see what I must do and I will go ahead and do it."

Now this talking about oneself to another person is what I call self-disclosure. It would appear, without assuming anything, that self-disclosure is a factor in the process of effective counseling or psychotherapy. Would it be too arbitrary an assumption to propose that people become clients *because they have not disclosed themselves in some optimum degree to the people in their life?*

An historical digression: Toward the end of the 19th century, Joseph Breuer, a Viennese physician, discovered (probably accidentally) that when his hysterical patients talked about themselves, disclosing not only the verbal content of their memories, but also the feelings that they had suppressed at the time of assorted "traumatic" experiences, their hysterical symptoms disappeared. Somewhere along the line, Breuer withdrew from a situation which would have made him Freud's peer in history's hall of fame. When Breuer permitted his patients "to be," it scared him, one gathers, because some of his female patients disclosed themselves to be quite sexy, and what was probably worse, they felt quite sexy toward him. Freud, however, did not flinch. He made the momentous discovery that the neurotic people of his time were struggling like mad to avoid "being," to avoid being known and, in Allport's (1955) terms, to avoid "becoming." He learned that his patients, when they were given the opportunity to "be"—which free association on a couch is nicely designed to do—would disclose that they had all manner of horrendous thoughts and feelings which they did not even dare disclose to themselves, much less express in the presence of another person. Freud learned to permit his patients to be, through permitting them to disclose themselves utterly to another human. He evidently did not trust anyone enough to be willing to disclose himself vis-à-vis; so he disclosed himself to himself on paper (Freud, 1955) and learned the extent to which he was himself self-alienated. Roles for people in Victorian days were even more restrictive than today, and Freud discovered that when people struggled to avoid being and knowing themselves, they got sick. They could only become well and stay relatively well when they came to know themselves through self-disclosure to another person. This makes me think of Georg Groddeck's magnificent *Book of the It (Id)* in which, in the guise of letters to a naive young woman, Groddeck shows the contrast between the *public self*—pretentious role playing—and the warded off but highly dynamic *id*—which I here very loosely translate as "real self."

Let me at this point draw a distinction between role relationships and interpersonal relationships—a distinction which is often overlooked in the current spate of literature that has to do with human relations. Roles are inescapable. They must be played or else the social system will not work. A role by definition is a repertoire of behavior patterns which must be rattled off in appropriate contexts, and all behavior which is irrelevant to the role must be suppressed. But what we often forget is the fact that it is a *person* who is playing the role. This person has a self, or I should say he *is* a self. All too often the roles that a person plays do not do justice to all of his self. In fact, there may be nowhere that he may just *be* himself. Even more, the person may not *know* his self. He may, in Horney's (1950) terms, be self-alienated. This fascinating term, "self-alienation," means that an individual is estranged from his real self. His real self becomes a stranger, a feared and distrusted stranger. Estrangement, alienation from one's real self, is at the root of the "neurotic personality of our time" so eloquently described by Horney (1936). Fromm (1947) referred to the same phenomenon as a socially patterned defect. Self-alienation is a sickness which is so widely shared that no one recognizes it. We may take it for granted that all the clients whom we encounter are self-alienated to a greater or lesser extent. If you ask anyone to answer the question, "Who are you?" the answer will generally be, "I am a psychologist," "a businessman," a "teacher," or what have you. The respondent will probably tell you the name of the role with which he feels most closely identified. As a matter of fact, the respondent spends a great part of his life trying to discover who he is, and once he has made some such discovery, he spends the rest of his life trying to play the part. Of course, some of the roles—age, sex, family, or occupational roles— may be so restrictive that they fit a person in a manner not too different from the girdle of a 200-pound lady who is struggling to look like Brigitte Bardot. There is Faustian drama all about us in this world of role playing. Everywhere we see people who have sold their soul, or their real self, if you wish, in order to be a psychologist, a businessman, a nurse, a physician, a this or a that.

Now, I have suggested that no social system can exist unless the members play their roles and play them with precision and elegance. But here is an odd observation, and yet one which you can all corroborate just by thinking back over your own experience. It is possible to be involved in a social group such as a family or a work setting for years and years, playing one's roles nicely with the other members—and never getting to know the *persons* who are playing the other roles. Roles can be played personally and impersonally, as we are beginning to discover. A husband can be married to his wife for 15 years and never come to know her. He knows her as "the wife." This is the paradox of the *"lonely* crowd" (Riesman, 1950). It is the loneliness which people try to counter with "togetherness." But much of today's "togetherness" is like the "parallel play" of two-year-old children, or like the professors in Stringfellow Barr's (1958) novel who, when together socially, lecture *past* one another alternately and sometimes simultaneously. There is no real self-to-self or person-to-person meeting in such transactions. Now what does it mean to know a person, or, more accurately, a person's self? I don't mean anything mysterious by "self." All I mean is the person's subjective side—what he thinks, feels, believes, wants, worries about—the kind of thing which one could never know unless one were told. *We get to know the other person's self when he discloses it to us.*

Self-disclosure, letting another person know what you think, feel, or want is the most direct means (though not the only means) by which an individual can make himself known to another person. Personality hygienists place great emphasis upon the importance for mental health of what they call "real-self being," "self-realization," "discovering oneself," and so on. An operational analysis of what goes on in counseling and therapy shows that the patients and clients discover themselves through self-disclosure to the counselor. They talk, and to their shock and amazement, the counselor listens.

I venture to say that there is probably no experience more horrifying and terrifying than that of self-disclosure to "significant others" whose probable reactions are assumed, but not known. Hence the phenomenon of "resistance." This is what makes psychotherapy so difficult to take and so difficult to administer. If there is any skill to be learned in the art of counseling and psychotherapy, it is the art of coping with the terrors which attend self-disclosure and the art of decoding the language, verbal and nonverbal, in which a person speaks about his inner experience.

Now what is the connection between self-disclosure and healthy personality? Self-disclosure, or should I say "real" self-disclosure, is both a symptom of personality health (Jourard, 1958, pp. 218–21) and at the same time a means of ultimately achieving healthy personality. The discloser of self is an animated "real-self be-er." This, of course, takes courage—the "courage to be." I have known people who would rather die than become known. In fact, some did die when it appeared that the chances were great that they would become known. When I say that self-disclosure is a symptom of personality health, what I mean really is that a person who displays many of the other characteristics that betoken healthy personality (Jourard, 1958; Maslow, 1954) *will also display the ability to make himself fully known to at least one other significant human being.* When I say that self-disclosure is a means by which one achieves personality health, I mean something like the following: It is not until I *am* my real self and I act my real self that my real self is in a position to grow. One's self grows from the *consequence of being.* People's selves stop growing when they repress them. This growth arrest in the self is what helps to account for the surprising paradox of finding an infant inside the skin of someone who is playing the role of an adult. In a fascinating analysis of mental disease, Jurgen Ruesch (1957) describes assorted neurotics, psychotics, and psychosomatic patients as persons with selective atrophy and overspecialization in various aspects of the process of communication. This culminates in a foul-up of the processes of knowing others and of becoming known to others. Neurotic and psychotic symptoms might be viewed as smoke screens interposed between the patient's real self and the gaze of the onlooker. We might call the symptoms "devices to avoid becoming known." A new theory of schizophrenia has been proposed by a former patient (Anonymous, 1958) who "was there," and he makes such a point.

Alienation from one's real self not only arrests one's growth as a person; it also tends to make a farce out of one's relationships with people. As the ex-patient mentioned above observed, the crucial "break" in schizophrenia is with *sincerity,* not reality (Anonymous, 1958). A self-alienated person—one who does not disclose himself truthfully and fully—can never love another person nor can he be loved by the other person. Effective loving calls for knowledge of the object (Fromm, 1956; Jourard, 1958). How can I love a person whom I do not know? How can the other person love me if he does not know me?

Hans Selye (1950) proposed and documented the hypothesis that illness as we know it arises in consequence of stress applied to the organism. Now I rather think that unhealthy *personality* has a similar root cause, and one which is related to Selye's concept of stress. It is this. Every maladjusted person is a person who has not made himself known to another human being and in consequence does not know himself. Nor can he be himself. More than that, *he struggles actively to avoid becoming known by another human being.* He *works* at it ceaselessly, 24 hours daily, and it is work! The fact that resisting becoming known is *work* offers us a research opening, incidentally (*cf.* Dittes, 1957; Davis and Malmo, 1950). I believe that in the effort to avoid becoming known, a person provides for himself a cancerous kind of stress which is subtle and unrecognized but none the less effective in producing, not only the assorted patterns of unhealthy personality which psychiatry talks about, but also the wide array of physical ills that have come to be recognized as the stock in trade of psychosomatic medicine. Stated another way, I believe that *other people come to be stressors to an individual in direct proportion to his degree of self-alienation.*

If I am struggling to avoid becoming known by other persons then, of course, I must construct a false public self (Jourard, 1958, pp. 301-2). The greater the discrepancy between my unexpurgated real self and the version of myself that I present to others, then the more dangerous will other people be for me. If becoming known by another person is threatening, then the very presence of another person can serve as a stimulus to evoke anxiety, heightened muscle tension, and all the assorted visceral changes which occur when a person is under stress. A beginning already has been made, demonstrating the tension-evoking powers of the other person, through the use of such instruments as are employed in the lie detector, through the measurement of muscle tensions with electromyographic apparatus, and so on (Davis and Malmo, 1950; Dittes, 1957).

Students of psychosomatic medicine have been intimating something of what I have just finished saying explicitly. They say (*cf.* Alexander, 1950) the ulcer patients, asthmatic patients, patients suffering from colitis, migraine, and the like, are chronic *repressors* of certain needs and emotions, especially hostility and dependency. Now when you repress something, you are not only withholding awareness of this something from yourself, you are also withholding it from the scrutiny of the other person. In fact, the means by which repressions are overcome in the therapeutic situation is through relentless disclosure of self to the therapist. When a patient is finally able to follow the fundamental rule in psychoanalysis and disclose everything which passes through his mind, he is generally shocked and dismayed to observe the breadth, depth, range, and diversity of thoughts, memories, and emotions which pass out of his "unconscious" into overt disclosure. Incidentally, by the time a person is that free to disclose in the presence of another human being, he has doubtless completed much of his therapeutic sequence.

Self-disclosure, then, appears to be one of the means by which a person engages in that elegant activity which we call real-self-being. But is real-self-being synonymous with healthy personality? Not in and of itself. I would say that real-self-being is a necessary but not a sufficient condition for healthy personality. Indeed, an authentic person may not be very "nice." In fact, he may seem much "nicer" socially and appear more mature and healthy when he is *not* being his real self than when he is his real self. But an individual's "obnoxious" but authentic self can never grow in the direction of greater maturity until the person has become acquainted with it and begins to *be* it. Real-self-being produces consequences which, in accordance with well-known principles of behavior (*cf.* Skinner, 1953), produce changes in the real self. Thus, there can be no real growth of the self without real-self-being. Full disclosure of the self to at least one other significant human being appears to be one means by which a person discovers not only the breadth and depth of his needs and feelings, but also the nature of his own self-affirmed values. There is no necessary conflict, incidentally, between real-self-being and being an ethical or nice person, because for the average member of our society, self-owned ethics are generally acquired during the process of growing up. All too often, however, the self-owned ethics are buried under authoritarian morals (Fromm, 1947).

If self-disclosure is one of the means by which healthy personality is both achieved and maintained, we can also note that such activities as loving, psychotherapy, counseling, teaching, and nursing are impossible of achievement without the disclosure of the client. It is through self-disclosure that an individual reveals to himself and to the other party just exactly who, what, and where he is. Just as thermometers and sphygmomanometers disclose information about the real state of the body, self-disclosure reveals the real nature of the soul, or self. Such information is vital in order to conduct intelligent evaluations. All I mean by evaluation is comparing how a person is with some concept of optimum. You never really discover how truly sick your psychotherapy patient is until he discloses himself utterly to you. You cannot help your client in vocational guidance until he has disclosed to you something of the impasse in which he finds himself. You cannot love your spouse or your child or your friend unless those persons have permitted you to know them and to know what they need in order to move toward greater health and well-being. Nurses cannot nurse patients in any meaningful way unless they have permitted the patients to disclose their needs, wants, worries, anxieties, and doubts, and so forth. Teachers cannot be very helpful to their students until they have permitted the students to disclose how utterly ignorant and misinformed they presently are. Teachers cannot even provide helpful information to the students until they have permitted the students to disclose exactly what they are interested in.

I believe we should reserve the term inter*personal* relationships to refer to transactions between "I and thou" (Buber, 1937), between *person* and *person*, not between role and role. A truly personal relationship between two people involves disclosure of self one to the other in full and spontaneous honesty. The data that we have collected up to the present time have shown us some rather interesting phenomena. We found (Jourard and Lasakow, 1958), for example, that the women we tested in universities in the Southeast were consistently higher self-disclosers than men; they seem to have a greater capacity for establishing person-to-person relationships, inter*personal* relationships, than men. This characteristic of women seems to be a socially patterned phenomenon which sociologists (Parsons and Bales, 1955) refer to as the *expressive* role of women in contradistinction to the instrumental role which men universally are obliged to adopt. Men seem to be much more skilled at *im*personal, *instrumental* role playing. But public health officials, very concerned about the sex differential in mortality rates, have been wondering what it is about being a man which makes males die younger than females. Do you suppose that there is any connection whatsoever between the disclosure patterns of men and women and their differential death rates? I have already intimated that withholding self-disclosure seems to impose a certain stress on people. Maybe "being manly," whatever that means, is slow suicide!

I think there is a very general way of stating the relationship between self-disclosure and assorted values such as healthy personality, physical health, group effectiveness, successful marriage, effective teaching, and effective nursing. It is this. A person's self is known to be the immediate determiner of his overt behavior. This is a paraphrase of the phenomenological point of view in psychology (Combs and Snygg, 1959). Now, if we want to understand anything, explain it, control it, or predict it, it is helpful if we have available as much pertinent information as we possibly can. Self-disclosure provides a source of information which is relevant. This information has often been overlooked. Where it has not been overlooked, it has often been misinterpreted by observers and practitioners through such devices as projection or attribution. *It seems to be difficult for people to accept the fact that they do not know the very person whom they are confronting at any given moment.* We all seem to assume that we are expert psychologists and that we know the other person, when in fact we have only constructed a more or less autistic concept of him in our mind. If we are to learn more about man's self, then we must learn more about self-disclosure—its conditions, dimensions, and consequences. Beginning evidence (cf. Rogers, 1958) shows that actively accepting, empathic, loving, nonpunitive response—in short, love—provides the optimum conditions under which man will disclose, or expose, his naked quivering self to our gaze. It follows that if we would be helpful (or should I say *human*) we must grow to loving stature and learn, in Buber's terms, to confirm our fellow man in his very being. Probably, this presumes that we must *first* confirm our *own* being.

REFERENCES

ALEXANDER, F. *Psychosomatic Medicine.* New York: Norton, 1950.

ALLPORT, G. *Becoming.* New Haven: Yale University Press, 1955.

ANONYMOUS. "A New Theory of Schizophrenia," *Journal of Abnormal and Social Psychology,* Vol. 57 (1958), pp. 226–36.

BARR, S. *Purely Academic.* New York: Simon & Schuster, 1958.

BUBER, M. *I and Thou.* New York: Scribners, 1937.

COMBS, A. and SNYGG, D. *Individual Behavior.* 2nd ed. New York: Harper, 1959.

DAVIS, F. H. and MALMO, R. B. "Electromyographic Recording during Interview," *American Journal of Psychiatry,* Vol. 107 (1950), pp. 908–16.

DITTES, J. E. "Extinction during Psychotherapy of GSR Accompanying 'Embarrassing' Statements," *Journal of Abnormal and Social Psychology,* Vol. 54 (1957), pp. 187–91.

DUNN, H. L. "High-Level Wellness for Man and Society," *American Journal of Public Health,* Vol. 49 (1959), pp. 786–92.

FREUD, S. *The Interpretation of Dreams.* New York: Basic Books, 1955.

FROMM, E. *Man for Himself.* New York: Rinehart, 1947.

———. *The Art of Loving.* New York: Harper, 1956.

HORNEY, K. *The Neurotic Personality of Our Time.* New York: Norton, 1936.

———. *Neurosis and Human Growth.* New York: Norton, 1950.

JAHODA, MARIE. *Current Concepts of Positive Mental Health.* New York: Basic Books, 1958.

JOURARD, S. M. *Personal Adjustment: An Approach through the Study of Healthy Personality.* New York: Macmillan, 1958.

JOURARD, S. M. and LASAKOW, P. "Some Factors in Self-Disclosure," *Journal of Abnormal and Social Psychology,* Vol. 56 (1958), pp. 91-98.

MASLOW, A. H. *Motivation and Personality.* New York: Harper, 1954.

PARSONS, T. and BALES, R. F. *Family, Socialization, and Interaction Process.* Glencoe, Ill.: Free Press, 1955.

RIESMAN, D. *The Lonely Crowd.* New Haven: Yale University Press, 1950.

ROGERS, C. R. "The Characteristics of a Helping Relationship," *Personal Guidance Journal,* Vol. 37 (1958), pp. 6–16.

RUESCH, J. *Disturbed Communication.* New York: Norton, 1957.

SELYE, H. *The Physiology and Pathology of Exposure to Stress.* Montreal: Acta, 1950.

SKINNER, B. F. *Science and Human Behavior.* New York: Macmillan, 1953.

ANALYSIS AND TYPOLOGY OF PERSONALITY MISINTERPRETATIONS*

G. *Ichheiser*

THE TENDENCY TO OVERESTIMATE THE UNITY OF PERSONALITY

The following three examples will serve as illustrations of the mechanisms which fall under this category:

We are passing by the army barracks and see how a sergeant is handling his subordinates. He barks his commands, snaps at any attempted questions on the part of his men, listens to no excuses or explanations, and is downright rude. Now, confronted by this type of behavior, we are not, as a rule, inclined to say to ourselves or to others, "This man is performing certain social functions defined by the context of military regulations and standards. He is behaving in a way which corresponds to expected and stereotyped norms of behavior in this type of social role." Rather, we tend to react in a way which, on the verbal level, would sound something like this: "The man is rude," or "The man has such-and-such personality characteristics which make him behave in this way."

A second example: A teacher complains to a mother that her boy behaves in an intolerable way and continually disturbs the class. The mother retorts angrily that this cannot be, for of her several children this particular boy is the nicest child one can imagine. The teacher thinks, "Something is wrong with this mother; she is either blind or she feels that she has to defend her child even though she knows that what she says is not true." The mother thinks, "Something is wrong with the teacher, he is obviously prejudiced, and this bias distorts his judgment." As a matter of fact, both the teacher and the mother are victims of an unconscious misinterpretative assumption which prevents for each of them a correct understanding of the situation. Their false assumption is related to the tendency to overestimate the unity of personality. This tendency blinds mother and teacher to the "obvious" fact that the boy has, as do

---

*Reprinted from *American Journal of Sociology*, Vol. 55, No. 2 (September, 1949), pp. 27–31, 40–43, 47–49, 51–53.

many other people, two or more "characters," each coming to the surface, depending on the situation in which he finds himself, and also that there might exist a very complicated under-the-surface connection between these "characters" which cannot be defined in a too simple manner.

A third example: A man is under suspicion of murder. During the investigation certain definite abnormalities of his sexual behavior come to light even though there is no evidence that they are related in any way to the committed murder. Again, the frequent reaction in many people, if verbalized, would read something like this: "This man whose sexual life deviates so strangely from the norm can also be expected to deviate from other social norms in any other respect." However, here again the overestimation of personality unity has probably misled their interpretative reaction. The sexual behavior might function in an individual according to a very specific sexual dynamics, either not affecting other areas of behavior or affecting them, but in a much more complicated way than simply in terms of an assumed interdependence between sex deviations and propensity toward criminal behavior. Thus, again, the tendency to overestimate the unity of personality might operate as a source of misinterpretations and misevaluations.

If the mechanisms which control our perception of other people would function simply in terms of registering only certain ways of behavior, then, in the case of the sergeant mentioned in our first example, we would say only that he behaved in a certain situation, at a certain time, in a certain way. This, however, is not the way in which our social perception and its mechanisms actually do operate. Rather, they function so as to transcend in many ways and many directions the pure raw material and to construct out of this material a more or less well-organized and integrated image of the given personality. This image construction is usually endowed in our minds with only those alleged characteristics which promise to help us explain, as a manifestation of the underlying personality, the behavior with which we are confronted. In other words, we have the tendency to consider a partial structure of personality which happens to be visible to us as if this partial structure were the total personality "itself."

Here we are faced with an obvious distortion in our social perception. Additional ones will be pointed out as we proceed in the consideration of other types of personality misinterpretations. Many of these distortions appear so obvious that one must ask how we can remain so unaware of them. It is as if we were not aware of what we ought to be aware. To explain this seeming paradox, we must return to a concept of "secondary mechanisms." These mechanisms veil and prevent us from seeing our "obvious" misconceptions as, for example, the overestimating of the unity of personality. The following discussion demonstrates the chief ways in which the secondary mechanisms operate in thus preventing the recognition and correction of our misconceptions.

a) Once the image of another person, shaped by primary mechanisms of one kind or another, is fixed in our minds, we tend either to overlook all factors in the other person which do not fit into our preconceived scheme or else we misinterpret all unexpectedly emerging factors in order to preserve our preformed misconceptions. In the teacher-mother example presented above, the expectations and interpretations both of the mother and of the teacher were dominated by the misconception that the aspect of personality of the boy which they had the opportunity to observe is identical with his total personality or, at least, that this aspect represents his "real" personality as compared with which all other aspects are either superficial, or insignificant, or artificial, or have even the outright character of a simulation. Thus, in order to prevent the disintegration of our preconceived image under the impact of contradicting experiences, we ascribe to one aspect of personality the character of "reality," to other aspects the character of superficial, or artificial, "roles."

b) As a rule, we meet and enter into personal relations with other people in certain more or less definite situations, playing certain more or less definite roles. Even though we often are not aware of it, we ourselves are a very important factor in the total situation which determines and evokes the type of behavior the other person is expected to play in the given relation. The father, as a rule, sees his son in this latter's role as a "son," for his (the father's) mere presence usually is bound to evoke this aspect of his son's personality and to eliminate, or to suppress, any other aspect. The employer sees, as a rule, his employee, in the role of an "employee," that is, behaving as one is expected to behave toward the boss. The teacher sees his pupils in the role of "pupils"; and similar examples. It is our own presence which either evokes or suppresses the manifestations of certain personality aspects of other people. Quite frequently we remain completely ignorant as to how they behave, or how they would behave, without our being present. To gauge correctly what in the observed behavior of other people has to be interpreted as reaction to ourselves and to our own characteristics is one of the most essential conditions of having psychological insight.

Now, if we happen to see a person whom we believe we know very well acting in a manner which is at variance with our expectations, either we are quite shocked and confused or we try to save our own false conception by declaring, "Something is wrong with the person." It does not frequently occur to us that something might be wrong with our own assumptions and interpretations.

We can well illustrate the peculiar situation we confront here by using a metaphor. Let us image a room with several doors for entrance. When closed, the room is dark. Each door, when opened, automatically switches on a different kind of light. Depending on whether you enter the room through the first, the second, or the third door, you will find yourself placed in a "red," or "blue," or "green" room. Now, let us assume that you would enter, or would even be expected to enter, the room always through the same, let us say, through the third door. What would be the consequence of this kind of procedure for your conception about the room? You would, obviously, come to believe that the room is always illumined by a green light, and you might even be inclined to call the room "the green room." The fact would remain concealed from you that the room is not always green and that its green illumination is caused by your entering it always through the same door. You would probably be extremely perplexed as to how it is possible for other people who enter the room by other doors to be so thoroughly foolish, or ignorant, or dishonest, as to declare that the room is not green but red or blue. Endless arguments might ensue as to who is right. Is the room "really" red, or "really" blue, or "really" green? Only someone who knows the secret of the various doors would be able to understand and to explain why different people are seeing the same room "in a different light."

It is a similar story with the different aspects of personality of other people, each of which is, unwittingly, evoked as reaction to our and other's behavior.[1] Many disagreements about interpreting and evaluating other people could be resolved easily if we would re-

---

[1] This metaphor was used by the author in his article, "Die Überschätzung der Einheit der Persönlichkeit als Täuschungsquelle," *Zeitschrift für angewandte Psychologic*, Vol. 33 (1929), 273–87. In discussing a similar type of problem, Gerard L. DeGré, in his monograph *Ideology and Society* (New York: Columbia University Press, 1943), is using a graphic presentation which follows a similar pattern.

alize that those disagreements are simply the result of our not being aware that we ourselves are "switching on" different aspects of other people's personalities by the mere fact of our presence.

c) There is still a third factor which, acting as a secondary mechanism, helps to perpetuate our distorted images about other people, in spite of the illusory character of those images. It is the tendency of other people, whether consciously or unconsciously, to anticipate and to adjust their behavior in some degree to the expectations and images we hold in our minds about their personalities. Consequently, the images we hold of other people are not only mirrors which reflect, whether correctly or not, their personalities, but they are also dynamic factors which control the behavior of those people. As a matter of fact, the images turn out often to be stronger than the realities which they represent. In case of a discrepancy between the socially accepted image of personality and the personality "itself," it is often the personality itself which has to adjust to its distorted reflection in the "mirror." Thus, in human relations the image often gets taken as the "real thing," and frequently the individuals concerned are forced to play the roles assigned to them by the perplexing reflections in the mirrors of social perception.

The ex-convict is frequently one of these. Although he may return to his community with a new view of himself and a determination to become a good citizen, the opinions the people of the community hold of him and ex-convicts in general often prevent his accomplishing his good aims. Instead, in bitterness and resentment, he often gives up the struggle and becomes what the community expected—a hardened criminal. Sometimes, too, the situation is reversed. The ex-convict comes back hardened, embittered, and with his worst characteristics emphasized. Some one or several persons take an interest in him, play up his better qualities, and through encouragement he comes to be what they see him as—a good citizen. In either case, although other factors are also involved, the ex-convict has found himself impelled to live up to an image of himself held by others.

d) Finally, in closing this discussion of secondary mechanisms making possible the perpetuating of our misconceptions, we note that sometimes our experiences with other people turn out to be so totally at variance with our preconceived images about their personality, and consequently with our expectations as to their behavior, that it is utterly impossible to maintain our images which have been based on misinterpretation operating within our social perception. Thus, eventually we might be compelled to give up our illusory construction. Even then the change will frequently be restricted to our conscious interpretations "in principle," leaving the more deep-seated interpretations "in fact" unaffected by the occurring transformations.

We return now to further consideration of the tendency to overestimate the unity of personality as a source of misinterpretations and wish to mention here one characteristic "disunity" in the personality makeup of the modern man. We have in mind the disunity and tension between the private and the occupational aspects of our personalities. As a result of several historical developments, particularly as a result of the specialization and depersonalization of our occupational activities, the tension and disunity between these two aspects of our personalities have dangerously increased. This state of affairs is symbolized in spatial terms by living in one place and working in another. The split is an important source of many conflicts and dilemmas in our modern life. The more depersonalized our occupational activities are growing, the more urgently do we feel the need to save the threatened deeper meanings and values of life by finding a home for them in the area of our private relations.

An important question relative to the fact of disunity in a personality might be raised at this point. It is the question: Which of the partial "sides," or "aspects," or "roles" of the disunited personality should be considered as something like its "core"? Or, to put it another way: Which characteristics of an individual constitute his "real" personality as over against the "roles" he is only "playing"? Does it or does it not make any sense to ask this kind of question?

Our answer is that it does make sense to ask this question, provided we approach the problem from different angles. Thus, first, we might ask with which "aspects," or "sides," or "parts" of his personality has the individual identified himself. If we ask this first question, the answer has to be given in terms of the conception of the individual about himself. Second, we might ask, in terms of a sociopsychological approach, which aspects or roles played by a given individual are considered by other people as representing his "real self." Again, we might ask, in terms of personality dynamics, in which parts or roles the greatest amount of the psychological energy of the given individual is involved.

This means that the question as to which aspects, parts, or roles have to be considered as the "core of personality" of an individual can be answered only in terms of one of these three or other significant perspectives. It means also that it cannot be answered in any absolute terms. In other words, it does not make any sense to ask questions about the "core of personality," or about the "real self," without having in advance defined explicitly the point of view from which the question is being asked. Otherwise, we are not facing a meaningful problem but rather a pseudo-problem which we cannot solve.

✲   ✲   ✲   ✲   ✲

As a matter of fact, we have distorted, and even perverted, in our modern world not only the idea of liberty, but also the idea of equality. We are paying a terrible price for it, and the end of our self-inflicted sufferings is not yet in sight. We have distorted and perverted the idea of liberty by calling insecurity, amounting in its consequences sometimes to an outright slavery, "freedom." Of this first perversion many intelligent people in our time are well aware. It seems rather doubtful whether there is as much awareness of the second ideological distortion—the distortion of the idea of equality— for what equality means, or rather ought to mean realistically and intelligently, is that people should have equal opportunities in life in spite of the fact that they are in many respects different. We tend, however, again and again to confuse and to distort this idea by declaring, or silently assuming, or implying, that "people are alike" and that "there are essentially no differences between men." This, of course, is disastrous nonsense.

We have distorted, however, not only the idea of equality but also its counterparts and shadows, the concepts of inequality and of prejudice. Since people are different, considering people as being different is not "prejudice." The prejudiced are not those who insist that people are different, in various respects and by various reasons, but those who deny it. Insisting that people who are different are not different means making propaganda for misunderstanding each other. Since we are different, we can only understand each other if we admit and are aware in what respects and why we are different. Prejudice comes in only if we misinterpret the existing differences in terms of inferiority and the like.

This ambiguity in the concepts of equality, inequality, and prejudice, this confusion of "being different" and "being inferior," is probably one of the most characteristic features of the American scene and is highly responsible for the peculiar confusion of human relations in this country. In drawing a comparison with Europe (a com-

parison which serves only the purpose of illuminating the issue involved and does not imply any evaluation), we might say that in the
United States the tensions between groups which are "different" are
less intense but more confused than in Europe. The culturally different European groups are identifying each other overtly as being
different, this all the more that, by and large, they are citizens of different countries and, with some few exceptions, are geographically
segregated from each other. The intercultural tensions, therefore,
take in Europe the form of open, external, international conflicts,
whereas in this country the intercultural (and interracial) tensions
operate in the more repressed forms of "prejudice" and "discrimina-
tion." Applying a medical metaphor to those two types of tensions,
we might say that Europe, as far as intergroup relations are concerned, is suffering by intermittent, but violent, attacks of pneu-
monia, whereas the intergroup tensions in this country might rather
be compared to a mild but chronic tuberculosis.

The misinterpretations which have their roots in the distortions
of both the concept of equality and inequality become clearly visible
in the dilemma which the minorities are facing when confronted by
a majority which is trapped in the maze of this conceptual confusion. Several possible avenues of adjustment are open to minority
group members under these circumstances, but no one or several
of them offer complete satisfaction, and all exact a price.

On the one hand, minority members may attempt to escape the
situation they are confronted with by trying to conceal the existing
differences in appearance, language, behavior, and other significant
aspects of personality. They may do this by propagandizing that
"there are no differences at all," or, if there are any, that "they are
not significant," and that to say something else "is prejudice." This
solution—the history of the Jews proves it so conclusively that only
the blind can disregard it—obviously does not work. It does not work,
first, because the existing differences do not disappear by the magical
procedure of being denied but rather remain and sound through all
disguises, pretenses, and concealments. The majority feels, therefore,
that the minority tries to solve the problem by a kind of deception,
which certainly does not improve the situation. And, second, this
solution does not work, because the mimicry has to be paid for at
the very high psychological price of repressing and distorting real
personality. Hence it becomes true that it is indeed the most honest
and most sensitive members of minorities who either refuse to pay

this price or, if paying it, are most heavily frustrated and disturbed by its burden.

On the other hand, the minorities can try to solve the dilemma by admitting being different. Those who are choosing this second way feel that, even if this choice should lead to being rejected as a kind of a "stranger," it is still more honorable to be rejected for what one really is than to be accepted for what one really is not. They prefer to preserve the integrity of their personalities and are willing to pay the price of not being accepted.

There are, of course, many types of intermediate solutions or pseudo-solutions through which members of minorities might try to adjust, or even partly succeed in adjusting, themselves superficially, on the level of external behavior, still preserving the integrity of their inner personalities. It will depend largely on the personality type which solution different members of minorities will be inclined to choose and which price they will be able to pay.

It is the perversion of the idea of equality which prevents us from understanding people who are different from ourselves and from being tolerant about their being different. Since we start with the false assumption that "people are essentially alike" and then find by experience that they are unlike, we confuse all issues involved and denounce as well as persecute each other because we are different.

This apparent paradox that the idea of equality actually does not engender the expected "brotherhood of man" but, on the contrary, intolerance and persecution should not arouse in us too great a surprise. In fact, it is only a modern version of another historical paradox, namely, that monotheism, in spite of its all-embracing meaning, turned out in the past to be one of the most powerful sources of intolerance. Both cases are essentially similar, for in the same way as the "one world" is inevitably seen differently by different people, each claiming to see it correctly, so also the "one God" was conceived and imagined by different religions in a different way. Each of them felt called upon to fight for the "one God" against infidels who, misled by false prophets, became so thoroughly blinded that they were unable to recognize the one God "as he really is."

Since it is obviously a basic fact that the range of our psychological insight is always limited in scope; since we tend to misinterpret what we are unable to understand because it lies beyond the threshold of our comprehension; since we are trying, by an unconscious defense

mechanism, to overcome our perplexity in the face of our disagreements and to maintain our belief that it is we, and not the others,
who see the things "as they really are," it is clear that, of all types
of people, the one most likely to avoid this kind of misinterpretation
is the type of personality which contains within its own makeup as
many diverse potentialities as possible. In other words, the "born"
psychologist, sociologist, anthropologist is the "marginal man" who,
split within himself, is fully aware that the world is not as "we" see
it but that "we" see it as we do because we are as we are. It is simply
not true that anybody can be "trained" to be a good psychologist,
sociologist, or anthropologist. This naïve assumption is, unfortunately, at the bottom of many striking defects and forms of social
blindness in our standardized and mechanized social science. Do we
wish to cure our sick society which reflects itself in a distorted way
in the broken mirror of a sick social science? If so, we should indeed
admit, and even insist, that only a rich personality, possessing
various and contradictory psychological, cultural, and situational
experiences, is or can be really equipped with the indispensable
inner potentialities to approach the job of social analysis. Only such
a personality can have adequate insight into the different forms of
motivation, the different cultural patterns, the different types of
situational dynamics in terms of what they mean to those who are
directly involved and not in terms of what they mean, or how they
look, to a spectator who is unaware of his own hidden and silent
frame of reference dominating and biasing his social perception.

Since the concept of prejudice is quite particularly responsible
for preventing a realistic approach to the problems centered around
the "limits of insight" and the "distortions of the idea of equality,"
we wish to conclude this section with some critical comments concerning the silent presuppositions of this concept. It is our contention that the validity of these presuppositions is open to serious
question. The concept of prejudice tends rather to camouflage than
to illuminate the essential factors in intergroup tensions. It reveals
sometimes more interesting facts about the bias of the particular
social scientist than about the attitudes of the "prejudiced" common
man who is the object of the investigation.

In order to make our position very clear, we are listing in two
parallel columns what we consider to be the silent presuppositions
of the current theory of prejudices on the one hand and the suggested corrections for these presuppositions on the other. We do not
contend that in all interpretations based on the concept of prejudice

SILENT FALSE ASSUMPTIONS	SUGGESTED CORRECTIONS
1. People are essentially alike; to insist that they are different is prejudice.	1. People are in important respects, by various reasons, different, individually and collectively; to deny differences which are actually there is prejudice.
2. All people can be subdivided into those who are and those who are not prejudiced.	2. All people are prejudiced, in one way or another. To assume that being prejudiced is a specific characteristic of certain people is prejudice.
3. "They" are prejudiced, but "we" are not.	3. We perceive the prejudices in others but fail to perceive them in ourselves.
4. The common man is prejudiced, but the social scientist is not.	4. The prejudices of social scientists consist in the silent assumptions with which they approach the problem of "prejudices"—not to mention many others.
5. The stereotypes concerning characteristics of cultural and racial groups are entirely false.	5. The stereotypes concerning characteristics of cultural and racial groups are a combination of truth and falsehood.
6. The prejudices are the main cause of intergroup tensions.	6. The main thing is that people are different, and identified with different groups, and not that they are "prejudiced."
7. Intergroup tensions which are not based on conflicts of economic interests are not "real"; they are artificial or the result of propaganda or "rationalizations."	7. Intergroup tensions which have their origin in differences of inner or external personality, i.e., cultural and racial tensions, are as real as tensions which have their roots in conflicts of interests.
8. Prejudices are acts of aggression.	8. Prejudices are acts of defense by which people defend the integrity of their own personality, their own culture, their own group.
9. People are (or ought to be) rational; all irrational factors are prejudices.	9. There are many meanings and values of life which are not rational in the utilitarian sense of this term. To call all nonrational or irrational factors prejudices is a prejudice. Societies without basic irrational beliefs tend to disintegrate.

10. If our dislikes refer to individual characteristics of other people, then this is antipathy; if they refer to collective characteristics, this is prejudice.

10. Our likes and dislikes operate on two levels; we may like or dislike other people either because of their individual characteristics or because they represent a certain type. This type may be cultural, racial, or simply psychological.

11. People are prejudiced against one another because they do not know one another well. If they knew one another better, the prejudices would automatically disappear.

11. To say the least, it works both ways. Very often the difficulties in human relations develop and are aggravated if people get closer acquainted with one another.

12. Prejudices are the only, or at least the most important, form of collective distortions of social perception.

12. There are many other collective distortions of social perception; some of them are much more important than the so-called prejudices.

all silent presuppositions listed in the left column are operating and effective. We insist only that, in all interpretations and theories of this sort, some of these presuppositions are playing an important, disturbing, as well as distorting, role. We insist also that, once these silent, hidden presuppositions are made explicit, their illusory character becomes indisputably and obviously clear.

There are, in all probability, still other "silent assumptions" at the bottom of the current theory of "prejudices" which will require some further clarification and rectification. Let the reader add to the list if he can, but in the meantime let us take cognizance of at least these and of the misinterpretations and confusions to which they lead.

＊　　＊　　＊　　＊　　＊

Now, even though personality and its behavior are obviously and decidedly codetermined by social situations, and even though we often know "in principle" that this is the case, our unconscious interpretations "in fact" do not reckon with this basic state of affairs and function as if personal traits alone, or at least predominantly, do determine the dynamics of human behavior. We all have in everyday life the tendency to interpret and to evaluate the behavior of other people in terms of specific personality characteristics rather than in terms of specific social situations in which those people are placed. More than that—the whole system of our sociomoral concepts such as "merit" and "guilt," "success" and "failure," "responsibility," and the like, as accepted and applied in everyday life, is based on the assumption of a personal rather than situational causation of human behavior. In interpreting actions as manifestations of personal characteristics, under disregard of the all-important role played by social situations, we chronically misinterpret the actual underlying motivations. Again and again, instead of saying that Dan or Tom or Sam behaved (or did not behave) in a specific way because he was placed in a specific situation, we are prone to believe that he behaved (or did not behave) in a certain way because he possesses (or does not possess) certain specific personal characteristics.

The impact of this type of misinterpretation is especially aggravated by a fact the significance of which can be clearly understood in the light of our analysis of the role of visibility in social perception. With reference to the problem we are discussing here, the important point is that in perceiving and observing other people we do see the spatial situation in which they act, but as a rule, we are not in the position to see and to evaluate correctly the dynamic meaning of the social, invisible factors in the total situation controlling the behavior of those people. This total situation includes such all-important factors as social opportunities and social barriers, relations of dependence and expectations of others, the bank account we possess and the hostilities we meet, which situational factors, as well as many others, are in their very nature "invisible." Consequently, if other people react to certain situations which are to them highly real but are not visible to us from our point of view, we fail to understand why they behave as they do even though in terms of those invisible factors their behavior is perfectly understandable and "reasonable." What really happens is that, not being aware of our own social blindness, we misinterpret (and usually denounce) their behavior as "unreasonable," or "abnormal," or "aggressive."

It is hardly possible to exaggerate the importance of this type of social blindness in the crisis of our age. The complete, tragic blindness of the privileged concerning the life situation of the underprivileged is the result of just this kind of not seeing the invisible factors in the situations of others. Reaction, revolt against invisible social chains, is being misinterpreted by blind spectators as "aggressive behavior." Many things which happened between the two world wars would not have happened if social blindness had not prevented the privileged from understanding the predicament of those who were living in an invisible jail. It would be good perhaps if our justified horror about visible concentration camps would not blind us to the horrors of "invisible concentration camps," of which there are a great many in our modern society—and, also, if our moral revolt against visible atrocities would not blunt our awareness of the invisible atrocities which insidiously poison and destroy human relations. Finally, we should try to understand better than we do that those who commit visible atrocities are often only taking revenge for invisible ones of which they themselves were (invisible) victims. If the author were not a social scientist but a preacher, he would say at this place, "Let us pray. . . ."

Certain clarifications about the concept of "abilities" will help us understand and to penetrate the peculiarly involved and confused relations between "personality traits" and "social situations." At first glance the concept of "abilities" in terms of being able, or not being able, to do something appears to be a neutral concept, far removed from any complicated distortions and misinterpretations. However, if we examine it a little deeper, it becomes clear that this concept contains a peculiar ambiguity which is a symptom of an underlying confusion concerning the role and function of social situations in motivating human behavior. This ambiguity and confusion, which do not arise by chance, consist in ascribing to the individuals certain potentialities for action as their "own," even though these potentialities are actually only a concomitant, or correlate, of certain situational factors. In other words, we are confronted here again with one of those basic illusions of social perception which operate both within our perception of other people and within our self-perception.

As a result of this peculiar illusion of self-perception, we experience as our "own" those of our potentialities which we owe, let us say, to money we possess, in the same way as we experience those we owe to intrinsic psychological and physical characteristics. The same kind of illusion permeates our perception of other people. These illusions operate in such a way that the share of situational factors in endowing us as well as others with certain potentialities remains concealed from our awareness. To put it another way, the actual conditions and determinants of our potentialities ("abilities") reflect themselves in our consciousness in a distorted way.

The inevitable consequence of this illusion is that disturbances which occur in the field of social situations in which we have to act are often misinterpreted as intrinsic defects of personal endowments. Hence, the unemployed is ashamed of being unemployed, even if his being unemployed is obviously due to a general encomic depression, for he is correctly aware that, on the level of the emotionally all-important unconscious interpretations "in fact," his misfortune is being ascribed to him as a manifestation of his alleged personal defects. Actually he is often himself a victim of this same illusion.

The traumatic experience of being unemployed is intensified by the invisibility of the situation and its associated conditions. If an individual is drowning in a lake, then other people present can see that he is drowning, and at least some of them will try to help him. If, on the other hand, an individual is "drowning" in the "invisible ocean" of unemployment, his predicament will not mobilize in others, even if they are present spectators, the attitudes of immediate helpfulness, for they are not aware in terms of an effective social perception that a fellow human being is drowning. Thus, in a way, the situation of the man who is in danger of drowning in the "invisible ocean" of unemployment is more desperate than the situation of a man who is drowning in the real ocean. (It might be of some interest to mention that the author was discussing this type of disturbing problems with a well-known American woman psychologist shortly after he arrived in this country and was somewhat surprised at finding in her a complete and very responsive understanding. A few years later this woman psychologist committed suicide. Possibly, she understood too much about the factual and moral dilemmas of our time.)

The consequences of the illusion that minimizes or excludes the role of situational factors are particularly aggravated by the fact that, as in other cases discussed previously, the misinterpretative mechanism not only influences the image of personality but often also influences the structure of the personality "itself." Here again the false image can eventually produce those personality characteristics which it, at first, only falsely reflected. The unemployed, to take up this example again, will often, under the all-pervading influence of collective misinterpretations, come to ascribe to himself the consequences of his unfortunate conditions as his own fault. This can and does happen, even if originally he understood the true role of the situational factors. He will become more and more insecure; the continuous failure to cope with a situation he is unable to control will seemingly justify his feeling of inadequacy. Finally, the destructive psychological process penetrates into the strata of his intrinsic abilities; his imposed inactivity not only undermines his self-confidence but, through lack of training, actually destroys his abilities "themselves."

✻   ✻   ✻   ✻   ✻

THE MOTE-BEAM-MECHANISM[2]

We shall analyze and clarify this final mechanism by comparing it with the mechanism of projection with which it is often confused. Both mechanisms have in common that their operation results in a distortion of self-perception and perception of other people, and the two (as Socrates already knew) are always closely interrelated. However, the lack of an adequate conceptual distinction makes us overlook a significant difference between the two types of false social perception.

The first of the two, projection in the specific, psychiatric sense, consists in attributing to other people certain characteristics which we do, but they actually do not, possess.[3]

The second consists in perceiving certain characteristics in others which we do not perceive in ourselves and thus perceiving those characteristics as if they were peculiar traits of the others.

Projection can be, or easily become, *pathological* in nature and is one of the sources of paranoid developments. The second type is, unfortunately, by no means pathological but rather, individually and collectively, almost a universal feature of human nature. We all tend, therefore, to perceive (and to denounce) in others certain characteristics, for example, prejudices, or blind spots, or ideologies, or ethnocentrism, or aggressiveness, which, strangely enough, we ignore in ourselves. This lack of insight is obviously so widespread that its counterpart, namely, the ability to perceive in ourselves those characteristics which we notice and disapprove in others, must be considered as a sign of an unusual detachment and almost "abnormally" keen insight.

Although in both cases we are dealing with types of false social perception, the distortion, as mentioned above, is in the two cases

---

[2]This section is a somewhat changed version of my article, "Projection and the Mote-Beam-Mechanism," *Journal of Abnormal and Social Psychology,* Vol. 42 (1947), 131–33.

[3]See the definition of "projection" in *Psychiatric Dictionary* (New York: Oxford University Press, 1940): "*Projection.* As used by psychiatrists, this means the process of throwing out upon another ideas and impulses that belong to oneself. It is the act of giving objective and seeming reality to what is subjective. . . . The person who blames another for his own mistakes is using the projection mechanism."

significantly different. In case of projection, in the specified narrow sense, the resulting falsification refers to the content of the perception. If A, being suspicious himself, instead of being aware of it, believes that it is he who is suspected (observed, persecuted) by B, this means that he misperceives certain characteristics in B as well as in himself, for actually it is A who is suspicious and not B. The projection consists, therefore, in falsely attributing certain characteristics to another person which this person actually does not possess.

In the case of the second mechanism with which we are dealing, the content of the perception, that is, the perception of certain characteristics in other persons, is correct. The prejudice, the ideology, the ethnocentrism are not "projected" by us but are actually there in the other person who is the object of the given perception. And the falsification consists only in the silent assumption that those characteristics are particular to the other person or persons and that we ourselves are free of them.

Now, it might be argued that the second type of false perception does not involve a distorted perception of other people but only a distorted self-perception. However, such an interpretation would not be correct and would miss an essential element in our distinction. Actually, the distortion involves not only the self-perception but also the perception of others, and it is just this falsification of social perception in which we are at present mainly interested.

If a member of a certain group declares that the members of a second group are prejudiced and overlooks or ignores that the members of other similar groups, including his own, have the same characteristics, this means that he ascribes to the members of the second group "being prejudiced" as their particular characteristic. Thus, even though the content of his perception is correct insofar as this characteristic is actually there in the members of the second group, the implied interpretation is false. If we use here the conceptual framework of the sociology of knowledge, we would say that in such a case the members of the first group perceive certain characteristics of the members of the second group in a "false perspective."

Consequently, if the members of the first group would (and could) be made aware of the nature of their false perception, the change would involve not only a transformation of the self-perception but also a transformation of the perception of the members of the second group. On the verbal level this change would reveal itself in replacing the statement "Look how prejudiced they are" by "Look, they are as prejudiced as all other people including ourselves, although the content of their prejudices seems to be somewhat different."

Once the distinction between projection and this second type of false social perception is made explicit, it must become clear that in terms of interpersonal and intergroup relations of everyday life this second type plays a role incomparably more important than the mechanism of projection in the specific sense of this word. Especially in times as confused as ours, the tendency to perceive in others as something peculiar to them certain characteristics which we are unable (or unwilling) to perceive in ourselves assumes truly gigantic proportions. The author of this study is under the impression that research and theory of interhuman antagonisms tend at present to exaggerate the role of such mechanisms as projection, displacement, and frustration-aggression and to neglect or even to ignore the highly disturbing role of the mechanism which we discuss in this section. In order to have a name for it, let us call it the *mote-beam-mechanism*.

It follows from what we have said that projection in the specific sense of "throwing out upon another the ideas and impulses that belong to one's self" is mainly a problem of abnormal psychology. The mote-beam-mechanism, on the other hand, is a problem of social psychology and sociology of knowledge. Since the mechanism of projection, under the predominant influence of psychoanalysis, is actually at present in the focus of scientific attention, the mote-beam-mechanism is the main victim of the lack of an adequate conceptual distinction. This means that we either ignore its operation in many cases where it actually occurs or misinterpret its nature in terms of projective (or other) mechanisms.

The approach of psychological and sociological research and theory to such collective phenomena as stereotypes, prejudices, ideologies, aggressiveness is seriously vitiated by the fact that the personal and social conditions of perceiving those phenomena are, naively, not taken into account. And, still, this is actually the crux of the problem. Not only the common man but also the social scientist is not enough aware that, as a rule, he notices only those stereotypes, prejudices, etc., which, by one reason or another, he does not share and that he does not see those stereotypes, prejudices, etc., in which he himself is deeply involved. The more deep-seated they are, the more does he take them for granted. It would be better for theory as well as for practice if we were more aware of this fact than we usually are and would realize more keenly than we frequently do that this kind of sociopsychological blindness is one of the most important causes of the intellectual and moral confusion of our age.

THE NATURE OF COMPETENCE-ACQUISITION ACTIVITIES AND THEIR RELATIONSHIP TO THERAPY*

Chris Argyris

I have been asked to discuss the objectives and nature of the group work that is called laboratory education (T-groups or sensitivity training). This is not an easy task because there is a great variety of learning activities that go under the same label. Another problem is that the underlying theory has only recently begun to be developed.[1]

The most useful solution seemed to be to focus on the theory that underlies much of these dynamics, a theoretical framework which may be called *competence acquisition*.[2]

The objective of competence acquisition is to provide the participants with opportunities to diagnose and increase their interpersonal competence. Interpersonal competence is the ability to cope effectively with interpersonal relationships. Three criteria of effective interpersonal coping are:

a) The individual perceives the interpersonal situation accurately. He is able to identify the relevant variables plus their interrelationships.

b) The individual is able to solve the problems in such a way that they remain solved. If, for example, interpersonal trust is low between A and B, they may not have been said to solve the problem competently unless

---

*Invited paper for Association for Research in Nervous and Mental Diseases, December, 1967, New York.

[1] Edgar H. Schein and Warren G. Bennis, *Personal and Organizational Change through Group Methods* (New York: Wiley, 1965), and L. P. Bradford, J. R. Gibb, and K. D. Benne (eds.), *T-Group Theory and Laboratory Method* (New York: Wiley, 1964).

[2] Such a differentiation is discussed in Chris Argyris, "On the Future of Laboratory Education", *Journal of Applied Behavioral Science* (June, 1967).

and until it no longer recurs (assuming the problem is under control).
c) The solution is achieved in such a way that A and B are still able to work with each other at least as effectively as when they began to solve their problem.

The test of interpersonal competence therefore is not limited to insight and understanding. The individual's interpersonal competence is a function of his ability (and the ability of the others involved) to solve interpersonal problems. This criterion implies that to test the interpersonal competence developed in a learning situation, the individual(s) must show that the learning has transferred beyond the learning situation. The aim, therefore, is to change behavior and attitudes in such a way that observable changes can be found in solving interpersonal problems outside the learning situations. Transfer of learning is a central aspiration in competence acquisition.

REQUIREMENTS FOR THE TRANSFER OF LEARNING

Providing the conditions for the maximum transfer of learning is extremely difficult in the interpersonal area. First, it takes much practice to develop interpersonal skills because they are complex and because much unfreezing is usually required. If the individual is to be internally committed to the new learning he must have come to the conclusion that his old modes of behavior were no longer effective. This conclusion needs to be based on actual experiences in the learning situation where he used his old modes of behavior and found them wanting.

Second, the individual must develop new modes of behavior that are also tested and found more effective than the old. These new modes of behavior must have been practiced enough so that the individual feels confident in his ability to use them.

Third, the individual must develop new modes of adjunct behavior that may be called for if he uses the new modes of behavior. For example, if the individual learns to express his feelings of anger or love more openly, he may also have to develop new competence in dealing with individuals who are threatened by such openness.

It is important, therefore, for the individual to learn how to express these feelings in such a way that he minimizes the probability that his behavior will cause someone else to become defensive, because then the environment could become threatening. This suggests a fourth criterion: namely, the probability that A will behave in an interpersonally competent manner is not only a function of his own confidence in his abilities to do so; it is also a function of the others' confidence and willingness to behave in an interpersonally competent manner. For example, the writer's interpersonal competence scores have been found to vary immensely, depending upon the situation in which he is placed. Quantitatively his scores have ranged from 150 to 390 where the lowest score obtained is 10 and the highest 390.[3] Interpersonal competence, therefore, is an interpersonal or situational ability and not simply an individual or personal ability. This does not mean that each individual cannot learn skills that will help him behave more competently. It means that such skills are necessary but not sufficient.

Finally, the probability is very low that an individual can be taught everything he needs to know in order to behave competently in most situations in which he will be placed. The variance and complexity of life is too great to predict it adequately ahead of time. Therefore, *the most important requirement in obtaining transfer of learning is to generate, along with the knowledge of any specific behavior, the basic skills needed to diagnose new situations effectively and those needed to develop co-operation with others involved to generate the competent behavior appropriate to the situation.*

Experience in, and theory relevant to, competence acquisition suggest that there are several key elements in the learning situation if these five requirements are to be fulfilled. The individuals must learn how to (1) communicate with each other in a manner that generates minimally distorted information; (2) give and receive feedback that is directly validatable and minimally evaluative; (3) perform these skills in such a way that self-acceptance and trust among individuals tends to increase; and (4) create effective groups in which problem solving may occur.

MINIMALLY DISTORTED INFORMATION

It seems self-evident to state that the information needed for competent problem solving should not be distorted. Altering behavior on the basis of distorted feedback would tend to make the individuals distorted, which, in turn, would tend to increase the probability that future feedback would be given or received in a distorted manner.

---

[3]Chris Argyris, *Organization and Innovation* (Homewood, Ill.: Irwin, 1965).

Self-Awareness and Self-Acceptance

The minimum requirement that each individual must meet if he is to provide minimally distorted information is to manifest a relatively high degree of *self-awareness* and *self-acceptance*. The more an individual is aware and accepting of those aspects of his self which are operating in a given situation, (1) the higher the probability that he will discuss them with minimal distortion, and (2) the higher the probability that he will listen with minimal distortion. For example, if A is aware and accepting of his predisposition to control others, he will tend to listen to the impact that he is having upon others without distorting what others are saying. Moreover, he will also tend to provide another controlling individual with feedback that is minimally distorted by his own similar problem in that area.

How is the individual to increase his self-awareness and self-acceptance? By receiving minimally distorted feedback from others about his impact upon them and their willingness to be accepting and understanding of his behavior, even though *he* may not be. Thus we have an interpersonal bind. Helpful feedback depends partially upon self-awareness and self-acceptance, yet these two factors depend upon helpful feedback!

How is this circular process broken into? This is a key task of the educator. Presumably he has (relatively speaking) a higher degree of self-awareness and self-acceptance against which the individuals can interact. His bind is that if he is not careful he can easily become the focus of attention. Everyone will tend to turn to him for valid information. This dependency could lead to awareness but hardly to confidence on the part of the learners that they can create their own conditions for self-awareness and self-acceptance. The educator strives to create conditions such that the learners will turn to each other as resources. In doing so, the educator makes two important assumptions about each individual. Each is assumed to have a constructive intent. Each is capable of learning from others *if* he receives the kind of information that is helpful and *if* the proper group atmosphere is developed.

Acceptance and Trust of Others

One of the major initial tasks of the educator is to create conditions under which the learners can become aware of and test the validity of these two assumptions. If these two assumptions are not validated for each individual in the learning situation, the processes of competence acquisition will not be highly effective. This test is very difficult to make during the early stages because most of the learners are expecting the educator to control their learning, to tell them what to do, to provide them with agendas, etc. If he behaves in any other way, he may easily be perceived as hostile, noncaring, or ineffective.

One reason a T-group experience usually begins with the withdrawal of the expected directive leadership, agenda, status, etc., is in order that the staff member may emphasize that he really means to help them come to trust in each other's intention to be constructive, in their capabilities to learn, and to develop an effective group. The point is made forcefully at the outset, not because the educator enjoys the drama of his apparent withdrawal and the resulting social weightlessness, but because he has learned that such behavior on his part is so strange that individuals do not tend to believe him unless he behaves this way with purpose and thrust. The educator strives not to be seduced from this stance by accusations of being perplexing, cruel, or ineffective. His major response during this period is, in effect, "I can understand that you may feel that if I have any concern for you I will help you out of this predicament. But may I point out again that I am assuming that a deeper predicament is to learn to rely on all of our strengths and not to become focused primarily on me?"

As soon as the learners realize that the educator means what he says, they usually turn to each other for help "to get the group moving." Those who begin to take the lead also expose their behavior, which becomes the basis for learning because it provides material to be diagnosed and discussed. Thus Mr. A may dislike the initial social weightlessness and may appoint himself as chairman. He may, somewhat demandingly, begin to define an agenda. The educator may eventually use this "here and now" situation to help the members explore their feelings about Mr. A. This could lead Mr. A to realize the impact he has had on others. It could also help the others to explore their different reactions to Mr. A (some welcome his behavior and some dislike it), as well as their feelings about beginning to be open. Another task would be for the members to explore the group process. For example, how was the decision made to develop an agenda? Did Mr. A check to see if he had the commitment of the members? What happens to decisions made unilaterally?

The point is that no matter which approach is taken, the educator uses the "here and now" to maximize their feelings of responsibility for their learning. It is primarily *their* behavior that they explore. It is *their* behavior that defines the goal. It is *their* responsibility to choose whether they will learn from the situation and if so, how, and how much. To be sure, early in the history of this type of learning, some people resent the fact that the educator does not prevent them from going in what he "knows" will be an ineffective direction. However, as the members see the importance of being self-responsible, as they feel the internal confidence that is developed from experiencing self-responsibility, as they come to trust others in the group, they become much more understanding of the educator's strategy not to interfere. Indeed, by the end of the first week, it is not uncommon for group members to caution an educator against too early intervention on his part to "pull them out of a difficulty." They have come to trust their capacity to do this and to value the intrinsic satisfaction that goes along with such learning. Moreover, they may have also begun to learn how it is for them, in another situation, to "withdraw" in order to help others help themselves.

Conditions for Psychological Success

The word "withdraw" is placed in quotation marks because it is not true that the educator withdraws in the sense of becoming uninvolved or being nondirective. The withdrawal from the expected leadership style is purposive action. The educator is deeply involved in creating the kind of environment which, if the learners decide to enter, will lead to important learning. What is that environment? The answer to this question identifies one of the underlying characteristics of competence acquisition mentioned at the outset. *No matter what is being learned substantively, it should be learned in such a way that it is accompanied by feelings of psychological success and confidence in self and others, and the group.*

The educator manipulates the environment (*never* the people) so that the individuals, if they decide to enter the environment, are offered frequent opportunities to (1) define their own learning goal, (2) develop their paths to the goal, (3) relate the goal and the paths to their central needs, and (4) experience a challenge in achieving the goal that stretches their present level of abilities.[4]

---

[4]Kurt Lewin, Tamara Dembo, Leon Festinger, and Pauline Sears, "Levels of Aspiration" in J. M. V. Hung (ed.), *Personality and Behavior Disorders* (New York: The Ronald Press, 1944), pp. 333–78.

The educator is actively striving to create the learning conditions which will lead them to an increase in trust and confidence in themselves and in their group. As the trust of self, others, and group increases, the probability of giving and receiving valid information increases and so does the probability of self-awareness and self-acceptance, which in turn increases the predisposition for more experiences of psychological success.

GIVING AND RECEIVING HELPFUL INFORMATION

Feedback may be undistorted but not very helpful in creating behavioral change, self-acceptance, and an effective group. In order for information to be most helpful it should be directly verifiable and minimally evaluative.

Directly Verifiable Information

It is important to distinguish between information that can be verified directly by self and others versus information that can be validated by reference to some conceptual scheme. The first type of feedback includes categories of behavior that are directly *observable;*[5] the second utilizes categories that are inferred. The more the information used in the learning situations is composed of *inferred categories* that refer to a conceptual scheme, the greater the dependence of the individuals upon the conceptual scheme if they are to verify the information that they are using. If, for example, the conceptual scheme is a clinical framework, then the individuals must turn to the educator for help because he knows the scheme. (Indeed, is not a great part of therapy learning the conceptual scheme of the therapist?) This dependence *decreases* the *probability* of experiencing psychological success, trust in others and in the group, because the key to success, trust, and effectiveness lies in knowing the conceptual scheme, which is in the mind of the therapist. For example, if B learns from the therapist that his hostility is probably an attempt to deal with authority figures and that the transference phenomenon is actively present, he will be unable to verify these inferences unless he learns the conceptual scheme used by the therapist. Moreover, even if he learns the scheme, B will soon find that he is using inferred categories for which relatively unambiguous tests are not available. He is being diagnosed, "interpreted," and advised with the use of concepts that he understands vaguely

---

[5] I am indebted to Dr. Alvan R. Feinstein (Yale Medical School) for clarifying this distinction and recommend to the reader his book, *Clinical Judgment* (Williams and Wilkins, 1967).

and which have minimal operational actions to test their validity. He may indeed come to feel that the very process of testing the therapist's inference could be interpreted as resistance.

Information, therefore, should be as far as possible directly verifiable. However, to generate information that is directly verifiable by nonprofessionals as well as professionals requires that it remain as close to observable data as possible. For example, B learns that when he behaves in X manner (asks questions, evaluates others), A feels attacked. B then can turn to the group and check to see if they see him behaving in X manner and, if so, whether they also feel attacked. He may learn that some see him behaving in X manner and some see him behaving in Y manner. He may learn that some feel attacked and some do not. Finally, he may learn that, of those who do *not* feel attacked, several feel this way because X type of behavior is not threatening to them. Others may find Y type of behavior threatening.

One of the crucial learnings that B obtains is that his behavior is rarely perceived in a unitary fashion and that its impact varies widely. He may then ask the members to describe what kind of behavior they would not have found threatening. This information may lead B to alter his behavior. It may also lead him to decide to behave in X or Y manner but, the next time, show awareness that his behavior is having a differential impact.

In the section above we distinguished two kinds of inferred categories. One that was related to a formal theoretical framework (he is projecting; she is ambivalent) and the other that was related to the personal values of the individual (he is nice; she is sweet). There is a third way that formal or personal theory may be used.

There are many writers who are beginning to stress the use of more directly observable categories. For example, the therapist may say to the client, "I think you are kidding yourself; it sounds like you would like to kill that individual, you are so angry."

The function of such *attributive* interventions is to attribute something to the person, which the therapist infers exists, about which the client is more or less unaware. Such an intervention may use relatively observable categories, but they are based upon a theoretical framework. Thus, if the patient asks, "Why do you say I am kidding?" he may receive a reply, "Because you are denying such and such." Or, if he asks, "Why do you think I want to kill so and so?" he may receive a reply "You sounded very angry, and I felt that you were afraid to say what you truly felt." It now becomes apparent that the former intervention was based upon the concept of denial, the latter on a concept of some category of psychological blockage.

Any intervention that attributes something to the client that he has not already mentioned (in some directly verifiable form) is based upon the therapist's inferences about the inner states of the client. Such an intervention is also of the inferred variety even though it may be initially placed in the language of observed categories.

Telling the client what may be "inside" himself, "causing" his problems, even if *correct*, will tend to lead to psychological failure, because the client, if he is to be rational and self-responsible, must assign the primary responsibility for the insight to the therapist. It was the therapist who guessed correctly what was "in" the client. If the therapist, however, intervenes and gives the raw data from which he infers the client is unaware or not expressing openly that he is kidding himself or wants to kill someone, then the client is able to judge for himself the possible validity of the inference.

This comment should emphasize that the meaning of "here and now" in competence acquisition is significantly different from the meaning of "here and now" in many psychotherapeutic activities. Some psychotherapists tend to use the "here and now" to help the client discover the unconscious structure active in the present but created in the past. Others use "here and now" data to help the client see that he uses the relationship to involve the therapist as a more or less unconscious object. Finally, others use the "here and now" data to generate enough evidence to make an interpretation to the patient, such as that he may be projecting, or that he may be identifying with such and such a person, etc.[6]

In all these examples the "here and now" data are used to help the professional generate interpretations that go much beyond the directly verifiable, observed category. This point cannot be made too strongly. To date, the overwhelming number of psychotherapists' works read by the author has led him to the conclusion that, unlike his emphasis on observed categories, they use interpretations of the "here and now" variety which are composed of *inferred* categories.[7]

---

[6]For illustrations, see Henry Ezriel, "Notes on Psychoanalytic Group Therapy: II. Interpretation and Research." *Psychiatry*, Vol. 15 (May, 1952), pp. 119–26.

[7]William Glasser may be closer to this view, but he gives examples in terms of "there and then." *Reality Therapy* (New York: Harper & Row, 1965), p.. 75 ff.

Minimally Evaluative Feedback

The second major characteristic of helpful information is that it is minimally evaluative of the recipient's behavior. There are two reasons for this. First, such information reduces the probability of making the receiver defensive, thereby creating conditions under which accurate listening will be increased. Thus, laboratory education does not value the communication of all information. It values that openness which will help the individuals receiving feedback to learn. Second, minimally evaluative information describes how the receiver feels about the sender's messages without describing them as good or bad. This places the responsibility for evaluation, if there is to be any, on the individual trying to learn about himself. He, and only he, has the responsibility of deciding whether he plans to change his behavior. Again, placing the responsibility on the individual increases the probability that if he changes, since it is his decision, he will tend to experience a sense of psychological success.

This does not mean that evaluation is harmful. Evaluation of behavior and effectiveness is necessary and essential. The point is that one ought, as far as possible, to create conditions under which the individual makes his own evaluation and then asks for confirmation or disconfirmation. If the individual first makes his own evaluation, then even if it is negative, a confirmation by others of his negative quality can lead to growth and inner confidence in one's capacity to evaluate oneself correctly.[8]

This implies that an individual should take the initiative in seeking confirmation and that he should "own up" with his evaluations before others do so. "Going first," if it is to be successful, requires that several conditions be met. First, the individual should be unconflicted and accepting about his evaluation of himself. If he is not, others will sense it and may tend to withhold their true feelings. This tendency to withhold, in turn, will be a function of their view of the individual's strength to receive accurately and use effectively the evaluative comments that he is requesting. Thus, "going first" requires less courage and more competence. The individual has created, by his behavior, the conditions under which others would trust him to use their evaluative feedback competently.

THE EFFECTIVE GROUP AND ITS USE FOR INDIVIDUAL CHANGE

A careful analysis of the activities described above will suggest

---

[8]Chris Argyris, *Interpersonal Competence and Organizational Effectiveness* (Homewood, Ill.: Irwin, 1962), pp. 140–43.

that competence acquisition requires the development of effective groups. For example, the individual requires minimally distorted and immediately validatable feedback. If he is to understand his impact upon others, then he needs to receive valid information from others. In order to obtain valid information, the others should be minimally defensive. Assuming that the selection process has eliminated those who are so defensive that they cannot learn from others (see next section), then the major source for defensiveness becomes the group. If the members cannot decide on a sequence of topics acceptable to all—who will receive the first feedback—or if they are unable to judge the constructive intent of the members, then their problem solving could become so ineffective that they would become frustrated with, and angry at, each other. Under these conditions, minimally distorted, immediately verifiable information will rarely be generated. *Although competence acquisition focuses on helping individuals become more interpersonally competent, the very nature of personality (its incompleteness without others, the need for consensual validation, etc.) makes an effective group central to the learning processes.*

This conclusion leads naturally to two questions. What is an effective group? How can one utilize an effective group to facilitate individual growth?

Beginning with the former question, four major dimensions of group effectiveness are:

1) The members focus on defining group goals that "satisfy" the needs and utilize the important abilities of the individual members. Adequate time is spent to make certain that the goals represent a challenge to the group as well as to the individuals and that the members are internally committed to the achievement of the goals.

2) Attention is paid, whenever it is necessary, to the group processes. For example, are the members' contributions additive? Do the members focus on the history of the group in order to learn from its successes and failures, from its internal conflicts, from its problem solving? Are the members owning up to their ideas and feelings? Are they open to new ideas and feelings? Are they experimenting and taking risks?

3) Norms are generated that reward the individuality of each member, that show respect and concern for the members' ideas and feelings, that facilitate and maintain a sense of trust.

4) Leadership is shared so that each member is leading the group when his skills are the most pertinent to the achievement of the group goals.

The next question is, how may an effective group be used as a medium for individual behavioral change? Cartwright, on the basis of a review of the literature, suggests several conditions under which a group may be a more effective medium for change.[9]

There needs to be a strong sense of belonging to the same group, including a *reduction* of the normal gap between teacher and student, doctor and patient, etc., so that the faculty and students feel as members of one group in matters involving their growth. This means that the staff member must strive to become a member of the group without giving up his expertise. This is a difficult task because, as we have seen, so many of the members come to the group with different expectations. As was pointed out above, the staff member strives to develop membership by withdrawing initially and dramatically creating a situation in which the members must turn to each other as resource people. As their trust and confidence in themselves and in their group increases, their need to see the staff member as a godlike, distant figure decreases.

A second way to earn genuine membership was also described above. The staff member makes as many of his contributions as possible be minimally distorted, at the level of observed categories, and focused on how he sees the world (and not what is "in" others, or what "the" group is doing). This makes every one of his contributions subject to verification by the other members. The point is that every other member must learn how to use effectively both of these strategies. As they do, they will begin to feel closer to each other, including the staff member. Indeed, one of the crucial ways in which a staff member earns his membership is by making several interventions which are not verifiable or are found to be in error. This helps the group to realize that he is not infallible and that the staff member needs *them* to check his own effectiveness.

As the members begin to trust their selves and each other, as their group functioning becomes more effective, the group becomes more attractive to each member. As the group becomes more attractive, it meets the second conditions defined by Cartwright. The more attractive the group is to its members, the greater is the influence that the group can exert on its members.

Cartwright also suggests a third condition; namely, that a strong pressure for change in the group can be established by creating shared perceptions by the members of the need for change. Again,

---

[9]Dorwin Cartwright, "Achieving Change in People: Some Applications of Group Dynamics Theory," *Human Relations*, Vol. 4 (1951), pp. 381–93.

examples of how a staff member creates opportunities for these pressures to develop were described in the previous section. If the staff member creates, at the outset, an opportunity for the members to "take over," and if in behaving they exhibit interpersonally incompetent behavior, it will lead to their becoming frustrated. If they feel a need to be competent and their intent is constructive, then these experiences will become a major source of shared perception of the need for their change.

If the staff member follows the strategy of helping the members develop their own plans, define their own learning goals, generate their own level of aspiration (psychological success), then we have created the fourth condition mentioned by Cartwright. Information relating to the need for change, plans for change, and consequences of change must be shared by all relevant people in the group.

We conclude, therefore, that individual learning cannot be separated from group effectiveness, and (happily) the conditions required for each are overlapping but highly consonant. This suggests that the arguments of individual versus group learning may be off the mark. Moreover, it may not make much sense to plan a learning experience that focuses on only one level of learning. Both levels of learning must be experienced to some degree of effectiveness if learning is to occur at either level. One may wish *to begin* at the group or individual level, but if a whole learning experience is to be developed, the interdependencies of each on the other must be brought out and mastered. This is especially relevant if we think of the criterion of transfer of learning. When an individual finds himself in a situation outside of the learning context, the members of that situation will not focus on individual or group phenomena simply because that is what *he* learned to do in *his* laboratory. Under these conditions the individual may feel frustrated and experience a greater sense of failure than the members who had never attended a laboratory, since their level of aspiration, related to their interpersonal competence, may be realistically lower than his.

Another implication is that the learning experience should last long enough and be designed in such a way that the learners can be exposed to "pairs" of interpersonal and group phenomena. Moreover, one may predict that if the staff chooses to ignore the individual or the group phenomena during the learning experiences, the learners will have to make up the deficiency in their own informal way. For example, a recent delegation to a Leicester-Tavistock conference reported that they spent many off hours discussing their learning about their personal competence and about the usefulness of the experience: two topics never scheduled formally (and rarely informally) by the faculty. A group experience recently conducted by the writer, which never got to group phenomena during the formal sessions, led many members to spend many of their informal hours focusing on that subject.

COMPETENCE AND SURVIVAL ORIENTATION LEAD TO OPEN AND CLOSED SYSTEMS

At the beginning of this paper two assumptions of competence acquisition were defined. They were that the individuals have (1) a constructive intent and (2) a genuine desire to learn, to become interpersonally more competent. It was noted that the less the constructive intent to learn, the less the conditions of competence acquisition apply. Why would individuals have different degrees of willingness to learn?

A detailed discussion of this question would lead beyond the main thrust of this paper. However, a brief note is necessary in order to build the position. Individuals can be described as predisposed or oriented toward increasing their competence or toward protecting themselves in order to survive. Maslow describes the former as growth motivation, the latter as deficiency motivation.[10] The more the individual is competence-oriented, the more he will tend to focus on those activities that enlarge his self and increase his self-acceptance and confidence. The individual becomes more an *open* system. In the area of interpersonal relations, the activities involved in the growth and acceptance of self may be conceptualized as the seeking of a sense of interpersonal competence.[11]

Developing a sense of interpersonal competence is intrinsically satisfying; it provides much of the motivation for growth and learning in interpersonal relationships. However, the individual will tend to be free to focus on competence acquisition only to the extent that he feels his survival problems are resolved (i.e., they do not control his present behavior). Thus human beings "graduate" into and, once having done so, strive to maintain, competence acquisition orientation. They will return to survival orientation only when they experience threat. A survival orientation is primarily one of the protection

---

[10]A. H. Maslow, *Personality and Motivation* (New York: Harper & Row, Pub., Inc. 1954.

[11]Robert W. White, "Motivation Reconsidered: The Concept of Competence," *Psychological Review*, Vol. 66 (1959), pp. 297–334.

of the self. The individual, through the use of defense mechanisms, withdraws, distorts, or attacks the environment. In all cases the end result is to reduce the probability that the individual will learn from the environment. This, in turn, begins to make the individual more closed and less subject to influence. The more closed the individual becomes, the more his adaptive reactions will be controlled by his internal system. But since his internal system is composed of many defense mechanisms, the behavior will not tend to be functional or economical. The behavior may eventually become compulsive, repetitive, inwardly stimulated, and observably dysfunctional. The individual becomes more of a *closed* system. The greater the proportion of the individual's behavior that falls into this category (closed), the more he approximates the condition that Kubie has described as neurotic behavior.

It is important to emphasize that individuals are *not* being viewed as either closed or open. People are not open or closed. Nor is all openness effective and all closedness ineffective. An individual may be quite open in learning about his authority relationships but not his capacity to create mistrust. Another individual may be open to learning more about how to express his feelings and suddenly become closed when he realizes he has reached the point that further expression of feelings could lead to an uncontrollable state. He prefers to postpone further expression of feelings until he has learned to manage the new feelings that he has expressed.

The important point, from a theory of learning, is that the educator and the client need to be able to differentiate between that learning which evolves around problems and issues about which the individual is more or less open or closed. Each state of affairs requires different interventions with which to encourage learning. Thus, as we shall see in a moment, it may be necessary to use inferred evaluative interventions under certain conditions if the individual is to gain insight and unfreeze. However, if one is to go beyond insight and unfreezing, then one will have to utilize competence-oriented learning conditions. These learning conditions may be inhibited if mixed with too strong a component of interventions designed to unfreeze closed (survival-oriented) behavior. The problem is *not* that it may be difficult for the educator to cope with; he may be competent to shift from one level of intervention to another. The problem is the group. Until the members become much more competent, they will find the mixture confusing. One of the basic reasons is that interventions designed to unfreeze closed behavior tend not to create conditions for psychological success, directly verifiable information, minimally evaluative feedback, and effective group functioning. The members will feel challenged enough to learn how to be competent in terms of these conditions. Moreover, they will feel the pressure stemming from the reality that their learning experience is limited in time.

Openness and closedness are affected by:

1) The situation in which the individual is placed. If the situation is confirmably threatening, then closedness may be a functional response. Individuals may become more closed for social reasons. Empirical evidence has been presented that there seems to be a general tendency for people to create social systems that are closed and reward survival orientation.[12] It is therefore possible for the individual to behave in a closed manner because it makes sense; it is functional in a closed system. This type of closedness we will call *external* to indicate that it comes primarily from the social system. An individual who is closed for external reasons has not internalized the systemic values to such a point that he cannot differentiate closedness from openness. He is able to go back and forth from more open to more closed behavior depending upon the situation. In a T-group, for example, an externally closed individual will resist openness initially until he can assure himself that the T-group is truly an open system.

The individual whose survival orientation stems from personal reasons may be called *internally* closed. This individual is unable to become open when he is provided with a situation in which openness is relevant and functional. He generalizes that the world is threatening far beyond the situation where threats have existed or do exist.

2) The duration of the threat. A threat could produce momentary closedness if it is of short duration, or it could produce long-lasting closedness if it lasts for a long period of time.

3) The parts of the personality affected by the threat. The degree of closedness will tend to vary if the source of threat is related to inner, peripheral, or central aspects of the self. Peripheral aspects are those that have a low potency for the individual, while inner aspects tend to have a high potency. We assume that one must pass through the peripheral in order to arrive at the inner aspects.

---

[12]Chris Argyris, *Interpersonal Competence and Organizational Effectiveness* (Homewood, Ill.: 1962); *Organization and Innovation* (Homewood, Ill.: Irwin, 1964); and "Interpersonal Barriers to Decision Making," *Harvard Business Review* (March-April, 1966), pp. 84–97.

The central aspects can be peripheral or inner. The key differentiating property is that change in a central part will tend to create changes in the surrounding parts, be they inner or peripheral.

4) Whether or not the source of the threat is from within or from without. The problems in dealing with threat that an individual faces are very different when the threat emanates from within than when the threat comes from the external environment.

5) Finally, the degree of control the system is able to manifest (in our case, individuals) over the threat. The less the control over the threat, the greater the probability that the individual will become closed. Closedness will also increase as the potency of the parts involved increases and as the duration of the threat increases.

It should be clear, therefore, that it is a gross oversimplification to think of open and closed individuals. What is more likely is that individuals are more or less closed or open, both in terms of degree and in terms of time. The more an individual seeks the processes of competence acquisition, the more open he may be said to be. The more an individual resists these processes, the more closed he may be said to be. *The point to be emphasized is the hypothesis that the more open an individual can be, the more he can learn from competence-acquisition activities; the more closed, the more he may need therapy, at least as the initial step toward competence acquisition.*

To summarize, the probability of learning to behave more competently *and* to transfer this learning beyond the learning situation increases:

1) *as the client's* self-awareness and self-acceptance increases; as his acceptance and trust of others increases.

2) as the *educator* is able to create, in the learning situation, conditions of *(a)* psychological success, *(b)* directly verifiable information, *(c)* minimally evaluative feedback, and *(d)* effective group functioning (group goals are congruent with member needs, attention to group processes, norms of individuality, concern, trust, and shared leadership).

3) *as these conditions for effective learning* feed back to help increase and strengthen the individual's self-awareness and self-acceptance and his acceptance and trust of others, which, in turn, increase the probability that

4) the *members* will take increasing responsibility and manifest greater competence in creating conditions of effective learning which

5) provide the *members* and educator opportunity to practice

and deepen their competence as well as their confidence in creating the conditions elsewhere.

Some readers may wonder if we are suggesting that feelings of pain, fear, self-accusation should not occur in the learning session. Is this learning experience one that emphasizes "sweetness and light"?

One of the problems is that we are limited by space. However, two points should be made. Anyone who has experienced, either as an educator or a member, the difficulty in creating conditions for effective learning, the embarrassment of realizing how incompetent one can be, the blindness of one's own impact upon others, or the capacity to unintentionally prevent the reception of valid feedback can testify to the existence of feelings of pain, fear, and confrontation of reality.

The second and more important point is that the strategy presented in this paper suggests that the educator should not focus directly on creating such feelings as pain, fear, etc. He should focus, as much as possible, on creating the conditions described above. If, while he does this, fear, pain, anguish, and frustration occur (and they will occur), he helps the members to express these feelings and to understand the basis of such fears. Past experience suggests two important causes of these feelings are (1) the awareness of one's blindness to (2) the degree of one's interpersonal incompetence. The awareness of such conditions provides internal motivation for further work on increasing one's interpersonal competence.